Marketing
Phrase
Book

Professional
Edition

Gail Hamilton

Hamilton House

Hamilton House, 630 County Road 14
RR3 Demorestville, Ontario, Canada K0K 1W0

Library and Archives Canada Cataloguing in Publication

Hamilton, Gail (Margaret Gail)
Marketing phrase book / Gail Hamilton. – Professional ed.

ISBN 978-0-9680853-9-4

1. Advertising – Terminology. I. Title.

HF5825.H35 2009   659.103   C2008-906452-6

Contents

Introduction

Your business depends on successful marketing. Whether you are the local plumber or a huge multinational, you must get your message across effectively.

The *Marketing Phrase Book* puts the language of the marketplace, the language that sells, right at your fingertips!

The *Marketing Phrase Book* contains a huge, infinitely versatile collection of phrases designed solely for marketing. The kind of phrases selling millions of dollars worth of products and services every day. No matter what your business, this unique, easy-to-use resource will put sizzle in your advertising, boost your results and practically create promotions for you.

How does it work?

Easy! Just look up your key words and you'll find a lavish array of ways to use them. Find what you want to say but can't put your finger on. Discover the "trigger" words that set customers reaching for their pocketbooks.

The phrases provide a springboard for your imagination, helping you come up with exciting new ways to get your message across. And, above all, they are dynamic construction blocks to build high-powered advertising and promotions tailored exactly to your needs.

Small Business Owners

If you produce your own advertising, the *Marketing Phrase Book* is a must. It's the easy way to increase your sales and free up more precious time to develop your business. Get more attention faster, reach more people and never struggle for words again.

New Entrepreneurs

You've got a great idea. You've taken that scary, thrilling leap out on your own. Now you have to make it work. The *Marketing Phrase Book* lets you quickly learn the language that attracts customers and racks up sales. Add instant professional polish to your promotions and pizzaz to your everyday selling techniques without hiring expensive outside expertise. Most important of all, get a head start on success when you need it most.

Salespeople and Executives

Does your livelihood depend on your ability to promote your company's product or service? The *Marketing Phrase Book* helps you turn out terrific letters, persuasive proposals and reports, compelling speeches and sales talks, and dynamite presentations. Give yourself that crucial competitive edge and let others wonder what your secret is.

Marketing Professionals

Whether you're part of an advertising agency, a public relations firm or the company marketing department, the *Marketing Phrase Book* remains an endlessly valuable resource. When you're expected to repeat your last triumph with something equally brilliant, only different, you and your staff can have all the red-hot advertising language on your desks for speedy reference. And you can mine the phrases for seed ideas that spark whole new campaigns. Make the *Marketing Phrase Book* a solid foundation for your own creativity. Revitalize and update your work. Save valuable time and come out on top when you're under pressure to perform.

Hot Marketing Phrases

The bulk of the book provides a huge selection of marketing phrases you can use to supercharge your promotional material. In addition, you get even more terrific resources to add sizzle to your marketing and profits to your bank account.

The Internet and Technology

The Internet is today's white-hot information and selling medium, linked to practically every aspect of doing business. Technology advances at a dizzying speed. Take advantage of the lively lingo that gets things done in a constantly changing digital reality.

Contests and Sweepstakes

Everyone loves a chance to win. Whether you're holding a contest with a toaster as a prize or playing in the big leagues, boost your chances with a marketing win here.

Telemarketing

The telephone remains one of the most potent, versatile tools to draw in customers and build business. Polish your telephone technique and dial up increased success every day.

Saying No

Saying no tactfully is an essential skill in any enterprise. Use the phrases to do so with courtesy and grace.

Apology

A warm, sincere apology will clear the air, clear your name and keep your valued customers. Learn to apologize with the best.

Name that Sale

1) Select anything from Part One. Such as **"Blitz"**.
2) Use it alone or
3) Match with anything from Part Two, such as **"Holiday"**.
4) Combine to produce **"Holiday Blitz"**.

Exclamations

Need to get your big selling point noticed? Choose the right exclamation and put it where it really stands out. Listen to the cash register ring.

Beginnings and Transitions

This exceedingly useful section provides you with all those vital words and phrases you need to tie your thoughts together and make your letters, speeches, proposals and promotions flow effortlessly and convincingly.

Reply Coupons

Your reply coupon is all-important. Check out this section to make sure you word it just right.

Colors

Have fun picking out a name for that vivid new color so important to your product, service or company.

Power Words

Here is the crucial core vocabulary of advertising, the words that pack the punch and pull in the dollars. Plunge in and get to know them. Words of similar meaning are loosely grouped together to rev up your imagination and fill you with bold new ideas. It's the quickest way to get the impact you need for all your promotions and advertising.

How To Use The Phrases

Step One

Decide on your purpose. For instance, you wish to promote the sale of roses from your florist shop.

Step Two

The phrases are arranged alphabetically by key word. When you see the word **"product"** or **"service"**, that is your cue to insert the specific product or service you are promoting.

Look up **"FINE"** and choose a phrase, such as **" when only the finest will do"**.

Look up **"AFFORDABLE"** and choose a phrase such as **"far more affordable than you think"**.

Look up **"GUARANTEE"** and choose a phrase such as, **"great low prices guaranteed"**.

Look up **"SELECT"** and choose as phrase such as **"will help you select exactly the product you need"**.

Look up **"CARE"** and choose a phrase such as **"show that special someone how much you care"**.

Step Three

Combine the phrases into a powerful marketing appeal that brings the customers and the money rolling in:

"When only the finest will do, send red roses. An armful of lush, fragrant blooms is **far more affordable than you think**. For the month of June, **great low prices are guaranteed.** Our friendly staff **will help you select exactly the roses you need** to **show that someone special how much you care**. Order by phone or come in and see for yourself at any of our convenient locations."

Sample Entry

COST
- Now you can beat the high cost of
- The low, low cost will surprise you
- What's the start-up cost to you
- Does anyone need to know it costs nearly nothing to produce
- Less costly than ever
- Provided at no additional cost
- You would expect it to cost more but it doesn't
- All these terrific extras included at no extra cost
- At no cost or obligation to you
- By far the most cost effective way to
- Reduced cost while improving strength and safety
- At absolutely no extra cost to you
- Lower costs mean more of your money can work for you
- Helping you keep your costs in line
- So you can keep the lid on costs
- Twice the value at no extra cost
- We know you have to keep your costs down
- Helps lower overall costs by

Cost: price, value, worth, market value, amount, figure, valuation, quotation, demand, asking price, appraisement, appraisal, dollar value, expenditure, expense, charge, rate, hire
See also: CHARGE, DOLLAR, EXPENSE, MONEY, PRICE, SAVINGS, VALUE

"COST" is the key word present in every phrase.

Where appropriate, a number of alternative words for **"cost"** are suggested below the bulleted list of phrases.

"See also: CHARGE, DOLLAR, EXPENSE, MONEY, PRICE, SAVINGS, VALUE" indicates that under these entries you will find even more phrases closely related to the meaning your are looking for.

Section One

Marketing

ABILITY

- Because of our ability to provide a high level of service
- Just one of our many fine abilities
- With proven ability to
- With the ability to do anything you want
- We're famous for our ability to
- Acclaimed for its amazing ability to
- Increasing your ability to enjoy

Ability: aptitude, artistry, bent, craft, competence, capacity, command, facility, flair, forte, genius, instinct, knack power, prowess, proficiency, wit, skill
See also: CAN, CAPACITY, COMMAND, CRAFTSMANSHIP, GENIUS, POWER, SKILL

ABOUT

- That's what we're all about
- It's all about you
- Find out what all the shouting is about
- When you're wondering what to do about a big problem
- There's no doubt about it

See also: CONCERN

ABOVE

- A cut above the rest
- Standing out above all competitors
- Imagine being above it all
- Far above ordinary expectations

See also: BEST, EXCEPTIONAL, FINE, OVER, SUPERIOR

ACCENT

- A great accent equals a lasting impression
- Putting the accent on
- The accent is on quality
- Use it to accent
- Assorted colorful accent items
- Accent on total delight

ACCEPT

- Accept only the finest
- Accepted everywhere as the leader of the pack
- Totally accepted wherever you go

See also: CHOOSE, TAKE

ACCEPTANCE

- Why we've won such overwhelming acceptance
- Acceptance is instant
- Act as soon as your acceptance comes through

ACCESS

- We give you access sooner
- You'll have preferential access to
- And you enjoy easy access anywhere in the country
- Can be accessed by phone, email or
- With quick and personal access
- Providing access day or night
- Now you can have unlimited access to all these services plus
- For immediate access
- Convenient access, 24 hours a day
- With instant access
- Request access today
- Gain direct access to a new world of wonder
- Make sure you have the access and support you need to
- Access is the issue
- Gives you immediate access to essential information
- Unlimited access, no questions
- Access in an instant
- That no one else can access
- Giving you even faster access to

Access: approachability, admission, admittance, entry, entree
See also: ADMISSION, ENTER, ROAD, PATH, WAY

ACCESSIBLE

- Easily accessible
- Are you looking for something a little more accessible
- Making this service accessible to you
- When you're up against the clock, accessibility is everything

Accessible: approachable, familiar, friendly, informal, genial, inviting, open, manageable, on hand, convenient
See also: AVAILABLE, READY

ACCESSORY

- And, of course, it's accessory to
- The accessory that makes all the rest of it work
- Accessorize with style

- Comes with a wide variety of accessories
- The ultimate accessory
- Complete with all accessories
- All accessories included

See also: **EXTRA. OPTION**

ACCIDENT

- Dramatically reducing risk of accident
- It's certainly no accident that people are choosing us
- Accidents happen
- Some people call it a lucky accident, but you know better

See also: **CHANCE, FORTUNATE, OPPORTUNITY**

ACCLAIM

- Nationally acclaimed
- No product has been more honored and acclaimed in its field
- You'll quickly understand why experts acclaim it

See also: **CELEBRITY, PRAISE, TRIBUTE**

ACCOMMODATION

- In the best accommodation available
- Always happy to make accommodation for your special needs
- To appreciate the luxurious accommodations

See also: **AGREEMENT**

ACCOMPLISH

- Doing what has never been accomplished before
- Showing just how much we were able to accomplish with
- Well-known for accomplishing things others can't

Accomplish: perform, execute, achieve, bring off, succeed in, carry out, do, effect, realize, make happen, work out, negotiate

See also: **ACHIEVE, SUCCEED**

ACCOMPLISHMENT

- We believe the greater accomplishment lies in
- An accomplishment we're justly proud of achieving
- Our biggest accomplishment yet is

waiting for you

See also: **ACHIEVEMENT, SUCCESS**

ACCORD

- An idea that will promote civil accord
- Striving to be in accord with your wishes
- In accord with the most advanced ideas of the time
- Always in accord about quality

See also: **AGREE, MATCH**

ACCOUNTABLE

- Always accountable to you
- You want a company that's accountable
- Accountability is at the core
- And you can hold us strictly accountable

See also: **GUARANTEE, RESPONSIBLE**

ACCURATE

- More accurate, more valid than ever
- It would be more than accurate to say we are the finest
- We aim for the utmost accuracy
- An accurate estimate the first time
- Faster, more accurate, lighter weight

Accurate: precise, exact, correct, on the mark, right on, faithful, in conformity, true, authentic, perfect, faultless, meticulous, particular, rigorous, strict

See also: **CORRECT, RIGHT, PRECISION, REAL**

ACHIEVE

- Rarely does someone achieve such rapid advances
- A combination of advantages never achieved before
- How you can achieve instantly
- There's no limit to what you can achieve with

See also: **ACCOMPLISH, ACT, CREATE, BUILD, DO, PERFORM**

ACHIEVEMENT

- Our greatest achievement just may be gaining your confidence
- Our most amazing achievement yet
- Not only do we get to boast proudly of our achievements
- Recognized for our achievements and ability to
- The secret behind every great achievement

- Our proudest achievement is your happiness

See also: ACCOMPLISHMENT, BREAKTHROUGH

ACT
- All so you can act more efficiently
- But you must act immediately
- You soon realize it's no act
- Act now before it's too late
- Act out who you really are
- Time to stop talking and start acting
- There are four good reasons why you should act today
- Act today if you haven't already done so
- So please act quickly
- A hard act to follow

See also: ACCOMPLISH, ACHIEVE, DO, MOVE, PERFORM

ACTION
- The action is legendary
- Actions speak louder than words
- Come in and watch the action
- Designed for those who want a little more action
- See all of the action all of the time
- Triple action works swiftly to
- Getting you breathtakingly close to the action
- Built to see action
- Helping you develop an action plan
- It's easy to find where the action is
- Catch all the action with
- Visit us to watch the action

Action: act, deed, transaction, adventure, effort, endeavor, enterprise, dispatch, handiwork
See also: ACTIVITY, ADVENTURE, EXCITEMENT, FUN

ACTIVITY
- Our sole activity is serving you
- As we step up our activities
- Just about the most fun activity you'll ever find
- All our activities have been directed toward pleasing you

See also: ACTION, ADVENTURE, EXCITEMENT, FUN

ADAPT
- Adapt to meet a fresh attack
- Quickly adapt to meet changing conditions
- Helping you adapt to a changing, exciting, modern world
- Can be easily adapted to your particular needs

See also: CHANGE, FIT, FLEXIBLE, VERSATILE

ADD
- Nothing added but excellence
- Please add us to your list
- Making the right things add up
- Just add our product
- It all adds up to satisfaction
- Add-on value
- Inspires you to add something to your
- Want to see your savings really add up

See also: ACCESSORY, ATTACH, BONUS

ADDITION
- A fabulous addition to your own collection
- A sensational addition to
- This freshest addition will inspire
- A great new addition today
- Come and see the most recent additions to our line
- A terrific last-minute addition
- With this latest addition, it's easier than ever to

ADJUST
- Adjusts to several different sizes
- You'll be amazed at how quickly you can adjust to comfort
- Adjusted exactly to your requirements
- So easy to adjust

Adjust: adapt, fit, regulate, fine-tune, focus, bring into line, settle, resolve, compromise
See also: ACCOMMODATION, ADAPT, COMPROMISE, FIT

ADMINISTRATION
- Benefit from excellent administration
- Administration you can trust
- Sound administration has paid off

See also: MANAGEMENT

ADMIRE
- If you've admired other people's
- It's time for others to admire you

- You no longer have to admire from afar
- We know you'll admire our
- Something new for them to admire

See also: CHOOSE, LIKE, PREFER

ADMISSION
- Free with admission
- For one low, low price of admission
- There is absolutely no admission charge
- Gets you instant admission to the greatest
- Merely the price of admission gets you all this and more

See also: ACCESS, JOIN

ADMIT
- Okay, we admit it
- Admit yourself to the front ranks
- Even our fiercest competitors have had to admit
- It's time to finally admit how good you are
- Admit how much you want it, then indulge yourself
- Admit one to an amazing future

ADVANCE
- One advance after another keeps us in the forefront
- Advancing with incredible speed
- Stay on top of the latest advances
- Advances in techniques give you
- Combines the latest advances
- The most advanced you could use

Advance: progress, headway, improvement, creation, invention, finding, breakthrough
See also: BREAKTHROUGH, LEAP, PROGRESS, STRIDE

ADVANTAGE
- Take advantage of this once-in-a-lifetime opportunity
- Take of advantage of the rewards and benefits of
- If you're looking for a definite advantage, come to us
- It's to your immediate advantage
- Take advantage of savings up to
- The plan advantage is clear
- You're already at an advantage because
- Consider the many advantages of
- Members rely on the flexibility, reliability and credit advantages
- Wide range of significant business and personal advantages
- It's advantages like these that have made us the first choice
- Has the added advantage of
- Lets you enjoy all these advantages
- All the advantages without the pain
- Here are some of the hidden advantages
- Able to take full advantage of our low prices
- Includes all the advantages you already enjoy
- The advantage is convenience and cost
- Get yourself an advantage today

See also: BENEFIT, BOOST

ADVENTURE
- Concerned with day-to-day adventures
- For those who long for adventure
- Live the incredible adventure
- Since life is full of adventure
- The adventure takes flight
- Join the adventure
- There's an adventure for everyone
- Uncommon adventures
- Planning an adventure is easy
- The adventure is all yours
- We've got just the adventure you're looking for
- An adventure in excellence
- An adventure like this comes calling only once in a lifetime
- Creating an adventure unlikely to be seen again
- Exploring it is an adventure for the whole family

Adventure: feat, exploit, hazard, danger, chance, gamble, deed, tour de force, plunge, enterprise, speculation, trial, experiment, dare, stake, try one's luck
See also: CHALLENGE, DARE, GAMBLE, RISK, VENTURE

ADVERTISE
- We have the best advertised prices on
- This week's advertising feature
- The best advertised prices on
- If you do not wish to receive further advertising from us, please do the following
- This sale will not be advertised
- Advertise where buyers and sellers meet
- Red-hot advertising campaign
- Proof that it pays to advertise

- As advertised
- Watch for our advertised sales
- Come in for our advertised specials

Advertise: publicize, bill, announce, broadcast, make known, publish, declare, promulgate, proclaim, herald, trumpet, ballyhoo, advance, promote, push, call attention to, boast, vaunt, post, display, circulate, distribute, propagate, spread, scatter, disseminate, disperse, point out
See also: ANNOUNCE, PROMOTE, PROMOTION, SELL, SALE

ADVERTISING
- See how your advertising dollars compound
- Supercharge your advertising dollars
- Finally, advertising you can believe
- Make your advertising work twice as hard

ADVICE
- Advice directly from the top
- Here's just one word of advice
- We include expert advice
- Call our advice line anytime
- The best advice for smart folks like you
- You'll continue to get expert advice
- Get advice either in person or by phone
- We offer advice that meets your needs today
- If it's time for some advice, you can turn to us
- Great prices and friendly advice
- Here's just a little sage advice
- Count on us to provide focused, forward looking advice
- Where to find essential and free advice
- The most helpful buying advice
- When you're searching for advice you can rely on
- Information and advice you just won't find anywhere else
- Free technical advice when you need it, day or night
- You get straight advice you can trust
- Plenty of practical, reliable advice
- The kind of advice that saves you time and money
- Filled with ideas and advice to help you create

See also: COMMUNICATE, COUNSEL, CONSULT, EXPERT, GUIDANCE, HELP, INFORMATION, INSPIRE, IMPACT, PLAN, PRESENTATION, PROFESSIONAL, SCOOP, SELL, SHOW, WISDOM

ADVISE
- Will gladly advise you on choice
- When you need someone to advise you, come to us
- Advise us of your wishes

See also: CONSULT, WISDOM

AFFAIR
- Have a love affair with
- Not just a temporary affair
- The nation has been having an affair with our product for fifty years

See also: RELATIONSHIP, VENTURE

AFFORD
- Prices you can afford
- And you'll still be able to afford
- So easy to afford
- Now everyone can afford the best
- Okay, so you can't afford the most expensive

See also: GENERATE, MANAGE, MEANS, SUPPORT, SUPPLY

AFFORDABILITY
- This degree of prestige and affordability
- Tops for affordability
- Attracted by affordability, staying for the value
- If affordability is your first concern
- Affordability is a given

See also: BUDGET, COST, VALUE

AFFORDABLE
- More affordable than ever
- For the surprisingly affordable price
- Easy and affordable
- Far more affordable than you think
- Now made even more affordable
- Very affordable
- Firmly in the affordable price class
- Let us help you find the must suitable and affordable
- Not to mention, of course, more affordably

- That's how affordable it is to join
- Way more affordable than you expect
- Offering affordable peace of mind

See also: **BUDGET, CHEAP, INEXPENSIVE, VALUE**

AFOOT
- Great things are afoot
- When this kind of excitement is afoot how can anyone resist
- Tremendous savings are afoot
- Visit us to discover what thrilling changes are afoot

See also: **HAPPEN, PLAN**

AGAIN
- You'd definitely do it again
- We keep you coming back again and again, happy and satisfied
- We've done it again
- Once again we've outdone ourselves

See also: **DUPLICATE, REPEAT**

AGE
- It's a coming of age
- Is it time you came of age
- Regardless of age
- Appeals to any age
- Now that you've reached the age of wisdom
- Makes age disappear
- Youth is not a matter of age
- Reverse the aging process
- Whatever your age or ability
- Our most advanced age-fighting formula
- More for all ages
- Suitable for every age

Age: seniority, maturity, epoch, era, season, mature, ripen, mellow

See also: **ERA, MATURITY, TIME**

AGES
- Practised through the ages
- Wisdom of the ages is yours
- Cultures and customs of humankind through the ages

See also: **HISTORY, TIME**

AGREE
- You've got to agree
- We're sure you'll agree they're extra special

- Apparently, the rest of the country agrees
- I think you'll agree
- At last, something we can all agree on
- Once you've tried them, we think you'll agree
- We think you'll agree right away
- At last, style you can agree with

Agree: concur, harmonize, allow, approve, accept, consent, acknowledge, fit, conform, tally, go together

See also: **ACCORD, MATCH**

AGREEMENT
- A clear and concise agreement
- A far better agreement than
- In total agreement with your desires
- To quickly and easily come to the best agreement
- It's yours the moment you sign the agreement

See also: **ACCOMMODATION, ALLIANCE, CONTRACT, GUARANTEE**

AHEAD
- How to get ahead and save at the same time
- Helping you forge ahead
- Gives you more of what you need to get ahead
- Get ahead and stay ahead with
- Full steam ahead
- We're always looking ahead
- Here's a look at what you'll see in the weeks ahead
- And that's because we look ahead of the trends
- Light years ahead
- Before we get ahead of ourselves
- We began thinking ahead a long time ago
- When everything else is equal, our `product puts you ahead
- Light years ahead of the competition
- Putting you way ahead of the game

See also: **FIRST, FOREFRONT, FUTURE, LEADER**

AIM
- Aim higher
- We aim to please
- Taking dead aim at
- We know what you're aiming for
- Helping with all your aims

- Take aim at better performance

See also: GOAL, HIT, OBJECTIVE, TARGET, TASK

AIR

- Like a breath of fresh air
- Imparting an air of confidence and style
- Fresh and airy as ever
- We'll have you walking on air
- Give you such an air of distinction
- Give yourself some airs

ALERT

- Bargain alert
- Always alert to the possibilities
- Red alert for huge savings
- On the alert for
- Wake up sharp and alert

See also: COMMUNICATE, NEWS, NOTICE

ALIVE

- Become more radiantly alive
- So exciting it makes you glad you're alive
- Comes alive with pleasure
- Come alive to the promise
- When it 's so wonderful to be alive
- We'll have you feeling more alive than ever

Alive: living, active, vigorous, energetic, dynamic, busy, full of life, vital, vibrant, astir, animated, brisk, frisky, sprightly, spry, exciting, bubbling, sparkling, vivacious, zippy

See also: ENERGY, ENTHUSIASM, PASSION, POWER

ALL

- But that's not all
- If you think it's all or nothing – it is
- That's all there is to it
- For the person who wants it all
- That's all there is to it
- Yes, you can have it all
- It's all right here, waiting for you

See also: COMPLETE, EVERY, TOTAL

ALLIANCE

- Just about the smartest alliance you could make
- Alliances with the very best all across the

country
- With strategic alliances to win

See also: ACCOMMODATION, AGREEMENT, CLUB, GROUP, PARTNERSHIP, TEAM

ALLURE

- Makes a woman alluring
- Everyone has their own special allure
- Turning it into a very alluring idea
- Double your allure
- The allure is irresistible
- Gives you the secret of its legendary mystery and allure

See also: ATTRACTION, BEAUTY, CHARISMA, SEDUCTION

ALONE

- Instantly becomes yours alone
- You are not alone
- Why keep going it alone when you can call in the professionals
- Can virtually stand alone
- Success is rarely achieved alone
- Stand on the peak of success alone
- Alone in the field, we can do this

ALREADY

- If you don't have one already
- Already on its way to you
- You may already know how good our product is
- You might already qualify for

See also: NOW

ALTERNATIVE

- Can also offer you alternatives
- The affordable alternative
- Shouldn't you consider the alternative that's already been chosen by thousands of others
- A credible alternative to the usual leaders in the field
- The handy and secure alternative
- Now there's an alternative
- The truly simple alternative
- There simply is no alternative
- It's the only sensible alternative
- At last, a reasonable alternative
- Now, the perfect alternative is here
- Looking for an alternative
- Basic alternatives give you choice

See also: CHANGE, CHOICE, RAIN

CHECK, OPTION, PICK,
PREFERENCE, SELECTION

ALWAYS
- Always there when you need it
- Always on the job
- You know we're always ready
- Service you can always count on
- You can always turn to us
- Always looking out for you
- When it's for always

AMAZE
- It astounds and amazes you
- Continues to amaze us all
- Come and see our amazing stuff
- You'll be amazed at the quality
- Just how amazing is this

See also: MARVEL, SURPRISE,
WONDER

AMENITY
- In addition to the numerous other amenities normally associated with
- Behold a world of sophisticated amenities
- Providing you with all the amenities of a much larger
- The amenities most people really want
- The best amenities for you, our best customer

See also: COMFORT, CONVENIENCE,
FACILITY, PLEASURE, SERVICE

AMOK
- Running amok with delight
- Once you see the savings, you're liable to run amok
- Our price tags will make you think we've gone amok
- In this staid, boring corner, something has really gone amok

See also: CRAZY, NUTS

ANALYSE
- Takes the time to analyse
- After analysing and comparing hundreds
- Made for people who love to analyse

See also: CONSIDER, PLAN, THINK

ANALYSIS
- Free in-depth analysis
- Call today for your free analysis and

price quotation
- In the final analysis, you'll find we're the best

See also: GUIDANCE, HELP,
INFORMATION

ANGLE
- Angling in on
- We've got all the angles covered for you
- Consider all the angles on
- We always look at it from your angle
- What's your angle
- See from a brand new angle

See also: CHOICE, OPTION, PLAN,
TAKE

ANNOUNCE
- We are pleased to announce that
- The first to announce a reduction
- We are proud to announce
- Our company is delighted to announce that we are now offering
- Announcing big changes

See also: ADVERTISE, FLYER,
INFORM, NOTICE

ANNOUNCEMENT
- Here is an important announcement
- The announcement everyone's been waiting for
- Get ready for a stupendous announcement from

See also: COMMUNICATION,
INFORMATION, MESSAGE

ANOTHER
- Definitely not just another
- And we'll give you another one free
- You won't want to choose another product after you've seen ours
- You'll ask for another one right away

ANSWER
- You already know the answer
- Giving you a clear, unmistakable answer
- Because we're here to answer your questions
- The answer to all your woes
- Here's the best answer to
- Nobody knows the answer like we do
- We answer to you
- The fastest way to get the answer you're looking for

- Answering the big questions
- The answer is already in your hands
- When you need answers that work, look to us
- We have the answers to your questions
- We're making it a lot easier to get straight answers
- The place to go for answers to
- Giving you honest answers about
- We've got more answers than you have questions
- If you've got questions, we've got answers
- Get solid answers to all the questions you have about
- Answering dozens of the most frequently asked questions about
- Take the time to answer any questions you might have about
- Answer in plain and simple language
- We do have the answers you need about all your concerns
- Filled with straightforward answers

Answer: acknowledgement, confirmation, reply, response, return, solution, explanation, justification, reason, key, clue, satisfy
See also: APPROACH, ANALYSIS, INFORMATION, KEY, REASON, REPLY, RESPONSE, SOLUTION

ANTICIPATE
- It's time to anticipate that delicious feeling of
- Anticipate a high degree of satisfaction
- The more you anticipate it, the better it gets
- The most anticipated sale of the year

See also: AHEAD, FUTURE

ANXIOUS
- We are anxious to become
- Anxiously awaiting the newest breakthrough in
- No need to be anxious any more

See also: BUM, CONCERN, WORRY

ANYBODY
- Anybody can do it
- It isn't just anybody that can
- Almost anybody can create this
- Because you're not just anybody
- More than anybody else, we strive to

serve you
See also: PEOPLE

ANYTHING
- Anything goes
- Go anywhere, do anything
- Anything can happen with
- You can have anything you want
- Ask us anything

ANYWHERE
- Ready anywhere, anytime
- Anywhere there is a need
- Put it anywhere, watch it perform
- Goes anywhere you want
- Works anywhere

APART
- Another thing that sets us apart from other
- Together or apart, we're always ready to help
- Looking for something to set you apart
- Apart from the savings, there are many other reasons to

See also: UNIQUE

APOLOGIZE
- We apologize for the inconvenience
- No need to apologize
- Never apologize again

See also: GUILT, MISTAKE, REGRET, SORRY, WRONG

APPEAL
- There's no denying the subtle appeal
- Rich history and lasting appeal
- The perennial appeal of
- Surrender to the appeal of
- The real appeal lies in
- The appeal of breaking the rules
- Nothing could be more appealing than this

Appeal: attraction, attractiveness, interest, allure, charm, fascination, entice, invite, tempt
See also: ALLURE, ASK, ATTRACTIVE, ATTRACTION, BEAUTY, TEMPT

APPEAR
- Appears even larger and brighter
- Now you can choose how you want to appear

- Always appear at your best
- Appears as good as it is

APPEARANCE
- Can improve your appearance many times over
- Keeping up appearances is easier than ever
- Dramatically minimizes the appearance of
- Can greatly improve the appearance of
- Would you like a classic appearance
- Appearances can be deceiving
- Finally, performance that matches appearance

See also: ASPECT, FACE, FACADE, LOOK

APPETITE
- Will satisfy the hungriest appetite for
- The opportunity to indulge your appetite for playfulness and improvisation
- Will give you an appetite for the best
- Our appetite for change and improvement is endless

APPLICATION
- After only one application, you'll see a big difference
- Your application will be accepted immediately
- Gives you a huge choice of applications
- All you have to do is make application

See also: FUNCTION, USE

APPLY
- Plus, you can apply right over the phone
- Easy to apply
- We really apply ourselves to serve
- Once you apply it, you'll never again go back to
- You're invited to apply
- Apply for yours today by calling
- Apply early to avoid the rush

See also: USE, UTILIZE

APPOINTMENT
- Book an appointment now
- Call today for your appointment or walk in anytime
- You appointment is waiting
- No appointment needed
- Same-day appointments guaranteed

- By appointment only
- One appointment you can't afford to miss
- Book an appointment and we'll set it all up for you

See also: CONSULT, MEET

APPRECIATE
- We appreciate you
- A price you'll appreciate
- You'll appreciate the outstanding quality
- Appreciate the savings for years to come
- It's all about appreciating the little things in life
- You'll appreciate the value
- For those who appreciate the best
- To show how much we appreciate your patronage
- We deeply appreciate your patronage
- We appreciate your business and wish you every happiness
- A way to show just how much we appreciate your consideration
- The faster your life moves, the more you'll appreciate

See also: SECTION FIVE, SAYING THANKS

APPRECIATION
- A growing appreciation is developing
- Appreciation changes and increases
- Just one more way to show our appreciation for your business
- There's never a better time to express our appreciation
- In appreciation of our continued association
- Showing a keen appreciation for
- This is the kind of appreciation you get when you come to us for
- Constant appreciation in value is only one benefit of

Appreciation: recognition, thanks, comprehension, gratitude, thankfulness, thanksgiving, acknowledgement, tribute, praise, applause
See also: CELEBRATION, GRATITUDE, LOYALTY, THANKS, TRIBUTE

APPROACH
- A rational, balanced approach
- An approach that loudly declares
- A completely different approach to

- A safe, effective approach
- We offer a dynamic new approach to
- Learn more about our disciplined approach
- A very rational approach
- Ultimately, our risk-averse approach pays off big time for you
- Finding the approach that works best for your needs

See also: ANSWER, DIRECTION

APPROVAL
- Held up for your approval
- We get your approval for every step
- You approval is our license to sell
- Meeting your approval in every way

See also: APPRECIATION, ENDORSEMENT, TESTIMONIAL

AREA
- Serving your area with complete coverage
- You won't find a better in the whole area
- This is one area where we can't be beaten
- An entire area devoted to
- In this area we're tops

AROUND
- What goes around, comes around
- We'll still be around when the others have faded away
- Look around you and compare

See also: ENVIRONMENT

ARRANGE
- Makes it so simple to arrange
- We can arrange it while you wait
- Takes only a very short time to arrange
- We can also arrange everything from
- You'll be surprised at how quickly we can arrange

See also: ORDER, ORGANIZE, PLAN

ARRANGEMENT
- For the sake of comfortable arrangements
- We make all the arrangements for you, no matter how complex
- What better arrangement than this
- For the kind of arrangement you want

See also: PLAN, SYSTEM

ARRAY
- Available in a wide array of colors and textures
- Come and see our lavish array of
- Offering an interesting array of
- Choose from a vast array of
- Add to this our astonishing array of choices

See also: CHOICE, RANGE, DISPLAY

ARRIVAL
- Intriguing new arrivals from around the world
- Announcing the arrival of
- The minute our new arrivals get here
- An arrival worth waiting for
- Includes new arrivals

See also: APPEARANCE

ARRIVE
- Has just now arrived in our store
- Now you can be here when they arrive
- For those people who have finally arrived
- Arriving just in time for your
- Show the world you've finally arrived

See also: HIT

ART
- Mastering the art under the expert guidance of
- The delicate art of
- Always state of the art
- We've turned this service into an art
- An impressive work of art created by

See also: CRAFT, SKILL

ASK
- We ask you what your needs are
- Yours for the asking – free of charge
- If you don't see it, please ask
- Ask for our full-color brochure
- Remember to ask about
- Just ask our helpful staff
- What more could you ask
- The only thing you'll need to ask for is
- Funny you should ask
- Ask about our new reward program
- Ask for it by name
- Ask about how you can get
- For complete details, ask or visit
- We asked you how we're doing
- Plus – be sure to ask about
- The names smart shoppers ask for

Ask: inquire, query, question, request,

petition, plead, apply to , turn to, solicit, clamour for, beg, beseech, supplicate, entreat, implore, cry to, demand, call for, invite, beckon, test, pump, grill, expect, count on, require, order, command, inspire, encourage, induce
See also: COMMAND, DEMAND, QUESTION, REQUIRE

ASPECT
- Fascinating look at every imaginable aspect
- Introducing a luxurious aspect to any
- And this is only one aspect of
- From whatever aspect you look at it
- The increasingly exciting aspects of

See also: APPEARANCE, DETAIL, FACT, LOOK, PARTICULAR

ASSET
- Protect your assets
- Turn your problems into assets
- The biggest asset is you
- Sit back and watch your assets grow

See also: BENEFIT, PROFIT

ASSIST
- We will be happy to assist you
- We have assisted thousands to
- Standing ready to assist you at any moment
- If we can assist you in any way
- Tell us how we may assist you
- We'd love to assist you in

See also: HELP, SERVE

ASSISTANCE
- That's why you can reach us for immediate assistance
- We're talking hands-on assistance here
- Providing you with personal assistance
- Assistance before you even ask for it
- Whatever assistance you need, we are ready to provide

Assistance: help, aid, boost, relief, service, benefit, lift, protection, friendship, backing, care, helping hand, sustenance, advocacy, sponsorship, advancement
See also: COMFORT, HELP

ASSOCIATE
- Our associates can help you find
- Just call one of our expert associates
- We have trained associates to help you whenever you wish
- Our associates are the best in the business
- Our sales associates are fully trained to answer all your questions
- Become an associate in one easy step
- Our fully-trained associates are eager to help
- Just ask an associate for anything you need or desire

See also: CONSULTANT, EXPERT, FRIEND, PROFESSIONAL, SALESPERSON, STAFF

ASSORTMENT
- A fabulous assortment of
- We offer a full assortment of
- Save on our complete assortment of
- Offering an assortment of delectable products
- You'll find a stunning assortment
- A diverse assortment rolled into one
- Have just the assortment you want

See also: BLEND, MIX, SELECTION, SPECTRUM, VARIETY

ASSURANCE
- Your absolute assurance that
- Gain more self assurance
- Your assurance of quality and care
- Just one more comforting assurance
- Our name is your best assurance

See also: CERTAINTY, CONFIDENCE, GUARANTEE, WARRANTY

ASSURE
- You'll also be strongly assured of
- Rest assured that the very best
- You can always be assured that
- One look will assure you

See also: CERTAINTY, GUARANTEE

ATHLETIC
- For the athletic types
- Sleek and athletic, just like you
- And for the more athletic among you

See also: OUTDOORS, SPORT

ATMOSPHERE
- An unassuming, comfortable atmosphere
- An unexpectedly relaxing atmosphere

- Embracing an intimate atmosphere of
- Add lots of atmosphere with
- Above all, the atmosphere is one of refinement and sophistication
- Famous for its friendly atmosphere
- Splendid atmosphere of joy and mutual understanding
- An atmosphere of casual elegance and privacy

Atmosphere: environment, medium, milieu, setting, surroundings, mood, ambiance, air, sphere, tone, aura, tenor, character, spirit, temper, feeling, vibration, vibes, sense
See also: CLIMATE, SPIRIT

ATTACH

- It's easy to get attached to
- Comes with a guarantee of quality attached
- We know you attach a lot of importance to this issue
- The accessories are so easy to attach

See also: ACCESSORY, ADD

ATTACK

- To quickly neutralize the attack
- Guarding you against attacks
- When you're having an attack of
- Attacking the problem from all directions
- No longer need fear an attack
- Attacks your problems head on
- Always on the attack
- Guards you against every kind of attack

See also: BATTLE, FIGHT, WAR

ATTENTION

- Someone has finally paid attention to the fact that
- Nothing draws attention like a
- Getting a lot of attention right now
- Enjoy a level of personal attention that surpasses anything you've previously experienced
- At last, getting the attention you deserve
- The product that's getting all the attention this year
- Lets you focus your full attention on
- Requires very little attention
- Starting to attract a lot of attention
- Because that's how you get attention
- And give you welcome added attention
- Your timely attention will be greatly

appreciated
- All statements and inquiries should be directed to the attention of
- Please turn your attention to

Attention: awareness, heed, mindfulness, consciousness, concentration, scrutiny, publicity, consideration, public eye, spotlight, deference, respect, regard
See also: CONCERN, INTEREST

ATTITUDE

- You could use an attitude adjustment
- We've got the proper attitude
- It takes more than the right attitude
- Lose that by-the-book attitude
- It's attitude that counts
- Along with it comes a whole new attitude
- We give you some attitude

ATTRACT

- Will attract you instantly
- When you want to attract the opposite sex discreetly
- Choose the one you're attracted to most
- It's what attracted you in the first place
- Attracting customers in droves

See also: BECKON, CALL, DRAW, URGE

ATTRACTION

- The list of attractions is as diverse as it is long
- Here's what the big attraction is
- Offering more attractions for less money
- Give in to the attraction
- Feel an irresistible attraction drawing you into its spell
- At our place, you are the main attraction

Attraction: interest, fascination, charm, magnetism, allure, enticement, temptation, enchantment, bewitchment, witchery, glamour, captivation, seduction, draw
See also: APPEAL, BEAUTY, INTEREST, SEDUCTION

ATTRACTIVE

- Because we're offering extremely attractive
- Look as attractive as you feel
- When you want to be at your most attractive
- A very attractive offer

● You can be even more attractive with

Attractive: pleasing, appealing, charming, engaging, winsome, winning, fascinating, interesting, captivating, enchanting, bewitching, inviting, enticing, alluring, tempting, seductive, delightful, pleasant, agreeable, dainty, pretty, cute, sweet, fetching, stunning, beautiful, lovely, good looking, flattering, enjoyable, delectable

AUSTERITY

● There's a cool austerity to this year's hottest designs
● You don't have to go on an austerity program to take advantage of
● Projecting a lean, stripped-down austerity
● A little awed by the imposing austerity

See also: BUDGET, THRIFT

AUTHENTIC

● Historically authentic
● One look tells you it's authentic
● The only genuinely authentic product on the market
● When authenticity really counts

See also: GENUINE, REAL

AUTHORITY

● A leading authority on
● Make your move with authority
● Speaking with authority
● Each one of our representatives is an authority

See also: EXPERT, PROFESSIONAL

AUTOMATE

● Fully automated
● Automate your entire business
● Our new automated process
● Fast and automated for same-day service

AUTOMATIC

● After that, everything is almost automatic
● Approval is automatic
● You will automatically receive all the benefits of
● In this uncertain world, nothing is automatic except

AVAILABLE

● Available only at one location
● Available only through
● They're already available in our spring collection
● All items featured here are available at
● Products exclusively available at
● Available in a wide range of
● This quality product is available exclusively through your local dealer
● It's all available right now at
● Now available at an unbelievable low price including
● Quite simply the most comprehensive set available
● Not available in all markets
● Now available to our elite customers
● Available for a limited time only
● Only available until
● The finest available anywhere
● Available anywhere in the country

Available: handy, of service, usable, on hand, accessible, on tap, convenient, reachable, at one's fingertips, on command

See also: ACCESSIBLE, READY

AVOID

● Avoid costly errors
● Helping you avoid added expense
● Here's away to avoid those dreadful

See also: ESCAPE, PREVENT

AWAIT

● As eagerly awaited as
● Come see what thrills await you
● Could you have guessed such wonders await

See also: EXPECT, WAIT

AWARD

● With award-winning service, year after year
● Consistently winning industry and consumer awards
● With our reputation, awards come easily
● Nobody has won more awards than

See also: APPRECIATE, EARN

AWARENESS

● Raising awareness in all fronts
● Awareness of our product has been steadily increasing
● By now, awareness is penetrating the farthest corners

See also: COMMUNICATION,
EDUCATION

AWAY
- Now you can really get away from it all
- Helping you get away in style
- Take away all the frippery and here's what you get
- By far and away the best

See also: ESCAPE, GONE, VACATION

BABY
- For all your baby needs
- Your baby is so important
- Baby yourself for once
- No one is more important than your beautiful new baby
- So simple even a baby could use it

Baby: infant, newborn, babe, toddler, tot, tiny top, preschooler, juvenile, adolescent

See also: CHILD, FAMILY, KID, YOUNG

BACK
- Backed by one of the strongest
- It's back, bigger and better
- Now you can pat yourself on the back
- If you're not satisfied, send it back

- It's back
- Now there's no need to hold back
- We're willing to back it one hundred percent
- We're back
- Great prices are back
- Bound to keep you coming back for more
- You'll always come back to
- You also get the confidence of being backed by

See also: GUARANTEE, RETURN, SUPPORT

BACK-TO-SCHOOL
- Hundreds of back-to-school savings
- In the great rush for back-to-school shopping
- Back-to-school and back to basics
- It's back-to-school time again
- Beat the back-to-school blues

BACK UP
- Always gives you a back up plan
- Backed up with solid service

- Count on us for back up when the going gets tough

See also: ALTERNATIVE. SUPPORT

BACKYARD
- Excellence right in our own backyard
- Look no further than your own backyard
- Turn your backyard into a
- Backyard convenience
- As comfortable as your own back yard

See also: COMMUNITY, HOME, NEIGHBORHOOD

BALANCE
- A wonderful balance of form and function
- Generates balance and endurance
- Striking the right balance
- We balance your needs against your
- When you want a balanced approach
- Helping you keep your balance

Balance: poise, equilibrium, aplomb, steadiness, assurance, confidence, coolness, common sense, wisdom

See also: CONSIDER, MEDIUM

BALL
- Keeping your eye on the ball
- To keep you from getting all balled up
- Making sure you're on the ball
- Don't end up behind the eight ball
- The ball is in your court now
- Your invitation to the ball

BANDWAGON
- Time to jump on the bandwagon
- Not just another bandwagon
- Hey, the bandwagon is here

See also: JOIN

BANK
- Bank on us
- Buy our product and put all your savings in the bank
- You'll be laughing all the way to the bank
- It's just like money in the bank
- Watch your bank account fill up fast

See also: DEPEND, RELY, TRUST

BARBEQUE
- Here's how to make your barbeque sizzle

- Now that barbeque season has finally arrived
- Gather round the barbeque and enjoy
- Everything you need to barbeque all summer long
- As casual as a July barbeque

BARGAIN

- Walk away with a bargain
- You can always find a bargain
- The biggest bargain ever
- Bargains galore in our store
- The everyday bargain shop
- It could be the bargain of the century
- Bargain hunters' paradise
- When you're hunting bargains, the chase is half the fun
- It's a real bargain, no kidding
- Top quality at bargain basement prices
- Bargain, anyone
- The best bargain you'll find for miles
- It's not a bargain if it doesn't do what you want it to
- Where you love to shop for bargains

Bargain: agreement, understanding, contract, settlement, bond, discount, reduction, good deal, buy, giveaway, steal, barter, trade, swap, traffic, peddle, vend, sell, exchange, dicker
See also: DEAL, OPPORTUNITY

BARGOON

- Big, big bargoons
- Bargoons for everyone
- Hunt yourself up a real bargoon
- Bop, bop, bargooneroony

BARRIER

- Breaks the price barrier too
- Surmounting just about any barrier
- Provides a natural barrier to protect
- Now all the barriers are gone
- There's no barrier any more to
- Everywhere, barriers are coming down

See also: CHALLENGE, OBSTACLE

BASE

- We're based here because
- Building from a strong base
- Our base is wide and deep
- Helping to establish a firm base
- Has become a thriving base for

See also: FOUNDATION, ROOT

BASH

- How to make your bash a smash
- Come to our big price bash
- Watch us bash the competition

See also: EVENT, OCCASION, PARTY, SALE, SPREE

BASIC

- Basic to every program we back
- When you're looking for something basic
- Starting with your basic needs
- So many options to add to the basic plan

Basic: primary, meat-and-potatoes, vital, radical, elementary, underlying, intrinsic, supporting, substantive, necessary
See also: AFFORDABLE, ESSENTIAL, FUNDAMENTAL, NECESSITY, NEED, STAPLE

BASICS

- Back to basics
- Better basics for you
- First, we get the basics right
- The best priced basics
- Return to basics for
- Start with the basics
- Have all gone back to the basics by

See also: BOTTOM LINE, FOUNDATION

BATTLE

- Let the next battle we win be yours
- Now you no longer need to battle
- Getting the best needn't be a battle

See also: ATTACK, FIGHT, RESIST, STRIVE, WAR

BEAT

- We'll beat any current advertised price
- We'll meet and beat any lower prices
- We haven't missed a beat
- You can't beat our
- Our prices can never be beat
- We will beat any advertised price by

See also: CONQUER

BEAUTIFUL

- We can help make it beautiful
- Beautiful choices for beautiful people
- As beautiful as it is useful

- Just happens to be the most beautiful
- Be more beautiful than ever before
- Beautiful things always fill you with delight
- So beautiful the world stops in its tracks
- Giving form to a beautiful idea

Beautiful: comely, attractive, handsome, lovely, becoming, eye-filling, good-looking, shapely, glamorous, sexy, charming, engaging, captivating, enthralling, enchanting, alluring, fascinating, winsome, winning, bewitching, enticing, tempting, seductive, ravishing, personable, pleasant, divine, elegant, graceful, artistic, dainty, delicate, exquisite, superb, matchless, gorgeous, first-class, first-rate, dazzling, radiant, resplendent, shining, lustrous
See also: ALLURE, ATTRACTIVE, HANDSOME, LOVELY, SEXY

BEAUTIFY

- Does more than beautify
- Guaranteed to beautify your
- For those who want to beautify
- One of the most beautiful cities in
- You too can do even more to beautify your home

Beautify: adorn, improve, grace, prettify, smarten, dress up, embellish, elaborate, enhance, heighten, set off, enrich, sweeten, ornament, bedeck, deck, deck out, array, decorate, emblazon, furbish, restore, doll up, dude up, preen
See also: BETTER, IMPROVE

BEAUTY

- Gives years of lasting beauty
- Treat yourself to unsurpassed beauty
- And the beauty of it is
- Rediscover your own natural beauty
- Provides a more concentrated beauty
- The beauty that lasts a lifetime
- Adds beauty and elegance
- Add exciting new warmth and beauty
- Combines natural beauty with the finest in service
- Lasting beauty, lasting enjoyment
- We create beauty year round
- Order this versatile beauty today
- The unabashed beauty of
- Discover the beauty of the night
- Give the gift of exquisite beauty

- Truly capturing the beauty of
- Taking care of your inner beauty too
- Real beauty comes from within
- Order today and enjoy colorful, carefree beauty at its best
- When you want lasting beauty

See also: ALLURE, ATTRACTION, BEAUTIFUL, CHARM

BECKON

- Beckoning you to
- When the far horizon beckons
- See the bargains beckoning to you
- An irresistible temptation is beckoning to you

See also: ATTRACT, CALL, DRAW, URGE

BEEF

- Beef it up
- Whatever your beef is about, we can take care of it
- Our new, beefed-up operation puts muscle into
- Now you can do more than listen to them beef

See also: ADD, COMPLAINT, CONCERN, IMPROVE

BEFORE

- No matter what you've tried before
- Never before has there been such a
- Even if you've never done it before, it's so easy
- Before you even look at another choice
- Before you choose, see us

BEGIN

- To begin with
- So before you begin, visit us
- One very smart way to begin is to
- We help you begin and keep you on track
- We always begin with you
- Always begin with the best

See also: INITIATIVE, START

BEGINNER

- Perfect for beginners
- Cash in on beginner's luck
- Even if you're just a beginner, you can do it easily
- We cater to beginners
- Beginners need not fear

- Go from beginner to expert in record time

Beginner: neophyte, novice, tyro, amateur, rookie, newcomer, initiator

BEGINNING
- It's beginning to dawn on people that
- And this is just the beginning
- More than merely a great beginning
- A scrumptious beginning
- With you from beginning to end
- Low prices are only the beginning
- From such modest beginnings

See also: DAWN, NEW, FRESH, START

BEHIND
- Everybody is behind you
- Behind you all the way
- Put your problems behind you
- When you're feeling a little behind, we can help
- So that you'll never get behind in

See also: BOOST, HELP, SUPPORT

BELIEF
- Belief that only a woman can truly understand
- It's one of our core beliefs that
- Firmly founded on the belief that
- More than just a belief
- Always in tune with your beliefs
- If you subscribe to these beliefs, we're the folks you want to come to

See also: FEELING, IDEA, OPINION, PHILOSOPHY, PRINCIPLE

BELIEVE
- You just gotta believe
- Yes, we firmly believe that anyone can do it
- It's hard to believe that
- Standing together for the things we believe
- Now you know who to believe
- At our company, we believe
- Let us help you believe
- Standing tall for what you believe
- Helping you believe in yourself even more
- Seeing is believing
- You won't believe it until you actually come and see for yourself

- It's something we all believe in
- When it comes right down to the things you believe in
- Talk to the people who believe in you
- We have always believed in offering the best

See also: THINK, UNDERSTAND

BELIEVER
- I'm a believer
- We'll turn you into a believer
- Believers flock to the source
- Join thousands of new believers in
- You don't have to be a believer to try

See also: FAN, FOLLOW

BENCHMARK
- Establishes a new benchmark within
- We've always been the benchmark
- Benchmark products and benchmark services
- The test of a real benchmark has always been
- Benchmark performance

See also: MEASURE, STANDARD

BENEFIT
- To benefit for as long as possible
- Shop with us and double your benefits
- Pleased to enrol you for this valuable benefit
- Both benefits are automatic
- Benefits and privileges include
- Excited to introduce you to a new benefit
- Allows you to benefit more from every purchase you make
- Also enjoy a number of premium benefits
- Benefits quickly add up
- For an outline of benefits available, please see our brochure
- Additional benefits for as low as
- As someone who understands the benefits of
- Imagine these exciting benefits
- Another nice benefit is
- You'll be bowled over by the extra benefits
- You could benefit quickly from
- One more hidden benefit becomes obvious when
- Its benefits are far more profound that any such product on the market to date
- Just one more added benefit available

through
- Yet another direct benefit comes from
- Something that can benefit everyone
- Outstanding benefits for years to come
- The most benefits for both of you
- Of course you'll enjoy the same benefits as before
- Including benefits usually reserved for top executives
- You too can benefit from
- You'll also get many other exceptional benefits
- And money-saving financial benefits
- Benefits that go far beyond
- The benefits are endless
- The benefits add up daily
- More benefits for you and your family with only a little
- Just add up the terrific benefits
- Only a few years ago, nobody could have imagined benefits like these
- And tons of other fabulous benefits
- With it come the benefits you want
- Provides benefits right from the start

Benefit: advantage, well-being, betterment, improvement, advancement, promotion, gain, help, aid, service, profit, advance, assist, contribute to
See also: ADVANTAGE, BLESSING, FEATURE, HELP, IMPROVE

BEST
- The best for everyone
- When only the best will do
- Bringing the best to you
- Doing whatever it takes to bring you the best
- Find the one that's best for you
- Inspired every day to be the best
- The best has gotten even better
- The biggest, fastest and best can be found right here
- For those who desire only the best
- You'll know instantly it's the best
- And best of all
- Best in the industry
- Settle for nothing less than the best
- Be sure you have the best
- The best for your peace of mind
- You deserve the very best
- Next best thing to
- The best thing since

- The best is not the most expensive
- Our best ever selection of
- The best deals are at
- The best in town
- We've saved the best for you
- Bringing you the very best available
- Best of all
- Why let it get the best of you
- Don't let it get the best of you
- Simply the best
- One of the very best things about it is
- You want the best for yourself and your family
- Serving the best since
- Get our best deal ever
- Very simply, the best savings we've ever offered
- The best of all possible worlds
- The best you've ever seen

Best: excellent, unexcelled, unparalleled, unsurpassed, fine, superfine, first-class, first-rate, crack, superior, choice, select, top, tip-top, tops, paramount, capital, outstanding, foremost, preeminent, venerable, highest, peerless, perfect, superlative, consummate, pure, genuine, sterling, gilt-edged, sound, wholesome, golden, advantageous, best-suited, right, correct, fitting, apt, enviable, covetable, supreme
See also: CHOICE, EXCELLENCE, PREMIUM, SUPERIOR, TOP

BEST-SELLER
- Catapulted into best-seller position
- A real best-seller
- We have more best-sellers in one location than any other
See also: LEADER, TOP

BEST-SELLING
- Has been the best-selling product in its class for years
- There's a good reason why this product has become the best-selling phenomenon it is
- This is our best-selling product

BET
- Your best bet for total satisfaction
- We're betting on you to
- All bets are off
- Bet on your best instincts

- You don't have to bet any more
- When half the country is betting on us we can't afford to

See also: CHOICE, DARE, GAMBLE, GUESS, OPTION

BETTER

- Better service and better results
- Better by miles
- Two are better than one
- Nobody knows it better than us
- Products that let you make better use of
- Nobody does it better
- Better than anything else
- It just keeps getting better and better
- And its gets even better
- By making better things, we are making things better
- Better performance, better value
- For better or for worse
- And that makes us feel a whole lot better too
- This better enables us to
- Usually do better for
- Brighter, bolder, better than ever
- Our best selling product just got better
- We're always one better
- Now we have a better way to
- Doesn't get any better than this
- We get better every year
- You can't get a better product than
- Gets better and better by the day

See also: BEST, DIFFERENCE, IMPROVE, SUPERIOR

BIG

- No matter how big we get, we never forget to
- The big one is here
- Be a part of something really big
- Bigger, better, cheaper
- Don't have to be big to be better
- Our biggest yet
- It's not just big that counts
- Gets even bigger
- Time to join the big girls
- Too big to stay a secret any longer
- We've just gotten bigger than ever

Big: large, huge, enormous, giant, whacking, prodigious, immense, colossal, monstrous, gigantic, tremendous, towering, great, vast, extensive, voluminous, grand, grandiose, majestic, august, massive, gargantuan, significant, weighty,

See also: GIANT, LARGE

BILL

- Really fills the bill
- We'll gladly bill you
- No more outrageous bills
- We'll bill you later – after you've decided
- You won't faint when you see the bill

See also: COST, DEMAND, INSTALLMENT, NEED, PAYMENT

BITE

- Don't worry, it won't bite
- At last, something with real bite to it
- Don't let problems bite into your profits
- Don't let trouble put the bite on you
- Take a bite out of

See also: ATTACK, FIGHT

BLAHS

- Beat the beauty blahs
- Blahs begone
- Banish the blahs
- Do you find you have the blahs
- Chase the blahs from you life

BLAST

- Prepare for a blast
- A big blast of value
- Blast-off with
- Come and have a blast
- Rocked by a blast of real flavor

See also: BLITZ, HIT, STRIKE

BLEND

- Creates a unique product by blending the best of each
- Built for easy blending
- A contagious blend of
- A unique blend of
- Won't just blend in
- Conspicuous blend designed to stand out
- Blends in beautifully with any
- Be sure to try our special blend of
- Seasoned with a delicate blend of
- Each blend contains a unique
- An affordable blend of luxury and performance

See also: COMBINE, INTEGRATE, MIX

BLESSING
- Will make you count your blessings
- And an even bigger blessing still is
- A blessing we don't think about very often

See also: ADVANTAGE, BENEFIT

BLINK
- Quick as the blink of an eye
- Be with you in a blink
- Will have you blinking in disbelief

See also: FAST

BLITZ
- Sales blitz
- The blitz is on
- The blitz is about to hit
- You've been blitzed

See also: BLAST, BLOWOUT, EFFORT, SALE

BLOCKBUSTER
- Look inside for more blockbuster savings
- A real blockbuster of a sale
- A blockbuster is coming

See also: BIG, GIANT

BLOOM
- In full bloom
- Blooming with values
- And then just watch yourself bloom
- Sure puts some bloom in your cheeks

See also: BOOM, EXPAND

BLOSSOM
- Rapidly blossoming into
- What started out small has really blossomed
- Blossoming into a beautiful young woman

BLOW OUT
- Value blow out
- Don't miss our summer blow out sale
- Blow out prices
- Blow out values rocking the whole industry
- The biggest blow out of all

See also: BLITZ, OPPORTUNITY, PROMOTION, SALE

BLUE
- Right out of the blue

- Chase away the blues with
- You don't have to be blue any longer
- The excitement of just blue-skying it

BLUEPRINT
- Your blueprint for
- Turned the blueprints upside down
- A step-by-step blueprint for success

See also: PLAN

BOARD
- Get on board now at the start
- Board the progress express
- Everyone's jumping on board

See also: JOIN

BOAST
- Boasts some of the finest
- Soon you'll be boasting about
- It's no idle boast that
- Even if you don't want to boast
- Nothing else boasts so many choices

See also: BRAG, CELEBRATE, PRIDE

BODY
- Proud of a healthy, toned body
- A highly responsive extension of your mind and body
- Just look at our body of achievements
- A wide range of body enjoyment
- Turn your body over to the joys of
- You'll feel your body responding

See also: ATHLETIC, FIT, SKIN

BOIL
- Excitement has reached a rolling boil
- A hot concept coming to a boil
- Our creative juices are on the boil
- Something to get your blood boiling

BOND
- Bonded, licensed and insured for your peace of mind
- Break the bonds of
- Bonded into an unbreakable unity
- It's our bond to you
- Employees are insured and bonded for your protection
- The bond will be instant
- No more bonds to hold you back

See also: CLICK, GUARANTEE, PROMISE, WORD

BONUS
- Plus a special bonus offer
- Free blockbuster bonus
- Another added bonus is
- Welcome bonus for all new customers
- You'll receive a free bonus of
- Get your extra bonus instantly
- Get one of our most popular products plus this great bonus

Bonus: reward, award, prize, gift, present, endowment, largess, freebie, dividend, extra, plus, surplus, gain, fringe benefit, prerequisite, perk, compensation, recompense, remuneration, emolument, repayment, premium, bounty, inducement, encouragement, stimulation, bribe, bait, payment, pay off, jackpot
See also: **EXTRA, GIFT, PREMIUM**

BOOK
- We wrote the book on
- Book now to ensure your place
- We go by the book
- Look in the book to find us
- For real assurance, book ahead
See also: **INFORMATION, RESERVE**

BOOM
- Grab your part of the boom in
- Join a booming industry
- Business is booming
- The biggest boom ever has just hit town
- Boom times are here

Boom: progress, prosper, thrive, flourish, luxuriate, burgeon, mushroom, explode, spring up, burst forth, rise, grow, increase, gain, add to
See also: **GROW, INCREASE**

BOOST
- With a little boost from
- We give you the boost you need
- Boosts performance amazingly
- Often it only takes the smallest boost to help you
See also: **ASSIST, CRANK, HELP, OVERDRIVE, PROMOTE**

BORN
- Born with it
- Born to succeed
- Some people are just born to be the best

- and you're one of them
- For those of you who weren't born yesterday
- You don't have to be born with the ability
- Born to win
- Now do what you were born for

BOSS
- Be your own boss
- Now no one can boss you around any more
- With us, you're the boss
- The best boss is yourself
- No more bosses to keep you jumping
See also: **COMMAND, LEADER**

BOTH
- Now you can have the best of both
- For the both of you
- Both of you will want to try it
- Both are winners

BOTTOM
- Got you covered from top to bottom
- Let's start from the bottom
- A complete overhaul from the bottom up
- Start on the bottom and work your way up
See also: **END, FINISH, LESS**

BOTTOM LINE
- Concentrate on the most important bottom line of all
- Because results are the bottom line
- The truth always shows up in the bottom line
- Translates into a strong bottom line
- Nothing does more for your bottom line than the right people with the right skills to get the job done
- The bottom line is your top priority
See also: **BASIC, PROFIT**

BOUNDARY
- Pushing the boundaries of taste
- No one crosses your boundaries
- Boundaries just melt away
- Leaping boldly over the old boundaries
See also: **EDGE, END, LIMIT**

BOUNTY
- A bounty that finds its way into all our

- Beauty from the bounty of
- The bounty of the land comes right into your home
- Coming to you from the bounty of
- Bounty enough for everyone

See also: **BONUS, GIFT, PLENTY, PROFIT**

BRACING

- The gently bracing quality of
- Bracing as a brisk, bright morning in spring
- Gives a bracing boost just when you really need it
- Savor the bracing tang of

BRAG

- Pardon us for bragging
- Giving you something to brag about
- Our bragging days have just begun
- Our customers are bragging about

See also: **BOAST, CELEBRATE, PRIDE**

BRAIN

- Brain power is featured
- The brains of the operation
- First, we use our brains
- The most brain power per square yard
- Now, more brains than brawn

See also: **INTELLIGENT, SMART**

BRAND

- The most reliable brand to look for is
- Thousands of different name brand products in stock
- Save on all our brand name products
- Brand names, low prices
- The kind of national brand quality you can trust
- We stock only the quality brand names
- Top quality brand names in
- Your value brand
- National brand quality at our great prices
- Bringing your more famous brands
- Brand names for less
- The brands you want
- Best brands available
- Put your trust in a brand doctors have been recommending
- We carry all brand name products
- More famous brands
- Great quality, brand names
- You'll find most popular brand name products
- Great savings on these great brands
- The brands kids love
- Carries all top brand names
- Amazing savings on best brands
- Nationwide, we sell only the best brands
- When it comes to customer loyalty and satisfaction, no other brand comes even close
- Name brand materials only
- Great prices on brand names
- Put your brand on it now

See also: **KIND, NAME, SORT**

BREAK

- Take a break from your daily routine and visit us today
- Give yourself that well-deserved break in your day
- Visit us for a great break on your
- You worked hard for this break
- Today you finally get your big break
- Take a break with something you can relate to
- Break out now
- Make the break
- Break away to freedom
- This time, you get the breaks

See also: **ESCAPE, REWARD**

BREAKAWAY

- Treat yourself to a breakaway today
- Breakaway prices let you break out of your doldrums
- For your biggest breakaway ever

BREAKFAST

- Breakfast doesn't have to be boring
- Gather round for a scrumptious breakfast
- A breakfast worth getting up for
- Eats competitors for breakfast

See also: **COOK, DINE, EAT, MEAL**

BREAKTHROUGH

- A technological breakthrough
- Dramatic new breakthrough
- We make the breakthroughs first
- This could be your big breakthrough
- The biggest breakthrough in a hundred years
- Showing you our breakthroughs in design and performance

See also: **ACHIEVEMENT, ADVANCE,**

INFORMATION, LEAP, PROGRESS, RESEARCH, STRIDE

BREATH
- Eventually, you have to catch your breath
- We'll take your breath away
- Giving you a chance to catch your breath
- You'll catch your breath at your first sight of
- The only thing more breathtaking than
- For a real breath of fresh air

BREATHE
- Breathe a little easier with
- Gives you room to breathe
- Just breathe deeply and relax
- Now you can breathe again
- Wins you real breathing space

BREED
- A forward-looking breed
- A whole new breed has just thundered over our horizon
- A breed with a wild streak
- Are you part of a different breed

See also: **KIND, SORT, SPECIES**

BREEZE
- Breezing their way into your life
- Light as a summer breeze
- Lets you breeze right through
- With our help, it'll be a breeze
- Breezing through what used to take hours

See also: **EASY, SIMPLE**

BRING
- We are pleased to bring you
- Want to bring you a delightful surprise
- Bringing you only the best
- Nobody brings you better
- Bringing you for the very first time

See also: **CARRY, PRODUCE, PROVIDE**

BROCHURE
- Present this brochure at a participating location
- Also includes an information brochure
- Call today for our in-depth brochure
- Be sure to pick up a brochure
- Details in the accompanying brochure

See also: **ADVERTISE, FLYER, INFORMATION**

BROKE
- Go from broke to
- Go for broke
- You'll never end up broke if you follow these principles
- If it ain't broke, don't fix it
- Come in even if you're broke
- You don't have to be broke any more
- Tired of being broke all the time

BROWSE
- Drop by to browse through
- Come in and browse
- You're always welcome just to browse
- You'd be surprised what you'll find just by browsing
- Browse as long as you wish
- Browse through and find valuable information

See also: **CHOOSE, LOOK, SEE**

BUCK
- Making the best use of your hard-earned bucks
- Buck buster
- Looking for someone who bucks the trends
- More bucks for the bang
- Puts big bucks in your pocket
- Get bucks back on
- Saves you big bucks on
- Soon you'll be the person with the bucks
- Looks like a million bucks

See also: **CASH, DOLLAR, MONEY, SAVE, SAVINGS**

BUDGET
- Slides under any budget
- One for every sized budget
- Everyone has a budget
- Add value without straining your budget
- When you're on a tight budget
- Also available to suit your budget
- For all tastes and all budgets
- A huge selection of styles for every home and budget
- Something to please every budget
- Tailored to fit your budget
- Choosing the product that best suits your budget
- Even your budget approves
- We always keep your budget in mind
- Kind to your budget

- Squeeze even more from your budget
- You don't need a big budget to
- Matches your needs and your budget

Budget: estimate, financial statement, costs, operating expenses, overhead, plan, blueprint, program, allowance, share, allotment, percentage, quota, cost out
See also: AUSTERITY, PLAN, PROGRAM, THRIFT, VALUE

BUILD

- Will build what others call the best
- Building toughness and dependability into the fabric
- Building a lifetime of knowledge, values and confidence
- Build on what you've begun
- Together, we're building something no one could construct alone
- Nobody builds them as well as we do
- If you can dream it, we can build it
- What you can imagine, you can build
- Build for trouble-free operation
- So thoughtfully built that
- Not everyone is built alike
- Built for action
- Built tougher and stronger

Build: make, construct, assemble, raise, erect, manufacture, fabricate, put úp, put together, form, model, shape, fashion, rear, create, originate, put together, forge, devise, increase, develop, speed up, quicken, accelerate, physique, frame body
See also: CREATE, DEVELOP, MAKE, MANUFACTURE

BULK

- We carry bulk products
- Bulk up your bank account
- Bulk savings every day
- Ask about our bulk prices
- Buy in bulk and save big
- Bulk quantities available
- Bulk buying cuts your costs

See also: BODY, QUANTITY

BUM

- Don't get bummed
- Such a bummer
- Stuck with a bum rap
- Don't let anyone hand you a bum steer

See also: ANXIOUS, WORRY

BUSINESS

- Because we value your business
- A business growing through excellent communications
- We appreciate your business
- Profit from repeat business
- We mean business
- This business actually runs itself
- Generating business for you as fast as possible
- One of the strongest aspects of our business
- Our business is built on satisfied customers
- Taking your home business to the next level
- Now you can be in business for yourself
- Want to perk up your business
- No matter what business you're in, you need
- In business you've got to control costs
- No matter what business you're in
- Ready to do business with you
- Help you manage the business you've always dreamed of
- Working to gain a deep understanding of your business
- On the right track for business
- This is not a business measured in
- A business measured in minutes
- You don't get anywhere in this business by standing still
- Best for business, best for you
- No business was lost to
- See what you can do for your business
- Best for your growing business
- Lets you concentrate on doing business
- Investing time in your business pays off big
- Can handle serious business
- Helps you do business faster and more professionally
- Understanding the unique and specialized needs of your business
- This fabulous business opportunity
- Let's do business together
- You'll like the way we do business
- We're open for business
- Not only do we offer your business a winning edge
- Working harder for your business
- Direct application in your day-to-day business

- Committed to helping your business take off quickly
- Get to know businesses like yours
- Where business is bound for
- Give your business a big advantage
- Responds to the needs of business today
- Designed to help your business grow
- Primed and ready to take your business to a higher level than ever before
- For vital savings on everyday business needs
- The big solution for small business
- It's not business as usual any more
- The best of part of business is working with special people like you
- We get right down to business
- An affordable way to grab more business
- Providing customized business opportunities

Business: occupation, profession, trade, line, vocation, avocation, career, following, calling, pursuit, craft, metier, employment, job, work, living, livelihood, means of support, bread and butter, industry, enterprise, barter, exchange, commerce, interchange, dealings, truck, intercourse, traffic, transaction, affairs, ventures, negotiation, bargaining, merchandising, selling, promoting, company, corporation, firm, house, establishment, shop, store, partnership, team, concern, affair, question, issue
See also: ACTIVITY, COMMERCE, MARKETING, SELL, TRADE

BUTTON
- At a touch of a button
- Cute as a button
- Push-button convenience
- We pushed all the right buttons
- Hit the hot button today
- Does it push your buttons

BUY
- Special buy, priced to sell
- Buy with confidence
- We'll spend the time to help you get the best buy
- When it comes to buying and selling, nobody comes close to
- It's a real buy
- You don't have to buy into

- Super buy on
- Your best buy
- Best buy anywhere
- You won't get a better buy than this
- Buy now, pay later
- Smartest buys in town
- Nothing to buy and no obligation whatever
- We buy and sell
- See and buy
- Best buy price
- Unbeatable buy
- Find out just how much you can buy for only
- Don't buy from anyone else until you talk to us
- You can be confident about buying from
- The best time to buy is now
- Nothing else to buy
- There's no obligation to buy anything else
- Before you go rushing out to buy
- That's why you've got to buy a
- How do you buy success
- Your absolute superior buy on
- Huge buying power working for you
- Know your needs before you buy
- The more you buy, the more you save
- The friendliest place to buy your
- Nothing more to buy, ever
- More great buys at half the price
- Buy once, love us forever
- Rush out and buy one now
- Buy two, get one free
- Buy two, get one half price
- Run right out and buy
- You can now buy and sell with confidence
- You can buy what you need when you need it
- Buy more, save more

Buy: purchase, pick up, pay for, get one's hands on, invest in, come by, acquire, put money into, obtain, get, procure, secure, hire, engage, take on, snap up
See also: CHOOSE, GET, INVEST, PAY, PURCHASE, SELECT

BUYER
- International buyers come regularly
- Offered for the privileged buyer who will take advantage

- Today's buyer must be educated
- For the buyer who knows what she wants
- Attracts potential buyers withing hours
- Our buyers are the shrewdest
- Appealing to a wider range of savvy buyers
- We get more serious buyers than any other

See also: CUSTOMER

BUYS

- Great buys on selected
- More fabulous buys inside
- We've rounded up the top buys from all across our stores
- The most tempting buys are sitting on our shelves waiting for you
- Hottest buys
- Incredible birthday buys
- Check out these sizzling buys
- You won't want to miss any of these super buys

See also: BARGAIN, VALUE

CALCULATE

- Precisely calculated for you by our computers
- After you do the calculations, you'll see why we're the best
- Calculated to please you
- You might call us the calculating sort
- We've done all the calculations for you

See also: ADD. FIGURE, MEASURE

CALL

- One call fixes it all
- Please call me at your convenience
- Just call and see how much you save
- Ordered just seconds after your call
- Choose when you want to call
- We don't charge for a service call
- Go ahead, make the call
- No matter when you call
- Why not call us today
- Heed the call to
- You'll never have to make another call
- Call right away
- For a good, old-fashioned service call
- If you're interested, please call us at
- We'll be awaiting your call
- That's why you might seriously consider giving us a call
- Calling all buyers

- Call today for prompt, professional service
- Call on us, day or night, to
- Please call ahead
- One call lets you do all this
- We're waiting for your call
- One call is all it takes
- It'll take only a minute to call and book your appointment
- Call for your nearest
- The moment we get your call, we're on our way
- Please call us
- Call to find out about
- The best hours to call are
- On call, twenty-four hours a day
- With one phone call, all this could be yours
- Call us in advance
- It all starts with one phone call
- Give us a call at
- It's your call
- You've called upon us to
- You are invited to call
- Or make a quick call to
- Has just issued a wake-up call to
- Answer the call
- Just call our toll-free number today
- So you'll never miss another important call again
- Call, write, email or fax us for more information today
- Just call, toll-free, for more information
- Call now for free information
- So give us a call
- Always at your beck and call
- Call now for faster service
- Call ahead and beat the rush
- You'll soon discover why we call
- This is your wake up call
- One call gets it all
- Make the call right now
- Call us today and save big
- Call us first
- Save time and money with a single call
- Call now for great prices on our
- All with one simple phone call
- Call us soon and start enjoying all these amazing features, including

Call: shout, exclaim, roar, sing out, halloo, yell, holler, ask, summon, signal, muster, convene, communicate, assemble, call

together, ring up, buzz, proclaim, announce, designate, name, phone
See also: ASK, COMMUNICATE, TELEPHONE, TOUCH

CALLER
- Experts to answer out callers' needs
- If you're a first-time caller we will give you a bonus
- Every tenth caller earns a free product
- Each caller is treated with the utmost respect and courtesy

CAN
- Of course you can
- Do it because you can
- If you can do this, you can do anything
See also: ABILITY, CAPACITY

CANCEL
- Just write "cancel" on your bill and owe nothing
- Cancel anytime at no extra charge
- Easy to cancel should you change your mind
See also: PREVENT, STOP

CAPABILITY
- Increasing your capability
- Integrates all of these full-featured capabilities
- Our design capabilities are endless
- With the rugged capabilities of
See also: ABILITY, SKILL

CAPACITY
- Now we have the capacity to
- With a bigger than ever capacity to
- We've increased out capacity to serve you better
- No one else has this kind of capacity
See also: ABILITY, CRAFT, ROOM, SKILL

CAPITAL
- irtually no effort and very little capital
- Use our capital to make money for you
- Very little capital investment needed
See also: INVESTMENT, MONEY

CAPTURE
- That captures it all
- Capture the feeling
- Nothing else captures the joy of
- Capture this special moment forever
- We capture smiles
- Now you can capture
- Captured now by
- Who better to capture
See also: GRAB

CARD
- To order, please return the order card
- And now use your new credit card and receive
- Apply for our credit card today
- The only card that counts
- When you use your card
See also: CREDIT, COUPON, FORM, MEMBERSHIP

CARE
- So we can take even better care of you
- We care about your complete satisfaction
- It's important to know how to care for
- How you take care of yourself says a lot about you
- We care about what you have to say
- You want to be able to take care of yourself
- Easy-care convenience
- Care, convenience and confidentiality
- Show him or her how much you care
- We show how much we care
- We care about
- Visit our care centre for
- We care about the way our product works for you
- Show that special someone how much you care
- When you really care, you want nothing but the best
- Caring for you, day and night
- Clearly care about quality
- Still made with good, old-fashioned care

Care: attention, vigilance, caution, watchfulness, concern, regard, mindfulness, consciousness, prudence, awareness, circumspection, care for, watch out for, look after, be concerned for, be solicitous, attend to, deal with, take up, take action on, cherish, protection, safeguard,
See also: ATTENTION, CONCERN, THOUGHT

CAREER
- Now it's time for your career to take off
- We've made a career of it
- A career of caring for our customers
- We know how much your career matters to you
- Don't put your career on hold any longer
- Preparing you for an exciting, multifaceted career
- Build your own career with these exciting
- Make the best career choice for you
- For every stage of your career
- Put your career into overdrive
- For a career that's really going places

See also: ACHIEVEMENT, FUTURE, POSSIBILITY

CAREFUL
- Please be careful out there
- Very careful with your precious treasures
- For a careful buyer like you
- Careful service is our hallmark
- Careful to make the best choices

CARESS
- The sweet caress of
- Gentle as a caress
- Feel it caress your skin
- The caress of the wind in your face
- Save all your caresses for

See also: CHERISH, EMBRACE, HUG. LOVE, TOUCH

CARNIVAL
- Carnival of savings
- Turns life into a merry carnival
- Join the carnival
- Turn your life into a carnival
- The carnival of value starts today

See also: CELEBRATION, MERRY-GO-ROUND, PARTY

CARRY
- We also carry a great selection of
- We carry everything you're looking for
- We carry an excellent selection of
- Cash and carry
- Carrying out studies to show you

See also: DO, PROVIDE, SUPPLY

CASE
- Read the case studies for yourself
- Every case is treated specially
- Just in case you need one
- Come in and case the joint
- In your case, we've got just the right

See also: CONDITION, NEED, SITUATION

CASH
- Safer and more convenient than cash
- Cash savers
- You pocket cash
- Get cash back with the purchase of any item
- Cash savers
- Heard about cash back
- Cash in today
- Putting more cash in your pocket immediately
- You can even get cash back
- Selling for cash
- Cash on the barrel head
- Turn your products into cash
- More flexibility in managing cash flow
- Cash in literally overnight
- Not redeemable for cash
- Start generating cash for you and your family
- Receive cash in your mailbox immediately
- Keep your cash event profitable
- No cash value
- Earns easy cash every time you use it
- Start collecting cash right away

See also: BUCKS, CAPITAL, DOLLAR, MONEY

CASUAL
- Casual and really reasonable
- Let's have a casual relationship
- Casually yours
- Relaxed and casual
- Casual but oh-so-stylish
- Just the right casual touch
- There's nothing casual about our service
- Making more than just a casual acquaintance
- Not too formal, not too casual
- Casual never looked this good

See also: COOL, EASY, INFORMALITY, LOOSE, RELAX

CATALOGUE
- Reply now for our new full color

catalogue
- Call for a complete product catalogue
- Catalogue of fabulous bargains
- Many items also available in our catalogue
- See them all in our catalogue, then call direct to order
- Your biggest catalogue of savings

See also: CLASSIFY, COLLECTION, GUIDE, INVENTORY, LIST

CATCH
- A very long way to go to catch up to
- Catch the latest news and views
- Catch the brass ring today
- The excitement is catching
- Catch a falling star
- No catches or hidden charges
- Everyone is catching on

See also: CAPTURE, GRAB, NOTICE

CATEGORY
- Having invented the category
- Climb up a category or two
- Puts you in a whole different category
- We have more categories of
- A category above all the rest
- In a category all your own

See also: CATALOGUE, KIND, SORT, SPECIES

CATER
- Catering to the growing need for
- We cater to your every need
- Nobody caters better to
- Sit back and be catered to

See also: PAMPER, SERVE, SPOIL

CAVE
- Unless you've been living in a cave, you'll know that
- Time to come out of your cave and look around
- Others might cave in to

See also: HIDE

CELEBRATE
- A great buy to celebrate our birthday
- In plenty of time to celebrate
- We're celebrating
- It's your time to celebrate
- Celebrate triumphs and set new goals
- Celebrate in a memorable way

- We're celebrating
- Come help us celebrate
- Celebrating with some of our hottest prices ever

See also: CHRISTMAS, EASTER, HOLIDAY

CELEBRATION
- Bring the celebration home with
- Join the celebration today
- It's our anniversary celebration
- In celebration of love and laughter
- The celebration fun just goes on and on

See also: CARNIVAL, FESTIVE, HOLIDAYS

CELEBRITY
- For the years the most famous celebrities have trusted
- Meet our most popular celebrity
- You become an instant celebrity
- The celebrity of our company is well founded
- Enjoying well-earned celebrity

See also: FAMOUS, LEADER, STAR

CENT
- Don't waste another cent on
- Where every cent counts
- Costs cents, saves dollars
- Your money's not worth a cent here

See also: MONEY, PENNY

CENTER
- Where you are always the center of attention
- Puts you front and center
- Come to the biggest center of all
- Now you are center stage
- We're the center for the entire city

See also: HEART, HEARTLAND, HOME, HUB

CENTURY
- Has been used for centuries throughout the world
- Made our mark on a brand new century
- Now we're growing into the new century
- The new century will be our century
- The only product designed for the twenty-first century

See also: AGE, ERA, TIME

CERTAINTY
- That's the certainty
- You can say it with absolute certainty
- The certainty will always remain
- Your satisfaction is a certainty

See also: GUARANTEE, WARRANTY

CERTIFICATE
- Purchase any time and receive a gift certificate
- Have you considered a gift certificate
- Everyone loves the surprise of a gift certificate
- You'll get your certificate in mere weeks
- Upgrade your certificate easily

See also: COUPON

CHALLENGE
- The sort of challenge our people have always delivered on
- Challenges the status quo
- Rising to the challenge
- Meeting today's challenges
- A team of experts to help you overcome the toughest challenges
- Thriving on new creative challenges
- Responding to these challenges is no easy thing
- Finding fresh challenges in looking at
- Solving tomorrow's challenges
- An even greater challenge than that faced by
- Know how to rise to a challenge
- Take the challenge
- Exceptional challenges require exceptional people

Challenge: invitation, dare, call, summons, venture, hazard, risk, puzzle, knot, barrier, defy, stimulate, excite, inspire, spur on, invigorate, jog, fan, propel, strive, fight
See also: FIGHT, HURDLE, NEED, OBSTACLE, PROVOCATION, PROBLEM, RISK, VENTURE

CHAMPION
- A shining litany of champions
- A champion in the global battle for supremacy
- Turn yourself into a champion
- Stand with the champions
- Have a champion in your corner
- The real champions are often unexpected
- Champions at your service
- Listen to the voice of champions

Champion: protector, defender, guardian, friend, winner, victor, leader, champ, hero, knight, supporter, advocate, backer, fighter, guard, booster, ace, title holder
See also: BATTLE, HERO, PROTECT

CHANCE
- This is your last chance to buy
- The longer you wait, the less chance you have
- Doesn't happen just by chance
- Here's your chance
- Now's your chance
- Grab your big chance to
- Where, for the first time, you had a chance to buy
- As changes work their way up
- Get ready for the main chance
- Finally giving everyone a chance to
- Automatically give you the chance to
- We leave nothing to chance
- Not a thing should be left to chance
- Don't take chances with
- Know they shouldn't take chances
- Take a chance with us

See also: ODDS, OPPORTUNITY

CHANGE
- Are you due for a change
- The only change will be more great benefits
- Come and see the changes we've made
- Which you can change as often as you like
- Can change all that in a hurry
- But things change fast
- You'll see amazing changes start to take place
- Things have certainly changed
- Very soon you'll notice a real change
- Devoted to bringing change to
- We listened and we changed
- Are you looking for a change of scene
- Have changed a lot over the years
- It's time for a change
- A truly substantive change
- Constitutes a major change
- Major changes at all levels
- The biggest change you'll have to deal with is

- This change of mind set has just begun
- We have changed
- You have the freedom, the power to change
- And you don't have to change a thing
- The costs change to stay in step with
- We're changing to respond better to emerging needs
- You'll notice some real changes
- We've made some exciting new changes

Change: transform, moderate, temper, alter, correct, modify, convert, mutate, transfigure, retool, remodel, switch, replace, exchange, translate, reconstruct, reorder, recast, reorganize, innovation, novelty, revolution, transition, evolution, barter, trade, swap
See also: ADAPT, COMPROMISE, DIFFERENCE, FLEXIBLE, MODIFY, VERSATILE

CHARACTER
- Add true character to your living space
- You can sense the character
- Now that's a product with character
- Founded on strength of character
- You can tell just by the character of
- Changing character to suit you

See also: FEATURE, INDIVIDUAL, UNIQUE

CHARGE
- When it's time to take charge
- Show them who's in charge
- Leading the charge to
- Charges payable at time of purchase
- No extra charge for
- Taking charge of your
- Decide to charge head-first into the fray
- We'll give it to you free of charge
- There are no service charges for this service
- All this at no extra charge
- Charge for work well done
- No hidden charges or catches
- You may return everything at no charge
- Slash your monthly interest charges

Charge: ask, expect, ask a price, levy, assess, appraise, tax, exact, bill, debit, defer payment, buy on the layaway/installment plan, take on credit and account
See also: COST, PRICE

CHARISMA
- Amazing talent and irresistible charisma
- You, too, can have this kind of charisma
- Feel the charisma

See also: ATTRACTION, CHARM

CHARM
- And the quainter charm of a traditional setting
- Experience the subtle, sophisticated charm
- Experience the unique charm of
- Accomplished with charm and skill
- Acquire the charm of
- This charm can fill your home

See also: BEAUTY

CHART
- Chart the course you need to succeed
- Charting new paths into the future
- Help you chart your way through the reefs and shoals of life

See also: GUIDE, PLAN, VISION

CHEAP
- Cheaper than dirt
- Cost-effective, not cheap
- Cheap at the price
- Cheap price, huge value
- No place cheaper

See also: BUDGET, ECONOMICAL, INEXPENSIVE, SAVE, THRIFT, UNDERSOLD

CHECK OUT
- Dive in and check out these great values
- Check out our
- Check out the following
- Check us out today at
- Every time you check out
- And check out the more than

CHERISH
- Cherish the simple dreams of
- Something to cherish
- Make them feel cherished
- We cherish your patronage

See also: CARESS, LOVE, VALUE

CHIC
- It doesn't get any chicer than this
- Looking crisp and incredibly chic
- It's pure chic

- Arrive with breath-taking chic
- Chic that cannot be imitated
- You too can achieve this kind of chic

See also: CLASS, ELEGANT, FASHION, STYLE

CHILD

- A delightful selection appealing to the child in everyone
- Pamper your inner child
- Even a child could do it
- For the child in you waiting to come out and have fun
- Makes it child's play to
- Designed with your child in mind

See also: BABY, FAMILY, KID, YOUTH

CHILDHOOD

- Cherish the special time of childhood
- Relive your childhood with
- The joy of childhood can be repeated here
- What is more precious than a happy childhood

CHOICE

- Let us be your choice
- Knowing they are the best choice
- We offer a choice of additional benefits
- Consumer's choice
- Gives you your choice of
- It's always an easy choice
- It's your money and your choice
- Working hard to become your first choice
- The first choice of champions
- And now you have even more choices
- Your choices say a lot about you
- And the choices only get better
- Makes the choice pretty simple, doesn't it
- It's your choice
- Make the right choice
- Equipping you to make a better choice
- A far easier choice
- By choice, not default
- Your choice is perfectly clear
- For so many, the choice includes
- The authentic choice
- Plus your choice of
- More choice than anywhere else in town
- The best choice for you
- Your obvious best choice

- Shouldn't you have a choice
- Customer's choice
- The smart choice for the ultimate
- Your first choice for
- Your choice for only
- Gives you a multitude of choices
- The perfect choice for do-it-yourselfers
- There is no better choice than
- The intelligent choice in
- It's the clear choice
- The finest choice for discriminating shoppers
- First and only choice
- There's only one choice
- The one with the most choice
- Here are some healthy choices
- Now you can make informed choices about everything we have to offer
- A world of choices
- Some choices are more important than others
- There are lots and lots of choices
- Providing more choices than any other
- When it's choice you want

Choice: selection, alternative, option, decision, commitment, possibility, answer, solution, way, substitute, discrimination, vote, equivalent, preference, pleasure, taste, wish, desire, inclination, elect, select, elite, pick, best part, prize, best, rarest, prime, treasure, gem, cream of the crop, paragon, nonesuch, nonpareil, one in a million, champion, prodigy

See also: ANGLE, ARRAY, BEST, CHOOSE, DECIDE, OPPORTUNITY, OPTION, PICK, RAIN CHECK, SELECT

CHOOSE

- We can help you choose the right product or service for you
- Here's how to choose
- You'll never have to choose between
- Smart people choose us first
- Helping you choose the product that is right for you
- Why choose when you can have it all
- To help you choose wisely and well
- Why not choose
- Choose from an incredible selection
- You get to choose
- Designed to fit whatever you choose to do

- Hard to choose
- Easier than ever to choose the product that's right for you
- To help you choose the right one
- Smart people choose
- No matter which product you choose
- Now you don't have to worry about choosing the right product yourself
- Right away you see how easy it is to choose
- You'll be able to choose one or all of five amazing offers

Choose: select, pick, draw, sort, fancy, favor, desire, balance, weigh, discriminate, judge, decide, opt, see fit, embrace, elect
See also: CHOICE, DECIDE, PICK, SELECT

CHOP
- Chop your bill in half
- When you really need to chop your costs
- Chop time, chop effort, increase your return
- Chopper specials
- The price chopper

See also: CUT, REDUCE, SLASH

CHRISTMAS
- Get what you want for Christmas
- A Christmas-time double bonus
- Come to us for all your Christmas gifts
- Let the Christmas season light up your heart
- The finest Christmas gift anyone could receive
- This Christmas, don't miss out
- Want to jingle somebody's bells this Christmas
- Give someone a memorable Christmas
- For someone special on your Christmas list
- As much as part of Christmas as decorating the tree
- Christmas is an important time for your family
- Christmas is the season of giving
- Make Christmas magic for someone on your list
- Make a Christmas wish come true
- For a very merry Christmas
- Lots and lots of Christmas cheer for everyone

- Make Christmas merry
- A Christmas treat that's jingle-licious
- A welcome Christmas gift
- Celebrating isn't just for Christmas and the New Year
- With Christmas just around the corner

Christmas: Yule, Yuletide, Noel, holiday season, Christmastime, Christmastide
See also: CELEBRATE, FESTIVE, HOLIDAY

CHUNK
- You don't have to pay it all in one chunk
- Keep a big chunk of cash for yourself
- When you've invested a chunk of time
- A bigger chunk of savings

See also: PART

CIRCUMSTANCES
- Extraordinary circumstances
- Under the circumstances, the wisest choice
- Fitted to your circumstances
- You need it even in the very best of circumstances
- No matter what your circumstances

See also: CONDITION, OCCASION, REASON, SITUATION

CITY
- To get away from city life
- For big city people
- Take convenient city life with you anywhere you go
- The country has come to the city
- Big city quality, small town warmth

See also: COMMUNITY, LOCATION, NEIGHBORHOOD

CIVILIZATION
- You're never far from civilization
- One of the big advances of civilization
- Make civilization a little kinder

CIVILIZE
- Civilized but not tame
- Exerting a civilizing influence
- The truly civilized way to do things

See also: EDUCATE, INFORM

CLAIM
- Good luck finding another product that

can claim that
- All our claims are true
- After you've checked out the claims of the competition, come back to us

See also: ANNOUNCE, DEMAND

CLASS
- Add class and distinction
- In a class of its own
- The largest in its class
- A whole new class of
- Go to the head of the class
- The best in its class
- In a class of your own
- Sets it in a class by itself
- Executive class all the way
- Each new model is tops in its class

See also: GROUP, LEAGUE

CLASSIC
- Every fit is a classic
- Power and prestige mixed with classic authority
- Always a classic
- New classics created now
- Clean and classic
- From classic to dramatic
- One of the classics that's been around forever
- A classic in its own time
- A classic has just become more contemporary
- Numerous classics ranging from

See also: STANDARD, TIMELESS, TRADITIONAL

CLASSIFY
- Very hard to classify
- Nobody can classify us
- Can change the way you classify yourself
- Classified as the very best

See also: CATALOGUE, DEFINE, SORT

CLEAN
- Clean up today
- You'll clean up
- Cleaner, more comfortable and healthier
- Clean value
- Starting with a fresh, clean slate
- Clean up on savings
- Clean, quick and easy
- Make a clean break with the past
- For gentle cleansing

- Clean as new
- Come clean about true value

CLEAR
- Everything must be cleared for new products
- The answer is strikingly clear
- The message is clear
- One thing becomes crystal clear
- We want to be perfectly clear about
- It's the clear choice
- Quickly becomes clear to you
- Nothing could be clearer

See also: OBVIOUS, PURE, SIMPLE

CLEARANCE
- Inventory clearance
- Warehouse clearance
- The clearance of the year
- A special clearance of
- Monster clearance
- First quality at clearance prices
- Factory outlet clearance
- The final clearance
- Semi-annual floor clearance
- Factory direct clearance sale

See also: BLITZ, BLOW-OUT, MARKET, SALE

CLICK
- Really clicks for
- This will click with you
- When something clicks inside your head
- The mental click is deafening

See also: BOND, REALIZE, WORK

CLIENT
- As a valued client, your business is important to us
- Your clients will love the addition
- Have been pleasing the most demanding clients in the world
- Our program works for each client
- Every one of our clients has unique needs
- Our clients are people just like you
- So that we can better serve our ever-increasing client base
- Serving an increasingly diverse clientele
- Our clients built our business
- Here's what our clients say
- Your clients will never know the difference
- Our clients love us

- Our clients know they can count on
- Our complete dedication to our clients' success
- Seizing opportunities on behalf of our clients

Client: customer, patron, regular, buyer, buyer, purchaser, shopper, consumer
See also: CONSUMER, CUSTOMER

CLIMATE

- In a climate fraught with constant change
- Creating the right climate for
- A climate of friendliness and cooperation
- In today's tough climate, you need

See also: ATMOSPHERE, ENVIRONMENT

CLINICAL

- The only one clinically proven to
- Clinically, it's the best
- Emerged triumphant from extensive clinical tests

See also: RESEARCH, SCIENTIFIC

CLOCK

- Round-the-clock service
- Enjoy round-the-clock access to
- When you have to beat the clock
- You don't have to be afraid of the clock
- Turn the clock into a friend, not an enemy
- No longer have to watch the clock

See also: COMPLETE, FAST, TIME

CLOSE

- Conveniently close by
- Close at hand for today and the future
- Closer than you think
- Get close to the best
- So close you can almost smell it
- View up close
- For those moments when you're really close
- Up close and personal
- Nothing comes close to
- We're close to where you live

See also: CONVENIENT

CLOTHES

- Clothes that work
- Your clothes say it all
- Clothed in honesty

- Clothes make the woman/man

See also: APPEARANCE, FASHION

CLUB

- Value club
- Join the club - it's free
- Become an instant member of the club
- Get all the benefits of joining a very exclusive club

See also: GROUP, TEAM

COAST

- From coast to coast
- The coast is clear at last for
- To prove we aren't just coasting along on our laurels

COINCIDENCE

- It's no coincidence that there's something a little different
- More than just a coincidence
- A lucky coincidence help you to

See also: CHANCE

COLD

- This season, come in from the cold
- Beat the cold rush
- Save cold cash on hot values
- You don't have to be cold any longer
- Come in from the cold

COLLABORATE

- We collaborate with you to
- When you're looking for the best people to collaborate
- An outstanding collaborative effort

Collaborate: cooperate, work together, partner, act jointly, pull together, stand shoulder to shoulder, team up, join forces
See also: JOIN, TEAM

COLLABORATION

- The result of inspired collaboration
- Replaced with a newfound collaboration
- This collaboration is a real first
- A historic collaboration has taken place
- Is the result an inspired collaboration

See also: PARTNERSHIP, TEAMWORK

COLLECT

- Start collecting the benefits
- If you hurry, you can collect every one

- Finally, you get to collect
- Collect your savings now

Collect: accumulate, heap up, pile, stack up, compile, amass, cumulate, squirrel away, hoard, stow away, gather, pull in, harvest, reap, garner, store up, stock up, lay by, lay up, lay in, stash away, reserve, set aside, save, stash
See also: GATHER, RAKE, SAVE

COLLECTIBLE

- Dozens of other fascinating collectibles
- More collectibles in one place
- Becomes more collectible every passing year

See also: GEM, TREASURE

COLLECTION

- Keep your collection up-to-date with
- Don't forget about these useful collections
- Presenting our premium collection
- Presenting the only collection of its kind ever
- An extraordinary collection of
- A must-have addition to your collection
- Some of the hottest pieces in the collection
- A collection like no other you've seen
- Presenting our designer collection
- Part of the newest collection available
- A fascinating collection comprised of
- We've put together a careful collection
- This outstanding collection is guaranteed to please

See also: CATALOGUE, GOODS, INVENTORY, LIST, MERCHANDISE, STOCK

COLLECTOR

- A true collector's edition
- The best put together into a collector's edition
- The smartest collectors get here first
- Designed for collectors of fine items everywhere

See also: CONNOISSEUR

COLOR

- Excellent quality, assorted colors
- With so many colors to choose from
- Leap into a kaleidoscope of color
- Designed in vivid color
- Color that stays true to
- Gives you living color
- Put some color into your life
- Drenched in rich, luscious color
- In the colors you want
- Show your colors proudly
- Colors that wake you up fast
- Nothing looks newer than layers of color
- A shimmer of color
- Color that lasts and lasts
- For subtle color, a lighter shade of pale
- Are you becoming color-wary
- Fashion colors for spring
- Available in assorted designer colors
- Add a splash of color to your
- In subtle color blends
- In all these new colors
- All-new colors, patterns and styles
- Lets your colors come out bright, not dull

Color: hue, tinge, tint, tone, cast, shade, tincture, pigment, dye
See also: HUE, SHADE
See also: SECTION ELEVEN: COLORS

COMBINATION

- Find your combination
- Finding the right combination for you
- The perfect combination for
- A potent combination of
- Make a combination to fit your needs
- An unbeatable combination of
- Sample exotic combinations of
- One impressive combination
- The most extraordinary combination
- The winning combination
- Choose any combination of
- What an outstanding combination of
- A knockout combination of first class
- You get an outstanding combination
- Combination of exceptional personal service and
- Hundreds of design choice combinations

See also: BLEND, MIX

COMBINE

- All of which combine to give you the greatest possible chance
- Combining the best of each
- What do you get when you combine
- You can combine as many as you please
- Now you have a chance to combine

- Combined especially for you

See also: BLEND, INTEGRATE, MIX

COME
- Only the finest come from
- Come and get it – for less
- We hope you'll come in soon
- Come and select that special gift
- Come in today
- You've got to come and see for yourself
- Come in and view
- Act now to keep this product coming

See also: VISIT

COMEBACK
- We're on the comeback trail
- They're staging a spectacular comeback
- The biggest comeback in years
- Now making a spectacular comeback

See also: RETURN

COMFORT
- Comfort and savings exclusive to
- Gifts and comforts from near and far
- It's really comforting to know we're there
- A whole new level of comfort doesn't necessarily require
- This kind of comfort is very easy to get used to
- A comfort zone you won't get elsewhere
- You'll find great comfort in knowing
- Takes you to the next level of comfort
- Your quest for comfort is finally satisfied
- Slip on casual comfort
- Comfort like you've never felt before
- Surround yourself with comfort
- We can all use little comfort to get us through the final days of winter
- The quintessential comfort
- Comfort and pleasure you desire need not be at odds with prices
- Get into comfort now
- Enter the comfort zone
- Comfort has never been so reasonably priced
- Highlights all the comforts of home
- Counting on comfort, again and again
- With all the amenities and comforts

Comfort: ease, tranquillity, luxury, opulence, security blanket, soothing, pleasure, cheer, peace

See also: AMENITY, CONVENIENCE, EASE, PLEASURE, SOFT

COMFORTABLE
- You'll feel comfortable and in control
- So comfortable you won't want to leave
- In the supremely comfortable
- Faster and more comfortable
- Whatever you're comfortable with
- We know you're comfortable

Comfortable: homey, cosy, warm, snug, room, ample, loose-fitting, commodious, luxurious, at ease, contented, congenial, agreeable, fit for a king, serene, in clover, bed of roses, cordial, gratifying, sufficient, satisfactory

See also: COSY, EASY, FIT

COMMAND
- Precisely at your command
- Puts you in total command of
- Your wish is our command
- In command of more services at once than any other
- For you, it's a command performance

See also: COMPEL, CONTROL, ORDER, WISH

COMMENT
- When you make a comment, we listen hard
- Your comments keep us in touch with your tastes and expectations
- So please feed us with your comments

See also: SUGGESTION

COMMERCE
- Continually improving the means of commerce
- Affordable solutions for commerce
- Turning to commerce for solve so many current problems

See also: BUSINESS, MARKETING, SELL, TRADE

COMMIT
- Committed to saving you money
- Committed to helping you maintain
- A lot more than others will commit to
- Committed to quality, value, selection and service
- Professional, knowledgeable, committed

to you

Commit: entrust, commend, confide, vest in, charge with, assign, authorize, pledge, promise, swear, covenant, vow, bind, engage, undertake, attest, certify, guarantee, vouch, answer for, oblige
See also: PLEDGE, PROMISE

COMMITMENT
- A combination of creativity, commitment and caring
- We'll show a commitment you can really depend on
- Is our commitment to deliver the best service available with the results you expect
- Attest to the versatility and commitment
- Considering a quarter of a century of commitment to
- For people who hate commitments
- Our commitment to you includes
- No commitment necessary

COMMODITY
- The single most precious commodity
- What's the hottest commodity today
- The most sought-after commodity in
- Offering you a very valuable commodity
See also: ITEM, PRODUCT, TRADE

COMMON
- Has a lot in common with the real thing
- We all have one thing in common
- Sharing common values
- Solving a very common problem
- We seem to have a common thought in mind
See also: NORM, ORDINARY, PLENTY

COMMUNICATE
- Communicate faster
- A new way to communicate
- Communicate instantly
- You need more ways to communicate
- You only have to communicate your needs and we'll be there for you
- Working to communicate with you

Communicate: inform, tell speak, advise, notify, mention, point out, bring to attention, let know, enlighten, clue in, announce, publish, convey, get across, say, voice, utter, reveal, divulge, make known, uncover, lay

open, impart, pass along, interface, chat, talk, get in touch, contact, call, telephone
See also: ADVERTISE, TALK, TELL, SAY, SPEAK, VOICE

COMMUNICATION
- Opening more lines of communication
- Honest and open communication
- Growing through good communication
- Communication is everything
See also: DATA, FLYER, INFORMATION, NEWS

COMMUNITY
- Connects you to the fastest growing community in the world
- Flocking to a safe new community
- Join a community of people and resources
- Owned and operated by a member of your own community
- Caring about our community
- A terrific part of your community
- Proudly serving your community for more than
- Proud to play a role in the community
- Putting us well ahead of the average community
- Speaking about its integration into the world community
- Proud to have served the community for the past number of years
- Everything we do is community based
- Find instant community
See also: CITY, NEIGHBORHOOD

COMPACT
- Compact, durable and powerful
- Able to get more into a compact space
- All in one handsome compact package
- Compact enough to go with you everywhere
- An even more compact model
See also: FIT, SMALL, TIDY

COMPANION
- The ideal companion for
- What better companion
- Designed as stunning companion pieces
- And there's always room for a companion
See also: FRIEND

COMPANY
- You're in good company
- A good, solid company that will really help you to
- The company that's been trusted for years
- Company's coming
- Keeps you company every day
- A company you can trust

See also: BUSINESS, FRIEND, VISITOR

COMPARE
- Compare the savings
- Compare our low prices
- We invite you to compare
- Dare to compare
- Compare our price and quality
- Compare at
- Only when you compare will you understand
- Just compare
- You'll love how easy it is to compare
- Compare us with any other
- Nothing compares with

See also: MATCH

COMPARISON
- That's why we invite comparison
- We're all for comparisons
- Standing up under the most exacting comparison
- Stands up to any comparison
- Comparison shop to find the best deals

COMPATIBILITY
- You'll get optimum performance and compatibility
- Engineered for compatibility with
- Compatibility with your needs is the first thing we take into account

COMPATIBLE
- So compatible with
- Find the one that is compatible with you
- Handsome and compatible
- Every item is compatible with
- You'll find it a very compatible fit

See also: FIT, MATCH, PARTNER

COMPEL
- A compelling, mesmerizing beauty
- One compelling argument after another
- The most compelling item of the moment

See also: COMMAND

COMPETE
- Our experience and skill can help you compete more effectively
- To compete and succeed today, you need the right tools
- With our help, compete successfully
- Competing fiercely for your business
- Competing better than ever
- Helping you compete at your best

Compete: contend, struggle, fight, wrestle, jockey, spar, participate, contest, challenge, play against, challenge, strive, engage, participate, toss your hat in the ring, grapple, pit yourself against

See also: BATTLE, CONQUER, FIGHT, SUCCEED, WIN

COMPETITION
- Everyone loves us except the competition
- It doesn't matter what the competition's got
- Everyone loves us except the competition
- Giving you an edge on the competition
- It's all about staying competitive
- Gaining a competitive advantage means setting yourself apart
- We offer something the competition doesn't
- Blow the competition away with
- Got what it takes to stay ahead of the competition
- Working harder to help you stay ahead of the competition

COMPETITIVE
- Competitive prices supported by over 100,000 satisfied customers
- Also proud of our high-quality, competitively priced products and services
- Eminently competitive
- Able to bring you consistently competitive pricing
- Staying competitive to keep your business
- Confident you will find our prices competitive
- Prices are always competitive

COMPETITOR
- We will beat any competitor's price

- Leaving competitors behind in the dust
- We'll match any competitor's offer
- We won't be undersold by local competitors
- Has proven a worthy competitor for the world's leading
- Two things our competitors don't want you to see
- Why customers buy from us eight times as often as they buy from our nearest competitor
- Our competitors don't think so
- We go way beyond our competitors in terms of performance
- After careful comparison with our competitors

Competitor: rival, opponent, opposition, foe, enemy, challenger, contender, candidate, contestant
See also: CONTENDER, RIVAL

COMPLAINT

- You will have absolutely no complaint about
- All complaints are handled promptly and with complete discretion
- We've never had a complaint

See also: BEEF, CONCERN

COMPLETE

- Now you can do a complete
- No other product offers more complete
- Complete service round the clock
- Get it immediately, whole and complete

Complete: entire, finished, whole, self-contained, independent, self-supporting, unabridged, comprehensive, thorough, perfect, flawless, total
See also: ALL, TOTAL, WHOLE

COMPLETION

- Serving you from concept to completion
- The satisfaction of total completion

- Guiding you to completion
- The completion of a brilliant idea

See also: END, FINISH

COMPLEX

- It's unique complex of
- Helping you with the most complex problems
- Sometimes choosing can be very complex

- Giving a complex life the appearance of utter simplicity
- Taking the complexity out of

See also: DIFFICULT, MULTI

COMPLEXION

- Keep your complexion looking more beautiful every day
- Putting the best complexion on it
- Delight in a glowing, youthful complexion

See also: APPEARANCE, BEAUTY

COMPLIMENT

- With our compliments
- To enhance and compliment your
- The ideal compliment to
- The natural compliment to
- When you're looking for something to compliment
- A perfect compliment to any occasion
- Here are some of the compliments we've been getting
- The best compliment is your business
- Enjoy it compliments of
- Accept it with our compliments
- Our compliments on your latest achievement

COMPLIMENTARY

- Get your complimentary copy
- A brand new complimentary service
- Even more complimentary and elegant

See also: FREE

COMPONENT

- Giving components the ultimate test
- Become essential components
- The biggest component in your success

See also: PART

COMPREHENSIVE

- Making it as comprehensive as possible
- Look to us for the most comprehensive coverage
- Comprehensive service is our secret

COMPROMISE

- Why compromise when you can easily get the best
- A comfortable compromise between
- Built without compromise

- No compromise
- Without compromising one iota
- The one thing you won't find is a compromise
- No compromise in quality, reliability or service
- There will never be a compromise between

CONCENTRATE
- Allowing you to concentrate on what's important to you
- Offering concentrated value
- So you're free to concentrate on the important stuff

See also: FOCUS

CONCEPT
- A concept dedicated to keeping you well-acquainted with
- The concept is now being rediscovered
- Here's the baseline concept
- I know that's a wild concept
- Terrific service is not exactly a new concept
- Based on a proven concept
- A brilliant new concept that's turning old ideas upside down
- The guiding principles of the concept
- Introducing a new and exciting concept
- That is the breathtaking concept
- One of the best appreciated concepts

See also: IDEA, INFORMATION, INSPIRATION, PLAN

CONCERN
- We answer affirmative to all your concerns
- What are your biggest concerns today
- Your concerns are valid
- The natural choice for anyone who is concerned about
- It's only natural to be concerned about your
- We can help with all your concerns
- Turning complicated concerns into simple solutions

See also: CHALLENGE, CARE, PROBLEM

CONCLUSION
- Based on our conclusions
- You'll soon come to your own conclusions about
- The result of carefully arrived at conclusions
- Don't jump to conclusions right away

CONDITION
- All in top condition
- Creating the conditions you need to thrive
- Withstands the toughest conditions imaginable
- Subject to certain conditions

CONFIDENCE
- Moving with confidence
- Adding a new dimension of confidence to the process
- Quickly, efficiently and with confidence
- You can have confidence in us
- Giving you confidence to

See also: PRIDE, TRUST

CONFIDENTIAL
- Every consultation is strictly confidential
- Can actually provide you with confidential
- All transactions are confidential
- Complete confidentiality just for you
- Your comments will kept completely confidential

See also: SECRET

CONFUSE
- Not to be confused with just any old
- Making the right choice can be very confusing
- Now you can stop being confused about
- The end of product confusion forever

See also: ERROR, MISTAKE, UNSURE, WRONG

CONNECT
- Inviting you to connect with
- We'll do our best to connect you with
- It keeps you connected with family and friends
- Connect with amazing value
- Connecting people to people
- Get connected
- Connecting everything into one convenient bundle

See also: JOIN, INTERFACE, LINK

CONNECTION
- To form a lasting connection with
- All the connections you need are right here
- People are starting to make the connection
- Make the most of your connections
- Giving you the connections to
- We've got the connections you need

CONNOISSEUR
- Become an instant connoisseur
- Especially for connoisseurs like you
- Built for connoisseurs
- Join the best connoisseurs

See also: COLLECTOR

CONQUER
- Have already conquered the world of
- Feel like a conquering hero
- Ready to conquer those stubborn problems that

See also: BEAT, VICTORY, WIN

CONSIDER
- If you've always been reluctant, consider this
- You are invited to consider purchasing
- If you're considering
- Before you buy, please consider these facts

See also: BALANCE, THINK

CONSISTENT
- Helping you be more consistent
- Producing consistently good results year after year
- Our service is consistent and consistently excellent

See also: RELIABLE

CONSTRAINT
- Instead of having to work within the constraints of
- Finally free of the constraints of
- Break loose from old constraints

See also: BOUNDARY, LIMIT, RESTRICTION

CONSTRUCTION
- Of extremely durable construction
- Great care is lavished on every stage of construction
- Just take a look at the fine construction and know you can have confidence

CONSULT
- You can always consult us with confidence
- We consult you all the way
- When you're looking for someone to consult
- Always consult the best

See also: ADVISE, WISDOM

CONSULTANT
- Skilled consultants will help you
- Try our friendly and knowledgeable consultants
- Maybe you should try the consultants the consultants consult.

See also: EXPERT, EXPERTISE, PROFESSIONAL, STAFF

CONSULTATION
- Call for consultation or visit our showroom
- For consultation or booking, please call
- Offering ongoing consultation with your staff
- Call today for a no-cost, no-obligation consultation
- Free in-home consultation
- Unlimited free consultation

See also: ADVICE, COMMUNICATE, MEET

CONSUMER
- Happy to respond to consumer demand for the best
- An integral part of today's consumer mix
- The most important consideration is you, the consumer
- Consumers' choice
- From the consumer point of view
- You're a very informed consumer

See also: BUYER, CUSTOMER

CONTACT
- We will contact you immediately
- For information, contact
- Contact us at any time
- Giving you the contacts you need to
- Contact our friendly staff today

See also: CALL, REACH

CONTENDER
- Are the strongest contenders for
- With this product you could be a contender too
- Easily beating out all other contenders for the prize of

See also: COMPETITOR, RIVAL

CONTENT
- Beefed up our content on
- Making more customers content
- You'll be truly contented with
- Once you try it, you won't be content with your old one

See also: MATERIAL, PLEASE

CONTEXT
- Providing a grand context for
- Helping you put your needs in context
- But when you look at it in another context

See also: ENVIRONMENT, SETTING

CONTINUAL
- Held continually throughout
- Continually available for your benefit
- Continual service for forty years

CONTRACT
- No long term contracts
- A contract you can live with
- Your safety is built right into the contract
- Stick to the letter of the contract
- Protected by an iron-clad contract

See also: AGREEMENT, ALLIANCE, GUARANTEE, WARRANTY

CONTRAST
- A place of astonishing contrasts
- Contrast it with the others and you'll be convinced
- Stands out in startling contrast

CONTROL
- When it's something you need to control
- Now you can take control over all your
- The easy way to stay in control
- For the first time, we're able to control
- Control is something you're really interested in
- Now you can take control
- Always under your control
- Be in control at all times

- If controlling the outcome is important to you
- Develop instinctive control
- Wouldn't it be nice to feel more in control

See also: COMMAND, POWER

CONVENIENCE
- For greater safety, convenience and pleasure
- Unequalled savings and convenience
- In addition to the added convenience of prepaid
- Crammed it with conveniences
- The ultimate in convenience
- Minor investment, major convenience
- The convenience of compact size
- Every possible convenience
- For your convenience
- The dawn of a whole new era of convenience
- The best in quality, price, service and convenience
- Open for your shopping convenience
- Country values, downtown convenience

Convenience: utility, leisure, ease, free, freedom, spare time, advantage, accommodation, service, amenity

See also: AMENITY, COMFORT, EASE, SIMPLE

CONVENIENT
- What could be more convenient
- Find out how quick and convenient
- Designed to be fast, easy and convenient
- Not to mention all the convenient services thoughtful extras
- Always working to make it more convenient for you
- It's much less expensive and more convenient than

See also: EASY

CONVENTIONAL
- Your reliance on the conventional is about to change forever
- Nothing is conventional here
- You're not a conventional person, so why use a conventional product
- Escape the conventional
- A very long way from the conventional
- Suitable for all conventional uses

See also: **REGULAR, STANDARD**

CONVINCE
- There's only one sure way to convince you
- Very convincing data
- You'll never again have to convince anyone of anything
- Let us convince you about
- You'll be convinced that
- We can state this incredible new conviction

Convince: persuade, reassure, affirm, bring round, win over, sell, satisfy, assure, prove to
See also: **PERSUADE, SELL**

COOK
- Find out what's cooking
- We're cooking up a storm
- Too tired to cook
- Cooking up something hot with you

See also: **DINE, EAT, KITCHEN, MEAL, PREPARE, RECIPE**

COOL
- Totally cool
- Cool off after a hard day's work
- Stay cool all the time
- Keep your cool
- Too cool for words
- The ultimate in cool
- Cooler than cool
- We'll help you keep your cool all summer long
- For cool people like you
- Frighteningly cool and comfortable

See also: **COLD, HIP, FASHION**

COOPERATION
- You have the assurance of our full cooperation
- Now in cooperation with many of the nation's most prestigious
- Always working in cooperation with you
- A masterpiece of cooperation
- Your cooperation is essential

See also: **PARTNERSHIP, PATIENCE**

COORDINATE
- All the better to coordinate
- A coordinated effort which not only links
- We do all the coordinating
- Everything coordinates beautifully after you've been to our experts
- Making it so very easy to coordinate all you
- Coordination for every room
- Improving the coordination of

See also: **MATCH**

COPY
- Something anybody can copy
- You can copy this success
- You don't want to be just another copy
- We don't copy anybody
- Always an original, never a copy

See also: **DUPLICATE, MATCH, REPEAT**

CORNERSTONE
- Trust, integrity and truth are the cornerstones
- Your satisfaction is the cornerstone of our business
- Our guarantee is our cornerstone
- Built upon a solid cornerstone

See also: **BASE, BASICS, FOUNDATION, STAPLE**

CORPORATE
- Springs from our unique corporate spirit
- Another example of our corporate imagination
- Take advantage of our corporate strengths
- Fine corporate skills that have taken decades to hone

See also: **BUSINESS, ORGANIZATION**

CORRECT
- Do whatever is necessary to correct
- You've made the correct choice
- Correct the cause of your dissatisfaction

See also: **PERFECT, RIGHT**

COST
- No hidden costs
- It won't cost you a thing
- Let's compare costs
- Costs are determined by you
- Are you fed up with the high cost
- Beat the high cost of
- The low cost will surprise you
- What's the start-up cost to you
- Does anyone need to know it cost nearly

nothing to produce
- Less costly than ever
- Provided at no additional cost
- You would expect it to cost more but it doesn't
- Included at no extra cost
- At no cost or obligation
- Cost effective
- Costs almost nothing
- Buy sooner and the cost is less
- Reduced cost while improving strength and safety
- At no additional cost to you
- Twice the value at no extra cost
- Lower costs mean more of your money can work for you
- Helping you keep your costs in line
- So you can keep the lid on costs
- We know you have to keep your costs down
- Helps lower overall costs by
- There is no hidden cost to you
- With no increased costs
- At less than the cost of
- You know in advance exactly how much it will cost
- It only costs a little pocket change to
- The least costly of them all

Cost: price, value, worth, market value, amount, figure, valuation, quotation, demand, asking price, appraisement, appraisal, dollar value, expenditure, expense, charge, rate, hire
See also: CHARGE, DOLLAR, INSTALLMENT, MONEY, PAYMENT, PRICE, SAVINGS, VALUE

COSY
- Curl up and get cosy
- Surrounding you with cosy warmth
- Cosiness that warms the cockles of your heart
- Cosy up to great value

See also: COMFORTABLE, FRIENDLY, WARM

COUNSEL
- Ready to counsel you about
- When you're looking for trustworthy counsel
- Get the best counsel available
- Counselling you about your most urgent requirements

See also: ADVICE. CONSULT, EXPERT, WISDOM

COUNT
- Count yourself in today
- Every day thousands of people like you count on us to
- You can always count on us
- Naturally, we can count you among
- Count on us for more
- Where it counts the most
- You can count on us for everyday low prices
- Find out what really counts
- When you have to count the costs
- An organization you can count on all the way
- You don't count the cost when

See also: CONSIDER, VALUE

COUNTERFEIT
- Beware of counterfeits
- All others are counterfeits
- Don't accept counterfeit pleasure
- Beware of a counterfeit sense security

See also: CONFUSE

COUPON
- Only one coupon per customer
- Coupon must be presented at time of purchase
- Free coupons and special offers inside
- Look for additional coupon savings in store now
- Send us the coupon below or call our order desk at
- If the coupon is missing, write to this address or call
- Free with coupon
- Be sure to bring the coupon of your choice
- Look at these additional coupon savings in store now
- Special coupon offer
- Your next purchase with this coupon and a minimum purchase
- Plus valuable free coupons
- Receive a coupon redeemable at
- Just complete and mail the coupon
- Valuable coupons inside
- Save money with valuable coupons included
- In partnership with retailers, we're

bringing you these valuable coupons
- Look for major coupons inside
- Save more when you use our in-store coupons
- Just send in the coupon now
- Visit our website for more coupons online
- This coupon entitles you to
- Use instant-saving coupons to
- Look inside for coupon discounts
- Valid upon presentation of this coupon

Coupon: certificate, voucher, ticket, freebie
See also: CARD, CERTIFICATE, FORM, TICKET

COURSE
- Chart your own course
- Go for the best as a matter of course
- Of course you'll choose it
- The shortest course to success

See also: METHOD, ROAD, WAY

COURTEOUS
- Pleasant, intelligent and courteous
- Courteous service from start to finish
- You'll appreciate our helpful and courteous staff

COVER
- You can cover yourself with this program
- We've got everything covered
- Covers twice the area
- Making sure you're covered
- We've got every angle covered
- We've got you covered
- Nobody covers more

See also: CLASSIFY, PROTECT

COVERAGE
- The most comprehensive, up-to-date coverage in the world
- Just the right amount of coverage
- Offers a wide range of coverage
- For a little extra coverage
- Unrivalled coverage for
- No matter what coverage you need

See also: PROTECTION

CRAFT
- So finely crafted you'll gasp
- Quality-crafted
- Crafted with the care you've come to

expect
- Crafted with quality and love
- Wait till you see how well-crafted our product is

See also: ART, SKILL

CRAFTSMANSHIP
- And the consummate craftsmanship you'd expect from
- A level of craftsmanship as yet unsurpassed
- The craftsmanship is everything

See also: ABILITY, SKILL

CRANK
- Now you can really crank it up
- Don't be afraid to really crank
- Crank out the profits day after day
- Now you're cranking

See also: BOOST, PRODUCE

CRAZY
- Get crazy with
- People are crazy about
- If this problem is making you crazy
- Everyone is crazy to get their hands on this new product
- The savings are just plain crazy
- You'd have to crazy to pass up this

See also: AMOK, MADNESS, NUTS, WILD

CREATE
- Taking great pride in what we create
- Allows you to create a whole new
- You can create it for yourself
- Created with you in mind
- We set out to create an all-new
- Now you can easily create a dramatic
- Creates new value
- That's why we've created the new
- Can be created in seconds
- When it comes to creating

See also: ACCOMPLISH, ACHIEVE, ACT, BUILD, DO, MAKE, PERFORM

CREATION
- Exciting new creations
- Splendid creations inspired by Nature herself
- Sizzling creations zap your taste buds and your imagination

CREATIVITY
- The height of creativity
- Fostering creativity among our staff
- Combine your creativity with our expertise
- Creativity is priceless
- Do you know how much your creativity is worth
- Gets your creative juices flowing
- Unlock your own creativity

See also: IMAGINATION

CREATOR
- From the creators of
- Join the other creators of
- You can be the creator of your own life

CREATURE
- A fun-loving creature
- The most luxurious of creature comforts
- You're not a creature of habit
- Go where the wild creatures play

CREDENTIALS
- Outstanding credentials for
- We'll be happy to present our credentials for your inspection
- No one has better, more extensive credentials than us

See also: ASSURANCE, CERTIFICATE, GUARANTEE

CREDIBILITY
- Gives you instant credibility
- Our credibility is enormous
- Just look at our credibility and make your decision
- Nobody has more credibility when it comes to

See also: BELIEF, GUARANTEE

CREDIT
- Orders subject to credit approval
- Protect your good credit
- Give yourself the credit you deserve
- There's plenty of credit to go around
- Your credit is always good at
- Proud to take credit for
- Will be automatically credited to

See also: BELIEF, RESPONSIBILITY

CREST
- Have been riding the crest
- And interest has far from crested
- As good as stamping your family crest upon it
- You too can reach the crest of the wave

See also: BEST, PEAK, PINNACLE, SUPERIOR, TOP

CREW
- Not to mention a topnotch crew
- Become a part of the whole merry crew
- Our crew can be on the job within hours
- Highly trained crews descend upon

See also: STAFF, TEAM

CRITERIA
- Based on the criteria you set
- Measured against the most exacting criteria
- Keeping up when criteria are changing every day

See also: BENCHMARK, MEASURE, STANDARD

CROWD
- Above the crowd
- You're not a part of the crowd
- Standing apart from the crowd
- Join the crowd flocking to
- There's a reason why crowds are coming to see us
- A crowd pleaser every time

See also: PEOPLE

CRY
- Enough to make a grown man cry
- A need crying out to be filled
- No longer a voice crying in the wilderness
- Cries of delight greet the sight of

CUISINE
- Exquisite international cuisine
- Cuisine to die for
- Be sure to try our unusual and scrumptious cuisine

See also: COOK, DINE, FEAST, KITCHEN, MEAL, RECIPE, TASTE

CULTURE
- A culture deeply attuned to nature
- One of the most important cultural events
- For those to whom culture is important and irreplaceable

- Become more cultured quickly
See also: **SOPHISTICATION**

CURVE
- The most challenging curve
- It's called the learning curve
- When life throws you a curve, we can help
- Sleek curves gleaming in the sun
See also: **BEAUTY, FORM, SHAPE**

CUSHION
- Further cushioned by
- Providing you with a cushion of safety
- Cushions the shock of
- Cushioning you from any rude fluctuations in
See also: **EXTRA, PROTECT**

CUSTOM
- Quality custom crafted
- Manufacturers of custom products since
- Custom-made for you
- It's our custom to please
- A world famous name in custom products
- We value your custom enormously

CUSTOMER
- To ensure our valued customers can take advantage of
- From the very beginning of a customer relationship
- To better serve our customer needs
- Steadily improving customer service
- You can count on us for dedicated customer care
- We enjoy a very high customer return rate
- We're giving customers what they want – quality and value
- The satisfied customer specialists
- Building customer satisfaction
- Because ultimately, this business is about customer service
- Customer service is our top priority
- Offering exclusive products to a wide range of customers
- We go right where the customer lives and works
- Offer limited to new customers
- For nearly half a century, we've worked closely with our customers

- Thank you to all our loyal customers
- Customers are demanding more and faster service every day
- Keeps customers coming back year after year
- Certainly be a hidden treasure for our customers
- We satisfy the most demanding customers
- Finding new customers is easy
- Our customers come first
- The endless process of finding new customers
- Taking care of our regular customers first
- You'll find new customers faster and easier than ever before
- Our customers always come first
- Most of our business is satisfied repeat customers
- Satisfying an unlimited number of customers
- Giving customers a good impression is critical to
- All our customers love us
- We value you as a customer
- Our customers are very special to us
- To ensure that our valued customers can take full advantage
- Thanks for being a customer during this new and exciting time of change
- We couldn't do it without special customers like you
- As a loyal and valued customer
- Enjoy a very high customer return rate
- If we don't please our customers, somebody else will
- Appreciate loyal customers like you
- First 100 customers only
- Get preferred customer rates
- Gaining a customer for life
- You'll see why more and more satisfied customers are choosing
- You'll be a satisfied customer too

Customer: patron, client, clientele, buyer, shopper, purchaser, vendee, marketer
See also: **BUYER, CLIENT, CONSUMER**

CUSTOMER SERVICE
- Customer service information
- Our concern with quality can be seen in our customer service
- Customer service is our middle name

- The fastest, finest customer service in the business
- Let's talk customer service
- When you shop, you're also looking for customer service

CUSTOMIZE
- Helps you customize
- Customized to your exact specifications
- And don't forget to ask about our customized models

See also: INDIVIDUAL, PERSONALIZE

CUT
- Cut through the clutter
- A cut above the rest
- Not just cutting it any more
- Make the cut
- No one cuts it like us
- We cut our prices to the bone
- Come to us for cut-rate service and products
- Cost-cutting is the name of the game

DAMAGE
- Dramatically reduces risk of damage
- Very fast damage control
- Call us before the damage is done
- Protects against loss or damage
- Sometimes it's impossible to prevent damage to
- Guard against damage from

See also: DEFECT, RISK

DARE
- Dare to be beautiful
- For those who dare
- If you're one of the daring ones
- Make the daring choice
- Double dare, double pleasure
- We dare you to try it

DAREDEVIL
- Maintaining your daredevil image
- Even daredevils would be pleased
- The place where daredevils shop
- You don't have to be a daredevil to enjoy

See also: HERO, ICONOCLAST, INDIVIDUAL, MAVERICK

DARK
- You'll never be left in the dark again
- If you're in the dark about
- Are you being kept in the dark
- Come on out of the dark

See also: CONFUSE, ERROR

DATA
- Just massaging your data
- Actually getting your data into some kind of shape
- Providing the data you need to decide
- Get more data here than anyone else give on

See also: FACT, INFORMATION

DATABASE
- Inside every underfed corporate database
- Once you're part of our database, you benefit from
- A gigantic database at your service
- Choose from our huge database of
- Take advantage of the biggest database in the business

See also: INFORMATION

DATE
- We'll arrange for a convenient time and date
- Put an asterisk beside this date
- Mark a new date on your calendar
- We've got a date with you
- The most important date for renewing
- To confirm your choice of dates

See also: ERA, TIME

DAWN
- Dawn of new value
- The dawn of a new era is upon us
- The enormous value of this product is just beginning to dawn on the world
- A new day is dawning for you

See also: BEGINNING, INNOVATION, MORNING, START

DAY
- We look forward to the day when
- Just knowing you're getting the most out of each day
- Make it part of your day
- Start your day with
- Make us part of your day
- After just one day
- This could be your lucky day
- A bright new day is dawning
- Since the grand old days of

- Perfect for any day
- Right for that special day
- Allowing you to manage your day with added
- Every day is an opportunity to
- A day like no other
- Every day is different
- Some days are made for
- Today is the day
- Nothing beats a day in the sun
- Day-to-day benefits for the whole family
- Makes any day special
- Choose a convenient time and day

See also: **TIME**

DAZZLE
- Dazzling with brightness
- Dazzle them
- Just has more dazzle
- Look past the dazzle and see the solid quality
- Don't be dazzled by false claims
- With dazzling speed and efficiency

See also: **PIZZAZZ, SHINE**

DEADLINE
- Set your own deadlines for
- When deadlines are chasing you
- Don't let deadlines get you down
- We always finish within deadline

See also: **LIMIT**

DEAL
- Hurry! These deals won't last
- Plus the best deal in town
- The kind of deals you want to take home
- Always figure on a great deal
- Buy two, get one free deal
- You choose the deal
- All kinds of deals
- Heavyweight deals from
- You won't get a better deal
- Always a square deal
- A fabulous deal now
- You can deal direct with
- Everything you need to know to make a great deal
- We have your best deal
- Let's make a deal
- A hot deal every day
- Wake up to a terrific deal
- Check out this deal
- Double, double deal

- Here's the straight deal
- When problems seem more than you can deal with
- Come in and make your best deal
- The right deal, the right protection for you
- It's a done deal
- Hurry in for the deal of the century
- When you have a great deal riding upon
- A deal worth talking about
- Come in for outstanding deals
- Check out these deals
- More sweet deals from
- Back page deals
- Just a few of this week's unbeatable deals
- You'll find incomparable deals here
- Best deals in town
- We will beat any competitive deals
- Family deals to save even more
- The best deals are made when
- Exclusive deals on selected merchandise
- The finest deals ever
- Unbelievable deals in
- Humungous deals on all the best
- Hot deals on hot products

See also: **BARGAIN, BARGOON, COST, PRICE, SCOOP, VALUE**

DEALER
- Get to know your neighborhood dealer
- Dealer inquiries welcome
- Below dealer cost
- We've sold more products than any other dealer
- Strong dealer support is a priority
- Call today to order or for the name of the dealer nearest you
- We're a fast, reliable, full-service dealer
- Call your dealer right away and schedule an appointment
- See your dealer for a wide variety
- Only at your product dealer
- See your local dealer now
- More dealers recommend us than any other
- The only dealer offering this unique
- Dealers wanted
- Ask your dealer about it today
- Now at dealers everywhere

See also: **SALESPEOPLE**

DEALERSHIP
- Stop by the dealership anytime

- Better service from our dealership
- There's sure to be a dealership in your neighborhood
- Drop into our dealership and see for yourself
- A dealership that always stands behind its customers

See also: RETAILER

DECIDE

- You decide when and how
- We decided right off the bat
- When you have to decide in a hurry
- Helping you decide which is the best for you
- Deciding ahead of time saves money
- Look at our low, low prices before you decide
- But you have to decide today
- We make it very easy to decide
- So much to choose from, we make it hard to decide

Decide: determine, settle, arbitrate, referee, evaluate, consider, judge, deem, form an opinion, negotiate, arrange, conclude, resolve, settle upon, fix upon

See also: CHOOSE, CONSIDER, SELECT

DECISION

- I look forward to your decision about
- Please don't delay your decision
- A decision must be made sooner or later
- The business decision of a lifetime
- We leave the decision to you
- The most important decision you may ever face
- Decisions, decisions, decisions
- The best decision is the one that's right for you
- We're here to help you make a very important decision
- A whole new approach to decision-making
- The right decision is obvious
- Make that decision, take that action
- This could be the best decision you ever made
- Make your own decision about the need for
- Making your buying decisions the right ones

- Sound decisions to ensure a strong future
- To help you make a more informed decision about
- A decision everyone has to make
- Sooner or later you'll come up against this decision
- When your decision hangs in the balance

See also: CHOICE, OPTION

DECOR

- Available to suit your decor
- You can tell from the decor that
- A decor that expresses the inner you
- Time for a change of decor
- More than just the decor

See also: ATMOSPHERE

DECORATE

- Decorating with
- Your most important decorating decision
- It's easy to decorate when you choose our products
- When you decide to decorate, come to us

See also: BEAUTIFY, IMPROVE

DECORATIVE

- The decorative appeal and color
- For a truly whimsical decorative effect
- The fine decorative piece can be yours for only
- Useful and decorative at the same time

DECORATOR

- Decorator-inspired
- The most talented decorators are consulted
- Everyone will think you hired a decorator
- A decorator's dream
- Our decorator will coordinate it all specially for you

See also: EXPERT

DEDICATE

- We are dedicated to providing you with the best service, knowledge and advice
- Find out just how dedicated we are
- We dedicate this product to you
- Dedicated service people at your beck and call

See also: COMMIT

DEDICATION

- With the same dedication to quality and

style
- The result of awesome dedication on the part of
- The same dedication goes into producing
- Find out what dedication is all about
- A result of pure dedication to
- Putting dedication to excellence ahead of all else
- You could call it dedication, we call it love

DEFECT
- In the event of defects, we will replace the entire product
- Produced without defects
- To catch defects before they reach you

See also: **DAMAGE, ERROR**

DEFENCE
- Also improves the defence of
- Stimulates your body's natural defences
- Your first line of defence
- You best defence is
- We take defence against disease very seriously

See also: **FIGHT, PROTECT**

DEFINE
- Who has helped define
- The defining moment has arrived
- The product that has defined all the rivals
- Shows how you define yourself

See also: **CLASSIFY**

DELAY
- Please don't delay
- Delivered to you without delay
- No delays – we promise
- Each delay is a loss of money

See also: **LATE, SLOW, STOP**

DELICIOUS
- Simply delicious
- Are you dreaming of dangerously delicious
- So delicious, it's hard to believe they're
- Deliciously yours

See also: **GOOD, TASTE**

DELIGHT
- Chosen to make you experience sheer delight
- It's just another word for delight

- Guaranteed to fill you with delight
- Feel the delight rippling through your body
- You won't be able to contain your delight
- A little pocket of delight
- If you are not delighted in every way
- We think you'll be delighted
- Carries you into exotic and sensory delights

See also: **ENJOY, FUN, PLEASURE**

DELIVER
- Delivered free to your door
- We know how to deliver
- Delivered fast and fresh
- That's a promise we deliver
- Delivering cost-effectively under remarkable pressures
- Delivering more than
- For a nominal fee, we'll deliver right to your door
- Delivered to every home
- We never promise more than we can deliver
- We deliver every day
- We deliver to your home or job site
- We deliver quality and service
- Delivered straight to you
- Now delivering to your area
- We over-deliver just to make sure
- And that's exactly what our product delivers
- Ready to be delivered
- Continues to deliver the best

Deliver: transfer, provide, hand over, fork out, transmit, send, discharge, grant, concede, direct, convey, supply

See also: **BRING, CARRY, GIVE, PROVIDE, SEND, SUPPLY**

DELIVERY
- Comes with convenient home delivery
- Most items available for immediate delivery
- Free next-day deliver
- Save fifty percent off the regular home delivery price
- Free next-day delivery
- Plus free delivery on all major
- Competitive pricing, fast delivery and high-quality work

- Even faster delivery
- Delivery anywhere on the planet
- Free delivery day or night
- Increasing the speed of delivery via increased efficiency
- Ask our staff about our delivery service
- No extra charge for delivery
- Delivery is available
- Your free delivery is ending

DEMAND

- Due to unexpected demand, stock is temporarily depleted
- We expect a heavy demand
- Demand is so great we have to train more people
- Thanks to popular demand, our offer is back
- Back by popular demand
- We understand your demand for excellence
- Held over by popular demand
- Meeting the growing demand for
- Huge market demand
- Filling the exacting demands of our customers
- To handle the exploding demand
- Sky-high demand for
- Back by popular demand
- Just as demanding as you are
- Responding vigorously to demand wherever possible
- The extreme demands of
- To satisfy the growing demand

Demand: need, solicit, order, require, ask, call for, seek, want, in vogue, fashionable, people's choice
See also: ASK, CLAIM, COMMAND, INSIST, ORDER, REQUIRE

DEMEANOR

- Shed your ladylike demeanor
- Projecting an authoritative demeanor
- The improvement in demeanor is tremendous
- Don't be intimidated by our fierce demeanor

See also: APPEARANCE, LOOK

DEMONSTRATE

- Demonstrate what is excellent about
- We'd love to demonstrate it for you
- Our staff will be happy to demonstrate

See also: SHOW

DEMONSTRATION

- Call today to arrange a demonstration
- Free demonstration on request
- For the best demonstration, come in and see it in operation
- There's no better demonstration
- One demonstration will have you hooked
- Happy to give a personal demonstration

Demonstration: exhibit, show, display, example, presentation, retrospective, case, proof, exposition, evidence, proof, confirmation, verification
See also: DISPLAY, SHOW

DEPARTURE

- A departure from the ordinary
- The most radical departure since
- Get ready for your departure from Planet Earth
- You departure into a future world of

DEPEND

- You know you can depend on yourself
- When you have to depend on
- You can always depend on us for
- Finally, a product you can depend on

See also: RELY, TRUST

DEPENDABILITY

- A reputation for rugged dependability
- Top-class dependability in a tough world
- We know the first thing you look for is dependability
- Putting dependability first

See also: RELIABILITY

DEPENDABLE

- Rugged and dependable
- For dependable and durable performance, depend on us
- Always dependable, no matter what the conditions
- Beautiful and dependable, what a match

Dependable: reliable, trustworthy, honest, above board, trusty, unfailing, sure, steady, firm, hardy, steadfast, true blue, strong, abiding, secure, faithful, accountable
See also: RELIABLE, STRONG

DEPOSIT

- No deposit required
- Your deposit is returned at once
- For just a small deposit

DESERVE

- You deserve the same as
- Your family deserves the best
- Come down and get what you deserve
- Giving you the service and quality you deserve
- You've earned it and you deserve it
- You deserve more than just a

See also: EARN, MERIT

DESIGN

- Designed especially for you
- Delivers unmatched design and flare
- Yours to design
- A variety of wonderfully imaginative designs
- Magnificent design prevails
- To achieve design not found in any other
- Unparalleled in graceful, meticulous design
- The heart of contemporary design
- Your best design resource
- Inspired by the designs of
- Representing the very best in design
- A very intelligent design
- Have spent a great deal of time to design the perfect
- Design a product capable of fulfilling the demand potentials buyers will put on it
- Providing complete design and construction
- Innovative design combined with quality
- Hot design, hot looks, hot value
- A plan designed specifically for you
- Committing ourselves to fine design and workmanship
- Exclusive design from our own workshop
- Eye-catching designs
- Designed to make you happy
- Your machine was designed for it
- Allowing you to explore alternatives in design
- Unmistakably distinctive design

See also: AIM, ENGINEER, GOAL, OPINION, PHILOSOPHY, PLAN, PRINCIPLE, SYSTEM

DESIGNER

- Visit our designers today
- A designer, not just a decorator
- Designer quality at off-the-rack prices
- Looks as though a great designer just created it
- Our designers are always on call
- It took an outstanding designer to create something this elegantly simple
- Our professional designers created this delightful

See also: DECORATOR, EXPERT, PROFESSIONAL

DESIRE

- Something you may dearly desire
- Gratify your every desire
- See it and desire it
- Unabashed in our desire to pamper you
- Eloquently expressing a desire
- All you need is the desire to
- Built to fulfil your fondest desire

See also: NEED, WANT, WISH

DESTINATION

- Your fashion destination
- Has become a popular destination
- The destination of choice for
- The first destination is your home
- Has always been a favorite destination
- Providing excellent destinations
- A truly marketable destination for your clientele

See also: GOAL, PLACE, STORE

DETAIL

- Every detail reflects an integrity of design that is unmatched
- Beautifully detailed
- Every electrifying detail is captured
- Detail captured in true-to-life perfection
- Intricately detailed
- We take care of every detail for you
- One more detail you won't have to think about
- In every finely engineered detail
- For more details, call anytime
- See full details at your nearest area
- Just ask for more details when you call
- Here's how to get full details quickly and easily
- With all the delicious details provided
- Watch for more details

- Among the most delightful details are
- Ask your store for details
- Call for friendly, no-pressure details
- Our details make the difference
- There's a good reason for this great concern with detail
- Attention to detail shows in every
- Getting the details right is more vital than ever
- Just call, write, email or fax for details on how you can team up with
- Call for complete details today
- Leave the details to us
- Get all the exciting details
- Full details available
- See inside for details

Detail: item, particular, factor, point, element, fact, accessory, aspect, feature, unit, attitude, circumstance, specific

See also: ATTENTION, FACT, FACTOR, ITEM, PARTICULAR, POINT

DEVELOP
- Developed in order to provide you with the best
- We'll continue to develop exciting new products just for you
- Carefully developing a relationship with you
- Come and see what develops
- Working hard to develop better and better products and services

See also: BUILD, CHANGE, CREATE, EVOLVE

DEVELOPMENT
- One of the primary participants in the development of
- Actively involved in the development
- Everyone involved in this dramatic development
- This development directly impacts you
- Benefit immediately from this exciting new development

See also: ADVANCE, EVENT, PROGRESS

DIFFERENCE
- Can make a dramatic difference to you
- Try them and notice the big difference
- Compare the difference
- That's the difference between

- A difference you'll remember
- You'll sense the difference the very first time you
- Feel the difference
- And this makes all the difference
- The difference quality makes
- Just look at the difference
- Experience the difference
- Making all the difference in
- The difference between merely correct and truly inspired
- Delivers a difference you can feel
- Our true point of difference
- See, hear, feel, savor the difference
- The difference is in the details
- See and feel the difference as soon as you try it
- There is a definite difference
- Let us prove the difference
- You can hardly tell the difference between
- You can spot the difference right away
- For people who want to make a difference in the world
- Double the difference, double the fun

See also: CHANGE, CONTRAST, IMPROVEMENT, MODIFY

DIFFERENT
- Different from anything else you've experienced
- What's different is
- Determined to be different
- Truly different
- For those who want to be stylishly different
- For those who prefer something a bit different
- Dramatically different
- You're an individualist, you want to be different
- How different can you get
- A dramatically different way of thinking
- Remains wholly different from
- Giving you the chance to try something totally different

DIFFICULT
- We know how difficult it can be
- No longer need be difficult to
- A difficult problem with an easy solution
- When you're wrestling with a really difficult decision

See also: CHALLENGE

DIGITAL
- A whole new digital era
- Now completely digital
- Now that everything is going to even faster digital, leap ahead with
- Giving the speed of digital design

DILEMMA
- The answer to a modern dilemma
- A problem that could throw you into a real dilemma
- Gets you out of your dilemma in a jiffy

See also: CHALLENGE, PROBLEM

DILIGENT
- Has always been diligent about
- Diligently taking care of all your needs
- Diligent research has turned up exciting new information

DIMENSION
- Has just doubled the dimensions
- A brilliant new dimension in
- To provide an extra dimension in the continued growth of
- Gives added dimension at an affordable price
- A dimension undreamed of before
- Elevating the product to a new dimension
- Of awe-inspiring dimensions
- Enter a different dimension today
- Brings an amazing new dimension to

See also: FORM, SHAPE, SIZE

DINE
- Two can dine for the price of one
- Dine out every day
- Imagine dining in such splendor
- For your fine dining pleasure
- Delicious dining at a more affordable price

See also: COOK, EAT, FEAST, TREAT

DIRECT
- Buy direct from the manufacturer
- Direct from Europe and beyond
- Directing every critical stage of the operation
- The savings go directly to you
- Up-front and direct
- You deal with us direct, not an agent

- Order direct and save even more
- You can direct the entire process
- Direct savings to you

See also: FAST, OPEN

DIRECTION
- A big step in the right direction
- Under the direction of new owners
- We'll point you in the right direction
- Takes you in a brand new direction
- Have taken an entirely new direction
- We try not to go in one direction
- A direction you haven't thought of yet
- Our directions are a lot easier to follow

See also: APPROACH, CONTROL, MANAGEMENT

DISCONTINUE
- We'll never discontinue this vital service
- Great deals on discontinued stock
- Save on a huge selection of discontinued items

See also: END, FINISH

DISCOUNT
- We will give you a discount equal to
- Now discounted
- Special offer discount
- Huge discounts for a limited time only
- Special discount for special customers
- Get the biggest discount here
- Over and above any discount
- Just call our service to enjoy further savings and discounts
- Not to be combined with any other offer or discount
- Ask how you can get a big discount
- You understand the value of big discounts
- Save over and above any other discount
- We would like to offer you a special discount
- Bring the special discount coupon
- For an extra discount on your purchases
- Every item offered at a discount
- This program give you exclusive discount rates and privileges
- Not valid with any other discount offer

See also: DEAL, PRICE, SAVINGS

DISCOVER
- Discover that this means to you
- Millions have discovered how very easy

it is
- Discover how easily you can
- I think you'll soon discover that
- You'll be amazed to discover
- Helps you discover a better way
- Discover what it's all about
- Discover the world of
- Just waiting for you to discover them
- You'll also discover
- Discover a smart new way to
- Come, discover this and much more
- Sailing the world to discover
- Visitors delight as they discover

See also: FIND

DISCOVERY
- The unmatchable thrill of discovery
- The biggest, most exciting discovery yet
- A discovery that could really change your life
- Working on new discoveries every day
- Taking a passage of self-discovery
- Join a captivating voyage of discovery

See also: ADVANCE, DEVELOPMENT, LEAP, RESEARCH, SCIENTIFIC, STRIDE

DISCREET
- Our service is expert, discreet and entirely confidential
- A discreet professional will call on you
- Information comes in a discreet, unmarked envelope
- Always reliable, always discreet

See also: CONFIDENTIAL, HIDE, SECRET

DISCRETION
- Completely at your discretion
- Always handled with discretion
- You can always count on taste and discretion

DISPLAY
- See our fantastic display
- Displaying all the signs of a real winner
- Our display model explains it all
- Don't miss our display at

See also: ARRAY, CHOICE, DEMONSTRATE, SHOW, SHOWROOM

DISTANCE
- We go the distance
- Finally able to put some distance between yourself and
- Shortening the distance significantly between you and your goal

See also: FAR, ROOM, SPACE

DISTINCTION
- Maintaining a firm distinction between
- Performing with distinction for the last twenty years
- Adding that indispensable touch of distinction to

DISTINCTIVE
- Refreshingly distinctive
- As distinctive as those who use it
- A very distinctive touch
- A distinctive style no one could miss

See also: INDIVIDUAL, UNIQUE

DISTINGUISH
- Only one of the things that distinguish
- Has distinguished itself once again
- Can satisfy even distinguished tastes like yours
- Rapidly distinguishing ourselves from the rest of the pack

DIVIDEND
- To help build your dividend even faster
- With dividends you never expected
- Reliable service is another huge dividend

See also: BENEFIT, BONUS, EXTRA

DO
- It's not that we do, it's how we do it
- You can do it at home in your spare time
- The power to do more and do it better
- Here's what we'll do for you
- Look what you can do in just one day
- Here's what we do
- Now you can do virtually all of your
- We're doing something about it
- You've got better things to do than
- All you have to do to join the party is
- Nobody today knows how to do it better than
- Does it all, all at once
- Who else is doing that for you
- How do we do it
- Suddenly, you have to do it
- You'll know exactly what to do
- You don't do anything halfway

- Learn the do's and don'ts of
See also: ACT, ACTION, ACHIEVE, ACCOMPLISH, PERFORM

DO-IT-YOURSELF
- You can do it yourself easily with help from our experts
- We're the place for the do-it-yourselfer
- Fast help for the do-it-yourselfer
- Great for the ambitious do-it-yourselfer
- For the beginning, intermediate and expert do-it-yourselfer
See also: CRAFTSMANSHIP

DOCTOR
- Safe, gentle, doctor-recommended
- Just what the doctor ordered
- No spin doctors involved
- Ask your doctor to find out
See also: CLINICAL, SCIENTIFIC

DOGFIGHT
- Successfully engage in a dogfight with some of the best
- If you don't want to find yourself in a dogfight
- When life seems like one huge dogfight

DOLL
- All dolled up and plenty of fun places to explore
- No more effective than a doll
- Cute as a doll
- Turns you into a living doll

DOLLAR
- A way to get top dollar for
- Savings by the dollar
- Earn an honest dollar
- Useful methods to maximize your dollar
- Make your dollar go further than ever before
- Dollar days are here again
- Dollar for dollar, feature for feature
- Squeeze more from your dollar
- Special dollar buys
- You'll be saving yourself a few more dollars
- Don't let dollars trickle away unnoticed
- Benefit from yet another source of dollars
See also: BUY, CASH, DEAL, MONEY,

SAVINGS, VALUE

DOMESTIC
- Both domestically and internationally
- Improves domestic management
- The best domestic product you can buy
- A big player in your domestic affairs
See also: FAMILY, HOME, LOCAL

DONE
- Help get things done with
- And we've done just that
- No longer just done in
- Now you can be finally done with
See also: END, FINISH

DOOR
- Just outside your door is an exclusive world
- You'll never have to knock on another door
- Come knock on our door
- Right at your door
- Delivered to your door day or night
- Opens doors you never dreamed possible
- Now a new door is open for you
- Keeping doors open for
- Opening the door to
- Your doorway to discovery
- Opens the door to a richer experience
See also: ENTER

DOORCRASHER
- Doorcrasher specials
- You can't beat a doorcrasher like this
- Come early for our doorcrasher deals

DOORSTEP
- Is now available right on your doorstep
- Savings right on your doorstep
- The help you need could be standing on your doorstep
- Doorstep to doorstep in record time
See also: HOME

DOSE
- Give yourself a dose of
- A strong dose of reality
- Providing a bigger dose of fun

DOUBLE
- Double your dollars, double the value

- Double your fun with
- Double value for half the effort
- This week only you get double

See also: DUPLICATE, INCREASE, PAIR

DOUBT
- Beyond a shadow of a doubt
- Putting all your doubts to rest
- If you had any doubts, this will finish them off

See also: CONFUSE, ERROR, MISTAKE, UNSURE

DOWN
- You won't be able to put it down
- It won't let you down
- Pick the one that never lets you down
- Goes down good
- Get down and dirty
- As prices go down, value shoots up
- Prices are dropping down, down, down
- No money down

DOWN PAYMENT
- A small down payment will hold these items until you need them
- No down payment until
- And we won't even ask you for a down payment
- The smallest down payment you'll ever find
- The down payment is easily negotiable

See also: INSTALLMENT

DOWNTIME
- Reduce your downtime
- Get yourself more downtime
- Makes even downtime productive
- You can do it all in your downtime

See also: REST

DOWNTOWN
- Shop downtown at
- Just minutes from downtown
- Now you can bring downtown home with you
- Downtown chic

DRAMA
- With all the drama of
- Capture total drama in
- Share the drama by

- You won't fine better drama than this
- Caught up in the drama of
- Famous for creating high drama

See also: ADVENTURE, EXCITEMENT, THRILL

DRAW
- Draws upon the vast resources of
- A look, a style that draws upon
- Do we have to draw you a picture
- Draw more profits to you

DREAM
- The countdown to your dream
- The stuff that dreams are made of
- More than you ever dreamed possible
- Build your own dream
- You've been dreaming of this ever since
- You can make your life's dream come true
- If you've ever dreamed of
- Why just dream when you can actually do it
- Sets you on your way to building your dream
- A place to dream about
- Dream about what to do with all the money you've just saved
- With a lot of other people who share your dream
- It's what you've always been dreaming about
- Plan your dream now
- Now is the time to create your dream
- Fulfil a different dream
- The possession that others can only dream about
- Dreams can come true anytime
- People like you have been turning dreams into reality for years
- Don't put your dreams on hold
- People who believe that dreams really do come true
- Dress up your dream with
- No such thing as a small dream
- For those who dream big
- See, dreams do come true
- Will seem like a dream come true
- If you've been dreaming of
- Passionate about fulfilling our customer's dreams
- Could actually change the way you dream

- Just like a dream come true
- Today your dreams are coming true
- Making your dream come to life

See also: DESIRE, IMAGINE, VISION, WISH

DRESS

- Dress up your home with
- We don't have to dress it up with fancy words
- Dressy in a very comfortable way
- Dressing up an old idea with a whole new twist

See also: BEAUTIFY, IMPROVE

DRIFT

- Results in sweeping drifts of
- Drift off into a world of delights
- Keeps you from drifting off track

See also: FLOAT, MOVE, SHIFT

DRIVE

- With enthusiasm and drive you can
- Barely an hour's drive from
- Have the foresight and drive to
- To arrange a test drive, call
- It's worth the drive to

See also: FUEL, INSPIRE, MOTIVATE, POWER

DROP

- Shop till you drop
- Drop in to see us soon
- Prices are dropping rapidly
- Just watch our prices drop
- You're always welcome to drop in
- Inviting you to drop in and chat
- Drop in throughout the week
- More and more people are dropping in to take a look at our product

See also: AVOID, DUMP, FINISH, VISIT

DRUM

- An even better way to drum up business
- The drums are rolling, the flags are flying
- Step to a different drummer

DUE

- Now get your just due
- Get your deliveries exactly when they're due
- Due to skyrocketing interest in
- Everyone gets their dues

- Finally getting your due
- You've paid your dues, now get your reward

Due: payable, in arrears, mature, outstanding, receivable, owing, unpaid, rightful, proper, correct

See also: DESERVE, OWE

DUMP

- It's time to dump that old
- Send that outdated contraption to the dump
- When you're down in the dumps, here's the cure

See also: DROP

DUPLICATE

- Once again we've duplicated our previous triumph
- Now you can duplicate this success
- Has never before been duplicated

See also: COPY, REPEAT

E-NEWSLETTER

- Receive our e-newsletter filled with exciting new products, trends and offers
- And you get our e-newsletter too
- Our e-newletter saves paper

EARLY

- Early bird special
- It's never too early to
- Get here early to make sure you get your
- Early results are astonishing
- The earlier you make your decision the more you'll save

See also: DAWN, MORNING, SOON

EARN

- You start earning right away
- Not only do you earn valuable
- Earn with every purchase you make
- We'll earn your business
- You've earned a rest
- Keep what you've earned by
- Earn big money by
- You've earned it, now enjoy it
- Gives you lots of ways to earn

Earn: gain, acquire, obtain, secure, get, profit, benefit, avail, procure, gather, garner, glean, reap, make, clear, pocket, pull down, bag, gross, net, take home, make a pretty

penny, bring home the bacon, bring in, pull in, merit, deserve, win, cause, bring about, yield

See also: COLLECT, DESERVE, GAIN, HARVEST, WORK

EARTH
- Nourished by the elements of Earth
- You wonder where on Earth we'd be without it
- Earth-friendly
- Like no other place on earth
- Kind to the Earth we live on

See also: ENVIRONMENT, GLOBE, WORLD

EASE
- To gently ease away
- The unstudied ease of a classic
- Now you can do it with the greatest of ease
- Travelling with ease
- To help ease the strain of daily expenses
- Ease your way with

See also: COMFORT, CONVENIENCE

EASTER
- Parade of Easter values
- The Easter bunny has arrived
- Easter Carnival
- Easter on parade
- Easter hunt for value
- Whopper eggs for Easter
- A joyous Easter to all our clients
- The Easter bunny follows the signs to great bargains
- Take a look in our Easter basket
- Hop to it Easter deals
- Easter savings on
- Have a safe and happy Easter
- Special treats for Easter enjoyment
- Make this Easter holiday weekend a memorable event for the whole family
- Egg-cellent Easter deals
- Every Easter bunny loves a bargain
- Easter specials all week
- Surprise some bunny special for Easter
- Look at these Easter specials
- Easter greetings to everyone
- Hop in for your Easter basket
- A tisket, a tasket, a yummy Easter basket
- Come join us for Easter
- Stroll in for Easter savings

- Some bunny special deserves a big Easter treat
- Egg-ceptional Easter savings
- Easter egg-stravaganza
- Hop on in for a Happy Easter

See also: CELEBRATE, FESTIVE, HOLIDAY, RITE

EASY
- Discover just how easy it is
- Makes it easy for you to become successful
- The quick and easy solution
- It's as easy as one, two, three
- Makes for easy eating
- Taking it easy with
- That's so easy to get into
- Yes, it's easy to
- Makes it very easy for you to
- It's the smart, easy way to
- We make saving money as easy as
- It's that easy
- We work hard to make it easy
- Always easy on your pocketbook
- Easy on your bank account too
- As easy as turning on your PC
- See how easy it is to
- To find out just how easy it is to
- Simple instructions make it easy
- Everything is so easy it can be done while
- Easier and quicker
- This task has never been easier
- It's never been easier to
- We could tell you how fast and easy it is to benefit
- If you don't agree that this is the quickest and easiest, most enjoyable you've ever tried, you can wave goodbye to
- To make things even easier for you
- It isn't always this easy to
- Easier and more enjoyable
- Easier to use than ever before
- We make it so easy to save
- Comfortable and easy to use
- Easy-to-follow instructions
- As easy as possible to order
- The easiest money you've ever made

Easy: simple, plain, obvious, effortless, hands-down, smooth sailing, pushover, piece of cake, picnic, breeze, duck soup, child's play, no sweat, comfortable, carefree, casual,

lenient, indulgent, natural, flowing, suave, leisurely, unhurried
See also: **COMFORTABLE, CONVENIENT, SIMPLE**

EAT
- Ready to eat
- Eat or be eaten
- All you can eat every day
- Why eat out when you can serve delights like this at home
- Make eating an even greater pleasure
See also: **COOK, DINE, FEAST, KITCHEN, MEAL, TASTE, TREAT**

ECOLOGY
- Ecologically wise use
- And you're also taking care of the ecology
- Ecology is always factored in first
See also: **ENVIRONMENT, NATURE, OUTDOORS**

ECONOMIC
- Regardless of economic conditions
- Take advantage of an economic upturn
- In today's tough economic climate you
- need extra protection
- When you make economic decisions, consider this
See also: **FINANCIAL**

ECONOMICAL
- But it's an economical and effective way of getting what you want
- Economical value
- Popular and economical to dress up your
- When you want to make the most economical choice
- Economical and beautiful at the same time
Economical: thrifty, economizing, saving, sparing, prudent, careful, conservative, frugal, money-saving, cost-effective, high-yield, low-cost, budget, low-budget, low-income
See also: **BUDGET, CHEAP, INEXPENSIVE, LOW COST, SAVING, THRIFT, UNDERSOLD**

ECONOMY
- Meeting the challenge of today's global economy
- Don't let the economy get you down
- No matter what the economy is doing, you can thrive
- We can give you economies of scale
- Sooner or later, everyone has to make economies
- When quality and economy are your prime concerns
See also: **BUSINESS, SAVINGS, TRADE**

EDGE
- Relish the driving edge
- Even those who live on the edge know
- If you like your items to be on the leading-edge
- Moving ahead at a fever pitch
- Adding an edge or spark to your newest
- We give you an edge
- Your edge on the future
- You'll be on the leading edge of
- The right look gives you the edge
See also: **ADVANTAGE, BOUNDARY, LIMIT, RESTRICTION**

EDITION
- After this edition closes, no more will ever be made
- This highly desirable limited edition is going fast
- Register today to get the latest edition

EDUCATE
- Educating your customers about the benefits of your product
- Educating the world about
- Educate yourself the easy way
- We service as we educate
See also: **INFORM, LEARN, TEACH**

EDUCATIONAL
- Will prove highly educational
- Your children need educational toys
- Visiting our store can be a very educational experience

EFFECT
- Creating a more intimate effect
- Now you can get the desired effect from merely
- You'll be amazed at the effect
- For best effect, use it often
- The beneficial effects will delight you

Effect: consequence, outcome, result, conclusion, issue, end, upshot, event, sequel, aftermath, fallout, side effect, punch, vigor, strength, potency, impact, influence, meaning, sense
See also: IMAGE, IMPRESSION, RESULT, USE

EFFECTIVE

- Here's what makes it so effective
- Fast and effective
- An effective plan you can put into action right away
- You want a product that's effective and economical
- You'll be amazing by its effectiveness
- The secret of its effectiveness is
- Is more effective and costs less
- These low prices effective only until

Effective: capable, competent, effectual, efficient, adequate, sufficient, useful, serviceable, practical, real, valid, striking, telling, impressive, pointed, moving, arousing, powerful, potent, forcible, influential, efficacious, able, good
See also: USEFUL

EFFICIENCY

- More efficiency is something we don't take lightly
- Tooled for efficiency, not effect
- For modern efficiency, we win hands down
- Gives greater efficiency with less
- Efficiency has increased dramatically in the last few years

See also: CONVENIENCE, SAVING

EFFICIENT

- Runs more efficiently
- The fast, safe, efficient way to
- Simple and efficient
- Always striving for greater efficiency
- The most efficient product you can find on the market
- This efficient system pays off for you right away

Efficient: effective, valid, active, productive, high-powered, competent, fit, on the ball, qualified, eligible, proficient, adept, accomplished, polished, practised, experienced, clever, deft, adroit, talented,

economical, thrifty, saving

EFFORT

- Part of a broad-based effort to
- We've put a great deal of effort into
- We know how much effort it takes to
- Honoring the effort you've put into
- One of the first organizations to combine our efforts with
- The first to actually put a coordinated effort together
- Combining efforts to enhance
- After a lot of hard work and effort
- The combined efforts of
- Does not take a lot of skill and effort on your part

See also: BLITZ, STRIVE, WORK

ELEGANCE

- Captures all the stately elegance
- Elegance is the social tone here
- Timeless elegance
- A look of sleek elegance
- Inspired by the elegance and charm of old world
- The purest form of elegance
- A touch of elegance at your fingertips
- The height of understated elegance
- Embodies timeless, streamlined elegance befitting

See also: BEAUTY

ELEGANT

- It is extremely elegant
- Breathtakingly elegant
- A supremely elegant solution to
- The cool, elegant way to
- For a more elegant good time, don't miss
- Wait until they see how elegant you've become
- Such a simple way to be elegant

Elegant: luxurious, posh, sumptuous, grand, fine, rich, swank, gorgeous, ornamental, ornate, excellent, choice, superior, select, exquisite, tasteful, well-made, urbane, sophisticated, polished, chi-chi, stylish, fashionable, cultured, cultivated, well-bred, debonair, dapper, charmer, polite, charming, courteous, genteel, gracious, correct, discriminating, refined, intelligent, well-proportioned, balanced, harmonious, aesthetic, artistic

See also: BEAUTIFUL, CHIC, STYLE

ELEMENT
- The primary element is
- One of the essential elements in your
- Here are the elements to watch for
- Finally, you're in your element

See also: BASIC, COMPONENT, NECESSITY, STAPLE

ELIGIBLE
- You may be fully eligible for
- Making you eligible for even bigger benefits
- We're contacting all eligible people

ELIMINATE
- Now you can eliminate many of the effects of
- Every item must be unconditionally eliminated
- Virtually eliminates the competition
- Eliminate worry and stress with

See also: PREVENT, REMOVE

ELITE
- Join a very special elite
- Make yourself one of the elite
- Where the elite shop
- The very few elite who get to the top
- Part of an elite group of products

See also: CLUB, EXCLUSIVE, GROUP, SPECIAL, RARE

EMBRACE
- You'll love the way it embraces
- Embrace the future with enthusiasm
- Embraces you with pure pleasure
- Make yourself embraceable

See also: CARESS, HUG, JOIN

EMOTION
- Teases your emotions with
- Stimulating all sorts of warm and pleasant emotions
- Let your emotions tell you what to do

ENCHANTRESS
- Turn yourself into an enchantress fast
- Fit for an enchantress
- A spell woven by an enchantress
- Look in the mirror and find an enchantress

See also: ALLURE, MAGIC, SEDUCTION

ENCOURAGE
- We encourage you to watch for
- The results are so encouraging that
- A very encouraging sign
- You'll be really encouraged to know

See also: BOOST, HELP

END
- It all ends this week
- Where you come to make sure of a storybook ending
- The perfect end to
- Marks the beginning of the end of
- And it doesn't end there
- The end is near
- Just no end in sight
- End your search here
- Just when you think there is no end
- The end of all your troubles is now within your reach

See also: AIM, COMPLETION, DISCONTINUE, EXPIRE, FINAL, FINISH, GOAL, GONE, LAST

ENDORSEMENT
- Our personal seal of endorsement
- Satisfied customers have been sending us endorsements
- Just look at these endorsements and see how good

Endorsement: stamp, seal, approval, authorization, attestation, promise, word, commendation, patronage

See also: ACCEPTANCE, APPRECIATION, PATRONAGE, SUPPORT, TESTIMONIAL

ENDURE
- Offering excellence that will endure
- Enduring long after the others have crumbled away
- Something that endures the tough stuff

See also: LAST, RELIABLE

ENERGIZE
- You'll feel energized
- Energize yourself with
- Refreshing and energizing
- Your life will be energized immediately

See also: INSPIRE, INVIGORATE, REJUVENATE, REVIVE

ENERGY
- You could discover more energy, joy and satisfaction
- Gets that extra energy from
- High energy products
- Provides you with plenty of energy to cope with stress and feel great
- For everyone who needs more energy
- Embraced by the energy of
- Beside saving energy, you'll be saving money too
- You'll feel the energy surge
- Replenish your energy after
- So energy-efficient you will actually save
- Energy to spring into
- Gives you the energy to
- Save time, energy and money
- Gets that extra energy from
- Try some high-energy moves

Energy: vigor, vitality, brio, get-up-and-go, force, power, guts, nerve, potency, drive, push, muscle, ambition, enterprise, spirit, dash, vivacity, verve, flair, fire, zing, glow, fervency, ardor, bounce, sprightliness, buoyancy, cheer, ebullience, sparkle, effervescence, vim, zip, zeal, passion, pep, exuberance, enthusiasm
See also: ALIVE, ENTHUSIASM, PASSION, POWER, STRENGTH

ENGINE
- An engine of growth for any business venture
- Like the purr of a powerful engine
- The engine that drives it all
- Turn yourself into a powerful engine
See also: DRIVE, HARNESS, POWER

ENGINEER
- Engineered for dependability and beauty
- Engineered to provide the best
- Our engineers have worked for years to create
- The engineering is simply superb
- An engineering marvel for your home
See also: DESIGN, PLAN

ENGLISH
- Give it to you in plain English

- Spelling it out in everyday English
- In a very readable English version

ENHANCE
- Enhances without overpowering
- The idea is to quickly and easily enhance
- To enhance and maintain
- Enhanced profits and sales are the result
- And to further enhance your
See also: ADVERTISE, HELP, IMPROVE, PROMOTE

ENHANCEMENT
- Their timely enhancement through
- It's an enhancement you can't do without
- Enjoy even further enhancements
- A number of enhancements quickly improve your
See also: IMPROVEMENT

ENJOY
- Settle down, tune in and enjoy
- Enjoy it year round
- Will be enjoyed again and again
- Let's you enjoy more of your favorite
- Something the whole family can enjoy
- Enjoy it in the privacy of your own home
- You'll soon be enjoying the finest
- Young and old will be able to enjoy
- We trust you enjoy our products
- Making them a pleasure to enjoy
- Dream of enjoying
- Everything you need to enjoy
- Go on, enjoy the goodness of
- Do you enjoy working with
- So you can enjoy it even more
- Do something you really enjoy
- If you enjoy working with
- Then sit back and enjoy a full year of

Enjoy: take pleasure in, rejoice, revel, riot, groove, luxuriate, bask, savor, appreciate, indulge, love, fancy, benefit from, profit, make the most of
See also: BENEFIT, DELIGHT, ENTERTAINMENT, EXPERIENCE, FUN, JOY, PLEASURE

ENJOYABLE
- Make getting there as enjoyable as being there
- Reward yourself with a truly enjoyable
- For a genuinely enjoyable experience

- Something both enjoyable and useful

See also: PLEASURE

ENJOYMENT

- An entirely new world of enjoyment to explore
- Your enjoyment gets greater every day
- Working hard to create enjoyment for you
- Just watch the enjoyment on their faces
- Continue the enjoyment you've come to expect from
- There's a wonder of enjoyment waiting for you
- Add to your enjoyment all year long

Enjoyment: delight, gladness, cheer, pleasure, gratification, satisfaction, zest, relish, gusto, exhilaration, transport, ecstasy, mirth, glee, merriment, jollity, gaiety, happiness, elation, bliss, felicity, contentment, ease, comfort, kick, bang, thrill, amusement, entertainment, diversion, recreation, delectation

See also: FUN, HAPPY, NICE

ENOUGH

- Just can't get enough
- If all this first class service isn't enough
- One is often enough
- More than enough for
- Now there's enough for everybody

See also: PLENTY, SATISFY

ENRICH

- Enrich your life with
- One of the most enriching experiences you can have
- Uniquely enriched with

See also: IMPROVE, INCREASE

ENROL

- Delighted to enrol you for this excellent benefit
- You are among the first to be invited to enrol
- Enrol today by calling
- Enroll now for your free trial
- Call to enroll before the deadline
- If you haven't yet enrolled yet, call now
- Now you can enroll in our exclusive

See also: JOIN, REGISTER

ENSURE

- Ensure the job is done to your satisfaction
- To ensure you are satisfied with the work
- We can ensure that
- We have ensured that only the best
- Ensure your pleasure with
- Ensure your future benefits now
- A staff of hundreds all working to ensure the utmost quality

ENTER

- Enter now to win one of these great prizes
- You can enter today
- Enter a dazzling new realm of
- You're invited to enter the open door of opportunity

See also: ACCESS, ADMIT, JOIN, PENETRATE

ENTERPRISE

- Reap the benefits of free enterprise
- Become part of a magnificent enterprise
- No limit to the possibilities of this thrilling enterprise

See also: ADVENTURE, GAMBLE, RISK, VENTURE

ENTERTAIN

- As entertaining as it is enlightening
- An enthralling, immensely entertaining look
- One of the most brilliantly original and entertaining
- Entertaining made easy with
- A highly entertaining way to spend an evening
- Take a moment to entertain a totally new idea
- Makes entertaining a snap

See also: CELEBRATE, ENJOY, HOST, PARTY, PLEASE

ENTERTAINMENT

- It's also great entertainment
- A treasure trove of marvellous entertainment
- More for your entertainment dollar
- If it's entertainment you're looking for, you've come to the right place

See also: ENJOYMENT, PARTY, SHOW

ENTHUSIASM
- We hope you share renewed enthusiasm
- The amount of enthusiasm generated is astounding
- Lighting a fire of enthusiasm
- Given with pleasure and enthusiasm
- The overwhelming enthusiasm shows

See also: DELIGHT, ENERGIZE, ENJOYMENT, FUN, PASSION, PLEASURE

ENTHUSIAST
- For the enthusiast in the family
- Offers enthusiasts a whole range
- For amateurs and enthusiasts alike
- We'll turn you into an enthusiast
- Formulated for the true enthusiast

See also: FAN

ENTITLE
- Here's what you're entitled to
- Entitles you to save on every purchase
- And you're entitled to even more big savings when you buy two

See also: DESERVE, EARN

ENVELOPE
- Promised to push the envelope even further
- One of the things that expand the envelope
- Enveloping you in warmth and softness

See also:, SETTING, SURROUND

ENVIRONMENT
- New, environmentally friendly
- In a highly professional environment
- Now you can do your part for the environment by
- Require specific knowledge, skills and attitudes in this environment
- Thrive in a safe and challenging environment
- A highly protective environment
- We care about the environment
- Adds up to an environment of excellence
- Thrive in a challenging and ever-evolving environment
- Effectiveness with the environment in mind
- While going easy on the environment
- Protecting the environment has never been easier

- In an exciting and growing environment
- Finding the right environment for you
- Environmentally-triggered
- We share your concern about the environment

Environment: milieu, conditions, surroundings, mood, setting, aura, scene, background, medium, element, ambiance, atmosphere, habitat, ecology

See also: ATMOSPHERE, EARTH, ECOLOGY, HOME, NATURE, SETTING

ENVIRONMENTAL
- Makes it a sound environmental choice
- Environmentally friendly
- Up to the highest environmental standards
- Passes all environmental tests with flying colors

See also: CLEAN, NATURAL

EQUAL
- Not every product is created equal
- Equal to the very best
- All things being equal
- More than equal to the job

EQUIP
- Equipping you for the job ahead
- Equipped with everything you need
- Specially equipped with
- Comes fully equipped with
- One of the largest and best-equipped
- The finest equipped in the city

See also: GEAR

EQUIPMENT
- You just need the right equipment
- Better equipment means better results
- We have all the equipment to help you
- Reducing the equipment you have to have to
- Major equipment supplied

See also: GEAR, MACHINE, STUFF

ERA
- Promising a whole new era in
- The era of total comfort has arrived
- It's our era now
- Be in at the start of a new era of
- Don't be stuck with the baggage of a

bygone era
- A bright new era begins

See also: **AGE, TIME**

ERGONOMIC
- All ergonomically designed and perfectly placed
- Shaped ergonomically for your health and comfort
- Ergonomic design will boost your productivity

See also: **COMFORT, EASE, HEALTH, NATURAL**

ERROR
- Reserve the right to correct pricing errors
- No more errors when you choose us
- Error-free and so simple to use
- Makes errors vanish like magic

See also: **CONFUSE, DEFECT, MISTAKE, WRONG**

ESCAPE
- Options in planning your great escape
- Escape from the ordinary
- Don't let a bargain like this escape
- Just when you think there's no way to escape
- Providing a lot more than one way to escape from
- Dream of the escape you long for

See also: **BREAK, GETAWAY, VACATION**

ESSENCE
- The essence of a great item
- We offer you the very essence of
- The essence of all your dreams rolled into one
- Get straight to the essence of it

See also: **HEART**

ESSENTIAL
- Absolutely essential to your success
- Start with the essentials
- Enterprising essentials
- It's really essential that
- The essentials are all here
- All the essentials you need for worry-free

Essential: basic, necessary, vital, requisite,, important, main, material, substantial, intrinsic, characteristic, chief, element, root,

nitty-gritty, primary, bottom line, attribute

See also: **BASIC, COMPONENT, ELEMENT, FUNDAMENTAL, NECESSARY, NECESSITY, NEED, REQUIRE, STAPLE**

ESTABLISH
- Now firmly established in
- Helping to establish you as
- Establishing our superiority for all to see
- Establishes you at the top

See also: **BEGIN, SET-UP**

ESTEEM
- Enhance your self esteem with
- The most esteemed establishment in the city
- We hold our customers in the highest esteem

See also: **PRIDE, VALUE**

ESTIMATE
- Free in-home estimates
- For a free, no obligation estimate, contact your nearest representative
- Call right now for a free estimate
- Call today for a complimentary estimate
- For a free, no-obligation, phone estimate
- Call for our no-obligation, in-home estimate
- For a free, no-obligation phone estimate, contact our rep
- We beat any major competitor's written estimate
- Ask for a professional, no-cost, in-home estimate
- All estimates done by owners

Estimate: guesstimate, ball park figure, reckoning, figure, appraisal, estimated value, valuation, assessment, price

See also: **CONSULTATION**

ETHICS
- Adhere to strict standards and code of ethics
- Unbreakable code of ethics
- And the ethics look great too

See also: **BELIEF, RIGHT, VALUE**

EVALUATION
- Call today for a free evaluation of
- We let you make the evaluation

- Our experts will give you a detailed evaluation
- Standing highest in the evaluation of all the professionals

See also: ESTIMATE

EVENT
- The event you don't want to miss
- Warehouse sale event
- The event of the year is back
- Making every event more successful
- Piggy-back on the success of another event
- This truly inspiring event happens only once
- An event everyone has been eagerly waiting for
- One of those really grand events when
- The biggest event of the season
- Join in this incredible event

See also: DEVELOPMENT, ENTERTAINMENT, OCCASION, PARTY, SALE, SPREE

EVERYBODY
- Everybody's doing it
- Something for everybody
- Join everybody else in
- A superior product not for everybody

EVERYDAY
- Not an everyday event
- Step out of your everyday life
- A sale every day
- Our today, everyday, sale rolls on
- Use it every day
- Come for our everyday low prices

EVERYONE
- Something for everyone
- Everyone is doing it
- Join everyone else in
- Not for just everyone

EVERYTHING
- That price includes absolutely everything
- Everything you love about
- Has everything to do with
- Comes with everything included
- Find out everything you need
- Everything to make your job easier
- You have to have at least one of everything
- Leads to everything else
- Everything to make your home and garden look its best
- Everything you need is here
- Everything is maximized
- Everything must go
- Everything to make your life better
- Where you'll find everything else too

See also: ALL, COMPLETE, TOTAL, WHOLE

EVERYWHERE
- You'll take it with you everywhere
- Compact enough, light enough to go everywhere
- And you'll find it everywhere you look
- Available just about everywhere

EVOLVE
- Steadily improve to meet evolving customer needs
- We evolve as you evolve
- Always evolving towards excellence

See also: CHANGE, DEVELOP, MODIFY

EXAMINATION
- No-risk examination
- Come in today for a free examination
- Completely open for your examination

See also: CONSIDER, LOOK

EXAMPLE
- Came up with this extraordinary example
- Just one example of the great many useful items you'll find
- Here's just one wonderful example
- Examples galore
- A stunning example of today's active person
- Includes examples by
- A fine example of the progress that can be made

Example: sample, specimen, test, model, pattern, standard, paradigm, ideal

See also; MODEL, TEST

EXCEL
- We strive to excel
- To help you excel more quickly
- In this, we truly excel
- Check out how we excel in this field

EXCELLENCE

- Our commitment to excellence doesn't stop here
- Excellence in service because we care
- The culmination of years of dedication to excellence
- You'll find our standard is nothing less than excellence
- A tradition of excellence since
- Committed to a higher standard of excellence
- Our goal is excellence
- We've created a new standard or excellence
- Built upon excellence that lasts
- Your search for excellence ends here

Excellence: superiority, greatness, distinction, fineness, quality, worth, merit, perfection, supremacy, preeminence
See also: BEST, EXCEPTIONAL, FINE, MERIT, TOP

EXCEPTION

- Some exceptions may apply
- Make yourself into the exception that proves the rule
- A brilliant exception in a long, boring line of blah
- When it comes to quality, we make no exceptions

EXCEPTIONAL

- Producing exceptional, award-winning products
- Providing you with exceptional value at a cost you can afford
- The exceptional will always stand out
- Exceptional quality lets your rest assured

See also: EXTREME, SPECIAL

EXCHANGE

- Return your purchase for exchange or refund
- Exchange it, no questions asked
- Exchange your old one for new
- You can always exchange it

See also: TRADE

EXCITE

- We're excited to bring you
- To delight you and excite you
- People are getting really excited about

- It's exciting intense interest from all quarters
- Something exciting is on the way
- More exciting than ever this year
- We've found even more wonderful ways to excite you
- Telling you about exciting new developments
- Exciting can't begin to describe it
- There's nothing more exciting than
- Exciting news is about to break
- Do something big and exciting

Exciting: thrilling, electrifying, galvanizing, spine-tingling, hair-raising, far out, rip-roaring, rip-snorting, stimulating, stirring, bracing, rousing, inspiring, invigorating, moving, impelling, compelling, affecting, soul-stirring, heart-moving, overpowering, overwhelming, overcoming, starting, astonishing, mind-boggling, mind-blowing, alluring, inviting, enticing, tempting, tantalizing, irresistible, charming, captivating, provocative, intriguing, fascinating, entrancing, beguiling, intoxicating, bewitching, enrapturing, attractive, interesting, appealing, piquant, seductive, sensuous, desirable, toothsome, mouth-watering, sexy, ravishing, voluptuous, glamorous, luxurious, rousing, sizzling, hot
See also: BLITZ, DELIGHT, ENERGIZE, FABULOUS, JOY, THRILL

EXCITEMENT

- Could it be the sheer excitement
- Feel the excitement of creating
- Our excitement was been regenerated
- Caught up in the excitement of
- Can you stand the excitement
- You won't believe the excitement you and your family will have
- We sell excitement
- Now you can be part of the excitement

Excitement: motive, impulse, desire, stimulation, spur, call, urge, infection, exhilaration, thrill, seduction, beguilement, intoxication
See also: ACTION, ADVENTURE, ALLURE, DRAMA, CHARISMA, ENTHUSIASM, FASCINATION, FUN, MAGIC, PIZZAZZ, ROMANCE, SPLASH, SPOTLIGHT, SPREE

EXCLUSIVE
- Found exclusively at
- Exclusive to better stores everywhere
- Now you can have access to exclusive
- Each comes with an exclusive
- Made exclusively of
- Enjoy these exclusive benefits
- The exclusive perks you deserve

Exclusive: select, particular, picky, choosy, limited, selective, posh, elite
See also: POSH, SELECT, PRIVATE

EXHILARATE
- For a wildly exhilarating experience
- Nothing can exhilarate you more
- Designed solely to exhilarate you

See also: ENERGIZE, THRILL

EXHILARATION
- How much exhilaration can a body take
- Taste the sheer exhilaration
- Never-ending exhilaration

See also: EXCITEMENT, THRILL

EXOTIC
- Why not choose something a little exotic
- Exotic and familiar at the same time
- Exotic and entrancingly beautiful
- Exotic scents, sights and sounds carry you to a faraway world

See also: JUNGLE, RARE, UNIQUE, UNUSUAL, WILD

EXPAND
- Our program has just been dramatically expanded
- All while letting you expand
- Now expanding to include
- Expanding into your neighborhood
- In the midst of a vigorous expansion phase

See also: DEVELOP, EVOLVE, GROW, INCREASE

EXPECT
- Expect to be surprised
- Not nearly as costly as you might expect
- Expect only the best
- The value you expect from
- Delivers precisely what you'd expect from a fine establishment
- Why expect less from

- You expect the best
- If you've come to expect the most from
- Would you expect this much
- You may not expect
- Expect more than you expected
- Expect the unexpected
- Here's what you can expect from
- Along with everything else you would expect from a luxury product like this

Expect: await, anticipate, look forward to, foresee, contemplate, hope for, rely on, trust, require, demand, believe
See also: ANTICIPATE, BELIEVE, DEMAND, RELY, REQUIRE, TRUST

EXPECTATION
- For those whose expectations are higher than their budget
- Even surpassed the critics' expectations
- Living up to the highest expectation
- We can meet all of your expectations
- The greater your expectations the more you need our service

See also: ANTICIPATE, BELIEF, STANDARD

EXPENSE
- At absolutely no expense to you
- We know you've got to keep expenses down
- Another expense you don't need
- Helping you with your biggest expense
- Cuts your expenses in half
- Full value at half the expense

See also: COST, SAVINGS, VALUE

EXPENSIVE
- Feels like a more expensive item
- Are your tired of forking over for expensive
- Need not be expensive at all
- Better than more expensive products
- Avoid expensive mistakes with

Expensive: costly, dear, high, high-priced, steep, stiff, exorbitant, excessive, unreasonable, valuable, precious, lavish, prodigal, extravagant, priceless
See also: COST, LUXURIOUS, PRICELESS, RICH

EXPERIENCE
- No experience necessary

- Protected by unparalleled experience
- Helping people with no experience to
- An experience that will turn your head around
- Would experience such highlights as
- An exciting, richly rewarding experience
- Bringing your personal experience on
- Giving you hands-on experience
- You've never experienced anything like this
- Introducing a totally new experience
- We have immense experience in
- Come to us for an experience like no other
- Come on in today and experience
- My experience has been terrific
- We've banked a lot of experience
- Delivers a much more personal experience
- You'll find a wealth of experience in
- Your own experience proves it special
- For a truly unique experience
- Join us for a whole new experience
- Duplicate the experience without leaving home
- We have the people with experience
- Experience the reward you deserve
- Trust our experience
- Building on fifty years of experience
- Unlike anything you've ever experienced
- Now experience this exceptional
- Experience the most glorious products
- Experience can save you a great deal of money
- We'll apply our considerable experience
- In these increasingly complex times, you can benefit from our years of experience
- We offer many different ways to experience it
- An experience truly unlike any other
- You'll soon know from personal experience
- A totally luxurious experience
- Experience the pleasure first hand
- No previous experience or special talent required
- Enjoy hands-on experience

Experience: wisdom, knowledge, perception, observation, common sense, sophistication, enlightenment, learning, cognizance, know-how, *savoir faire*, understand, discover, realize, discover, appreciate, absorb, take in

See also: **ENJOY, FEEL, FEELING**

EXPERIMENT
- Join an experiment in better living
- Dare to experiment
- A little experimentation could jazz up your life
- An experiment in living well
- Calls for all-out experimentation

See also: **CLINICAL, EFFORT, SCIENTIFIC, TRY**

EXPERT
- Experts working to help you reach that goal
- Get expert help immediately
- More than a hundred experts on call just for you
- Our experts can enhance your home with a complete new
- Meet experts who will challenge, instruct and inform you
- We have carefully chosen and trained our experts
- Experts available to work with you at your request
- Here's a sample of what the experts have to say
- Our experts have carefully studied
- We have experts in every department
- Our experts provide you with the highest level of customer service
- Our expert associates are ready to help
- Ask the experts
- Our experts will show you how
- Our experts can help you choose
- Let our experts show you the way
- Experts agree that
- Our experts will be glad to coach you
- Directly from the experts
- Approved by the experts at

See also: **ASSOCIATE, PROFESSIONAL, STAFF, SALESPEOPLE, SPECIALIST**

EXPERTISE
- Has a depth of experience and expertise
- Has combined many years of expertise to bring you
- Giving you real-world expertise
- We possess the expertise and sophisticated capability that is truly essential

- A lot of expertise has gone into this wonderful product
- A whole new world of expertise

See also: EXPERIENCE, KNOWLEDGE, SKILL, WISDOM

EXPIRE

- This offer expires soon
- Get here before the discount expires
- Has your old machine expired

See also: END, EXTINCT, FINISH

EXPLORE

- Cut you loose to explore
- Explore a whole new way of
- You'll want to explore this thrilling new
- Come and explore

See also: DISCOVER, EXPERIENCE, SEARCH

EXPONENTIAL

- Exponential value
- Growing at an astounding exponential rate
- Exponentially expanding as demand explodes

See also: EXPAND

EXPOSURE

- Providing ultimate exposure
- A delicious way to extend your exposure
- Increased exposure has resulted in increased
- More exposure for a fresh idea

See also: SHOW

EXPRESS

- Express yourself with
- A very useful means of expressing
- Our records show you have expressed an interest in
- Express your wildest desires

See also: COMMUNICATE, SAY, SHOW, SPEAK

EXTINCT

- Making sure you don't become extinct
- All your problems will become extinct
- And you thought superb service was extinct

See also: DONE, END, EXPIRE, FINISH, GONE

EXTRA

- Could you use an extra
- Giving you the extra attention you require
- Enjoy all the thoughtful extras we provide
- We provide extras such as
- Give yourself an extra treat
- We've added something extra to
- Because you demand extra from yourself

See also: INCREASE, MORE, OVERFLOW

EXTRAORDINARY

- A chance to do something extraordinary
- Extraordinary quality right in your own neighborhood
- And you'll suddenly understand how extraordinary this product is

See also: SPECIAL, UNUSUAL

EXTREME

- Get extreme
- Get ready for some extreme enjoyment
- Extreme comfort, extreme delight
- So long as it goes to extremes
- Not afraid to go to extremes

See also: END, EXCEPTIONAL, MAXIMUM

EYE

- Catches your eye and grips you with its power
- Made under the watchful eye and steady hand of
- And very pleasing to the eye
- Irresistibly eye-catching
- And once your eyes have witnessed
- Done with a very creative eye
- Delights the eye and the mind
- The apple of your eye
- Sure to please your eye
- You won't believe your eyes

See also: LOOK, NOTICE, SEE

FABULOUS

- So just how fabulous is it to be
- Offering you a fabulous opportunity
- Weaving a fabulous tale of

See also: MARVEL, WONDERFUL

FACADE

- Not just another pretty facade

- Behind the lovely facade, the real thing
- Behind the magnificent facade is an even more magnificent product
- Breaking down the facade to reveal

See also: **APPEARANCE, ASPECT, FACE, LOOK**

FACE

- Talk face-to-face with those who really know
- A new face, a new concept, a new era
- We're putting a beautiful new face on an old friend
- Forever changed the face of
- So come and see the many faces
- A great way of saving face
- There's more to a flawless face than
- Wakes your face over with a tingle
- At last, a fresh face
- Behold the new face of
- The face of our service has been changed forever
- Let's face it
- Squarely facing the future

See also: **ASPECT, FACADE, LOOK**

FACELIFT

- Giving your whole house a facelift
- Like having a facelift without the hassle
- When your plan needs a bit of a facelift
- Amounts to an instant facelift

See also: **CHANGE, IMPROVEMENT, MODIFY**

FACILITY

- This facility offers everything you need
- Better facilities than any other place
- Giving you the facility to

See also: **EASE, ORGANIZATION, PLACE**

FACT

- Just the facts, ma'am
- That fact remains unchanged today
- For more facts, call our experts
- When you're thinking of buying, you want the facts
- Laying out the hard facts of
- Get the facts you need before you negotiate
- All the facts, please
- First, you want the hard, cold facts
- Get the facts and get them fast

- At least check out the facts for yourself
- You can't argue with the facts
- The facts speak for themselves

See also: **DATA, INFORMATION**

FACTOR

- A distinguishing factor
- The factors that make us a wise choice for you
- More than all other factors combined
- No matter how many factors you have to consider
- The biggest factor of all

See also: **ELEMENT**

FACTORY

- Continues to sell below factory prices
- We manufacture everything in our state-of-the-art factory
- Direct from the factory
- Factory direct savings
- Buy direct from the factory
- Rushed from the factory to your door
- Factory open to the public

See also: **MANUFACTURER**

FAIL

- You cannot fail when you follow
- Fail-proof no matter who you are
- For those of you who have failed to notice
- When other systems fail, ours soldiers on
- Will never fail you in a crunch
- Our no-fail formula outdoes all the rest

See also: **BREAK, MISS, OUT**

FAIR

- It's easy to play fair
- If life were fair, we'd all have one
- Fair to say that ours is the best
- You'll always get a fair deal at
- Great value at fair prices
- The rustic feel of a country fair

See also: **HONEST, RIGHT**

FAITH

- Renewing faith in
- Put your faith in us
- A lot more than just blind faith
- Take a flying leap of faith
- Keep the faith

See also: **BELIEF, TRUST**

FALL

- Last call for fall
- Making it all fall into place
- Fabulous fall fashion
- Those first days of fall really make you come alive
- The news in products this fall is
- It's what's in store for fall
- In all the colors of fall

See also: SEASON

FAMILIAR

- A seductively familiar
- Comfy and familiar as your favorite slippers
- It's easy to get familiar with
- Right from the start, we're familiar with all your needs
- Instantly familiar to you
- The name that's familiar to you

See also: COMFORT, EASY, SAFE

FAMILY

- Will keep your whole family busy
- A family to serve your family
- We're just like one of the family
- Far transcends basic family requirements
- For the entire family
- Something for everyone in the family
- We understand how important the time your family spends together is to you
- Discover an investment in family fun
- One all the family can enjoy
- Perfect for all your family's growing needs
- Room for the whole family
- Foremost family product
- Your family has been cooped up to long
- For you and your whole family
- You're like family to us
- Helping families find what they need
- A surefire family favorite
- Become part of the family
- Get more time with your family
- Make it a family affair
- Family owned and operated
- Help you make the most of your family life
- Join the thousands of families who already enjoy
- You can see how important this is for you and your family

See also: COMMUNITY, HERITAGE,

FOLKS, PEOPLE

FAMOUS

- Famous name, famous value
- For the most famous name in
- We're famous for our
- Try some of our famous product for free
- You'll feel like you're famous

See also: CELEBRITY, KNOW, REMARKABLE, RENOWN

FAN

- If you're a fan of
- Everything for the die-hard fan of
- Deliciously fanning the flames of desire
- Will make a fan out of you

See also: ENTHUSIAST

FANCY

- Fancy free
- How does this strike your fancy
- Indulge your fancy
- For something a little fancier
- What tickles your fancy today

See also: IMAGINATION, WISH

FANTASY

- Has created a fantasy world for you to play in
- Fulfilling your wildest fantasies
- No matter how extravagant your fantasy, we can satisfy you

See also: DREAM, IMAGINATION

FAR

- Going too far isn't a problem any more
- A far cry from the old methods
- Taking you farther up the scale
- Choose us and you'll go far

See also: DISTANCE

FASCINATION

- Encouraging an ongoing fascination
- Become an object of fascination
- Increasing fascination every day with

See also: ALLURE, ATTRACT, EXCITEMENT, INTEREST

FASHION

- Here's your fashion secret
- Fashion and more
- Selected fashions for the whole family
- A way for fashion's new wave

- Will you follow fashion's lead away from ordinary
- High fashion, low cost
- Keeping you always in fashion
- The fashion choice of millions
- Fashion isn't just for the young
- Newest fashions come here first
- Understanding fashion is our business
- First chance at a fashion first
- Join the fashion revolution
- We proudly fashion
- A fresh infusion of fashion

Fashion: style, rage, trend, craze, look, fad, vogue, latest thing, mode, convention, decorum, etiquette, high society, elite, manner, system, approach, form, shape
See also: CHIC, CLASS, CREATE, ELEGANCE, LIFESTYLE, METHOD, PIZZAZZ, STYLE, WAY

FAST

- Faster and easier than ever before
- Go as fast or as far as you wish
- You move fast
- They really move fast
- Fast track your life
- They'll go very fast
- It's as fast and easy as
- These babies are really going fast
- First, fast and fun
- Is fast becoming
- It's never been easier or faster to
- Get it faster at
- So much faster today
- Getting it faster and smarter through
- Not only is it fast and easy – it's free
- Are we going too fast for you
- Fast forward into
- Better, faster, higher
- They're gonna go fast
- Look how fast
- For people in the fast lane
- Fasten your seat belts
- They really move fast

Fast: quick, rapid, swift, speedy, express, expeditious, accelerated, fleet, nimble, spry, brisk, light-footed, hasty, post-haste, expeditious, lickety-split, with dispatch
See also: INSTANT, SPEED

FAT

- Think low fat
- Shed that ugly, unhealthy fat
- Live off the fat of the land
- Fat is not where it's at
- Melts fat quickly
- How about a nice fat bonus
- More delicious, with less fat than any other
- Give yourself a nice fat raise
- Fatten up your profits

See also: BIG, ENRICH, GIANT, OVERFLOW, WEIGHT

FATE

- More than just a twist of fate
- You are fated to succeed
- Staring fate in the face
- When fate brings you to our door

See also: FORTUNE, FUTURE

FAVOR

- Do yourself a favor and
- As a personal favor to you
- We have a favor to ask
- Ask any favor you like

See also: BENEFIT, SERVICE

FAVORITE

- See why we're the nation's favorite
- Here's a few of your favorites
- A perennial favorite
- The world's favorite
- Dig into this honest-to-goodness favorite
- An all-time favorite
- We hope our favorites will become yours too
- With so many choices, it's hard to pick a favorite
- Everybody's favorite
- Traditional favorites
- We stock all your old favorites
- Favorites any time of the year
- Here's more of your favorites
- A favorite with young and old alike
- We have all your very favorites
- Trying to decide which is your very favorite

Favorite: choice, preference, hero, star, predilection,, apple of one's eye, pet, chosen, preferred, selected, welcomed, popular, to one's taste
See also: CHOICE, PREFERENCE, SELECT, WELCOME

FAX
- Fax is faster
- Please fax your order to
- Email, fax and a phone give you instant access

FEAST
- A sumptuous feast of
- Feast your eyes on this
- A feast for every one of your senses

See also: DINE, EAT, ENJOY

FEATURE
- You'll appreciate these fine features
- Feature value on
- For a short time we're featuring a hot selection of
- These features, combined with the latest technological advancements and world-class engineering
- Featuring some of today's top draws
- Feature of the month
- Another specified feature is
- Having this feature doesn't hurt either
- A specific feature is built to conform to the recommendations
- Featuring a full year of
- Check out the outstanding performance features that make
- Gives you even more key features to
- Features we personally think are the best in the business
- Added standard features
- Plus value-added features and applications
- With many luxury features such as these
- Other famous features include
- You'll fine plenty of other fine features, too
- A superior collection of standard features
- A dazzling number of standard convenience features
- The great features add up to a truly outstanding product
- Includes additional features that quite simply
- Have unique features that make them virtually

Feature: looks, appearance, shape, configuration, aspect, look, hallmark, trademark, earmark, trait, specialty, keynote, attribute, property, characteristic, quality, peculiarity, idiosyncrasy, quirk, special attraction, headliner, leader, number one, highlight, outstanding, focus, cream of the crop, spotlight, play up, star, emphasis, distinguish, accent, underline, point out, call attention to, outline, portray, set off, loss leader, drawing card

See also: BENEFIT, CHARACTER, HIGHLIGHT, LOOK, PART

FEE
- For an extremely low fee of
- Compare it to the fees you already pay
- No initiation fees
- You might think such benefits carry a high fee
- No hidden fees or commissions mean you'll save more money
- No enrollment fees or hidden costs
- Call today and we will waive all fees
- No startup fee and no management fee
- Low fees that won't eat up your profits

See also: ADMISSION, COST, EXPENSE

FEEDBACK
- Thank you in advance for your feedback
- Your feedback tells us exactly what you need
- Shaped by your feedback

FEEL
- You'll love the exceptional feel and consistency of
- Nothing else feels like
- You'll love the look and feel of it
- You can almost feel the
- Think about what feels good
- You'll feel better every day you
- Another chance to feel wonderful
- Feel the way you want to feel
- At your best when you feel most comfortable
- Nothing else feels like
- Feel good about what you do
- Just the feel of it will tell you
- Just feel the pleasure of it
- Nothing feels better than
- You can feel it instantly
- Feels good in every way
- Feels simply fabulous
- You can feel the difference
- Feel the difference for yourself
- Such a spirited feel

- Keep on feeling great
- Now you can have that same happy, healthy feeling
- Has a very pleasant feel
- You'll love how soft it feels
- You've never felt anything like it

See also: EXPERIENCE, TOUCH

FEELING

- A sensational feeling
- There's no feeling in the world like it
- Feeling is believing
- There's always been a feeling that
- For those of us at our company, it's a feeling we hold dear
- A feeling that's part of who we are
- Nothing compares to the feeling of
- A delicious feeling of tranquillity and order
- Let the feeling wrap around you
- For a more sensuous feeling
- You know the feeling
- Giving you that certain feeling
- You know the feeling
- Oh, what a feeling
- You'll agree that the feeling is heavenly
- The feeling is expansive but warm

Feeling: sensation, emotion, ardor, sense, impression, intuition, inkling, hunch, hint, premonition, tingle, quiver, throb, palpitation, vehemence, heat, attraction, affection, warmth, response, reaction, consciousness, awareness, perception, sensibility, sensitivity, consideration, discrimination, tact, empathy, sympathy, fellow feeling, identification, vibe, notion, idea, sentiment, conception, thought, estimation, theory, opinion, outlook, viewpoint, point of view, attitude, stance, position, posture, way of thinking, intense, ardent, passionate, receptive

See also: EMOTION, EXPERIENCE, MOOD, OPINION, THINK

FEET

- Keeping your feet on the ground
- Making sure you land on your feet
- Planted firmly on your feet

See also: FOUNDATION, ROOT

FEMININE

- Basics with a really feminine feel
- A surprisingly feminine mix
- For your feminine side
- Experience all the deliciously feminine joys of
- Fabulously, fascinatingly feminine

See also: WOMAN

FESTIVAL

- A festival to celebrate almost every weekend
- Come to our festival of values
- Turns your life into an ongoing festival

See also: CARNIVAL, CELEBRATION, FIESTA, PARTY

FESTIVE

- It's easy to make your home look festive with
- The real joy of the festive season
- Feisty, festive and full of fun
- For that truly festive feeling
- Everyone loves a festive event

See also: CELEBRATION, CHRISTMAS, EASTER, HOLIDAY

FEW

- If you're one of the few who still hasn't tried it
- You can't eat just a few
- Many are called but few are chosen
- Be one of the fabulous few who

See also: LESS, RARE, SELECT

FIELD

- Leading in the field
- Because this is a new, fast-growing field
- A field that's wide open to you
- Get ahead of the field with a boost from us
- Our company is the best in the field

See also: AREA, EXPERTISE

FIESTA

- Come join the fiesta
- When the party turns into a fiesta
- It's a big fiesta every day

See also: CELEBRATION, PARTY, SPREE

FIGHT

- Helps fight
- Fight back with
- Ready to help you fight the fight

- When you know you've got a fight on your hands
- Fights even the worst problems

See also: ATTACK, BATTLE, RESIST, WAR

FIGURE
- Flaunt your figure instead
- Figured out a way to make
- If you're dying to figure out what makes
- Full figure value
- Enhances you figure like no other

- Figure on our help
- Letting you figure out how

See also: FASHION, RELY, SHAPE

FINAL
- Final ten days
- All sales final
- Your final chance to
- It's final, we're the best
- And for your final need
- Now you can finally find
- Final notice

See also: END, FINISH, LAST

FINANCE
- Our financing program measures up
- Ask about our easy financing plan
- Choose no-limit financing
- Finance it in ten easy payments
- We arrange financing for you
- Don't worry about how to finance
- When it comes to finance, we're out front
- Just look at the simple financing
- And we arrange all the financing too
- No matter what your record, you can finance
- Let us help you finance
- Three different ways t o finance your purchase
- Finance is no problem
- Gives you a chance to finance something even bigger
- High finance made easy

See also: COST, ECONOMIC, MONEY, PAY, PAYMENT, SAVINGS, VALUE

FINANCIAL
- Reach a new level of financial power
- Taking financial responsibility for ourselves

- You can't afford to leave your financial future to someone else
- Now, all your financial needs taken care of with confidence
- Taking good care of you financially
- Make out your own financial success
- Invest precious financial resources in other priorities
- And we've got top financial ratings to back us up
- The financial world is a jungle
- Makes the greatest financial sense
- Financially speaking, we're the best
- The end of financial worries for you
- Talk to us about all your financial concerns
- The best financial decision you could make

See also: COST, ECONOMIC, MONEY, PAY, PAYMENT, SAVINGS, VALUE

FIND
- You won't find a better selection anywhere else
- Find out for free
- Funky and fabulous finds
- Something you won't find just anywhere
- Haven't found exactly what you're looking for
- You're sure to find that each and every one is
- If it's unusual, exceptional and charming, you'll find it here
- We can help you find
- What better place to find out than here
- Find out from the pros themselves
- Definitely worth finding out
- We'll help you find what you need
- What a find
- Need help to find it
- Find it fast
- Helping you find just about anything
- Only here will you find
- Call to find out about
- To find out how to save on
- Finding the item you want has never been so easy
- Looking for a product and can't find what you want
- We'll find it for you
- Where else would you find
- Find yourself in unfamiliar waters
- Why don't you find us

- Only here will you find great
- Find exactly what you're looking for and save money too
- Find what you're seeking
- You can find out more fast

See also: DISCOVER, EXPLORE, RETRIEVE, SEARCH

FINE

- For lovers of fine quality everywhere
- The fine difference between good and superb
- Those who appreciate the finer things in life will understand
- Finer than all others

See also: BEST, EXCELLENCE, PREMIUM, SUPERIOR

FINEST

- The finest is yours to enjoy
- The finest product we've ever made
- When only the finest will do
- The finest products come from
- The finest product we've ever made
- It's what makes our products unquestionably the finest

FINGERTIPS

- Now you can have it at your fingertips
- Putting more at your fingertips
- Complete information at your fingertips

See also: CONVENIENT

FINISH

- An uncompromisingly beautiful finish
- You're not completely finished without
- Finished off with
- And to finish, the grand finale
- And we're not finished with you yet
- Buffed to a lasting finish

See also: COMPLETION, END, FINAL, LAST, OVER, SHINE,

FIRE

- Fire it up and see
- Forged in the fire of your imagination
- Put some fire in your belly
- All fire and ice and enchantment
- We've really lit a fire under the competition
- On fire to experience it

See also: DRIVE, PASSION, START, URGE

FIREWORKS

- Get in on the fireworks
- Make some fireworks
- Find out what the fireworks are all about

See also: ENTHUSIASM, PASSION

FIRST

- We've placed first among all
- Always think of us first
- Call us first for a successful event
- Now we bring you another first-of-its kind
- Be one of the first to get
- As well, our company was one of the first to bring in such advanced thinking
- The world's first and only
- Just the beginning of a long line of firsts
- A real first for
- Make sure we're the first people you call
- It's a first
- Be among the very first

See also: BEGIN, FOREFRONT, LEADER, PIONEER, PREMIERE, START

FIRSTHAND

- Explore it firsthand today
- You know from firsthand experience
- Nothing beats firsthand testing

FIT

- We've got your fit
- Fit for an emperor
- Great look, great fit
- Beauty, comfort, fit – they're all here
- Combined, they ensure an extraordinary fit
- Designed to fit perfectly
- Engineered to fit smoothly into all sorts of lives
- Fitting into your plans no matter how
- You'll love the fit
- The individual fit makes them the most comfortable for you
- You've never experienced fit like this
- Fits nicely into
- It's only fitting that you have the finest
- See, it all fits
- Fit for a palace
- The fit that counts
- Fit is everything at
- Fit for a queen, fit for you
- It fits in a compact space

Fit: well-fitted, proper, suitable, harmonious, seemly, decorous, right, correct, fitting, apt, relevant, adequate, meet, due, prepared, equipped, up to grade, hardy, robust, strong, vigorous, healthy, befit, suit, equal, match, adjust, modify, fashion, adapt, rig, supply, provide, alter, calibrate, deck out, garb, attire, apparel, dress, invest, size
See also: ATHLETIC, COMFORT, FASHION, RIGHT, SHAPE, SUIT

FITNESS
- Maintain your mental fitness with
- Has an inevitable fitness to it
- Financial fitness the same as physical fitness
- Increase your fitness level safely and easily
- Glowing with health and fitness
See also: ATHLETIC, HEALTH, RIGHT, STRENGTH

FLAIR
- Express yourself with your own special flair
- Develop a flair for life
- We've got a flair for pleasing you
- A real flair for beauty
See also: ABILITY, IMAGINATION, PIZZAZZ, SKILL, STYLE

FLAMBOYANT
- Full-blown, flamboyant
- You may be more flamboyant than you think
- Release the flamboyance inside you
See also: CRAZY, GLAMOROUS, PASSION, WILD

FLAUNT
- Flaunt your good fortune
- If you've got it, flaunt it
- For those who don't want to flaunt their superiority
See also: BOAST, PRESENT, PRESENTATION, SHOW

FLAVOR
- With old-fashioned flavor
- Adding a continental flavor to
- A whirlwind of flavor
- Experience the flavor

See also: DELICIOUS, DINE, EAT, TASTE

FLEXIBILITY
- The financial flexibility to work with
- Provides you with more purchasing power, convenience and flexibility
- But also gives you the flexibility
- A little extra flexibility for
- Not only gives you the flexibility
- Flexibility to meet individual needs
- The flexibility to accommodate your changes, whatever they are
See also: ADAPT, CONVENIENCE, EASY, INNOVATION

FLEXIBLE
- Flexible enough to meet your demands tomorrow
- You want a company that's really flexible
- A flexible plan to suit your every scenario
- Our products are so flexible
Flexible: adaptable, adjustable, comfortable, malleable, tractable, compliant, cooperative, docile, biddable, obedient, manageable, easy, willing, yielding, ready, amenable, agreeable, receptive, predisposed
See also: ADAPT, CHANGE, MODIFY, VERSATILE

FLIGHT
- Let your imagination take flight
- More flights to more places than any other
- A wonderful flight of fancy

FLOAT
- It floats effortlessly
- The best always floats to the surface
- That wonderful floating feeling
- Float on a sea of delight
See also: DRIFT, FLOW, MOVE

FLOCK
- People are flocking to
- The flocks are gathering at
- Separate yourself from the common flock
See also: CROWD, GATHER, GROUP, PEOPLE

FLOOR
- Get in on the ground floor
- The bargains will floor you
- Terrific buys on every floor and in every department

See also: BASIC, BOTTOM, GROUND

FLOW
- Free-flowing as the sea
- Creating a feeling of flow
- Watch the money flow toward you

See also: DRIFT, MOVE

FLYER
- Look for your flyer in
- This week's flyers tell it all
- Take a flyer on a brand new venture
- Plan your shopping around these great flyers

See also: ADVERTISE, CATALOGUE, COMMUNICATE, INFORMATION

FOCUS
- Our entire focus is on providing you with the best
- A brand new focus that allows you to
- So you can focus on the most important thing
- Future-focused
- Are you out of focus
- Also happens to be the focal point for
- Intensely focused on bettering

See also: CONCENTRATE, INTENSITY

FOLKS
- C'mon folks
- Designed for smart folks like you
- Discover that we're just folks too
- And something for the little folks

See also: PEOPLE

FOLLOW
- Then we follow through with complete service
- All you need to do is follow each step
- Then follow up with
- The leader others follow
- Making it easier to follow
- Always following your lead
- Simply read it and follow it faithfully

See also: COURSE, LEADER, PATH, WAY

FOND
- Demonstrating a fondness for
- For people you're fond of
- The stuff fond memories are made of
- We've got all the items you're so very fond of

See also: LIKE, LOVE, PREFER

FOOL
- Without feeling like a fool
- Don't let the richness fool you
- Don't be fooled by
- Holding back when fools rush in

See also: CONFUSE, CRAZY, GIMMICK, TRICK

FOOT
- Starts you off on the right foot
- Helps you put your best foot forward
- Puts you on a solid footing to
- More than just a foot in the door
- We can help put you on an equal footing
- On an equal footing with the big girls

See also: BASE, FOUNDATION

FOR
- No longer just for
- One for all and all for one
- Just for you
- Helping you make a change for the better

FORECAST
- The forecast is always sunny
- Change the forecast of your life
- Forecasting fabulous savings and great delight
- We forecast pleasure for you

See also: AHEAD, BET, FUTURE, PREDICTABLE

FOREFRONT
- Remaining at the forefront of
- Puts you in the forefront
- Inspiring those at the very forefront
- We've always been in the forefront

See also: AHEAD, FIRST, LEADER

FOREVER
- It lasts forever
- But hurry, it won't last forever
- Forever searching for something even better

See also: ENDURE, LAST

FORGE
- Already forging another future
- Boldly forging ahead of the pack
- Forged from sweat, determination, vision and imagination
- Forge a new image

See also: CREATE, MAKE, SHAPE

FORGET
- We should not forget that
- Don't forget about these evocative
- Don't forget to check these out first
- How could anyone forget
- An experience you won't forget

See also: LOSE

FORGIVE
- The endlessly forgiving nature of
- You'll never forgive yourself if you miss out
- You can be forgiven for indulging yourself a little

FORM
- Exquisitely formed
- Just complete the attached form
- Stay in top form
- Form made-to-order
- Great form, great substance, all for you

See also: FIT, MAKE, SHAPE

FORMAT
- This format will produce raw, spontaneous
- Presented in an all-new format for easier
- Formatted to suit you best
- And you'll love the format too

See also: ORGANIZATION

FORMULA
- It's patented formula lets you
- This naturally balanced formula
- Have created the most advanced formula possible
- We challenged ourselves to create a formula that
- It's our most effective formula ever
- The proven formula for success
- Amazing new breakthrough formula
- This exclusive formula is currently the only one with everything you need
- The amazing formula that

See also: INFORMATION, PLAN,

RECIPE, SYSTEM

FORMULATE
- Exclusively formulated with our unique, advanced
- Carefully formulated for
- Specially formulated to
- Formulated to today's demanding standards
- A plan formulated specifically for you
- This unique formulation has been designed for those who are looking for something very unique

See also; CREATE, DESIGN, MAKE

FORTUNATE
- We've very fortunate to have
- An extremely fortunate find
- You can be one of the fortunate ones

See also: ACCIDENT, CHANCE, LUCKY

FORTUNE
- Discover a secret that could make you a fortune
- An investment that's already worth a fortune
- Doesn't have to cost you a fortune
- Better than fame and fortune
- Good fortune is right in front of you
- Making it easier for you to seek your fortune

Fortune: assets, capital income, treasure, revenue, worth, riches, wealth, affluence, destiny, fate, success, prosperity
See also: EXPENSIVE, MONEY, WEALTH

FORWARD
- Fast forward
- Looking forward to
- The treat the whole family looks forward to enjoying
- Always moving forward
- Never stop moving forward

See also: AHEAD

FOUND
- Found only on
- Now that you've found us, let's stay together
- Founded by people who believed that
- Staunchly true to our founding principles

- The saving amounts to found money

See also: DISCOVER

FOUNDATION
- Provides a foundation for
- Acquire a solid foundation for
- You've got the foundation for
- A strong foundation of memory and experience
- Always start with a firm foundation

See also: BASE, FOOTING, GROUND, ROOT

FRANCHISE
- Franchise opportunities available
- If you've never looked into a franchise before
- Producing so much happiness we ought to franchise it

See also: LICENSE

FREE
- Try it for free
- You're finally free of
- Buy one, get one free
- You will receive a free
- You've finally broken free
- Free tryout
- Is absolutely free to you
- Yours free with
- And you get all this free
- Feel free as a bird with
- Like getting every third one free
- A freebie too good to ignore
- Set yourself free with
- Buy this and get this free
- It's easy and free
- Discover our free
- Get more free benefits
- Includes a free gift
- Get your free, no-obligation information
- It's yours free – with no obligation
- We all love getting things for free
- The best is that it's free
- How to get free bonuses
- Buy one, get one free
- Call today for your free
- Free with every purchase

Free: independent, autonomous, at leisure, uninhibited, relaxed, unbound, unchained, untrammelled, unimpeded, unhampered, unbridled, unrestrained, unrestricted, laissez-faire, no holds barred, wild, unconditional, released, exempt, clear, generous, liberal, lavish, unstinting, gratis, on the house, without cost, free of charge, for free, for nothing, at no cost, let loose

See also: BONUS, COMPLIMENTARY INDEPENDENT, WILD

FREEDOM
- The freedom to enjoy the exceptional pleasures of
- Namely, freedom
- Giving you total financial freedom
- Finally, the freedom to take charge of your future
- Experience pure freedom
- Making freedom roar
- The freedom you're looking for
- Listen to the call of freedom
- The freedom machine
- Freedom can be habit-forming
- Experience real freedom
- The intoxicating freedom of being able to choose any one you want
- Gives you true freedom of expression

Freedom: liberty, autonomy, independence, self-determination, self-direction, emancipation, release, relief, discretion, right, privilege

See also: CHANCE, LIBERTY, LOOSE, OPPORTUNITY

FRESH
- Alway new, always fresh
- Fresh products every day
- Giving you a fresh new outlook
- You can't get fresher than this
- Fresher by far than
- You can always use a fresh angle
- The freshness you want in
- Seals in quality and freshness
- Freshness first
- Freshen up your life
- Freshly made to order
- Fresh, hot and ready to enjoy
- Only the freshest ingredients will do
- Get a breath of fresh air

Fresh: recent, new, latest, modern, brand-new, just-out, new-fashioned, novel, unconventional, energetic, youthful

See also: NEW

FRIEND
- Let's be friends
- A friend to customers for fifty years
- A girl's best friend
- Say hello to an old friend
- You probably know friends or neighbors who love
- Friends will want to know your secret
- Ask your friends and family about
- With a little help from your friends
- Meet new friends
- Come where your friends are
- We want to make a friend out of you
- Buy one for yourself and one for a friend
- Favorite friends are always waiting

Friend: companion, sidekick, pal, buddy, chum, ally, assistant, helper, partner, patron, benefactor, advocate
See also: ASSOCIATE, COMPANION, CONSULTANT, HELPER, PARTNER

FRIENDLY
- Friendly and helpful
- Friendly service is our hallmark
- A savings-friendly solution
- Come see the friendly folks at
- Who could be friendlier than us

FRIENDSHIP
- Join a whole world of friendship
- Make hundreds of new friendships
- Your friendship means a lot to us
- A lasting friendship based on trust
- Your friendship and support mean everything to us

See also: CARE, HELP, LOVE, PARTNERSHIP

FRONT
- This year's front runner
- Putting you way out in front
- We're always clear and up-front about

See also: BEST, LEADER

FRONTIERS
- Join us on the frontiers of
- Fresh from the frontiers of science and into your home
- Pushing the frontiers and discovering new horizons

See also: BOUNDARY, EDGE, LIMIT

FRUIT
- Seeds planted may now bear fruit
- Allowing you to enjoy the fruit of your labors
- Bearing the seeds of complete satisfaction
- Your efforts bear fruit right away

See also: RESULT, SATISFACTION, SUCCESS

FUEL
- Providing the optimum fuel for healthy body and mind
- Fuelling hopes and expectations
- The fuel your business success runs upon

See also: DRIVE, FIRE, INSPIRE, MOTIVATE, POWER

FULL
- Stuffed deliciously full
- Value to the fullest
- Full of delights for you

See also: COMPLETE, TOTAL, WHOLE

FUN
- Time to have fun
- So you can have fun even faster
- The fun's not over yet
- The fun's just beginning
- Fun, natural and you
- Have fun without worrying about
- Having fun never goes out of style
- Imagine all the fun you can have
- It's fun and easy
- Or if you just want to have fun
- Plenty of fun for everyone
- Just for the fun of it
- If you're looking for fun
- What could be more fun
- The package spells fun
- Interested in having a little more fun
- Simple, affordable and fun
- Life is fun
- Having fun never goes out of style
- Bonding together all the elements of fun
- Up close and personal with your fun side
- We're willing to bet you're a fun person
- There'll be lots of fun for everyone
- Makes living fun
- If it's not fun, why do it
- Just plain fun
- Products that put some fun back into your life

- The most fun you've had in years
- More than just the fun choice
- You make our work fun
- Everything you need to know about having fun

Fun: glee, merriment, enjoyment, play, sport, amusement, zest, gaiety, mirth, entertainment, delight, celebration, high spirits, jollity, cheerfulness, hilarity, pastime, distraction, clowning, horseplay, tomfoolery, playfulness, exhilaration
See also: CELEBRATION, DELIGHT, ENJOYMENT, HAPPINESS, JOY, PLEASURE

FUNCTION

- Discussing how you will function in the new
- You'll be impressed with how well it functions
- Many more functions than you expect
- Helping you function in a tough situation
- Fun and functional
- Which aid in the proper functioning and maintenance
See also: ACTION, FORM, USE

FUNDAMENTAL

- Discover the fundamentals of
- Absolutely fundamental to
- Fundamentally better
- Giving the fundamentals easily and quickly
- Addressing your fundamental needs
See also: BASIC, NECESSARY, STAPLE

FUNNY

- Drop-dead funny
- A funny way to win
- If you think this if funny, wait until you see
See also: ENJOYABLE

FURTHER

- Taking you further every day
- Further on the path toward your dreams
- The further you go, the happier you become

FUSS

- Without the fuss of
- No fuss, no bother

- Find out what all the fuss is about
- Enjoy them with a minimum of fuss
- No need to fuss with messy
See also: HASSLE, TROUBLE

FUTURE

- Kick start your future today
- The future begins at
- Positively futuristic
- Gives you the tools you need to design a solid future
- Give them the future you didn't have
- Get your future rolling
- Welcome to the future
- The future is here
- The future starts today
- The future is now
- The future is in the bag
- The future is waiting for you at
- But the real future is
- If you want to see the future, visit us
- Investing in your future
- Helping to position you for the future
- One of the ways we're keeping our eyes on the future
- We're leading the way into the future
- For the past fifty years, we've been delivering the future
- It's not hard to predict the future
- Your future depends upon it
- Decisions that have your future in mind
- Don't gamble with your future
- To better anticipate your future needs
- New for the foreseeable future
- Unlocking the future for you
- A bright future to come
- Ensuring a strong future for
- Products of the future
- Call today for answers to your future
- Better value, brighter future

Future: time ahead, tomorrow, prospect, offing, expectation, outlook, anticipation, probability, likelihood
See also: AHEAD, ANTICIPATE, FATE, PREVIEW

GAIN

- All gain with no pain
- You'll experience some astonishing gains
- A net gain for all
- Just look at what you stand to gain
- Get bigger, better gains with

- With so much to be gained by
- You have nothing to lose and everything to gain

See also: ADD, BENEFIT, GOAL

GALLERY
- A veritable gallery of
- And joining our gallery of proud successes
- A huge gallery of fine products

See also: SHOWCASE

GAMBLE
- Takes the gamble out of choosing
- You don't even have to gamble a stamp
- It's not a dangerous gamble
- Don't gamble with your health
- Choosing doesn't have to be a gamble
- A gamble you know you can win

See also: BET, CHANCE, DARE, ENTERPRISE, OPTION, VENTURE

GAME
- This is no kid's game
- Beat them at their own game
- Join the ultimate game
- We're part of the game
- We've changed the way the game is played
- Improves the way young athletes play the game
- It's more than just a game
- Get with the game plan
- When you need a whole new game plan
- To some, it's just a game
- Let the game begin
- Staying ahead of the game with

See also: ATHLETIC, GIMMICK, PLAY, TRICK

GATHER
- A favorite gathering place for
- A gathering of superb products for your convenience
- You'll be able to gather up benefits like candies

See also: COLLECT, JOIN, RAKE

GEAR
- We gear our services to you
- Gear you gotta have
- The most important piece of gear you have is

- Gear up for
- Watch us go into high gear
- We'll install and test your entire checklist of gear
- Gear up for less
- Always operating in top gear
- If you've got the game, we've got the gear
- Designed to really get you in gear

See also: EQUIPMENT, MACHINE, STUFF

GEM
- You'll find that they're real gems
- A glittering gem of a product
- Scattered like gems across the land
- This little gem does it all

See also: NUGGET, TREASURE, VALUE

GENERATE
- Generating millions of dollars for you
- Able to generate more excitement than any other
- Generating spinoff and profits in every direction

See also: CREATE, GROW, MAKE, MOVE

GENERATION
- The next generation is here
- Celebrating a generation of
- For generation after generation of
- Call the greatest of this generation
- Simply the best of its generation
- A new generation takes over
- Join the smart generation
- You'll discover a whole new generation
- Quality has been passed on from generation to generation
- A new generation works to renew

See also: AGE, FAMILY

GENERIC
- There's nothing generic about
- Name quality in a generic brand
- Save on excellent generic products

See also: BASIC, BRAND

GENIUS
- Genius at work
- Challenge our resident genius to
- A stroke of genius

- It doesn't take a genius to figure out what's best
- Your friends will think you're a genius
- Turns you into a genius overnight

See also: ABILITY, BRAIN, CAPACITY, SMART

GENTLE
- Gentle enough for
- A gentle boost could be all you need
- Gentle and soft to surround with cosiness
- Gentler on your system than
- Gentle but firm

See also: CARESS, SOFT

GENUINE
- If you're looking for genuine value
- And every bit of it is genuine
- Genuine materials, genuine value
- It's the genuine deal

See also: AUTHENTIC, REAL

GESTURE
- A caring gesture that
- More than just a gesture
- Even if you only make a gesture toward
- More than just a gesture
- A gesture we deeply appreciate

See also: INVITATION, MOVE, OFFER

GET
- Now go out and get it
- What you get at this location
- Here's what you get when you
- Get it easily
- Get in on the savings, get in on the fun
- Here's what you get
- You can get it all from a
- Get into it
- What to get when you don't know what to get
- Here's what you get when you buy
- Get what your want when you want it

See also: ACHIEVE, OWN

GETAWAY
- This summer, treat yourself to a getaway
- For a fast getaway, call us
- Great getaways are waiting
- Instant getaways always available

See also: ESCAPE, TRAVEL, VACATION

GIANT
- We're the product giant
- A giant of a sale
- One of the giants of the industry
- You can walk with giants
- Giants have opened the way to

See also: BIG, FAT, IMPORTANT

GIFT
- Hard-working gift ideas for
- Come in and select that special gift
- Don't forget, this product makes a wonderful gift for a friend
- We'll send a card announcing your gift
- A truly uplifting gift for
- Guaranteed to please the many friends on your gift list
- Perfect gift for yourself or a loved one
- Makes a thoughtful and welcome gift
- The ideal place to find a memorable gift
- An uplifting gift for
- Treat someone you love to a special gift
- Pick up valuable gifts for nothing
- Your gift with a purchase of
- A truly original and practical gift
- We supply gift certificates
- You deserve a specials gift from
- Gifts straight from the heart
- Gift-giving made easy
- Give a gift and save up to
- Our biggest gift ever
- Give it as a gift
- A gift means so much more when
- Our gift to you
- Call today and get your free gift
- Select the gifts you want from
- Come to us for all your gifts
- Gift boxed or wrapped at no extra charge
- Choose a gift with spirit
- Give a gift that will be enjoyed for years
- Great gift ideas that work for everyone in the family
- A great gift idea
- Gifts and comforts from near and far
- We offer gifts only a man/woman would enjoy
- The gift that sparkles all year long
- The more you buy, the more gifts you may select
- We will give you one of these valuable gifts
- Free gifts and prizes
- Great gifts in store for all the family

- Gifts to entertain and instruct

Gift: present, favor, endowment, bequest, legacy, heritage, inheritance, bounty, largess, prize, giveaway, contribution, donation, benefit, blessing, boon, gratuity, honorarium, grant, aid, allowance, subsidy, presentation
See also: ABILITY, BONUS, BOUNTY, PREMIUM, PRESENT, REWARD, SKILL, TALENT

GIFT CERTIFICATE
- Our gift certificates make giving even easier
- When you're not sure what to get, pick up a gift certificate
- A gift certificate is always welcome
- Friends and family love getting gift certificates
- A gift certificate might be the most appropriate
- Buy a gift certificate for a friend

GIMMICK
- No catch, no gimmicks
- Don't fall for gimmicks
- This is no gimmick
- We have no gimmicks, only solid value
See also: FOOL, PLAY, TRICK

GIVE
- It not only helps give you a better
- No other product gives you
- With more to give than
- Giving you the very best
- Giving you more
- The emphasis is on giving back to you
- Give a helping hand with

Give: present, bestow, donate, contribute, turn over, award, hand over, vouchsafe, grant, leave, supply, shell out, pay, dish out, allot, allocate, mete out, distribute, apportion, dispense, off, manifest, yield, consign, surrender, relinquish, furnish, endow, entrust, provide, afford, impart, communicate, deliver, confer, empower, enable, authorize, expend, put out, pass on
See also: AFFORD, DELIVER, PROVIDE, SUPPLY

GIVEAWAY
- Enter the dream giveaway
- Don't miss this huge giveaway
- The biggest giveaway in our history
See also: GIFT, PRESENT, PREMIUM

GLAD
- You'll be glad you did
- Always glad to be of service
- Our staff is glad to see you
- A way to fill your heart with gladness
See also: FUN, HAPPY, JOY

GLAMOROUS
- Glamorous, commanding, larger than life
- Be more glamorous today
- You deserve to be glamorous
- A brighter, more glamorous self

GLAMOUR
- Add that touch of glamour to your home
- A metaphor for modern glamour
- Glamour shimming under the moon
- The passionate search for real glamour
- Slip into something more glamorous
See also: ALLURE, BEAUTY, ELEGANCE, ENCHANTRESS, STYLE

GLANCE
- Now at first glance
- Shows you at a glance
- Certainly merits a second glance
See also: LOOK, PEEK

GLITTER
- Come to glitter paradise
- Now you can glitter too
- All that glitters may not be gold
- Glittering with beauty
- A glittering promise of
See also: GOLD, LUSTRE, SHINE

GLOBAL
- A global response to a global problem
- Competing successfully with other global centers
- Able to seize global opportunities with confidence
- It's all about global commerce
- Making you truly global in reach
- Poised to meet global needs
See also: INTERNATIONAL, WORLD

GLOBE
- At home or around the globe
- Sending the message shooting round the

globe
- Putting the globe in the palm of your hand

See also: **EARTH, PLANET, WORLD**

GLORY
- These are the glory days
- Relive the glory
- Shoot for glory while you can
- Share in the glory of

See also: **ACHIEVEMENT, POWER, PRESTIGE**

GO
- Will keep you going strong
- We're just rarin' to go
- Never go anywhere without it
- Go where no other product has gone before
- Go for it
- Go straight to the head of the class
- On your mark, get set, go
- With some real get up and go
- When you're on the go, it goes with you

See also: **MOVE, TRAVEL**

GOAL
- Help you safely achieve your goal
- Working with only one goal in mind
- Our goal from the beginning was to provide you with the best
- Set goals for yourself
- Our goal is to delight and satisfy our customers
- You'll discover new ways to reach your goals
- We take the time to understand your goals

See also: **AIM, CHALLENGE, INTENTION, TARGET**

GODDESS
- Looking like goddess
- Like a gift from a goddess
- Turning yourself in a goddess

See also: **FEMININE, WOMAN**

GOLD
- Catch gold fever
- Fulfilling a golden promise
- Worth it's weight in gold
- Good as gold
- A golden hour has arrived

See also: **GLITTER, LUSTRE, VALUE, WORTH**

GONE
- Get them before they're gone
- Soon they'll be gone for good
- Going, going, gone
- Gone down a different road
- Once they're gone, they're gone

See also: **END, FINISH, LOSS**

GOOD
- Find out how good you can be
- Look good and feel good
- Know it sounds too good to be true
- Has never looked this good
- A product can only be as good as its
- We've come up with something pretty good
- Good for so much
- You'll discover plenty of good things about us
- Nothing else looks and feels quite as good
- So good to your
- It's got to be good
- You're only as good as your last
- A good time was had by all
- Good as gold
- Good things are brewing at

Good: honest, moral, virtuous, noble, wholesome, pure, unsullied, untainted, satisfactory, all right, acceptable, superior, extraordinary, first-class, ace, topnotch, first-rate, correct, proper, right, sterling, excellent, courteous, mannerly, upright, well-behaved, kind, benevolent, respectable, reliable, secure, sound, safe, authentic, genuine, real, valid, delicious, delectable, scrumptious, flavorful, tasty, appetizing, yummy, likable, competent, quality, prime, choice, best, grade A, finest, full, complete, entire, straight

See also: **BEST, CHOICE, EXCELLENCE, FINE**

GOODBYE
- Don't make it a final goodbye
- Say goodbye to all your troubles with
- Goodbye to boredom, hello to thrills and fun

See also: **END, FINISH, PART**

GOODNESS
- Bursting with natural goodness
- Gets all the goodness to you
- You can just see the goodness
- Goodness that really satisfies
- Goodness to keep you healthy

GOODS
- Get the goods here to
- Get your hands on the goods
- The finest of goods and services
- A wide selection of goods
- Goods must be satisfactory or your money refunded

See also: **COMMODITY, INVENTORY, ITEM, MERCHANDISE, PRODUCT**

GOODY
- Hey, check out these goodies
- Just one goody after another
- Showering you with goodies
- Smart people go straight for the goodies

See also: **DELIGHT, TREAT**

GOTTA
- Gotta have it
- Gotta see it
- Gotta want it

See also: **MUST**

GRAB
- So grab yours now
- Grab hold of the ultimate
- Grab all the pleasure your can
- Grabs you and holds you
- What better way to grab attention

See also: **GET**

GRACE
- A fluid grace
- A wonderful saving grace
- Adds grace and charm to any
- With all the grace of a long tradition
- This lovely piece can grace your home for only

See also: **BEAUTY, ELEGANCE**

GRADE
- Really makes the grade
- Want to make the grade
- Make the grade in style
- Top grade service says it all
- Only the best grade
- Grade A all the way

See also: **CLASS, RATE, STANDARD**

GRADUATE
- Great gifts for grads
- Graduate to a higher level of product
- Helping you graduate to a whole new

GRANDMA
- Even grandma would love this
- From grandma to the littlest tot, everyone loves to
- Just do what your grandma always told you

See also: **FAMILY, WISDOM**

GRATIFY
- Working to gratify your every wish
- Gratify your desire to
- Gratifying more customers than ever before
- Instantly gratifying

See also: **DELIGHT, PLEASE, SATISFY**

GRATITUDE
- Sincerest gratitude to all those who have helped make our success possible
- In order to express our gratitude, we're making a very special offer
- Our loyal customers have earned our deepest gratitude

See also: **APPRECIATION, THANKS**

GREAT
- The greatest thing since sliced bread
- Great on its own or combined with
- Goes great with
- The greatest yet
- A brush with greatness

See also: **BIG, FAT, GIANT, MAGNIFICENT, SPLENDID**

GREEN
- Green products, bigger savings
- Start going green now
- Make them green with envy
- Greener technology is our biggest priority
- We know how important green products are to your family
- Safer, greener, better for the planet
- Helping you choose greener alternatives and save money too

Green: safe, healthy, environmentally friendly, organic, natural, earthy
See also: **ECOLOGY, ENVIRONMENT**

GREET
- Where you're greeted like a friend, not a stranger
- You'll be greeted by a welcome smile
- Warmest greetings from
- Greeting you at the door

See also: **HELLO, MEET, WELCOME**

GROOVE
- A new groove
- Get in the groove
- Definitely the grooviest
- Groovier than ever
- And lots of groovy new

See also: **AREA, ZONE**

GROUND
- Start from the ground up
- Breaking new ground every day
- Get in on the ground floor
- With feet firmly planted on the ground
- Stay grounded in reality
- You're never on shaky ground

See also: **BASE, FOUNDATION**

GROUP
- You become part of a unique and influential group
- A small, select group is being invited to try it
- We specialize in large group orders
- A very select group of
- Our group has an outstanding record
- Choose from our large group of
- Grouped together for easy access
- Join an advanced group today

See also: **CHOICE, SALESPEOPLE, SELECTION, STAFF, TEAM**

GROW
- We continue to grow, thanks to
- Grow with us
- One of the fastest growing
- Helping you grow more rapidly
- All of which has made us one of the fastest growing companies in the world
- Helping you grow your business
- We grow on you

- The appeal grows on you fast
- Join one of the most rapidly growing
- It's how we've grown to become

Grow: increase, develop, swell, fill out, enlarge, augment, reinforce, extend, supplement, stretch, widen, magnify, amplify, spring up, flourish, mushroom, thrive, prosper, advance, get ahead, progress, generate, nurture, cultivate
See also: **ADVANCE, BOOM, DEVELOP, EXPAND, GENERATE, INCREASE**

GROWN-UP
- Grown-up value
- Join the grown-ups
- Play like a kid, save like a grown-up
- You're really grown-up when you can finally appreciate

See also: **MATURITY**

GROWTH
- Getting excited to see the growth
- So future growth is all gain, no pain
- Identified tremendous growth potential
- Giving the highest growth rate
- Be part of a growth industry
- A sign of your personal growth is your increasingly discriminating taste
- No end in sight to the phenomenal growth of
- One of the reasons for this phenomenal growth is
- Take advantage of the explosive growth
- Poised for further vigorous growth

See also: **INCREASE**

GUARANTEE
- Backed by a 60-day satisfaction guarantee
- Plus a top-notch product guarantee
- Better than money-back guarantee
- No nonsense guarantee
- With a guarantee like that, you never need worry again
- Satisfaction guaranteed or double your money back
- We guarantee service, quality and dependability
- This guarantee has no time limit except for some conditions
- Guaranteed by law
- Guaranteed forever

- Money-back guarantee
- Remember, we guarantee it
- With our unconditional guarantee there's absolutely no risk on your part
- We guarantee it no matter what happens
- Unconditionally guaranteed for one full year or your money back
- We guarantee that every item has been made to the highest standards
- A ninety-day lowest price guarantee
- Lower prices guaranteed
- Our price guarantee lets you relax
- Price match guarantee
- Satisfaction guaranteed
- Best prices guaranteed
- Your complete satisfaction guaranteed or your money back
- Unconditionally guaranteed for life
- We guarantee your satisfaction
- Great low prices guaranteed
- Remember, everything is backed by our famous guarantee
- We offer an unconditional one-year guarantee
- Guaranteed to please
- No-nonsense guarantee
- Each item guaranteed to provide satisfactory service
- Unconditional guarantee
- There's now only one way to guarantee
- Backed by our famous guarantee
- For guaranteed success
- Lifetime guarantee, lifetime satisfaction
- Best guarantee in the business
- Unparalleled guarantee with written references
- Wear guarantee
- You're guaranteed to find what you need
- Our guarantee is your satisfaction
- The best price guarantee you'll ever find
- Our products are guaranteed for life
- Unconditional money-back guarantee
- Our guaranteed savings
- You're guaranteed to benefit from
- All work guaranteed
- A guarantee like no other
- Guaranteed to blow you away
- You get it at guaranteed low prices
- We offer the best guarantee in the business
- Guaranteed to warm your heart
- Can be guaranteed for a limited time only
- We guarantee you'll be satisfied

- All work is 100% guaranteed
- Money-back guarantee – quick results
- Guaranteed in writing
- In fact, we guarantee it

Guarantee: warranty, protection, indemnity, certification, certainty, pledge, promise, assurance, word, agreement, contract, recommendation, covenant, endorsement, collateral, ensue, secure, vouch, certify, sponsor, underwrite, countersign, swear to, affirm
See also: AGREEMENT, ASSURANCE, CERTAINTY, CONTRACT, PROTECTION, WARRANTY

GUESS
- Guess again
- We don't make you guess
- Don't guess, call us
- Guess what that can lead to
- Takes the guessing out of
- Now you don't have to guess about
- Guess what you can do to
- Don't you hate it when you have to guess
- It's anybody's guess how
- Keep them guessing with
- You don't want to need to guess about something this important
- Get rid of the guesswork

Guess: reckon, estimate, surmise, postulate, hypothesize, conjecture, take a stab at, figure, speak off the top of one's head, shot in the dark, guesstimate, fancy, suppose, deem, judge, daresay, assumption, inference, pot shot, crack, whack, shot, forecast, prediction, theory, prophesy, presupposition
See also: BET, CHOOSE, ESTIMATE, GAMBLE, SURPRISE

GUEST
- Your guests will do a double take
- You are always our most important guest
- You're always an honored guest at
- All our guests are pampered shamelessly
- We invite all our guests to
- A product your guests will love
- Extends an invitation to guests from all over the world.

See also: HOTEL, VISITOR

GUIDANCE
- You need expert guidance from the

people who
- Guidance is provided free
- Look to us for guidance
- Always under the firm guidance of our professionals
- Search no further for the guidance you need to

See also: ADVICE, EXPERT, HELP, PLAN, PROFESSIONAL

GUIDE
- Gently guides you through difficult
- An excellent guide to achieving
- An invaluable guide to finding success
- A common sense guide to
- Your guide to the best new products
- Let us be your guide
- A really handy guide to
- Let your inner voice guide you
- Your easy-living guide
- It's your guide to new delights
- Your complete shopping guide to
- Using this indispensable guide, you can
- Easy-to-read how-to guides, updated regularly
- Full-color, troubleshooting guide based on the advice of experts

Guide: lead, lead the way, conduct, usher, pilot, drive, navigate, hold the reins, take the helm, direct, steer, head toward, show the way, put on the right track, escort, advise, counsel, teach, supervise, oversee, preside, manage, superintend, handle, govern, rule, control, example, model
See also: CHART, COUNSEL, DIRECT, EXPERT, LEAD, LEADER, SPECIALIST

GUILT
- With absolutely no guilt about
- Guilt-free self indulgence
- Fling guilt to the winds and plunge in

See also: APOLOGIZE, REGRET, SORRY

GUY
- For the big guy
- It's a guy thing
- Guys really understand it
- For that special guy in your life
- Guys go for it
- Here's one guy who won't let you down

See also: MAN

HABIT
- Develop a powerful profit-building habit
- Make it a habit to visit our store
- Our service can be habit-forming
- Shake off old habits, get a sharp new
- Your habits will change forever

See also: CUSTOM

HALF
- Half off
- It's a half and half deal
- And then there's the other half
- Don't go home half-satisfied
- Deciding which store is half the battle

HALLMARK
- Dedication that has truly become our hallmark
- Our hallmark is on it
- Look for this famous hallmark
- Look for these hallmarks of
- The hallmark of success stands out
- Service that's the hallmark of
- One of the hallmarks of a successful leader

See also: BENCHMARK, GUARANTEE, MARK, SIGN, SYMBOL, STANDARD

HALO
- You've earned your halo
- So good you have a halo
- Your halo is showing

See also: GLITTER, HERO, LUSTRE

HAMMER
- Hammering away at it
- Facing the mighty hammer of change
- Getting rid of the stresses hammering away at you

See also: ENDURE, PERSEVERANCE

HAND
- It's a comfort to know we're here to lend a hand
- Get your hands on it now
- Give yourself a helping hand
- Giving you a hand up
- Reaching out a hand to you
- All you have to do is hand us your
- The benefit is handed directly to you
- Keeps problems from getting out of hand

- Every item is hand-selected
- If you've got your hands full
- It's in your hands
- Join hands with
- Build it with your own two hands
- We understand the importance of what you've placed in our hands
- Don't be afraid to place your future in our hands
- You may need the help of an experienced hand

See also: **ASSIST, FRIEND, HELP, PARTNER, REACH**

HANDCRAFT

- We meticulously handcraft each one
- Individually handcrafted from the finest
- Only a handcrafted product could be this beautiful

See also: **CREATE, MAKE, SKILL**

HANDLE

- Handled beautifully by
- You'll love the way it handles
- We know you can handle it
- Helps you handle high speed change
- Can you handle this much fun
- So you can handle anything

Handle: lift, touch, feel, hug, caress, direct, manage, administer, supervise, rule, head, govern, boss, take the helm, guide, pilot, drive, trade, deal in, buy and sell, peddle, market, truck, control, oversee, superintend, transact, execute, swing, regulate, run, take charge

See also: **CONTROL, MANAGE, ORGANIZE, PLAN**

HANDS

- If you've got your hands full
- It's in your hands
- In hands you can trust
- Join hands with
- You can't beat hands-on experience
- Build it with your own two hands
- We understand the importance of what you've placed in our hands
- Don't be afraid to place your future in our hands

HANDS-ON

- If you're ready for a hands-on experience

- Real hands-on instruction walks you through it
- It's a hands-on thing with your financial planning
- You can't beat hands-on experience

See also: **CLOSE, DIRECT, INTIMATE**

HANDSOME

- It also happens to be remarkably handsome, too
- You can make a very handsome profit
- We do handsomely buy you
- Handsome is as handsome does

See also: **ATTRACTIVE, BEAUTIFUL, LOVELY**

HANGOUT

- Always a great hangout
- Has long been a hangout for the stars
- We'll show you the hippest hangouts in the country

See also: **CAVE, CLUB, ESCAPE, GET AWAY, HOME, PLACE**

HAPPEN

- Make it happen
- When it comes to happening
- It could happen to you too
- We help it happen for you
- We're seeing it happen throughout the country
- You can see what will happen when
- Showing you how it really happens
- That's what happens when you experience
- It could happen to you
- Can actually make it happen as promised
- This doesn't happen every day

See also: **ACT, EVENT**

HAPPINESS

- Happiness is a great product
- Turns into pure happiness
- We love to see the happiness on your face when
- We're the happiness store
- The happiness of our patrons is our first concern

See also: **DELIGHT, JOY, PLEASURE, SATISFACTION**

HAPPY

- You'll always go away happy

- We want to make you happy
- We're always happy to help
- Whatever makes you happy makes us happy
- We won't stop until you're happy with our product
- They all make someone, somewhere happier
- You'll walk away happy
- What makes you happy and brings you joy
- Have a happy
- We love to see your happy smile
- The happier you are, the happier we are
- You'll also be happy to know that

Happy: delighted, glad, pleased, contented, gratified, satisfied, thrilled, elated, well-pleased, tickled, euphoric, cheerful, cheery, gay, sunny, blithe, in high spirits, blithesome, light-hearted, buoyant, optimistic, positive, upbeat, debonair, free and easy, happy-go-lucky, carefree, breezy, easy-going, jolly, mirthful, hilarious, laughing, smiling, joyful, joyous, jubilant, rejoicing, gleeful, exhilarated, lucky, fortunate, auspicious, favorable, beneficial, profitable, opportune, valuable, gainful, lucrative
See also: **DELIGHT, FUN, GLAD, JOY, PLEASURE, SATISFACTION**

HARD

- It isn't as hard as you think
- We're playing hard to get
- Such a little thing shouldn't be this hard
- We don't make things hard for you
- If you think it's hard to do, think again
- We work harder than anybody else to

See also: **CHALLENGE, DIFFICULT**

HARMONIZE

- Our quest was to harmonize
- Harmonizing all the disparate parts for your convenience
- A harmonization of all the different programs

See also: **BLEND, INTEGRATE, MIX**

HARMONY

- Creating a harmony of color and form
- We've created the perfect harmony of
- Living in harmony with
- Always in harmony with your wishes

- Working in harmony with you

See also: **PEACE, TOGETHER**

HARNESS

- Harnessing all this power
- Harnessing our know-how to your ambition
- We'll show you how to harness everything

See also: **MOTIVATE, USE**

HARVEST

- Country harvest good
- Time to harvest the benefits of
- When your investment yields a bountiful harvest
- Come harvest the profits of
- Straight from the harvest to you

See also: **COLLECT, EARN, RAKE, RESULTS, REWARD, SUCCESS**

HASSLE

- Hassle-free
- Who says it has to be a hassle
- Yours to use without the hassle
- Saves time and money and hassles
- No more hassles with
- Say goodbye to hassles forever
- Discover the hassle-free guaranteed way
- No hassle and no negotiating

See also: **FUSS, TROUBLE**

HAVE

- When you just gotta have it
- Come and see what we have
- You really can have it all
- Become one of the "have" people

HEAD

- Head-spinning value
- Puts you at the head of the line
- Go straight to the head of the class
- Straightens out your head about
- Finally, your head and your heart can agree
- If you've got a head for business, you'll know

See also: **REASON, THOUGHT**

HEADACHE

- Will take you away from the headache
- No more headaches on account of
- Gets rid of the headache

- Banish the headache of

See also: DIFFICULT, HARD, HASSLE, TROUBLE

HEADQUARTERS
- Your improvement headquarters
- Headquarters for
- Come to the headquarters for
- Make us your headquarters for
- Your price and value headquarters

See also: ADMINISTRATION, COMPANY, HOME, OFFICE

HEADY
- These are heady days
- Success can be a pretty heady experience
- You never dreamed it could be this heady

See also: CRAZY, INTOXICATE

HEALTH
- In blooming good health
- Widely used by people who are health conscious
- Protecting the health of your family
- Better health for your pocketbook
- Yet more healthy choices
- Particularly important for healthy functioning of
- Deserves to be kept healthy
- Another chance to feel healthy
- Look better and feel healthier too
- The healthier alternative
- Giving your style a healthy lift

Health: well-being, good condition, good shape, fitness, tip-top shape, vigor, glow, bloom, heartiness, robustness, vitality, strength, potency, get up and go, energy, zing, liveliness, wellness, vim, brio, verve
See also: STRENGTH, VITALITY

HEAR
- Get ready to hear praises
- We hear you
- You've heard it all before
- You haven't heard this before
- Make yourself heard
- We heard you right from the beginning
- Heard all across the land
- You'll like what you hear
- Get it fast before everyone else hears about it
- Here's why you may not have heard

about it before
- The sooner we hear from you the sooner you benefit
- We really like to hear from you

See also: LISTEN, UNDERSTAND

HEART
- Sliding straight into your heart
- Let it take a place in your heart
- At the heart of things
- Bringing right into the heart of
- At the heart is
- Poured our heart and soul into it
- Young at heart
- Will always hold a special place in your heart
- Is there room in your heart for
- At the heart of this success is
- At the heart are professionals who thrive
- Open your heart and have fun
- Go with your heart
- Your heart will choose
- To your heart's content
- Real people, making decisions of the heart
- Have romanced the heart for years
- Guaranteed to warm your heart
- Will warm even the coldest of hearts
- Designed to take your heart

Heart: feeling, sympathy, spirit, soul, emotion, gut feeling, sensibility, understanding, concern, kindness, goodness, love, graciousness, humanity, magnanimity, good will, bravery, daring, courage, valor, guts, fearlessness, dauntlessness, pluck, mettle, gumption, core, center, seed, kernel, substance, essence, nitty-gritty, essential
See also: CARE, EMOTION, ESSENTIAL, FEELING, HUB, LOVE, SPIRIT

HEARTLAND
- Come to the heartland of
- Born in the nation's heartland
- Bringing the heartland right to your home
- Now, brought to you from the very heartland of

See also: CENTER, HOME, HUB

HEAT
- Lick the heat

- Now your item can take the heat
- Give heat the cold shoulder
- Turning up the heat with
- The savings are heating up
- Beat the heat
- Heat rising
- When things heat up
- Before things really heat up
- Are you feeling the heat

See also: DESIRE, HOT, PRESSURE

HEAVEN
- Heaven on earth
- This corner of heaven is perfect
- You'll find it's nothing but pure heaven
- Heaven knows – but do you
- Simply seventh heaven
- Experience heaven on earth
- You are about to experience a little piece of heaven

See also: BLESSING, GETAWAY, PARADISE

HEIGHT
- Take your choice to new heights
- Aspire to greater heights
- The very height of good taste and style
- Soar with us to the highest heights of

See also: BEST

HELLO
- Say hello to happiness
- After we say hello, we'll show you the best
- We'd just love say hello to a new customer

See also: GREET, INTRODUCTION, MEET

HELP
- I know we can help you
- Have helped hundreds of people to help themselves
- You can call for help 24 hours a day
- Guaranteed to help or you pay nothing
- Helps you get things done
- Here's some help with
- We're here to help
- Let us help
- We helped get it there
- A rare gift for helping people to
- With a little help from your friends
- Well, it's part of our job to help you

- Need a little help in livening up
- Nothing helps like
- Actually helps prevent
- To help you, we've introduced
- How can we help you
- Helping to make your day
- Let us help you
- Looking for some help
- We're standing by, ready to help
- Help yourself to
- We've been helping people like you for years
- Pleased to help you with all your needs
- Helping people, one at a time
- Need help
- Our representative is there to help you
- In short, you may need a little help
- We'll help you to
- We've made calling for help easier than ever
- We're ready to help you
- When you really have to have help with something important
- We are committed to helping you

Help: aid, assist, accommodate, oblige, abet, befriend, contribute, join in, chip in, lend a hand, boost, lift, cooperate, team up, take part, join forces, support, combine, sustain, maintain, endorse, stand by, save, rescue, deliver, facilitate, ease, expedite, accelerate, speed up, quicken, clear the way, underwrite, enhance, promote, advocate

See also: ACCOMMODATE, ASSIST, BOOST, IMPROVE, PROVIDE, SERVE, SERVICE, SUPPLY

HELPFUL
- Friendly and helpful
- Our helpful staff is always on hand to
- Always striving to be more helpful
- It's always helpful to compare
- Tell us how we can be even more helpful

See also: BENEFIT, USEFUL

HELPLINE
- The helpline is designed to answer your questions
- We put in the helpline specifically to make it easy for you to
- Call our helpline with confidence any time of the day or night

See also: CALL, SERVICE, SUPPORT

HERE

- Getting here is easy
- Here when you need us
- Everything you need is here
- Everything's right here close to you
- Here's how you get your copy
- Here's what you need to
- Firmly rooted in the here and now

See also: **LOCATION, PLACE**

HERITAGE

- A wonderful pioneering heritage
- Ensuring your family heritage lives on
- A racing heritage that translates from track to traffic
- Come into your true heritage
- Adding to your heritage with
- Part of your heritage

See also: **GIFT, HISTORY, LEGACY, TRADITION**

HERO

- You'll be a hero when you
- Fit for a hero
- Truly heroic in proportion
- Giving heroic portions of
- Everyone wants to be a hero to their children
- Do you dream of being a true hero

See also: **CHAMPION, DAREDEVIL, FAVORITE, ICONOCLAST, LEADER**

HESITATE

- Don't hesitate any more
- Don't hesitate for a moment to
- If you hesitate, they'll all be gone
- You can't afford to hesitate, not even for a day

See also: **CONFUSE, MISS, UNSURE**

HIDE

- Forget about trying to hide
- Absolutely nothing to hide
- There's no longer anywhere to hide
- Hides imperfections, enhances strong points

See also: **DISCREET, SECRET**

HIGH

- Just about as high as you can get
- High quality, high value
- Held up to the highest standard
- Taking you higher than ever before

See also: **BEST, FINE, GOOD, TOP**

HIGHLIGHT

- To highlight the splendid work our professionals do
- Highlighting just a sample
- Highlight on savings
- We just want to highlight one of the better
- Style highlighted by
- One of the highlights of

See also: **FEATURE, NOTICE, SPOTLIGHT**

HINT

- Notes and hints to help you
- For those who can take a hint
- If your loved one has been hinting for

See also: **SUBTLE**

HIP

- Something hip, hot and cool
- Can come out with something hip
- So ya wanna be hip

See also: **COOL, HOT, YOUNG**

HISTORY

- Help us preserve history
- Seasoned with history
- Changing the course of communications history
- Change the course of history
- Making history as you watch
- The rest is history
- Buy a piece of history
- Just look at our history
- Create some history with
- Opening up a whole new chapter in product history
- You're attending a historic occasion

See also: **HERITAGE, LEGACY, PAST, TRADITION**

HIT

- A hit on the runways
- Get the quality you need without taking a financial hit
- A really big hit with the little people
- Hit the pavement running
- You'll be a hit when you show up with
- Now hitting the stores
- Hot hits
- Just the biggest hit of the season

See also: **ARRIVE, JOY, PLEASURE, SUCCESS**

HOLD
- Now take hold bravely
- An idea that is taking hold everywhere
- Helping you to hold on to all your gains

See also: **GRAB**

HOLIDAY SEASON
- Wishing you all the best during this holiday season
- Sending warm wishes for the holiday season and the coming year
- Warmest wishes for a happy holiday season
- May you enjoy a wonderful holiday season
- A safe and prosperous holiday season
- Bringing you good tidings this holiday season
- Wishing you a truly magical holiday season
- As the holiday season approaches, we extend our thanks
- All of us join in wishing you a splendid holiday season
- Joy throughout the holiday season
- The holiday season is about to get a lot easier
- Just in time for the holiday season
- Bringing you the best for the holiday season

See also: **CELEBRATE, EASTER, FESTIVE**

HOLIDAY
- Holiday gift offer
- The holidays are for making people happy
- The holidays are right around the corner
- Wishing you peace and happiness during the holidays and throughout the coming year
- Do your holiday shopping the easy way
- Enjoying the warmth and goodwill of the holidays
- Spend less time preparing for the holidays
- You can find everything you need for the holidays right here
- You'll see just how easy holiday shopping can be
- Fill your home with a holiday atmosphere
- In the joyful spirit of the holidays
- Putting you in a holiday mood
- Super holiday specials
- In the spirit of the holidays, we're offering you this special
- You'll find a lot of holiday cheer
- Take it easy during the holidays
- For the most important holiday of the year
- Take a break from the holiday rush
- Check your store for holiday hours
- Our best to you during the holidays and throughout the new year
- May your holidays be filled with joy and happiness
- May only good things fill your holidays
- We treasure the joy of the holidays
- The holidays are filled with special moments like this
- Wishing you the best of everything during the holidays ahead

Holiday: day off, vacation, time off, respite, recess, breather, sabbatical, red-letter day, gala, event, occasion, birthday, jubilee, anniversary, fete, lark, treat, whirl, carnival, fair, junket, folic, spree, feast day, good time, merry, joyous, convivial, gleeful, gay, sportive, festive, festival, fiesta, in holiday spirits, break

See also: **CARNIVAL, CELEBRATION, CHRISTMAS, EASTER, ENJOY, EVENT, FESTIVE, FIESTA, FREEDOM, FUN, HOLIDAYS, OCCASION**

HOMAGE
- Paying homage to centuries of
- The homage that is your due
- We're paying homage to a master

See also: **KUDOS, PRAISE, RESPECT, TRIBUTE**

HOME
- Every home should have one
- Get it at home in your spare time
- Arrange for a convenient time and day to visit your home
- Call for free shop at home service
- Enhance the comfort and beauty of your home for years to come
- Found in any dream home

- What does your home say about you
- So good to come home to
- So close to home
- Making you feel perfectly at home
- Brighten your home
- What you need for your home – for less
- To meet the needs of every home
- It's what makes a house a home
- Come home to
- A need just now hitting home
- Now you can shop without leaving home
- To help your house feel like a home
- Perk up your home with
- Help is close to home
- Welcome to our home
- Take it home with you today
- Free shop-at-home service
- Do it in your own home
- Another home run from
- Take home some incredible deals
- Comfort to come home to

Home: dwelling, residence, domicile, habitation, accommodations, quarters, hearth, family circle, home sweet home, household, homestead, shelter, retreat, refuge, den, environment, hometown, destination
See also: ACCOMMODATION, DOORSTEP, ENVIRONMENT

HONEST
- We're being completely honest
- Nothing but honest value and hard work
- You want the honest truth
- Honest work, honest value
- Always honest about the real costs

Honest: upright, upstanding, incorruptible, ethical, moral, principled, high-minded, truthful, veracious, trust-worthy, trusty, reliable, dependable, tried and true, faithful, loyal, staunch, steadfast, true-blue, honorable, worthy, right, decent, good, fair, impartial, equitable, fair and square, level, square-dealing, plain-dealing, square-shooting, straight-shooting, unbiased, open-minded, valid, legitimate, rightful, proper, candid, frank, forthright, foursquare, direct, straightforward, straight-from-the-shoulder, genuine, sincere, aboveboard, up front, unequivocal, real, sterling, bona fide, sure enough, authentic, reputable, creditable, straight-arrow, unvarnished
See also: FAIR, GUARANTEE,

RELIABLE, RELY, RIGHT, TRUE, TRUST, WARRANTY

HONESTY
- Our honesty and patience serve you, year after year
- Treated with honesty and respect
- Honesty is like gold to us
- A carefully nurtured reputation for honesty
- Founded on honesty
- Above, we value honesty and integrity

See also: NAME, RELIABILITY, REPUTATION

HOOK
- Designed to get you hooked on
- Get hooked on
- You'll be hooked from the start
- Swallowing it hook, line and sinker

See also: ATTRACT, GRAB, INTEREST

HOP
- Positively hopping with life
- Hop to it and get down here
- Hey now, hop on the bandwagon
- Just a hop, skip away

See also: ADVANCE, JOIN, LEAP

HOPE
- There is help and hope
- Stop hoping, start doing
- Before you give up hope, let us introduce you to
- Hope springs eternal
- Sharing your hope that
- Everything you hoped for and more
- Your best hope for

Hope: expectation, longing, desire, want, fancy, wish, eagerness
See also: DESIRE, WANT, WISH

HOSPITAL
- Hospital studies show
- More hospitals use this product than
- Think of it as a hospital for
- Avoid a trip to the hospital

HOSPITALITY
- Enjoy our warm hospitality and more
- Hospitality is our middle name
- Hospitality demands it

- Showering you with lavish hospitality
See also: **ENTERTAIN, GUEST, HOST, HOTEL, VISIT**

HOST
- Will once again hosting
- So that you can now host any size party
- Turns you into the most genial of hosts
- The host with the most
See also: **ENTERTAIN, VISIT**

HOT
- Give a red hot welcome
- Hot doings in the old town tonight
- Hot off the
- Look hot, feel cool
- For a product that's really hot
- Any more and it would be too hot to handle
- It's the hottest thing going
- Here's the hot spot
- What's hot, what's not
- This is really hot.
- Hot and fresh
See also: **COOL, HEAT, HIP, SIZZLE**

HOTEL
- The perfect hotel for the perfect vacation
- In the tradition of great hotels everywhere
- At our hotel, everything is just as you imagined it
See also: **ACCOMMODATION, HOSPITALITY, STAY, VISITOR**

HOTFOOT
- Hotfoot it over to our store
- Have them all hotfooting it in your direction
- Give them the hotfoot for
See also: **FAST, SPEED**

HOURS
- There just aren't enough hours in the day
- To provide our customers with the most convenient hours possible
- You'll save the hours and hours it takes to
- Very flexible hours of service
- Takes less than an hour to
- Now on extended hours for your shopping convenience

See also: **OPEN, TIME**

HOW
- Here's how it works
- How to get any item you want
- Find out how with no money down
- You'll find out exactly how to
- Packed with information on how
- Now you really know how to
- Find out how right now
- An excellent way of discovering how
See also: **METHOD, WAY**

HUB
- Now is the hub of activity for
- The hub around which everything revolves
- Make your home a hub for
See also: **CENTER, HEART, HEARTLAND**

HUE
- Prettiest hues we've seen in years
- Certainly putting a different hue on
- Adding a rosy hue of possibility to all your dreams
See also: **COLOR, RAINBOW, SHADE**

HUG
- Soft, cuddly, ready to hug
- So good you'll hug yourself
- Like a warm, comforting hug
See also: **CARE, CARESS, CLOSE, COMFORT, EMBRACE, INTIMATE,**

HUMAN
- If you need help from a human, our staff is on hand
- It's only human nature to
- A totally human desire to
- Wake up feeling a little more human
See also: **PEOPLE**

HUMOR
- The saving grace of a fine sense of humor
- As necessary as a good sense of humor
- Come where folks have a sense of humor
See also: **ENJOYMENT, FUN**

HUNK
- Hey, it's hunk-hunting season
- Drop a big hunk of luck on you
- You, too, can be a hunk

- If you're sighing over some unattainable hunk

See also: GUY, MAN, PART, SHARE

HUNT
- Hunt down some totally new
- Your long, exhausting hunt is over
- Always on the hunt for something better
- Calling all bargain hunters

See also: SEARCH, SUBTLE

HURDLE
- You won't have to jump any hurdles
- Take the hurdles easily
- Sweeping the hurdles out of your way
- No longer a hurdle in your path
- Clears the last hurdle out of your way

See also: CHALLENGE, OBSTACLE

HURRY
- You better hurry though
- But hurry because they won't last
- Hurry on over and take a look
- They're going in a hurry
- See what the hurry is all about
- Hurry in today

See also: FAST, HOTFOOT, SPEED

HYPE
- Amid the endless hype about
- You'll find it's much more than just hype
- Find out what the hype is all about
- Underneath the hype, the real story

See also: ADVERTISE, BOOST, JAZZ, PIZZAZZ, PUMP

ICON
- Behind every icon there is a powerful idea
- For the past forty years, an icon of quality
- Choose your icons carefully

See also: SIGN, SYMBOL

ICONOCLAST
- A true iconoclast at work
- An explosion of iconoclastic ideas
- Proud to be an iconoclast

See also: DAREDEVIL, INDIVIDUALIST, MAVERICK

IDEA
- One of the nicest things about the whole idea is
- It's your idea of what really matters
- Everything about this idea is perfectly simple
- Now all of this should give you a pretty good idea of just what it takes
- Here's a crazy idea
- That's why we took the idea beyond
- A classic idea of
- An idea whose time has truly come
- An idea you should consider seriously
- Perhaps it's time you heard an entirely new idea
- The heart of the idea behind it all
- To act on your ideas immediately
- Here's a bright idea
- It's the basic idea behind
- Where the idea originated
- An incredible idea from
- Not just another wild idea
- One smart idea after another
- Add our latest idea to your repertoire
- Does more than just give a general idea

Idea: notion, thought, belief, concept, conception, perception, surmise, observation, theory, conjecture, guess, plan, design, dream, vision, intention, object, end, aim, goal, impression, assumption, opinion, view, feeling, conviction, persuasion, philosophy, outlook, principle, teaching

See also: AIM, BELIEF, CONCEPT, DESIGN, FEELING, GOAL, IDEAS, INSIGHT, INSPIRATION, NOTION, OPINION, PHILOSOPHY, PLAN, PRINCIPLE, SYSTEM

IDEAL
- Turning it into more than just an ideal
- Ideal for all your needs
- Firmly committed to these ideals
- Living up to the very highest ideals

See also: AIM, GOAL, PERFECT

IDEAS
- Offers beautiful and creative ideas
- Bright ideas don't come cheap
- Encourage people from different disciplines to interact and exchange ideas
- Brilliant ideas cost more
- Enjoy great ideas for
- Ideas you can use immediately

- You supply the ideas, we'll
- Connect with powerful ideas
- Good ideas for you
- Created from the ideas you bring
- Amazing ideas for small business
- Ideas that last
- Sure to spark lots of ideas for
- Here are even more inspired ideas
- The source of pioneering ideas
- Get some sizzling new ideas for
- We've got all kinds of great ideas and smart solutions for
- Do you need more ideas
- Taking your ideas very seriously
- Go out of our way to come up with ideas to help you
- Helping to bring your ideas to life
- We're open to any of your ideas
- Dozens of ideas to get you going
- For more ideas, visit our store

See also: IDEA

IDENTIFY

- In order to help you better identify
- Identified as one of the leaders in the industry
- Identifying you as one of the most desirable customers
- Identifying those who need our services the most

See also: RECOGNIZE, SPOT

ILLUSION

- You might think it's an illusion
- It's certainly no illusion that
- The reality behind the illusion
- More than just a beautiful illusion

See also: DREAM, CONFUSION, FOOL, TRICK

ILLUSTRATE

- To superbly illustrate the
- Let us illustrate exactly what we mean
- Illustrating just how easily you can do it and succeed

See also: DEMONSTRATE, SHOW

IMAGE

- Something that can help your image
- You don't have to spend millions to give yourself a million dollar image
- Your chance to fashion a whole new

image for yourself
- Will enhance your business image
- Create an image with impact
- When image is everything
- Living up to our image every day
- Intensify your image
- Your image is key to
- Boost your body image now
- Capturing a fresh new image

Image: appearance, semblance, aspect, form, shape, idea, concept, likeness, symbol, type
See also: APPEARANCE, ASPECT, IMPACT, IMPRESSION

IMAGINATION

- Anywhere your imagination takes you
- Exercise your imagination
- It takes real imagination to
- Enrich your imagination
- Facing the future with imagination and insight

See also: CREATIVITY, FLAIR, VISION

IMAGINE

- Going further than you ever imagined
- More beautiful than you ever imagined
- How could you have imagined that
- Imagine one of these in your home
- Now imagine what we'll do for an encore
- Imagine the time and money you'll save
- Imagine for a moment
- Take the time to imagine a different reality

Imagine: picture, envision, dream up, conjure up, visualize, rhapsodize, envisage, guess, conjecture, create
See also: DREAM, PICTURE, THINK

IMITATION

- Accept no imitations
- It's the real thing, not an imitation
- Imitation is the sincerest form of flattery
- No imitation can come even close to the quality of our product

See also: COPY, DUPLICATE, REPEAT

IMMERSE

- You can be completely immersed in
- Immerse yourself in sheer luxury
- For years, people have been immersed in the idea of
- Immerse yourself in comfort

See also: **COVERAGE, SURROUND**

IMPACT
- A major impact on a material world
- High-impact thinking
- Still reeling from the impact
- More impact for your buck
- Increase our personal impact with
- We're making a major impact on

Impact: force, shock brunt, pressure, impetus, momentum, energy, slam, bang, knock, blow
See also: **EFFECT, ENERGIZE, HIT, PUNCH**

IMPERATIVE
- It's absolutely imperative that we keep up with and deliver on those needs
- Imperative that we provide the service you need
- When it's imperative that you get action fast

See also: **IMPORTANT, REQUIRE**

IMPETUS
- Adds a powerful impetus to
- The whole impetus behind this product
- Get some impetus behind you ideas

See also: **DRIVE, IMPULSE, MOMENTUM, POWER, URGE**

IMPORTANCE
- Communicating the value and importance
- Attesting to its importance
- Your importance to us is enormous
- We understand how much importance your place upon
- Of particular importance ot you

IMPORTANT
- It is extremely important that
- We all know how important
- Just as important
- What's the most important thing you put on every day
- With this important difference
- The most important decision you'll ever make

Important: significant, critical, momentous, weighty, serious, grave, sober, crucial, urgent, pressing, imperative, necessary, essential, major, principal, prime, primary, big, major, main, substantial, considerable, formidable, imposing, commanding, high-level, superior, big-time, eminent
See also: **BIG, SERIOUS, SUPERIOR**

IMPOSSIBLE
- Absolutely impossible to put down
- What was once considered impossible is now yours
- Making the impossible possible is our business
- No longer impossible
- Win against impossible odds

See also: **HURDLE, OBSTACLE**

IMPRESSION
- The fast way to make a lasting impression
- Make a great first impression with
- There's no second chance to make a first impression
- The kind of impression you want to make
- Helping you create a great impression

See also: **IMAGE, IMPACT**

IMPRESSIVE
- But perhaps even more impressive is
- Presenting a really impressive amount of data in support
- Truly impressive results from very little effort

See also: **MAGNIFICENT, SPLENDID**

IMPROVE
- Always changing, always improving
- The time when you can most improve
- It's possible to improve on a good thing
- New and improved
- Measurably and visibly improved
- Helping you to improve your life
- Felt it could still be improved upon
- Always looking for ways to improve your shopping experience
- With an aim to expand and improve service through
- Improving through a joint initiative

See also: **BENEFIT, BETTER, BOOST, HELP**

IMPROVEMENT
- The improvement that pays you
- Adding improvement after improvement

to an already excellent product
- Helping your make improvements to
- Committed to constant improvement and success
- To find out how you can make improvements
- We're convinced you'll keep those improvements

See also: **ADVANCE, BETTER, PROGRESS, STRIDE**

IMPULSE
- Give way to a totally revolutionary impulse
- More than just an impulse buy
- Your impulses are right to
- Can indulge your every impulse
- Let your wild impulses out

See also: **DESIRE, IMPETUS, MOMENTUM, URGE**

IN-STORE
- Just a sample of what you'll find in-store
- Don't miss our in-store specials
- Great in-store values for the entire family

INCENTIVE
- Incentive to start saving early
- Providing the buying incentives you need
- Your business is our greatest incentive
- With even greater price incentives, you win all round

See also: **ALLURE, BENEFIT, PREMIUM, PRIZE, REASON**

INCOME
- The opportunity to earn a good income
- Powered by the desire to generate a large cash income
- It is possible to create a perpetual cash income
- The need for a successful income opportunity is perpetually in demand
- Generating income for you from day one
- Preserving more of your income to personal use
- You have to stretch your income a long way
- Take control of your income and time right now

Income: revenue, returns, receipts, gross, annuity, pension, subsidy, allowance, profits, gain, yield, interest, winnings, take, proceeds, net, gravy, pickings, wages, salary, pay, payment, hire, remuneration, stipend, fee, benefits, extras

See also: **MONEY. SECURITY, WEALTH**

INCORPORATE
- Incorporates so many improvements, enhancements and innovations
- Incorporate it immediately into your life and see the difference
- Easily incorporated into your overall plan for maximum results

See also: **BLEND, INTEGRATE, MIX**

INCREASE
- Increasing your efficiency, your customer base, your bottom line and your growth
- Before it has a chance to increase in value
- You'll notice a dramatic increase in

See also: **BOOM, DEVELOP, EXPAND, GROW**

INDEPENDENCE
- The easiest way to get the independence and satisfaction you want
- Helping you keep your hard-won independence
- What real independence is all about

See also: **CHOICE, FREEDOM, LIBERTY**

INDEPENDENT
- Your independent store
- You want to make an independent decision about
- Get the best service from your independent agent

INDESTRUCTIBLE
- Utterly indestructible no matter what the circumstances
- As nearly indestructible as we could make it
- A good idea is indestructible

See also: **ENDURE, LAST, RELIABLE, TIMELESS**

INDIVIDUAL
- Is very individual and very bold
- In our eyes, each individual is

wonderfully unique
- Each individual need receives concentrated attention
- Passionate about treating our customers as individuals
- Services structured to your individual needs

Individual: separate, sole, alone, complete, alone, particular, private, special, singular, custom, distinguished, select, different, rare, unusual, unparalleled, free, spirit, maverick, eccentric, original, nonconformist, uncommon
See also: DIFFERENT, RARE, SELECT, SPECIAL, UNUSUAL

INDIVIDUALIST
- For the rugged individualist
- Created by individualists for individualists
- Approach you in a very individualist manner

See also: DAREDEVIL, ICONOCLAST, MAVERICK

INDULGE
- Indulge yourself, day and night
- When you yearn to indulge yourself
- Indulge in the possibility of

See also: PAMPER, SPOIL, TREAT

INDUSTRY
- Placing us among the industry's best
- Industry leaders
- Remaking an industry
- Helping to make our industry a better one
- The finest in the industry

See also: BUSINESS

INEXPENSIVE
- A smart, inexpensive solution
- Excellent quality yet inexpensive
- Inexpensive enough to fit any budget
- A very inexpensive line of products

See also: CHEAP, ECONOMICAL, LOW COST

INFLUENCE
- The mediating influence of client's needs
- Has a wide-reaching influence
- Including all the new influences
- A far-flung, lasting influence

- Influenced only by the very best

See also: CONVINCE, MODEL

INFORM
- Be well informed
- While keeping you fully informed at all times
- Keeping you informed of the very latest
- Informed with a haunting beauty
- If you want to be well-informed
- Make valuable contacts and stay informed

Inform: advise, notify, let know, tell, relate, impart, acquaint, brief, proclaim, publish, broadcast, report, communicate, instruct, teach, enlighten, blow the lid off
See also: ANNOUNCE, COMMUNICATE, TELL

INFORMALITY
- An addictive informality
- Informality is the rule at our place
- A wonderfully relaxing informality reigns
- You'll really enjoy the informality

See also: CASUAL, COMFORT, EASE, FAMILIAR

INFORMATION
- Put together as a central source of information
- Getting the information you want is easy
- I'm talking about killer information
- Call now for up-to-the-minute information
- Is now the major source of information
- For your information
- Finding the right information takes time
- Our information specialists will
- Filled with valuable information
- You'll get full product information so you can compare
- Receive up-to-date information
- Assuring you accurate information
- Please check with your dealer for current information
- You'll have access to the most current business information and resources
- No one keeps vital information safe like
- Keep this information handy in case
- Keeps information at your fingertips
- Your trusted retailer has more

information
- For more information and reservations, call
- Handy for organizing information
- I'd like to send you more information about
- Providing practical information on
- For more information visit the store nearest your
- Information is just a phone call away
- Complete information at your fingertips
- Featuring the best ideas and information
- Now you can access a wealth of information on
- For twenty-four hour information, just visit our web site
- Information becoming more and more useful to you every day
- Call now for hot tips and solid information on
- If you're interested in some amazing information
- Providing the information you'll need to do just that
- Reorganize the information universe
- Call us and ask for free information
- Making it possible for you to send for more information
- When you need information right now
- Information is moving fast these days
- The key to your success is the best up-to-date information
- All the information you need to

Information: data, facts, knowledge, intelligence, background, report, communication, message, account, counsel, pointer, lowdown, inside story
See also: ADVICE, ANALYSIS, DATA, EXPERT, FACT, GUIDANCE, HELP, PLAN, PROFESSIONAL, REPORT

INGREDIENT
- A unique blend of the best classic and contemporary ingredients
- These aren't the usual ingredients of
- The really important ingredients are
- Combined with the purest, mildest, most natural ingredients possible
- Wholesome ingredients to
- Made of several highly effective ingredients

See also: FUNDAMENTAL,

INTEGRATE, MATERIAL, MIX, PART, SUBSTANCE

INHERITANCE
- Preserving a fine inheritance
- An inheritance of excellence
- Taking care of your precious inheritance

See also: BIRTHRIGHT, HERITAGE, LEGACY, TRADITION

INHIBITION
- Peel away your inhibitions
- Believe it or not, some people still have an inhibition about
- Say goodbye to inhibitions

See also: HURDLE, OBSTACLE

INITIATIVE
- A high degree of initiative
- To succeed, you need to take the initiative
- We've been taking the design initiative for years
- Just take a look at this price initiative
- Now it's time you took the initiative

See also: ADVANCE, BEGINNING, IMPETUS, START, STRIDE

INNOVATION
- Innovation means looking boldly ahead
- Innovation is about looking forward
- Making the leap from need to innovation
- Tradition meets innovation right here
- Innovation in product design and production methods are setting the pace
- Fifty years of innovation
- Innovations to give you a competitive edge

See also: ADVANCE, CREATIVITY, DREAM, FRESH, IDEA, NEW, VISION

INNOVATIVE
- Innovative designs for creating and updating your
- One of the finest and most innovative
- This innovative product will put you away ahead of your competition

INPUT
- We want your input
- Give you the input you want
- We took your input and created this fine product

See also: **GIVE, INFORMATION, SUGGESTION**

INQUIRY
- Inquiries invited from
- Quickly answer your inquiries
- In answer to your inquiry
- Serious inquiries only

See also: **ASK, QUESTION**

INSIDE
- Inside, you'll find
- Reaches deep inside you
- Take advantage of inside information
- It's what's inside that counts
- Beautiful inside and out

INSIDER
- Offering you a rare insider's view
- You too can be an insider
- Straight from the savviest insiders to your ear

See also: **CONSULTANT, EXPERT, SPECIALIST**

INSIGHT
- Providing you with the experience and insight to
- Insight and research has provided this advance
- Priceless insights struggling to get out
- Providing unique insights into the principles of
- There comes a dazzling moment of insight
- Providing a touchingly personal insight

See also: **EXPERIENCE, UNDERSTANDING, VISION**

INSIST
- Insist on the best
- We insist on serving you
- We insist on providing only the finest

See also: **ASK, DEMAND, NEED, PRESSURE**

INSPECTION
- Free home inspection
- Customer inspection prior to delivery is our long standing possible
- Standing ready for your inspection
- Inviting your closest inspection

See also: **EXAMINATION, OVERHAUL**

INSPIRATION
- The inspiration that enables us to make the leap
- Suits almost any inspiration you can have
- When you need inspiration, come to us
- Remains our lasting inspiration
- Sometimes you need a little inspiration
- Turning inspiration into ideas
- Your needs provided the inspiration to create

See also: **CREATIVITY, FLAIR, IDEA, IMAGINATION**

INSPIRE
- Countless people have been inspired
- Inspired and influenced by
- Inspired by the goodness of
- Something to inspire you
- Has inspired a legion of
- Something that will caress you and inspire you
- An inspiring place to visit
- We try to inspire you with

See also: **ENERGIZE, MOVE, MOTIVATE**

INSTALL
- Completely installed
- Neatly and expertly installed
- Save money by installing it yourself
- Easy to install
- Even a child could install it
- Comes ready to install
- We can install it right away
- You can easily install it yourself
- We can design, deliver and install your
- We install all products
- We can special order and install

See also: **BUILD**

INSTALLATION
- Free home installation any time you call
- Making installation quick and easy
- Installation services available by professionals
- Complete instructions for easy installation
- Fast and easy installation
- Will arrange installation by qualified contractors in most areas
- Installation has been made super simple

See also: **BUILD, SERVICE**

INSTALLMENT
- Buy it on the installment plan
- You'll be able to handle the installments easily
- Payable in convenient monthly installments

See also: PAYMENT, STAGE, STEP

INSTANT
- Instant value
- Designed for instant gratification
- Get results instantly
- Instant savings every time you buy

See also: BLITZ, FAST, SPEED

INSTINCT
- Some people know it instinctively
- Done almost by instinct
- Your instincts are superb
- Do what your instincts tell you
- A new way to hone your instincts

See also: FEELING, NOSE

INSTRUCTION
- Step-by-step instructions make it easy and fun
- Offers full-time, real situation instruction
- Always comes with step-by-step instructions
- All you need is the ability to follow simple instructions
- If you can follow these easy instructions for four weeks
- Follow simple instructions to get started
- Comes with complete instructions

See also: EDUCATION, INFORMATION, LEARN, ORDER, TEACH

INSTRUCTOR
- Providing instructors who know first hand
- Just call up one of our instructors and ask for details
- We hire and train the very best instructors

See also: EDUCATE, LEADER, TEACH

INSTRUMENTAL
- Definitely instrumental in helping you to build your portfolio
- Something that's been instrumental in developing
- A great concept is instrumental in

making

See also: KEY, NECESSARY

INTANGIBLE
- The intangible thing that turns heads
- The benefits are intangible but very real
- An intangible beauty that keeps them dreaming

See also: MYSTERY, SUBTLE

INTEGRATE
- Able to integrate easily
- We'll integrate it seamlessly with all your other
- Integrate it into your life

See also: BLEND, MIX

INTEGRITY
- Meets the highest standard of product integrity
- Just look at our shining record of integrity
- Our integrity means everything to us

See also: HONESTY

INTELLIGENT
- It's the intelligent thing to do
- The place where intelligent people come to shop
- A triumph of intelligent design
- The intelligent choice

See also: BRAIN, SMART

INTENSITY
- With a singular intensity
- The intensity of concentration is remarkable
- Forged with intensity and fervor
- Increasing the intensity of your experience

INTENTION
- Our intentions are pleasantly transparent
- Your intention is clear
- We have every intention of indulging you to the fullest

INTEREST
- In the midst of this flurry of interest
- Brought to you in the interest of
- Showing a healthy interest in
- Is quickly attracting world-wide interest
- Taking a real interest in you

- Deeply interested in
- Strive to keep your best interests at heart
- Who wouldn't be interested
- No interest, no payments for
- No interest for one year
- Low introductory interest rate
- Low interest financing
- Take advantage of an interest rate drastically lower

Interest: engagement, attention, notice, scrutiny, curiosity, heed, consideration, concern, consequence, hobby, diversion, pastime, stake, share, part, portion, equity, stock, claim, increment, increase, slice, right, cut, piece, benefit, profit, preference, gain, percentage, value, involvement, partiality
See also: HOOK, INCOME, MONEY

INTERFACE
- This is how we interface with
- A far easier interface than any other
- Interface with the world
See also: CONNECT, LINK

INTERNATIONAL
- Internationally acclaimed
- We start you thinking internationally
- Think international, think rich, think success
- Fortunate to have an internationally recognized name
- Internationally known
See also: GLOBAL, WORLD

INTERPRET
- Does such a fine job of interpreting
- Beauty needs no interpretation
- Able to interpret and satisfy your every desire
See also: UNDERSTANDING

INTIMACY
- The more you cherish the intimacy of
- Enjoy the quiet intimacy of
- Achieving an even greater intimacy
See also: CARESS, CLOSE, WARMTH

INTIMATE
- Roomy yet intimate
- Giving you that softly intimate feeling
- When it's time to get intimate, you need
- An intimate setting that releases all your

fantasies
- For those truly intimate moments
See also: CLOSE, FRIENDLY

INTOXICATE
- So fresh it fairly intoxicates
- Inducing a wildly intoxicating rush
- Let us intoxicate you with pleasure
See also: HEADY, WILD

INTRODUCE
- Here's why we introduced
- Proud to introduce
- Introducing the very latest addition to our product line
- Please let us introduce you to a new way of thinking
See also: MEET

INTRODUCTION
- Perfected for introduction this month
- Since it's introduction a decade ago
- Certainly needs no introduction
- The best introduction for you is
See also: CONTACT,, GREET, MEET

INTRODUCTORY
- Try them now at the introductory price
- And take advantage of an introductory
- We invite you to try our no-risk introductory offer
- Special introductory offer
See also: FIRST, NEW

INVENT
- This just might be the best that's ever been invented
- We invented it just for you
- Inventing a brand new life for you
See also: CREATE, INNOVATION

INVENTORY
- Get everything you need from our huge, in-stock inventory
- Huge inventory clearance
- More inventory than ever before
- We just have to clear all the extra inventory
- Too much inventory means big savings for you
- We must reduce our inventory of
- Giant inventory clearance
- Best prices on all our inventory

See also: CATALOGUE, LIST,
SELECTION, SPECTRUM, STOCK

INVEST
- Invest in your world
- The most important resource you can invest in is yourself
- We invest under a microscope
- Invest an hour of your time – get a great return
- Before you invest your money, let us invest our time
- Before we invest your hard-earned money
- We've invested years in building a strong customer base
- We invest in you
- Investing in the most dynamic sectors
- Invest in something with lasting value
- Invest in your future
- Invest your money twice

Invest: put money into, fund, subsidize, back, support, provide capital for, spend, expend, supply, contribute, equip, outfit
See also: BUY, CHOOSE, PAY, PROVIDE, SELECT

INVESTMENT
- Your investment continues to grow all year
- Meeting all your investment needs
- Watch your investment in action
- For a very low initial investment you can
- Your investment starts at
- All for a low investment
- Quick return on your investment
- Make a wise investment in yourself
- Make your investment back and then some
- Achieve the most mileage from your investment
- We look closely at our investments
- Investments that will help your money grow over time
- Protect your investment
- Make an investment in quality
- The best investment in today's economy
- Make your biggest investment your smartest investment
- For more information on this unique investment please call
- A growth investment with tax savings

- Strengthen your investment

Investment: venture, speculation, risk, endowment, empowerment
See also: MONEY, VENTURE

INVESTOR
- Largest investor-owned operation
- Turning you into a successful investor
- We take good care of our investors

See also: BUYER, CUSTOMER, PATRON

INVIGORATE
- Refreshes and invigorates your mind and body
- For an invigorating change
- Feel invigorated through and through

See also: ENERGIZE, REJUVENATE

INVITATION
- We're sending you a very special invitation
- Your invitation to special trade shows and seminars
- We continue to extend a warm invitation to you
- An invitation from the house of
- A remarkable invitation to enhance your life
- If you accept this invitation, you will join very select company
- Your invitation to this exclusive offer
- We hope you'll accept this invitation

See also: EVENT, GUEST, HOSPITALITY

INVITE
- Cordially invited to our grand opening
- You are warmly invited to a special open house
- For a limited time, customers are invited to enjoy
- We invite you to come every day
- You are invited to explore
- Respectfully inviting you to participate
- Inviting pleasure with every move

See also: ASK, INTRODUCE, MEET

INVOLVE
- Get involved
- Most often involve
- You are involved in every aspect of

development
See also: INVITE, JOIN

ISSUE
- Often a critical issue
- We know what your issues are
- A special issue filled with ideas
- A very important first issue
- Issued to you immediately upon

See also: CHALLENGE, CONCEPT, GIVE, IDEA, PROBLEM

ITEM
- Regularly come to seek out special items for clients
- Not all items, colors and sizes in this circular have been offered for sale in all stores
- Buy any item, get one at half price
- Many items are also available in our catalogue
- Among our most popular items this year

See also: COMMODITY, GOODS, PRODUCT

JAM
- Jam with the coolest
- When you're in a jam, come to us
- Jammed with value
- Just groovin' and jammin'

JAZZ
- We're jazzing it up
- Put some jazz in your life
- Jazz up the old homestead a bit

See also: FUN, HYPE, PIZZAZZ

JOB
- You've done a great job of
- A job no one thought was possible a few years ago
- Working quietly to get the job done
- We're here to finish the job
- Within reach for any job
- Can do the job handily
- If it's a tough job, it's a job for us
- For relaxing on the job
- Ensuring the job is done properly
- The job has never been easier
- Get the job done right
- It's a job for our company
- Cuts the job down to size
- We can begin most jobs immediately

- Always on the job
- Be job ready in four months
- We charge by the job, not by the hour
- Does four jobs at once
- Have the right person for the job
- Handle jobs others won't do
- Do all your small and medium-sized jobs

Job: work, undertaking, business, proceeding, task, chore, activity, exercise, performance, project, affair, venture, enterprise, effort, contribution, accomplishment, achievement, role, function, concern, duty, office, mission, trust, employment, occupation, livelihood, living, pursuit, vocation, calling, profession, field, metier, area, province, trade, craft, grind, contract

See also: BUSINESS, MISSION, TRUST, VENTURE, WORK

JOIN
- No cost to join
- Come join us in
- Join today, it's free
- There's never been a better time to join
- So join the millions who have already
- Join now and win
- Join us for all the excitement
- Isn't it about time you joined thousands of your fellows in

See also: CLUB, CONNECT, INTERFACE, LINK, PARTNER

JOURNEY
- This journey begins here
- With you every step of your journey
- Sometimes the journey can be long and tiring

See also: ODYSSEY, TRAVEL, TRAVEL, TRIP, VISIT, VOYAGE

JOY
- A joy to behold
- All the joy of the season to you
- Plunge into the joys of
- Discover the joy of
- Put some joy in your heart
- Feel the joy
- Rings with the sonorous joy of
- There's a certain joy that comes from

See also: COMFORT, DELIGHT, FUN, HAPPY, PLEASURE, SATISFACTION

JUDGEMENT
- Trust your judgement
- The judgement half the country trusts
- Judgement matured by many years of experience

See also: **CHOICE, DECIDE**

JUNGLE
- So it's a jungle out there
- Showing you how to find a path in the jungle
- Clearing away a jungle of misconceptions

See also: **EXOTIC, WILD**

JUSTIFY
- No one need justify doing anything that feels this good
- The savings alone will more than justify
- The excellent results justify any expenditure involved in

See also: **DEFENCE**

KEEP
- Will keep up with anything that comes along
- Yours to keep absolutely free
- Well kept and immaculate
- Whether you buy or not, keep the beautiful free gift we will include

See also: **PROTECT, STAY**

KEY
- The key is right in front of you
- Take your free key, unlock the door to
- Your key to peace of mind
- Singing in the key of freedom
- Your key to a successful future
- The key which unlocks
- Your key to greater happiness
- We put the key in your hand

See also: **ESSENCE, INSTRUMENTAL, NECESSARY, SECRET**

KICK
- Nobody kicks sand in our face
- With additional kick when you need it
- Get some extra kick
- Something with some kick to it
- Are you kicking yourself for not doing it when you had the chance

See also: **HAPPY, HIT, JOY, IMPACT, INTOXICATE**

KID
- We don't kid around when it comes to quality
- Kid stuff isn't our game
- And the kids can take part too
- Not just kid stuff
- Kids love it
- Bring the kids, they're welcome
- Plenty of fun for the kids
- Our best buys for kids
- Kids can have fun being kids
- Just for kids
- The kids will love it and so will you

See also: **CHILD, CHILDHOOD, FAMILY, YOUNG**

KIDDING
- Who are you kidding
- We're not just kidding around
- Are you kidding yourself

See also: **FUN, HUMOR**

KIND
- Largest of its kind in the world
- One of a kind and available only from
- The kind of benefit you're looking for
- Our way of paying in kind
- Will be kind to your pocketbook

See also: **GROUP, SORT**

KING
- The king is back
- Turns you into the king or queen
- When you're king of the mountain, you can do anything
- Feel like a king, pay like a pauper
- Be king for a day

See also: **BEST, CHAMPION, LEADER**

KIT
- Ask for our free information kit
- This kit shows you how to
- Comes with a complete kit
- We kit you out completely

See also: **EQUIP, EQUIPMENT, GEAR, SET**

KITCHEN
- Country kitchen comfort
- A kitchen where good things appear
- One busy kitchen you won't have to get out of

- **See also: COOK, EAT, MEAL, MEALTIME**

KITSCH
- Toss out the kitsch and put in classics
- Kitsch might be in somewhere, but not here
- A wickedly kitschy touch adds funk

See also: QUIRK, UNUSUAL

KNACK
- We've developed an uncanny knack
- You, too, can have the knack for
- We have a knack for making you happy
- You'll develop the knack pretty fast

See also: ABILITY, FLAIR, SKILL

KNOW
- You'll feel better knowing
- Want everyone to know about the many benefits
- You may or may not know that
- Invited to find out everything you need to know
- You may not even know you have it on
- The ten things you need to know before you buy
- Find out what you don't know about
- We invite you to get to know us better
- It's nice to know that
- Let us know how we did
- We always want to know we are satisfying you
- Just let us know what you think
- Created by people who know about
- So you'll always know exactly how much
- Nobody knows it better
- We know the product
- Everything you need to know about
- At your fingertips, everything you need to know
- Want to know more
- Did you know that
- Care to know more
- Know it all right now
- We know a thing or two about
- No one ever has to know
- Only you will know
- The more you know about it, the more you'll want to
- You probably already know
- Knows it works

- But you have to know what to do
- You'd never know you were in
- And you want to know more about
- As you may already know
- Includes everything you need to know about
- No one ever has to know
- Nobody knows it better than
- Five things you need to know before you buy

Know: comprehend, realize, grasp, get the hang of, understand, fathom, catch on, discern, make out, perceive, apprehend, recognize, see, get the picture, appreciate, distinguish, discriminate

See also: REALIZE, UNDERSTAND

KNOWLEDGE
- An unmatched knowledge of local conditions
- You also get years of accumulated knowledge along with your purchase
- It takes knowledge to win
- All our knowledge is at your service
- Test your knowledge
- New knowledge allows us to understand
- Knowledge is power

Knowledge: understanding, savoir faire, information, education, consciousness, awareness, enlightenment, scuttlebutt

See also: EXPERIENCE, EXPERTISE, INFORMATION, UNDERSTANDING, WISDOM

KNOWN
- That's known as
- Highlights a little known fact
- You've known it all along
- You've always known what you wanted

KUDOS
- Has received industry kudos for
- Kudos to them for all that
- More kudos for you, more savings for your company
- Every day more kudos come in
- Keep on earning kudos

See also: AWARD, CELEBRATION, PRAISE, TRIBUTE

LANE
- Puts you in the fast lane

- Won't leave you coasting in the slow lane
- The slow lane just turned into a superhighway

See also: COURSE, PATH, ROAD, WAY

LANGUAGE
- A whole new language has to be learned
- Speaking the language of love
- Put in language you can understand
- Language the whole world can understand

See also: COMMUNICATION, INTERPRET, SAY

LARGE
- Large sizes, large savings
- Standing larger than life
- Giving a far larger view of

See also: BIG, GIANT

LAST
- Longer lasting performance
- Lasts for years
- Lasts and lasts for hours
- Saving the best for last
- Designed to last
- Your last chance to
- Making it last
- Lasts longer than other

See also: END, ENDURE, FINAL, FINISH, TIMELESS

LATE
- Don't be late
- Buy now, pay later
- Introducing the very latest in
- Better late than never
- The latest, greatest innovations
- If you come late, you'll miss out

See also: DELAY

LATITUDE
- To give you even more latitude
- Providing the latitude to
- If it's more latitude you want

See also: ROOM, SPACE

LAUGH
- Now you can laugh at worries about
- Giving you a reason to laugh
- The last laugh is on

See also: ENJOY, FUN, HAPPY, JOY

LAUGHTER
- Just like a burst of laughter
- Brimming with laughter and enthusiasm
- Just to see the laughter in your eyes
- Lovely as the laughter of children

See also: FUNNY, HAPPY, JOY

LAUNCH
- And with the enthusiastic launch of
- Back in the market with the launch of
- With the launch so close, excitement is building
- Launching the lowest rates ever

See also: BEGINNING, START

LAVISH
- The lavish use of
- Plying you with lavish comforts and luxuries
- Lavishing attention on you from the moment you arrive
- Taking care of you lavishly

See also: LUXURY

LEAD
- Rest easy in the lead
- Only natural that we should take the lead in providing
- Will be on hand to lead you
- Taking the lead in providing you with the finest
- Making sure we're always in the lead
- Widely regarded as one of the leading

See also: FIRST, GUIDE, SPEARHEAD

LEADER
- Always the leader in quality
- Has always been a leader in
- The country's leaders in
- Find out why we've been a leader for four generations
- Always a leader in the field of
- We got what it takes to be a world leader
- There's only one world leader
- Is the acknowledged leader in
- Be the leader of the pack
- We're the new leader in
- The recognized leader in
- Leaders in award-winning
- Join the leaders in
- Taking a leadership stance

Lead: principal, head, chief, kingpin, boss,

director, dean, manager, supervisor, number
one, superior, warlord, commander, ruler,
master, pacesetter, trend-setter, ringleader,
motivator, bellwether, forerunner, advance
guard, vanguard, spearhead, pathfinder,
scout, trail blazer, explorer, groundbreaker
**See also: FIRST, FOREFRONT, HEAD,
KING, PACESETTER**

LEAF
- Turn over a new leaf
- To stop blowing about like a leaf in the
  wind
- Take a leaf out of our book

LEAGUE
- In a league of their own
- Now that you've moved into the major
  leagues
- Big league success with little league
  costs
See also: CLASS, CLUB, GROUP

LEAP
- This is the way to leap forward
- Making the leap from need to innovation
- We're here when you're ready to make
  the leap
- Advancing in leaps and bounds
- Not such a big leap after all
**See also: ADVANCE, HOP, PROGRESS,
STRIDE**

LEARN
- Discover what millions of others have
  learned
- Now is the time to learn more about
- To learn more about how you can
  become part of
- We learn everything we can about you
- Learning more every day about
- Learn firsthand what you need to know
- If we've learned anything, it's that
- Learn everything you need to know about
- Learn the ins and outs of
- Occasion to learn and relearn
- Introduce your child to a lifelong love of
  learning
**See also: EDUCATE, INFORM, TEACH,
UNDERSTAND**

LEASE
- Lease or own one of a limited number

- We lease for less
- For sale or lease
- It makes great sense to lease
- Buy or lease easily
- Leasing program available

LEGACY
- Part of their legacy to the world
- Restoring a legacy
- A legacy that has been carefully
  preserved for you
- Inheriting an unparalleled legacy
- Carrying a proud legacy of quality
- Our legacy is at your service
- All part of your natural legacy
**See also: BIRTHRIGHT, HERITAGE,
HISTORY, INHERITANCE,
TRADITION**

LEGEND
- Glamour befitting a legend
- Make them into local legends
- What legends are made of
- It's a modern legend
- Made it the legend it has become
- Putting myth and legend aside
See also: HISTORY, PAST, STORY

LEGION
- Join the legion of others who have come
  round to
- The reasons why are legion
- Marching in disciplined legions toward
- A whole legion of satisfied customers

LEGWORK
- We do the legwork for you
- A welcome end to the legwork
- Just imagine, no more legwork
- No matter how much legwork you do,
  you end up here
See also: RESEARCH

LEISURE
- Leisure living at its best
- Examine it at your leisure
- Promising more leisure time for these
  enjoyable activities
- Your leisure pursuits will fit right in
See also: EASE, TIME, VACATION

LENGTH
- Goes to incredible lengths to bring you

- Ranging the length and breadth of the land to find
- Just an indication of the lengths we'll go to for you

See also: EFFORT

LESS

- We always sell it for less
- To those who can accept no less
- Get the best for less
- Bringing you the finest for less
- You simply can't get it for less
- Nowhere else where you get it for less
- Pay less, get more
- Don't settle for less
- Less is more
- Get less of the things you don't need
- We sell for less every day
- For much less than you'd pay in a normal store
- You'll pay a little less for it

Less: not very much, a smaller amount, lower, fewer, not as much, little, reduced, limited, hardly any, minimum
See also: MINIMIZE, REDUCE

LET

- It's all about letting go
- There's no letting up
- You won't ever want to let it go
- Practically impossible to let go of

LETTER

- Your letter will receive personal attention
- Your instructions are followed to the letter
- Please read this letter to the end

See also: COMMUNICATION

LEVEL

- Taking you to a higher level
- Conducted at the most efficient level possible
- Provides its owner with an exceptional level of
- A level of luxury previously unheard of in this class

See also: CLASS, LEVEL, RANK, STANDARD

LIBERTY

- The exhilaration of liberty
- Taking the liberty of offering you
- Gives you more liberty to
- Are you longing for more liberty
- Win the liberty you deserve

See also: FREEDOM, OPPORTUNITY

LICENSE

- Licensed and bonded for your security
- Giving you a license to choose
- You don't need a license to really enjoy this

See also: ABILITY, FREEDOM

LIFE

- Has it changed your life
- Dress for real life
- Take control of your life
- Get your life back to normal
- A celebration of life
- Put some life in your
- Life can be a challenge
- You don't need that in your life
- Has a life of its own
- Giving new life to thousands of
- Has it changed your life yet
- Uncompromising quality helps you enjoy life to the fullest
- The quality of modern life depends upon
- New lives begin here
- Learn how to add life to your years
- The essence of life
- Makes life simpler
- A place where life happens
- Places value on how you choose to live your life
- Determine how you will live your life for years to come
- Life is a series of choices
- For once in you life, take a chance on
- There's more to life than
- Now a fact of life
- Here life is to be lived well
- An unhurried, casual way of life
- Giving it a life of its own
- Provides an enhanced quality of life
- Will bring to life
- One of the facts of life
- Get a hundred percent out of life
- Putting some life into
- Larger than life
- Stay that way for the rest of your life
- Simply makes life better
- Appreciate how it can enrich your life

- Will make all the difference in your life
- Life just gets better and better
- You deserve the finer things in life

Life: existence, being, human condition, creation, nature, vivacity, spirit, liveliness, verve, flair, zing, brilliance, airiness, dash, elan, warmth, fervency,, dazzle, effervescence, vim, zest, vigor, passion, zeal, enthusiasm, intensity, energy, sprightliness, fire, glow, buoyancy,
See also: ENERGIZE, REJUVENATE, REVITALIZE, VITALITY, WARMTH

LIFELINE
- It's your lifeline to
- Throwing you a lifeline at the crucial moment
- Much more than just a lifeline for the desperate
- Grab this lifeline fast
See also: HOTLINE

LIFESTYLE
- Everything you need to enjoy a healthier lifestyle
- Increase your ability to enjoy a healthier, more active lifestyle
- Contributes to a healthy, active lifestyle
- To help you meet the demands of today's fast-paced and hectic lifestyle
- You've worked hard for this lifestyle
- Changing your lifestyle can be easy and exciting

LIFETIME
- Assuring your family a lifetime of enjoyment
- Try it just once in your lifetime
- A once-in-a-lifetime chance to
- Providing you with a lifetime of productive
- Adding to your lifetime achievement
- You've got a whole lifetime to enjoy
See also: ENDURE, LAST, UNIQUE

LIFT
- Anyone in need of a lift can choose
- Give yourself a lift
- Gives your style a lively lift
- We do the heavy lifting for you
See also: IMPROVE

LIGHT
- Making light work to your advantage
- In harmony with light
- Super light, super strong
- Spreading a little light in the world
- Drenched in light
- Feels light as a feather
- Shedding some welcome light on a difficult subject
- Open the door, come into the light
- You'll feel light and euphoric when you try it

LIGHTNING
- Lightning strikes again
- Proving lightning can strike twice
- The lightning speed is just one of the many features
- Faster than lightning
See also: BLITZ, DAZZLE, HIT, IMPACT, STRIKE

LIGHTWEIGHT
- This is no lightweight in the business
- You don't want to deal with just lightweights
- Stronger and more lightweight than any other product
See also: CONVENIENT

LIKE
- If you like last year's
- Chances are you'll like
- You'll take a liking to
- We pay close attention to your likes and dislikes
- There's nothing quite like a good
- If you're someone who likes to
- Exactly the way you like it
See also: ATTRACT, CHOOSE, ENJOY, PREFER

LIMIT
- For a limited time, save an extra
- Designed to push your limits
- There's no limit on what you can do when you dream of
- We reserve the right to limit quantities
- This flyer contains limited-time sale values, special buys and items at our everyday low prices
- Limit is one per family
- Stretch your limits

- There's no limit on the ways
- Takes the limits off fast so you can get what you want
- There are no limits to where you can go or what you can experience

See also: BOUNDARY, DEADLINE, CONSTRAINT, EDGE, END, FINISH, RESTRICTION

LIMITED

- Fantastic limited time offer
- Do you feel limited on every side
- You won't be limited any longer
- Offer limited to the first fifty people, so hurry on down
- Stock is limited so don't miss out

LINE

- Sleek lines for simple styling
- We know when to draw the line
- More from the world's best-loved line
- Get the inside line on your favorite
- A new product line
- We manufacture a complete line of quality products
- Drop us a line today
- Starting with an entirely new line
- The most complete line of high quality products
- Proud to present a complete line
- Be first in line
- The lean, sleek lines of
- The latest in a long line of
- Helping you hold the line on
- A total line of products to let you make better use of
- Introducing our new line of
- It's time you discovered the full line

See also: CATALOGUE, CHOICE, SELECTION, STOCK

LINK

- Provides the missing link
- Your chance to link up with
- Links you to top notch support
- Your best link to the best
- Quickly establishing a seamless link between

See also: CONNECT, JOIN

LIQUIDATION

- Bankruptcy liquidation
- Don't miss our big liquidation sale

- Everything is in liquidation
- Our liquidation sale is your good luck

See also: SALE

LIST

- Do you find it reads just like your wish list
- A shopping list for
- We want to put you on our list
- You'll find a complete list of
- The list goes on and on

See also: CATALOGUE, GUIDE, INVENTORY, SELECTION

LISTEN

- We listened to you and made the changes you asked for
- We do it by listening carefully to your needs
- Listen every day for
- Actually listens to you
- You talk, we listen
- Looking for someone who will listen
- We listen to you before we act

See also: HEAR

LITTLE

- A little or a lot
- All this for as little as
- Giving you just that little bit more
- A little goes a long way
- You only need a little
- Little did you imagine you could go this far

Little: small, tiny, teensy, pint-size, wee, mini, short, itty-bitty, itsy-bitsy, peewee, baby, bantam, child size, toy, lightweight, petite, dainty, slender, slim, thin, skinny, midge, miniature, minute, atomic, infinitesimal, microscopic, brief, abbreviated, rarely, seldom, infrequently, snip, scrap, trifle, minuscule, weensy

See also: LESS, REDUCE, SMALL

LIVABLE

- Seriously livable
- Making your surroundings much more than just livable
- Geared to making your life more livable

LIVE

- The single thing you can't live without

- No matter where you live, you'll be able to enjoy
- It doesn't matter where you live
- Give so that others may live
- A comfortable place to live
- Live for today
- Luxury living at real life prices
- Means the living is easy
- The elegant refreshing way to liven up your day
- Makes it a whole lot easier to live with

See also: ACCOMMODATION, LIFE

LOAD
- Taking the load off your shoulders onto ours
- Fully loaded for your pleasure
- When the load is just too much
- Now don't have to carry the whole load by yourself

See also: OBSTACLE, PROBLEM, RESPONSIBILITY

LOCAL
- Buy products made locally
- Look what these local businesses are offering you
- Now one of our local stores can provide
- Now you can buy locally and save
- Locally owned and operated

See also: AREA, CLOSE, COMMUNITY, DOMESTIC, HOME

LOCATE
- You'll find us conveniently located throughout
- Accessibly located at
- We located here just to be near you
- Making us really easy to locate
- Our stores are handy and fast to locate

See also: FIND

LOCATION
- Now in ten great locations to serve you better
- Twenty years at one location
- Visit our other locations
- A friendly but upscale location
- A prime location for
- A wide range of products and services available at on convenient location
- Combing an excellent location with
- Watch for our new location
- Great savings at three convenient locations
- A new location to serve you
- Check the white or yellow pages of your phone book for the location nearest you
- One location only
- For all locations call
- To find out the nearest location, just call
- Now at a closer new location at
- Selected as the finest location for
- Only at this location
- A wealth of locations

Location: place, base, zone, area, region, territory, realm, district, neck of the woods, backyard, home ground, domain, spot, environment, situation, establishment
See also: AREA, COMMUNITY, HOME, PLACE, SITE, ZONE

LOCK
- Locks in vital juices
- Locks in the goodness
- Locked in instead of locked out
- We have a lock on value

See also: KEEP, PROTECT, SECURE

LONGEVITY
- Will feel fresh yet have longevity
- Increasing the longevity and costing you less
- You'll be impressed with the longevity

See also: ENDURE, LAST

LOOK
- Please look over this offer carefully
- You don't have time to look at hundreds of items
- It's worth a look
- Come give us another look
- If we don't have what you're looking for
- Look at it this way
- An exclusive, behind-the-scenes look
- Helping you build a brand new look
- Worth taking a closer look
- Built to accommodate different looks
- Will make you look fabulous
- Create a beautiful new look
- Giving a comfy, lived-in look
- Follow our step-by-step guide to getting your look
- The winning look is all about style, self assurance and personality

- Making your total look turn out right
- Give you your first look
- For a calm, unfussy look
- A crisp, tailored look
- Always look your best
- Whatever you're looking for, you'll find it here
- Beyond its head-turning look
- Everything looks good on
- Looks that really stand out
- Looks you'll love
- For a beautifully younger look
- For better looks
- Take a second look at
- Take a real close look at
- You'll never look twice at anything else
- Look for them in better stores nationwide
- Look for these terrific savings and buys throughout the store
- This season's most wanted look
- Look less forbidding
- Look to us for
- Take a closer look
- Just look around you
- Two ways to look at
- Create the look you desire
- Great looks every day
- Worth looking into
- Also, be sure to look for our
- You don't have to look any further
- Look no further
- Sure to have exactly what you're looking for
- Get the right look at the right price
- Look one way, change it the next
- They'll always know how good you look
- You look your best when
- A look defined by you
- You'll have a look that's very real
- The look of the moment
- The winning look is all about style
- Looking better is only part of it
- Looking smart is easy when
- Fun colors, fun looks
- You'll see the latest looks for
- Great looks at great prices
- Somebody to look up to
- All the hottest looks
- We invite you to take a look
- Take a look at the endless possibilities
- Look for more new products
- Take a good second look at
- So you can create whatever look you want
- Accentuate your look
- Look good while you do it
- A naturally beautiful look
- The look and feel of genuine
- Look forward to savings
- We look forward to seeing you
- Just can't resist the urge to take a closer look
- Made to give that professional look
- The sleek new looks feel right
- Looks aren't everything
- Looks are everything

See also: APPEARANCE, ASPECT, EXAMINATION, SEE, SEARCH, STYLE

LOOKER
- Not surprising that it's a real looker
- This one's a looker that'll attract attention wherever it goes
- You, too, can turn into a real looker

See also: BEAUTY, DAZZLE

LOOSE
- Helps you break loose
- The definition is pretty loose
- Cut loose from whatever has been holding you back
- If you long to get yourself loose from all your worries

See also: FREE, LIBERTY, RELAX

LOSE
- There's absolutely no way you can lose
- You just can't lose
- Lose that unwanted problem in record time
- What have you got to lose
- Lose the blahs, come to us

See also: END, FINISH

LOSS
- Stop those costly losses with
- At no loss to you
- With absolutely no chance of loss

See also: RED INK, REDUCE

LOVABLE
- More lovable than ever
- So lovable you won't be able to resist
- Hug this cuddly, lovable little pal
- So lovable your heart will go bump as

soon as you see

LOVE

- We understand your love affair with
- It might turn out to be love after all
- Are you ready to fall in love
- Love lessons
- Join the love connection
- Where love affairs begin
- There are many things to love about
- But you'll love the
- For those of you who really love life
- Improve your love life
- You love it, it loves you
- For when love blossoms
- Gotta love the
- They love what they do
- Love the work and love helping people
- If you liked us before, you'll love us now
- It's all about love
- You'll love it at first bite
- Love what you do and do what you love

Love: affection, fondness, warmth, cherishing, adoration, devotion, liking, adulation, esteem regard, attachment, regard, closeness, intimacy, passion, fancy, infatuation, concern, sympathy, caring, amity, concord, harmony, accord, relish, savor, enjoy, long for, worship

See also: ADMIRE, CARESS, DESIRE, EMOTION, FEELING, FOND, MOOD, PASSION, WISH, WANT

LOVER

- It'll bring out the product lover in you
- If you're a product lover, you'll be in heaven
- Real lovers ask for it
- Calling all lovers of

LOW

- For as low as
- Lowest cost for the best
- Never find it this low
- Prices hit a new low today

See also: BOTTOM

LOW-COST

- A low-cost solution to your need
- Low-cost but not low quality
- Everything is low-cost and designed to please you

See also: CHEAP, ECONOMICAL, INEXPENSIVE

LOW-DOWN

- Get the real low-down
- Getting low-down and dirty about
- When you want the real low-down on it, call us

See also: GOODS, INFORMATION

LOW TECH

- We've gone low-tech to provide
- A low-tech response to a high-tech problem
- Sometimes low-tech is the best

See also: SIMPLE

LOWER

- Think lower, aim higher
- Lower prices than any competitor
- We're lowering your costs every day
- The end of lowered expectations

LOYALTY

- We want to earn your loyalty
- Your loyalty shows that you always get what you need
- In deep gratitude for your continued loyalty
- Your loyalty says it all
- Your ongoing loyalty is deeply appreciated
- We work hard to earn your loyalty

See also: APPRECIATION

LUCK

- If your luck has been anything but great
- You won't believe your luck
- Your luck just got a lot better

See also: CHANCE, FORTUNE

LUCKY

- Hey, it's your lucky day
- Get lucky today
- You're not just lucky, you're smart
- Funny how the luckiest people seem to work the hardest

See also: FORTUNATE

LUSTRE

- Get instant lustre with
- Adding still more lustre to your reputation

- A lustre that almost glows in the dark
See also: GLITTER, RADIANCE, SHINE

LUXURIOUS

- Prepare for what can only be described as a truly luxurious experience
- Relax in sinfully luxurious surroundings
- Could you imagine that it was this luxurious

LUXURY

- Indulge in luxury
- Bringing you the ultimate luxury – peace of mind
- Satisfy your longing for luxury
- The finest luxury offer
- A benchmark of our commitment to classic luxury and sophistication
- Looking for luxury
- A long list of thoughtfully provided luxuries
- Offers a full measure of luxury and comfort
- A whole new level of luxury

Luxury: luxuriousness, luxe, sumptuousness, lavishness, opulence, splendor, abundance, profuseness, excessiveness, indulgence, ease, easy street, well-being, sufficiency, bed of roses, wealth, affluence, richness, epicureanism, sybaritism, hedonism, voluptuousness, sensuality, high living, *dolce vita*, pleasure, enjoyment, delight, extravagance, refinement
See also: ENJOYMENT, RICH, PLEASURE, WEALTH

MACHINE

- More machine for your money
- People have often described us as a well-oiled machine
- Not made by machine
- Thrill to a magnificent machine
See also: GEAR, EQUIPMENT

MADE

- Tell them you made it yourself
- You've got it made
- Made as well as a product can be made
- Better made, better price
- You'll swear we made it just for you
See also: BUILT, CREATE

MADNESS

- Midnight madness
- Super special madness
- Time out from all the madness
- Inventory madness gives you unbelievable prices
See also: CRAZY, FEELING, MOOD, NUTS, WILD

MAGAZINE

- Here's what newspapers and magazines are saying about
- You wouldn't believe it if you saw it in a magazine
- Pick up any magazine and read about it
See also: NEWS

MAGIC

- There's an aura of magic that
- It seems like magic
- Magic moments
- Do you believe in magic
- Makes you believe in magic
- There's always something magical about seeing
See also: AMAZE, MIRACLE, MYSTERY, ROMANCE, WONDER

MAGNET

- Attracts like an irresistible magnet
- Has become a magnet for
- Feel the powerful magnetic pull
See also: ATTRACT, DRAW

MAGNIFICENT

- M-m-m-magnificent
- In a stunningly magnificent setting
- Accessible and magnificent at the same time
- Making you a really magnificent offer
See also: GRAND, IMPRESSIVE, SPLENDID

MAIL

- Values in the mail
- Please hurry and mail the enclosed card today
- We can mail guides and brochures to your home
- Shop by mail
- Mail order madness
- We mail it the same day
See also: DELIVER, SEND

MAILBOX
- Look for a surprise in your mailbox
- Look for upcoming issues in your mailbox
- As close as your mailbox
- A whole new world in your mailbox
- Just open your mailbox and find

MAINSTREAM
- Now gaining a mainstream following
- Challenging the mainstream
- A far-out idea now entering the mainstream
- Jump into the mainstream with

MAINTAIN
- Able to maintain over the long haul
- To maintain and improve our service
- And it's so very simple to maintain
- Working to maintain a close relationship with you

MAINTENANCE
- And it's maintenance free
- Easy maintenance
- Simplest maintenance of all
- Goodbye to maintenance worries
- Which means it's extremely low-maintenance
- You can do a little preventative maintenance

Maintenance: preservation, upkeep
See also: KEEP, PRESERVE, UPKEEP

MAKE
- Everything we make is now available at great prices
- Help you make it to the top
- You can make as much as
- We stand behind everything we make
- Has the makings of something big

See also: BUILD, CREATE, FASHION

MAKER
- Makers of fine products
- Brought to you by the makers of
- For years, the makers of the very best products
- Just look who the maker is
- Makers you can really trust

See also: MANUFACTURER

MALL
- Why go to a mall and buy something mass-produced
- Find us at your favorite mall
- You won't find this at your local mall
- Come on down to the mall and participate

See also: SHOP, RETAILER, STORE

MAN
- Fashions for the big man
- Speaking to you man-to-man
- It's a man thing
- Designed for real men
- The man in your life will flip

See also: GUY, HUNK

MANAGE
- Helps you manage your time and your schedule
- Just when you're wondering how you'll manage
- Yes, you can manage it all
- Never more than you can manage
- Helping you manage your most valuable assets

See also: AFFORD, CONTROL, HANDLE. ORGANIZE

MANAGEMENT
- For much easier management of your
- Through careful management
- Now under the new ownership and management of
- Our management team personally meets with you

See also: ADMINISTRATION, DIRECTION, GUIDANCE

MANDATE
- Our only mandate it to
- Your confidence is our mandate to serve your needs
- You've given us a mandate to
- For years, our mandate has been

See also: GOAL, MISSION

MANUFACTURE
- Designed and manufactured exclusively for your needs
- Manufactured to exacting quality standards
- Manufactured in an environmentally

friendly manner
See also: CREATE, SUPPLY

MANUFACTURER
- Buy direct from the manufacturer
- Manufacturer's suggested retail prices
- Only one manufacturer is good enough
- Quality begins with the manufacturer
See also: FACTORY, MAKER

MARK
- Draws nearly flawless marks
- Helps you make your mark
- Purchase a specially marked
See also: BRAND, HALLMARK,
STANDARD

MARKET
- If you're in the market for
- You can cash in on a vast, untapped market
- Take advantage of a buyers market
- Successful in a very exciting market
- Specially trained for your market
- If you're in the market for
- Heralding our entry into the market
- The best value on the market
- Reach your goal in an increasingly demanding market
- The market is hot
- The market is reflecting that change
- With luck, the market takes off
- The only product on the market that provides
- Judging from our number one market share
- Finest on the market
- Now you can play the market safely
- The best value in the market today

Market: marketplace, mart, exchange, trading center, shopping center, commercial resort, mall, emporium, supermarket, trade, traffic, sale, transaction, commercialism, jobbing, brokerage, truck, dealing, barter, selling, negotiating, hustling, quotation, appraisal
See also: BARGAIN, BUYER,
CONVINCE, EXCHANGE, MALL,
MONEY, PRICE, SELL

MARKETING
- A marketing giant at your service
- Put our guaranteed marketing plan to work for you
- Join us in marketing this product across the country
- A marketing team outclassing all others

MARKETPLACE
- One of the best available in the marketplace
- Expanding your horizons in the world marketplace
- A genuine marketplace phenomenon
- Make it your marketplace for all your needs
- Exploding into view in the marketplace
See also: MALL, RETAIL, SHOP, STORE

MARRIAGE
- Here are the technical reasons for this triumphant marriage
- A happy marriage of grandeur and simplicity
- You'll think it's a marriage made in heaven
See also: BLEND, CONNECTION, LINK,
MEET, MIX, PARTNERSHIP, TEAM

MARVEL
- It's a marvel of skill and design
- Even more marvels lie in store for you
- Introducing you to one marvel after another
- Marvel at our range of merchandise
See also: AMAZE, MAGIC, MIRACLE,
ROMANCE, SENSATION, WONDER

MASTERPIECE
- A masterpiece with absolutely no waste
- Every masterpiece has to start somewhere
- Now you can own this masterpiece
- Each product is a masterpiece
See also: BEST, SUPERIOR, WONDER

MATCH
- Find an exact match easily
- We'll match the price
- You get a better match by
- Mix and match with joyous abandon
- The total match on all counts
- We can help you find the right match
- Matching as closely as possible
- We're the matchmakers

- The perfect match for you
- When you need to match

Match: twin, duplicate, pair, counterpart, look-alike, replica, copy, bird of a feather, spitting image, colleague, fellow, contest, game, equal, measure up, keep pace with, parallel, reproduce, compete, meet
See also: **COMPATIBLE, COORDINATE, DOUBLE, DUPLICATE, INCREASE, PAIR**

MATERIAL
- We use only name brand materials
- Quality materials at exceptional prices
- Utilizing only the very best materials
- The finest of materials go into making

Material: stuff, substance, staple, goods, component, element, unit, constituent, medium, factor, cloth, texture, weave, tissue, data, facts, information
See also: **INFORMATION, SUBSTANCE, STUFF**

MATTER
- It doesn't matter at all how young or old you are
- Much more than simply a matter of taste
- Your opinion really matters to us
- A matter of always having the best

See also: **CONCERN, ISSUE**

MATURITY
- We all look forward to the privileges of maturity
- Approaching it with maturity and style
- A dazzling new concept tempered with the maturity of experience

See also: **AGE, GROWN-UP, READY**

MAVERICK
- Specially designed for mavericks like you
- Calling all mavericks
- You never thought of yourself as a maverick before
- Appealing to your maverick streak

See also: **DAREDEVIL, ICONOCLAST, INDIVIDUALIST**

MAX
- Goes to the max for you
- Maxed out on pleasure

- When you're all maxed out
- Excites you to the max and saves money too

See also: **BEST, MOST, TOP**

MAXIMIZE
- Lets you maximize their savings more quickly
- Minimize effort, maximize results
- Helping you maximize your satisfaction

MAXIMUM
- Encourages maximum payoff
- For maximum satisfaction, call this number
- Putting in maximum quality

See also: **BEST, EXTREME, MOST**

MEAL
- Meal deal
- It's a full meal in itself
- Make a meal of it
- A meal you'll never forget

See also: **COOK, DELICIOUS, DINE, EAT, FEAST, KITCHEN, TASTE**

MEALTIME
- Make the most of mealtime
- If mealtime is getting humdrum
- You do most of your planning at mealtime

MEAN
- What does this mean for you
- Gives new meaning to
- You know exactly what it means
- You'll know what we mean when we say

See also: **UNDERSTANDING**

MEANS
- Providing a safe, clean, efficient means
- Giving you the means to do it now
- Always well within your means

See also: **METHOD, RESOURCES, WAY**

MEASURE
- Find out how you can measure up to
- Measures up to the finest
- Really measures up
- Showing you how we measure success
- It's the measure of your success

See also: **ENGINEER**

MEDAL

- You deserve a medal
- We've been winning medals since the day we opened
- A gold medal performance

See also: APPRECIATION, AWARD, PRIZE, REWARD

MEDIUM

- Now you can head for a happy medium
- Don't settle for medium when you can have the max
- Strikes a careful medium between too little and excess

See also: BALANCE. ,MATERIAL

MEET

- You never know who you'll meet
- Come in and meet the whole team
- A wonderful meeting place
- A meeting of great minds
- You'll meet them all at
- We can meet in the middle
- We look forward to meeting with you to discuss
- The meeting place for today's business

See also: CONNECT, CONTACT, INTRODUCE, JOIN, VISIT

MELLOW

- Delightfully mellow
- The most fun way to get mellowed out
- Mellow is out, energy is in

See also: RELAX

MEMBER

- As a member, you'll enjoy important benefits
- Become a member now
- As a member, you can visit as often as you like
- Consider becoming a member of the world's greatest
- You are a valued member of
- The easy way to become a member
- You become an instant member when you buy
- All the advantages of being a member are yours
- You'll automatically become a full member

See also: PARTNER

MEMBERSHIP

- Membership is absolutely free
- Applications and membership cards available to for immediate access to the program
- If you accept this membership offer
- Might be interested in other areas of membership
- So you can enjoy the privileges of membership without risk
- Membership entitles you to full access to all services
- If you have any questions regarding membership
- A lifetime membership is an added bonus
- Your membership is highly valued

See also: JOIN, PARTNERSHIP

MEMORABLE

- Definitely one of the most memorable
- Making your stay one of the truly memorable ones
- A product that will make you memorable
- Some of the most memorable people are the ones that

MEMORY

- Far more than just a beautiful memory
- Memories are made of this
- Share special memories
- Build a precious memory
- More than just a happy childhood memory
- A natural repository of memories
- Brings back memories of

See also: MEMORY, REMIND

MENTION

- And there's so much more I haven't mentioned
- Did we mention the savings
- No one mentioned how much fun it would be

See also: COMMUNICATE, SAY, SPEAK

MERCHANDISE

- Travelling the world to find extraordinary merchandise
- Great selection of merchandise
- For quality merchandise every day
- A wide selection of merchandise throughout the entire store
- Merchandise may vary by store

- Completely new merchandise every time you visit
- Very advanced merchandising policies
- Top quality merchandise at bargain prices

Merchandise: goods, commodities, stock, stock in trade, vendibles, produce, staples, supplies, dry goods, yard goods, cargo, freight, shipment, products, inventory
See also: GOODS, INVENTORY, ITEM, OFFER, PRODUCE, PRODUCT, STOCK

MERCHANT

- At better merchants everywhere
- Merchants of fine products for over fifty years
- Proud to be a respected merchant of
- Tops in the merchant class

See also: RETAILER, SELLER

MERIT

- Selections are based on merit alone
- Certainly merits a second look
- Outstanding merit
- Judge it on merit alone

See also: DESERVE, EARN, MEDAL

MERRY-GO-ROUND

- Hop on the merry-go-round
- Sometimes life can seem an endless merry-go-round
- A merry-go-round of happiness

See also: CARNIVAL, FUN, PARTY

MESS

- Success, without the mess
- No fuss, no mess and lots of fun
- When other messy products just won't do the job
- Gets rid of the mess you hate, gives you the results you love
- No more mess, no more worry

See also: CONFUSE, MISTAKE

MESSAGE

- Can mean the difference between a message that gets looked at and one that doesn't
- A product with a message
- We want you to get the message
- Our message to you is

- An opportunity to get your message out there
- Lets you rush messages anywhere
- I urge you to read this message to the fullest

Message: communication, news, tidings, dispatch, communiqué, postcard, word, information, report, intelligence, meaning, point, idea, intent, aim, announcement, notice, response, reply, answer, memo, note, bulletin, transmission
See also: ADVERTISE, COMMUNICATION, FLYER, INFORMATION

METHOD

- Other methods could be even more expensive
- Others have succeeded quickly using this exact method
- There's still the tried and true method
- We have developed the best method
- Using only the most modern methods
- The moment you put this method into action
- The latest methods at your disposal

See also: HOW, MEANS, PROCESS, STRATEGY, WAY

MILLION

- Be on your way to your first million
- You're one in a million
- A million reasons to

See also: MONEY, WEALTH

MIND

- Can't make up your mind
- For whatever your frame of mind
- It's a state of mind
- When you've got one thing on your mind
- Comes with built-in peace if mind
- Take your mind off other matters
- We take everything off your mind
- Mind power
- Where designing minds meet
- You should make up your own mind
- Tomorrow's finest minds are right here
- Bright minds at your service
- You're starting with an open mind
- Might not be the first thing that comes to mind
- Style is a state of mind

- Creating something new in your mind
- Whatever your frame of mind

See also: FEELING. THOUGHT

MINIMALISM

- The subtle minimalism that is the driving force
- If minimalism just isn't your style
- If you're a fan of minimalism, have we got the item for you

See also: LESS

MINIMIZE

- Minimizing imperfections
- Really helps to minimize
- Minimizing the risks and maximizing results
- When you want to minimize

See also: LESS, REDUCE

MINUTE

- In just one minute, you too can
- It takes only a minute to find out how
- Take a minute right now to
- Just minutes away
- Now takes minutes instead of ages
- You can do this in under a minute
- Making minutes count
- Only minutes from satisfaction

See also: INSTANT, MOMENT, SOON

MIRACLE

- A real miracle that
- Everyone said only a miracle could
- An amazing miracle you've been waiting for all your life
- Some call it a miracle
- Who says miracles don't happen any more
- Now, the miracle of
- It's nothing short of a miracle
- At our company, miracles happen every day
- Thanks to the miracle of
- A miracle of simplicity, clarity and power

Miracle: wonder, marvel, phenomenon, wonderwork, prodigy, curiosity, spectacle, portent, rarity
See also: AMAZE, MARVEL, SENSATION, WONDER

MIRROR

- All you have to do is ask your mirror
- Mirroring the changes in you
- Now look in the mirror and see the change
- You only have to consult your mirror to see the difference
- Your mirror will tell you the truth

See also: DUPLICATE, REFLECTION, REPEAT

MISS

- You can't afford to miss this
- We've missed you
- Able to tell what's missing from
- You may be wondering what you're missing out on
- This is not a hit or miss
- Don't miss out on
- You're missing out on something great
- Don't miss a minute of it
- You don't know what you're missing until you
- Look at what you're missing

Miss: fail to reach, miscalculate, bungle, goof, come up short, let slip through the fingers, blow the chance, overlook, disregard, pass over, slip up, be left at the starting gate, skip, forego, long for, regret, yearn for, lament, misunderstand, get wrong, lose out, screw up, fall short, fizzle, flunk out, oversight
See also: CONFUSE, OUT

MISSION

- Everything we do is part of our mission to improve the world around us and help more people to
- Gain the ability to focus on your mission
- Our mission has always been
- On a different kind of mission
- We need to carry on with our mission

Mission: calling, objective, pursuit, duty, business, assignment, charge, trust, task, concern, affair, position, object
See also: AIM, GOAL, MANDATE

MISTAKE

- Avoid a little known mistake that could wipe out
- Make no mistake
- Don't worry if you made a mistake

- It would be hard to make mistake if you tried
- Never a mistake to shop here
- No more expensive mistakes
- Don't make the mistake of imagining

See also: UNSURE, DEFECT, ERROR, WRONG

MIX
- No mixing required
- Mix and match
- They're all part of the mix
- Really mixes it up
- A really nice mix of

See also: BLEND, COMBINE, INTEGRATE

MODEL
- All major makes and models available
- Each is a working model of
- Have developed a model whereby
- All stock models reduced to sell
- The very model of perfection

See also: DISPLAY, EXAMPLE, INFLUENCE, PROTOTYPE, SAMPLE

MODERN
- Make a major modern impact
- Join the modern world with
- Using the most modern methods
- Turn it into the most modern

See also: INNOVATION, NEW

MODIFY
- Modified to meet your business needs
- We'll modify it any way you want
- A plan that can be constantly changed and modified

See also: ALTERNATIVE, CHANGE, FLEXIBLE

MOMENT
- Won't you take a few moments right now
- Things that preserve the moment
- It seems the right moment to
- Will bring a very special moment
- Never a dull moment with
- Relive the moment
- Shining moments in
- At a moment like this
- Life is full of special moments
- Make this moment golden
- A defining moment in

- Share a truly magical moment with someone you love
- Take a moment too ponder the difference

See also: INSTANT, MINUTE

MOMENTUM
- Giving you all you need to really build momentum
- The momentum is increasing as we speak
- Enough momentum to build up a good head of steam

See also: DRIVE, IMPETUS, MOVE, PROGRESS, URGE

MONEY
- Best value for your money
- Your money back
- Does not have extra money to spare
- A never-ending money supply
- The answer to all your money problems
- Start making some real money
- We can get you truly making money fast
- There's big money to be made
- Are you saving enough money
- How to get more for your money
- Helping you save time and money
- And, of course, you want genuine value for your money
- Has a healthy respect for money
- Money can flow out as easily as it flows in
- Earning more money than ever before
- Making your money work harder for you
- Don't you think it's time to save some money
- Committed to saving you money
- Send no money now
- The best for your money anywhere
- Save money, make money
- You'll be amazed at how much further your money will go
- Ask about our no-money-down option
- Watch your money grow
- It's a money machine
- Helping your money grow over the long term
- Saves you money every day
- Save your money the easy way
- When you want to save money
- Now that's easy money
- Offering you the finest money can buy at an affordable price
- Now make all the money you need

- Money will roll in fast
- Put more spendable money in your hands
- Make money the smart way with
- We'll show you how to save more money
- Make big money with
- Solve all your money problems
- Start making money right away with
- Send no money now
- We'll watch your money for you
- That will help you save money
- Saves you time, saves you money
- And much more that's right on the money
- The money you save could be your own
- Makes your money go far
- And when you really want to save money
- Or double your money back
- You can make this money with very little investment

Money: medium of exchange, standard of value, note, cash, cold hard cash, legal tender, greenbacks, coin, change, chickenfeed, folding money, almighty dollar, dough, moolah, mazuma, bread, loot, do-re-mi, gravy, wampum, bucks, mint, boodle, bundle, wad
See also: CASH, CENT, DOLLAR, FINANCE, INVEST, INVESTMENT

MONITOR
- Now you can monitor results instantly
- Designed to closely monitor
- Monitoring progress by the minute
- We monitor you long after you've
- We regularly monitor performance
See also: SEE, SHOW, TRACK, WATCH

MONTH
- Deal of the month
- This month only
- Big savings during anniversary month
- This is savings month at
- Don't pay for six months

MONTHLY
- Pay monthly – with no additional charges
- Low, low monthly payments
- Pay monthly and own soon
See also: INSTALLMENT, PAYMENT

MOOD
- Compliments your every mood

- The mood is at its most dramatic when
- You can always create the mood you want
- Puts you in the mood for
- Reflects your every mood
- Creates the mood for love
- Are you in the mood for savings
- Celebrate all of your moods
See also: EMOTION, ENVIRONMENT, FEELING

MORE
- No more will every be made
- Stand up and shout, "No more!"
- Start saving more than ever
- Plus so much more
- More quickly than ever before
- Don't pay more later
- No one does more to
- We give you more for a whole lot less
- Fewer items that do more
- What more could you ask for
- Expect to get a lot more than you pay for
- Helping you get more out of your
- Now save more
- Buy more, save more every day
- For whole lot more
- And start getting more out of your
- To find out more about any of our advanced
- More is better
- More is definitely more
- Need we say more
- And many more to come
- For those looking for more from their
- We always offer you more
- To find out more about the new
- More than just a
- More for less
- Expect more from our store
- No more when these go
- Get more of the things you need
- Count on us for more
- Gives you more everyday
- We came up with more
- More, please
- If it means more to you than something just to
- More than just ordinary
- Able to do much more with much less
- More than any other
- Made for a whole lot more than
- Giving you all this and more

More: additional, extra, plus, supplemental, supplementary, spare, fresh, new, added, addition, increment, increase, adjunct, again
See also: BIG, EXTRA, INCREASE

MORNING
- Jump start your morning with
- A morning sort of thing
- And they'll still respect you in the morning
- A new morning for you

See also: BEGINNING, DAWN, START

MOST
- When it comes to making the most of
- The most for the least
- That gets the most out of
- Squeezing the most from every
- Showing you how to get the most from your
- Make the most of
- Get the most for yourself out of

Most: greatest, largest, utmost, ultra, extreme, maximum, farthest, furthest
See also: EXTREME, MAXIMUM

MOTHER
- The mother of all
- No one is more important than mother
- First, get mother's approval
- Mothers everywhere adore it

See also: CHILD, FAMILY, WOMAN

MOTIVATE
- We keep you entertained and motivated
- Revitalize and motivate you
- If saving money motivates you
- A great deal can motivate you pretty strongly
- We understand what motivates you

Motivate: prompt, incite, provoke, fire up, light a fire under, move, stir, arouse, turn on, inflame, enkindle, set on fire, trigger, start, impel, egg on, urge on, encourage, coax, stimulate, encourage, influence, persuade, propel, energize, drive, cajole, push, cause
See also: DRIVE, ENERGIZE, IMPETUS, INSPIRE, MOVE

MOVE
- Before you make your move, make certain that

- Gets things moving
- The wisest move you'll ever make
- The smartest move you could make
- Get a move on
- Make your move today
- It's your move
- Move more of your business to us today
- Make the right move now
- The right move at the right time
- Can get you moving again
- Every move you make will be a success
- The best move you ever made
- Why it's the right move for you

See also: ACTION, ACTIVITY, CHOICE, PROGRESS

MUCH
- So much for so little
- And much, much more
- It's not too much to ask
- When you ask how much, you'll be amazed

See also: PLENTY, MORE

MULTI
- The sophisticated, multi-positional
- This multi-use product has been selling like hot cakes
- Multi-purpose uses and multi-purpose savings

See also: CHOICE, COMPLEX, PLENTY

MULTIMEDIA
- Gives you a rich multimedia experience you can't get anywhere else
- Multimedia is the latest way to
- A dazzling multimedia performance
- Using multimedia to interpret inmost feelings

MUSCLE
- No muscle required
- Easy, affordable ways to build marketing muscle
- We've added considerably more muscle
- Put some muscle into your
- Twice the muscle, half the price

See also: POWER, STRENGTH, STRONG

MUSIC
- Music that spills out onto the streets
- The huge savings will be music to your

ears
- Making music in hearts everywhere
- Just listen to the music

See also: DELIGHT, HARMONY

MUST
- A must for anyone who contemplates
- A must for those wanting to make it as independent entrepreneurs
- They're definitely must-haves
- It's a must for anyone planning to
- An absolute must

Must: necessity, requirement, need, prerequisite, essential
See also: ESSENTIAL, NEED

MYSTERY
- Taking the mystery out of
- Still remains a mystery
- Thrill to the mystery of
- Do you crave that touch of mystery

See also: DISCREET, MAGIC, ROMANCE, SECRET

NAME
- People whose name you can trust
- Just to name a few
- Because it's a name you can rely on
- A name for all seasons
- The name to remember
- Keeping your name in front of your customers every day of the year
- The best place to promote our name
- You'll see how the business got its name
- The most recognized name in
- Most trusted name in
- From the name you trust for quality
- No other name is so trusted
- Everyone loves to see their own name
- Certain names register better than others
- The number one name in
- A name that is accepted by
- Remember the name that tops them all
- Ask for these products by name
- It won't be the last time you hear this name
- More name recognition than ever
- It's already got your name on it
- Looking for names you can trust
- Taking on some of the biggest names in the industry

See also: BRAND, CALL, REPUTATION

NATURAL
- A choice that is only natural
- Works naturally with
- Now your choice is only natural
- Simply, safely, naturally
- A natural for
- The perfectly natural way to pamper yourself
- It's the perfectly natural thing to do
- Discover the natural benefits of
- For a smooth, natural look
- A natural high
- Looking your best, naturally
- It's the natural thing to do
- Only natural that
- Now you can enjoy a truly natural look
- Enhancing the natural beauty of
- Made of all-natural materials for your comfort
- What a natural
- It's natural to want more for your money
- A great natural way to promote
- Making it the natural center for
- So natural, in fact, that
- Naturally, it's better

See also: CLEAN, COMFORTABLE, EASE, ENVIRONMENTAL, ORGANIC, PURE

NATURALLY
- Some things just come naturally
- Doing what comes naturally
- Naturally better
- Impress them, naturally

NATURE
- Discover the true nature of
- Experience the power of nature
- Nature's most valuable gift to us
- Only nature could inspire so perfect a
- The way nature intended
- Back to nature the easy way
- A place in the heart of nature
- You just can't fool with Mother Nature
- We work with Mother Nature to
- The endlessly forgiving nature of
- Nature is generous
- A synergistic blend of nature's most potent
- Introducing nature's way

See also: EARTH, ENVIRONMENT, OUTDOORS, RUSTIC

NECESSITY
- Is now a household necessity
- First, we take care of the necessities
- Necessity really is the mother of invention
- This level of comfort and service is quickly becoming a necessity

See also: BASIC, ESSENTIAL, FUNDAMENTAL, MUST

NEED
- Whatever you need done
- This is what you need
- What you may need the most is
- We have everything you need to
- We have what you need most right now
- Needed on a daily basis
- Intelligent solutions for all your needs
- You don't need special equipment or an office
- It will give you whatever you need to
- That's all you need to
- We're always here if you need us
- The only product you'll need this season
- No matter what your needs
- Feature and performance you need at a price you can afford
- We designed it to meet the needs of
- The answer to all your needs and more
- Tailored to your very special needs
- To better identify and respond to your needs
- Committed to meeting the unique needs
- Our products are engineered to meet all of your needs
- We cover all your needs
- Save on everyday needs
- Finding services to fill your unique needs
- As we continue to meet your ever increasing needs
- Addresses your unrecognized needs
- Depending on your needs
- With us, your needs always come first
- After careful study of your needs

Need: demand, requirement, necessity, requisite, obligation, charge, duty, essential, indispensability, shortcoming, urgency, desire, hope for, desire, crave, yearn for, long for, want, wish, require
See also: DESIRE, ESSENTIAL, REQUIRE, WANT, WISH

NEIGHBOR
- We want to be your best neighbor
- Offering special prices for our neighbors
- What your neighbors are saying
- Meet your new neighbors
- It's just what neighbors do to help out

See also: COMMUNITY, FAMILY, FRIEND, HELP

NEIGHBORHOOD
- We're in your neighborhood
- Do it without even leaving your neighborhood
- Close to neighborhood shopping
- Right in your neighborhood
- Your neighborhood center for

See also: LOCAL

NERD
- Does all that nerdy stuff for you
- Where all the smart nerds gather
- You don't have to be a nerd to appreciate
- For the tech nerd in you
- No longer just for nerds

NESTLE
- All nestled in a bed of
- Nestle up to some real comfort
- Nestle snugly in the midst of

See also: CARESS, COSY, EMBRACE, FIT, HUG

NETWORK
- A network that grows with you
- Support for your entire network
- Delivering more on your network
- A network of more than
- A network of people at your command
- Become part of the network by filling in the enclosed reply form
- The most extensive network available today
- Part of a worldwide network
- Steadily expanding your business network
- Nobody knows networks like we do

See also: CLUB, COMMUNITY, CONNECTION, GROUP, MEMBERSHIP, PARTNERSHIP

NEVER
- Will never be the same again
- There's never been anything like this

- You've never seen an offer like this before
- Like never before
- When it's now or never

NEW YEAR
- May your New Year be filled with promise
- We look forward to serving you in the New Year
- Happy New Year to all
- The happiest beginning to your New Year
- Wishing you great joy in the coming New Year

See also: CELEBRATE, HOLIDAY

NEW
- Also new are
- We'll make it look new again
- Get the amazing new
- Look what's new
- Something new in the business of
- The brand new product you want
- A sensational new feeling
- Here's all the new stuff
- The newest and the best
- The shock of the new
- Why buy new
- Introducing the all-new
- Gets you into a brand new product fast
- Can allow you to move up to a new product more frequently
- New this year
- New on the market
- Will remain like new, year after year
- A mix of new and centuries-old
- Try something new
- New and improved

New: modern, late, recent, advanced, contemporary, topical, twenty-first century, present-day, hot, hot off the press, abreast of the times, up-to-the-minute, up-to-date, spanking, brand new, mint condition, late-model, newly arrived, futuristic, revolutionary, ahead of its time, far out, new-fangled, pristine, fresh, smart, current, hip, fashionable, stylish, all the rage, the latest thing, novel, original, untried, experimental, just hatched

See also: ADVANCE, BEGINNING, FRESH, INNOVATION, MODERN,

START

NEWCOMER
- A brash newcomer in the world
- Make room for an up-and-coming newcomer
- Providing free extra service for newcomers
- If you're a newcomer, you'll want to find out about

See also: PROTOTYPE

NEWS
- Start spreading the news
- News that could have a big impact on
- Keeping pace with the latest news
- News you've been waiting for
- And the best news is
- By now you've heard the news
- I've got good news for you
- Surprising news revealed inside
- Getting the news to you instantly
- Here's more good news
- The really good news is
- Good news for everybody
- Unbelievable news about
- I have some great news for you
- Here's wonderful news

See also: BLITZ, COMMUNICATION, DATA, INFORMATION

NICE
- Doubly nice for
- The very nicest
- Doing nice things for nice people like you
- A very nice touch is
- The nicest thing you can do for yourself right now
- What nicer way to

Nice: agreeable, pleasant, attractive, winning, winsome, delightful, likable, cheering, amiable, friendly, amusing, cordial, genial, charming, gracious, generous, sympathetic, understanding, gratifying, pleasing, pleasurable, good, enjoyable, satisfactory, proper, suitable, appropriate, decent, decorous, precise, accurate, detailed, flawless, scrupulous, careful, great, dandy, crackerjack

See also: ENJOYMENT, PLEASURE

NICHE

- A significant opportunity to carve a new niche in the market
- Has captured a specialized niche
- Niche marketing is coming into its own
- Now that you've found your niche
- Move to a better niche

See also: FIT, LOCATION, PLACE

NIGHT

- You'll never want the night to end
- You can reach us any time of the day or night
- Sun-drenched days and glorious tropical nights

NOBILITY

- Possesses a nobility that can't be imitated
- The austere nobility of line states its quality
- A nobility of purpose no amount of money can buy

See also: IDEAL

NOODLE

- Use your noodle
- Lets you just noodle about at your leisure
- It'll be the first thing that pops into the old noodle

See also: HEAD, MIND

NORM

- With things that aren't the norm
- A product very quickly becoming the norm
- Leaves the norm far behind in the dust
- When you become the norm

See also: STANDARD

NORMAL

- Now you can live a normal life
- Get's your life back to normal
- Nothing could be more normal than
- Excellence is just normal for us
- Will not disrupt your normal activities

See also: ORDINARY, REGULAR, STANDARD

NOSE

- From nose to tail, inside and out
- If you have a nose for value
- Nosing out the best deals
- A winner by much more than a nose

See also: FEELING, INSTINCT

NOTE

- Hit a high note with
- We also took care to note
- People are sitting up and taking note
- Make a note to
- One of the most noted
- Has just issued several noteworthy

See also: NOTICE, SEE, SPOT

NOTHING

- Nothing comes close to this
- Doing it on practically nothing
- Nothing does it better than
- There's nothing like it for your
- There's absolutely nothing like it
- We hold nothing back
- You ain't seen nothing yet
- There's nothing else like it

NOTICE

- You'll notice right away
- Notice anything new
- What you have to notice is
- We're giving notice right now, the future is here
- A special notice to all
- Make them sit up and take notice
- Everyone will notice when you

See also: DISCOVER, FIND, LOOK, NOTE, RECOGNIZE, SEE, SPOT

NOTION

- Puts to rest the notion that
- Someday, should you take a notion to
- A truly splendid notion that deserves

See also: CONCEPT, IDEA

NOURISH

- Nourished and cared for by
- This revolutionary product nourished your
- Tasty and nourishing

See also: EAT, PROVIDE

NOW

- When now actually means now
- Speaking of right now
- Do it now
- Now is the time to
- It's now or never
- There's no time better than now to

- Now you see it , now you don't
- Now, for a short time only, available

Now: immediately, at once, instantly, at present, at this time, right now, just now, nowadays, right away, straightaway, without delay, soon, presently
See also: ALREADY, HERE, INSTANT, READY

NUGGET
- Full of choice nuggets of
- Yielding a very precious nugget of information
- As much fun as finding nuggets of gold
See also: GEM, TREASURE

NUMBER
- This little number is strictly
- You've got our number
- We've got your number
- A smart little number going fast
- Our number is in the book
- Go ahead, check out the numbers
- The numbers don't lie
- Not just a numbers game
- We understand what it takes to be number one
- The numbers speak for themselves

NUTRITION
- Nutrition for the mind
- Did you ever think solid nutrition could taste this good
- Always putting nutrition first
- Without nutrition, taste is nothing
See also: DINE, EAT, HEALTH

NUTS
- You'll go nuts for
- Getting right down to the nuts and bolts of it
- Watch them going nuts over your brand new
See also: AMOK, CRAZY, FOOL, MADNESS, WILD

OASIS
- A hidden oasis of rare and wondrous
- Come to an oasis of pleasure
- A quiet little oasis in the midst of
- An oasis of peace and tranquillity amidst the rush

- Create your own private oasis
See also: ESCAPE, GETAWAY, PARADISE, RELIEF, SAFETY

OBJECTIVE
- Truly essential to achieving your long-term objectives
- If your objective is to improve
- Accomplish your objectives quickly and easily
- Our biggest objective is to ensure your satisfaction
See also: AIM, GOAL, MISSION, TARGET

OBLIGATE
- Does not obligate you in any way
- You will not be obligated to buy
- We're obligated to do better
See also: COMMIT, REQUIRE

OBLIGATION
- And you are assured, at no obligation
- No obligation to you now or ever
- Requesting this product puts you under no obligation
- Call today for a no obligation demonstration
- Taking care of your obligations can sometimes be difficult
- With no obligation to buy anything, now or in the future
- No obligation, no restrictions, no strings attached
- Under no obligation, no matter what
- With no obligation on your part
- There's no cost or obligation, of course
See also: COMMITMENT, NEED, PRESSURE, WARRANTY

OBSESSION
- To others, it's an obsession
- Our obsession is being the best
- Swept away by a glorious obsession
See also: DESIRE, FOCUS, MADNESS

OBVIOUS
- Beyond the obvious
- The superiority is obvious
- Great value isn't always so obvious
- Making us the obvious choice
See also: CLEAR, DIRECT, SIMPLE

OCCASION
- Of course we can't forget those special occasions
- Rise to the occasion with
- Great savings for every occasion

See also: EVENT, TIME

ODDS
- Improving your odds of
- Odds are you'll come to us in the end
- The easy way to beat the odds
- Your odds just got a lot better

See also: BET, CHANCE, LUCK

ODYSSEY
- Join us on the odyssey
- A tremendously exciting odyssey of discovery
- Cut the odyssey short, find the answer here

See also: DISCOVERY, JOURNEY, TRAVEL, TRIP, VISIT, VOYAGE

OFFER
- Exclusive offer for our readers
- Has so many things to offer
- Take advantage of fabulous half price offers
- Offering our most valued clients customers the very finest of
- Offer ends this month
- Limited time offer
- Choose the offer that's right for you
- Special, time-limited offer
- Hot offers every day
- Take advantage of this winning offer
- No other retailer can make you this offer
- We are pleased to offer our customers a wide range of
- Take advantage of this free trial offer
- We're happy to oblige by offering new
- One cool offer
- Incredible offer won't last
- Special designer offer
- Doorcrasher offer
- In-store bonus offer
- Cannot be combined with any other offer
- Some specified items not included in this offer
- This great offer ends soon
- You two can take advantage of this offer
- Incredible one-time offers
- Special offer today only
- Offers much more than just
- Free trial offer
- Take advantage of this special offer
- Simply an offer no one can refuse
- Offers something that's been sorely missing in
- Always has more to offer
- An exclusive offering of
- The offerings are spectacular
- Plus, you can save even more with these additional offers
- These special offers are exclusive
- Offers available to our valued retail customers only
- Take advantage of our best offer
- This very special offer includes
- This is a special, time-limited offer
- We are pleased to offer you
- We're making this unprecedented offer to a select group
- Offers like these don't come very often
- Hurry! Offer must be activated by
- Don't miss out on this limited offer
- We are making this generous offer because
- We cannot extend this unusual offer beyond
- Offer void where prohibited

Offer: deal, bargain, sacrifice, up for sale, on the market, on the block, bid, offering, proposal, proposition, advance, suggestion, presentation, overture

See also: BARGAIN, DEAL, GIVE, INVITE, MERCHANDISE, PROVIDE, SALE, SAVINGS

OFFICE
- Everything for the office of the future
- We'll have it at your office in an hour
- Today, your office has become your second home
- As easy as calling one of the offices listed
- Call the office closest to you

See also: ADMINISTRATION, HEADQUARTERS

OFTEN
- As often as you like
- Come often and enjoy
- Often more than enough to
- We like to see you often

OKAY
- Finally, it's okay to
- Giving you a big okay on
- Much more than just okay

See also: **APPROVAL, STAMP**

OLD
- Getting older doesn't have to mean getting old
- When what's old is what's best
- Out with the old and in with the new
- Trade in your old one for a bonus
- Old-fashioned value

See also: **AGE, MATURITY, VINTAGE, WISDOM**

ONCE
- Does it all at once
- You only have to do it once
- Once you had to do all it all yourself, but no more

See also: **TIME, TOGETHER**

ONE
- There's only one
- The one and only
- This is the one for you
- Right away, you know it's the one for you
- This is one magnificent product
- Buy one, get one free

See also: **UNIQUE**

ONE-STOP
- One-stop shopping for all your needs
- Providing one-stop service
- The result is one-stop shopping
- When you want one-stop convenience, come to us
- All at a one-stop service center

See also: **CONVENIENCE, LOCATION, TOGETHER**

ONE-OF-A-KIND
- Value-priced, one-of-a-kind treasures
- Own a one-of-a-kind work
- Be the one to cherish this one-of-a-kind marvel

See also: **ORIGINAL, PROTOTYPE, SPECIAL, UNIQUE**

ONLINE
- Online service 24 hours a day
- Get it faster online
- Go online for all the details
- Online speed at your fingertips

ONLY
- Only at these outlets
- The one and only
- The only product in existence that
- Only here can you find your dream
- Your only consideration should be
- Only at our store can you find

See also: **EXCLUSIVE, UNIQUE**

OPEN
- Open up to value
- We open early, close late, all for your convenience
- Always open to new ideas
- Open more hours than our competitors
- Ready as soon as we open

See also: **FREE, READY**

OPENING
- Our grand opening continues with
- Grand opening full of savings for you
- Only a limited number of openings available
- Incredible savings, free gifts and prizes to celebrate the opening of
- Thrilled to be opening our biggest

See also: **BEGINNING, START**

OPERATE
- Easy to operate
- Let us show you how we operate
- All operating instructions included
- So simple to operate
- If this is how you operate, take a look at our product

See also: **FUNCTION, MANAGE, USE**

OPERATION
- It's operation is simple and convenient
- Does it all in one quick operation
- Now a way you can streamline the entire operation
- In one easy operation

See also: **ADMINISTRATION**

OPINION
- We care about your opinion
- In our opinion, the best
- Changing opinions all across the country

- We want to earn your good opinion
- We have a different opinion of value

See also: BELIEF, CONCEPT, FEELING, IDEA, PHILOSOPHY,

OPPONENT
- No match for a formidable opponent
- An advantage no opponent has over you
- Leave all opponents behind in the dust
- Good opponents make us better

See also: BATTLE, FIGHT, RIVAL

OPPORTUNITY
- Expand your opportunities
- Can mean an opportunity lost or gained
- Rely on us to help them take advantage of opportunities to
- The opportunity to enjoy your dream
- Don't let this exciting and profitable opportunity pass you by
- The result is a unique an financially powerful opportunity
- Nothing to lose, everything to gain by learning about this brand new and unique opportunity
- Offering you this splendid opportunity for success
- Offering a tremendous opportunity for your whole family to
- Only those who realize this golden opportunity is waiting
- An opportunity to build a truly independent
- Knock on opportunity's door today
- Opportunity knocks
- Don't miss this glorious opportunity
- This is your best opportunity to
- Offering you the perfect opportunity to stop and take advantage of
- Giving you the optimal opportunity to enjoy
- Offering visitors and residents alike an opportunity to view
- A hot opportunity
- Don't let the opportunity fly away
- To find out more about the opportunity
- Opportunities abound
- Are you curious about opportunities
- International opportunities available
- Allows you more opportunities for
- Crank up the opportunities to
- Burgeoning business opportunities opening up all over

- Making opportunities easier and easier to identify
- Don't miss this once-in-a-lifetime opportunity
- Give you the opportunity to
- Take advantage of this opportunity
- Why should you let the best opportunity slip away
- The greatest opportunity of your life is yours now
- Never before have offered this kind of opportunity
- A professional, serious business opportunity
- Make the most of this opportunity

Opportunity: accident, serendipity, possibility, prospect, opening, likelihood, occasion, time, right occasion, favorable moment, good time, golden chance, contingency, chance, right circumstances, once-in-a-lifetime chance, break, stroke of luck, twist of fate, turn of events

See also: BARGAIN, CHALLENGE, CHANCE, CHOICE, DEAL, OFFER, SALE, OPTION

OPT
- And, if you want, you can opt for
- The one that people in the know opt for most
- So many more marvellous things you can opt to do

See also: CHOOSE, DECIDE

OPTION
- Select the best option to meet your needs
- The options are as varied as ever
- Explore your fashion options with
- If you wish to take advantage of this option
- You also have the option to
- You can choose from several appealing options
- Giving you the option to
- Take a look at all these options
- More options than you ever imagined possible
- Explore interoperability options
- You've got a lot of options to consider
- As you examine the options more closely
- Come to us for an even bigger menu of options

- Now you have more fabulous options
- There's plenty of sophisticated options

Option: choice, alternative, substitute, solution, replacement, equivalent, possibility, preference, selection

See also: CHANCE, CHOICE, CHOOSE, FEATURE, OPPORTUNITY, PREFERENCE

ORDER

- Simply complete the attached order blank
- We guaranteed delivery within two days of receiving your order
- We ship within 24 hours of receiving your order
- Your order will be filled before any others are accepted
- If you've already placed your order, please accept our thanks and disregard this notice
- To order yours, please see the attached order form
- The one reason among many to order
- Time is growing short, so order now
- Order at least one
- Why not order today
- Order one for every family member
- Orders subject to credit approval
- Rush your order to the address shown
- So we can include your order
- Ask about our special order process
- Filling a pretty tall order
- Order one for yourself and one for someone you care about
- Order today and see
- Order right away and find out how easy it is to
- Order yours direct from
- Ordering is so simple
- Return the order card and write
- Ask about our special order items
- We can special order virtually everything
- All special order items
- May we take your order
- Complete and mail the attached order form
- Everything is made to order
- Order at your store's customer service desk
- Order today for fastest service
- Please order today
- It's so easy to order

- It can save you money when you order
- See it before you order
- Frees you from any preconceived notions of order
- Personally inspect each order
- We encourage you to order early to avoid disappointment
- We're so certain you're going to be pleased with your order that we're going to give you extra
- Order before the end of the month and save
- Order online for faster service
- Simply complete and mail an order card today
- To place your order, call us at
- Four ways to order
- Let's talk about why you haven't ordered yet
- Two convenient methods to order
- Here's how to order without embarrassment
- Please rest assured that we have received your order
- We are processing your order in order to provide you with continuous service
- If you have not sent your order, it's not too late
- Order today and don't miss out
- If you've already sent your order, thank you

Order: command, mandate, direction, requirement, demand, request, bidding

See also: BUY, CALL, COMMAND, DIRECT, PURCHASE, SELL, SALE

ORDINARY

- Not your ordinary product
- This is no ordinary product
- Anything but ordinary
- Doesn't look or feel like ordinary items
- Go beyond ordinary

See also: FAMILIAR, NORMAL, REGULAR

ORGANIC

- Organically inspired
- Guaranteed safe and organic
- All in one organically united design
- Our product is organic to the whole process

See also: ENVIRONMENTAL,

NATURAL, PURE, RUSTIC

ORGANIZATION
- The comfortable organization of
- No other organization offers you so much
- An organization you'll be with for a long time
- You'll fit right into our organization

See also: CLUB, COMPANY, GROUP, NETWORK, PARTNERSHIP, TEAM

ORGANIZE
- Get organized today
- Helping you organize your priorities and your life
- Organized in a way that easy to use and understand

ORIENT
- Primarily information oriented
- Changing the way the world is oriented
- Totally oriented to pleasing you

See also: DIRECT, DIRECTION

ORIGINAL
- Even better than the original
- So faithful to the original that
- Own something as original as you
- The originals just got stronger
- If you're an original, you need us
- The original product, not an imitation
- The original is still the best
- Come to the original source of

See also: INNOVATION, PROTOTYPE, UNIQUE

OTHER
- Accept no other
- There just isn't any other that can perform this well
- Working with others is all-important to us
- What it's done for others, it'll do for you
- Wait until you've seen what it's done for others

See also: ALTERNATIVE

OUT
- Don't be left out
- Find out what's in, what's out
- Do you find yourself out in the cold
- Will keep the world out

See also: MISS, PROTECT

OUTDOORS
- Indoors or outdoors, you can use it everywhere
- Celebrate the great outdoors
- Outdoor fun for the whole family
- Spend more time outdoors with
- Bring the outdoors inside

See also: EARTH, NATURAL, ENVIRONMENTAL, PURE, RUSTIC, SPORT

OUTLET
- Value and quality at outlet prices
- Coming soon to an outlet near you
- Factory outlet
- The biggest outlet yet
- First rate quality at an outlet price
- Discount outlet prices

See also: FACTORY, MALL, STORE

OUTLOOK
- There's been a change of outlook
- Always a fresh outlook
- Time for a change of outlook
- It all depends on your outlook

See also: FEELING, IDEA, VIEW

OUTPERFORM
- Will greatly outperform any other
- We manage to outperform
- Helping you outperform
- Outperforms conventional products three to one

See also: BETTER, SUPERIOR

OUTRAGEOUS
- Twice as outrageous as
- The end of outrageous prices
- So outrageously delightful
- Feeling a little outrageous

See also: CRAZY, NUTS, WILD

OVER
- And it's not over yet
- Away over and above the competition
- Placing your needs over everything else
- Pushing the value over the top

See also: ABOVE, END, FINISH

OVERDRIVE
- Jumps into overdrive in an instant

- Put your advancement into overdrive
- When your life is in overdrive and your budget is not

See also: **MOMENTUM, POWER, SPEED**

OVERFLOW
- Overflowing with terrific products, ideas and inspiration
- Overflowing with value
- Can easily take the overflow

See also: **EXTRA**

OVERHAUL
- We've just undergone a major overhaul
- Come and let us give your priorities a complete overhaul
- Is it time for an overhaul

See also: **REPAIR, RESTORE**

OVERSTATEMENT
- It's no overstatement to say
- Some of our competitors are given to overstatement
- Tired of overstatement and underperformance

OVERVIEW
- For someone who can provide an overview
- Stop a moment and examine the overview
- Giving you a breathtaking overview of everything you need

OWE
- You owe it to yourself to
- You'll be surprised at how little you owe
- You won't find yourself owing huge amounts
- And you'll owe nothing

See also: **DESERVE, DUE**

OWN
- Why own anything less than a
- Designed to give you more choices in owning
- Now, for the first time, you can own
- Works with you to make it your own
- Don't miss this chance for you to own your own
- You'll be proud to call your own
- Own your own territory

- Locally owned and operated by
- Easy to own, easy to use
- You can own it today
- For your very own
- Something to call your own
- We make it easy to own
- Own them today
- Now you can own your own

See also: **BUY, PURCHASE**

OWNER
- Helping you feel more like an owner
- Once you become an owner, you'll never again go back to leasing
- More proud owners because of us
- Owner satisfaction has dramatically increases
- All estimates done by owners

OWNERSHIP
- Experience the pride of ownership
- Providing a lower cost of ownership
- Time to take ownership of your future
- For the best ownership experience
- A very unique ownership opportunity

See also: **RESPONSIBILITY**

PACE
- Keep pace with the smart set
- The pace is picking up
- You set the pace
- At whatever pace you want
- Keeping up with your pace
- Discover who is setting the pace

See also: **RATE, SPEED**

PACESETTER
- If you're a pacesetter
- We're the pacesetter for
- Keeping up with the pacesetters

See also: **LEADER, PIONEER**

PACK
- Packed with savings
- Always ahead of the pack
- Packed with exciting
- Packing in more value for less money

See also: **FULL, GROUP**

PACKAGE
- Good things come in small packages
- After you've read our detailed information package

- A part of your service package
- This excellent package features
- Means so much more when it's packaged beautifully
- So nicely packaged
- The best package for you
- This handsomely packaged item
- Complete package for the whole family
- Ask about our package deals
- Makes this your complete protection package
- Get many of the same features, at exceptional value, in a smaller package
- Our luxury package at no extra charge

See also: COMBINATION, KIT

PAGAN
- Project a pagan splendor
- Take a thoroughly pagan delight
- A wild, pagan freedom
- Inviting you to sample some truly pagan pleasures

See also: EXOTIC, GODDESS, LUXURIOUS, MAGIC, WILD

PAINLESS
- Looking for a painless way to
- Now borrowing money is completely painless
- Not just painless, but pleasant as well

See also: EASY, FAST

PAIR
- Pair the pieces with everything
- The power pair
- Pair up with us and see
- Get the pair for the price of one

See also: DOUBLE, MATCH

PALATE
- Sure to please any palate
- Even the most finicky palate will be delighted
- Created to appeal to your palate
- Discriminating palates all over the country enjoy

See also: CUISINE, TASTE

PAMPER
- Sit back, be pampered, and watch the world go by
- In pampering you, no detail has been overlooked
- Pampering you with relaxing comfort
- Pamper your family with love and attention
- A little romantic pampering is definitely in order
- You've never been pampered like this
- Pampering like you've never experienced before

See also: CARE, COMFORT, INDULGE, LUXURY, SPOIL

PARADISE
- Filling your particular definition of paradise
- A paradise awaits you
- Cruising paradise
- Paradise is waiting for you
- Shoppers' paradise
- Enjoy a little touch of paradise
- You'll think you've found paradise

Paradise: heaven, Eden, utopia, Xanadu, Shangri-la, happy valley, pie in the sky, bliss, celestial
See also: HEAVEN, OASIS, VACATION

PARE
- Pares it down to the extreme
- Pare expenses, increase effectiveness
- Pare your costs to the bone

See also: CHOP, CUT, REDUCE

PARKING
- Lots of free parking available
- Take advantage of our free parking
- Does your environment look like a parking lot

PART
- Always a part of the landscape
- Part of who we are
- And now you can be part of it all
- We want you to be part of it
- Look the part
- Something you'll never have to part with
- We're excited to be part of
- You'll be part of the fun
- Making it a growing part of your life
- Make it the best part
- Specializing in sales, service and parts

See also: CHUNK, ESSENTIAL, INGREDIENT, SHARE

PARTICIPATE
- And at participating outlets around the world
- At participating stores everywhere
- Available at participating locations
- Hundreds of participating items
- Visit your nearest participating store or dealer
- Here's how you can participate
- The best way to participate is
- Look what you get when you participate
- The whole neighborhood is participating
- Make your plans now to participate

See also: JOIN, PARTNER, SHARE

PARTNER
- A partner who works with you
- When you're looking for a partner to
- Your best partner in
- A good partner is always there to help
- Partners you can trust
- In something this important, you need partners you can rely upon

Partner: associate, colleague, coworker, right hand, helpmate, sidekick, confederate, helper, aide, henchman
See also: MEMBER

PARTNERSHIP
- Prepared in partnership with
- Establishing a solid partnership with you
- Another benefit is the result of our partnership with
- Our ongoing partnership helps you in every way
- A respected partnership for years
- Deeply appreciate a partnership with you

See also: COMMUNITY, MEMBERSHIP, NETWORK

PARTY
- Bringing the rest of the world to the party
- Having a party every day
- Let's have a party tonight
- Join the party
- Making you party to a great success
- Guess what, it's party time
- Brings the party to your home
- This country's largest party

See also: CARNIVAL, CELEBRATION, FESTIVE, FIESTA, SPREE

PASS
- You can't pass it up
- Don't pass this one up
- Passing savings value on to you
- Gets more than a passing grade
- Passing the torch to a new generation

PASSION
- Passion is the real power behind
- Offering irresistible opportunities to indulge a passion
- You'll soon develop a passion for
- Passion wins out
- Join the passion for
- Passion and mental stimulation
- We have a burning passion for
- Surrender to your passion for

See also: DESIRE, DRIVE, EMOTION, FEELING, FIRE

PASSPORT
- Your passport to international success
- Like handing you a passport to
- A passport to value and savings

See also: INVITATION, TICKET

PAST
- Rooted in the past, unmistakably contemporary
- Don't rest on past glory
- Make this problem a thing of the past
- Don't let this deal get past you
- Some people remain stuck in the past

See also: FINISH, HISTORY, LEGACY, OVER, TRADITION

PATH
- Setting you on the path to successful and fulfilling
- Offers an uncomplicated path to
- The path to financial and personal success
- Setting the path for the rest of your life
- Taking you off the beaten path to discover

See also: COURSE, JOURNEY, METHOD, ROAD, WAY

PATIENCE
- Patience goes a long way toward
- Now your patience is about to be rewarded
- Developed with infinite patience and care

to detail
- We'll never try your patience

See also: COOPERATION

PATIENT
- New patients and emergencies always welcome
- Now you don't have to be patient
- Always patient help and support

PAY
- Pay absolutely nothing
- Pay next year
- Are you paying too much
- It can pay for itself in
- You do not have to pay until you are totally convinced
- You don't even have to pay postage
- Will start paying off instantly
- Nothing else to pay
- Does it pay to
- Pay off your investment in less than
- Always pay yourself first
- You pay for only what you use
- Why pay more
- Pay now or pay later, but pay you must
- Don't pay until
- Don't pay for one full year
- Why pay for a costly new
- An easy way to buy now, pay later
- Choose from these easy ways to pay
- Doesn't it feel good to pay less
- Nothing to pay for six months on all our inventory
- Are you paying too much for
- You'll never pay less for
- A way to really make it pay
- Finally paying off for you
- Pays for itself the first time you use it
- And you'll pay less for it
- Two ways to pay, the choice is yours
- Why pay more when you can get a better deal from
- The easy new way to pay
- Don't pay more later
- Pay less, get more
- Twelve months to pay
- Pay as you play

Pay: compensate, remunerate, reward, recompense, refund, settle, satisfy, liquidate, discharge, clear, honor, square, meet, spend, expend, hand over, shell out, lay out, cough

up, ante up, contribute, chip in, advance, yield, return, profit, avail, benefit, help

See also: BUY, COST, MONEY, PROFIT, REWARD

PAYMENT
- Can save you huge amounts of money on monthly payments
- If you send payment now, you will receive
- All in one easy payment
- With this easy payment plan you can get as many as you want
- No interest, no payments for twelve months
- One payment plan
- No down payment, no monthly payments
- So you can maintain an affordable payment
- You won't even notice these low payments
- Your payments can be significantly lower
- The affordable payments allow you to
- Develop your personal payment plan

See also: BILL, COST, INSTALLMENT, MONTHLY

PEACE
- You can't put a price on peace of mind
- You'll enjoy peace of mind everywhere
- More peace of mind, less cost
- Here to give you the peace of mind you need
- It's a little extra peace of mind
- It is the very eve of real peace
- Finally, you can have some peace
- When you just want peace and quiet
- Complete comfort and peace of mind
- You'll have peace of mind just knowing
- Providing maximum peace of mind
- Means peace of mind while you plan your family's future security

See also: HEAVEN, OASIS, PARADISE, RELIEF

PEACH
- A peach of a value
- Making everything just peachy
- We're just peachy keen about

See also: DELIGHT, GEM, TREASURE

PEAK
- You, too, can have a peak experience

- Just now reaching its peak
- If you think you've peaked, just wait

See also: **CREST, PINNACLE, TOP**

PEEK

- A sneak peek at what's in store for you
- Here's a sneak peek at something really new
- Free advance peek

See also: **LOOK, PREVIEW**

PENDULUM

- The pendulum has swung
- Grab onto the next swing of the pendulum
- Protect yourself from the wild, unpredictable pendulum swings

PENETRATE

- Penetrates deep to reduce
- Has already penetrated deep into the marketplace
- Giving you an even more penetrating analysis of

See also: **ENTER**

PENNY

- Pinching pennies till they holler
- We look after your pennies too
- For just pennies a day, enjoy
- Finally available for pennies
- Just pennies each
- Everything you need for just a few pennies a day
- You'll never have to pay a penny back

See also: **CENT, MONEY, SAVINGS**

PEOPLE

- We're looking for people like you
- A service people want
- A service that smart people are willing to pay for
- Charming people make this a hit
- People are all different
- We care about people
- People are our business
- Naturally, its from the people who know about
- Everyday people are the best of all
- There to ensure the people you care about are provided for
- Improving your people skills
- The most outrageous people in the world

- For people on the go
- With our continual investment in people and technology
- To a very select group of people
- People like you are benefiting
- These are the people who will help you
- We love to deal with people like you
- Technology has changed but people haven't
- Trying to help as many people as possible get started
- Real people pleasers

See also: **ANYBODY, COMMUNITY, CUSTOMER, FAMILY, FOLKS**

PERCEPTION

- Changing your perception of
- Reshaping your perception of reality
- Perceptions have shifted and sharpened

See also: **UNDERSTANDING**

PERFECT

- Perfect for all your demands
- The search for the perfect
- You always feel perfect in
- That's perfect
- The perfect solution to all your needs
- We've spent years perfecting

See also: **BEST, IDEAL**

PERFECTION

- The search for perfection ends here
- The myth of perfection exploded
- The relentless pursuit of perfection
- It all depends on how you view perfection
- A mania for perfection
- Made by perfectionists
- Displaying a passion for perfection

See also: **IDEAL**

PERFORM

- Ready to perform
- Just watch the way it performs
- Able to perform even more services for you
- You will perform better when you have the help of

See also: **ACHIEVE, ACCOMPLISH, ACT, DO**

PERFORMANCE

- For peak performance

- For style and performance in one beautiful package
- Anticipating long-term performance
- Delivers legendary performance
- Unbeatable combination of power and performance
- Three ways to look at performance
- Treat yourself to a command performance
- Advanced performance never stops
- A really sporty performance
- It embodies quality and performance
- Good performance, good economy
- The perfect harmony of inspired performance
- Experience the exhilarating performance
- For longer performance life
- Performance you can trust down the road
- If you demand the ultimate performance
- With years of peak performance to offer
- Now that same performance can be found in a low cost model
- Most respected for performance
- Combine superb performance with unexpected luxury
- The smoothest performance yet
- Essential to peak performance
- Performance isn't just about

Performance: entertainments, show, drama, representation, spectacle, happening, execution, doing, accomplishment, attainment, completion, realization, achievement, work, deed, feat, act, exploit, enterprise, endeavor, undertaking, task, procedure, production, operation, transaction
See also: ACCOMPLISHMENT, ACHIEVEMENT, ENTERTAINMENT, JOB, TASK

PERFUME
- A delicious perfume
- The sweet perfume of success
- Float in a cloud of heavenly perfume
- Perfumed with pure delight

See also: PLEASURE

PERK
- Want to perk up your life
- Enjoy one of the perks of
- Watch them perk up when you walk in with

See also: BONUS, PREMIUM,

REJUVENATE

PERMANENT
- To ensure a successful and permanent job
- A professional and permanent
- The change for the better is permanent

See also: ENDURE, LAST

PERSEVERANCE
- A combination of hard work and perseverance
- Your perseverance is finally paying off
- When perseverance really counts

Perseverance: endurance, steadfastness, persistence, continuance, patience, stamina, courage, grit, pluck, zeal, ambition, application, tenacity, resolve, determination, decision
See also: ENDURE, LAST

PERSONAL
- For those of you who prefer the personal touch
- For the personal service that defines us
- Expect to receive uniquely personal service
- Experience the personal treatment you deserve
- Adding elegance and personal style
- It's an expression of personal freedom
- The personal touch is always there
- Your choice is a very personal thing
- We take excellence very personally

Personal: individual, private, close to one's heart, particular, exclusive, especial, special, intimate, familiar, chummy, one-on-one, secret, confidential, face-to-face
See also: CONFIDENTIAL, DISCREET, SECRET, SPECIAL

PERSONALITY
- Each with its own distinct personality
- A product with personality
- Designed to reflect your own personality

PERSONALIZE
- Custom personalization
- Offering a unique selection of personalized items
- Personalized for you and your family
- Personalized, confidential service

See also: CUSTOMIZE, INDIVIDUAL

PERSUADE
- If anything will persuade you, this will
- Persuade more customers to come
- Persuaded to make this decision

See also: ATTRACT, CONVINCE

PEST
- Rid yourself of these annoying pests once and for all
- Sometimes this problem can really be a pest
- Stop thinking of it as a pest

See also: HASSLE, PROBLEM

PHASE
- First phase sold out fast
- Carefully phased in to cushion the impact
- Helping you phase in a brand new system

See also: STEP

PHILOSOPHY
- Dramatically re-interpreted our philosophy
- A company with a global philosophy
- Working to fit in with your personal philosophy
- Shaped by a whole new philosophy of
- Supported by our philosophy of

See also: AIM, BELIEF, DESIGN, FEELING, GOAL, OPINION, PHILOSOPHY, PLAN, PRINCIPLE, SYSTEM

PHONE
- You are only a phone call away
- One quick phone call does it all
- One phone call away from saving
- The only cost is the phone call
- As easy as picking up your phone
- Last day to order by phone
- Shop by phone and save time and money
- Please phone for availability
- Visit your local store or shop by phone
- Just pick up the phone and it's yours

See also: CALL, COMMUNICATE, TELEPHONE, TELL

PICK
- Come in and pick up your windfall
- Fresh picked for maximum freshness
- Get the pick of the litter
- If you prefer, you can pick up too
- The pick of the crop

- Simply pick up a product today
- Let us be the one you pick
- Just pick out what you want and pick up valuable gifts

See also: CHOICE, CHOOSE, DECIDE, SELECT

PICTURE
- Gives you a complete picture of all
- Think about the big picture
- A critical part of the picture too
- Will stay in the picture for years
- Can you picture it
- Just picture yourself doing this
- Helping you get the picture

See also: IMAGINE, OVERVIEW, VIEW

PIE
- Get a bigger piece of the pie
- No longer just pie in the sky
- Slicing the pie in a creative new way

See also: REWARD, SHARE

PIECE
- In just one easy piece
- Put the pieces together to discover how easy it can be
- Giving you the last piece of the puzzle

See also: PART, SHARE

PILE
- Piling on the features
- Piling savings on top of value
- Puts you on top of the pile
- You won't believe the pile of benefits

See also: ADD, COLLECTION, RAKE, STACK

PINNACLE
- Taking you to the pinnacle of
- Reaching the absolute pinnacle of
- Perched on the very pinnacle

See also: CREST, PEAK, TOP

PIONEER
- Capture the pioneering spirit of
- The same pioneering spirit that drove
- You too can be one of the pioneers
- A pioneer in this field since

See also: DISCOVER, EXPLORE, ICONOCLAST, INDIVIDUALIST, LEADER

PITCH
- In perfect pitch with
- Fielding the wildest pitches
- Not just a pie-in-the-sky sales pitch

See also: HARMONIZE, PERSUADE, PRESENTATION

PIZZAZZ
- Add polish and pizzazz
- Make your point with pizzazz
- Put some pizzazz into your life

See also: ATTRACTION, GLITTER, HYPE, JAZZ

PLACE
- There's a place for you at
- Your place is at the front
- Quite simply, the place you love the most
- Will soon be your favorite place
- Coming to a place near you
- It seems fitting that the best place in town
- Always a very popular place
- A rather nice place to be
- Always placing you first
- The most charming place to be
- Perhaps no other place evokes such stirring images
- A friendly local place to
- You can reach more places from more places
- You'll never feel out of place
- Discover the people and places

See also: LOCATION, SITE

PLAN
- Under this one simple plan
- Planning ahead is time well spent
- We accept all plans
- And the satisfaction of a plan that's just right for you
- A detailed, A to Z plan to
- The plan is great
- It's always best to plan ahead
- You do the planning, we do the work
- It's time for a custom marketing plan
- Start planning today for
- Helping you determine which plan is best
- Make us part of your plans
- To get ahead, you've got to have a plan
- We have a better plan
- Planning carefully for the future
- Sensible, long-range planning is essential
- Detailed plans designed for you and you alone
- Your plans tell you how to
- Success is your when you follow these simple plans
- Follow easy, step-by-step plans
- Just follow the plans with their detailed instructions
- Introducing the plan that makes sense for you
- A plan that's the result of listening to you
- Currently planned are
- Choosing a plan can be pretty complicated
- Working with you to form a plan to suit your needs

Plan: scheme, arrangement, design, grouping, layout, organization, pattern, configuration, proposal, project, prospect, conception, purpose, view, intent, ambition, intention, hope, aspiration, map, ground plan, model, sketch, draft, chart, look ahead, arrange, line up, work out, schedule, block out, propose, strategize, devise, develop, frame, construct, envision, mastermind, contemplate, outline, draw up, plot, shape, connect, intend

See also: BLUEPRINT, DESIGN, INFORMATION, STORY, STRATEGY, SYSTEM

PLANET
- You might as well be on another planet
- And you'll be helping the planet too
- Taking care of Planet Earth by using

See also: EARTH, GLOBAL, WORLD

PLATE
- Talk about a full plate
- When you've got more on your plate than you can deal with alone
- Putting the best on your plate

See also: RESPONSIBILITY

PLAY
- Something the kids can play with for hours on end
- Would you rather play catch-up
- Are you ready to play
- Play time for everyone
- We don't play around with value
- Make it into child's play

- Play with the best
- Work hard, play hard and get your just reward
- Playing around with
- Play to your heart's content
- Great to play in
- You're not content just to play hard
- You play to win
- We always play to win

Play: drama, amusement, pastime, fun, entertainment, sport, enjoyment, whoopee, skylarking, joke, make-believe, liberty, activity, scope, compete, frisk, frolic, gambol, caper, rollick, romp, roister, whoop it up, clown, have a good time, horse around, fool around, josh, cut up, make merry, banter, make believe, affect
See also: **DRAMA, ENJOY, ENTERTAINMENT, FUN, GAME, HAPPY**

PLAYER
- We help you look like a player
- Some of the biggest players come to us
- Now you can be a real player
See also: **PARTICIPATE, PARTNER**

PLAYGROUND
- It's our ocean playground
- The whole city becomes your playground
- Grownups need playgrounds too

PLEASE
- You'll be especially pleased with
- Our only goal is to please you
- We're so confident you'll be pleased with
- Free to do as you please
- All geared to pleasing you
- A decidedly pleasing product
- Developed specifically to please you
- Extremely pleased to be able to offer
- Please the whole family with
- We've been pleasing customers for years
See also: **DELIGHT, GRATIFY, SATISFY**

PLEASURE
- A product that will keep on giving pleasure
- Blended with the smooth pleasure of a legendary

- The delightfully unsettling pleasure
- The ultimate pleasure principle
- Discover the pleasures of being
- Bringing pleasure to
- Alive with pleasure
- What a pleasure to share with
- So many pleasures at your fingertips
- The tempting allure of forbidden pleasures
- Boasts such pleasures as
- Discover unlimited pleasure
- Cherish the simplicity of its pleasures
- The pleasures are legendary
- Whether you come for business, pleasure or both
- Putting your pleasure ahead of everything else
See also: **AMENITY, COMFORT, DELIGHT, DESIRE, ENJOY, FUN, JOY, NICE**

PLEDGE
- Our pledge to you has always been
- Keeping the pledge
- We never go back on our pledge
- Making a solemn pledge to you
See also: **COMMITMENT, PROMISE**

PLENTY
- We've got plenty of
- There's plenty for everyone
- We give you plenty of choices
- There's plenty more
See also: **BOUNTY, MUCH, MULTI**

PLUNGE
- Take the plunge with
- Plunge in and enjoy
- If you've been afraid to take the plunge until now
See also: **CHANCE, DARE, RISK**

POCKET
- Puts money right in your pocket
- Needn't stretch this month's pocket money
- You don't need deep pockets to buy this product
- Now you can keep more money in your pocket
- Puts savings in your pocket as soon as you walk in the door
- Pocket money right away

- To suit every pocket

See also: SAVE, SAVINGS

POCKETBOOK

- Less painful to your pocketbook
- If you have the taste but not the pocketbook
- Suits everyone's needs and pocketbook
- Goes easy on your pocketbook
- Light on the pocketbook, heavy on value
- Hang onto your pocketbook, here we come

See also: BUDGET, WALLET

POINT

- I'll get right to the point
- Which, of course, is exactly the point
- This could be the turning point
- People are beginning to get the point
- You've made your point
- The point is big benefits for you
- Knows how to make a point
- A point well taken
- Reaching the point of no return

See also: REASON

POISE

- Gain popularity, confidence and poise
- Poised to become the industry leader
- You'll be poised to win

See also: GRACE, READY, SET

POPULAR

- Wildly popular and incredibly useful
- Ever wonder why our products are so popular
- Has never been more popular
- Once again the most popular item in
- That's why we've become so popular with so many
- One of our most popular items
- Giving you the perennially popular
- Popular, year after year
- One of the leading and most popular products

Popular: in demand wanted, desired, favored, in fashion, in vogue, fashionable, stylish, all the rage, *au courant*, well-liked, successful, beloved, easily understood, everyday

See also: DEMAND, DESIRE, PEOPLE, PLEASE

POPULARITY

- Popularity continues to grow
- It's not a popularity contest
- It's popularity it proof of its effectiveness

PORTFOLIO

- Best fits your investment portfolio
- A portfolio of value for you
- Expanding your portfolio in unexpected directions
- No portfolio required
- Let us plan a balanced portfolio for you

See also: CHOICE, COLLECTION, RANGE

POSITION

- Putting you in a great position to
- Uniquely positioned to
- You couldn't be in a better position
- An excellent competitive position that translates into
- We've earned our top position

See also: LOCATION, PLACE, SITE

POSITIVE

- Do something positive for yourself
- Positively painless for everyone
- Just wait until you see the positive results
- A very positive move for you all round
- Very positive, very popular

See also: sure, certain, sound, definite, unequivocal, categorical, indisputable, confident, assured, real, veritable, optimistic, hopeful, cheering, sunny, heartening, inspiring, encouraging, promising, favorable, propitious, profitable, good, affirmative, salutary, genuine, authentic, solid, substantial
See also: HOPE, SUCCESSFUL

POSSIBILITY

- Change it from a possibility to a reality now
- Think of all the possibilities
- Imagine the unlimited possibilities of
- Discover the mind-boggling possibilities
- Open your eyes to the possibilities
- Creating new possibilities and efficiencies
- From here, the possibilities are endless
- Wake up to the wild possibilities in store for you

See also: CHANCE, CHOICE,

OPPORTUNITY, OPTION

POSSIBLE

- Was made possible by
- Suddenly, anything is possible
- Making it possible for the very first time
- In a way simply not possible before
- For less than you ever thought possible
- With us, anything is possible

Possible: likely, probable, liable to, odds-on, feasible, workable, doable, practicable, achievable, within reach, attainable, affordable, thinkable, credible, conceivable

POST

- We keep you posted
- Posting results that are incredible
- Be first past the winning post

See also: INFORM, MAIL, SEND

POSTAGE

- We'll even pay the postage
- For a mere postage stamp, you'll receive all this
- All it costs is the price of the postage
- Postage is always included

POTENCY

- The greatest potency yet
- Increase the potency of
- Have bumped up the potency to the highest levels yet
- Test the potency of

See also: POWER, STRENGTH

POTENTIAL

- Helping people achieve their potential
- Letting you free to reach your full potential
- There is a huge potential for
- Packed with potential
- Increase your potential for
- All this incredible potential can be yours for only
- Most people don't even recognize the potential

See also: OPPORTUNITY, POSSIBLE

POWER

- All of the power with none of the problems
- Increase your purchasing power

- Designed to give you the power to do more
- Puts the power in your hands
- Delivers all the power and flexibility
- Experience the sheer, exhilarating power
- Powered by personal style
- Put all this power to work for you
- Feel the surge of power
- Along with increased value power
- Take the restorative powers of
- Concentrated power
- With real staying power
- The power is yours to

See also: ABILITY, CAPACITY, ENERGY, MUSCLE, STRENGTH, STRONG

POWERFUL

- More powerful than every before
- A powerful new force has appeared
- Powerful enough for all your needs

PRACTICAL

- Both practical and beautiful
- As practical as it is rewarding
- Tough, bright and practical
- Offering a practical solution to your
- A purely practical decision
- It's what practical people do
- The smartest, most practical thing to do
- Eminently practical and classically sound

See also: USEFUL

PRACTITIONER

- A savvy practitioner of
- Experienced practitioners are at your command
- You, too, can become an expert practitioner of

See also: EXPERT, CONSULTANT, PROFESSIONAL, SPECIALIST

PRAISE

- Many products inspire praise
- You'll soon be singing the praises
- Find out why people from all corners of the world have been praising this product

See also: KUDOS

PRE-APPROVED

- You are already pre-approved
- Because you're pre-approved, you start

benefiting right away
- Pre-approved and ready to roll

PRE-OWNED
- Great pre-owned specials
- Pre-owned but still in premium condition
- Get a fine pre-owned product for a fraction of the cost of new
- A great pre-owned item is waiting for you

See also: USE

PRECIOUS
- Something this precious deserves the best
- Your high regard is very precious to us
- Taking care of the things most precious to you
- Nothing is more precious to you than

See also: RARE, SPECIAL, UNIQUE

PRECISION
- Elegance and precision make an unbeatable team
- Built with studied precision
- Always buy a precision product

See also: EXPERTISE

PREDICTABLE
- Excellent results are always predictable when you choose us
- Who wants the boring and predictable when you can have this
- Take a break from predictability with

See also: FUTURE, RELIABLE

PREFER
- Or, if you prefer
- For those who prefer
- Or, if you prefer
- More people prefer our product than any other
- Most preferred product
- You'll prefer it to all others
- Preferred above all others

See also: CHOOSE, LIKE, WANT, WISH

PREFERENCE
- Keeps your preferences in mind when
- We're glad to alter our product according to your preference
- Your preference dictates everything we do
- Simply express your preference and the

deed is done
- The number one preference is

See also: CHOICE

PREMIERE
- Premiering exclusively at
- And you can be in on the premiere
- How rarely something this splendid premieres

See also: FIRST

PREMIUM
- Pay no premium
- The industry calls it premium
- Premium products always on hand just for you
- We put your patronage at a premium
- Premium values for premium customers
- Always at a premium

See also: BEST, EXCELLENCE, FINE, GIFT, OFFER, SUPERIOR

PREPARE
- You've got to prepare now for
- Takes only minutes to prepare
- Fully prepared, oven ready
- Helping you prepare for the challenge
- We've spent years preparing for this moment
- Not just well-prepared but tasty too
- Prepare yourself for a savings blowout
- Prepare for great savings
- Personally prepared with your wants and needs in mind
- All prepared with the finest, freshest ingredients
- The way is already prepared for you

Prepare: make ready, set up, fix up, lay the groundwork, set the stage, take steps, warm up, rehearse, practice, whip into shape, tune up, review, go over, outfit, equip, furnish, supply, provide, fit out, rig out, deck out, dream up

See also: COOK, PROVIDE, READY, SUPPLY

PRESENCE
- Sheer delight each time you are in it's presence
- Conjuring up the presence of
- The most striking presence

PRESENT
- Our company proudly presents
- Presenting the number one, most awaited product
- Makes great presents
- Always present your best side
- Proudly presenting
- Present yourself with pizzazz

See also: GIFT, PREMIUM, SHOW

PRESENTATION
- Fascinating information and artful presentation
- Dazzling presentation of a brand new
- Our feature presentation
- Come and let us make a presentation
- Excellence and exquisite presentation is reflected in all our services
- Inviting you to an innovative presentation
- Designed to give better protection and preservation

Presentation: display, show, exhibit, exhibition, representation, parade, spectacle, appearance, exposure, performance, offering, gift, present, legacy, bequest, prize, award, trophy

See also: DEMONSTRATION, PITCH, SHOW

PRESERVE
- In addition to preserving your precious things beautifully
- Some things are really worth preserving
- Preserving tradition and respect for

See also: ENDURE, KEEP, PROTECT

PRESSURE
- Put some pressure on
- Today, the pressure is building
- Pressure to squeeze out more productivity than ever before
- If you're feeling the pressure
- Taking the pressure out of

See also: CHALLENGE, HASSLE, HEAT, INSIST, OBLIGATION

PRESTIGE
- It's not just about prestige
- Do you want the prestige, satisfaction and security of
- Increase your prestige with
- Our prestige is very high in our community
- The most prestigious

See also: ADMIRE, ESTEEM, PRIDE

PRETTY
- Has you sitting pretty
- Pretty and popular
- A lot more than just pretty good
- Will save you a pretty penny

See also: BEAUTIFUL

PREVENT
- Helps prevent irritation
- And you can prevent it so easily with our product
- Something that is so preventable
- You can prevent this from happening
- Prevents problems before they start

See also: AVOID, SAVE, STOP

PREVIEW
- Free preview invitation
- You are invited to preview
- Don't miss this rare preview of
- Call for an exclusive preview
- Free preview for special clients
- See this special preview
- Enjoy a free one-week preview

See also: ANTICIPATE, FUTURE

PREVIOUS
- Previously sold for
- Previously loved and now a real bargain for you
- Better than all previous models

PRICE
- At the new low price of
- Name your price
- We will beat any advertised price
- All at a very affordable price
- Price pleasers
- Special introductory price
- Buy one, get one half price
- And that's not the only thing included in the price
- Outrageously low prices
- At a price you can afford
- And not only through price
- At a sweeter price
- The lowest price you've ever seen
- Irresistible, especially at this price

- At last, priced right
- No-haggle price
- Non-negotiable bottom line price
- Big in everything but price
- Our best-priced products
- At a price that's too good to pass up
- Three great items at one great price
- Lower priced guaranteed
- Value priced for quick sale
- Unbeatable quality and price
- At an amazing low price
- Everyone has their price
- Our price is just less
- Priced not to cost the shirt off your back
- Lowest price ever
- Price chopper
- Blowout price
- A price you can live with
- A price that's hard to copy
- A truly affordable price
- Low price leader
- Best price, best advice
- Huge price drops this week
- The lowest price is right here
- We'll meet the price and beat it
- Our price guarantee means
- For a price that won't cut into your holiday money
- Listed at a fabulous price
- At one low price every day
- It's competitively priced at
- A price that includes absolutely everything
- At an unbelievably low price
- Fit-any-budget price
- More than reasonably priced
- Now at reduced price
- Let's talk about price

Price: cost, expense, charge, fee, rate, check, tab, bill, payment, hire, rent, fare, toll, tax, levy, duty, assessment, consideration, recompense, remuneration, compensation, outlay, expenditure, value, worth, amount, figure, valuation, appraisal, quotation, demand, asking price, bounty, reward, prize, stipend, consequence, result, loss, cost, damage
See also: BUY, CASH, COST, INVESTMENT, MONEY, PAY, PAYMENT, PRICES, PRICING, PURCHASE, SAVINGS, VALUE

PRICELESS
- Positively priceless
- Some things are simply priceless
- We don't try to put a price on the priceless

See also: RARE, TIMELESS, TREASURE, UNIQUE

PRICES
- Allows you to receive great prices
- Budget-pleasing prices
- Direct-to-you low prices
- We have the lowest prices
- Where low prices are just the beginning
- Best prices in town
- Everyday low prices made better
- Prices guaranteed until
- At prices you just won't believe
- You'll find all the greatest prices
- Nobody beats our prices
- Great low prices guaranteed
- Everyday low prices
- Great prices, quality guaranteed
- Amazing miracle prices
- Really stunning prices
- Calls for special prices on
- New low prices on
- Prices in effect until
- Heavenly results at down-to-earth prices
- Rock bottom sale prices
- Low prices that just won't stop
- Everyday low prices made better
- Prices are low today and everyday
- Prices guaranteed until
- Prices will never be lower
- Best prices guaranteed
- Low, low introductory prices
- Nobody beats our prices
- Prices you can afford
- Putting our prices where our mouth is
- Low, low sale prices in effect until
- Prices will be lots of fun
- New lower prices
- Best prices, superior quality
- For some of the best prices yet
- Has it all – and for low, low prices
- The highest quality at the lowest prices
- If we advertise our low, low prices, the competition will have a fit
- Excellent prices on
- Sale prices in effect this weekend only
- Lowest prices every day
- Just stellar prices every day

- At highly competitive prices
- At prices you won't mind paying
- A unique opportunity to purchase at exceptional prices
- With prices this low, it may be too late by the time you read this
- New low prices daily
- At truly original prices
- Save even more on our already low everyday prices
- A month of locked-down prices
- Our lowest prices of the season
- Red hot prices on
- The absolute rock bottom prices on

See also: PRICE

PRICING

- Power pricing for power people
- Competitive pricing at all our locations
- We've put a lot of thought into pricing
- Downright enticing pricing
- Pricing is what it's all about
- The best pricing policy in the business
- And our pricing shows it

See also: COST, PRICE

PRIDE

- Take pride in the fine quality of our
- Something we do with pride
- Built with pride
- Our staff takes pride in the fine service they provide
- We take great pride in what we create
- Inviting you to look at our pride and joy
- Take a lot of pride in our work
- Our special ingredient is pride

See also: BOAST, CONFIDENCE, ESTEEM, FEELING, PRESTIGE, PROUD

PRINCIPLE

- The principle behind it is simple
- We stand firmly in the principle that
- Our founding principles remain the same
- Sticking to tried and true principles

See also: BASE, FOUNDATION, IDEAL, ROOT, STANDARD

PRIORITY

- Make your own priority list
- What's your priority
- People like yourself are always our highest priority

- Your priorities come first
- We have no other priority
- Always in line with your priorities

Priority: urgency, precedence, seniority, rank, preference, primacy, preeminence, superiority, supremacy, importance, weightlessness, consequence

See also: CHOICE, FIRST, IMPORTANT

PRIVACY

- With complete security and privacy within your own home
- Your privacy is guaranteed
- Offering complete and total privacy
- Protect your privacy with
- A feeling of privacy
- We absolutely guarantee your privacy

PRIVATE

- It's very private and very personal
- Available to private and public alike
- For a very private experience
- Everything takes place in private

See also: CONFIDENTIAL, SECRET, UNDISCOVERED

PRIZE

- Win the most coveted prize of all
- The real prize is financial security
- The most highly prized
- Take home fabulous prizes

See also: AWARD, GIFT, PREMIUM, WIN

PRO

- Go straight to the pros
- Find out from the pros themselves all about it
- What the pros urge you to do
- Lets you perform like a pro
- The name pros trust
- Be treated like a pro
- We've got everything for the pro
- The pros can tell you that
- The pro's choice
- Hot tips from the pros
- Come in and talk to the pros

See also: CONSULTANT, EXPERT, PROFESSIONAL, SPECIALIST

PROBLEM

- Thank you for calling our attention to

this problem
- Carefully checked for possible problems
- No problem
- Not only addresses these problems but any others as well
- Now you can solve problems the same way – right in your own home
- Tired of covering up your problem
- Helps you solve specific problems
- More than just solving problems in a routine way
- Alert you to your problems
- Watch problems vanish away
- Because of our excellent ability to solve problems

Problem: riddle, poser, question, mystery, predicament, quandary, plight, pickle, hornet's nest, difficulty, trouble, affliction, handicap, disadvantage, inconvenience, nuisance, pest, headache, bother, vexation, hassle, annoyance, intractable
See also: CHALLENGE, CONCERN, HASSLE, MYSTERY, OBSTACLE, QUESTION

PROCESS
- We can quickly and easily guide you though the entire process
- The process of turning your dreams into reality
- An evolutionary process that's a combination of
- Puts you in charge of the whole process
- For prompt processing
- The process is fast and pleasurable
- Due to system error, we are currently unable to process your request
- Makes the process much more effective

See also: METHOD, WAY

PRODUCE
- Makes it possible to produce
- For a product that really produces
- Produced to your satisfaction
- One of the leading producers of

See also: CRAFT, MANUFACTURE

PRODUCT
- This product sells itself
- A valuable product or service that's always in great demand
- Our product is already used by most

manufacturers of
- Do you have energy, imagination and a great product
- We make it easier for customers to get hold of our product
- People love our product
- To help you choose the best product
- A product best suited to your needs and lifestyle
- Selected as the most desired product
- Our latest product improvement
- It's products like these that help
- Products you need in the colors you want

See also: COMMODITY, GOODS, ITEM, SAMPLE

PRODUCTIVITY
- Maximizing productivity and minimizing downtime
- Just watch productivity shoot up
- Productivity has increased every year
- High productivity means savings on
- Can boost your productivity with

See also: ACTIVITY, MAKE, SUCCESS, WORK

PROFESSIONAL
- All are designed for a professional look
- Giving you serious professional capacity
- We have professional quality products
- Do it like a professional
- A really professional level
- Designed with the professional in mind
- Help you to obtain professional results
- Committed to providing prompt, professional service
- We're listening to the professionals
- Now you can select the industry's most professional company
- Fast, professional service
- Let an experienced professional take care of everything for you
- Give yourself the professional advantage
- You need a professional to help you
- Find out what the professionals are thinking and doing when it comes to achieving
- Staffed by experienced professionals
- Our professionals believe that serving a client well means more than just a lot of talk
- Should only be done by professionals
- Knowledgeable service professionals

guarantee expert advice and superior customer service
- Our world-wide team of professionals is waiting to help you
- Demands the highest degree of professionalism
- All done in a professional manner
- Making your documents look as professional as possible
- We provide professional service
- Professionals insist on our products
- Let the professionals do it properly

Professional: skilled, knowledgeable, experienced, pro, veteran, seasoned, trained, adept, dextrous, adroit, accomplished, able, apt, gifted, talented, polished, expert, proficient, masterful, masterly, topnotch, top-flight, crack, best
See also: CONSULTANT, EXPERT, PRO, SKILL, SPECIALIST

PROFICIENT
- The most experienced and proficient
- You, too, can become proficient in no time at all
- Become more proficient in a short time with our product
See also: ABILITY, CRAFT, SKILL

PROFILE
- Giving you a higher profile in
- Need a higher profile
- Increase your profile where you need it most
See also: CHARACTER, RECOGNITION

PROFIT
- Proven low risk and all profit
- Guaranteed to explode your profits
- Translates directly into profit for you
- An opportunity you can profit from immediately
- High profit margins
- How would you like an even bigger profit
- Profit from inside information
- Your partner in profit
- Everyone can profit from
- Attracts profits from every direction
- Incredible profits can be yours
- Now your profits are your own
- Adds up to profits for you

- How to develop profitable results

Profit: gain, return, yield, interest, income, revenue, net, bottom line, winnings, proceeds, remuneration, recompense, surplus, excess, gravy, advantage, benefit, help, aid, service, good, efficiency, use, usefulness, furtherance, improvement, betterment
See also: BENEFIT, BOTTOM LINE, BOUNTY, GAIN, IMPROVEMENT, INTEREST, SAVINGS, VALUE, WIN

PROGRAM
- Thousands of people have used the program to
- Able to participate in this highly profitable program
- A proven, cash generating program
- The program offers significant savings
- Invest in your own money-building program
- We tailor our program to meet your specific needs
- Easier to program
- We have designed this program specially for you
- Ask about our program to
- We offer a self-starting program
- Examine the entire program to see
- Discover why we offer a complete program
- One of the most comprehensive programs ever introduced
- The diversity of programs available
- Programs to meet your individual performance requirements
- Our most popular, full-featured care program
- Consider the economical, effective programs offered by
- Properly designed programs are the key to controlling
- A richly varied program of
See also: DESIGN, INFORMATION, PLAN, SYSTEM

PROGRESS
- We've made great progress to date
- Join the march of progress today
- Riding the leading edge of progress
- Progress has arrived
- Described as a work in progress
See also: ADVANCE, CHANGE,

FUTURE, LEAP

PROJECT
- For every project, big or small
- Taking care to plan the project in every detail
- We manage and complete the entire project for you
- Now you can complete your project
- Our associates can help with your projects
- Plus exciting new projects
- Big project promotion
- Whatever the size of your project

PROMISE
- That's a promise
- We don't just promise, we deliver
- Deliver on the promise of quality and value every day
- That's a promise we always deliver
- Our promise to you
- Fulfilled the promise that
- No longer just a promise, but a dazzling reality
- We do everything exactly as we have promised or you don't pay a penny
- The joy and satisfaction of a promise kept
- Helping people keep their promises
- Making good on the promise of
- Showing so much promise
- You'll find it's a promise kept
- We keep our promises faithfully
- Fulfilling every bit of promise

Promise: pledge, assurance, word of honor, vow, oath, declaration, testimony, affirmation, obligation, guarantee, warranty
See also: GUARANTEE, PLEDGE, WORD

PROMOTE
- Promoting itself as the highest standard
- There's really only one place to promote
- Everything it's promoted to be
- Rightfully promoting this product as the very best

Promote: encourage, hearten, boost, build up, raise, lift, support, sanction, back, sustain, uphold, hold up, maintain, improve, strengthen, amend, make better, upgrade, help, develop, enrich, enhance, augment, contribute to, benefit, advance, facilitate, foster, nourish, nurture, aid, help, abet, advocate, advertise, introduce, make known, persuade, convince
See also: ADVERTISE, BENEFIT, BOOST, ENHANCE, HELP, MARKET, PERSUADE, PUSH, RECOMMEND, SELL

PROMOTION
- Big project promotion
- Our most exciting promotion of the year
- Take advantage of this huge promotion
- The best value promotion
See also: PROMOTE, SALE

PROMPT
- Please do it promptly
- Promptly performed and reasonably priced
- Assured of prompt and courteous service every time
- We'll prompt you when you need it
See also: FAST, SOON

PROOF
- Just look at the proof
- Here's proof from people who have succeeded
- Offers solid proof that
- Give you the proof you need to choose us
- If you need any more proof, just watch
- Simply proof that we're the best

PROTECT
- A smart, simple way to protect
- Protect your investment
- Protect your family first
- Relax, you're protected 24 hours a day
- Two ways to protect the things you buy
- Protects beautifully
- Nothing protects better
- Protect yourself with total coverage
- Nothing else protects your investment quite as well
- Protect it with
- To preserve and protect
- Now you'll be fully protected
- Protect your dearest with the best
See also: LOCK, SAVE, SECURE

PROTECTION
- Get the ultimate protection

- Give your loved ones protection for life
- That means better protection
- Protection against theft or damage
- Protection for your peace of mind
- A professional level of protection
- There's no better protection than
- For the protection you need
- For added protection
- When you need protection against
- Provides quality protection for
- This research has led to one of the most powerful protection programs
- Treat yourself to the added protection
- Total body protection
- For more concentrated protection
- Delivers excellent protection
- Giving you all-season protection
- Take protection with you
- In short, if you still don't have proper protection
- Protection against the inevitable
- Don't take chances when you can get the ultimate protection with
- Offering the highest level of protection possible

Protection: preservation, conservation, care, safekeeping, maintenance, upkeep, safety, security, defence, guard, safeguard, shield, bulwark, barrier, wall, cover, screen, sanctuary, asylum, safety zone, shelter, refuge, haven, harbor, precaution, preventative measure, insurance
See also: SAFETY, SECURITY

PROTOTYPE
- Developing proof-of-concept prototypes
- The very prototype of
- The prototype is available for viewing
- Springing from the most advanced prototype ever to

See also: BEGINNING, EXAMPLE, MODEL, SAMPLE, START

PROUD
- Proud to help keep it that way
- You'll be proud of what you're doing
- You have every reason to be proud
- As much as we are proud of our service and product
- Make them proud of you
- That's why we're so proud of
- **See also: BOAST, CONFIDENCE,**

PRIDE

PROVE
- That's why studies prove that this product does more in less time that
- To prove it to you, we'll let you try it free
- Prove it yourself
- Let us prove to you what our professionals can do
- Over and over again, our customers prove that
- Now you can prove conclusively that our product is better
- Let us prove to you just how much we have to offer
- Now is a great time to let us prove

See also: CLINICAL, PROVEN, RESEARCH, SCIENTIFIC, TEST

PROVEN
- We've proven it with quality
- The proven one
- Proven time and time again
- One of nature's most time proven

PROVIDE
- Always pleased to provide
- Providing the finest service to valued customers like you
- We can provide you with instant
- Taking care to always provide the best

Provide: furnish, supply, contribute, accommodate, equip, outfit, afford, yield, produce, present, serve, give, bestow, endow, attend to, take care of, render
See also: GIVE, SERVE, SUPPLY

PROVIDER
- The leading provider of
- Welcome to the world's premier provider of high-quality
- The most qualified provider in business today

See also: SUPPLIER

PROVING GROUND
- Think of it as a proving ground
- A proving ground for client/server applications
- Has long been a proving ground for the toughest

See also: PROVE, TEST

PROVOCATION
- Pure provocation from
- Do you consider it a provocation or a challenge
- Wear it as a glorious provocation

See also: CHALLENGE, DARE

PSYCHE
- Fast, strong, psyched
- Designed for extroverted psyches
- Appealing to the wildest part of the human psyche

See also: CHARACTER, MIND, PSYCHE

PULL
- Keeps pulling you back
- You'll be amazing at the pulling power
- Pulls in more profits for less output
- Give in to the powerful pull of

See also: ATTRACT, DRAW

PUMP
- We're totally pumped for
- Keeping you pumped up and hot for action
- Pumping out more excitement than ever before

See also: BOOST, ENHANCE, HYPE, IMPROVE

PUNCH
- More punch than ever
- Just punch out this number
- The punch delivered in everything from
- Pumped up to give it some punch
- Adds some real punch to your
- Punched-up value

See also: BLAST, BLITZ, HIT, IMPACT, STRENGTH, STRIKE

PUNCTUAL
- Punctual and professional
- Our service people are always punctual
- Being punctual is one of our virtues

See also: TIME

PUNISHMENT
- Can take all kinds of punishment
- Stands up to the worst punishment you can give
- Built for the punishment of

See also: ENDURE, STRENGTH

PURCHASE
- Nothing else to purchase
- Save on virtually every purchase
- Purchases are made at today's prices
- You are invited to purchase
- Good for one purchase only
- We made an incredible purchase from one of the leading names in
- Remember, you get a free gift with every purchase
- No minimum purchase
- Purchase this fine product for only
- The convenience of being able to make purchases just about anywhere
- We arrange to have your purchases delivered
- Call this number now to purchase
- With every purchase you make
- Purchasing our products is convenient and secure
- Free with your every purchase
- Free with any purchase
- Take advantage of this special purchase
- A huge special purchase
- Now you can purchase it so easily
- Actually available to you for purchase
- Save on all your purchases

See also: BUY, MERCHANDISE, OFFER, SALE

PURE
- There's something so pure about
- Only the purest and finest
- Nothing but pure enjoyment

See also: CLEAN, NATURAL

PURPOSE
- We have products for every purpose
- Designed with a purpose
- Our purpose is to please you
- Made with a single purpose in mind
- Never wavered from our set purpose

See also: AIM, FUNCTION, GOAL, MISSION

PURVEYOR
- The exclusive purveyor of
- For a hundred years, purveyors of fine products
- Now your local purveyor of
- Your neighborhood purveyor will be glad to help you

See also: PROVIDER, RETAILER,

SELLER, SUPPLIER

PUT
- We put a lot into our product
- We really want your input
- We always put you first
- Putting your needs ahead of everything else

See also: **PLACE, PROVIDE, SUPPLY**

QUALIFY
- Listen to discover whether or not you qualify
- You qualify instantly for
- Listen to find out if you qualify
- As one of an exclusive few qualified to serve you
- You may be already qualified for
- Reply now to qualify

See also: **APPROVAL, CLASSIFY, MEASURE, WIN**

QUALITY
- You can always trust the quality
- Professional quality
- Until you are totally convinced of its quality
- Convinced of the high quality and value
- Provider of quality worldwide
- You won't find better quality anywhere
- Pleased to announce the highest level of quality and service
- Unbeatable quality and service at a price you'll love
- Offer superlative quality for the price
- Where quality is an important factor
- Lowering prices, not quality
- When it comes to quality, you just can't beat
- Qualities we'd all like to have
- We refuse to give in on quality
- First quality all the way
- Just feel the quality
- Good quality doesn't have to be expensive
- Quality assurance
- Offering quality without compromise
- The quality you want at the price you need
- Providing you with the best quality at great prices
- The ultimate in quality
- Now offering a wide range of quality products
- Quality you can trust at the nation's lowest prices
- Exudes quality in every respect
- Preferring quality over quantity
- Quality guaranteed
- Experience the difference quality makes
- Quality manufactured from
- Quality from start to finish
- Quality products at warehouse prices
- We have all the top quality products you're looking for
- Because quality takes precedence over quantity
- You'll love the homemade quality of
- Quality is a non-negotiable concept
- Hospital quality
- Best quality ever
- Our concern for quality can be seen in our customer service
- Exceptional quality at an amazing low price
- Compare our quality and price anywhere
- Quality and value are guaranteed
- Unbeatable quality and price
- Committed to quality, value selection and service
- Full line of quality
- You'll love the quality
- Finest quality ever
- Enables us to provide you with a top quality product
- Handcrafted quality
- Far less than what you would expect to pay for this great quality
- Start at an unprecedented-for-quality-price of just
- For consistent quality insist upon the best
- Now you find all the same qualities in the exciting new

Quality: characteristic, property, attribute, distinction, note, cachet, feature, trait, virtue, quirk, nature, kind, grade, sort, style, particular, element, personality, disposition, tendency, bias, leaning, penchant, predisposition, innate, endowment, gift, talent, genius, faculty, knack, badge, earmark, trademark, forte, strong point, selling point, merit, advantage, superiority, excellence, class, eminence, preeminence, greatness, nobility, fineness, worth, value, supremacy, perfection, status, standing, notability, elite,

privilege
See also: BEST, EXCELLENCE, MERIT, NATURE, PROOF, VALUE

QUANTITY
- Always putting quality before quantity
- Limited quantities available
- Due to anticipated high demand, quantities will be limited to
- While quantities last
- Preferring excellence over quantity
- Quantities may not last long enough to satisfy every customer

Quantity: amount, substance, measure, extent, content, capacity, sum, whole, lot, lots and lots, share, portion, quota, batch
See also: BOUNTY, MUCH, PLENTY

QUEEN
- Truly fit for a queen
- Now you can be the queen of your domain
- A queen would be proud to wear it
- Makes you feel like a queen

See also: COMMAND, GODDESS, LEADER, RULE, WOMAN. WISDOM

QUENCH
- Quench your thirst for
- Tart, quenching and thoroughly pleasurable
- Quenching a raging need for

See also: SATISFY

QUEST
- A passionate statement about our quest
- Supporting your quest for the perfect
- The answer to your quest for

See also: JOURNEY, RESEARCH, SEARCH, VOYAGE

QUESTION
- Always available to answer your questions
- Now on hand to answer all your questions
- Happy to answer any questions you may have about
- If you have any questions, just call
- Ask these key questions to help you choose
- Your local center will be happy to assist

you with any questions you may have
- If you have any specific questions, ask to speak to
- Ask yourself these questions
- Wave goodbye, no questions asked
- When you have the right questions, we have the answers

Question: query, inquiry, problem, issue, enigma, puzzle, riddle, mystery
See also: ASK, DEMAND, INFORMATION, INQUIRY, MYSTERY

QUICK
- Quick 'n easy
- The quick way to
- Does it even quicker
- Nothing is quicker than
- You really can get rich quick
- Ten times a quick as the old method

See also: FAST, INSTANT, SPEED

QUIET
- To preserve the calm and quiet of
- Very flamboyant in a quiet way
- Quietly becoming the best
- The quiet look is deceiving

QUIRK
- Quirkiness at its best
- Takes all of your quirks into account
- No unexpected quirks or kinks
- Take advantage of this quirk in the market

See also: TRICK

QUOTATION
- Phone for a free quotation
- We'll beat any written quotation
- Always the most competitive quotation
- We'll match and better any quotation you bring us

See also: ESTIMATE, EVALUATION, PRICE, VALUE

QUOTE
- No-obligation, hassle-free quote right over the phone
- Call now for a fast, no-obligation quote
- Call for a quote and be pleasantly surprised
- Guaranteeing a fair and reasonable quote
- We can have a detailed quote for you

within a day
See also: ESTIMATE, MEASURE

RADIANCE
- Enhancing your own individual radiance
- Seem to shine with a special radiance all their own
- The real radiance has to come from the inside

See also: GLITTER, LUSTRE, SHINE

RAIN CHECK
- We are pleased to provide a rain check on any item not available during this promotion
- You can always get a rain check
- If an item is out of stock, take a rain check

See also: ALTERNATIVE

RAINBOW
- A pot of gold at the end of this rainbow
- Paint it with rainbows
- This rainbow is just for you

See also: COLOUR, HUE, SHADE

RAKE
- Rake in the savings
- You, too, can rake in the profits
- Raking up some new ideas

See also: COLLECT, GATHER

RANGE
- This is made possible through a range of
- We offer an even wider range of
- Only our product comes with a full range of options
- Enjoy a complete range of
- Choose from our huge range of
- Noteworthy for the wide range and quality of its
- That's why we've developed a range of premium quality products
- Offering a comprehensive range of products and services to meet your needs
- Get the complete range of benefits

See also: ALTERNATIVE, ARRAY, CHOICE, COLLECTION, DISPLAY, OPTION

RANK
- Ranked as one of the best
- Constantly ranked as the top
- We've earned top rankings
- When you're ranked among the top
- Call now to join the ranks of successful
- Always in the top ranks
- Ranked by relevancy
- Now ranked at the pinnacle

See also: LEVEL, POSITION, TIER

RARE
- Have become exceedingly rare and valuable
- If you believe good service is rare
- It's that rarest of things
- A thing of rare delight
- A rare pleasure at your fingertips

See also: UNIQUE

RATE
- Find the best rate available
- Thousands have switched for lower rates
- At a very competitive rate
- We offer reasonable rates
- Up front flat rate pricing
- To lock in these great rates
- Continue to save with an ongoing rate
- If your rates haven't gone down
- Translate into the best rate in the business
- Rated number one more times than any other
- Scrambling to keep up with the rate of change
- Our best labor rate is
- Our success rate is well above the average
- Offering more than just competitive rates
- Rates take a tumble
- Hurry – bonus rates available only on
- You get preferred rates
- Rates shown subject to change
- The most comprehensive, all-inclusive rates
- Have always received the highest possible ratings for
- Rated tops for strength and security
- Highly competitive rates
- Call today for rates and additional information
- Call for discounted rates

See also: CASH, GRADE, INTEREST, MONEY, PACE, PRICE, SAVINGS, SPEED, VALUE

RATHER
- What would you rather be doing
- When you'd rather be golfing
- We know there's a dozen things you'd rather do
- We'd rather be helping you save money
- Rather than wait
- Wouldn't you rather enjoy

See also: ALTERNATIVE

RE-ENGINEER
- Thoroughly re-engineered to
- Working to re-engineer it to your specification
- A reliable program re-engineered

RE-INTERPRET
- Dramatically re-interpreted for
- Have to re-interpret some old, familiar ideas
- Come and see your world re-interpreted

RE-OPENING
- Grand re-opening party
- Re-opening after extensive renovations to better serve you
- Re-opening better than ever
- Re-opening under new management

REACH
- Reach us fast
- Reach for the best
- Reach more people faster with
- It's all within your reach
- If your reach exceeds your grasp, we can change all that
- Reaches you faster than any other
- Giving you ways to reach millions of new customers
- Now within your reach
- Reach out and take hold of
- You only have to reach out

See also: CONTACT, COMMUNICATE, TOUCH

REACTION
- The reaction has been overwhelming
- We can't wait to see your reaction
- Your reaction says it all
- Faster reaction, faster solutions
- Just watch the reaction of your friends
- A natural reaction to seeing the best

READ
- Read on to discover how
- Read all about it
- Don't believe everything you read
- You've been reading the glowing reports, now come see for yourself
- Easy to read and understand

See also: UNDERSTAND

READY
- We're not quite ready for you yet
- Always ready for you
- Ready or not, here they come
- So get ready for our all new
- Ready to go
- Get ready for
- We're getting ready to
- Are you ready for this
- Ready to rock and roll
- We'll be happy to get you ready now
- Primed and ready to
- You've been ready for this for a long time
- Now you're ready for anything
- Ready for rain or shine
- Ready when you are
- Get ready to shake, rattle and rock

See also: EXPECT, NOW, PREPARE

REAL
- Nothing feels as real as
- Just real products for real people
- Make it real by getting a
- Get real with
- Nothing beats the real thing
- When you're looking for real value and savings, come to us

See also: AUTHENTIC, GENUINE, TRUE

REALISM
- Enjoy the spirited realism of
- Giving an even greater sense of realism
- Total realism is our goal

REALISTIC
- Most realistic ever
- Meeting very realistic expectations
- It's completely realistic to expect top quality from

REALITY
- Get used to the new reality

- Making your dreams a reality
- Is it time for a reality check
- Now it can be a reality for you
- It's often a hard reality that
- Nothing comes closer to reality than

REALIZE

- Do you realize what this means
- Realize your dreams sooner
- As soon as you realize the advantages, you'll choose us
- It's that realization that separates us from the rest

See also: UNDERSTAND

REASON

- Just one more reason why
- The reason is delightfully simple
- Count the reasons
- The reason is simple
- A great reason to get it now
- Really good reasons to come
- Seeming to defy reason
- The reason is simple
- All these things add up to some very good reasons why
- People tell us the number one reason
- Just another reason people trust us
- Seeming to defy reason
- As good a reason as any
- There's no reason to let
- The number one reason why
- It stands to reason that it's the one thing you shouldn't scrimp on
- Now there's no reason not to
- Ten reasons why we're number one
- The top ten reasons to
- Giving you more reasons to buy
- More great reasons to shop at
- It's for these reasons and many more that we've
- Do it for all your own reasons
- Here are just a few of the reasons why people buy

See also: CHOICE, GOAL, MISSION, PURPOSE

REBATE

- Mail-in rebate saves you big
- Our rebates are bigger
- Big rebates available on
- Worth it for the rebate alone

REBORN

- Reborn for peace
- A familiar product totally reborn
- You'll be utterly reborn

See also: RENEW

RECIPE

- A surefire recipe for success
- The recipe is simple
- We add a lot of love to the recipe
- Spectacular in your favorite recipes

See also: FORMULA, INFORMATION

RECKON

- Something to reckon with
- Maybe you didn't reckon on something like this
- We reckon you're right
- Better by anybody's reckoning
- You reckon right when you choose our service

See also: CONSIDER, CHOOSE, INVOLVE, MEASURE

RECOGNITION

- Increasing the recognition factor
- The opportunity to gain recognition
- Basking in international recognition
- We've earned the recognition of

See also: KNOW, PROFILE

RECOGNIZE

- That smart people have learned to recognize and seek out
- Recognized as being number one
- Widely recognized in the industry
- You may not even recognize the new, improved
- Something you'll recognize instantly
- Recognized as the best

See also: SPOT, UNDERSTAND

RECOMMEND

- Would gladly recommend to others
- Highly recommend this business
- Not recommended for those afraid to
- Recommended by professionals
- More experts recommend our product
- Very proud to recommend
- Highly recommended everywhere

Recommend: approve, commend, promote, speak well of, put in a good word for,

sanction, favor, plug, tout, cry up, endorse, uphold, second, vouch for, underwrite, back, guarantee, suggest, offer, propose, advance, prescribe
See also: ADVANCE, PROMOTE

RECONFIGURE
- Reconfigure spaces to better suit your
- It can be an easy matter to reconfigure your
- Reconfigured regularly to keep on the cutting edge
See also: CHANGE, IMPROVE, RENEW

RECORD
- Once again the industry leader has broken the record for
- With a proven track record
- A proven track record for quality and reliability that assures
- An impressive record for
- Nobody can compare with our track record
- Our record speaks for itself
- Makes it even easier to record
See also: INFORMATION

RECOVERY
- Less shock, faster recovery
- You can make a quick recovery from
- A recovery system that saves you more

RECRUIT
- Now recruiting experienced workers
- We want to recruit you
- First, we recruit the very best
- Recently recruited and loving it
See also: ATTRACT, JOIN

RED INK
- Mops up red ink
- Get rid of red ink immediately
- Never have to look at red ink in your accounts
See also: CHALLENGE, HASSLE, LOSS, PROBLEM

REDEFINE
- You can see why it redefines
- Redefine your needs
- Helping you redefine yourself
- Redefining excellence

REDESIGN
- We have completely redesigned
- Every component has been redesigned to increase efficiency
- Now you can redesign your life today
- Redesigned into a brand new

REDUCE
- And the cost has recently been reduced
- Some models reduced up to
- Goes straight to work reducing
- Prices reduced yet again to save you money
- Now we're able to reduce costs even more
- Designed to greatly reduce
- You'll find we've reduced the price on many items
- Reduced the price to make them more appealing
See also: CHOP, LESS, LOSS, MINIMIZE, SALE SAVE

REDUCTION
- Further reductions now in effect
- Drastic reductions
- Don't miss these huge price reductions
- Reductions of up to
See also: SALE, SAVINGS

REFERENCE
- A handy reference tool
- Changing all your points of reference
- Just ask for our references, they're impressive
- References always supplied
See also: KNOWLEDGE

REFINEMENT
- It's all about the refinement of things
- A further refinement is
- For people of refinement and taste
See also: ELEGANCE, SMOOTH

REFLECTION
- Get an honest reflection of
- There's no more accurate a reflection of the times than
- A reflection of your tastes and needs
- A reflection of today's hottest trends
See also: MATCH, MIRROR

REFRESH
- Helps to refresh the body and the mind
- Wake refreshed, not tired
- Always refreshing, always fresh
- Refresh your whole body with
- Refresh your point of view
- For a truly refreshing change

See also: REGENERATE,
REJUVENATE, RENEW, REVITALIZE

REFUND
- If you're not satisfied, we'll refund your money completely
- Call us for a full refund
- We'll issue you a complete refund
- If you are not satisfied for any reason, just return the product for a complete refund
- We'll refund your money on the spot
- Return it for a refund on
- We'll not only refund your money, we'll also
- Prompt refunds for your convenience
- Fully refundable and can be changed at any time
- Always a guaranteed refund if you're not satisfied in any way
- We'll issue you a complete refund
- If you are not completely satisfied, return it for a full refund

Refund: restore, replace, return, repay, give back, pay back, recompense, compensate, remunerate, reimburse, remit, make compensation, satisfy, adjust, settle, square, make amends, redress, make good, make restitution, cover, indemnify, redeem, rebate, repayment, reimbursement, allowance, cut, discount
See also: COUPON, PROFIT, RETURN,
SALE, SATISFY, VALUE

REGENERATE
- Able to regenerate growth quickly
- Regenerating interest in a big way
- Regenerate business no matter how big your setback
- Thanks to natural regeneration

See also: REFRESH, REJUVENATE,
RENEW, RENOVATION, REVITALIZE

REGISTER
- Register now and get a gift coupon
- As soon as you register, you get all this
- Register and win
- Register all your friends too
- Thank you for registering

See also: JOIN

REGRET
- Don't be fooled into something you'll regret
- You'll never regret your decision
- Make a no-regrets purchase

See also: APOLOGIZE, SORRY

REGULAR
- Saves you money on a regular basis
- Save even at regular prices
- Regularly excellent

See also: CONVENTIONAL,
ORDINARY, STANDARD

REINVENT
- Reinventing ourselves every day
- Helping you reinvent yourself to stay ahead of the curve
- Do it without having to reinvent the wheel

REJUVENATE
- Because it helps rejuvenate
- Watch it rejuvenate your
- A wonderful rejuvenating influence
- We all need a little rejuvenation now and then

See also: REFRESH, REGENERATE,
RENEW, RENOVATION, REVITALIZE

RELATIONSHIP
- The key to a meaningful relationship
- Launching a glorious relationship between
- Plans include a relationship marketing program
- The relationship can seem almost mystical
- We value our relationship with you enormously
- Hope this will be the start of a longstanding relationship

See also: FRIEND, FRIENDSHIP,
PARTNERSHIP

RELAX
- Why not relax

- Relax in a quaint and cosy atmosphere
- Just sit back, relax and leave the rest to us
- When you really want to just relax and have fun
- Finally, you can relax
- You'll enjoy relaxing
- Now you can be relaxed about
- Gives you more time to relax and
- So relax and enjoy without worry

See also: COMFORT, EASE, FREE, FREEDOM, MELLOW, REDUCE

RELEASE
- Releases extra burst of
- Just released this week
- The latest release is being snapped up from the shelves
- Get advance notice of new releases
- Announcing the release of a spectacular new product

See also: FREE, UNLOCK

RELIABILITY
- Over a century of rock-solid reliability
- Improving the reliability of your
- Proven reliability
- Rest assured about the reliability
- Reliability is our middle name
- Reliability you can count on

See also: DEPENDABILITY, TRUST

RELIABLE
- Nothing proves so reliable as
- Everything should be this reliable
- The most reliable in the business
- Designed for people who depend on reliable performance
- Reliable service, reliable prices
- You just can't get more reliable than this

See also: ENDURE, LAST, SAFE

RELIEF
- I'm so relieved to be able to tell you
- Bringing instant relief for
- Natural relief within reach
- Transform discomfort into blessed relief
- Puts natural relief within reach
- For fast-acting relief
- Giving you quickest relief
- For fast relief from
- You won't believe the relief
- What a wonderful relief to

- Isn't it a relief to

See also: COMFORT, EASE, FREEDOM

RELY
- You can always rely on us
- Someone you can rely on
- That's why so many successful people like you rely upon
- One thing you can always rely upon
- That's why so many people, just like you, rely on
- We're the company folks have always relied on to take care of
- You can rely on dozens of
- Thousands rely on us every day

See also: BANK, CONFIDENCE, DEPEND, FAITH, TRUST

REMARKABLE
- Truly remarkable
- It's remarkable that so many
- Making all the difference between the ordinary and the remarkable
- A remarkable change in

See also: FAMOUS, NOTE, NOTICE, SPECIAL

REMEMBER
- Why not remember this day by
- Remember your loved ones with the best
- Make it a night to remember
- Remember how lovely it was to
- Someone people remember
- Always remembering your individual tastes and needs

See also: MEMORY, REMIND

REMIND
- Time to remind yourself of the benefits
- We don't need to remind anyone of the need for
- Will always remind you of your happiest moments
- Take a moment to remind yourself about the importance of
- There to remind you
- Reminds you when to renew

See also: REMEMBER

REMINDER
- Just a reminder that
- A constant reminder that no matter how far you

- When you need a little reminder
- Give them a beautiful reminder that you care

See also: NOTE

REMINISCENT

- A sense of scale and detail reminiscent of a grander age
- Reminiscent of the great masters
- You don't have time for reminiscences

See also: COPY, REMIND, VINTAGE

REMOVE

- It even removes
- Removes even the toughest
- Just one remove from paradise
- Removes your biggest worry

See also: AVOID, ELIMINATE, PREVENT

RENEW

- Renew your acquaintance with an old friend
- Renewed just for you
- Renew yourself with
- Please renew now
- Automatically renewed for your convenience
- Feel renewed all day
- A very renewing experience

See also: REFRESH, REGENERATE, REJUVENATE, RENOVATION, REVITALIZE

RENOVATE

- Renovate with a company you can trust
- Renovate with confidence
- Helping you renovate from the start of your project to the end

RENOVATION

- Your quality renovation specialists
- When complete renovation is called for, trust us
- Celebrating with these incredible renovation deals
- Low-cost renovations with topnotch quality

See also: REFRESH, REGENERATE, REJUVENATE, RENEW, REVITALIZE

RENOVATOR

- Our renovators will help you determine

which kind you need
- Even the inexperienced renovator can handle it easily
- A magnet for renovators

RENOWN

- Internationally renowned
- A quickly spreading renown for
- Renowned for quality and service
- Only adding to our renown

See also: CELEBRITY, FAMOUS, NOTE

REPAIR

- Repairs almost any kind of damage
- We'll repair it for you free
- For exchange or repair
- Repairs are included

See also: OVERHAUL, RESTORE

REPEAT

- Repeat of a sell-out
- Get repeat business every time
- There's certainly no need to repeat the importance of
- And now back for a repeat performance
- We're about to repeat the miracle
- An even grander repeat of last year's blowout

See also: COPY, DUPLICATE, REPRODUCE

REPLACE

- Replaced, free, with no time limit
- We'll replace any damaged item
- If it breaks, we'll replace it fast
- We'll replace it free
- It's time to replace your clunky old product with something new

See also: DUPLICATE, REFUND, RENEW

REPLACEMENT

- A replacement will soon be in your hands
- You'll certainly find a replacement among our vast selection
- When you need a fast replacement, come to us

See also: DUPLICATE

REPLY

- Reply today to be sure to get
- We're eagerly awaiting your reply
- We reply to your query with one business

day
See also: ANSWER, RESPONSE

REPORT
- We're happy to report that
- Here's what you'll discover inside this invaluable report
- Our customers are reporting a lot of pleasure and satisfaction
- When you report back to us, we pay attention

See also: INFORMATION, RECORD

REPRESENT
- Always representing the best
- Represented a breadth of products and services unequalled by any other retailer
- There is no better way to represent your business
- Representing ourselves as exactly what we are – the best

See also: DEMONSTRATE, IMITATION, SHOW

REPRODUCE
- Have been scrupulously reproduced
- Reproducing the wonderful experience again and again
- Reproduced for half the cost
- Makes it so easy to reproduce

See also: COPY, DUPLICATE

REPUTATION
- Built a reputation for excellence over the years
- Our reputation keeps customers coming back
- Reputation based on an unchanging formula
- Living up to its reputation is this splendid
- Nothing can tarnish our reputation
- We put our reputation on the line every day
- With a reputation as solid as your own
- A reputation built upon the trust and confidence of customers like you
- Our reputation is built on solutions
- We bet our reputation
- Reputation for offering quality and value is renowned

Reputation: name, repute, regard, standing, status, rank, station, position, good name, respect, esteem, honor, laurels, fame, renown, celebrity, notoriety, prestige, authority, influence, importance, acclaim, recognition, noteworthy, distinction, lustre, approbation
See also: CELEBRITY, ESTEEM, FAMOUS, NAME, RENOWN

REQUIRE
- Requires nothing more than the right
- Providing you with everything you require
- Whatever you require, we have
- Just tell us what you require and we'll custom order

See also: ASK, DEMAND, NEED, OBLIGATE

RESEARCH
- Developed through scientific research
- Take advantage of our outstanding research team
- Extensive research is an absolute necessity
- It's called research
- Our research never stops
- Enhancement through ongoing research
- Through this extensive research, we find
- Advances in research now enable you to do something about

Research: investigation, inquiry, analysis, study, scrutiny, fact-finding, probe, exploration, assessment, appraisal, search, quest, survey, review, examine, seek
See also: ADVANCE, BREAKTHROUGH, DISCOVER, INFORMATION, REPORT, SEARCH

RESERVATION
- No additional booking or reservation fees
- Your reservation is waiting
- You'll have no reservations about performance or quality

RESERVE
- Always reserved for you
- Reserve the very best for your family
- Reserve yours now
- Hurry, you must reserve before
- Call now to reserve
- A reserved seat is waiting for you
- Continually keeping something in

reserve for you
See also: BOOK

RESIST
- Sometimes you just can't resist
- Resist if you can
- Don't even try to resist
- Won't be able to resist you when you wear
- Who can resist
- To resist is futile
- One temptation you don't have to resist
- Better able to resist the damaging effects

See also: BATTLE, FIGHT, WAR

RESOURCE
- This invaluable resource is the most authoritative
- The largest resource for
- Your resource guide to
- Your resource center
- You can't afford to be without this invaluable resource any longer
- Link up to a national resource
- Discover the latest in resources and services
- Providing the kind of resources you'll find valuable
- Are your resources spread too thin
- Telling us about the kind of resources you'll find valuable

Resource: asset, support, help, reserve, source, cache, storehouse, savings, wealth, property, real estate, goods, possessions, holdings, income, revenue, profits, gains, money, bucks, funds, finances, belongings, capital, cash, wherewithal, effects, estate, accounts receivable, securities, bonds, stocks, notes, inventory, goodwill, skill, know-how, knowledge
See also: ADVANTAGE, MONEY, INFORMATION, KNOWLEDGE, PROFIT, SKILL

RESPECT
- Respect and honesty are foremost
- One of the largest and most respected
- A highly-respected
- The world's most respected
- Determined to gain your respect
- Someone the competition respects
- With some of the most respected

products in the world
See also: ESTEEM, REPUTATION

RESPOND
- Respond to your request within an hour or less
- It costs you nothing to respond
- If you respond right away
- Respond now and receive extremely low interest rates
- Responds instantly
- Responding to all your needs
- We respond faster than anyone else
- We respond to what you want
- We're responding to what you've been telling us
- Watch people respond to you in a whole new way

See also: ANSWER, REPLY

RESPONSE
- To instantly select the optimum response
- We expect a tremendous response to this offer
- Elicited a boisterous response
- Measuring success by the huge response
- Everything depends on your response
- Giving you a better, quicker response
- Your response is important to us

See also: ANSWER

RESPONSIBILITY
- Bearing full responsibility for
- We see this as a great privilege and responsibility
- You don't have to carry the responsibility all alone when we're nearby to help
- We'll take all the responsibility

RESPONSIBLE
- Has been consistently responsible
- Responsible for your success
- We're the responsible party
- Responsible directly to you
- A very responsible organization
- Responsible for more happy customers than any other

See also: ANSWER, LOAD

RESPONSIVE
- Our most responsive ever
- Very responsive to your needs

- With till you feel the responsiveness
- You also get the improved responsiveness you need

See also: AWARENESS, SENSITIVE

REST
- The best of the rest
- And the rest is history
- Get deep, peaceful rest
- Just leave the rest to us
- And we'll do the rest

See also: COMFORT, RELAX, SLEEP

RESTORE
- Restore rather than replace
- Will restore your confidence instantly
- Restoring excellence

See also: DUPLICATE, OVERHAUL, REPAIR, REPLACE

RESTRICTION
- Some restrictions apply
- Absolutely no restrictions upon
- Lifted the restrictions on
- Avoid all those annoying restrictions
- Certain restrictions may apply

See also: BOUNDARY, EDGE, ENVELOPE, LIMIT

RESULT
- Produced a truly amazing result the first time out
- For top results
- Helping you achieve great results
- Visible results begin in
- Blazing fast results
- Providing immediate results
- Results which intensify over time
- To measurably increase results
- Compare our performance results with that of
- We are results-oriented
- You can swear by the results
- For optimum results
- Helps give you professional results
- You'll be very satisfied with the results
- Best possible results will be achieved
- Simply heavenly results
- There simply isn't a more cost-effective way of obtaining guaranteed, professional results
- You get great results
- Results that pull ahead of the pack

- Guaranteed permanent results
- If you want results, come to us
- Promising early results
- The result may well be the most exciting product to date
- You'll see these results in just days
- Yes, you can really see results this soon
- Giving you the results you want
- Because every case is different, your results are unique for you
- The result was incredible
- Guarantees better results
- You'll see the results in days
- With truly extraordinary results
- You'll love the results
- Giving you better results every time
- We guarantee results or money back

Result: outcome, conclusion, effect, issue, end, upshot, consequence, spin-off, development, harvest, crop, resolution, feedback, answer

See also: PROFIT, RETURN, SUCCESS

RETAIL
- The best place to buy it retail
- Offering you a huge number of retail outlets
- The best deal in the retail world

RETAILER
- Available at most major retailers
- Your local retailer is eager to serve you
- Carried by selected retailers

See also: MALL, MERCHANT, SELLER, STORE

RETREAT
- A comfortable, informal retreat
- Sometimes you need a retreat from the hurly burly
- Relax in your own private retreat

RETRIEVE
- Looking for a quick way to retrieve vital data
- When you retrieve more, there is much less waste
- Retrieving more of your money from

See also: FIND, RETURN

RETURN
- You may return it if you are not satisfied

- We make it easy to return
- Return your purchase easily
- Simply return it for full credit
- Just return your purchases within 10 days
- You may return everything at no charge
- If you're not happy with any item you order from us, simply return it
- Return it for a full refund or replacement, whichever you prefer
- If your purchase is not what you expected, just return it for a replacement, refund or credit
- Satisfied people are returning again and again

See also: BACK. COMEBACK, REFUND, SATISFACTION

REVENUE
- Increasing your self-generated revenue
- Each year, increasing revenue has shown the value of
- Watch revenues shoot skyward
- You'll enjoy it when the revenues start rolling in
- More revenues mean more benefits for you
- One of the easiest ways to increase revenue is

Revenue: income receipts, funds, money, remuneration, allowance, yield, gain, return, fee, finances, wealth, substance, means, wherewithal, capital, cash, proceeds
See also: CASH, MONEY, SAVINGS, VALUE

REVERSE
- Immediately reversing
- Often, it's just the reverse
- Quickly reversing any downward trend
- Time to get out of reverse

See also: CHANGE

REVITALIZE
- Visibly revitalizing
- Revitalize your skin
- Refreshing, revitalizing, relaxing, wonderful
- You can revitalize your entire self
- Revitalize your body, your spirit and your bank account

See also: REFRESH, REGENERATE, REJUVENATE, RENEW

REVIVE
- Helps to visibly revive
- Taking advantage of swiftly reviving interest in
- Widely credited with reviving traditional
- Reviving a fine old-fashioned idea

See also: REFRESH, REGENERATE, REJUVENATE, RENEW

REVOLUTION
- It's a revolution in your closet
- A revolution that's still turning heads
- A revolution was born
- Thanks to our revolutionary new design
- To produce one of the most revolutionary systems in the history of
- Revolutionary inside and out
- The people who revolutionized

See also: CHALLENGE, CHANGE, SHAKE

REWARD
- Enjoy the rewards of your good record
- Reward yourself with
- Can be very rewarding for you
- Reward yourself with
- It's only your just reward
- Low investment, big rewards
- The rewards add up
- Free rewards
- You will be able to enjoy the rewards
- To find out how your company can realize the rewards of
- You'll be getting great rewards faster
- Enjoy the rich rewards of
- You can earn rewards every time you
- Bringing you more rewards for less
- Reap the rewards of low prices
- Get your free rewards faster
- Reward yourself
- Earn even more free rewards
- It's never been easier or more rewarding

Reward: award, prize, return, payment, emends, compensation, payoff, honor, tribute, compliment, testimonial, bonus, premium, bounty, profit, gratify, remember. repay, fee, satisfy
See also: AWARD, BENEFIT, CASH, MONEY, PRIZE, SAVINGS, VALUE

RHYTHM
- Get with the rhythm

- You'll find everything has its own rhythm here
- The rhythms of change and excitement

RICH

- Rich enough to arrive in a limousine
- Your own ideas can make you rich
- A rich array of choices and benefits
- Get rich quick
- A deal rich in benefits
- An experience this rich

See also: MONEY, WEALTH

RIDE

- Riding on the coattails of
- Ride with the wind
- Enjoy the ride
- Don't let any fly-by-nighter take you for a ride
- The ride of choice

See also: MOVE, SPEED

RIGHT

- We have the right one for
- The right products for your needs
- Suddenly they feel so right
- We're sure to have the right one for you
- The key is knowing how to do it right
- Just right for you
- Do it right the first time
- Finally, you've got it right
- Ask which is right for you
- Do it fast, do it free, do it right
- Offering the right products, the right service and the right price
- That's right
- Right to your door
- The right thing to do
- Choose the one that's right for you
- Right on the money
- Products that are right for
- It's your right to
- Right place, right products, guaranteed low prices
- You'll know how right you were to choose
- Right to start early
- Your customers' bill of rights
- We do it right the first time
- We take the time to do the job right
- Concerned with doing the right thing

See also: ACCURATE, CORRECT, STRAIGHT

RISE

- A reason to rise and shine
- Can easily rise to the challenge
- Visit us and your expectations will rise
- We always rise to the occasion
- Guaranteed to get a rise out of your kids
- Keeping up with rising new technology

RISK

- Risk nothing
- We take all the risks
- Absolutely no risk on your part
- The greatest risk is resting on our laurels
- At absolutely no risk
- We're in business to minimize your risks
- Doing business can be risky
- Minimizing risk takes building relationships
- Leave the risk behind
- The risk is almost zero
- Practically risk free
- Absolutely no risk on your part
- Helps protect you against risk better than others
- Because we understand more kinds of risk
- An arrangement that takes the risk out of the decision
- Without risk to the user or the environment
- The risk and rivalry is fierce

Risk: peril, hazard, danger, vulnerability, jeopardy, insecurity, unpredictability, chance, liability, imperilment, unpredictability, plunge, long shot, speculation, endanger, expose, menace, threaten, play with fire, venture, gamble, attempt, go for broke, hazard all, throw caution to the winds, take a flier, speculate

See also: ADVENTURE, CHALLENGE, DARE, VENTURE

RITE

- It's become a rite of passage
- One of the rites of the season is
- A necessary rite of adulthood

See also: TRADITION

RIVAL

- Simply has no rival
- We'll take on any rival
- Our rivals can't possibly match it

- Check out our rivals, then come back for the best

See also: COMPETITOR

ROAD
- Get on the road with
- One for the road
- Find your own road
- On the road and off
- There are no road maps
- All roads lead to our store
- Helping you find your own road

See also: ACCESS, PATH, WAY

ROCK
- Rockin' and rollin' to better
- We like to rock the boat
- Solid as a rock and just as dependable

ROCKET
- We've rocketed to the top
- Take a rocket to success
- Demand has been rocketing upward
- Ride the rocket to

See also: ACHIEVE, SPEED

ROLE
- Proud to play a role in
- New rules, new roles
- Will play a very big role in
- We'd like to play a bigger role in your life
- Tell us how you see your role in
- Helping to enhance your role in

See also: ACTION, ASPECT, FACE, FUNCTION, PLAY

ROMANCE
- Making sure there's romance in the air
- Just the right touch of romance
- For the sheer romance of it all
- Swept away by romance
- Step into a world of romance
- The product that whispers romance

See also: EMOTION, FEELING, LOVE, MAGIC, WONDER

ROMANTIC
- Here's the romantic way to
- From the designer of the world's most romantic
- Receptive to romantic possibilities
- When you're in a romantic mood

- So romantic, you could swoon
- Light-hearted and romantic

See also: EMOTION, FEELING

ROOF
- The city's best values are all here under our roof
- Thousands of items under one roof
- Puts a better roof over your head
- Raising the roof with joy

ROOM
- Great for any room in the house
- Brighten any room with
- And, of course, there's plenty of extra room for
- Standing room only
- Giving you room to breathe

See also: DISTANCE, LATITUDE, SPACE

ROOT
- Very quickly put down roots
- The real root of all success is
- Rooting out inefficiencies
- Get to the root of the matter

See also: FOUNDATION

ROUGH
- A diamond in the rough
- When the going gets rough, call us
- Helping you over the rough spots
- Rough and ready, that's us

ROUND
- Designed to round out
- You don't have to go round in circles any more
- A well-rounded solution to your needs
- Eventually, smart people come round to our product

See also: COMPLETE

ROUTINE
- Dramatically reduces routine costs
- Get away from the routine of
- There's nothing routine about
- Break out of boring routine
- Will never be routine again

ROYALTY
- A product worthy of royalty

- We treat you like royalty
- Treating you like royalty by looking after your every need
- Feel like royalty for once in your life
- Fit for royalty

See also: SPECIAL

RULE

- Get ready to rule
- Break all the rules
- Our rules are pretty simple
- We stick to the rules
- Rules are made to be broken
- Keep breaking the rules by

See also: COMMAND, STANDARD

RUMBLE

- Creating such a rumble
- Hear the rumble of approaching success
- There have been rumblings about it for years

RUSH

- Experience the ultimate rush
- Rush in today and buy yours
- Everyone is rushing to
- Find out what the mad rush is all about
- We'll rush you your free product immediately
- The rush is on
- Beat the rush today

See also: FEELING, HURRY, SPEED

RUSTIC

- Rustic charm and affordable price
- With a genuine rustic look
- Rustic in look, modern in function

See also: ENVIRONMENTAL, NATURAL, OUTDOORS

SAFE

- There's never been a simpler way to stay safe
- Remarkably safe for
- When you want to be really safe
- Safe and convenient
- Safe and effective for everybody who needs it
- Safe for all uses
- A very safe way to
- Now safer than ever before
- Feel relax, safe and secure

See also: CERTAINTY, SECURE

SAFETY

- We care about your safety
- Your safety choice
- An impressive safety feature
- No substitute for the best safety feature of all
- Legacy of safety innovations
- More of a safety net for you and your family
- Increased safety, increased peace of mind
- More built-in safety features than any other

See also: GUARANTEE, PROTECTION, SECURITY

SALE

- Now on sale at
- Sale starts today
- Sales have gone sky-high
- The sale the country waits for
- Everything in the store is on sale
- Our entire selection is on sale
- The sale continues, so hurry in today
- Get it for him/her sale
- Weekly sales never stop
- One sweet sale
- Special sale prices on
- One-of-a-kind sale
- Sale ends before you know it
- Items return to regular price when the sale ends
- Famous brand sale
- Kick-off sale
- Sale starts today
- Great weekly sales
- Sales have never been better
- For more sales
- This sale won't be advertised to the general public
- We invite you to join us for a special neighborhood sale
- More for less sale
- A honey of a sale
- All on sale
- Our biggest sale of the year continues
- This is our annual seasonal sale
- Plus great weekly sales
- Wow, look at the sales
- Don't pay a cent until you make a sale
- Our biggest sale ever
- Never lose a sale again

Sale: blitz, clearance, doorcrasher,

extravaganza, liquidation, special, selling, vending, trade, traffic, exchange, bargaining, jobbing, auction, reduction, cut, discount, markdown, closeout
See also: BENEFIT, BUY, EVENT, MONEY, PURCHASE, PROFIT, SAVE, SAVINGS, VALUE

SALESPEOPLE
- Thanks to all the wonderful and knowledgeable salespeople
- The best trained salespeople
- Our salespeople are the very best
- Speak to one of our salespeople immediately
- Enthusiastic salespeople are always on hand to help you

See also: ASSOCIATE, EXPERT, MERCHANT, PROFESSIONAL, RETAILER, SALESPERSON, STAFF

SALESPERSON
- A knowledgeable salesperson is at your command
- Important to choose the best salesperson for the job
- Easy to judge the professionalism of the salesperson
- A friendly salesperson is always close at hand

Salesperson: salesman, saleslady, shopman, clerk, salesclerk, seller, vendor, middleman, agent, drummer, solicitor, door-to-door salesperson

SALVATION
- This could be the salvation of
- The prospects for salvation is closer than ever
- Has been the salvation of small business for the last decade

See also: CERTAINTY, SAFETY, SOLUTION

SAMPLE
- Try a sample – free
- Feel free to sample
- Filled with valuable gifts and samples
- For a limited time only we are offering a generous free sample
- Order your free sample now
- This week, test these free samples
- A free sample with any purchase
- Call today for a free sample
- A free sample treatment is yours for the asking
- Provides a splendid opportunity to sample the many different
- We'll even send you a free sample
- This is just a small sample of what you'll find at

See also: MODEL, PRODUCT, PROTOTYPE, TASTE

SANCTUARY
- We give you sanctuary from
- A seaside sanctuary
- Designed to be your sanctuary

See also: ESCAPE, SAFETY

SATISFACTION
- Satisfaction assured
- Try it, your satisfaction is guaranteed
- If, for any reason, your purchase is not to your complete satisfaction, just return it to us for a replacement
- Your satisfaction is fully guaranteed
- Your satisfaction is unconditionally guaranteed
- We guarantee your satisfaction
- Satisfaction guaranteed or your money back with a smile
- We simply won't compromise your satisfaction
- Your satisfaction matters to us
- Backed by our pledge of satisfaction
- You are entitled to continuous and complete satisfaction
- Always to your total satisfaction
- Satisfaction is a must
- Your satisfaction assured or your money cheerfully refunded
- Ensures your satisfaction on all purchases

Satisfaction: fulfilment, gratification, contentment, pleasure, enjoyment, joy, delight, happiness, comfort, assurance, belief, acceptance, trust, reparation, compensation, repayment, remuneration
See also: COMFORT, ENJOYMENT, PLEASURE

SATISFY
- If not completely satisfied

- If, for any reason, you are not satisfied
- Over one million satisfied customers
- Satisfies the discerning eyes of
- Experience the joy and pleasure of satisfying your needs
- It's very satisfying for everyone
- We want to be sure you're totally satisfied with
- And if, for whatever reason, you are not satisfied, just return the item
- Our customers are the most satisfied of all
- We've learned how to satisfy

See also: GRATIFY, PLEASE, QUENCH

SAVE

- See how much more you'll save
- Show you how much you can save
- How much can you save
- This alone can save you more
- See how much you can save
- Nothing saves like
- The sooner you decide, the sooner you save
- Save an additional percentage on
- Great ways to save and get the most from
- Save more with
- Now you can save in more ways than one
- Save on everything you need to
- Save on products for the whole family
- You always save more at
- Save, save, save
- Everyone loves to save money
- Come save with us
- Try the intelligent way to save
- Ask us how you can save even more
- Stop and save
- People come here to enjoy themselves and to save
- Shop and save
- Save money by using less
- You can save even more by
- You'll save automatically
- Come save up to
- Try a new way to save
- You'll save on all your
- Save instantly on
- Now you can save fifty percent on the price and get
- Save on our super savers

Save: rescue, redeem, liberate, protect, safeguard, guard, secure, shield, screen, keep, preserve, conserve, maintain, sustain, carry over, reserve, husband, withhold, save for a rainy day, hold in reserve, set/put/lay aside, put away, lay by/in/aside, stow away, salt away, squirrel away, store, store up, hoard, stockpile, amass, accumulate, pick up, economize, scrimp, scrape, pinch pennies, tighten one's belt, cut costs, cut expenses, reduce, buy wholesale, bring down, cut back
See also: BENEFIT, COLLECT, PROTECT, SECURE, STORE, WIN

SAVER

- Free benefits for smart savers
- This program is for serious savers
- Don't miss our terrific, weekly super saver specials
- Turn yourself into an expert saver

SAVING

- Get serious about saving
- See how close you are to saving big
- Now you're saving bigtime
- You'll enjoy saving additional cash on
- Saving you the trouble of
- Even if you have been saving for years
- Saving you time and money
- We've been saving the best just for you
- Just think about all the money you'll be saving
- When your goal is saving money
- Will provide customers with an additional saving on

See also: SAVINGS

SAVINGS

- You'll receive unbelievable savings
- Preferred savings and service from
- Receive substantial savings and discounts on services you already use
- But the savings don't end there
- Just compare the savings
- Reduced costs let us pass more savings to you
- Direct savings to you
- We're simply passing the savings on to you
- Huge end-of-season savings
- Our savings are terrific
- Really, really big savings
- Score big with savings
- Helping you identify substantial savings
- Look to us for vital savings on everyday

needs
- Savings like you've never seen before
- More savings on the latest
- Opens the door to value and savings
- You'll see the savings
- Aisle after aisle of savings
- Carnival of savings
- Get the savings you want
- Fill up on savings
- Get in on the savings
- You'll see the savings in
- You'll be astounded at the savings
- Packed with sensational savings
- Unbeatable everyday savings
- It's all about incredible savings
- It's all about great savings for you
- You must shop during our exclusive savings weekend
- Joins us as all our stores offer incredible savings
- Savings you want on
- Choose the savings you need
- Locks in savings longer
- Special savings on
- Stupendous savings Saturday only
- Power savings
- Big savings over the cost of buying elsewhere
- Super savings on our entire selection
- Savings available until
- Look inside for more blockbuster savings
- Just look at the potential savings
- Amazing savings
- Hurry in and check out these savings and values
- Hurry in for special savings
- Savings quoted off regular price
- There's no limit to the savings
- Savings available until
- Super savings on items for your home
- All at substantial savings
- Day-to-day savings
- Direct savings to you
- You'll see the savings on
- Treat yourself to these great savings
- More savings now
- Shop with us for fashionable savings
- Three days of savings at
- It's savings week at
- You've never seen savings like this

See also: BENEFIT, CASH, MONEY,
PURCHASE, SAVE, SAVING, VALUE

SAVVY
- How savvy are you about
- The store for smart, savvy people
- Cool and savvy
- Savvy buyers have known the secret for a long time
- Join the ranks of the super savvy
- Savvy folks know where to find us

See also: SCEPTICAL, SMART

SAY
- Here's what people like you have to say about it
- What more can we say
- We can confidently say that
- You can say that again
- Just say the word
- We listened to what you had to say and we got better
- What you say really counts with us
- Listen to what people are saying
- Which is no more than might be said about

See also: COMMUNICATE, TALK,
TELL

SCARY
- That's downright scary
- A decision this big can be pretty scary
- Making the right choice doesn't have to be scary

See also: DAREDEVIL

SCENE
- Making you part of the scene
- Giving a complete change of scene
- Step into a truly happening scene
- Moving on to a totally fresh scene

SCEPTICAL
- I know you're sceptical
- You're right to be sceptical about
- We win over the most sceptical of folks
- We like sceptical people

See also: SAVVY, SMART

SCHEDULE
- Now you can work on your own schedule
- Everyone deserves a break from busy schedules
- Our extensive schedule includes
- We scheduled it for your convenience
- Call today to schedule

- We have the product for any schedule or budget
- We can always fit you into our schedule

See also: PLAN, PROGRAM, TIME

SCHOOL
- For school and play
- From the old school of service
- Your one stop for school supplies
- No matter what kind of school you go to, you'll find it useful

See also: EDUCATIONAL, LEARN, TEACH

SCIENCE
- Has now become an exact science
- Bringing you the latest science has to offer
- The benefits of both art and science
- We've got service down to a science

See also: KNOWLEDGE, RESEARCH

SCIENTIFIC
- The scientific approach to
- Backed by major scientific studies
- Proven through rigorous scientific testing
- More scientific studies show our product is best for you
- The scientific way to improve your life
- Behind this gorgeous exterior is a major scientific breakthrough

See also: CLINICAL, RESEARCH

SCOOP
- Get the scoop on
- Here's the inside scoop on
- Here's the big scoop
- Get the scoop on saving money
- Scoop up the value and the savings
- We've got the scoop on our competitors

See also: FIRST, NEWS

SCORE
- Get more than the score delivered
- What exactly could you score
- Find out what you could score
- You know the score
- Score a winner
- Know the score, buy smart
- Come to someone who really knows the score
- We want to score big with you

SCRATCH
- Scratch and save
- Gets you started from scratch
- Starting from scratch is easy
- Ours are made from scratch
- Scratch and save
- Does a lot more than scratch the surface

See also: BASE, BEGINNING, START

SCREEN
- Must go through a screening process to ensure skills
- Screen out those who are not completely serious about success
- Carefully screened so that only the best reach you

See also: EXAMINATION, PROTECT

SEAL
- Earning your seal of approval
- Our seal is excellence is upon it
- Always look for this seal on the product
- Signed, sealed and delivered before you know it.

SEARCH
- Your final search starts here
- Your search is over
- We've got what you've been searching so hard for
- Have you been searching for this
- We'll do your searching for you

See also: DISCOVER, FIND, LOOK, RESEARCH

SEASON
- The season's best new look
- The best deal you'll find all season
- Each season has its color
- Season's greetings to you and all your family
- This special season of celebration
- The season to remember special people like you
- Wishing you all the joys of the season
- Wishing you the season's best from your friends at
- Smack in the midst of a season of
- This season's most important trend
- There's no better time to prepare for the season ahead
- All-season versatility
- Take advantage of special seasonal rates

- Here's the best deal you'll find all season
- Gigantic end-of-season savings

See also: CHRISTMAS, HOLIDAYS, FESTIVE, TIME

SEAT
- Doesn't have to take a back seat to anyone
- Puts you firmly in the driver's seat
- Puts you in the driver's seat
- Fasten your seat belts
- Giving you the best seat in the house
- Taking a back seat to no one
- Guaranteed to keep you glued to your seat
- Take your seat with the best
- The best seat is right in your own home
- Visit the whole world without leaving your seat
- Saving you the best seats in the house
- Front row seats for great action
- You'll always have a front-row seat

See also: PLACE

SECOND
- Make sure there's enough for seconds
- Right this very second
- Second to none
- A second one at no extra cost of all
- There are no second choices
- Don't hesitate another second

See also: BEST, INSTANT, MOMENT, TIME

SECRET
- The secret is out
- Take advantage of the country's best kept secret today
- Learn trade secrets directly from
- Learn the secret to big savings
- It's no secret that
- The secret is incredibly simple
- A secret that will change your life completely
- This secret is incredible
- You can put this simple secret to work for yourself right away
- Discover the sweetest little secret
- This secret will change your life too
- You'll prove to yourself that this amazing secret can work for you
- Before you buy, you should know this secret

- For the first time, the secret is revealed
- The secret to naturally healthy
- What's the secret to
- Nature's ultimate secret
- Unlocking new secrets of
- Finally yielding up the secrets of
- Ten secrets the government doesn't want you to know
- Your secret is safe with us

Secret: under wraps, masked, hidden, concealed, in the dark, undercover, veiled, camouflaged, shrouded, covered, covert, clandestine, under one's hat, private, confidential, hush-hush, intimate, personal, remote, mysterious, arcane, cryptic, mystery, puzzle, riddle, enigma

See also: CONFIDENTIAL, INFORMATION, MYSTERY, PRIVACY, UNDETECTABLE

SECTION
- Special pullout section
- The whole section is packed with savings
- A section completely devoted to your needs

See also: PART

SECURE
- The feeling of being in a really secure place
- Assures you of years of secure
- All to make sure your investment remains secure
- Very secure, you can be sure
- Secure in the knowledge that
- Doing whatever it takes to make you feel secure

See also: CERTAINTY, GUARANTEE, SAFE

SECURITY
- An extra measure of security
- Address security concerns
- If security is your first concern
- Surround yourself with a welcome sense of security
- Enjoy the added security of
- You too can enjoy the security of
- Includes extensive security features to ensure privacy

See also: CERTAINTY, GUARANTEE, SAFETY, WARRANTY

SEDUCE
- Let yourself be seduced
- One look will be enough to seduce you
- Shamelessly seduced by

See also: ALLURE, DRAW

SEDUCTION
- Timeless seduction
- It's outright seduction
- Surrender to the seduction of

See also: ALLURE, APPEAL,
ATTRACTION, SEXY

SEDUCTIVE
- Endlessly rich and seductive
- A seductive appeal that cannot be duplicated
- Instant wealth is a very seductive idea

SEE
- If you like what you see
- Easy to see up close
- With so much to see and do around every corner
- If you don't see it, call
- What you see is what you get
- You can't see it but you know it's there
- Just wait until you see this
- See your world more clearly
- Even though you can't see it, you'll love what it does
- Now's the time to see
- See for yourself
- Don't miss seeing all our
- You have to see it to believe it
- We see what you see
- Finally, something you've never seen before
- Drop in and see for yourself
- Seeing is believing
- We have it, even if you don't see it
- See and be seen
- You've got to see it in action
- Come in and see
- You can see why more people choose the quality of

See also: LOOK, NOTICE, SEARCH

SELECT
- You have been specially selected to receive
- That's why we won't select just any
- Only a select group of agents carry and sell this fine product
- Select quality for special customers
- Every item has been hand selected
- Will help you select exactly the product you need
- Select the one that's right for you
- Makes it easy to select
- Selected from thousands across the country
- Lovingly selected from our best
- Now available at selected outlets
- The reason we're so selective is

See also: CHOOSE

SELECTION
- You won't believe the selection – or the savings
- Nobody comes close to the selection and service offered by
- An unrivalled selection of
- Premium selection and quality
- We've got selection and service
- Nobody beats our selection
- We have a large selection of styles and colors to choose from
- Selection may vary from store to store
- Hurry – for best selection shop early
- You get great selection when you come in to our store
- Our entire selection is now on sale
- Expanded selection just in
- More than just the best selection of
- We have a huge selection of
- With plenty of selection at
- We've got the right selection for you
- Knowledgeable salespeople will help you with your selection
- Choose from an unbeatable selection
- Come in and see our selection of
- Make your selection from thousands
- New, extended selection
- Offering a better selection than any competitor
- See our massive selection of
- The most diverse selection of
- Just one of the many selections our staff is proud to recommend
- Our best selection of
- Widest selection of merchandise in town
- A large selection is waiting for your perusal
- Choose from a vast selection of
- Widest selection of models and brand

names
- Our entire selection is now on sale
- Our selection doesn't stop here
- The largest selection in the area
- The proper selection is very important
- Unrivalled selections of top-quality
- Only as good as the selection offered
- All the names, the looks, the selection you could ever hope for
- Save on a selection of
- More selection, more brand names, more savings
- Great selection and terrific prices
- With a selection second to none
- More selections every day at
- We have an incredible selection
- We offer the most extensive selection
- No one can match our giant selection

Selection: choice, preference, option, assortment, line up, group, bunch, batch, set up, series, offering, spread, pick
See also: CATALOGUE, CHOICE, INVENTORY, RANGE, SPECTRUM, STOCK

SELL
- Leave the selling to us
- We skip the hard sell
- Hard sell just isn't our style
- And that's exactly what we sell
- We don't do hard sell
- Before we sell anything to you, we make sure
- Sell yourself first, your product second
- Almost sell themselves

See also: ADVERTISE, BUY, OFFER, PURCHASE, PROFIT, SALE, SAVINGS, VALUE

SELLER
- It's our top seller
- You've turned this product into one of our all-time best sellers
- Our top super seller
- We've dropped the price again on our best seller
- People are snapping up our best seller
- Such a top seller it will soon be gone

See also: MERCHANT, PURVEYOR, RETAILER, SALESPEOPLE, SALESPERSON

SEND
- Send no money now
- Send today for
- We look forward to sending you
- We urge you to send immediately
- Please do not send any money now
- Send the card now before you forget
- Send no money – we'll bill you later
- Take the time to send for
- Send for yours today
- We'll send it immediately
- Send in your order now before supplies run out

See also: CONTACT, FORWARD, MAIL

SENIORS
- Great advantages for seniors over sixty
- Seniors' day bargains
- Free gift for seniors
- Great advantages for seniors
- Calling all seniors
- Take advantage of our great seniors' discounts

SENSATION
- A remarkable new sensation
- A sensation you haven't felt before
- The new sensation sweeping town
- A whole new sensation for

See also: MARVEL, WONDER

SENSE
- A sense of grace and warmth
- Leaves you with a sense of the tropics
- Finally, something that makes sense
- A little old-fashioned common sense works wonders
- It makes sense to call us today
- An admirable sense of
- It just makes sense to do it now
- Makes more sense than ever
- Simply shows your good business sense
- Experience an overwhelming sense of relief
- Doing our very best in every sense
- An intuitive sense of each other's
- All you need is a little common sense and the ability to
- A delight for the senses
- Let your senses make your decision
- Meant to stir the senses
- Some things must be measured by the senses

- Should stimulate the senses
- All your senses will thrill to
- Will arouse all your senses

See also: EMOTION, FEELING, REASON, SMART

SENSIBLE

- Used by sensible people worldwide
- The sensible thing to do
- It's what sensible people choose
- A sensible person like you can easily see the benefit

See also: REASON, SENSE, SMART

SENSITIVE

- Pampering the most sensitive
- Always sensitive to your needs
- The most sensitive of all
- Taking care of sensitive issues

See also: AWARENESS, EMOTION, FEELING, RESPONSIVE

SERIES

- This exciting series features
- First in a series from
- Get the whole series
- There's never been a series like this
- This best-selling series is
- A creative, stylish series of

See also: RANGE, SELECTION, SPECTRUM

SERIOUS

- Is nothing if not serious
- We're serious about providing you with
- If you're serious, take a serious look at this
- And because we take this matter so seriously
- Now for some serious savings
- Get down to serious satisfaction
- We're serious about helping you to
- Before things get serious

See also: SENSIBLE

SERVE

- We look forward to serving you in the year to come
- Proudly serving you with stores across the land
- Just warm and serve
- All we want to do is serve you
- Serving you from coast to coast

- To serve you better and faster
- Just make yourself at home and serve yourself
- Waiting to serve you right now
- We take the time to serve you right
- Here's what we've done to serve you better
- We're here twenty-four hours a day, seven days a week to serve you
- Serving up savings and value

Serve: wait on, attend, minister to, care for, give service, help, render assistance, lend a hand, oblige, accommodate, abet, assist, be of service, work for, respect, honor, perform, function, do the duties of benefit, contribute to, boost, advocate, support, recommend, assist, aid

See also: BENEFIT, HELP, INSTALL, PROMOTE, RECOMMEND

SERVICE

- Best service, lowest prices
- We look forward to giving you outstanding service for years to come
- One-time or occasional service is available
- Providing you with a very special level of service
- Speedy service every day
- We pride ourselves on our unparalleled service, friendly smiles and good advice
- Offering many different services to make your life easier
- Warm, caring service
- Committed to providing outstanding service
- Providing an essential service for
- A new dimension in full and self-service
- Does a real service for
- Providing you with loyal service wherever your business takes you
- Offering comprehensive services, including
- There is no charge for this service
- City knowledge, country service
- You'll find real friendly service
- All-new service begins now
- Warm, attentive service is as famous as the name
- Around-the-clock service
- Service that will catch your eye and your attention

- Romantic elegance combines with gracious service
- Service is unquestioned
- Guaranteed service
- You gave our services and staff top marks
- Service in a class of its own
- We hope you will find this an invaluable service
- Service while you wait
- For professional service you can trust
- We service what we sell
- Established as a service to
- Service makes it simple for you to
- Low prices, superb services
- At your service, every day
- Worry-free service
- Keep on giving you the same excellent service you've come to expect
- Great prices, superior services
- Best price and service since
- Information to help you make the most of this new service
- Safe, fast service seven days a week
- Fast, friendly service
- Not to mention the attentive service one can only find at
- Providing a very valuable service
- Fantastic service seven days a week
- Includes the exceptional service of
- Where service is an art
- The art of fine service
- Providing services in just the areas you require
- Additional products and services you won't find anywhere else
- We also give you value-added services such as
- We'll continue to search for new services to full your needs
- With a broad range of customized service to manage
- Knowing where to go for better services
- An exploding demand for these services
- Superior service and personal attention
- The following services are available from
- Sales and service since
- We're at your service
- We're proud of our facility and service
- Dedicated to outstanding service
- You are assured of prompt and professional service
- Fast 60 minute service

- Service maintenance programs available
- Committed to reliable and courteous service to our customers
- Confident you will find our service outstanding
- Famous for prompt and gracious service
- Offering services that fit your unique needs
- A revolutionary new service is now available
- We service all makes and models

Service: assistance, good turn, favor, leg up, contribution, boost, aid, support, backing, system, organization, job, work, duty, function, capacity

See also: ASSISTANCE, BENEFIT, FUNCTION, HELP

SET
- No matter which set you choose
- Get set for
- Setting the scene for savings
- We're all set to serve you
- This innovative gift set includes

See also: COLLECTION, READY

SET-UP
- For a one-time only set-up fee
- You'll love our convenient set-up
- The best set-up for you

See also: ESTABLISH

SETTING
- All the advantages of the setting
- You won't find a more perfect setting
- A truly intimate setting
- A great addition to any family setting
- Creating a setting you'll really feel comfortable in
- Relax and enjoy yourself in a setting that
- Dramatic setting and stimulating surroundings

See also: ENVIRONMENT, LOCATION, PLACE, SITE

SETTLE
- If you don't want to settle for just any
- The perfect product to settle down with
- Don't settle for second best
- Whatever choice you settle on, you'll be pleased
- If you're the type who will settle for

nothing but the best
See also: CHOOSE

SEXY
- The sexiest products going
- Sleek, sexy and slinky
- A sexier, brasher look
- For a sexier you

See also: ALLURE, BEAUTIFUL, FEELING, SEDUCTION

SHADE
- Sizzling shades of
- A more delicate shade of
- Puts competitors in the shade

See also: COLOR, HUE, RAINBOW

SHAKE
- Shake things up
- Get down to where things are movin' and shakin'
- We shake up old ideas
- Watch us shake up the competition

See also: ACTION, CHANGE, REVOLUTION

SHAPE
- You have dozens of shapes and sizes to choose from
- Shaping up to be so exciting for us
- Could suddenly start to take on a whole new shape
- Shape up now for
- Your future could have whole new shape
- Behold the shape of things to come
- They'll stay in peak shape when you
- And now available in a variety of different shapes and sizes

See also: CONDITION, FORM

SHARE
- Share in these savings
- Share the benefits
- We want to share all this with you
- Get your fair share
- Sharing is part of our value
- Nothing is more satisfying than sharing
- Nothing's cozier than sharing everyday things
- When you see what we have to share
- Get your full share now

See also: BENEFIT, HELP

SHARP
- Show you how sharp your mind really is
- Sharpen your competitive edge
- Look sharp
- Back in the game and sharper than ever

SHEEN
- A lustrous sheen
- Comes with a beautiful sheen to it
- You can tell how healthy it is just by the sheen

See also: LUSTRE, RADIANCE, SHINE

SHIFT
- Whenever there's a major shift like this
- There's been a major shift recently
- The balance of power has shifted to you
- Keeping you abreast of all the shifts in marketing
- The ground can shift right under your feet any day

See also: CHANGE, MOVE

SHINE
- It's your turn to shine
- Add a special shine to your day
- Your reason to shine
- You'll take a shine to our product
- We've taken a shine to you
- It's time to shine
- You're about to take a real shine to

See also: GLITTER, LUSTRE, RADIANCE, SHEEN

SHIP
- Your ship has come in
- Watch your ship arrive in style
- All shipping charges are included
- We will even pay for return shipping
- We ship the moment we receive your order
- Shipped the same day

See also: DELIVER, FORWARD, SEND

SHIPMENT
- You will be billed at time of shipment
- The shipment will arrive the very next day
- Shipment after shipment of customer satisfaction

SHOE
- Step into someone else's shoes

- Let us stand in your shoes for a while
- Now the shoe is on the other foot

See also: PLACE

SHOP

- The place where you love to shop
- So you can shop for the best price and quality
- You are free to shop around
- Shop around for the best deals
- Where else would you shop for
- You can shop in style for
- Shop early for best selection
- Shop till you drop
- Why shop anywhere else
- All you have to do is shop
- Find out what shopping is all about
- Shop at your local store for these great values
- You probably know why millions shop at our store
- The smart way to shop
- You'll see just how easy shopping can be
- Plan your shopping around
- To make your shopping experience even better
- Providing you with one-stop shopping
- We're your one-stop shop for all your needs
- A good place to shop
- Now there's a whole new way to shop with
- It's our job to make your shopping easy
- A really interesting way to go shopping
- Makes shopping twice as interesting

Shop: be in the market for, look for, look to buy, window shop, browse, search for, hunt for, retail outlet, workshop, studio, factory, business, office
See also: BUY, MONEY, MALL, OUTLET, PURCHASE, STORE

SHOPAHOLIC

- Sending shopaholics into a frenzy
- We cater to shopaholics
- Calling all shopaholics
- Enough to turn anyone into a shopaholic

See also: BUYER

SHOPPER

- A shoppers' paradise
- For the discerning shopper
- More shoppers flock to us than to any other
- Be one or our satisfied shoppers
- We strive to make our shoppers happy

See also: BUYER, CUSTOMER, PATRON

SHORT-CUT

- We never take short-cuts
- Able to show you short-cuts you never imagined existed
- The fastest short-cut is in our store

SHOT

- Why not give it a shot
- Go ahead, give it a shot
- Sometimes you only get one shot at the brass ring
- We always give it our best shot
- More than just a shot in the dark
- Please give us a shot at it
- You've earned your shot at the top

See also: TRY

SHOUT

- Shout out loud and clear
- The value shouts at you
- We give you something to shout about
- Shout with joy
- We don't have to shout it out

See also: COMMUNICATE, TALK

SHOW

- We can show you how to
- Showing what we're made of
- Showing once again why
- We can show you how easy it is
- Showing you how to double your
- Best in show
- Show off
- You can be forgiven for showing off a little
- We'll show you how easy it is
- We can do it or show you how
- Helps you get on with the show
- Putting in a spectacular show
- Show your brilliance with
- Steal the show with
- Real show-stealers
- Let us show you the way to
- We show you a superb collection of options

See also: DEMONSTRATE, DISPLAY,

DEMONSTRATION, PRESENTATION

SHOWCASE
- A stunning showcase for
- A veritable showcase of value and style
- What better showcase for your/our talents than
- Turning your home into a showcase

See also: DISPLAY, SHOWROOM

SHOWROOM
- We're your product showroom
- Call now or visit our showroom
- Visit our showroom for many unique design ideas
- Look past the showroom glitter
- Visit our new showroom and save

See also: DISPLAY, SHOWCASE

SHUTTLE
- Shuttle your way between
- Tired of shuttling back and forth
- Our shuttle bus will shuttle you to the door in a jiffy

SHY
- There's nothing shy about this
- Some people are a little shy about asking
- Don't be shy about going after what you want
- Your shy days are gone

SIDE
- Show your sensational side
- Lets your wild side come out
- A product with many sides
- Showing another side of you
- It's a good thing we're on your side
- We refuse to take sides

See also: ASPECT, PART, PROFILE

SIGHT
- We set our sights on a brand new challenge
- Set your sights on something higher still
- Set your sights on the best
- A sight you will hardly believe
- It's called love at first sight
- New arrivals have just been sighted

See also: AIM, GOAL, SEE, TARGET

SIGN
- Sign up today

- Use it at the first sign of
- Sign up now and check out
- Sign up and take advantage of our early bird discount
- A good sign that you've gotten it right
- Visit us and sign up for big value
- All the signs of
- Reducing the signs of
- Here's why you should sign up now
- And maybe the best sign that it's working is
- Just sign up and take your pick
- When you sign up you can earn up to
- Sign up for this fantastic offer before
- Please sign me up
- Sign up now before it's too late

See also: BRAND, ICON, SYMBOL

SIGNAL
- You've been sending all the right signals
- Yes, your signals have been getting through
- Celebrate a signal victory with us

See also: SIGN

SIGNATURE
- Our exclusive signature series
- It's easy to recognize our signature products
- All it takes is your signature to
- It's easy to recognize our signature item
- Gives it its signature look
- As soon as we have your signature, we swing into action

See also: BRAND, NAME, REGISTER

SIMMER
- Been simmering for a long time now
- Give you time to let your best ideas simmer
- Slowly simmered over an open fire

See also: COOK

SIMPLE
- Such a beautifully simple solution
- It's the simple things that count
- Simple and safe
- Pure and simple
- Keeping things simple
- Nothing could be simpler
- It's that simple
- You asked us to keep it simple and we did

- We understand how to put simple thing together beautifully
- Plain and simple
- The joy the simplest things can provide
- Makes it really simple to use the service
- What could be simpler
- It's so simple and so profitable

See also: ORDINARY

SIMPLICITY

- A totally mysterious simplicity
- Will let you do it with ease and simplicity
- In keeping with your insistence on simplicity
- Designs share an appealing simplicity
- You'll love the sleek simplicity of
- We've reduced it all to an elegant simplicity

See also: EASE, EASY

SIMPLIFY

- Simplified and streamlined
- Simplifies your life for you
- Let us help to simplify things for you

See also: EASY

SIREN

- Listen to the siren song of
- Don't have to listen to sirens going off
- Loud as a siren

SIT

- Don't just sit there
- We aren't just sitting on our laurels
- You don't have to sit this one out
- Leave you sitting pretty
- Sit in the catbird seat

SITE

- An ideal site for you
- A site chosen with a great deal of care
- Everything starts with the site
- On a site close to you

See also: LOCATION, PLACE

SITUATE

- Perfectly situated to
- We've situated ourselves to help you
- Choose the one situated best to

SITUATION

- See how you can better your situation

- We will do whatever is necessary to correct this situation
- Can handle just about any situation

See also: CASE, CONDITION, NEED

SIZE

- Discover why we've doubled in size
- Huge size range
- Any size, one price
- In exactly the size you want
- No matter what size you're looking for, we can help
- May be shown larger than actual size
- Just my size, just your size
- With standard and custom sizes available
- For every size and shape
- Now available in a wide selection of shapes and sizes

See also: BIG, CHOICE

SIZZLE

- Put a little sizzle in your
- For some sizzling good times
- Come to you sizzling hot
- As soon as you hear the sizzle your mouth will water

See also: HOT

SKILL

- You'll also find skills you need to better evaluate
- It takes a certain skill to
- Exhibiting superb problem-solving skills
- Use your valuable skills and experience to work with us
- A company with people skills
- We have all the required skills to
- Expand your skills with
- Ensure skills are at the highest level

See also: CRAFT, EXPERT, INFORMATION, PROFESSIONAL

SKIN

- Rejuvenate your skin
- End dry skin forever
- Imagine your skin actually looking better with time
- Makes your skin more beautiful from the very first time you use it
- Defend skin against exposure that can lead to signs of premature aging
- The moisture in your skin keeps building
- Skin looks better and better

- Designed to minimize visible signs of aging in your skin
- The beauty of healthy looking skin
- Improves skin texture
- It's already gotten under your skin
- Gives your skin just the right amount of moisture

See also: BODY

SKY

- We do more than blue sky it
- The sky's the limit
- Reach for the sky today
- We're not just offering pie in the sky

See also: IMAGINE

SKYROCKET

- Has absolutely skyrocketed
- Demand has been skyrocketing lately
- Rapidly skyrocketing to the top

See also: ROCKET

SLEEP

- Works while you sleep
- More than just a place to sleep
- Sleep with complete peace of mind
- Helps you get a good night's sleep

See also: ESCAPE, RELAX, REST

SLIP

- Is quietly slipping back into
- Give your troubles the slip
- Slip into something gorgeous

See also: RETURN, WEAR

SLOW

- Don't let it slow you down
- Sure won't slow you down
- In a slow and leisurely matter
- Time to slow down and take a look around you

Slow: unhurried, dawdling, moderate, leisurely, slow-paced, paced, methodical, deliberate, relaxed

See also: EASE, PACE, RELAX

SMALL

- Small is beautiful
- It's small wonder that
- And you can start small
- It's the small things that count

See also: LITTLE, SIZE

SMART

- A lot cheaper, simpler and smarter
- Get smart with
- It's the smart way to do things
- It's so smart it even
- Get smart quick
- It's the smart thing to do
- Found to be the smart way to
- Smart folks shop at
- What may well be the smartest
- Smarter, faster, better-priced
- The smartest move you'll ever make
- Go where the smart people go
- You've got the smarts to recognize
- You got where you are by working smart
- It looks like a smart buy and here's why
- Nothing could be smarter than
- It's the smart choice too

See also: INTELLIGENT, SAVVY

SMILE

- Gets you smiling
- Why are they smiling
- Find out why they're smiling
- Smiles appear right before your eyes
- You leave with a smile
- We pride ourselves on friendly smiles and good advice
- Something to smile about
- Let us put a smile on your face

See also: GLAD, HAPPY, JOY, PLEASURE, SATISFACTION

SMOOTH

- Starts to smooth and soften in an instant
- Satiny smooth
- Smooths and refreshes
- Making the transition smooth and trouble-free
- Get the smooth moves and the cool duds
- Glides more smoothly
- Elasticity, resilience and smoothness increase significantly
- A smoothness that comes from

See also: EASE, EASY

SMORGASBORD

- Generating a high-energy smorgasbord
- Offering you a lavish smorgasbord of choices
- Belly up to the great smorgasbord of life

See also: CHOICE, DINE, SELECTIO, SPECTRUM

SMOTHER

- Smothered in loads of delicious
- Don't smother your better instincts
- Do you feel smothered and backed into a corner

See also: END, FINISH

SNACK

- Take a snack break
- When you want a healthy snack
- A snack that satisfies your craving for
- Time out for a snack
- Some snacks just don't cut it

See also: DINE, EAT, TREAT

SOAR

- Makes you soar like an eagle
- Get ready to soar
- Really starting to soar
- A burning desire to soar higher

See also: FLIGHT, RISE

SOCIETY

- So prevalent in our society
- Move up in society
- Society's best

See also: CIVILIZATION

SOFT

- Ultra soft to pamper your whole body
- Softer than soft
- Softer than anything that touches you
- You've never felt anything as soft as this
- Softness that's pure heaven

Soft: pliable, pliant, flexible, bendable, plushy, malleable, squishy, tractable, stretchable, plastic, shapable, lithe, supple, smooth, silky, velvety, satiny, creamy, kissable, fuzzy, downy, furry, fleecy, cosy, warm, mellow, muted, understatement, heavenly, tranquil, low, pastel, fluid, curved, gentle, genial, temperate, tender, sweet, mild, indirect, light, dainty

See also: COMFORT, GENTLE, PAMPER, SMOOTH

SOLD

- We expect to be completely sold out by morning
- Get sold on our service
- Everything must be sold
- Must be sold for
- Sold down to the bare walls
- Before you know it, you're sold on it
- Sold by the dozens every week
- Get sold with
- Just one look and you'll be sold
- You'll be sold on a brand new idea

See also: BUY, CONVINCE, PURCHASE, SELL

SOLUTION

- The most comprehensive solution
- The simple solution to these kinds of headaches
- The solution that works for you
- Providing the total solution for all your needs
- Introducing your newest, best solution
- Common sense is the best solution to
- An enormously scalable solution
- The most economical solution to
- Willingness to look for solutions wherever they might exist
- A safe, gentle solution
- You can't find a better solution to your needs
- It's the only real solution to
- The number one selling solution worldwide
- A lively, affordable solution
- Be part of the solution
- The easy solution for our
- An array of upgradable, customer-focused information management solutions
- Intelligent solutions for all your needs
- Innovative and practical solutions for all your problems
- In business to find the right solutions for our customers
- Finding the right solutions for you
- Dedicated to finding solutions for you
- Providing solutions for every level of your organization
- Solutions to help you compete and succeed in the years ahead
- We can create a custom-designed solution
- The seasonal solution to
- Solutions are shaped by
- Knowing it was the best solution
- We have the solutions
- Do you have a problem that needs a solution

See also: ANSWER, RESULT

SOLVE
- Perfect for helping you solve your not-so-small problems
- No matter what the problem, we can solve it for you
- Solving problems like this is our business
- When you're looking for someone to solve
- Our ability to solve problems boosts our value even beyond that of price
- There's nothing you can't solve so long as you

Solve: work out, resolve, figure out, crack, answer, untangle, unravel, translate, decode, unlock, penetrate, fathom, get at, clear up, explain, interpret, elucidate, make clear, account for
See also: DISCOVER, HELP, RESEARCH, UNLOCK

SOMEONE
- For that special someone
- Someone, right now, is waiting for you
- When you really want to impress someone

SOMETHING
- Now you can make something out of nothing
- Something comes over you when
- A little something for everybody
- Something you really ought to know
- The start of something big

SOON
- The sooner you call, the more you save
- Sooner costs less
- Coming soon to a store near you
- Soon to be in your neighborhood
- Getting it to you sooner
- Get yours sooner than anyone else

See also: EARLY, FAST, SPEED

SOPHISTICATED
- For the most sophisticated system in the business
- Just a little more sophisticated than
- Sophisticated people know

See also: CIVILIZE, CLASSIC, SMART

SOPHISTICATION
- Coming out with a fresh, modern sophistication
- With more sophistication than ever before
- You don't see this kind of sophistication just anywhere
- Earthy sophistication that draws you in
- Blending sophistication with business savvy

See also: ELEGANCE, SAVVY, WISDOM

SORRY
- You won't be sorry
- Don't be sorry later
- You'll never be sorry you bought from us

See also: APOLOGIZE, GUILD, REGRET, WRONG

SORT
- Sort it out with
- See the light and sort out your life
- Products of the better sort
- We have just the sort you're looking for

Sort: make, kind, type, class, line, grade, quality, genre, category, list, lot, style, manner
See also: BRAND, KIND, NAME, TYPE

SOUGHT
- Some of the most highly sought after
- Have sought a solution like this for years
- Much sought, rarely found

SOUL
- Designed to delight the soul
- You want something that includes a soul
- Is the guts and soul of
- Soothes the soul
- Expresses the very soul of
- True beauty comes from the soul
- We haven't lost sight of the heart and soul of

See also: FEELING, HEART, SPIRIT

SOUND
- Alive with the sound of
- Based on thoroughly sound knowledge
- A really sound idea
- Sounding off for
- Now you can really sound off about
- We'll like to sound off a little

- You'll like the sound of it when you hear

See also: **RELIABLE, TRUST**

SOURCE
- We're your best source for
- We're your source of
- Your unfailing source for
- Go straight to the source
- Relying on a uniquely qualified source
- It's your best source for discovering
- The premier source is now available

See also: **BEGINNING, RESOURCE**

SOUVENIR
- Makes a great gift or souvenir
- Perfect souvenir for you and your family
- Mecca for souvenir hunters
- A souvenir you'll never part with

See also: **KEEP, MEMORY, REMEMBER**

SPACE
- To give you maximum breathing space
- You create the space
- Create a great outdoor/indoor space
- Create a brighter, more inviting space
- But space is limited
- Excellent utilization of space
- Space age value
- Makes you want to head for the open spaces
- A space to live, a space to grow
- Limited space available for
- Maximize your space and your savings
- Space is still available
- A space you can really live with
- We have much more to say than we can squeeze in this small space
- Even the smallest spaces have potential
- Designed to save space
- Time to head for open spaces
- Space is limited we suggest you reserve immediately

See also: **LATITUDE, ROOM, STORAGE**

SPEAK
- Speak volumes
- Our products speak for themselves
- We're not just speaking figuratively
- Speaking up about value

See also: **COMMUNICATE, CONTACT, TALK, TELL**

SPEARHEAD
- Spearheading change
- Spearheading the move to
- Now you can help spearhead

See also: **FOREFRONT, LEAD**

SPECIAL
- With a special thank you from
- You'll agree they're extra special
- Ask about our special orders
- Special pre-release price when you
- We've got the special things you're going to be wanting
- If you'd like to do something special for someone special
- Something very, very special
- There's always something special happening
- Low price special
- Makes it just a little bit more special
- Grand opening special
- Yes, we're back with another one day special
- Our special has been extended
- Early bird special
- Check out these early opening specials
- What makes this so special
- This week's specials
- Coming soon is something very special
- You need something special
- Early morning specials
- Super specials on
- Don't miss these awesome specials
- Because you're so super special

Special: particular, specific, certain, distinct, distinctive, individual, singular, one of a kind, different, unusual, uncommon, rare, unique, out-of-the-ordinary, unconventional, unorthodox, novel, new, important, significant, memorable, momentous, great, earthshaking, foremost, predominant, primary, paramount, chief, principal, prime, notable, noted, outstanding, celebrated, well-known, private, select, elite, exceptional, incredible, spectacular, dear

See also: **BEST, BARGAIN, NEW, RARE, SALE, SAVINGS, UNIQUE, VALUE**

SPECIALIST
- Call a specialist
- Your product specialist
- For those times when you really need a

specialist
- That's why our teams of specialists get to know you
- Our specialists are waiting to talk to you
- Go with a specialist

See also: EXPERT, INSIDER, PROFESSIONAL

SPECIALIZE
- For those who want to specialize
- We also specialize in
- Specializing in the best
- We also specialize in
- We specialize in providing detailed information

SPECIES
- A whole new species of
- A brand new species has just appeared
- Time to try a superior species of
- You might wonder just what kind of species is this

See also: KIND, SORT, TYPE

SPECTRUM
- Solutions that cross the spectrum
- Wherever you are on the spectrum, we can help
- Covering the broadest spectrum of all

See also: CHOICE, RANGE, SELECTION

SPEED
- Built for speed
- You'll be awed by the speed at which we can act
- Making their way to you at warp speed
- The speed will make your head spin
- Advanced features for simplicity and speed
- Speediest service in town
- Speed and simplicity all rolled into one

See also: FAST, INSTANT, PACE, STREAMLINE

SPEND
- Spend less on
- No matter how much you spend
- Make more, spend less
- Spend the day/night, not your savings
- Do it without spending a cent
- Spend less on the best
- Cuts your spending by half

- Now you don't have to spend a ton of money on
- You'll be enjoying yourself more and spending a lot less
- Not just a convenient way to increase your spending power

Spend: shell out, outlay, expend, ante up, lay out, lavish, fork out, disburse, pay out, splurge, profligate, spend like a drunken sailor, squander, dissipate, use up, consume, exhaust, deplete, empty, finish

See also: BUY, PURCHASE, PAY, SAVE, SAVINGS, VALUE

SPICE
- Add extra spice to
- Spicing things up
- Spiced with excitement
- When you really need a some spice in your life

See also: ATTRACTION

SPILL
- Spilling the beans about
- The benefits spill over into all other parts
- And don't forget the great spillover effect

See also: INFORM

SPIN
- Take one for a spin
- Put your best spin on it
- Changing fast enough to make you head spin
- When the choices leave you spinning
- We don't leave you spinning in the wind

See also: DAZZLE, TRY

SPIRIT
- Choose a gift with spirit
- Applauding the independent spirit of so many of you
- Lifts your spirit
- Has given it real spirit
- Born with the spirit
- That same spirit guides everything we do today
- Embodies the spirit and passion of
- A product with spirit
- There's no better place to get into the spirit than at
- It all springs from our unique corporate spirit

- Spirit of the west/east/north/south
- Breathe in the spirit of adventure
- Breathing more spirit into
- Get into the spirit
- In the spirit of our hardy pioneer ancestors
- Our tribute to the spirit of
- It is precisely in this spirit that
- Born-to-run spirit
- Our ingenuity and entrepreneurial spirit will keep us reaching out
- Reputed to have special spiritual powers
- Feel a whole new spirit of
- Performed with a joyful spirit

See also: ATMOSPHERE, energy,
FEELING, FREEDOM, HEART, SOUL

SPLASH
- We'll help you make a splash
- All you need to make a splash
- Making a major splash in the world of
- The splash of savings
- Splashdown for excitement
- Make a big splash today

See also: IMPACT, IMPRESSION

SPLENDID
- They're splendid on their own
- What a splendid opportunity to
- What could be more splendid than
- A very splendid idea

See also: EXCELLENCE, FINE, GOOD,
GREAT, SUPERIOR

SPOIL
- Ready to spoil you
- Could very well spoil you for anywhere else on earth
- We spoil all our customers
- Come and be shamelessly spoiled today

See also: PAMPER

SPONSOR
- Why we're honored to sponsor
- One of the founding sponsors of
- Delighted to be a sponsor of
- Brought to you by the sponsors of
- Sponsoring the finest
- Proud sponsor of
- We're very happy to sponsor
- Just look at who our sponsors are

See also: BACK, PAY, SUPPORT

SPORT
- No matter what your favorite sport is
- To counter the wear and tear of high impact sports
- Try it just for the sport of it
- Are you the sporting type

See also: ATHLETIC, GAME

SPOT
- We've got a soft spot for
- If you have a soft spot for
- This is the spot
- Saving the best spot for you
- One of the wittiest, most sought-after spots
- Hits the spot
- The new spot for
- Spot-on value
- Spot check on value

See also: LOCATION, NOTICE, PLACE,
SEE

SPOTLIGHT
- Leap into the spotlight
- Grabbing the spotlight
- Turning the spotlight on
- Now seizing the spotlight
- Turning the spotlight on
- The spotlight is pointing at
- Today the spotlight is on you

See also: FEATURE, HIGHLIGHT

SPREE
- The city's best shopping spree
- You don't have to go on a spending spree
- You'll feel like you've just been on a spree

See also: INDULGE, PARTY, WILD

SPRING
- Spring into action
- Spring savings are here
- We spring into action instantly
- New spring colors
- Our new spring collection features popular
- Come in for a touch of springtime
- Will once again be hosting a spring celebration of
- Spring spectacular
- Hot spring deals

- Spring into summer
- Say goodbye to winter, hello to spring
- April showers of great spring values
- Bring on spring
- Spring into savings
- Experience an early taste of springtime
- Spring shopping spree
- Spring into action where the savings are
- Get a jump on spring
- Helping you snap into spring
- Just right for spring
- Returns just in time for spring

See also: **LEAP, SEASON, YOUTHFUL**

SQUEEZE
- Squeeze more from you
- Putting the squeeze on you
- Great gifts for your main squeeze
- Squeezes more from your shopping dollar
- Are you feeling really squeezed

See also: **HASSLE, PRESSURE**

STACK
- Nothing stacks up to
- Stacking up the savings
- Stacks and stacks of great values

See also: **PILE, PLENTY**

STAFF
- Knowledgeable staff
- We have whizzes on staff to help you
- Knowledgeable staff always on hand to help you with your selections
- The friendly staff is waiting to
- Just ask any member of our staff
- Our staff is always standing by to
- Our helpful staff can show you how
- One of our cheerful staff will answer your questions
- With the help of our very professional staff

See also: **ASSOCIATE, CREW, EXPERT, HELP, PROFESSIONAL, TEAM, SALESPEOPLE**

STAGE
- Healthy choices for every stage of life
- For your transitional stage
- No matter what stage you are in
- Come and see the next stage of

See also: **INSTALLMENT, STEP**

STAIN
- Ensures stain-resistance for easy care
- Proudly maintaining our stainless reputation for
- Stains just disappear

See also: **SPOT**

STAND
- Stand up and be heard
- Stands up to wear
- We want you to know where we stand
- We stand right behind you all the time
- A product that can stand the heat
- Stand tall

See also: **ENDURE**

STANDARD
- The true value of establishing unbeatable standards
- Exceeding the highest standards daily
- Sets professional standards for
- Setting the standard for
- You choose the standard, we deliver the results
- And control the standard of service you receive
- The highest standards of value, quality and excellence
- An exceptional standard of quality and service
- The standard by which the others are measured
- Standards that work hard for you
- A proven approach to developing high standards
- Will be remembered for impressive standards
- The highest standards of excellence
- Setting our own standard of ease-of-use
- Find out who is setting the standard
- Our enviable standards of quality
- Doing it to the highest quality standards in the business
- Making sure the highest quality of standards are consistently met
- Sets the standards others aspire to
- Subject to the same design standards
- Working to set the finest standards of

Standard: model, pattern, example, paradigm, ideal, mirror, prototype, archetype, rule, principle, guideline, rule of thumb, regulation, precept, order, gauge, guide,

touchstone, measure, criterion, axiom, foundation, norm, average, par, rank, median, grade, recognized, accepted, approved, orthodox, official, definitive, classic, authoritative, established, sure, reliable, common, widespread, prevalent, popular
See also: CONVENTIONAL, GUIDE, MEASURE, MODEL, MARK, NORM, POPULAR, PRINCIPLE, RULE, VALUE

STAPLE
- A tried-and-true staple
- A product that has always been the staple
- Always stocking plenty of our staple merchandise

See also: BASIC, ESSENTIAL, NECESSITY

STAR
- You could look like a star
- Catch a rising star
- Reach for the stars
- Bring out your star quality with
- Inside every person is a star
- Play among the stars
- You can bet the stars will be out
- Where stars are born
- Hot stars
- The star of our show is
- You be the star
- Here, you're always the star
- Meet the newest star in our galaxy
- Just one of the stars of our

See also: BEST, CELEBRITY, TOP

START
- Can usually start work right away
- Start saving money right now
- We'll start you off with
- Always start with the best
- Start here for a winning
- Off to a flying start
- Get a head start with
- Starting today, you can
- Gets you off to a running start
- Get off to a flying start with
- The start of something beautiful
- It's easy to start
- Don't start until you've seen
- Start your own home-based
- Starting at just
- Getting started is simple with
- To get you started right away

- For starters
- The best possible start
- Getting started is so easy
- Start smart
- A thrilling start to
- And that's just the start
- Get ready for a strong start next year
- Great results start at
- Give yourself a head start
- Try starting over
- Now you can start over with
- It doesn't cost a lot to get started
- We start you off with
- Know how to start from the ground up
- Everything to get you started
- From start to finish
- So don't get a late start
- Get your free starter kit today

Start: begin, commence, go ahead, embark, set sail, set about, take off, jump off, kick off, blast off, get going, take steps, get a move on, get on the stick, start off, start out, move out, get the show on the road, plunge in, dive in, get one's feet wet, get down to it, get to it, arise, dawn, break out, spring up, crop up, initiate, instigate, set in motion, start the ball rolling, take the first step, break the ice, open, pioneer, lead off, institute, inaugurate, found, establish, set up, organize, break ground, lay the foundation, introduce, launch, usher in, create, beget, engender, give birth to , give rise to, sow the seeds of
See also: BEGINNING, CREATE, INNOVATION, LAUNCH

STATE-OF-THE-ART
- Chosen to make a state-of-the-art product
- State-of-the-art solutions for space age problems
- Confident that you'll always be getting state-of-the-art components
- You can be sure it's state-of-the-art construction

See also: ADVANCE, EDGE, MODERN

STATEMENT
- Makes a strong statement
- You can make a statement with
- A cool, confident statement
- An individual statement
- Making a statement without saying a word

- Making a powerful statement for

See also: COMMUNICATE, MESSAGE, SAY, TALK, TELL

STATUS
- Reserved for those who know there are more important things in life than just status
- Your status just shot up
- A simple, inexpensive way to increase your status
- Everybody could use a little more status
- Just won't stand for the status quo

See also: RANK, PLACE, POSITION

STAY
- If you're looking for a product that works, and one you'll stay with
- To make your stay more enjoyable
- Ensure that it stays that way
- And to make sure our customers stay with us, we're offering
- We stay with you all the way

STEER
- Steers you clear of
- Steering you on a course to success
- Just when you're wondering which way to steer
- Will never stick you with a bum steer
- We steer you right – and that's no bull

See also: GUIDE. LEAD

STEP
- Take a giant step forward today
- Keeping you in step with the world
- We're at the first step of a splendid journey
- Always several steps ahead of
- Take your first step now
- Step away from boring
- Leads you every step of the way
- Take a big step towards
- You'd better step on it because
- Helping to make a swift step forward
- Two simple steps to help you to
- Taken one step further
- Stay in step with the world of change
- Take this step today
- Here are some easy steps to
- Ten steps to a cleaner, healthier
- Check out these easy steps

See also: ACTION, INSTALLMENT,

METHOD, STAGE

STIR
- In a real stir over
- Has been stirring hearts and imaginations since
- For a truly stirring experience
- Go ahead, cause a stir

See also: EXCITEMENT

STOCK
- Due to unexpected demand, stock is temporarily depleted
- Stock up and save
- All stock will be sold
- Always in stock, round the clock, day-in, day-out
- Dozens in stock, reserved just for you
- A time for taking stock
- Stock up on these fine items
- Stock up on essentials
- Stock up now
- Stock up today on
- All new stock on our shelves
- New stock is arriving daily
- Day in, day out – always in stock
- We stock hundreds of
- Not every item may be stocked by
- We stock everything you'll need for
- Stock up while you can
- Stock up while quantities last
- New stock means new value
- All stock will/must be sold
- With these great prices, it's time to stock up on
- Building up our stock to coincide with
- Time for you to take stock
- We put a lot of stock in
- Open stock bonanza
- Stocking a vast selection of
- Making room for new stock

See also: CATALOGUE, INVENTORY, MERCHANDISE, STUFF

STONE
- Where no stone is left unturned
- The rules aren't carved in stone
- Help when it seems you've come up against a stone wall
- Are others stonewalling you

STOP
- Hundreds of ways to stop

- Stop by your nearest
- Why not stop by and
- Stop the problem dead in its tracks
- But we won't stop there
- Designed to stop problems before they start
- But we didn't stop at just
- One stop gets you everything you need
- Make our site your first stop every day
- Please stop by again
- Thanks for stopping by
- Why don't you stop by and
- Lots of people like you stop easily
- Stop by on Saturday
- That's why we'll never stop doing our level best to serve you

Stop: halt, arrest, prevent, repel, repulse, deny, avert, discontinue, conclude, end, withdraw, knock off, shut down, complete, finish, pause, cease, desist, quit, slow down, break off, wind up, run out, run its course, rest, terminate, close, silence, subdue, lower the boom, squash, scotch, check, nip in the bud, overpower, cut off, shut off, prevent, delay, postpone
See also: AVOID, CHANGE, DISCONTINUE, FINISH, HELP, PREVENT

STORAGE
- Designed for easy storage
- For all your storage needs
- Doubles your storage space
- Storage is one more problem you don't have to think about
- Everybody needs more storage
- Abounds with convenient storage
See also: ROOM, SPACE

STORE
- Every store guarantees low prices on
- You store's savings are sizzling on
- The company store people look to for the very best
- We want to be your one-stop store
- Celebrate our hundredth store opening
- See store for details
- Now at fine stores everywhere
- A truly unique store for you and your family
- Shop the store with more
- Your savings store

- Your friendly neighborhood store
- Not only does your store bring you top quality merchandise
- Hurry into your store for this super special on assorted designer items
- Your store brings you only the best
- Coming soon to a store near you
- More surprises in store
- Now in a store near you
- The best in store for you
- Our superstores are now bigger than ever
- Simply store your information right at your fingertips
- The only store that sells
- Great area stores to serve you
- A different selection in each store
- Here's what's in store for you when you buy
- Available at selected stores only
- Plus more great deals in store
See also: KEEP, MALL, MARKET, OUTLET, RETAILER

STORY
- We'll never be without the full story
- Now that's the whole story
- We can tell you a pretty interesting story
- Don't be satisfied with only half the story
- The inspiring story behind
- This could be your story
See also: INFORMATION, PLAN, STRATEGY, SYSTEM

STRAIGHT
- Straight as a stripe
- From us you get the straight goods
- Helping you get everything straight
See also: CORRECT, RIGHT

STRANGER
- Is no stranger to
- Hoping to turn you from a stranger into a good friend
- No one is a stranger here

STRANGLEHOLD
- Breaking the stranglehold of
- Has old-fashioned thinking got a stranglehold on you
- Sometimes you can't even feel a stranglehold
See also: POWER

STRATEGY
- Conducting strategy sessions
- Helping you develop the right strategy
- Here's the best strategy
- Whatever your personal financial strategy

- Giving you breakthrough strategies
- For up-to-date strategies

See also: INFORMATION, PLAN, SYSTEM

STREAMLINE
- Also a great way to streamline
- Streamlining service for your convenience
- Our entire operation has been streamlined to lower costs to you

See also: FAST, SPEED

STREET
- Street smart, street sleek
- The look is street-smart
- Has made its way down to the street
- Street-level glamour

See also: COMMUNITY, NEIGHBORHOOD

STRENGTH
- Strength is inspiring
- Industrial strength value
- To add strength for within, we have
- Add to your strength by
- Extra strength provided by
- Driven by strength and performance
- Combines the strength of
- Multiplying your strengths
- Increasing your strength of purpose
- Combines the tremendous strength of
- Key strengths are timing and know-how
- Dozens of ways to strengthen your

See also: MUSCLE, POWER, STRONG

STRESS
- To combat fatigue and stress
- All this contributes to reducing stress
- You can't put enough stress on getting quality for your money
- Stands up to whatever stresses you put on it

See also: HASSLE, INHIBITION, PRESSURE

STRIDE
- Finally hitting your stride
- Find your stride
- Will take it all in stride
- Striding with you boldly into the future

See also: MOVE, STEP

STRIKE
- Don't strike out again
- Striking out in bold new directions
- Has your old machine gone on strike

See also: HIT, IMPACT

STRING
- No strings attached
- Following up on a spectacular string of successes
- Now you get to pull the strings
- Tired of people just stringing you along
- No strings attached
- A no-strings offer

See also: INHIBITION, CONDITION

STRIVE
- Striving each day to provide our customers with quality service and quality products
- We strive to have the items you want
- Striving every day to please you
- Working longer, striving harder

See also: EFFORT, TRY

STRONG
- We made it strong enough to
- Turn to the strong one
- Strong as steel
- Strong enough for
- Strong on savings, strong on value
- Getting stronger every day
- Putting a strong emphasis on
- Become stronger than you ever thought possible

Strong: mighty, powerful, sturdy, tough, virile, robust, red-blooded, hearty, hale, fortified, durable, heavy-duty, cast-iron, substantial, enduring, long-lasting, permanent, solid, sound, firm, resolute, unyielding, unbending, emphatic, intense

See also: POWER, STRENGTH

STUDIO
- Available through selected studios

- Studio quality done right in your home
- Just like having your own studio

STUDY
- Acting as a case study
- Let us do the studying, you the enjoying
- Time and time again, studies have shown the superiority of

See also: EDUCATE, LEARN, RESEARCH

STUFF
- The right stuff
- Where people know their stuff
- Here's some terrific stuff, and it's free
- Get great stuff for only
- More stuff, better stuff, cheaper stuff
- Very exciting stuff
- Where you get good stuff cheap
- For people who know their stuff
- Great stuff in every department
- Terrific stuff on every floor
- The right stuff at the right prices

See also: INVENTORY, MATERIAL, MERCHANDISE

STYLE
- A little extra gives a lot of style
- Style that captivates
- All of the absolutely latest styles
- Something sure to fit your distinctive style
- Professional style and convenience
- Capturing your singular style in an exclusive
- A product that fits your style
- Our best-selling styles
- Style that will rock your world
- What better way to mix style and individuality
- A real sense or style
- Making a difference in style
- You can create any style with
- Luxuriant texture and style
- Accessorize with style
- Decorate your home with timeless stylings
- Your style store
- Celebrated styles you've admired for excellence
- Come in and see our assorted styles
- Country style, city smarts
- Special style features

- It's an energetic style that's all about
- The height of style
- Now learn what style is all about
- The singular style of
- Your style is real
- Real style, comfort and great colors
- We have many other/more sizes and styles for you to choose from
- Designer styling combines elegance and comfort
- Offering distinctive styling and outstanding value
- Stock up on these best-selling styles at one low price
- And should you decide this just isn't your style, we'll give a full refund

Style: mode, vogue, look, taste, approach, rage, fad, craze, form, shape, design, flair, dash, pizzazz, tone, spirit, character, brand, stamp, wording, elegance, refinement, outline
See also: CHIC, ELEGANCE, FASHION

STYLISH
- Setting is stylishly apart from the rest
- Anyone can be more stylish
- Sleek and stylish choice
- Decidedly stylish
- A more beautiful, stylish you

Stylish: smart, natty, modish, flashy, dressy, dapper, spruce, ritzy, suave, urbane, cosmopolitan, sharp, trim, neat, fashionable, snazzy, sophisticated, all the rage, hip, nifty, trendy, popular, in style, up-to-the-minute, tony, posh, elegant, luxurious, sharp as a tack, swanky, high-class, fancy, chi-chi, current, in fashion, chic, high-toned

SUBSTANCE
- Giving shape and substance to
- At last, a claim with some real substance
- We get straight to the substance of the matter

See also: INGREDIENT, MATERIAL

SUBTLE
- The difference can be very subtle
- The changes are subtle, not jarringly sudden
- Moved towards a kind luxurious subtlety

See also: INTANGIBLE, MYSTERY, UNDETECTED

SUCCEED

- Do you have a desire to succeed
- Succeeds where others fail
- Keeps you succeeding every step of the way
- Get out of your way and let you succeed
- Nothing succeeds like success
- At last, we've succeeded in creating

Succeed: accomplish, complete, do, work out, carry through, make good, prosper, thrive, grown, advance, get ahead, succeed with flying colors, triumph over, win, conquer, prevail, luck out, strike it rich, hit the jackpot, make the grade, turn out, be victorious
See also: ACCOMPLISH, ACHIEVE, WIN

SUCCESS

- Fiercely dedicated to our customer's success
- Following success with even greater success
- What's your definition of success
- Success naturally achieved
- To ensure your success
- Flushed with success
- The opportunity for success you've been seeking
- Sharing the secrets of success
- Guarantee you success by
- Become an overnight success
- Ongoing commitment to your success
- Already a great success
- When your success depends on us
- Have made this week a huge success
- For guaranteed success
- The success of your business depends on you
- Join the voyage to success
- Ensuring your success requires clear direction
- Steering you toward success while keeping your costs down
- The real foundation of our success is our people
- Find success right in your own back yard
- We believe in success, pure and simple
- The size of your success is totally up to you
- Success totally redefined
- It's hard to improve on success

- Your success depends solely on you
- Information that is critical to your success
- How to achieve success right in your own backyard
- Join us on the road to success
- Fuel your success

Success: smash, accomplishment, victory, sensation, winner, hit, sockeroo, coup, triumph, boffo, sellout, grand slam, tour de force, good fortune, stroke of genius, stroke of luck, master stroke, fame, wealth, money, affluence, celebrity, renown, high repute
See also: ACCOMPLISHMENT, ACHIEVEMENT, CELEBRITY, TRIUMPH, MONEY, WIN

SUCCESSFUL

- To ensure you remain successful
- Used successfully by
- Successfully serving customers for twenty years
- Shows you how you can do it and be very successful at it
- Why so many successful people introduce their friends to us
- All the earmarks of a successful business

Successful: money-making, gainful, cost-effective, profitable, booming, sitting pretty, out in front, ahead of the game, on top of the world, on easy street, in clover, in the catbird seat, up-and-coming, hotshot, flourishing, thriving, growing, mushrooming, productive, rewarding, prosperous, fruitful, paying, best-selling
See also: POSITIVE

SUFFER

- Why suffer from
- Now you don't have to suffer the agony
- Have you been suffering in silence until now

See also: ENDURE

SUGGESTION

- We take your suggestions seriously
- Please take a few moments to jot down your comments and suggestions
- We listen to every suggestion you give
- We have a few suggestions for you
- Special suggestions

See also: COMMENT, INFORMATION,

INPUT, PLAN, STORY, STRATEGY, SYSTEM

SUIT
- So ideally suited to you that
- It'll easily suit your
- Suit yourself – beautifully
- Suiting up is easy with

SUMMER
- Summer's here already
- Super values and buys make summer even better
- Put some sizzle in your summer
- Enjoy it all summer long
- Spring into summer
- Summertime fun at big savings
- Great summer value on
- Summer is here and so are super savings
- Shape up for summer now
- With summer just around the corner
- We'll help you keep cool all summer long
- Summer wouldn't be summer without
- Sizzlin' summer deals
- A summertime favorite
- We've got a hot summer deal on a cool
- Lots of summer shortcuts
- Summer spectacular
- Summer's sunsational savings
- Think summer
- Summer value days
- A new slant on summer
- Signaling summer's new direction
- Try our taste-of-summer
- Summer sales heat up
- Look hot all summer long
- Call about our sizzling summer specials
- There's still a whole summer to enjoy
- Party along to a swinging summer
- Cool off this summer with
- Heating up this summer
- Endless summer sale
- This summer's hottest
- Get set for summertime
- Get summer's coolest

See also: SEASON, SUN

SUN
- Give yourself some fun in the sun
- Perfect for sun lovers
- Have fun in the sun
- Discover your place in the sun

See also: FUN, SUMMER, WARMTH

SUNSHINE
- Bask in the glory of year-round sunshine
- Put some sunshine in your life
- Basking in the sunshine of your smile

SUPER
- Changes it from pretty good to super
- It's extra super
- Super values, super savings
- Our service is super
- We think you are super
- Supercharged with value

SUPERIOR
- Superior by design
- At superior stores everywhere
- A genuinely superior product
- When you see how superior our service really is
- Turning in a superior performance
- First in strength and superiority

See also: BEST

SUPERSTORE
- Your neighborhood superstore
- Your brand new superstore
- Get all the advantages of a hometown superstore
- A superstore with everything you want

See also: OUTLET, MALL, STORE

SUPPLIER
- We have been a leading supplier for years
- We want to become your exclusive supplier of
- After you've seen what other suppliers have to offer, come to us
- Proud supplier to

See also: SELLER, SUPPLIER

SUPPLY
- Supply the industry for
- Stocks an endless supply of
- The supply is shrinking
- Our supply is limited
- Order now while the supply lasts
- We have a complete line of supplies
- While supplies last

See also: GIVE, PROVIDE, RESOURCE

SUPPORT
- Providing you with all the support you need
- Support offered night or day
- Offering full-scale support
- To help support your
- Provides perfect support for
- With unmatched support to help you explore
- Ranks are united in our support for
- Lending real support to
- We'll give you the information, guidance and support your need to
- Supporting you every step of the way
- Outstanding support

Support: elevate, bolster, uphold, enhance, buttress, shoulder, keep up, reliever, comfort, sympathize, assure, hold up, hang in, maintain, sustain, cherish, nurture, nourish, foster, provide for, take care of, look after, watch over, tend, mind, finance, subsidize, pay for, fund, sponsor, underwrite, capitalize, put the money up for, set up, meet the expenses, encourage, abet, accommodate, hearten, advocate, promote, vouch for, endorse, make good, adopt
See also: BEHIND, HELP, NURTURE

SURE
- In fact, we're so sure that
- You can be sure of one thing
- Not sure what to do
- That's why we've made sure we have what you want
- You have to be sure that
- They'll make sure that
- A sure way to
- When you've never been more sure
- It's a sure thing
- To be sure you get exactly what you want

See also: CERTAINTY, DEPEND, GUARANTEE, RELIABLE

SURPRISE
- Don't be surprised if
- Surprise that someone special tonight
- Not surprisingly
- You'll be surprised at just how good our product is
- Surprise him/her with a top quality
- Someone with everything can still be surprised

- And much to the surprise of many
- No surprise that
- And a very pleasant surprise to find
- It's all about complete surprise
- So that there's no surprises
- Our excellence is no surprise at all
- There are no price surprises
- The last thing you need are surprises

Surprise: stun, flabbergast, amaze, astonish, blow away, overpower, overwhelm, throw for a loop, floor, bowl over, hit between the eyes, catch off-guard, jump, ambush, bushwhack, swoop down upon, blitz, out of the blue, pounce, take unawares
See also: AMAZE, BLITZ, UNEXPECTED

SURROUND
- Surround yourself with the ultimate in luxury and comfort
- Surrounds you instantly
- The more you surround yourself with pleasure you deserve

See also: ENVELOPE, IMMERSE

SURVIVAL
- Always worked and planned for your survival
- To you, it means survival
- In today's tough world, it's survival of the fittest

SURVIVE
- Surviving beautifully
- Helping your survive in a rough world
- Survived the hardest conditions

See also: LAST, LIVE, SUCCEED

SWEAT
- For another reason not to sweat
- Don't sweat the small stuff
- You've put a lot of sweat into getting ahead

See also: EFFORT, WORK

SWING
- You don't have to swing to
- We're swinging
- Opinion is swinging in our direction
- Get into the swing of the new

See also: CHANGE, CHOOSE

SWITCH
- Switch to freedom
- Now you don't have to constantly switch between
- Switch and save
- Switch to a better brand of
- Isn't it time you switched
- More people than ever are switching
- Switching couldn't be simpler
- Switch today and start enjoying
- Switch over now
- Make the switch today
- To convince you to switch to
- Switch now and save hundreds
- Thousands have made the switch

See also: CHANGE, CHOICE, CHOOSE, TRADE

SYMBOL
- Just look for this symbol
- For years it's been the symbol of quality
- This symbol means the very best
- To symbolize the preservation of

See also: ICON, MARK, SIGN

SYMPTOM
- Goes beyond just treating symptoms
- Just one more symptom that has to be dealt with
- You can't afford to ignore the symptoms

SYSTEM
- Anyone who follows this incredible new system can
- You can't buy a better system
- Our proven system can quickly adds up to profits
- No other system even begins to come close
- It does just that via an innovative system
- A system that lives up to everyone's expectations
- All to make sure your system remains intact
- Identify ways to expand your system down the road
- Beating the system is a snap with
- Makes other systems look like ninety-eight pound weaklings
- Works effortlessly with your other systems
- Ask for the system that works fast and easily

- A superior system for
- A totally personal system for you
- All because of our advanced system
- A durable and economical system
- Most advanced system on the market today
- Total systems designed to being people closer together

System: organization, arrangement, order, method, process, procedure, technique, custom, means, practise, scheme, design, pattern, outline, rule, policy
See also: DESIGN, GOAL, IDEA, INFORMATION, PHILOSOPHY, PLAN, PRINCIPLE, PROCESS, PROGRAM

TACKLE
- Now it's time to tackle the big challenges
- When you're ready to tackle the big one
- We can tackle anything you throw at us
- Helping you tackle what life brings

See also: CONQUER, FIGHT, HELP, TRY

TACTILE
- A very tactile experience
- Sensuously tactile, beautifully shaped
- Richer, more tactile and full of delight

See also: FEEL, TEXTURE

TAILOR
- We tailor it especially for you
- Custom-tailored to your needs
- Impeccably tailored
- Tailor-made for

See also: DESIGN, FIT, SERVE, SHAPE

TAKE
- We do more than just take you there
- Here's our take on
- Who says you can't take it with you
- Something we don't take lightly
- A completely different take on things
- Taking you farther and higher than ever before

See also: ANGLE, CARRY, MOVE

TALENT
- Alive with the voices and vision of today's brightest talents
- Brings out the sleeping talent deep within you

- Call upon the many and varied talents
See also: **ABILITY, CRAFT, SKILL**

TALK
- Talking to more people every day about
- Now you're talking
- We're talking about
- This is a good time to talk about
- We're talking products and services
- We're talking lots of it, folks
- We hope to talk to many of you through these venues
- Feel free to talk to our staff about
- Talk of the streets/town/land
- You should be talking to us
- Now you're talking
- And we're not just talking about
- Straight talk on
- We take the time to really talk to you
- Looking for someone you can talk to
- We've got the time to talk
- Can we talk
See also: **CALL, COMMUNICATE, CONSIDER, SPEAK, TELL**

TAME
- Anything but tame
- Are you tired of tame designs
- Will tame the most intractable problems
- When you don't want to be tame any more
See also: **COOPERATION, PEACE**

TARGET
- Don't be a target this winter
- A sale that targets you
- Need not be mutually exclusive targets
- To reach your/our target customers quickly
- Advanced options help you target what you want
- Targeting a whole different kind of
See also: **AIM, GOAL, MISSION, PURPOSE**

TASK
- No longer find the task so daunting
- Multi-tasking is our specialty
- So many tasks are simple enough to be performed on your own
- Getting all your tasks done satisfactorily
- Organizes your tasks efficiently
See also: **JOB, VENTURE, WORK**

TASTE
- Better taste. better value
- Great taste, great price
- To suit your individual taste
- Exactly to your taste
- Wherever your tastes take you
- Products to suit every taste
- A product for everyone's taste
- With a taste all their own
- For a taste that's out of this world
- All taste, no waste
- Quick and tasty
- Giant taste, tiny price
- Good taste remains constant
- Points out users who share your tastes
- Giving you a taste for the very best
- Taste the best
- For the cultured taste you crave
- A rich, rewarding taste
- Taste the difference
- Tastes better too
- Put your taste buds on full alert
- Terrific tasting
- Taste the freshness
- If you have a taste for
- Without taking the bite out of taste
- Low in fat doesn't mean low in taste
- Puts the taste back in
- Get a taste now
- Taste the warmth
- Taste the best of both worlds
- Have you tasted it yet
- Topped off with the great taste of
- Out-of-this world taste starts here
- Savor these other tasty products
Taste: relish, savor, experience, encounter, sample, appetite, discernment, perception, acumen, finesse, grace, discrimination, polish, cultivation, elegance, style
See also: **CHOICE, COOK, ELEGANCE, FLAVOR, LIFESTYLE, PREFER, STYLE, TRY**

TEACH
- We'll teach you the ABC's of
- As you teach us your needs
- Gladly teaching you everything you need to know to
- We don't need to teach you how to
See also: **EDUCATE, INSTRUCTIONS, LEARN, SHOW**

TEAM
- Team up beautifully with
- Recognizing the team effort required for the creation of
- A real exercise in team building
- Join the team
- You can join our leading team
- To join the winning team, call
- Because we've got the best team
- Determining who will fit in best with your team
- A strong team player
- Working with a team of leading people from around the world
- You count on your team to succeed
- Make us part of your team
- The most successful team in history

See also: CLUB, CREW, GROUP, PARTNER, SALESPEOPLE, STAFF

TEAMWORK
- By encouraging respect for teamwork
- For better work and better teamwork
- Excellent teamwork is key to our success
- You'll be impressed with our teamwork

See also: COOPERATION, PARTNERSHIP

TECHNICIAN
- A friendly, trained technician is always ready to help you
- A trained technician arrives as scheduled
- An expert technician is always on hand to answer your questions
- Let our technicians do the work do all the work for you
- Our technicians are the best in the business

See also: EXPERT, PRO, PROFESSIONAL, SPECIALIST, STAFF

TECHNIQUE
- The secret techniques of
- Covers step-by-step techniques for creating
- Created using the most advanced techniques
- Developing ever better techniques of
- Spent decades perfecting the technique

See also: METHOD, TECHNOLOGY, WAY

TECHNOLOGY
- Enjoy the challenge of conquering new technology
- Pushing technology to the limit
- We've been advancing technology in the areas of
- Applying technology to some of the world's most difficult problems
- How quickly technology becomes ancient history
- Led us to the development of many innovative technologies to help you
- Ensuring today's technology won't be obsolete tomorrow
- Uses the most advanced technology
- Connects you to the extraordinary technology of
- And this same technology allows you to do much more than just
- The result of a new generation of technology
- An impressive combination of advanced technology and ease of use
- Breakthrough technology
- Compares state-of-the-art technology
- Integrating new technologies
- To better technology alternatives
- Your lifeline to the latest technology
- As the latest technology becomes available
- The most technologically savvy way
- Actively involved in the development of new-age technologies
- Every one a technological marvel

See also: ADVANCE, GEAR, INNOVATION, INVENT, MACHINE

TEETH
- A product you can really sink your teeth into
- A service with some teeth in it
- No longer do you have to grit your teeth and face

TELEPHONE
- Limited time only – telephone today
- As close as your telephone
- Pick up your telephone right now
- Order it over the telephone
- All done via your telephone

See also: CALL, CONNECT, ORDER, PHONE

TELL

- We'd like to tell you firsthand
- Here's why we're telling you about our
- Let me tell you more about this fascinating secret
- We keep telling you about
- Please tell us what you think
- Telling it like it is
- Tell your friends about the things you've discovered
- Anyone will tell you that
- We are very pleased to tell you that
- Doesn't just tell you, it shows you step-by-step

See also: COMMUNICATE, SAY, TALK, TELL

TEMPT

- We love to tempt you with
- You can't help but be tempted
- Let us tempt you with this terrific selection of
- More people are tempted by
- A very tempting offer

Tempt: entice, allure, seduce, lure, fascinate engage, infatuate, carry away, enamor, excite, captivate, charm, attract, appeal, enthral, enrapture, bewitch, hypnotize, mesmerize
See also: APPEAL, ATTRACT, DRAW

TEMPTATION

- Embrace temptation
- Sweet temptations
- Give in to the temptation of
- Nothing but wall-to-wall temptations

See also: APPEAL, SEDUCTION

TERROR

- Take the terror out of
- Some people have an irrational terror
- Need not strike terror to your heart

TEST

- Take them for a test run
- The real test is how the product has been tested
- Because these solutions have been thoroughly tested
- This product has been clinically tested to be safe and effective
- Give us a test run
- Just wait till you see the test results

- Put us to the test and see how well we do
- Could what you're using now pass this test
- Developed without animal testing
- You're eager to test your
- The test results are in
- Everything you do has already been tested

See also: RESEARCH, TRY

TEXTURE

- Improves the texture of
- Altogether better in flavor and in texture
- All in the texture of your choice

See also: APPEARANCE, FEEL

THANK

- Thank you for your business
- Thank you for your order
- We're thanking our loyal customers with this fabulous, limited-time offer
- We have what they'll thank you gratefully for
- We've made it big, thanks to you
- Thanks to your support and encouragement
- Thanks to you
- Thanks for thinking of us
- Just wanted to say thanks
- Our way of saying thank you
- Thanks to new technological advances
- Thanks a million
- Just one more way of saying thank you for choosing us
- Thanks for the opportunity to serve you
- Thanks for your deeply valued business
- It's thanks to you for this success
- It's our way of saying thanks for being a customer
- Thanks again for choosing us
- We send a heartfelt thank you to
- A special thanks to all our clients
- With great pride we say thank you to
- Thank you for making us your first choice

See also: APPRECIATE, APPRECIATION, GRATITUDE

THAW

- Thaw n' serve
- Finally thawing out relations between
- Tired of waiting for something to thaw

THEORY
- Describes the latest, most exciting theory behind
- Here's the most exciting, most powerful theory of all
- It worked in theory, now it works in practice too

See also: IDEA

THERE
- That's why there's nothing like being there
- You finally know you're there when
- We put it there just for you

See also: PLACE

THING
- We think the neatest thing about it is
- It's the real thing
- We've got a thing about quality
- Means only one thing
- The most wonderful thing to offer
- Starting with one of the things that made us famous
- Naturally, you like nice things

See also: FEATURE, STUFF

THINK
- You probably don't think about these things very often
- If you're thinking of
- Just think of it
- Just when you're wondering what will they think of next
- Think again
- This is how we think
- Think big
- Start thinking of your future
- Taking the time to actually stop and think
- Why didn't they think of this before
- See what you think
- You probably think you'd never be able to afford
- Discover a whole new way of thinking
- We know you'll never think of our product the same way again
- It's smart thinking like this that's made us the choice of
- So that you don't have to think twice
- It's all part of the thinking behind our
- A place where all forward thinkers turn

See also: CONCEPT, CONSIDER, IDEA

THOUGHT
- Collect your thoughts with this lovely item
- You never need to give it a second thought
- Here's some thoughts on
- You probably never thought you'd even need a
- We'd like to hear your thoughts

See also: CONSIDER, IDEA, THINK

THREAT
- Threats can come from many directions
- Now your biggest threat is gone
- Get rid of the threat of

See also: POSSIBILITY, RISK

THRIFT
- For those of you with thrift in mind
- Thrift doesn't have to mean deprivation
- Thrift is coming back into style
- Thrift is a virtue often overlooked
- Designed for thrifty souls like you

See also: AUSTERITY, BUDGET, SAVE

THRILL
- Give them the thrill of a lifetime
- Nothing is more thrilling than the kick of a new
- Thrills and chills and an altogether wonderful time
- Feel the thrill

See also: ENJOY, EXHILARATION, EXCITE, PLEASURE

THROUGHOUT
- We'll find what you want throughout
- Throughout the experience, we're at your side
- The greatest care all throughout production

THROW
- We'll even throw in an extra bonus
- Can take whatever life throws at it
- Don't let the idea throw you
- Just look at all the other goodies we throw in

TICK
- Figure out what makes them tick
- Lest it turn into a ticking time bomb
- Keeping you merrily ticking along

See also: FUNCTION, WORK

TICKET
- Your one-way ticket to the hottest
- Giving you a ticket to success
- Hurry and get your ticket today
- Your ticket to the next stage of
- Just the ticket
- Your ticket to a better life

See also: TICKET

TIDY
- Stays completely neat and tidy
- And makes you a tidy profit
- Tidy savings when you plan ahead

See also: ORDER

TIER
- Moving you into the top tier of
- Tiers upon tiers of bargains waiting for you
- Moving upward from tier to tier

See also: LEVEL, RANK

TIME
- Any time, day or night
- It's time for a change
- No matter what time you call
- Giving you the ability to manage time
- Time for a fresh approach
- And that takes time you don't always have
- Can put you back in control of your time
- If you don't have the time, tools or talent
- Don't pay for time you don't use
- Why waste your time when you can get
- Putting time on your side
- Now time is definitively on your side
- In business, you don't have time to waste
- An don't waste any more time
- Isn't it time you
- Too much to do and not enough time
- Your time together is precious
- So time won't tell
- Just another way to save you time
- Really prime time
- Do it any time you wish
- We invest our time
- There's no better time to
- Save time and money
- It's that time again
- Now would be a very good time
- The perfect gift, the perfect time

- For the first time in
- Just a matter of time
- On time and on budget
- Great if you're really pressed for time
- Right place, right time for
- The time is right/ripe for
- Do it now because time is running out fast
- The latest time and money saving service
- We're there when the time comes to
- Just in time for
- Once upon a time
- Before time runs out
- Now is the time to
- Save time and effort
- Limited time only
- For a limited time, take advantage of our optional
- Thanks to all who dropped in to
- The time we save you makes a huge difference in cost and efficiency
- So this time around, we are
- In times that are changing ever faster
- Helps fight the effects of time
- Your time is valuable
- Takes you on a pleasurable journey back through time
- It's only a matter of time until we see
- Take some time off for good behavior
- There's never enough time to
- Timing is everything
- The most precious commodity these days is time
- Only a matter of time before
- Not the first time that
- Time waits for no one
- Time spent with us is time well spent
- It's been a long time coming
- Finally, time to do what you want
- Regularly, good times and bad
- Timing is now perfect for
- In these fast-moving times

Time: juncture, instant, moment, point, hour, day, stretch, spell, span, interval, tenure, interlude, break, pause, hiatus, watch, tour, duration, age, date, epoch, leisure, freedom, occasion, rhythm

See also: AGE, CLOCK, FREEDOM

TIMELESS
- Capture timeless beauty of
- The over-all feeling is of timelessness

and enchantment
- Timeless beauty at your fingertips
- Soak in the timeless feel of
- A place of timeless serenity and peace

Timeless: ageless, everlasting, undying, eternal, deathless, never-ending, immortal, immemorial
See also: CLASSIC, TRADITION

TINGLE
- Feel the healthy tingle of
- Makes you tingle all over
- Gets you tingling with excitement

TIP
- How-to tips you won't get anywhere else
- Gain invaluable tips, techniques and shortcuts
- Want a hot tip on
- Tip of the week
- Tips on everything from
- For interesting tips and information, tune in to
- Here you can find insider tips on latest
- Tips on how to improve and maintain
- For more great tips, call
- Paved with golden tips

See also: HELP, INFORMATION

TITLE
- Lives up to its title
- You win the title
- It's like you've just won the title fight
- And the title goes to you
- Much more than just a fancy title

See also: NAME, PRIZE

TODAY
- Today on the eve of
- Starts today
- Do it today
- Today is the day when you finally
- It's easy and you can do it today
- Today's products at yesterday's prices

See also: NOW

TOE
- Starts your toes a-tingling
- Feel the thrill all the way down to your toes
- Keep on your toes
- Now you don't have to toe the line for

anyone
- A top-to-toe makeover
- Feel terrific from top to toe

See also: EVERYTHING

TOGETHER
- Always looks pulled together
- Work effortlessly together
- Shows you how to put it all together
- Never got together before
- Some things go together naturally
- Achieving more together
- Together, we can do it
- Bringing together some of the most famous
- The first time so many have come together to
- We pull it all together
- Together, we can see it through
- Getting it all together
- Working effortlessly together
- Bringing together some of the country's most respected experts

See also: PAIR, PARTNER, PARTNERSHIP, TEAM, TEAMWORK

TOLERANCE
- Developed a very high tolerance for
- Zero tolerance for the mediocre
- Rapidly increasing the tolerance level

TOMORROW
- The product of tomorrow is here today
- Ready to answer tomorrow's needs
- Tomorrow's product and service today
- Striding boldly into tomorrow
- Don't wait until tomorrow
- Tomorrow may be too late
- Building a firm foundation for tomorrow
- Tomorrow is another day
- Tomorrow's abilities today

See also: FUTURE

TOOL
- This valuable tool helps you organize
- A wonderful new tool for people who are searching for
- Don't forget the tools you'll need
- Creative tools for personal expression
- Are you getting the tools you really need
- The right tools for
- Giving you the tools you need to get the job done right

- All the tools you'll need to
- Bright ideas need smart tools
- A tool you won't want to be without
- You need the right tools

Tool: instrument, device, invention, gadget, contraption, gimmick, machine, time-saver, convenience, vehicle, agency, means, agent, medium, go-between, implement, channel
See also: INFORMATION, METHOD, WAY

TOP

- To top it all off
- Climb to the top with our expert help
- Putting you at the very top of our list
- Has raced to the top
- Let them try to top this
- A product you can't top
- Takes you all the way to the top
- We're tops at
- Showing you how to come out on top
- Helping you stay on top of
- Go to the top of the class
- There are no shortcuts to the top
- Direction coming from the top

See also: BEST, PEAK, PINNACLE, SUPERIOR

TOPIC

- The hot topic for today is
- A topic everyone is interested in
- We can't say enough about this topic
- Whatever topic you choose
- For more on this topic, check out
- A topic for a very lively discussion

See also: CONCEPT, IDEA

TOUCH

- Keep in touch effortlessly
- It's those little touches that make it so enjoyable
- Touches the entire
- You will some to recognize this as our touch
- Keeping in touch with you
- Staying in touch with the people who matter most
- Other ways to get in touch with us
- We provide the human touch
- For that special touch
- Just the right touch
- The soft touch

- Touchably soft
- Next time you touch down, visit us
- Come in for a touch of
- We help you keep in touch with
- Gives it that sweet finishing touch
- And for the final finishing touch
- Add the perfect crowning touch
- You can't afford to be out of touch
- Systems that keep you in touch
- Acquire the golden touch
- For the personal touch
- Keeping you in touch and up-to-date

See also: COMMUNICATE, CONNECT, EFFECT, EXPERIENCE, FEELING, REACH, SKILL, TALK, TELL

TOUGH

- Two parts beautiful, one part tough
- Tough as nails
- Tough on problems
- A tough act to follow
- A tough nut to crack, but we cracked it
- When you're this tough, you don't bother with
- We built it tough and strong so that you can
- So you think you're tough
- Built for the world's toughest

See also: STRENGTH, STRONG

TRACK

- On the right track for
- Now you can keep track of your entire
- Delightfully off the beaten track
- How to get back on track
- The easy way to keep on track
- What better way to keep track of
- Get on track for big savings

See also: FOLLOW, PATH, ROAD, WAY

TRADE

- Trade secrets directly from the professionals
- Buy, sell and trade
- Now running a special trade-in campaign
- Trade and save
- Best trade-in values in town
- No trade offs
- Trade in your old items for new

See also: BUY, CHANGE, PURCHASE, SELL, SWITCH

TRADITION
- The tradition must go on
- But the tradition continues
- A wonderful tradition since
- A great new tradition is born
- Committed to time-honored traditions
- There is no substitute for tradition and craftsmanship
- Thoroughly steeped in tradition
- Following in the successful tradition
- Today, that tradition continues
- Tradition for a modern world
- Drawn by a rich artistic tradition
- The meaning and tradition behind
- Building quality in a time-tested tradition
- We know what it means to break with tradition
- Maintains the highest standards of traditional service
- Continuing in the great traditions of

See also: HERITAGE, HISTORY, INHERITANCE, LEGACY

TRADITIONAL
- As traditional as they come
- There's nothing traditional in our approach
- Traditional reproductions and unparalleled modern selections
- Not so traditional is the idea that you can
- Traditional savings are here again
- Isn't it time you stepped out of the traditional and into the modern
- The timeless beauty of traditional style

See also: CLASSIC, HERITAGE

TRAFFIC
- Join the traffic in the fast lane
- Let us increase your traffic dramatically
- Stop traffic with
- Buy one of these traffic-stoppers and you'll be a hit
- And you don't have to fight traffic to get to our store
- Tie up traffic with
- Let us increase your traffic dramatically

TRAIN
- You're not just training bodies, you're shaping minds
- Our trained staff is waiting to help you
- We provide all the training necessary
- You don't need special training
- Quality training at an affordable cost

See also: EDUCATE, LEARN, TEACH

TRANSFORM
- Is instantly transformed into a bright and welcoming
- Transformed into something you'll be proud of
- Instantly transforms into
- Few have the energy, talent or resources to transform
- You'll feel transformed

Transform: transfigure, renew, convert, alter, modify, permutate, remodel, remold, rearrange, reconstruct, revolutionize, recast, translate metamorphose

See also: ALTERNATIVE, CHANGE

TRANSITION
- Thousands of people, just like you, have successfully made the transition
- You can make the transition too
- The transition is very easy

See also: CHANGE. SWITCH, TRADE

TRANSPORT
- Folds for easy transport
- Created to transport you to
- Transporting you to a whole new world of wonder
- Improved transport means improved value

See also: CARRY, MOVE

TRAVEL
- You don't have to travel any farther than your local store
- Make us your travel destination
- Let's travel together down this exciting new road
- Experience the sheer comfort of travelling with

See also: JOURNEY, MOVE

TREASURE
- Want something you'll treasure forever
- Will be treasured for years and years
- A real treasure waiting for you
- A store packed with treasures
- We treasure your good opinion of us
- A unique treasure to delight almost any age

See also: GEM, SPECIAL, UNIQUE

TREAT
- A real treat for your feet
- Treat yourself or a special someone
- Time to give yourself a treat
- A simple, effective way to treat
- The best treat of all is
- It's always a treat to
- Treat your family to health and happiness
- Treat yourself to something really special
- Treat yourself to a quality product at a surprisingly affordable price
- For this festive season a variety of delectable treats

See also: EAT, PAMPER

TREMENDOUS
- Only then can you appreciate the tremendous amount of
- Simply tremendous
- When you find something as tremendous as this, you grab it fast

See also: BIG,

TREND
- Designed to help you take advantage of the trend to
- A trend we're determined to dispel
- One of this year's key trends
- Trends come here first
- Starting a whole new trend to
- We create trends
- Trendy and smart

See also: FASHION, STYLE, TASTE

TRIAL
- Enjoy it for a 10 day home trial
- Why we're making this no-risk trial offer
- Three months free trial
- Do not wait for your free trial
- Give it a trial and see how well it works
- Try it on a trial basis
- Take advantage of our one month free trial offer

See also: OFFER, TRY

TRIBUTE
- Pays glorious tribute to
- Paying tribute to fifty years of
- As a tribute to our customers, we're offering
- We want to pay tribute to you with this
- A tribute to honor your loyalty

See also: APPRECIATION, GIFT, HOMAGE, KUDOS, PRAISE

TRICK
- Learn all the tricks of the trade
- You'll soon see that it isn't any trick
- And it does tricks too

See also: ILLUSION, MAGIC

TRIMMINGS
- Comes with all the trimmings
- Gives you even more trimmings
- Of course you want all the trimmings

See also: BONUS, EXTRA

TRIP
- Promise it will be worth the trip
- A trip your family will never forget
- Easily worth the trip to
- One trip to our store and you'll realize

See also: JOURNEY, MOVE, TRAVEL, VISIT, VOYAGE

TRIUMPH
- Total triumph
- A triumph of engineering
- Triumph over all rivals

See also: CONQUER, SUCCESS, VICTORY, WIN

TROUBLE
- Double trouble for
- It's no trouble at all to help you
- Taking the trouble to make sure
- Getting you out of trouble in double quick time
- No amount of trouble is too much

See also: CHALLENGE, EFFORT, HASSLE, PROBLEM

TRUCKLOAD
- Savings by the truckload
- Truckloads of bargains are arriving every day
- Now you can get them by the truckload

TRUE
- What was true then remains true today
- Tried and true
- True value, true quality
- See what true beauty looks like
- It's amazing but true that

- Is this chance too good to be true

See also: AUTHENTIC, GENUINE, REAL

TRUST
- Quality products and services you can trust
- Nothing is more important than the trust and confidence you place in our company
- Gives trust a whole new meaning
- Complete trust in
- The store you trust
- Earning your trust every day
- People trust us
- Trust is what it's really all about
- More reasons to trust
- We give you a reason to trust
- Use it once and find out why it's trusted most
- There's no other product that's more trusted
- If trust is important to you, read on

Trust: surety, faith, certitude, belief, confidence, assurance, conviction, security, reliance, positiveness, dependence, reliability, credit, credibility, trustworthiness, solvency, guardianship, responsibility, commitment, obligation, count on, rely on, believe in, hope, entrust, invest, empower, swear by

See also: CONFIDENCE, FAITH, GUARANTEE, RELY, WARRANTY

TRUTH
- A new truth for
- Get the straight truth about
- Sometimes it can be hard to get to the truth

TRY
- This way, you can try it out yourself
- Try it, then buy it
- Come in and try it out
- It's time you tried a
- You just can't wait to try
- If you haven't tried our product recently, you're missing out on something great
- A must-try product
- We are pleased to offer you one more reason to give us a try
- Beauty without even trying

- Isn't it time you tried it
- Give it a try for free
- Try it today
- Don't take our word, try it yourself
- You can try it before you buy it
- Just try it yourself
- Instead, we'll invite you to try it
- Try it today and experience the tempting
- You owe it to yourself to try

Try: attempt, endeavor, undertake, take a shot/crack at, strive, essay, make an effort

See also: EFFORT, TRIAL

TUCK
- You'll find it tucked cosily away
- With extra value tucked in
- Great convenience all tucked into one

TUMMY
- To satisfy a growling tummy
- A real tummy pleaser
- You'll feel good with this in your tummy
- Making tummies happy everywhere

TUNE
- A first-time opportunity to tune in to what's happening
- Tune up for
- Tune in, turn on to
- Totally in tune with you
- Listen to a different tune
- Tunes you completely to the rhythm of
- Carry a tune with
- Time for your spring tune-up
- We'll have you playing to a whole new tune

See also: CONNECT

TURN
- When you feel there's nowhere else to turn
- Turn to us when you really need
- Make life take a turn for the better

TWIST
- That gives it a fresh twist
- When things take an unexpected twist
- Giving you the familiar, but with a twist

TYPE
- Almost every conceivable type of
- A brand new type of

- Definitely your type

See also: KIND, SORT. SPECIES

TYPICAL
- For those who don't want to be typical
- Such excellent results are typical of our company
- Not just another typical product

ULTIMATE
- The ultimate in value
- The ultimate in comfort
- Will ultimately lead to a beautifully

See also: EXTREME, FINAL

UNBELIEVABLE
- Unbelievable value
- Something unbelievable has just happened
- It's simply unbelievable
- The unbelievable has just come true

See also: AMAZE

UNCHANGED
- Virtually unchanged since
- Unchanged no matter how turbulent the times
- The product is new, the quality and value unchanged

UNDERSOLD
- We refuse to be undersold
- Never undersold by competitors
- We will not knowingly/willingly be undersold
- We will not be undersold by anyone

See also: LESS, REDUCE

UNDERSTAND
- Understands your desire to look and feel your absolute best
- You know how critical it is to understand
- Customers come to us because we understand
- We understand very well that
- Come to someone who really understands
- It really helps that our people understand your needs
- Helping to understand what you're doing
- Specially trained to help you understand
- We understand your needs and desires

- Taking the time to understand your goals
- And because we truly try to understand the needs of
- We understand that not everyone's needs are the same
- So you'll understand how easy it is
- To understand what this can do for you

Understand: comprehend, fathom, penetrate, figure out, grasp, recognize, see through, perceive, discern, make out

See also: KNOW, INFORM, RECOGNIZE

UNDERSTANDING
- A greater understanding of
- For those who want a clearer understanding of
- Bringing deep experience and understanding to
- Working to increase your understanding

Understanding: comprehension, consciousness, cognizance, knowledge, realization, awareness, conception

See also: CONCEPT, IDEA, INFORMATION, KNOWLEDGE, WISDOM

UNDERTONE
- Warm, woodsy undertones
- A quiet undertone of comfort and security
- Delicately undertoned richness

See also: HINT, SUBTLE

UNDETECTABLE
- It is completely undetectable
- Undetectable when you're wearing it
- Confidential, personal and completely undetectable

UNDISCOVERED
- Still largely undiscovered
- A lovely undiscovered nook is waiting for you
- Discover the undiscovered

See also: DISCREET, HIDE

UNEXPECTED
- Always the unexpected
- Such excellent results are not exactly unexpected
- Providing you with unexpected, built-in

value
See also: SURPRISE

UNIQUE
- Discover an incredibly unique
- Is what makes this fine product truly unique
- Embraces all that is unique and fascinating about
- You bet we're unique
- What makes this product unique is our amazing use of
- Unique and well-established
- Unique and invaluable
- Unique limited edition creation
- Always looking for ways to meet your unique needs

See also: ONE, ONE-OF-A-KIND, ORIGINAL, RARE, SPECIAL

UNIVERSAL
- Is ageless and universal
- Universally loved and admired
- Universally accepted standards
- The timeless and universal appeal of

See also: CLASSIC, EVERYWHERE, TIMELESS

UNLIMITED
- Just imagine the unlimited
- Tap into unlimited possibilities
- An unlimited offer for people just like you

UNLOCK
- Unlock the door to financial freedom
- Unlock the secret of success
- Unlocks the door to a whole new universe
- Unlock your hidden beauty
- Unlock the inner you
- Unlock sizzling potential you never knew you had

See also: FREE, RELEASE, SOLVE

UNMISTAKABLE
- Unmistakable and irresistible
- The unmistakable look and feel of quality
- The signature is unmistakable
- Unmistakable for anything else

UNPRETENTIOUS
- Handsome but unpretentious
- Unpretentious goodness and solidity
- Straightforward unpretentiousness to relax in

UNSIGHTLY
- Prevents unsightly
- No longer do you have to put up with unsightly
- Removes unsightly problems before they escalate

UNSURE
- If you're still unsure about which
- You don't need to be unsure any more
- A sure thing in an unsure world

See also: CONFUSE

UNTHINKABLE
- We just did the unthinkable
- Unthinkable just last year
- Such advances used to be unthinkable

UNUSUAL
- So unusual and striking
- For unusually big benefits
- Want to tell you about unusually splendid savings

See also: EXCEPTION, RARE, UNIQUE

UNWIND
- Stretch out and unwind
- What better way to unwind than
- Now you can unwind in style
- Relax and unwind with

See also: PAMPER, RELAX, REST

UP
- Up, up and away
- Are you up for it
- Bounding up to another level
- Take us up on our offer

See also: ACCEPT. RISE

UPDATE
- We are continually updating our
- Constantly revised and updated to keep you currant
- You'll receive updates on new products every week
- Call us for an update on
- Free updates as often you wish

See also: INFORMATION

UPGRADE
- Upgrading fine minds since
- And it's so easy to upgrade when you're ready
- Buy something you can upgrade when you want
- Continually upgraded

See also: IMPROVE

UPKEEP
- Carefree upkeep
- Very low upkeep costs
- And the upkeep takes no time

See also: MAINTENANCE

UPLIFT
- A wonderful uplift of spirits
- Feel the uplift as soon you arrive
- A real mood uplift

See also: RISE, SOAR

URGE
- When the urge hits to
- A urge that cannot be denied
- The urge to excellence is never-ending
- I strongly urge you to act now

See also: DESIRE, DRIVE

USE
- If you've got it, use it
- Making it faster than you can use it
- Best with daily use
- You can always use a few great
- Thousands like yourself use
- Use it year after year
- Use it as much as you like
- Easy to use and even easier to
- Both for everyday and specialized uses
- However you intend to use it
- Unlike any you've ever used before
- Easy to use, easy to afford
- Makes exceptional use of
- Anyone can use it
- Designed for ease of use
- Another great use was born
- Handy products you'll use every day
- You won't find anything that's easier to use
- A hundred handy uses
- Simple to use and useful at the same time
- Another great use is born
- Yours to use whenever you want
- Always ready to use

- Use them immediately to
- Designed for instant use
- Why would you use anything else
- Use it every day
- Easier to use than any other product
- You only pay for what you actually use
- Hundreds of daily uses
- Use it anywhere, any time
- Would definitely used and recommend
- Actually pays you for using it

See also: APPLICATION, FUNCTION, METHOD, SERVE

USEFUL
- Widely useful in
- You'll find it very useful for
- A very useful addition to you
- Of almost unlimited usefulness

See also: PRACTICAL, HELPFUL

USER
- Very user friendly
- Our customers are repeat users of our service
- Creates a very satisfied end user

UTILIZE
- We utilize the best
- Helping you to utilize
- Now you can utilize all of you talents and options

See also: FUNCTION, USE

VACATION
- Discover the vacation of adventurers
- Treat yourself to a whole new vacation experience
- Go on a dream vacation this winter
- Like having a vacation every day
- Feel as though you're on vacation
- Now you can have vacation sooner than you thought
- Have the vacation of a lifetime

See also: ESCAPE, GETAWAY, HOLIDAY, TRAVEL, VISIT

VALUABLE
- For quick, easy and valuable information
- You can't put a price on something so valuable
- Plus you can get valuable
- Is immensely valuable
- Providing something unique and

valuable
- Quite likely the most valuable available
- Your valuables are protected
- Giving you valuable experience with

See also: PRECIOUS, TREASURE

VALUE
- Get it before it has a chance to increase in value
- Values to hundreds of dollars
- Will not only increase in value with time
- Making it an even better value than before
- Adds value in a variety of ways
- One of the most highly valued, highly used
- You appreciate the enduring value of
- Bringing you value that far exceeds the price
- Your best value is
- If you value quality of life
- Continues to add value to
- Has the potential to increase in value
- Value really adds up
- Add up the value and save
- Long live value
- Hotline to value
- Rock solid value every day
- Value-packed
- Value-crammed
- Value-added
- Value you can really count on
- Big value power
- Economical value
- Value jammed
- Overflowing with value
- Double value
- Triple your value
- Creates new value
- Instant value
- Spot-on value
- Clean value
- Industrial strength value
- Open up to value
- Unbelievable value
- Exponential value
- Value blowout
- Explosion of value
- Grown-up value
- Space age value
- Old fashioned value
- Dawn of new value
- Out-of-this-world value
- How do you unearth value
- Exceptional value
- Fantastic values
- Experience incredible value
- Committed to quality, value, selection and service
- Add value to your home with
- Value-driven
- Our feature value
- An unprecedented value
- And perhaps nowhere else will you find such an exceptional value
- Strength, consistency and value
- With unbelievable value
- Spectacular values
- Enjoy values only a mom and dad could love
- More great values
- The values are outta sight
- Unbelievable values in-store
- More value than ever
- Shoot-for-the-top value

Value: worth, merit, utility, advantage, benefit, usefulness, gain, profit, avail, good, importance

See also: BENEFIT, BUY, MONEY, SALE, SAVINGS, USEFULNESS

VARIATION
- Each form comes in a slight variation
- Grow to love the variations
- Not even the tiniest variation is allowed

See also: DIFFERENCE

VARIETY
- Not your average variety of
- We bring a wide variety of
- Right now, our selection offers phenomenal variety
- A large variety of impressive
- A massive variety of styles and patterns
- A great variety of products to choose from
- A huge variety to suit your home
- Now reflects a wide variety of

See also: ASSORTMENT, CHOICE

VENDOR
- Good at all participating vendors
- Take it to your local vendor
- Honored by all our vendors

See also: PURVEYOR, SELLER

VENTURE
- Consider a new venture
- Nothing ventured, nothing gained
- Venture boldly into this exciting world
- Join in this enthusiastic and far-sighted venture

See also: **ADVENTURE, INVESTMENT, RISK**

VERDICT
- The verdict is in
- The only verdict that matters is the one you give
- The best verdict yet

See also: **DECISION, JUDGEMENT**

VERSATILE
- It's all quite versatile
- Year-round versatility
- Affordable, pretty and versatile
- Renowned for serviceability and versatility

See also: **ADAPT, CHANGE, FLEXIBLE, USEFUL**

VERSION
- An all-new version
- A completely unabridged version of
- Several versions to suit your needs

See also: **KIND, SPECIES**

VIABLE
- Makes them also commercially viable
- Always a viable choice
- Now giving you very viable options

See also: **POSSIBLE**

VIBRATION
- That wild vibration is probably your pulse
- Gives off great vibrations
- Just feel the vibrations

See also: **EXCITEMENT, THRILL**

VICTORY
- Prepare for victory
- And what makes the victory even sweeter
- A victory over
- Chalk up another victory for our side
- Victorious, year after year

See also: **BEAT, CONQUER, TRIUMPH, WIN**

VIEW
- Offers breath-taking views
- We'd love to hear your point of view
- Giving you a whole new view of
- A view we enthusiastically endorse
- Suggesting a very different point of view

See also: **IDEA, INFORMATION, PICTURE**

VINTAGE
- Vintage-inspired
- A vintage idea whose time has come again
- Of a very superior vintage

See also: **HERITAGE, HISTORY, LEGACY**

VISIBLE
- A visible transition
- It's visibly better
- The difference is clearly visible

See also: **SEE**

VISION
- Our vision continues to grow
- And because your vision is boundless
- Searching for your vision
- A wonderfully nostalgic vision
- A stirring new vision of
- Come share our vision
- A singular vision
- Share our vision for a better future

See also: **CONCEPT, IDEA, MISSION**

VISIT
- Visit us often at
- Visit us this month to enjoy
- Visit this website for more information
- An essential part of any visit
- It's sure to be a magical visit
- Here's your chance to visit
- Come and visit
- An exciting and educational place to visit
- We would like to invite you to visit us
- Please visit and enjoy
- We'd love to see you visit us
- To make sure you visit our store
- Our frequent visits and constant monitoring make certain

See also: **CALL, COME, HOTEL**

VISITOR
- Has drawn visitors from around the

world
- Will be on hand to give visitors a rare opportunity to view
- A cordial invitation to all visitors
- Treat all our visitors wonderfully
- We love to pamper visitors

See also: FRIEND, GUEST

VISUAL
- Tying them in visually
- Visual proof of superiority
- For those of you who want visual proof
- And also very pleasing visually

VITALITY
- Lends volume, depth and vitality
- Adds more vitality to your
- Glowing with vitality

See also: ENERGY, STRENGTH

VOICE
- The prevailing voice of great
- A powerful voice for
- Another strong voice speaks up
- Your voice at
- Now you can really make your voice heard
- Really listen when you voice your concerns

See also: EXPRESS, SAY, SPEAK, TALK, TELL

VOLUME
- Volume buying assures you of competitive prices
- How can you pump up the volume
- Bigger volume means bigger savings for you
- Pump up the volume for maximum fun
- The place to come for volume purchases
- More volume in our stores
- Our volume discounts allow us to offer you great savings

See also: QUANTITY

VOTE
- Thanks for voting us your favorite
- Cast your vote for
- Consistently voted the industry's best
- Vote with your feet and your pocketbook
- We want your vote of confidence

See also: CHOICE, CHOOSE

VOYAGE
- Come on a voyage of discovery
- A voyage few have taken before you
- A daring voyage straight into the unknown

See also: JOURNEY, ODYSSEY, QUEST, TRIP

WAIT
- And you don't have to wait until
- You'll never have to wait
- No waiting to save
- Improvement without the wait
- You don't even have to wait while
- You aren't just going to wait around for success, you're going to go right out and get it
- But wait, there's more
- No lag, no waiting
- Can't wait to tell you about
- Why wait any longer to
- Just wait until you see what's in store for you
- Alterations while you wait
- You've waited months or years for it
- Don't wait for
- No waiting around for
- Tired of waiting for hours to
- So why wait any longer

Wait: linger, remain, stay, rest, tarry, await, hang around, stick around, pause, hover, hesitate, anticipate, bide one's time, expect, look forward to, watch out for, lookout for, delay, postpone

See also: AWAIT, EXPECT, PATIENCE

WAKE
- Something to wake up to
- Wake up to big value
- The world is waking up to the excitement
- Wake up your senses with
- Wonderful to wake up to

See also: AWARENESS

WALK
- Within easy walking distance of
- Walk away with a great deal
- We walk in your footsteps
- Walk in anytime
- We warmly welcome walk-in traffic

See also: MOVE, STEP, VISIT

WALLET
- Without being hard on your wallet
- Now you can have a fat wallet too
- Saves your wallet
- Take care of your wallet by visiting us
- Your wallet will love it too
- Big on value, easy on your wallet

See also: BUDGET, POCKETBOOK

WANNABE
- Don't be just a wannabe
- All the wannabes can join in too
- Built for wannabes

See also: DESIRE

WANT
- Whatever you want, whenever you want
- For people who want it all
- There's only one person who really knows what you want
- Goes just where you want it to
- You're going to get even more of what you want
- When the only thing you want is
- We make sure you get exactly what you want
- Give them what they want
- Give it to them the way they want
- If you've always wanted to
- Everything you want in a
- Get what you want
- What you really need and want
- If you've ever wanted to
- Sooner or later, you're going to get what you want
- We really know what you want
- They all want this for school
- Get everything you want from
- Working hard to bring you more of what you want

See also: DESIRE, WISH

WAR
- Waging war on problem
- All-out war on
- This means war
- The war on prices is heating up
- Be part of the war on overpricing

See also: ATTACK, BATTLE

WAREHOUSE
- We are your product warehouse
- Lots and lots of warehouse specials
- A huge warehouse crammed with values

See also: SHOWROOM, STORE

WARM
- All warm and fuzzy
- Warmed up instantly
- Just warm and serve
- A sensuously warm feeling
- Warm up to value
- Lighthearted, warm and profound

Warm: toasty, snug, roasty, cosy, comfy, ardent, passionate, zealous, cordial, friendly, close, on good terms, genial, hearty, thick as thieves, open-hearted, glowing, heartfelt, earnest, sincere

See also: COMFORT, COSY, FRIENDLY, WELCOME

WARMTH
- Surround yourself with the warmth
- A whole new dimension of warmth
- A place full of warmth and welcome

See also: COMFORT, SOFT

WARN
- But be warned, it's wild
- We have to warn you about the excitement of
- All your warning alarms are going off
- The warnings have been coming in for some time now

See also: DANGER, RISK, THREAT

WARRANTY
- Lifetime warranty on
- Factory direct warranty
- And get extended warranty protection
- Ask us about our satisfaction guaranteed warranty
- A thoroughly comprehensive warranty
- We'll honor the replacement warranty
- Full season warranty available
- Lifetime warranty available
- We will honor all warranties
- Extended warranty without charge
- Under complete warranty
- Hazard warranty guarantee
- And it comes with a lifetime warranty
- Plus limited lifetime warranty
- Comprehensive warranty backed by an industry leader

See also: CERTAINTY, GUARANTEE,

OBLIGATION, PLEDGE

WATCH

- Just watch it get results
- The eyes that keep a close and constant watch on
- A steady watch on the well-being
- Watch for our
- Watch out for terrific values
- Watch what happens when
- The more you watch, the more you learn
- A product to be watched
- Always watching out for you

See also: LOOK, MONITOR, SEE

WATERPROOF

- Finally waterproof
- Sealed by a totally waterproof agreement
- And it's waterproof too

WAVE

- Make some waves
- Ride the wave of the future
- Carrying you up to the very crest of the wave
- Wave goodbye to problems with

WAY

- The intelligent way to
- What better way to
- Will never get in your way
- Choose from five ways to pay
- Coming your way soon
- One way to help maintain
- The best, fastest, most efficient, most technologically savvy way
- We have to find the way
- Discover a better way
- The best way to make sure
- A convenient, economical way for you to enjoy
- It's the easy way to
- The way to go, the way to save
- Once you see how many ways you can
- Looking for a way to
- The surest way to get what you really want
- Is there a better way
- The most impressive way to
- So you can discover a new way to
- One easy, revolutionary way to
- Simply your cheapest, most convenient way to

- It's the best way to be sure you
- There's more than one way to get
- A surefire way to
- Discover quick and clever ways
- Amazing new ways to
- Even more ways to save
- It's the smartest way to be sure you get exactly what you want
- There is no better way to
- Finding new ways to
- It's hard to imagine anything getting in the way of
- We wouldn't have it any other way
- Are you still doing things the hard way
- Stop doing things the tough way
- The new way is simple and easy
- We're behind you all the way
- Showing you there's more than one way
- Finding its way into all kinds of
- On their way to you in twenty-four hours
- A couple of great ways to

See also: COURSE, FORMULA, MEANS, METHOD, PATH, SYSTEM, TECHNIQUE

WEALTH

- As more and more people look for ways to create wealth
- Achieving greater wealth couldn't be easier
- Achieve wealth in your spare time
- Working to preserve and enhance your wealth
- Get the look of wealth
- Giving you a wealth of choice

See also: CASH, FORTUNE, LUXURY, MONEY, RICH

WEAR

- Since just about everything can wear out
- Wear it all by itself
- Refuses to wear out
- Coordinated wear collection
- Wears forever, almost
- Practically never wears out
- What you wear is just as important as how you wear it
- We make them very wearable
- Easy to wear
- Why not wear it head-to-toe
- Sheer pleasure to wear

See also: FLAUNT, SPORT

WEATHER
- Weather permitting
- Weather-proof
- Handles any kind of weather
- Will see you through all kinds of weather
- Untouched by the roughest weather

See also: AIR, ATMOSPHERE, WET

WEB
- Visit our website at
- Come see on us on the Web
- We'll tell you more at our site on the Web

See also: JOIN, NETWORK, PARTNERSHIP

WEEK
- This week's specials
- One week only
- Better get here before the end of the week
- This is the biggest week in
- In less than a week you can

WEEKEND
- Big savings for the long weekend
- Spend the weekend of your life at
- Have yourself a lazy weekend
- This weekend only
- This exciting weekend also includes
- You can do it in a weekend
- A weekend break to recharge your batteries
- Long weekend deals
- Your weekend just became unlimited
- Taking you right through the weekend

WEIGHT
- Boost energy, lose weight, take control
- Giving more weight to the idea of
- A very weighty matter
- Don't let weight get you down
- Watch the weight melt off

See also: LOAD

WELCOME
- Extending a warm welcome to
- Welcome in all kinds of places
- Softens and welcomes
- Welcome to our establishment
- We're welcoming even more of you
- Always open to welcome you
- Welcome to drop in on a casual basis
- Transformed into a bright, welcoming
- You'll be welcomed with open arms
- Everyone is welcome
- Now welcome at these fine stores
- Waiting to welcome you
- Our company welcomes you at any time
- Comfortable and welcoming
- Welcome to adulthood
- Time for a very welcome change

Welcome: greetings, salutations, hello, salute, hail, glad hand, open door, welcome mat, address, wave to, tip the hat, doff the cap, shake hands, press flesh

See also: COME, HAPPY

WELL
- Did it and did it well
- No one else does it so well
- Making sure you're well and happy
- Transforms discomfort into a state of well being
- Well ahead of all the rest

See also: GOOD

WEST
- The spirit of the west
- This is how the west was won
- Straight from the wild west
- Brings the west right into your home

WET
- The very wettest of wet looks
- Aren't afraid to get wet
- Looks even better when wet
- Now is the time to get your feet wet

See also: WEATHER

WHAT
- We've got what it takes to be number one
- Always wondering what if
- What to do if
- Just look at what we have to offer
- Doing whatever it takes

WHEEL
- Time to lose those training wheels
- Get on side without having to reinvent the wheel
- Putting wheels on your ideas
- Become one of the big wheels

WHERE

- Puts it exactly where you want it
- If you've been wondering where to go for the best
- Here's where you can get the best
- Where everyone is going these days

WHO

- Revealing who you are
- Who says you can't
- We're the people who are famous for it
- Let the world know who you really are
- Join the who's who of
- Somebody who can spot quality

WHOLE

- Composing a remarkably serene whole
- Now you can get the whole thing
- Seeing product and service as parts of a whole
- Feel peaceful and whole again

WHOLESALE

- Below wholesale prices
- Get it wholesale at
- You'll think it's wholesale, the prices are so low
- Selling wholesale to the public
- Our wholesale pricing is just the start

See also: SALE, SAVE, SAVINGS, VALUE

WHY

- Also why we proudly offer
- Here's why
- Why are you waiting
- Why not do it now
- Why not say "yes" today
- Why wait another day
- Why not order right away
- See why nothing works like
- See why we're the country's number one
- Which is why you need
- Come see why we don't call them
- Which probably sums up why
- You'll soon see why
- This is why everyone is coming to us
- Here's why you should choose us
- Value, quality and service is why

See also: REASON

WILD

- Answer the call of the wild
- Try something wild
- Lets your wild side loose
- For the wild thing inside you
- A way to go wild
- The latest breed of product goes wild
- So go wild
- Unspoiled, wild and free
- Drive them wild with

See also: CRAZY, DAREDEVIL, EMOTION, FEELING, FREEDOM, INTOXICATE, NUTS, OUTRAGEOUS

WIN

- We're determined to win you over
- Somebody will win; why not you
- How would you like to win a
- Get ready to win
- There's more to winning than just scoring points
- The difference between playing and winning
- If you want to win big
- You win no matter which you choose
- Winning big without losing big
- What you love most is winning
- What matters is how much you want to win
- Enhances your will to win
- Winning doesn't come easy

See also: BEAT, CONQUER, SUCCEED, VICTORY

WIND

- Get wind of what's to come
- A fresh wind is blowing through
- The winds of change are blowing through

See also: CHANGE, NEWS

WINDOW

- Becomes a window on the world for you
- A new window, a new view
- Rush down while the window is open
- Opens more than windows for you
- This window of opportunity won't last long
- Opening a window, letting in fresh air

WINNER

- You're a winner every day
- You could be our big winner
- Winner take all
- Go where the winners go

- You're a winner right from the start
- What will make your business a winner in the long run is
- We want to congratulate all the winners
- Feel like a winner all the time

See also: **LEADER**

WINTER
- Say hello to winter
- With winter fast approaching
- Now actually enjoy winter
- Don't let winter get you down
- Now you can laugh at winter

See also: **SEASON**

WIPE
- They simply wipe clean
- Wiping out your doubts about
- Now wipe out those pesty problems
- Wipes out your worries
- Wipe them all out at once

See also: **CLEAN**

WIRED
- If you're already wired
- Helping you learn to live in a wired world
- Wired for excitement

See also: **CONNECT**

WISDOM
- Ancient wisdom for a modern world
- Listen to the hard-won wisdom of
- We've accumulated a lot of wisdom over the years
- You need to find not only knowledge, but also wisdom
- The wisdom to make the right choices when they're most crucial

See also: **INFORMATION, KNOWLEDGE**

WISH
- You'll wish you'd done it sooner
- You'll wish you'd known about it years ago
- Whenever you wish
- Stop wishing and start doing
- Any time you wish, you can
- Bring us your wish list
- Ready to gratify your every wish
- Your wish is our command
- Send your heartfelt wishes with a

- Your fondest wishes realized
- Now you can realize your greatest wish
- See how easily your wish can come true
- Sympathetic to our client's wishes
- Best wishes for you and yours
- It's just what you wished for
- We know what you're wishing for

Wish: desire, long for, want, yearn for, hope for, sigh for, care for, covet, have a yen for, hanker, fancy, bent upon, inclined to, prefer, aspire, set one's heart on, leaning, relish, hunger for, fondness, liking, itch, appetite, inclination, preference, crave, have a mind for, pine

See also: **DESIRE, WANT**

WITHOUT
- Don't do without it
- No one should go without
- Without a doubt, it's the very best
- Don't be without
- Never find yourself without service

WOMAN
- The power of a woman
- Made for the woman in you
- Only a woman could truly understand
- Created specifically for women
- Women love it
- Designed by women for women

See also: **GODDESS**

WONDER
- Wondering where you go from here
- No wonder we're number one
- It's one of the wonders of
- Why wonder when you can know for sure
- Small wonder it's the number one choice
- You'll wonder how you did without it
- Waste no time in wondering
- If you're wondering how to get more for your money
- It's no wonder that we're the best
- The wonder of it is
- Is it any wonder that
- You might be wondering why we're doing this

See also: **AMAZE, MARVEL, MIRACLE**

WONDERFUL
- Wide and wonderful

- Just so wonderful
- The most wonderful product you'll ever come across
- A wonderful time of the year
- Try something wonderful
- The most wonderful thing about it is

WORD
- You have our word on it
- The word is out
- We keep our word to you
- But don't take our word for it
- So amazing we can't quite express it in words
- Meaningful words, wise sayings
- The result is too good for words
- Words can't do justice to
- Sometimes words are not enough
- There are not enough words to describe your love
- Words seem inadequate to describe
- Just wait until word gets around
- Once word gets out that
- Our word is our bond
- The operative word here is
- Words that truly inspire

**See also: GUARANTEE,
INFORMATION, PROMISE**

WORK
- Discover how to work smarter
- We make our product work harder because you do
- Cut your working time in half
- Clothes that really work for you
- Includes the works
- To find out how we work, just call
- For heavy-duty work, try
- People who believe that hard work deserves reward
- We think hard work should pay off
- Working closely with you to achieve
- Works together with your
- Make light work of
- Making this product work harder for you
- They all work together for you
- You can do it while you work to
- Works the way you've always wanted it to work
- Put it to work for you right away
- If you think it's about time someone worked harder for
- Make it work for you, not against you

- We'll have you working with the best
- The hardest working part of your
- It works so well we've actually
- The work has just begun
- It really works
- All the benefits with none of the work
- It works for you
- Making quick work of
- Together, we can get down to work
- Designed to work together to
- It only works if we all do our part
- It works, period
- Begins to work immediately
- We look forward to getting to work for you
- It works well on
- It has worked for millions all over the world
- Works best when you need it most
- The harder you play, the harder it works
- And it works right away
- It's easy and it works fast
- No work, we do it all
- Helps you do a lot of work in less time
- You just know it's going to work
- It's about making your work easier and more productive
- Makes easy work of even the most difficult
- Here's how it works
- For something that works better
- Will make your work a lot easier
- You'll know it's working when you see
- A very good place to work
- You'll enjoy working with us
- We know what works and what doesn't
- It takes a lot of hard work to
- Working side by side with you to
- So you too can put this amazing product to work for you
- The work is extremely easy
- And remember, we do all the work for you
- Work smart, not hard
- If you are willing to work hard
- All work is 100% guaranteed
- Work guaranteed in writing
- Guarantee our work to be satisfactory to you

Work: effort, toil, labor, endeavor, sweat, performance, function, act, enterprise, undertaking, occupation, industry, business,

trouble, pains, exertion, spare no effort, bring about, effect, attain, achieve, exercise
See also: EARN, EFFORT, FUNCTION, JOB, PERFORMANCE

WORKHORSE
- A workhorse that never quits
- A workhorse you never have to feed
- Stop feeling like a workhorse

See also: FOUNDATION

WORKOUT
- Give yourself the ultimate workout
- Won't give your pocketbook a workout
- Give our brains a workout
- As good as a total workout

See also: ATHLETIC

WORKSHOP
- Workshop helpers finish the job fast
- Manufactured in our workshops
- Our workshops are famous the world over

See also: EDUCATION, TRAIN

WORLD
- Makes your world go round
- No one in the world does more with
- We're world leaders in
- Can make a world of difference
- That's why the world's leading authorities recommend
- In today's fast-moving world you need
- Team up with world-renowned
- Explore new worlds
- Discover the exciting world of
- One of the largest in the world
- Where we go, the world tries to follow
- We select only the finest products from around the world
- Ushering onto the world stage
- Just because you're on the other side of the world
- Some of the world's most interesting
- The world is wide
- It's a dog-eat-dog world out there
- From virtually anywhere in the world
- Hold the world in your hand
- We'd like to hand you the world
- Enter a whole new world
- Thank you for inviting us into your world
- Already hard at work around the world

- Out-of-this world value
- Shut out the world
- Welcome to a brand new world
- Someone who made a real difference to the world
- Your introduction to the world of
- Anywhere in the world
- Bring this exciting world right into your home
- Taste the world
- Travel the world without leaving home
- Now you can enjoy one of the world's only
- It's the world's leading
- The brand new world of
- Flashing round the world
- The world's best is yet to come
- We've got the world covered
- Nobody in the world sells more
- Welcome to a whole new world
- From the world to you
- From recognized world class
- Organized into easy-to-explore worlds
- Get the best of both worlds
- World-class in every sense
- Welcome to a perfect world of
- It's a small world after all
- Means the world to us
- World's greatest
- They come from every corner of the world
- The world's most excellent
- We search the world to bring you
- It means the world to you
- Here is your own private world
- Backed by worldwide personal service
- No longer worlds apart
- The world's most popular product just got better
- The world is raving about it
- See the best in the world
- No matter where in the world you are travelling

World: sphere, planet, globe, earth, terra, four corners of the earth, humanity, humankind, everybody, general public, society, class, part, sector, realm, domain, kingdom, field, cosmos, universe, heaven and earth, firmament, space, macrocosm
See also: EARTH, GLOBAL, GLOBE, UNIVERSAL

WORRY

- One less thing to worry about
- Why worry about
- Takes the worry out of
- One more worry you don't have to think about
- Solving a worry that's been keeping you up at night

See also: HASSLE

WORTH

- It's time you got your money's worth
- For which you'll receive you money's worth
- We'd rather tell you what it's worth
- Undoubtedly worth the money
- Judged not by its price but by its worth
- Worth more than ever before
- Why it's worth holding onto

See also: SAVINGS, VALUE

WRAP

- Get wrapped up in
- Comes gift-wrapped and beautiful
- All wrapped up in savings
- We've been keeping it under wraps

See also: DISCREET, HIDE, SECRET

WRITE

- I'm writing to tell you about
- Please write today, you have absolutely nothing to lose
- You have only to write and ask
- People have been writing in enthusiastically from all across the country

See also: COMMUNICATE, CONTACT

WRONG

- You can't go wrong
- A million people can't be wrong
- All these people can't be wrong
- You're never wrong at our store
- Stopping you from making the wrong choice
- The customer is never wrong
- Just might be wrong for you

See also: ERROR, MISTAKE

YEAR

- As often as you like throughout the year
- Giving you year round satisfaction
- It's that time of year again
- Man/woman/idea/surprise of the year
- Every year for decades to come
- Enjoy more each year
- This is the year for you to
- Enjoy it for years to come
- Shaping up to be a very rewarding year
- Twenty years in business
- Now you can turn back the years

See also: TIME

YES

- Say yes to
- The answer is yes
- Yes, you can find it here
- We want you to say yes
- Finally, someone who says yes
- Get her to say yes

YESTERDAY

- A glimpse of the world of yesterday
- The grace of yesterday, the advances of tomorrow
- Don't get stuck with yesterday's ideas
- We get it to you, even if you wanted it yesterday
- The one you have may already be yesterday's news

YOU

- It's really up to you
- Thinking of you
- So it's up to you now
- Look in the mirror and see a whole new you
- Why can't it be you
- Find the real you
- Just knowing how important it is to you
- It's all about you
- We do it all for you
- So we'll be there when you need us
- We did it, and you can too
- Time to be you
- Designed for people just like you
- It's all just for you
- Lets you do all this
- All you have to be is you
- Lets you be you
- Just be you
- Just for you
- Now you don't have to
- You can do it
- You've got it so flaunt it
- Yes, this is the one for you

- You either have it or you don't
- You are who you are – be proud
- You give it your all
- We'll come to you
- You determine how much is spent

YOUNG
- No matter how old or young you may be
- For younger looking
- Not just for the young
- As young as you feel
- Making you feel young again
- Younger looking than you ever thought possible
- Feel younger than ever

Young: adolescent, teenaged, minor, juvenile, unfledged, callow, childish, puerile, inexperienced, green, wet behind the ears, unsophisticated, naive, innocent
See also: **CHILD, KIDS, FAMILY, TIMELESS**

YOURS
- It's yours for just
- Yours for the asking
- Get yours today
- Irrevocably yours
- Forever yours
- Something that's yours alone
- All yours for one low price
- Yours is the best

YOURSELF
- Doing it yourself will cost you more
- Treat yourself to the best
- Suit yourself
- Do it yourself for greater savings
- Always yourself
- Finally, put yourself first

See also: **YOU, YOURS**

YOUTHFUL
- Smooth, youthful appearance enables you to ward off
- Youthful freshness and energy
- You can be youthful no matter what your age

See also: **YOUNG**

ZAP
- Zap it before it starts
- Zap's problems instantly

- One zap and it's finished
- Never get zapped again

See also: **HIT, IMPACT, STRIKE**

ZERO
- Zero in on who's right for you
- Zeroing in on featured values
- Put zero down on
- Start at zero

See also: **DISCOVER, FIND, SEARCH**

ZING
- Put some zing in your life
- More zing in your swing
- You can tell by the zing
- More zing for your dollar

ZONE
- Puts you in a different time zone
- Move out of your comfort zone to forge ahead
- Puts you in the wild zone
- Entering the deal zone
- Zoned for progress, zoned for value

See also: **AREA, COOL, GROOVE, LOCATION**

Section Two

Internet
and
Technology

ABILITY

- An even more useful addition to your present abilities
- The ability to reach thousands, even millions, of people
- Extending your ability by amazing dimensions
- Increases your ability to do amazing things
- You've never had ability like this before
- Demonstrated and proven its ability to

ACCESS

- That means unlimited access
- Access code to your future
- The most competitive full access on the market
- Access it through several different
- Giving quick and painless access
- All access is not the same
- Access is guaranteed
- Everything you need to access the information you want
- Access to online services with amazing speed
- Now providing easy access to every area
- Now you can have instant access to
- Let us help you improve your access
- Such easy access could prove very attractive to many small and medium-sized businesses
- If you need to have quick access to a broad source of information
- For direct access to the Internet and thousands of other services
- One-stop access to the online world
- Gives you fingertip access to
- The easiest access anywhere
- Unparalleled access to information
- Gives you one-step access today
- Access to hundreds of continuously updated

ACCESSIBLE

- Make yourself instantly accessible to the world
- Making your information widely accessible on the Internet
- Accessible by millions of people on the Internet
- Bet you never imagined anything this accessible

ACCUSTOM

- Helping you get accustomed to this new high-speed world
- You'll very quickly become accustomed to this way of
- Soon accustomed to reaching you by a different route
- It's easy to become accustomed to using

ACHIEVE

- Now you can instantly achieve what you're looking for
- Achieve a sound working knowledge of this new technology
- Achieving even more electronically
- Computers will help you achieve far more than you ever dreamed possible
- Encouraging our customers to achieve more

ACTIVITY

- You determine where and when activities take place
- All the hottest activity happens right here
- Many ways to boost activity at your site

ADDRESS

- Your electronic address gives thousands more instant access to your business
- The address of our web site is your ticket to the best information
- Now including your web address everywhere

ADVANCE

- Part of one of the most advanced products yet
- You won't believe the advances in just this short time
- Leaping from one advance to the next
- More advances faster than any other company
- With today's technological advances

ADVANTAGE

- Hey, there's some serious advantages
- Experience the advantage of the Internet
- Now the electronic advantage is immeasurable
- Now the advantage is all yours
- As your business grows, you need the advantage of more web tools

ADVERTISE

- The Web is your hottest advertising platform
- Now you can advertise on the Web for next to nothing
- The best advertising right on your screen

ADVICE

- A world of expert advice and entertainment
- You can bank on sound advice at
- We sell the product; our advice is free
- We also give advice and personal service

AFFORD

- How can you afford not to
- You can't afford to miss this
- Now you can afford access to the world
- And you thought you couldn't afford it
- Nowadays, you can't afford to be without

AFFORDABLE

- Oh yeah, an it's affordable too
- Affordable and award-winning
- Growing more affordable every day

AHEAD

- Too far ahead of the pack to worry about competition
- The urgent need to stay one step ahead
- Puts your whole family ahead in today's race to

ALTERNATIVE

- A highly-affordable alternative to old-fashioned direct mail
- An alternative mode of communication exceeding all expectation
- It's time we tried this brand new alternative

AMAZEMENT

- Will leave you staring wide-eyed in amazement
- Much to the amazement of the competition
- Amazement now comes at half the price

AMAZING

- So easy it's amazing
- Now that's amazing
- Another amazing leap forward

ANIMATION

- Affordable animation finally arrives
- Animation is making a big impact on the entertainment world
- Wait till you see what animation will do for your web page

ANNOYANCE

- Stop this unwanted annoyance
- When lack of speed becomes an unbearable annoyance
- Gets rid of all those little annoyances that drive you nuts

ANSWER

- Finally, the answer to these problems
- Get answers when you need them
- Putting all the answers right in the palm of your hand
- Use your computer to find instant, easy, accurate answers to
- And the answer is
- We'll be happy to answer any questions you have about
- Finding the answer for you
- Find the answers faster
- The Internet is an answer you've awaited for years

APPEAL

- On the appeal of the Internet is compelling
- An appeal now reaching into the far corners of
- Increase your appeal with one of these terrific products

APPLICATION

- A half dozen great little applications
- Don't pay for applications you don't use
- Combines our most powerful, easy-to-use application with
- Gives you quick access to your applications
- Generates business applications automatically
- Setting up applications so you can find and work with them easier
- The Internet is a continually evolving set of applications
- Changing applications are now being driven by users and supporters
- The hottest emerging applications

- Start your applications up faster than ever before
- There's no faster way to get applications running than with
- Offering a significant performance advantage in computing application
- Dozens of new and well-known applications such as
- Top applications brought together seamlessly
- You'll only have to deal with a single application

APPLY
- So log on and apply right now
- You can apply your new knowledge instantly to
- Apply even more power to your

APPROACH
- To date, the most popular and successful approach has been to
- A new approach to online
- The trick is in how you approach new technology
- To experience this new approach, just see our home page at

AREA
- Expanding rapidly into all major areas
- Opening up undreamed of areas
- A new area of untold possibilities

ART
- Advancing the state of the art on the Web
- Where art and science become one
- Applying our art to your art

ARTICLE
- Search valuable archives and articles on the Internet
- Now everyone who is interested can have access to thousands of informative articles
- At last, the real article

ASK
- Ask us in your own words
- Now you can ask us your questions directly by email
- Ask it anything
- You can ask a lot of your new web site

ASPECT
- The most practical aspect of all is the most useful
- Every day there's another new aspect you haven't thought of before
- Just one more exciting and unexpected aspect
- Every single aspect is spread out before you

ASSEMBLE
- Proudly assembled in
- We don't just assemble it, we build every bit of it
- Where else could you assemble so many superior components

ASSURE
- And you can rest assured that
- Assured of top quality components
- The name that assures you of

AUDIENCE
- Helping you reach your target audience
- An audience you never knew existed
- Just one click and your audience is the world

AVAILABLE
- Available from your local retailer
- Now more available than ever
- A great many more applications are now available to you

BACKGROUND
- All this is happening against the background of
- No matter what your background, you should be able to relate easily to this
- Now you really don't need any background in

BARGAIN
- The quickest way to find bargains
- It's no bargain if it screws up your data
- The best bargains on the Internet are

BARRIER
- Removes all barriers
- Breaking down the barriers to entering cyberspace
- Smashing communications barriers
- Making sure there are no more barriers to

widespread use

capture the flag

BASIC
- Some basics about expanding business on the Internet
- First, you need the basic equipment
- If you want a system that's far better than basic

BELIEVABILITY
- Three ways you can increase your believability
- First in believability
- Believability is built right in

BENEFIT
- Gain bottom line benefits fast
- Great business-boosting benefits
- Wired for benefits

BEST
- Assurance that you have the best
- Bringing you the best of what's online
- Keeping all the best things, the ones you like
- Succeeds by being the first with the best
- You demand the best; we give it to you
- You can have the best and have it now

BETTER
- Nothing does it better than
- Getting better and better every day
- Connecting you faster and better to the world
- There's no better product available
- Always looking for better ways to help you do business

BLOG
- Visit our blog for the latest
- Appears first in our blog
- More visitors will read your blog

BLOW
- Blow them away with eye-popping new
- Blowing up old ideas about
- The future has just blown into town

BOARD
- Get on board now
- On board for a wild ride through cyberspace
- You've boarded the competition, now

BONUS
- An electronic bonus for everyone
- The Internet is a bonus you take very seriously
- And, as an added bonus, you get
- Built-in bonus with each key stroke

BOOKMARK
- Put a bookmark on that
- A site that's bookmarked more often than any other
- Your bookmarks tell the tale

BRAND
- A tool to enhance brand awareness
- Your brand of progress
- Pick the brand that always wins

BREAKTHROUGH
- Announcing a startling scientific breakthrough
- Two decades of experience in delivering breakthrough technology
- We'll also set you up with our breakthrough product which lets you
- Finally, the breakthrough you've been waiting for
- Advanced technology breakthrough

BROWSE
- Why not pop by and browse
- Be sure to browse our online catalogue
- Please take a moment to browse
- Just point your browser to
- You'll be browsing, creating and accomplishing more than ever before
- Try out a truly awesome browser

BUBBLE
- Isn't just some electronic bubble that will someday burst
- A swelling bubble of interest in
- The bubble is getting bigger and bigger
- One bubble that isn't going to burst

BUDDY
- Everyone can use a cyber-buddy now and then
- For when you really need a cyber-buddy
- It's like starting out on the buddy system

BUDGET
- Whatever your budget, our product won't put the squeeze on you
- Don't risk your Internet budget on untested strategies
- We have the best deals for your budget

BUILD
- Build your own musical library
- We've built it; they will come
- No, we don't build 'em like we used to

BUNDLE
- Comes bundled with
- We give you a bigger bundle
- Open up the bundle and have a look

BUSINESS
- Handling all your business like nobody's business
- Digital media fundamentally change the way the world does business
- Designed for a growing business like yours
- For a fully-wired business center
- It's easy to get down to business
- Get more business on the Web
- All the tools for fully secure business on the Internet
- Putting your home page in the middle of targeted business traffic
- Where businesses meet on the Web
- Focusing on the latest in web business trends
- The example of successful web-based businesses
- Dramatically changing the way business does business
- The hottest, coolest way of doing business this side of virtual reality
- Are you up for some online business
- Generating a brand new kind of excitement and a lot more business
- A new way to create worldwide business
- The Internet will prove a real boon to your business
- Businesses are flocking to use this new method
- Add the Internet to your business strategy
- Internet based businesses have increased dramatically recently
- The biggest foundation block of today's business world
- Working to develop a business survival guide to the Internet
- For more information on any aspect of business, please email us at
- Working to develop a powerful business presence on the Internet
- Your web site and Internet presence compliment your existing business effort
- Marrying business to the Internet in a happy union
- Conquering the right way to integrate business and the Internet
- A growing number of businesses are now transferring all activities to the Internet
- Putting corporate business online
- About to radically alter your business practices
- State-of-the-art computer-aided business is here
- Taking your business efforts onto the Internet
- No matter how big or small your business
- Redefining your business
- Whatever it takes to help you grow your business
- Take this opportunity to build your business fast
- Taking your business to the next level
- Your business will move even faster
- Easier than ever to supercharge your business
- Show them you mean business
- A tool to sell your business services
- Put the Internet to work for your business

BUTTON
- Click on the button for more information
- Offers touch-of-a-button power
- Press a button and it's done
- All at the touch of a button
- We push all your buttons
- A small button to a big, big world

BUY
- Buy with confidence online
- You're not just buying a system, you're buying a new way of life
- The number one thing to buy is

BYTE
- Will you byte
- Mission-critical bytes

- Doesn't take a big byte out of your pocketbook
- Harnessing the might of the byte

CALCULATE
- Calculate the savings
- Makes the most complex calculations a breeze
- Designed for calculating people

CALL
- For more information and a store near you, call
- Responding to a powerful call
- Call us for free literature and an authorized dealer near you

CAPABILITY
- Now you can discover the new Internet capabilities of your
- Wouldn't you like the capability to
- Expand your capabilities, expand your fun

CAPTURE
- Striving to capture the same power and versatility
- Capture the world in your keyboard
- So you can capture up-to-the-minute

CATCH UP
- Don't get caught playing the game of catch-up
- Everyone must catch up or be left in the dust
- We can do our catching up together

CHALLENGE
- We challenge you to find a more robust
- Success on the Internet can be a challenging process
- We also provide help for the Internet challenged
- There's never been a better time to challenge old ideas of communication
- Challenging all your assumptions about

CHANGE
- A fast, easy way to keep up with a rapidly changing world
- Everything is about to change
- It's really all about change
- A thrilling change sweeping the old ways

away
- Your world can change very fast
- Leading accelerated change into the next millennium
- Clearly explains the coming changes
- It's downright scary how fast things are changing
- Massive changes being mapped into society as a whole
- Your participation drives the changes
- Changing assumptions about how you work and make money
- Destined to dramatically change the way you do everything
- Where the agent of change will be found

CHEAP
- World's cheapest
- Progress isn't cheap
- Cheap at twice the price
- Dizzying power just got cheaper

CHECK
- Why not spend a few minutes checking out our website
- Cool stuff worth checking out
- So check out your favorite site
- Check us out on the Web

CHILDREN
- Children can now access a way to learn
- Children and computers take to each other naturally
- Computers helping children to learn more quickly
- Net-savvy children are now the norm

CHOICE
- Working hard to develop a full range of choice
- Your choice will be critical in determining
- It's today's best choice
- Still the number one choice to keep your office running smoothly
- Makes it the intelligent choice for everyone
- The choice is clear
- Here's why our product is your best choice
- Helping you make a more informed choice about

CHOOSE
- Offering so much to choose from
- An overwhelming amount to choose from
- Now you get to choose instantly online
- Need help choosing a computer

CLASS
- World class in every way
- Now in a class of its own
- Click your mouse and class is in session

CLICK
- Just click and go
- In just a few clicks, find a new career
- Give you one-click access to all your
- Easy-to-use point and click operation
- Just get clicking
- A single click automatically connects you
- Just point and click to obtain
- All you need to know is how to point and click
- With just one click, you grab it
- Click power at its greatest
- If you can click, drag, and drop, you can do it.

CLIENT
- Helps you reach your most profitable clients
- Perfect for helping your clients remember
- Clients will come flocking to the site

CLOSE
- Gets you even closer to your customers
- You can't get closer than this
- Close to perfect

CODE
- Now there's no code between you and your goal
- And you don't have to learn one bit of code
- Down with codes, up with freedom

COLOR
- Sample it in vivid, vicarious color
- It's really the color of fun
- Getting ever better color with

COMBINATION
- Offering you the exceptional and unique combination of
- In combination, they produce wonders

- Putting together the best combination
- Previously unimagined combinations now wait for you

COMBINE
- Look what you get when you combine
- Combining technological power with your imagination
- Combine your business with the versatility of the Internet

COMMAND
- The Internet will be yours to command
- Deciphering those crazy commands
- At a single command, it all springs to life
- With just a couple of simple commands, you can access this
- Technology puts you in command

COMMENTARY
- A huge selection of commentary now open to you
- Join the continuous running commentary on our web page
- Reading all the commentary, you begin to realize the breadth of
- Praises of our product make a continuously running commentary

COMMERCE
- Easing the move of commerce to the Internet
- Where commerce turns instantly to e-commerce
- The rules of commerce have completely changed

COMMITMENT
- Able to make an extraordinary commitment to you
- We've strengthened our commitment
- Our commitment is to top quality combined with ease of use

COMMON
- Becoming common on the Web
- Find out how much you have in common with the rest of the world
- Quickly becoming our common means of contact and communication

COMMUNICATE
- Communicate with customers round the

world
- Cost-effective, speedy way to communicate
- Communicate in a whole new way
- Giving you the power to communicate with potential customers you could never reach before
- To even more effectively communicate
- Now you can communicate daily
- New ways for you to communicate in a shrinking world
- Designed to communicate the latest information quickly
- We communicate excellence

COMMUNICATION
- The principles of communication remain the same whatever the technology
- The Web also provides excellent communication within your company
- Developing a new relationship with this unique form of communication
- Speed of communication is continually increasing
- The focus of communication is shifting radically
- A whole new way to handle communications
- Factoring in the future of personal communication technology
- It's still all about communication between people
- Becoming one of your greatest communication strengths
- Increasing your ability to quickly and effectively communicate
- The emphasis remains on genuine communication
- The communications solution for you
- Helping you understand a whole new means of communication
- Advanced communication technology connects you to
- Evaluate your communication needs at no charge

COMMUNITY
- Are you eager to join the rapidly growing world wide community
- Please become part of our online community
- The sense of community has been enormously expanded

- Taking the Internet community by storm

COMPANY
- Call the company with more than thirty years of experience
- Companies that move quickly gain customers faster than those who
- Keeping company with you on the journey into cyberspace

COMPATIBLE
- Guaranteed compatible with
- Also compatible with your pocketbook
- Give you the proven compatibility and reliability of
- Compatibility is guaranteed

COMPETE
- Helping successful companies compete
- Now you can compete with the big guys
- Competing for your business keeps us on our toes

COMPETITION
- Blows the roof off the competition
- Blasts the competition away
- Go to the competition to see just how good we are
- This product just has no competition
- So they'll choose you over the competition

COMPETITIVE
- Raises the industry competitive bar
- Gives you a sharper competitive edge
- Gets the competitive gigs flowing

COMPLETE
- Comes all complete
- Offering you the complete service you want
- To complete your connection, you need

COMPLIMENT
- Complimenting this unsurpassed attribute
- You'll be showered with compliments
- Each part perfectly compliments the next

COMPONENT
- Our unique components can be placed directly into just about anything
- Premium components ensure maximum

performance
- The smallest component may very well be the most important

COMPUTE
- Powerful enough to satisfy all your computing needs
- Non-stop computing is becoming more and more common
- Now you can take joyfully to full throttle computing
- Working with top-of-the-line computing capacities
- Power computing zooms ahead
- Where the cutting edge of computing really is
- As always in the world of computing, less is more
- The ultimate computing tool
- Take the next step in mobile computing
- As originally established by computer enthusiasts

COMPUTER
- A completely new way to use your computer
- One of the most important parts of your personal computer
- Your business needs faster computers
- Try out the latest and greatest in computer technology
- The quick way to get to know your computer
- Computers can really help your kids
- Calling all computer lovers
- Help for all those still intimidated and confused by computers
- Acquiring a whole new power and meaning when attached to millions of other computers on the Internet
- Computers are everywhere
- Use your personal computer to explore
- Using the computer has become second nature to you
- Your office computer can be transformed into a personal broadcasting station for your business
- Now computer-based programs allow you to expand the benefits to
- As long as you are familiar with your computer you can do it
- You don't have to be a computer genius
- It all happens at your computer

- Some things are best left to a computer

CONCEPT
- A great concept rediscovered and revitalized
- First you need to absorb a few concepts
- A concept that barely existed yesterday
- So you can reach a level of comfort with concepts, jargon and most-used applications
- Though the term is new, the concept is as old as
- A concept so new, you are the first to know
- Concepts unimagined only yesterday
- Race from concept to finished model

CONFERENCE
- By conferencing over the Web, you can get together with
- Now you can be in continual conference with
- A click of the mouse and you're in instant conference

CONFIGURATION
- Several configurations are offered
- Simply select the configuration that best meets your needs
- Automatic setup and configuration
- The configuration that suits you
- This configuration is designed to help provide
- Other models and configurations available
- No one could have imagined such a configuration
- In this configuration, you are central

CONFIGURE
- Getting your system configured can be a challenge
- Helping you plan carefully how to configure your system to your needs
- Your initial configuration will be all important
- The fastest and easiest to configure
- Dozens of accessories to configure
- Configure it exactly the way you want
- Easily configures to all your personal needs
- Configure it in minutes

CONFINE
- If you're tired of being confined
- Doesn't confine you to a boring
- Breaks down those confining walls
- Break out of what's been confining you

CONNECT
- Once you're connected, we'll help you
- If you're confused about how to connect
- You won't believe how quickly you get connected
- The simplest way to connect to the whole world at once
- No one can connect like us
- Now a fast, friendly way to connect with your favorite
- Lets you connect to almost anything from just about anywhere
- Everyone's getting connected
- Take advantage of our new Internet connectivity
- Are you connected enough
- Get well connected

CONNECTION
- Making the connection utterly seamless
- Forging connections in cyberspace
- Everyone's racing to get a better, faster Internet connection
- Provides your very own dedicated connection
- No more worries about an inconsistent connection
- You connection to the world

CONSTRUCTION
- We're sorry that this page is still "Under Construction"
- Please be patient while we're under construction and visit us soon
- Please come back; construction will be finished soon

CONSULTATION
- Just call and we'll send someone for immediate consultation
- Expert consultation any time you want
- Free online consultation

CONSUMER
- Driving more consumers online
- The heart of the consumer online market
- More and more consumers are connecting online
- Direct to the consumer

CONTACT
- Make key contacts fast
- Or contact us on the Internet
- Contact the whole world through the Internet
- Now the quickest way to make important contacts

CONTENT
- A great deal of original online-only content
- A unique combination of great content and stunning design
- Able to create compelling content
- Supporting a content-rich web site
- Web-only content that people can't get elsewhere
- Offering frequently changing and dynamic web content

CONTROL
- Giving you total control over
- And now you're at the controls
- All this control saves service and support time
- Controlled by a microprocessor for optimum accuracy

CONVENIENCE
- The convenience of receiving personalized news and information
- Convenience is everything
- Now that's convenience

COOL
- Which you can see is very cool
- It's the absolute coolest way to
- Cool just got a whole lot cooler
- The cool way to make a hot connection

CORPORATE
- Ideal for corporate strategy
- Now that the corporate world has finally discovered
- You too can look like a corporate giant

COST
- At less than half the cost of similar
- You want costs kept down and connectivity boosted

- Shedding the high costs of outdated technology
- In the end, it can cost you a lot more than you may have thought
- The cost has recently been reduced
- Have even lowered the monthly cost

COUPON
- For more coupons online, please visit
- Electronic coupons available
- Online coupons mean even more saving right in your computer

CREATE
- The fast and easy way to create and manage
- Creating your web site just got easier
- Create a solid presence for yourself
- Create with a click of your mouse

CREATIVE
- Giving you a more creative way to be heard
- Creative technology is changing lives and it could change yours
- Giving you the tools to get down and be creative
- Everything you need to unleash your creativity

CRISIS
- A much quicker way to deal with a crisis situation
- For when you really have a crisis on your hands
- For one less crisis in your office

CULTURE
- Becoming part of the electronic culture
- Joining in the digitalization of our culture
- Already we have a new culture
- Reacting quickly to changes in web culture

CURVE
- The training curve is lowered dramatically
- Does your computer system keep throwing you curves
- Jump to the top of the technological curve
- Practically abolishes the learning curve

CUSTOMER
- Customers can reach your site and begin purchasing your products immediately
- Targeting exact Internet locations where your customers would likely meet
- Plenty of customers are to be found on the Internet
- The trick is to get customers flocking to your web site
- Drive the right customers to your home page
- A means of giving potential and current customers information about
- Happily increasing your customer base through the Internet
- A value-added service to your customers
- Generating a large customer base via the Internet
- Using email as part of your campaign to reach prospective customers
- Putting customer preferences first
- A product to match customer interests
- Change the way you attract and retain customers
- Get thousands of new customers
- More visitors mean more customers
- Helping you gain a customer for life

CYBER-COMMUNITY
- The cyber-community beckons you
- We all meet in the cyber-community
- Letting the cyber-community know the real you

CYBERSPACE
- A place in cyberspace for
- Our appeal may be in cyberspace but our feet are firmly planted on the ground
- Be a buddy from cyberspace
- Daring to take a ground-breaking leap into cyberspace
- In cyberspace, the only boundary is your imagination
- Women are forging cyberspace
- Taking the fight against poverty into cyberspace
- Visit us in cyberspace
- Welcome to cyberspace
- Now we're expanding into cyberspace
- Develop your own niche in cyberspace

DATA
- Now handling your data with such ease

- Letting you update your data more quickly and ensure the best possible service
- Now using computers to analyse data in a very different way
- Comparing vast amounts of data in a millisecond
- Everything needed to safeguard your valuable data
- Handles all your data with enormous ease
- Helping you understand the underlying data relations
- Allowing you to customize, manipulate and query your data

DATABASE

- Seamlessly link your database to your web site
- The importance and use of database systems is crucial to your success
- Now you can search many more databases
- Accessing the immense usefulness of a truly customized database
- Database marketing has really come into its own

DAWN

- Marks the dawn of a new era in
- Is the difference beginning to dawn on you
- By the time it dawns on our competitors, we're way ahead

DEAL

- Fantastic deals
- Post it as a done deal
- You'll never again have to deal with headaches like
- Easiest of all to deal with
- Fantastic hi-tech deals are for real

DEALER

- At authorized dealers everywhere
- See your computer or electronics dealer today
- Dealers are rushing to get this great product in for you

DECISION

- It's an easy decision once you know what you're looking for
- All decisions should be this easy

- Helping you make one of the most crucial decisions for your office or your business

DELETE

- Delete this and always wonder
- Press delete and watch your problems vanish away
- As easy as hitting delete
- Stop them from hitting delete

DELIVER

- Delivered direct from the factory to your door
- Delivered at a price that can't be beat
- Delivers the features you want at the price you need
- Who also delivers on time
- Delivering the world to you at lightning speed
- Delivering exactly what you expect to get
- We deliver what we promise

DEMAND

- For the truly demanding, we present
- As demanding as you are
- When you demand only the finest
- Now get information on demand

DEMONSTRATION

- Come for a free demonstration
- Ask to see a demonstration
- Demonstrations models at greatly reduced prices
- After one demonstration, you'll be sold
- Glad to provide a full working demo

DESIGN

- With a radical new approach to design
- Designed for those demanding the impossible
- With a design this revolutionary
- Designed to be new from the ground up
- Designed to be more than just another
- Straightforward, easy-to-use design
- Design that comes fully loaded
- Take advantage of the latest design capabilities
- Designed using advanced software
- It's design makes even the most sophisticated features easy to use
- The design tool for the Net
- Technology has improved all aspects of

design
- Design and build it on the Web

DESKTOP
- Welcome to our desktop
- For all your desktop needs
- The power of the Internet sitting on your desktop
- Now your desktop is the world
- Fully customizable desktop

DETAIL
- For those who want more detail
- Making sure you know all the details of the system
- Sooner or later, you have get down to the technical details
- Using the Internet, you can now explain your service in full
- The place where the details really count
- For details on this or any other package, just call or visit our site

DEVELOPMENT
- Exciting developments are in the making
- And even bigger development is
- New, amazing technological developments every day
- The development of your business is paramount

DIFFERENCE
- Join those making a difference and those on the move
- Making a huge difference in cost and efficiency
- Finding ways to take advantage of the difference the Web is bringing
- The difference is the smile on your face

DIFFERENT
- What's different about this product is
- Recognizing that each individual need is different
- Swing to a totally different heading
- Taking you down a very different road

DIGIT
- All you have to do is punch these digits
- The most important digits are your fingers
- No more punching digits

DIMENSION
- Taking design to a new dimension
- Undreamed of dimensions are opening up every day
- Entering a vast new dimension
- Leaping from dimension to dimension

DIRECTORY
- The easiest, most comprehensive directory available for the Internet
- Just look in the directory to find
- Listed in more directories than any other

DISCUSSION
- Able to keep up a running discussion of topics of concern to you and your customers
- The discussion inevitably swings round to the Internet
- Your business will broaden dramatically once you create an email list

DISTANCE
- Working well over the longest distance
- Distance becomes nothing
- Distance is now completely irrelevant
- When distance suddenly becomes insignificant
- Distance doesn't make a difference

DISTRIBUTE
- The Web is an extremely effective way to distribute information
- Please distribute this message electronically to your friends, colleagues and other interested parties
- So much easier to distribute the facts and figures

DIVERSITY
- Learning about the incredible diversity now available
- Now reach a huge diversity of folks
- Diversity becomes one of your best tools
- Vast diversity in a single delivery system

DO
- When you can't figure out what to do next
- Showing your customers what to do and how to do it
- Able to do it in a whole new way
- Tons of exciting things to do

- Look what you can do with the new
- There's only one thing to do
- Doing it all while on the go
- Newest idea in do-it-yourself

DOWNLOAD

- You can download in seconds
- Gearing up for quicker downloads
- You can easily download them all to
- Available for downloading
- A downloaded copy is now available on the Web
- Download an evaluation copy now
- Download your future
- Once connected, you can download valuable ideas
- Now able to download the latest from
- Download some happiness

DREAM

- An online provider's dream
- It's your dream machine
- Watch your dreams take shape before your very eyes
- Your dreams are our commands

DRIVE

- Of course, you're welcome to test drive all our products
- Test drive a vaster, faster Web
- Get on what's driving all this change
- Driving the rush to get online

E-COMMERCE

- Today's progressive businesses are embracing e-commerce
- Transformed by e-commerce
- Join the e-commerce revolution

Email

- Without doubt, email is the most widely used Internet service
- Email marketing is making real inroads
- Constantly expanding email contacts
- Email brings friends and contacts right to your desk
- Get your email in many more ways
- Grasping the fact that email is more than just information
- Email us for the all the details
- Email messages turn from to trickle to a stream to a raging flood
- As your email technique changes and is refined

- For those who are picky about email

E-SHINGLE

- Hang out your e-shingle
- Get your e-shingle seen by the world
- Pride in your very own e-shingle

EASY

- It really is that easy
- Designed to lighten your load by making it easier than ever to
- Just got easier for one simple reason
- Just doesn't get any easier
- Easy to stack
- Yet it's extremely easy to use
- It's fast and easy
- It's so easy you don't have to know a thing about
- So easy you'll wonder what you did before
- Guaranteed easy to use
- Make things easy on yourself by
- It's so easy it's amazing

EDGE

- Now on the leading-edge of technology
- Great reports from the cutting-edge
- Keep your edge sharp with products from
- Gets you closer to the edge than any other product

EDUCATE

- To educate you about the latest
- First, you must educate
- Turn you educated guesses into certainties

EDUCATIONAL

- Packed with educational resources
- For educational purposes, nothing can beat it
- Part of your educational process too

EFFECT

- Helps get the effect you're looking for
- The effect will be to greatly improve
- Special effects are just the beginning

EFFECTIVE

- This technology is so effective
- Effectively encourage your customers to contact you
- More effective than any other

EFFICIENT
- Cost-efficient and speedy
- So efficient you're astonished
- Choose the efficient way
- Efficient in ways you've only dreamed of

EFFORT
- A totally re-engineered effort
- Spurred on by a tremendous effort to
- Making that extra effort to
- More results with much less effort

EGALITARIAN
- Putting you into a truly egalitarian mode
- Egalitarian and socially unstratified
- One of the most egalitarian mediums yet

ELECTRONIC
- Join the electronic gold rush
- The whole world is going electronic
- Electronic connections racing around the globe

ENCRYPT
- Our new secure servers mean your credit card details will now be even more effectively encrypted
- Superior encryption is taken for granted
- You can feel perfectly confident about our method of encryption

ENTHUSIAST
- Turning you into a Net enthusiast
- Where true enthusiasts can now meet each other
- More enthusiasts per square yard than

ENVELOPE
- Pushing the technology envelope
- Wrapping you in an envelope of security
- The envelope gets bigger every day

ENVIRONMENT
- Lets you do all this from the same environment
- Creating an environment of excitement and energy
- A pleasant environment conducive to

EQUAL
- Recognizing no equal
- Makes you equal to the biggest
- Get the great equalizer and put it to work

for you

ESCAPE
- Now there's a fast escape from the dull confines of
- Escape from the real world now
- Escape is at your fingertips
- When you thought there was no escape

EVENT
- Visit our customer service center online
- Make your news on the Internet an event
- Expanding web presence has been a big event for our business and our customers

EVERYONE
- Anyone and everyone with a product to sell, information to share, a point of view to voice
- Now giving everyone effective access
- Everyone now knows about

EVERYTHING
- Packed with just about everything you can imagine
- It's everything you can desire in a
- When you want everything in one neat package

EXPECTATION
- Has already far exceeded expectations
- It's time to raise your expectations again
- Meeting the biggest expectations
- Designed specifically for your expectations

EXPERIENCE
- Providing you with the same excellent experience
- Easily share your experiences together
- Nothing can replace hands-on experience
- Technical experience is not necessary
- A whole new experience for your staff
- Shaping your online experience
- Experience combined with the Internet and technical know-how
- To maximize your web and online experiences
- The Web is a thrilling experience
- No experience required
- Experience cyberspace advances with an experienced friend
- Tap into years of experience

EXPERT

- Without having to become the world's greatest Internet expert
- When you know it's time for expert help
- Turns you into an instant expert
- Highly recommend expert assistance with planning
- To be able to get expert attention exactly when you need it

EXPERTISE

- Necessary technology and expertise to assist your business in developing an ongoing Internet presence and strategy
- Pleased with our rapidly developing expertise in this area
- Expertise on the Net may be crucial to your success in the future

EXPLAIN

- Explaining the necessary commands to get you started
- Lucidly explains concepts, uses and low-level details
- It's very easy to explain to neophytes

EXPLORE

- It's the perfect way to explore
- You can choose to explore more web possibilities right away
- Exploring more and better ways to compliment your
- Now you can explore a lot more possibilities
- With a bit of patience and exploration, you can find out a very great deal about
- Now you can choose to explore all your other interests too

EXPRESS

- Most effective way to express yourself
- Now express yourself worldwide
- You'd be surprised who expresses interest

EXTRA

- Nothing extra to buy
- Get the digital extra
- Giving you the extras that really count
- The extra power will put you into orbit

FACTOR

- Decide what factor is most important to you
- Your new machine will be a big factor in your future
- Several different factors will enter into your decision

FAMILIAR

- As the frontiers of Internet use become increasing familiar to you
- As the Internet becomes more familiar, more people will use it more comfortably
- The Internet will be as familiar as a telephone
- Step out of familiar territory

FAST

- Wickedly fast connections
- Now faster than ever
- A fast, effective and convenient way
- Offering blazingly fast computing ability
- Helping you finish faster

FANATIC

- Welcome to an outpost of online fanatics
- Definitely fanatic about quality
- For online fanatics

FAST

- Get on the Net that fast
- Welcome to the fast lane
- Lifts the limits on how fast you can
- It moves even faster than you do
- Has hit the fast lane
- Twice as fast
- Feel the power of working with the fastest
- No matter what you're looking for, you can find it fast
- Fast even during peak hours
- In a very fast world, don't get left behind

FEATURE

- Get features that actually help you do your job
- With a host of other awesome features
- Introducing the first fully-featured product
- Lots of standard features that can hardly be called standard
- One of the most engaging features of the program is
- Please check out our feature of the month

- Discover the many new features of this exciting new operating environment
- One of our flagship features is
- You can add great features like
- All the powerful features you'll ever need
- A magnitude of dynamite features
- We're talking beefed-up features like
- You get the most potent features of any
- Confident you're getting cutting edge features

FEEDBACK

- Customer feedback greatly influenced how we developed our new product
- We have received such a lot of positive feedback when our site was launched
- Please keep the feedback coming
- Response to the activity at your site will provide continuous and vital feedback

FILE

- A complete electronic file cabinet
- Have your files where you can get at them when you want them
- When your life is all wrapped up in your files
- It's all right there, in your files

FIND

- It takes only 30 seconds to find out
- You can also find us on the Internet
- So they'll find you fast

FINGERTIPS

- You may have had the Internet literally under your fingertips and not known it until now
- The Internet puts most of the world at your fingertips
- Thousands more customers now at your fingertips

FIRST

- There is a first time for everything
- To be first onto the Web with this is to become a pathfinder
- Make this a major first for you
- The best was also the first

FOCUS

- With the focus on technology
- Will change your focus pretty fast
- Focus is now on an entirely different place

FORMAT

- Translating everything easily into this new format
- Placed in a very easy-to-use format
- Requiring a fresh and innovative format to get your message across electronically

FORWARD

- Forward this issue to your friends
- Propel your business forward at the speed of light
- Fast forward into the new millennium

FREE

- Providing vast numbers of services free for the taking
- All free of charge
- We'll even throw in the other things you need for free
- Frees you from the problems of old-fashioned
- Try it for free
- Providing a free, comprehensive
- Why pay for what you can get for free
- Try it free by downloading
- The free ride is over

FRIEND

- You'll make more than just friends
- Now friends to all the world
- When you've bought from us, you've also made a friend

FRONTIER

- Bulletins from the frontiers of technology
- Come with us into the next frontier
- As with any frontier, there are challenges and exciting unknowns
- Giving you a rich new frontier to conquer

FUN

- The fun begins immediately
- The technical word for fun
- And we've packed it with fun

FUNCTION

- Targeted toward those performing the day-to-day functions
- Prepare to function with increased competence
- Have added yet more functions than ever

before
- A glorious unity of function and design

FUNCTIONALITY
- Easy-to-use functionality
- This kind of functionality enables you to
- Increased functionality opens doors to the universe

FUNDAMENTAL
- Fundamental to understanding and getting the most out of your system
- Learn the fundamentals of operating your system quickly
- Getting the fundamentals down pat in a hurry
- Get up to speed on the fundamentals

FUTURE
- Kick start your future
- So that your success can continue into the future
- Show you have what it takes to take hold of the future
- Step directly into a brand new future
- Many future thinkers firmly believe
- Preparing you for the demands of a technologically advanced future
- Helping you gain the knowledge and skill to face the future
- The future has arrived dizzyingly fast
- Get the jump on planning for a technological future few of us could have foreseen
- Prepare for the future now
- Making Internet growth part of your comprehensive plan for the future
- Powerfully challenging your view of the future
- The future is coming at us so swiftly
- We can barely keep up with the future
- Take a ride into the future with
- Driving the future of how we do business
- The future of how we'll amuse ourselves
- Deciding to build a new future
- If you're wondering what the future might look like
- We'd offer you a glimpse of the future
- If you're serious about your future, give us a call

GEEK
- Now you don't have to call in the neighborhood geek to find out how
- Celebrate the triumph of the geeks
- No longer geek territory
- Dare to venture in among the geeks
- Geeks and mouse potatoes come alive

GENERATION
- The next generation is here
- Skip a generation
- Already we've designed the next generation of
- We're giving a sneak peek at the next generation
- Is your computer having a generation problem

GLANCE
- Does at-a-glance information turn you on
- Take the time to take a glance at
- A single glance will convince you

GLOBAL
- A global meeting point for
- A global leader in a wide range of technologies
- Your invitation to join the global community

GO
- Old methods go the way of the dodo bird
- Go modern, go electronic, go into cyberspace
- Gets you where you're going faster
- Clearly, there's only one way to go

GRAPHIC
- Extraordinary graphics at your fingertips
- See how easily graphics can now be sent out to vividly illustrate your point
- With graphics to spice up your presentations
- Good graphics have become vital to good business

GROW
- One of the fastest and easiest ways to grow your business
- The growth of the Web is phenomenal
- The growth has been explosive
- A new way to promote your continued growth and success
- Taking advantage of a wild growth period

GUIDE

- Plus a handy reference guide to help you get around the Web
- A guide to show you the best and brightest
- Let us be your guide
- Need a guide – click here
- Your guide in this uncharted new region
- For a guided tour of our company, click here
- Your original, one-stop guide to everything you need to know about
- A guide to cutting-edge ideas in
- Comprehensive guide with complete instructions
- Guide you through it, step by step

GURU

- Yes, we have plenty of resident computer gurus to help you
- Ask our guru about all your concerns
- Become your own media guru
- Even the gurus approve of

HAPPEN

- Can actually make the impossible happen
- Cutting you loose to make exciting things happen
- Make it all happen right in front of you
- Be there when it happens

HELP

- Virus? Media crash? Data loss? You could use help
- Providing lots of online help
- The fastest, friendliest way to help you when you need it
- You can get help faster by asking for it on the Internet
- Helping your business thrive in a networked world

HERE

- Yes, you can get there from here
- The best is right here so come and look
- Come alive in the here and now

HIGHWAY

- As you speed along the electronic highway
- Making sure the information highway leads right to your door
- Take a ride to the future on the information highway

HOME

- A home on the Web for
- A new home for your best ideas
- Now it can all happen right in your home
- Build a comfortable home in cyberspace

HOOK

- Means you can now hook up with any
- Hook up to the smart way
- Hooking you up the way you want

HORIZON

- Ever-changing horizons
- Now you can look right over the horizon and see
- New horizons are approaching fast

HOST

- Now you can get to any host on the Internet through
- Web hosting to provide your company with the independence and the recognition it needs
- Let us host your cyber-party
- This is web hosting made easy
- A whole host of new advances

HYPE

- Are you wondering what the hype is all about
- So important to separate the hype from reality
- Assuring you that it's not just hype
- You've heard all the hype
- Has lived up to all the hype
- The hype is all true
- There are real wonders behind the hype

ICON

- This icon points to places of wonder
- You may visit related home pages by choosing from the icons below
- Click on this icon for additional information

IDEA

- Helping you turn your ideas into reality
- Your ideas make a difference
- Click for the latest business ideas and opportunities
- Visit our research section for hundreds of

ideas in a huge array of subject areas
- Open up to new ideas
- Delivering rapid-fire ideas about the new techno culture

IDENTITY
- Think of it as a chance to create a whole new identity for your business
- Maintain your identity in a digital age
- Helping to maintain and enhance your business identity electronically
- Get leading-edge identity on the Internet
- Move quickly to establish your identity on the Net

IMAGE
- Images are finer than ever before
- Create images with impact
- Gripping images spilling onto the Web
- Choose just the right image for any situation
- Prepare high-impact images for your documents

IMAGINATION
- The only limit is your imagination
- Now you can do everything your imagination desires
- The greatest journeys take place in the imagination

IMAGINE
- Imagine teleporting to
- Imagine it, then do it
- Helping you imagine

IMMEDIACY
- The need for immediacy is steadily increasing
- The immediacy and ease of email
- Now even greater immediacy

IMPACT
- Has made a huge impact on the Internet
- Increase your impact without exploding
- The impact is rumbling across the entire cyberworld

INFORMATION
- Pick up hard-to-find information
- Find information on just about any topic
- Easier to find the information you want
- It's easy to receive free information about

- Put important information right on your
- Discover the valuable hidden information in your data
- Making it much easier to transfer information
- There's a flood of information out there
- How you keep important information with you
- Information is intoxicating
- For those of you who are information seekers
- We are superb information providers
- Providing even more dynamic information about
- For in-depth information about
- Finding only the information that is valuable to you
- Easy-to-read information enhanced with audio explanations, video clips, slide shows and animations
- Hundreds of pages of information, tools and discussion to help you get your job done more effectively and efficiently than ever before
- Now you can link to specific information with a single click
- Instant information for the truly fact-hungry
- Be among the first to convert to this new form of information transfer
- You too can be a leading global provider of information about your business
- Visit our one-stop information spot
- Get the latest expert information instantly
- The information is processed for you at lightning speed
- Information can now be offered in real time
- Your international online information center
- Now the easiest way to organize your information
- Plug in to a wealth of valuable information now
- Introducing you to the most current information about

INTERACT
- The Internet is revolutionizing how we interact with the outside world
- Turning around your interactions with the world at large
- Connecting and interacting with the

outside world in a whole new way
- Learn even more about people and how they will interact in the Internet
- To interact appropriately on the Internet
- Drawing more and more people into daily interaction with computers
- Blaze through our easy interactive program
- And speaking of interactivity
- Interactivity connects people to each other via the machine

INITIATIVE
- Announcing new Internet initiatives
- Now you can get customers to take the initiative
- Take the initiative and do it on the Net

INPUT
- Your input is very important to us
- Get more input for far less output
- Just sitting there waiting for your input
- Everything depends upon the quality of input

INQUIRY
- Due to the tremendous response, serious inquiries only
- So easy to make an inquiry online
- A single inquiry can make or break your online success

INSTALL
- Installs in minutes
- So easy to install
- Install it with a single click of the mouse
- Easy installation makes your job a breeze
- Self-installing, no hassle

INSTANT
- Brings instant awareness
- Connection is instant
- When instant isn't fast enough
- Instant just got faster

INSTRUCTIONS
- How-to instructions right on your screen
- You won't even need instructions
- Complete instructions are always included with
- Step-by-step instructions help you explore

INTEGRATE
- Seamlessly integrates with
- To integrate the Net into your operations
- Great because it's totally integrated
- Gives you all the integration you need

INTERACT
- Interact in real time with friends, associates and customers
- A truly interactive service that will bring them back for more
- Provides the ability to reach millions in an interactive way
- Such interactivity has long been a dream

INTERACTIVE
- Gives you a wide range of interactive
- Leading a completely interactive life
- Interactivity increases exponentially

INTERFACE
- It's the most natural interface of all
- Keeping the basic interface smooth and sophisticated
- Simple fill-in forms interface with
- The easiest and most effective interface available for
- Incorporates the familiar interface of
- An interface similar to the software you're already familiar with
- Interfaces naturally and easily with
- Leap into the interface between life and cyberspace

INTERNET
- Makes working the Internet into child's play
- The Internet can hook you up with
- The Internet will never be the same again
- Today's big buzz on the Internet
- The Internet at its best
- Designed specifically for the Internet
- Now Internet ready
- When it comes to making the most of the Internet
- The Internet is giving your whole operation a facelift
- The Internet is a friendly place
- The Internet is ready to provide a wildly entertaining and educational experience
- A weird place called the Internet
- Dazzling Internet sites abound
- Ideas and resources to help build and

improve your Internet presence
- Direct Internet access is yours for only
- Putting the Internet to work for you
- The Internet can be a rough and tumble place
- Increasing overall awareness of our presence on the Internet
- Is the massive power of the Internet working for you
- Working directly with anyone interested in developing a presence on the Internet
- The Internet is a huge and happening place
- You'll wonder why you're not making the most of the Internet already
- Now offered via the Internet
- Try an adventure on the Internet today
- The Internet itself can offer all kinds of excellent advice about
- The Internet is already producing substantial benefits in all areas of
- The best and brightest are racing onto the Internet
- Already have a demonstrated track record on the Internet
- Here's the real scoop on the Internet
- One of the great joys of the Internet
- Take a chance on the Internet
- Don't let the Internet leave you feeling helpless
- Gleaning a great harvest of information from the Internet
- Now featured on the Internet
- Why there is no free lunch on the Internet
- Take a test drive on the Internet
- Get to know the Internet a whole new way
- Use the Internet free for a month
- Get a free easy-to-use Internet starter kit
- If you're serious about Internet marketing
- Time you took advantage of this Internet craze
- The easy way for you and your family to enjoy the Internet

INTIMIDATE
- Sometimes the Internet can be truly intimidating
- No longer intimidated by the new technologies
- Those intimidated and confused by cyberspace will have to get over it
- The world is no longer intimidated by

computers and the Internet

INTRODUCTION
- Providing an easy introduction to the new possibilities of the Internet
- Making sure your web page is an effective introduction to your business
- What better introduction than a lively, informative web page

INVENT
- Please contact the people that invented
- Inventing new breakthroughs every day
- We invented it so you can invent

ISSUE
- Already coming to our web site to find out about the latest
- Exploring important new opportunities and issues created by the Internet
- Probing contemporary issues that affect us all

JOB
- The Internet is the fastest way yet to get your job done
- One of the jobs your computer can do for you is
- Boring jobs you won't even have to think about any more

JOURNEY
- A site that makes your cyber-journey something special
- Take a journey into the unknown and come back smiling
- Join us on a journey into the future

KEY
- The key is right in front of you
- Only you have the key
- Start with only the key components
- A couple of key strokes does it

KID
- Cool links for kids
- Designed to be kid-friendly
- Giving your kids a head start on the future
- The tech kids have grown up
- Even a kid can use it
- Introduce your kids to the Net safely

KNOW

- Everything you need to know but were afraid to ask
- A must-have for everyone in the know
- The easy way to get to know someone
- Know more faster with
- Providing everything you wanted to know about
- All to put you in the know
- Explaining what you need to know
- Everything you need to know to get started

KNOWLEDGE

- Even if you have little or no prior knowledge of how computers work
- You very quickly gain a working knowledge of
- The purpose is to enhance your knowledge of
- There when you want to update your knowledge
- You'll come away with the knowledge to bring the Internet to life

LAUNCH

- A launch pad for the latest technological advancements
- All ready to launch
- And you can be in on the launch of a wild new era

LEARN

- To learn more, first try
- You learn by doing and that's exciting
- Everything you need to learn what you need to know about
- Through the Internet, you can do most of your learning at home
- A flexible and accessible way to learn
- Has spurred interest in learning all about
- Hands-on, experiential learning cannot be replaced
- To learn more, call us at

LIBRARY

- Now you can crank out an entire library of web pages
- Puts an entire library at your fingertips
- Whole libraries have been compressed

LIFE

- Bringing the Internet to life for your business
- Helping you keep up with dizzying changes in your business life
- Put more thrills in your life with

LIGHT

- Have you seen the light
- Lighter, faster, more fun
- They'll never make light of you again
- Our lightest, most powerful yet

LIMIT

- Why limit yourself
- Always pushing to limits, opening up the world
- Seizing opportunity and leaping limits
- Get rid of your limits

LINK

- Time to hit the links
- Your link to the whole world
- Offers direct links to other exciting websites
- The best way to increase your link popularity
- Bubbles over with links to splendid pages
- Linking you only to information you can use
- Linking you to people with interests similar to your own
- Can easily update your links
- As simple as putting in a link to your site
- Simply your best link to real profits
- Link yourself to hundreds of interesting
- Simply your best link to everything necessary
- Hundreds of links to the world's best sites

LIST

- To be permanently removed from this list
- Not just one big list you'll get lost in
- Get a friend to join this list

LOG

- Or for more information, log on
- Waiting for you whenever you log in
- Every time you log on you'll see a change for the better

LOOK

- The product that all the others look up to

- Helping pinpoint what you're looking for
- Look no further for what you need
- Won't believe what you're looking at

MAGIC

- Can work the same magic for you
- You can be forgiven for thinking it's pure magic
- Putting magic in your keyboard

MAIL

- Sending mail is now so very easy
- No more trudging out to the mailbox
- The Web saves a fortune in printing and mailing costs
- A stratospheric improvement over old fashioned mail

MANAGE

- Helping you manage, innovate and motivate
- Looking for ever better ways to manage the flow
- Manual management provides the great advantage of personal service
- Managing your web site well becomes a major priority

MASTER

- Now you can master the newest Internet
- Mastering whole new worlds
- The undisputed master of

MATCH

- Matching people with common interests
- Can match, modify and create
- Matching you up with like-minded folk from across the globe
- Let the competition match this

MATERIAL

- Augmented by a wealth of original online material
- Store more material in far less space
- Giving you access to an unbelievable amount of material

MEDIA

- Providing superior media support
- Extends your media use
- More media, more sales
- For all your media needs

MESSAGE

- Carrying your message further than ever before
- Your message could be zapped into thousands of email boxes in mere minutes
- The stunning possibilities inherent in being able to exchange messages with anyone on the Internet
- A concise, punch and grabbing message works on the Internet
- Your message can say anything you want
- Making your message stand boldly out amongst the great mass of stuff
- An easy, effective way to get your message out
- Gets your message across in a cost effective manner

METHOD

- Using visionary methods to manage
- Appetite for new and creative methods
- Your previous method of doing business has finally outlived its usefulness
- Much easier than any of the other methods
- Learning new methods for a new era

MIND

- Created by the most brilliant minds in the country
- Make it into an extension of your mind
- Something you won't mind using

MODEL

- All models are shipped with
- An old model trashed by the Internet and the Web
- Setting up on an entirely new model

MODEM

- Commute by modem
- Your modem is a good place to start
- A simple modem has become a magic carpet to the world
- Ancient as a modem

MONEY

- Turning your web page into a conduit for money
- Set up to help you make money on the Internet
- Save money and make money at the same

time
- Looking for a way to make more money from the Internet
- Making money on the Internet just got easier
- If you're serious about making money on the Internet
- You can't help but make money

MORE
- When you want more, call us
- And, for those who want more, a wide range of tools
- Take a moment to see for yourself how much more there is to
- All this and much more for only
- Now you can see more, do more, learn more

MOUSE
- Lets you use your keyboard and mouse to adjust
- Help is just a mouse click away
- All it takes is a couple of mouse clicks
- Makes it easy as clicking your mouse
- A single mouse click lets you connect
- No more mousing around with
- Undreamed of uses for your mouse

MULTIMEDIA
- Pull the plug on multimedia woes
- Supports a rich multimedia experience
- Enhancing your multimedia performance
- More multimedia magic
- Enhancing the extraordinary multimedia experience available only from
- Get the most from your multimedia experience
- A creative process in multimedia
- Result in a great multimedia experience
- Gives you the multimedia power to sample
- Taking your multimedia experience to an all-time high

NAVIGATE
- Makes navigating the Net as simple as click, click, click
- To navigate you through the maze
- Navigate as easily as

NET
- Join the Net set

- It's simple to get it on the Net
- Fully experience the Net with a single button click
- Click here if you're new to the Net
- Turn on to one of the most comprehensive and extensive support areas on the Net
- Visit us on the Net at
- Make the Net work for your business
- Tools that will influence your Net experience well into the
- You want to be on the Net and you want to do it right
- The most wonderful part of the Net
- Putting the Net in your pocket
- Another amazing thing about the Net
- How about some Net profits
- Helping you make the Net work

NETIQUETTE
- Careful to follow the philosophy and netiquette of the Internet
- An offense against netiquette can bring down a royal flaming
- Netiquette codes are becoming much more flexible
- Taking care not to offend against netiquette
- Guards you against netiquette errors

NETWORK
- Vastly expand your networking possibilities
- Tap into a worldwide grid of networks
- Taking advantage of a worldwide network of supporters
- The mother of all networks is the Internet
- Setting out to take advantage of the world's largest computer network
- The larger the network, the more people you can make contact with
- Really a network of networks
- Networking technologies are revolutionizing business communications
- Networks are fast becoming critical to the daily operation of businesses
- Quickly learn what is involved in creating a successful communications network
- A network that is very large and useful
- The world's fastest growing communications network

- The best networking your business can do
- Network solutions for your business
- A fast and reliable network

NEW
- New technologies are included and used
- New every day at your web site
- Something new is going on in your computer
- Taking care to provide always something new to see

NEWBIE
- A guide for newbies and web wizards
- A red carpet welcome for newbies
- Even newbies can use it like pros
- You won't remain a newbie for long

NEWS
- Your free online source of news, information and resources
- Delivering the latest news about
- Now good news travels on the Internet
- Bringing personalized news about the latest programs to you
- Get red hot news immediately

NUMBER
- Even with the numbers staring you in the face
- The numbers say it all
- Now you can get their number

OFFICE
- We can equip your office more economically
- A whole office in your pocket
- You can leave your office, but you office won't leave you

ON
- It's always on
- Get on top fast
- Plug in, turn on, stay on

ONLINE
- Get ahead online before your rivals
- Be online the same day
- For those online and those who will be online soon
- Check us out online
- Our top professionals are now online

- Take advantage of this online world
- Follow us online
- Able to professionally represent your business in the online world
- If you've been considering getting online
- Putting kids in contact with heroes online
- An online way to support the future needs of your business
- A successful and profitable online business
- More online to enjoy
- Now so easy to do online
- Bringing your business to online, real-time, day-to-day transactions

OPPORTUNITY
- Hundreds of great opportunities right in your area
- Why not take advantage of this powerful opportunity
- Every change brings an opportunity
- Opportunities to have an online presence
- Opening up a world of new opportunities
- The Web is providing many more opportunities than you could possibly have imagined
- You could get dizzy just thinking about the opportunities
- A great opportunity to keep instantly up-to-date
- Opportunities are appearing in such different guises that we're even having trouble recognizing them

OPTIMIZE
- Helping you optimize operations
- When you need to optimize
- The best way to optimize
- Naturally optimizes system use

OPTION
- The only other viable option is
- Now your options are no longer limited
- Now the business world has another option
- Displays a list of available help options for your convenience
- Generating more options than ever before imagined
- Check out all the options, then choose

ORDER
- This is clearly the new order

- To order, call us toll-free at
- Order instantly by accessing our web site
- Place your order directly into our automated online system
- You can place your order right from our web site
- Secure online ordering
- Helping you fill a very tall order

ORGANIZE

- Customizing, organizing and rearranging
- The quickest way to capture, organize and use information from the Web
- The easiest way to organize your business
- The first necessity is to be well organized
- Organizing you efficiently on the Web

PACKAGE

- All combined in one easy-to-use package
- The package that has everything you need
- In one seamlessly integrated package

PAGE

- A simple web page housing so much information
- Visit our web page as soon as you can
- Now anyone can create an amazing web page
- Goes right onto your web page without wasting time on
- Learn the art of spinning a web page
- A great way to jazz up your web page
- Create unique and individual pages
- Making your home page the best it can be
- The official home page for

PATH

- Making your cyberspace path safer in every way
- Makes the path easy to follow
- New paths every day

PAY

- You'd probably expect to pay a lot
- Pay for it online with confidence
- Paying for it is so easy

PEOPLE

- There are millions of people online
- Find out what's happening with people around the world
- Cyberspace people are often very friendly and welcoming to newcomers

- The Internet is composed of the people who use it and the information residing in it
- A digital means of putting us in touch with real people
- Putting you close to the people that matter to you

PERFORMANCE

- Designed to offer a significant performance advantage in
- Designed to eliminate performance bottlenecks
- Tops in every performance category
- Getting a high performance result for you
- Enhancing your daily performance
- Now you can measure your daily performance
- Steadily improving our communication performance
- A whole new way to enhance your performance
- Optimum performance is our top priority

PERSONALITY

- Views of the leading Net personalities
- Express your personality dramatically
- A system with a whole new personality

PHONE

- Now you don't need a second phone line
- No more waiting on the phone
- Completely integrated with your phone, email and fax

PIONEER

- It's the pioneer of the Internet
- Now you, too, can be a pioneer
- Join the pioneers of cyberspace

PLACE

- This is an actually useful place
- Bring you the best places on the Web, bar none
- Find your true place on the Web

PLAN

- The excitement of learning to plan and create web pages
- The planning
- The Internet is central to all our plans
- Make us a part of your plans

PLANET

- Able to do business from the farthest reaches of the planet
- So it doesn't look like something from another planet
- Now the whole planet is yours

PLATFORM

- Flexible technology that works across any platform
- Customized, multi-platform support you're looking for
- Giving a wider platform for your operations
- With seamless cross-platform compatibility

PLAYER

- A huge opportunity to be a big player in a lucrative business
- Turns you into a player fast
- If you want to be a player, we'll set you up

PLUG

- Plug in to us and away you go
- Plug into practical ways to upgrade your business
- Now you're plugged into the entire world
- A way to plug ourselves into the biggest network of all
- A web site becomes a vehicle to show just how plugged in you are

POTENTIAL

- Helping you take full advantage of the Internet's potential
- Discover the enormous revenue potential of the Internet
- Wouldn't you like all this potential at your command
- Potential you haven't imagined before

POWER

- Power user's heaven
- Make your words power the Web
- All of the power with none of the problems
- How's this for an impressive display of power
- Which means you'll be sure to have the power necessary to respond
- Giving you the power to be your best
- Feel the raw power of
- You'll be blown away by the power
- For when you need more power
- What you need to power your
- Designed for the power hungry
- Then power up your
- Giving you power, knowledge and prosperity through the Internet
- Gaining a truly awesome power
- Now the power of the Internet is working for you
- Using the full power of the Internet
- Giving the credit to computing power
- The power is concentrated

POWERFUL

- Sink your teeth into something really powerful
- More powerful than ever
- Just how powerful does your computer make you
- A truly powerful new vision

PRECISION

- You rely on the precision of
- Precision starts with remarkable control provided by our
- Precision is our middle name
- Done with precision and class

PREPARE

- Designed to prepare you for a new age
- Working hard to prepare ourselves for this medium
- This Internet leap caught up with us before we were quite prepared for it

PRESENCE

- Call today to establish your presence on the Web
- A big-time presence on the Web
- Monitoring the effectiveness of our Internet presence
- Establishing an Internet presence is one of the most important next steps your business can take
- Working together to build the best possible Internet presence
- Web site giving you a presence on this astounding mass medium

PRESENT

- The future has suddenly become your

present
- Present your information with interest and pizzazz
- A totally new way to present your ideas, products and services to others

PRESENTATION
- Fine tune your presentation
- On the Web, presentation is everything
- Spiff up your presentation with no effort at all
- Presentation is everything

PRICE
- Check daily online price specials
- Prices are dropping at the speed of cyberspace
- Get the Web pricing advantage

PROBLEM
- Proven effective problem solvers
- Overcoming new problems, one by one
- Makes problems disappear like magic

PROCESS
- We can make the process even easier
- Helping you actually enjoy the process
- Processes all your work automatically
- You'll love the process
- Hooked on the process
- Every step of the process is made transparent
- We help you understand he process
- The process of learning is greatly speeded

PRODUCT
- Offering you a large array of products and leading-edge technology
- A wide selection of online products
- Hot products on the Net
- A new class of products is starting to hit the market
- Working furiously to one-up each other on products
- A product you must have on your machine
- A product round-up that has everything you want to know about

PRODUCTION
- Your production level will increase
- More production, less effort
- Watch your production zoom

PROFESSIONAL
- For professional use only
- Products for the creative professional
- Makes you look like a real professional

PROFIT
- So your site returns a significant profit
- Putting your profits first
- Profit from the Internet easily

PROGRAM
- Thousands of people have used the program to
- See how great this program really is
- Might be the only such program you'll ever run across
- To benefit from our program, please visit our website
- Get the program that gives you the speed, power and ease-of-use to
- A huge program with even more capabilities
- A program that meets your needs
- A program designed to run on your personal computer
- Works just like the programs and tools you already know

PROJECT
- Guiding you through your projects, start to finish
- Able to do all your projects
- Big projects need big computing power
- Produce projects sure to put you in the winner's circle
- Packed with information on how to get your project done

PROMISE
- We promise if any part has a problem, we'll replace it
- So promising, so confusing
- As promising as the Internet is
- More promising than ever before

PROMOTE
- Already promoting improvements in a broader, more innovative and more effective context
- Increasingly promoting your business on the Web
- Promoting your site is crucial to its

success
- When you promote yourself on the Web, results shoot up big time
- Start promoting your site the smart way

PROSPECT
- Your best online prospects
- Now reach prospects anywhere
- Your prospects just got a lot brighter

PROTECT
- Protect all the important stuff in your computer with
- Makes protecting yourself very easy
- All the protection you could want

PROTECTION
- Protection that gives you peace of mind
- Extra attention to your protection needs
- Protection always comes first
- Protection for all you've already achieved

PROVIDER
- One of the leading business-focussed global providers
- A provider of wonder and joy
- The provider providing you with the best

PUBLIC
- Technology just released to the public
- Make it public to the world
- Now everything is public
- So the public can reach you
- Now the public can easily participate

RATE
- At the best Internet rates anywhere
- Offering special rates to the cyber-savvy
- Keep up with the ever increasing rate of change
- Rated totally awesome
- You'll rate it very high

REGISTER
- Register your business and personal domain
- Register sooner for less cost
- Register your concerns instantly

RELATIONSHIP
- Forging a powerful customer relationship
- A relationship that can change every day
- Improve your relationship with the Web

RELIABLE
- Providing something that is even faster and more reliable
- Making even cyberspace more reliable
- Totally reliable is difficult on the Web, but we come close
- When reliability means everything

REPRESENTATIVE
- Representative on only a tiny fraction of what's available
- Let us be your representative on the Web
- For more information, talk to your sales representative today

RESEARCH
- Ideal for market research
- Enabling thorough research and insightful analysis
- Vastly expands your research capability
- All this research just to benefit you
- Successful research at an ever accelerating rate
- Our complete research really shows

RESELLER
- To buy direct or find your nearest reseller
- Authorized, value-added reseller
- The best reseller deal on the Web

RESOURCE
- The Internet itself provides you with so many resources
- Downloaded software provides resources
- Discover more resources at your fingertips than you dreamed possible
- Now providing access to resources around the clock
- These resources may be your best weapon
- Access to the same resources no matter where you are
- Guiding you to the resources you need
- It's your one-stop resource
- The most complete resource center in town and on the Net
- Remains a viable, useful commercial resource
- Your international online resource for
- Offering fast, easy access to dozens of additional resources
- A resource that never sleeps

RESPONSE

- Increase response exponentially
- Designed to help boost your response
- Creating a low cost, high response program
- Response rates shoot up
- Dramatically increase your rates of response
- The excitement of responses within moments of sending your message
- Take advantage of the newest kind of response devices
- Lower costs, faster response

RESULT

- Results that sound too good to be true – but they're not
- Better results demand more time and energy
- Terrific results from only a small amount of conversion effort
- Once on the Web, your results will increase dramatically
- Delivering results almost instantly
- More results faster

REVOLUTIONIZE

- The way we work has already been revolutionized
- Revolutionizing how we connect with you
- Now you can do the revolutionizing
- Revolutionizing everyone's thinking about personal communications
- Revolutionizing how you make money

ROAD

- Viewing the Net as a road to information
- Speeding your way down the road to
- Step onto the shining road into cyberspace
- The road to cyber-success starts here

RULE

- Contrary to the usual rule of thumb
- An area so new the rules haven't formed
- The rules are changing all the time

RUN

- You don't have to run faster to win
- Gets you up and running fast
- You'll be up and running in minutes

SALE

- Costing you only pennies per sale
- Helping you generate more sales
- Dramatically increase your sales with this system
- The ultimate sales tool of the future

SAMPLE

- Here is just a sampling of
- A sampling of what you can use with your software
- Here are just a few samples from what we have available
- Once you sample the speed and convenience

SAVINGS

- Get optimum performance, ultimate protection and the bottom line savings you need
- Just click to increase your savings
- Connect with cyber-savings
- Take your savings on the road with you

SAVVY

- Now it's easy to get savvy about
- Join other savvy folk in
- Helping you become much more tech-savvy
- So that your customers will know that you are electronically savvy
- The new and savvy way to reach one's customers
- Small, savvy and lightning fast

SEARCH

- Internet search engines are dotting the landscape
- A way to widen your search for customers
- Your customers no longer have to search for you
- Make the searches lead to you
- Search for us on the Net – we're easy to find
- The fastest, hungriest search engine
- Your search ends here

SECURITY

- You need to know about a few security concepts
- No more worries about security
- And the security is built in

- Adds even more security to your smart digital investment
- Keeping ahead of security concerns

SEE

- You've got to see it for yourself
- You've got to see it to believe it
- The place to see and be seen on the Web
- You're seeing only the tip of the iceberg

SELECTION

- Unbeatable selection at unbeatable prices
- Offering a wide selection of online products
- For a complete selection, please visit us

SERIOUS

- As serious about your business as you
- Get serious power through the Net
- One reason you should seriously consider

SERVICE

- Call us and find out why our service is better
- Providing local support, services and upgrades
- Where service is the difference
- Backed by our dedication to customer service
- Waiting for the service that's right for you
- Customers see no interruption in service
- We have a complete set of products and services to help you
- Special services instantly for preferred customers
- Now providing a full range of digital services
- Offering instant service over the Internet
- Online services continue to grow at a dizzying pace
- The most heavily trafficked online service
- Plus thousands of other services online
- You also want good service
- Providing 24 hour customer service and technical support
- The power to provide unsurpassed service
- The only service that gives you easy access to
- Now focussing primarily on online services

SET UP

- Easy to set up and use
- If you've got the right setup, you can
- Equipped for automatic setup and configuration

SHARE

- Now you never have to share
- Getting a bigger share of customers' attention through the Internet
- Solving the need for better ways to share information
- Increasing your market share via the Internet

SHIP

- And we ship to you the next business day
- Same day shipping guaranteed
- Same day shipping on all in-stock items
- Call for free shipping
- Free shipping with no minimum purchase
- We absorb the cost of shipping

SHOP

- Provides a unique shopping experience
- Shop conveniently online at
- Set up shop in the Internet
- Shop without leaving your keyboard
- Offering hundreds more shopping options
- A really interesting way to go shopping
- Makes your shopping virtually effortless

SHOWROOM

- Visit our showroom for in-store specials
- Now millions can come to your showroom
- Invite the world to your showroom

SIGNATURE

- Your signature logo on every web page
- Unmistakable as your signature
- Electronic signatures can then be added

SIMPLIFY

- Simplifies web-based tasks
- More ways to simplify things
- Simplify your life with some complex technology

SITE

- Something for everyone at this site
- A site designed with lots of attractive

features to keep people coming back
- Visit our site, find out more about what we can do for you
- Better yet, visit our web site and download a free demo
- Takes the mystery out of web site creation
- Your site will really come to life
- The whole site is searchable
- Distinguishes itself from other web sites
- Searching out star-quality sites
- Some of the best site-seeing cyberspace has to offer
- A source to the hottest web sites
- Cruise the web sites to find the best
- Now you can build an interactive site full of multimedia attractions
- Increasing your site's "stickiness"
- A site giving you the personal attention you need
- Intrigue them enough to visit your site
- Your own site is a great place to start
- Make your site a sizzling success

SKILL
- Picking up skills and knowledge they can share with
- Help you master online research skills
- Develop the skills essential to successful computer use
- Quickly building the skills that you need
- Internet skills are now in the highest demand
- Combined with skill development exercises

SOCIETY
- How is society affected by the Internet
- Raising new issues that have a new impact upon your business
- Now bringing diverse sections of society together on the Web

SOFTWARE
- With pre-installed business software
- The software you need to connect
- Super prices on software bundles
- Get software designed for this technology
- The world's best-selling software
- Comes with all the software you need
- The latest and greatest in software
- Check out our huge selection of clearance software

- Includes the software listed along with a special bonus offer
- You don't have to be a software programmer to
- Switching your software is a breeze
- Enhanced software applications
- Software bonanza
- Check out our free demo software
- The best software from leading companies is included
- All the software you need to easily set up, author and maintain your web site

SOLUTION
- There's a solution that won't put a dent in your bottom line
- Committed to bringing you reliable, leading-edge solutions
- A solution that works for any business
- Here's the smart solution
- To recommend the right solution
- For the easiest, most affordable solution
- Means you're getting the most easy-to-use, innovative and reliable solution
- A range of highly flexible solutions
- Available to help you determine which solutions are best for
- So when you're looking for the complete solution
- For a family Internet solution
- Has spurred the availability of technical solutions
- The perfect solution where space and budget is limited
- Designed to offer time-saving solutions
- A traditional solution for businesses of all sizes
- An accessible, easy-to-use solution for creating web sites
- Integrated telecommunications solution
- Become a leading solutions provider
- Advanced solutions for the next generation of
- Creating world class solutions every day

SPEED
- Satisfy your need for speed
- High speed and high service
- Getting your company up to speed
- For those who crave the ultimate speed
- Helps you break the speed limit
- Full speed ahead
- The blistering speed you need to

- You finally get all the speed you want
- Speed your way through

STAFF

- Our staff is trained and tested in the latest applications
- Staff upholding highest professional standards
- Instant access to highly trained staff
- Just ask our expert staff for any help you need

STANDARD

- Setting new standards in productivity
- A standard already being widely adopted
- Rapidly changing and improving existing standards

START

- Getting started is a breeze
- Getting started is so easy with
- This is where it all starts
- All you need to know to get started
- The start-up costs are surprisingly minimal
- Shows you how to get started fast

STATE-OF-THE-ART

- State-of-the-art interactive and animated programs
- State-of-the-art design and speed
- Always state-of-the-art
- You, too, can possess state-of-the-art technology

STEP

- Recognized as the next logical step beyond
- Taking that first nervous step into the cyber-jungle
- Letting you take as few extra steps as possible
- Very simple steps required to install the software
- Leads you carefully through every step

STRATEGY

- Need to adjust your strategy
- Sharpening your strategy significantly
- Tweaking strategy to accommodate
- Fits right in with your strategy

STRETCH

- When you're really stretching it to
- Stretching our capabilities in a new, exciting way
- Now you can stretch in every direction

SUCCESS

- It's very important to us that you succeed
- Why argue with success
- Backing your success all the way

SUPPORT

- Offering superior support with no surprise charges
- Support and expert advice whenever you need it
- A clear leader in Internet support
- Does your business suffer from lack of reliable support
- Providing a great deal of support through electronic means
- Cutting edge features and excellent support
- Count on fast, reliable support
- For support, call anytime, day or night
- All the software and support you'll need
- Knowledgeable technical support

SURF

- So if surfing off to a world of wonders sounds inviting
- Start surfing the wildest of the Web
- Your customers are already surfing the Internet in search of your product
- You'll be able to get more and more Web surfers to drop in
- Now you can surf right into the world
- Take a break from surfing for a moment
- Joining all the others blithely surfing the Internet without drowning
- Surf's up, let's go ride the wave to prosperity
- Allows you to surf and talk at the same time
- Speedier surfing at your fingertips

SURPRISE

- The surprising thing is that they haven't done it already
- Bringing you a world of surprises
- No more surprises
- Constantly surprising you with its ability

SURROUND
- We've got you surrounded
- Surround yourself with the best
- Surrounded, even when you think you are alone

SWAMP
- Suddenly, you're swamped by calls
- We've been swamped by your responses
- The information can swamp your system in no time

SWITCH
- There's never been a better time to switch
- Switch now, before it's too late
- The switch is in your hand

SYNERGY
- Feel that special synergy
- Bursting with synergy
- Feel the synergy carry you along

SYSTEM
- This superbly engineered system
- All systems are backed by
- We service all compatible systems
- Many systems have sprung up recently
- Why buy one of our systems
- Three easy steps to using this surefire system
- This is a foolproof system
- The system you can't live without
- Most advanced system on the market today
- Why buy an inferior system when you can have one of ours
- Aimed at getting best results without putting a huge load on your system
- The best system you can get
- We've configured a really hot system here.
- The heart of the system is
- Unique within the bounds of your system
- The fabulous thing is that it's a two-way communications system
- Understand the system networks use to communicate with each other
- So as not to end up engaged in hand-to-hand combat with the system
- Get around easily within the system
- Don't get boxed into a system that's not quite right
- Locking into a unique system that combines
- All systems go
- Now you can build your own system easily
- Pick a value-packed selection that's right for you
- Try out these new, completely innovative systems as soon as you can
- It's your dream system, configured the way you want it
- No other system now on the market can boast such
- No system is easier to learn

TALENT
- Reach hundreds of talented, motivated individuals
- Put your talent out for the whole world
- The technology behind the talent
- Letting you make full use of your talent

TEAM
- Our team is made up of specialists
- Come where artistry teams up with technology
- Team up with the entire world
- Excited about making a contribution as a member of the team
- A team that's invisible and instant

TEAMWORK
- Providing technology, talent and teamwork
- Makes teamwork easy even if you're not on the same team
- Lets you do teamwork with the whole world
- The best team comes with the box

TECHNICAL
- Unavoidably quite technical
- Dazzle them with your technical brilliance
- Technical advances are no longer so intimidating
- Able to start without any requirement for a technical background
- You don't have to be technical to
- Makes the most technical part the easiest
- The technical part has disappeared

TECHNOLOGY
- Technology makes you even more

resourceful
- Technology provides a compact, affordable way to enjoy
- Celebrating ten years of superior technology
- Capitalize on cutting-edge technology
- No technology has been spared in creating
- It's about rapidly changing technology
- We cater our technology to fit your needs
- The technology is built-in
- This technology just keeps on ticking
- Get in on the wide-spread adoption of this new technology
- Learn how these new technologies affect the way we live and work
- Technologies for communications, creativity and problem solving
- Taking you straight to the cutting edge of this technology
- Keeping up with changing technology
- Making first use of a pioneering technology
- Technology is making it easier to do just that
- Leading edge technology offering far faster service to you
- Technology is changing every aspect of our lives
- Testing the limits of wireless technology
- How well we use this new technology is up to us
- Helping you get savvy to current technologies
- You are encouraged to explore cutting-edge technology
- Setting you up in a great working relationship with the technology
- By this time next year we'll be discussing yet another exciting technology
- Converging technologies increase your pull
- Sophisticated technology has laid the groundwork for
- With technology moving faster than ever before, you need to keep on the ball
- Learn how to use the latest technologies from the experts in the field
- Examine the effect these new technologies have upon
- Today, technology is not only making new things possible

TECHNOPHOBES
- To accurately identify the technophobes in your company
- Ferreting out and retraining hardened technophobes
- Even a hopeless technophobe can deal with this
- Yes, technophobes still exist
- You may not be a technophobe after all

TECHSPEAK
- Not to fall into the trap of techspeak
- Guarding against creeping techspeak
- Techspeak and gobbledegook are not far apart
- Techspeak will turn your prospects off quicker than anything
- We won't pull techspeak on you

TERRITORY
- Those who venture forth into this uncharted territory tend to be adventurous
- Charting new territory
- Lay claim to your territory on the Web

TEST
- Take a test drive for free
- Bigger and more powerful and available for a test
- As soon as you test it, you'll want it
- Test drive the latest Internet tools
- Rigorously tested, amazingly reliable

THINK
- Recognizing that no two people think alike
- Will completely change your thinking
- Let us know what you think about this exciting new product
- Frees you to think about other things

TIME
- Crossing the barriers of time and space
- Is there a more opportune time than now to move onto the World Wide Web
- Getting you totally onto the Web in a nick of time
- Just click on the time line to find out
- Giving you the freedom to set your own timetable
- Save so much of your valuable time
- Get back control of your time

TOMORROW
- Engage in a journey into tomorrow
- Tomorrow has just arrived today
- Join the world of tomorrow
- Giving you a head start for tomorrow
- Stop waiting for tomorrow

TOOL
- More tools for the digital revolution
- Together, they're the only tools you'll need
- You gotta have toys, you gotta have tools
- If there's one thing you've learned about online tools
- Gives you the tools you need to manage
- But first, you need the proper tools
- Will rapidly become your tool of choice
- Tools to help you make sense of the mountain of information available
- Now giving you the straight tools
- Now, the tools you need to really help
- Has quickly become a fundamental tool
- Tools to manage your information base
- Now a powerful generative and analytical tool
- An compelling tool in facilitating effective learning
- A powerful tool with which to tailor information
- A tool we can use immediately
- Tips, tricks and tools for
- Get the right tool at the right price
- Put this useful tool to work for you
- The benefits make it an indispensable tool

TOUCH
- It's fun, easy and inexpensive to keep in touch with
- Now it's a one-touch universe
- Putting you in touch with the products and services you're looking for
- Happily in touch with the entire world

TRADITION
- Helping you continue the tradition in this very untraditional way
- Our tradition of outstanding service is carried on into cyberspace
- Starting a new tradition electronically

TRAFFIC
- Can mean more traffic for you
- Attract large volumes of highly targeted traffic
- There are many ways to increase traffic

TRAIN
- Get hands-on training to create your own
- We receive ongoing training on the latest products
- Trained to respond instantly
- Hands-on, results-oriented training
- The training is included free of charge
- Training you can afford
- Get the benefits of serious, accelerated training
- So easy you can skip the training

TRANSACTION
- Turn yourselves into a business prepared to accept even more secure transactions on the Web
- Encountering the most amazing transactions via the Internet
- Transactions speeded up astronomically

TRANSFORM
- Transform yourself into a viable player
- Transforming the way you think about just about everything
- Your entire life might just be transformed

TREASURE
- Proving a treasure trove to
- Helping you find treasures on the Net
- Ask anyone who treasures
- Finds you treasure in cyberspace

TRIALS
- Gamely facing the trials of keeping your business current on the Internet
- Now your electronic trials and tribulations are finally over
- Running continual trials to gauge the best approach
- Rigorous trials prove it to you

TRICK
- Learn all the tricks of smart Internet use
- Now we come to the tricky part
- Learn all the tricks to making it work
- Not just another clever trick
- Some people might wonder whether there is some trick to it
- Experts share their favorite tricks

- Fun computing tricks you can try
- Teaching you a few new tricks we've learned along the way

TRIP

- You'll find something new and interesting at every trip onto the Web
- Take a trip into the future right now
- Make contact with those taking regular trips onto the Internet
- What a trip

TRY

- Once you try it, it'll become part of your routine
- Come in and try it out today
- More people are trying it every day
- You can try it out yourself

TUNE

- Stay tuned for exciting new developments
- Puts you in tune with
- Tuning in on the whole world
- A finely-tuned communications plan
- Tune in to the delights of cyberspace

TUTORIAL

- Online interactive tutorials are provided
- Able to offer very specific tutorials
- To help you learn, there are in-depth tutorials
- The program offers a mini-tutorial whenever you need one

UNDERSTAND

- Helping you understand the ever-changing
- Break down barriers, build bridges of understanding
- Increase your awareness and understanding of
- Something momentous is happening to our traditional understanding of space and time
- First, people must develop a conceptual understanding of this new technology
- Striving to increase our understanding every day

UNIQUE

- Need something unique
- Equipped to fill your unique needs

- Recognizing that every customer is unique
- Astoundingly unique and advanced

UNLOCK

- Now unlocking undreamed-of possibilities
- Unlocking a gate you have only to step through
- Unlocking a vast new universe

UP-TO-DATE

- Providing the finest, most up-to-date information on
- Be up-to-date before the date
- We keep the most up-to-date products on hand to

UPDATE

- Check daily prices update at
- Continuously updated
- Get round-the-clock updates
- We intend to update this page regularly

UPGRADE

- And it can be upgraded instantly to
- Upgrading ways of selling
- Upgrading makes you feel so good
- Upgrading to a whole new level of
- Time to upgrade yourself onto the Web
- You won't find a quicker, cooler way to upgrade

UPLOAD

- Upload yourself into
- Uploading more value every day
- Upload it more easily than ever
- Not just another upload
- Simply upload your expectations

USE

- Get unparalleled ease of use
- Best of all, it's really easy to use
- Making creative use of the Web
- Bringing an unmatched ease of use
- Rapidly coming into common use
- We've only begun to figure out its many astonishing uses
- The power anybody can use

USER

- Striving constantly to make it more user-friendly and effective

- Turning Internet users into willing customers
- Designed to take new users through the basics
- Thirty million users can't be wrong
- Focusing closely on the user
- A smart choice for users
- For experienced users
- Your user base will spread contagiously
- Very user friendly
- Now connecting users everywhere
- The solution to increasing user costs

VENTURE
- Helping you make your venture a success
- Venturing out into uncharted worlds
- Venture beyond anything you've known before
- Turns your venture into a success fast

VERSATILE
- More versatile than any other
- Making you versatile where you need it
- Make this great versatility pay off for you
- Endlessly versatile, always up-to-date

VERSION
- Keep an eye out for the newest version
- Download the trial version from
- You get version updates instantly
- Offering you a new version of the future

VIEW
- Changing how you view things
- How you view things is important
- Information designed to be viewed after visiting our attractive home page
- A whole new way to view us
- How you view us is important to us
- Talk about a way to expand your world view
- Our world view has changed overnight

VIRAL MARKETING
- Get in on the viral marketing rush
- Viral marketing shooting through
- Makes viral marketing so easy
- The brand new tool in viral marketing

VIRTUAL
- Create a virtual marketplace instantly
- Turn virtual reality into real reality by selling

- A huge virtual party that everyone can join
- All this is virtually yours
- This virtual village is home to
- Visit our virtual showroom at

VIRUS
- Ruined by a virus sneaking onto your hard drive
- Nasty viruses don't have a chance
- On guard against the most insidious virus
- Don't catch a virus when you're not looking

VISION
- Changing your vision of the future
- Making your latest vision come true
- Where vision and reality become one
- Enhance your vision through the Internet

VISIT
- Visit our web site to see how it is
- Visit the real thing and see
- A terrific way to visit
- Visit the whole world from home

VISITOR
- Get your visitors back in seconds
- Get new visitors by word of mouth
- Make sure you can follow up on your visitors
- Getting value per visitor
- With so many guaranteed visitors, how can you lose

WAIT
- You've waited long enough to try this new way
- Don't even wait for a nonosecond
- Now you don't have to wait
- No more waiting when you want to participate
- So what are you waiting for

WATCH
- All you need to do is sit and watch
- We're the one to watch
- Just watch it go
- Keep watch with us
- Watch us get better every day
- They'll all be watching you
- Watch the future unfold on your desk

WAY

- Brings you the Web your way
- The non-threatening way to
- Easily the most cost effective and professional way to have a presence on the Web
- Unlike many of the old-fashioned ways of communicating
- We'll help you find your way
- Leading the way for Internet users
- Introducing a whole new way to
- A way to take greater control of
- The simplest, easiest way to scoop up the Internet is to
- The Internet is the fastest, most reliable way to move information
- Represents the easiest, more affordable way to
- Now there's a better way to
- Why go the long way around when a short-cut will get you there
- Totally changing the way you do things
- You've never travelled this way before

WEB

- Come to one of the Web's hot spots
- Time to really get on the Web
- Learning to be Web magicians
- Exploring reasons to buy on the Web
- Supplying access for almost as long as the Web has been around
- Women on the Web have felt disenfranchised until very recently
- Top-notch Web development to help your business
- The Web is building even more credibility for people like you
- The web sites are good and improving every day
- An uncluttered, easy-to-understand web page is essential
- Explore the fundamentals of sound Web authoring
- Helping you mine the Web for information
- So you don't get hopelessly tangled up in the Web
- Why buy something hawked all over the Web
- Spread knowledge of your existence over the Web
- Getting your point across on the Web
- Explode your profits on the Web

WEB PAGE

- Our web page is enjoying immense popularity among our customers
- If you are serious about designing documents and web pages that
- The all-in-one web page for
- Our web page in now considered the hub
- We hope our web page will be a big hit
- Taking you rapidly into advanced web page creation
- Proven enhancements increase the number of hits on your web page

WEB SITE

- A very attention-getting web site
- A complete web site service especially for all kinds of users
- Web sites are popping up right and left
- Transforming your web site into a virtual reality visitors can explore
- Never know who you will encounter at our web site
- Creating and managing your own home web site
- View our new and critically acclaimed web site
- This way to our web site
- The new web site everyone is rushing to view
- We have launched a hot new web site
- The purpose of your web site is to help
- Just visit our web site at
- A web site consistent with our organization's image
- Promoting your web site could be the key to promoting your business
- This web site provided in support of
- Have you visited our web site today
- Visit our web site for weekly updates
- Check our web site for details
- Thousands of items on our web site
- Please go directly to our web site to find out
- A web site generating dollars you never have to work for

WEBMASTER

- Join our webmaster's club
- Resources and ideas for webmasters
- Now we're developing shrewd webmasters
- Watch your webmaster get excited
- Now is the time to encourage your office

tinkerer to turn into your office webmaster

WHATEVER
- Whatever you're into, we've got it
- Do whatever is best for you
- Ask for whatever you want

WORD
- Don't take our word for it
- Stumped by an unfamiliar technological word
- No easier way to get word to the masses
- Now we're getting the word out electronically

WORK
- Will work without limitations for 60 days
- It's amazing how beautifully this works
- Here's how it works
- Real quality work on the Web
- Put the Internet to work for you
- Allowing us to work even more closely together
- Working hard to make the Web work for you
- A wonderful new way to work with you to help
- See it at work on the following sites
- Works seamlessly with your
- Stop working so hard to
- For work and play
- Works the way you think it should
- The quickest way to jump start your work

WORLD
- Around the world or across the street
- Turning the world upside down – yet again
- Your point of departure for the world of
- Built for today's high-tech world
- Making the world a healthier happier place to
- The world is changing faster than anyone imagined
- Mapping out a whole new world
- What in the world is going on
- Across the country and around the world
- Now you can give your family the world
- Take advantage of the online world with full connectivity
- Now giving you the world
- Now you can track the whole world

- Now suddenly confronted with people, places and ideas from around the world
- Join a close-knit world
- In the whole, volatile world of
- For those who think the world is changing too fast
- Enter a totally connected world
- Touch new worlds with
- Your world has changed
- When you need your project to touch the world
- Your world will probably change again tomorrow
- Brings worldwide attention to your home page

WORLDWIDE
- A local presence and worldwide exposure
- Gaining worldwide access and appeal
- Go worldwide from your desk
- Worldwide and personal

ZONE
- Turns your site into an instant hot zone
- Enter the future zone
- Puts your whole company in the zone
- Turns your desk into a place zoned for progress
- Customers no longer zone out

Section Three

Contests
and
Sweepstakes

ACTION
- Get in on the action
- Do it for the action
- It's all action here
- The most action for the least money
- Maybe more action than you can handle
- Nothing but action, action, action

ADVANTAGE
- Take advantage of unbeatable odds
- The advantage is all yours
- Get as many advantages on your side as possible
- Treat yourself to a winning advantage

ADVENTURE
- Join in the adventure
- Try out the adventure of winning
- Every ticket is an adventure in the making

BALLOT
- Drop in the ballot box for your chance to win
- Just fill out the attached ballot for a chance at big prizes
- Your ballot automatically enters you in the contest

BIG
- You could be the next one to hit it big
- The bigger the numbers, the bigger your chances
- This could be the start of something big
- Think big, win big

BINGO
- Bingo, you've won
- Bingo with a wild new twist
- You've never seen bingo like this

BUBBLE
- Hope of the big win continually bubbling
- Grab the great big bubble of hope
- As the pot gets bigger, excitement keeps bubbling up

BUY
- When you buy a ticket you're doing yourself a big favor
- Buying a ticket is the simplest way to win
- Find out why millions of people are buying tickets
- You know why you buy our tickets
- You're not just buying a lottery ticket, you're investing in
- All the excitement of buying a fresh new ticket
- You're really buying a chance to win double the usual prize
- The more chances you buy, the more chances you'll have to win big
- Avoid disappointment, buy your ticket now
- The more tickets you buy, the better your odds
- Every time you buy a ticket, you get a boost of excitement
- Buy your ticket today
- Buy a ticket now before they're all snapped up
- With every ticket you buy, the odds get lower
- When you buy a ticket, everybody wins

CALL
- You must call now to order your ticket in time
- Hear the call of the action
- Calling everyone to join in the fun
- Call now to enter

CARNIVAL
- A carnival of chance and fun
- Ticket-selling is turning into a regular carnival
- Join in the joyous carnival atmosphere

CASH
- The cash doesn't end here
- More cash prizes to be won
- Of course the cash doesn't stop there
- Largest ever cash prizes
- Mountains of cash to spend any way you like
- You'll be awash in cash
- Armfuls of cool, beautiful cash
- More than a thousand fabulous cash prizes to be won

CASINO
- Casino competition for the gaming dollar
- Come to the casino and join the fun
- Our biggest casino ever

CHANCE

- Giving you the chance to win big
- Plus a chance to win
- Your chances of winning are excellent
- Take a chance on instant wealth
- Chances are pretty good that
- Every time you take a chance the odds get better
- Take a chance on a sure thing
- Take a chance to bring Lady Luck into your life
- Take a chance, give a chance to
- Nobody gives you a better chance to
- Have you ever seen chances like these
- Now, your best chance ever
- There nothing chancy about the this kind of contest
- Getting and giving a fair chance at
- Yet another way to increase your chances
- Your best chance to win
- Take a chance, be a winner
- Take a chance now while tickets are still available
- This could be the biggest chance you'll ever take
- Not only will you be getting a great chance to win, you'll also

CHOICE

- The most comprehensive choice of tickets
- Choose the number one choice of millions
- More choices mean more chances
- Your choice, benefits all round
- Your best choice in lottery tickets
- The range of choices is exploding

COMPETITIVE

- There has always been a strong competitive element here
- A productive way to gratify your competitive urges
- We offer by far the most competitive odds

CONGRATULATIONS

- Congratulations, you may have just won
- Congratulations in advance
- You can hear the congratulations already
- Big, big congratulations could be in order
- Congratulations on reaching the top prize level
- Congratulations will come flooding in from every direction

CONTEST

- Contest runs for a limited time
- Contest runs this week only
- One contest you absolutely have to enter
- Enter the contest, win big
- Contest begins today
- A contest in which everybody wins
- Contestants must correctly answer a skill-testing question

DAY

- This could be your lucky day
- This could be the day you win big
- You winningest day ever
- You'll always remember the day you won
- Don't let another day pass without getting your ticket

DELIVER

- Delivering more fun and more action for your dollar
- We deliver more bang for your buck
- Delivers big prizes and plenty of chances to win

DISCOVER

- Discover how you can win a
- Just wait till you discover how big the prize can be
- Discover the fun of entering again and again

DOLLAR

- Imagine winning all those tax-free dollars
- You could be awash in dollars
- The best dollar you ever spent
- Just look what one dollar can do
- You could be showered with dollars

DRAW

- You will be automatically entered in our draw in celebration
- Conduct a major draw
- The big draw is today
- Take part in our draw for
- We'll conduct a random draw to select the grand prize winner
- Random draws for great prizes

- We've already entered you in the draw
- Richest draw ever
- Spectacular daily and weekly draws
- Every winning entry goes right back into the draw
- Draw gives you a chance to win again and again
- All valid tickets are eligible for all draws
- The draw order will be
- Our biggest draw yet
- Every draw is our biggest
- Don't miss this draw
- Drawing more and more participants every day
- Feel the excitement mount as the draw date approaches
- And that's just one of the draws we are able to offer during this event
- Chosen weekly from a separate drawing

DREAM

- You could make your dreams become reality
- Fulfil a dream
- The prize everyone dreams of winning
- Now – all you've ever wanted or dreamed of
- Do you dream of making it big
- Back up your dreams by buying a ticket
- Fulfil a dream today
- We could turn your dreams into actual life
- An unforgettable dream coming true
- Ways to make your dream of winning come alive
- Answer your dreams and enter

DRIVE

- Our biggest ticket drive ever is about to start
- You have a drive to win
- Participate in our latest drive by playing the game to win

DRUM

- The entry is then returned to the drum
- That's your ticket, your chance to win spinning round in the drum
- As the drum spins, feel that rush of excitement
- Can you feel your heart drumming with excitement

EASY

- It's so easy to enter and win
- The easy way to participate
- Easy winnings are at your fingertips
- The easiest money you've ever made
- It's easy, it's fun, it's delightful

EDGE

- The thrill of living on the edge
- Give yourself that winning edge
- You're always right on the edge of winning

ELIGIBLE

- Here is your eligibility confirmation
- You may be eligible to win big
- You ticket makes you eligible for the grand prize

ENJOY

- Something the whole family can enjoy
- Something that can be enjoyed by anyone who plays
- Enjoy the thrill of winning and the thrill of taking home big prizes

ENTER

- All you have to do to enter is send
- To enter, complete this official entry form and mail to
- Enter online to win
- Enter today to win your choice of prizes
- We can't urge you enough to enter soon
- Make sure you enter in time
- Do not hesitate to enter
- Automatically enters you

ENTRY

- Chances of winning depends on the number of entries received
- Send you entry today
- Every winning entry goes right back into the draw for a chance to win again
- As soon as your entry is selected as a winner
- Act now, make your entry a winner
- Your entry is automatically activated when
- Yours could be the winning entry

EXCITEMENT

- Taste the excitement
- Do it for the excitement and the prizes

waiting for you
- Come alive to the excitement

EXPERIENCE
- Once you experience the thrill you'll be back for more
- Treat yourself to a new experience
- The best experience ever
- Experience the fun, experience the freedom

FANTASY
- Fulfil a personal fantasy
- Create your wildest fantasy
- Winning big isn't just a fantasy
- A fantasy that could actually come true for you

FEVER
- Catch the fever
- Feeling the fever to buy and to win
- Lottery fever is sweeping the country

FIRST
- Now you can get there first
- Now you can be first when it comes to winning chances
- Be first in line to win
- If it's your first time playing, your in for a great surprise

FORTUNE
- Worth a fortune to you and your family
- A way to make your fortune – instantly
- A fortune in winnings is waiting just for you when you enter

FRIEND
- You and three friends could win
- Enter your friends too
- Bring a friend, earn a bonus ticket
- It's like playing a game with your best friends

FUN
- Join in the fun
- Play for fun, play to win
- This game is the most fun of all
- How much fun can a person stand

GAMBLE
- Does gambling give people the hope of being rich

- Gambling can be very exciting
- For those who think gambling is a waste of money
- Dealing with the possibility of gambling being addictive
- What are the positive aspects of gambling

GAME
- It's so much more than a game to us
- Play the game for fun and profit
- The trend is to increasingly interactive games
- Games requiring a greater reliance on technology are inevitable
- Game modifications must be carefully researched
- The hottest game in town
- The game's the thing
- It's much more than just a game
- Join in a game that fills you with delight
- Get in on the best game in town
- A friendly game for a very serious purpose
- Now everyone can join the game
- No better way to play the game

GAMING
- Join in a variety of gaming activities
- The growth in gaming has been phenomenal
- Spending an increasing percentage of income on gaming
- Predicting that legal gaming will grow
- Gaming now provides a significant amount of money to
- The problem of illegal gaming must be addressed
- Must accept that legalized gaming is here to stay
- Ensure that the gaming always contributes to the public good

GENERATE
- Generating millions in fantastic prizes
- A wonderfully fun way to generate pleasure
- Generate some luck for yourself by

GOAL
- If your goal is winning big, come see us
- Achieve your goals and our goals all at once

- The prize is big enough to fulfil all your goals in one big win

GRAND PRIZE

- Here's the clue that could win you the grand prize
- One lucky grand prize winner gets it all
- Imagine yourself carrying off the grand prize

HEARD

- It's time you heard about the action
- Have you heard about the big one
- The best way to help you've heard about

HIGH

- You too could be riding high
- The jackpot just mounts higher and higher
- Set your sights on a really high prize

IDEA

- Try out an entirely wild idea
- A whole new idea in lottery advances
- A fresh idea, a fresh way of winning

IMAGINE

- Imagine what you could do with a prize this big
- Imagine receiving such a fabulous sum
- Imagine the fun of deciding on your choice

INDULGE

- Indulge in luxuries you never thought possible before
- Indulge yourself, buy a chance to win
- You're not just indulging yourself, you're giving your family a chance for a rich future

INTEREST

- Something for everyone and every interest
- I bet we've got you interested now
- Just to pique your interest, take a look at this prize

INVOLVE

- A really fun way to get involved
- Buy your ticket and get involved in
- Now you can really enjoy getting involved in winning

- We want you to be involved

JACKPOT

- Hit the jackpot today
- Just look at the jackpot waiting for you
- You have a chance at more than one jackpot
- The biggest, best jackpot to date
- We've been pumping up the jackpot
- Is the jackpot bigger than your dreams yet

LIBERATE

- Liberate yourself
- Just the thought of winning can be very liberating
- With just one ticket, you could liberate all this money for yourself

LIFE

- You could be set for life
- Your whole life could be changed in an instant
- Imagine how your life would change
- Are you ready for the good life
- Life could suddenly get a whole lot better
- The win of a lifetime

LOSE

- You just can't lose
- Take us up on this can't-lose offering
- Please don't risk losing out

LOTTERY

- A mega-lottery offering mega-prizes
- A truly big-ticket lottery
- Lotteries are a hot new trend
- Odds in this lottery are
- Vast numbers of people brought lottery tickets last year
- To link the retailer to the lottery
- Develop a lottery that enjoys superior participation rates
- The first in town to try this kind of lottery
- No other lottery does so much for those who want to enjoy themselves
- Biggest lottery ever of its kind
- This lottery is a way to attract people
- Largest lottery ever to hit town
- Proud to announce the biggest ever cash lottery

LUCK
- Let this be your lucky day
- Try your luck
- Luck will be a lady for you
- Help your luck, let your luck help others
- You luck gets better every time you participate
- Luck is booming everywhere
- Your good luck has just got better

LUCKY
- Be one of the lucky few who
- Do you feel lucky today
- I know you're feeling lucky right now
- Today could be your lucky day
- Lucky you spotted our offer

LUXURY
- Indulge in luxuries you never imagined possible
- You could be living life in the lap of luxury
- This ticket is not just a luxury

MILLIONAIRE
- As a potential millionaire
- This could make you a millionaire
- Imagine would it would feel like to suddenly become a millionaire

NEED
- Tailored to everybody's need
- Fill your need for fun
- You want it, you need it, so do it
- You need to enter right away

NEW
- An entirely new line of lottery tickets
- All new, all terrific
- Are you ready for a new level of excitement
- A new way of winning

NOTICE
- No wonder so many are sitting up and taking notice
- This is one lottery you're going to notice
- Notice how owning a ticket makes people smile

NUMBER
- Is your lucky number coming up
- Play your lucky numbers
- No need to check your numbers
- Just imagine hearing your numbers called
- Your number could be the big winner

ODDS
- You're an odds-on favorite to win
- Buck the odds
- Incredible odds
- Great odds on every ticket
- You're smart to take advantage of our unbeatable odds
- Improving the odds for you
- You won't find better odds anywhere
- What better way to improve the odds
- The odds of winning will depend on the number of tickets sold
- With odds like these
- Fairest odds you can find
- The odds are dropping every day
- You've never seen odds this small on a prize this big
- Providing remarkably handsome odds
- Have you ever seen better odds than these
- Where the odds are all in your favor
- With great odds on every ticket
- With odds like these, we'll sell out quickly
- Our best odds yet

OPPORTUNITY
- Take advantage of this great opportunity
- A once-in-a-lifetime opportunity to
- The opportunity to win is right before you
- An opportunity of a lifetime
- An opportunity that comes once a decade
- I urge you to take part in this exciting new opportunity

PARTICIPANTS
- Remember, all participants have an equal chance to win big
- If you hurry, you too could be one of the participants
- We've been overwhelmed with participants

PARTICIPATE
- When you participate by buying a ticket
- Now is the time to participate
- You get more than one chance to participate

- If you don't participate, you can't win

PARTNERSHIP
- The real prize is in increased partnership
- Your ticket is your partnership with us
- Partnership with you is not just a game

PICK
- Just make your pick
- You know you can pick them
- Be on the list for our next big prize delivery

PLAY
- Designed to keep you playing
- Why not play
- Play just for the fun of it
- Now is the time to make your play
- You get to play and help at the same time
- Go for the really big play
- Jump into the play right now
- The more you play, the better your chance of winning
- Play and you could win big

PLAYER
- Pursuing a new player market
- You can be a player in something grand
- A way to feel like an important player

POSSIBILITY
- Swept away by the possibilities
- Think of the possibilities
- Just look at the possibilities
- More possibilities than ever before
- Join in the possibilities
- Winning big is a major possibility
- Treat yourself to some truly stupendous possibilities
- Have you ever seen possibilities like these

PRIZE
- Free info on the prize registry
- An incredible variety of prizes
- Still more grand prizes
- Proud to announce the largest cash prize ever
- Hundreds of prizes to win this month
- Buy more chances at an early bird prize
- Total grand prize package valued at
- Prizes must be accepted as awarded and redeemed by

- Don't just enter for the prizes
- I can almost see you holding that big prize check
- Even prizes for the hard to please
- A chance at the most exclusive prizes
- The real prize is help for others
- The prize you win is only a small part of money raised to help
- The prize grows bigger and bigger every day
- Spot prizes, door prizes
- Prizes that work for change
- Prizes that work hard for you
- Offering guaranteed jackpot prizes of
- Your chances of winning a major prize are excellent
- Research has shown that the most attractive kind of prize is
- The prize you win is only the beginning
- An incredible variety of prizes
- Over a million instant prizes

PROFIT
- A way for everyone to profit
- When you win, you profit big
- The profit isn't just money
- Ticket profits boost prizes for everyone

PROGRAM
- Time to get with the program and buy a ticket
- Our brand new lottery program has already been extended due to popular demand
- We've set up the program to give a chance to everyone

PROJECT
- Though the lottery, you too can participate in this vitally important project
- Projected lottery revenues could put us through the roof
- We project hundreds of happy winners

PURCHASE
- Purchase your ticket early for a chance at
- Tickets must be purchased before this date
- Free with your ticket purchase
- The purchase price is next to nothing

RAFFLE
- Have you got your raffle ticket yet
- We're about to raffle off some splendid dreams
- Raffling off everything but the kitchen sink

RESIST
- So hard to resist the allure
- Resist no more
- Why resist any longer
- Prizes you just can't resist

REVENUE
- Lottery revenues are soaring
- Revenues from gaming and lotteries will climb to
- Lotteries can become a very effective revenue source

REWARD
- Just for buying your ticket early, you could be rewarded
- Reward yourself today
- Your reward is a chance to win really big
- Winning big could be your reward for shopping at

RICH
- You could be rich tomorrow
- Do you think you would live the life of a rich person
- It's easy to be rich
- Buy a ticket, you'll be richer for the experience
- Riches for everyone
- All these riches could be yours for the taking

RISK
- Risky business
- Don't risk forfeiting a prize this big
- It's good for you to take a little risk now and then
- Where risk is kept to a minimum
- Experience the thrill of the risk

SCRATCH
- Scratch and match
- Scratch up a real challenge
- Start from scratch
- Are you up to scratch
- Scratch yourself a fortune
- One scratch and you could be rich
- Scratch 'n win

SELL
- Sure to sell out quickly
- The tickets are selling like hot cakes
- We want to sell you the winning ticket
- Selling you a chance at all your dreams

SIGN
- Don't forget to sign up to win
- When you sign up, you get a chance at these big prizes
- Lady Luck is waiting to sign you up
- Enter wherever you see this sign

SKILL
- Try your skill
- With the right combination of luck and skill, you could win
- Where your skill really counts for something

SOCIALIZE
- Gaming provides the opportunity for some friendly socializing
- People love to socialize around the gaming tables
- A lot of fun, a little socializing, a chance a winning big

SPIN
- Watch us put a different spin on things
- Spin the wheel and you could win
- Where the spinning stops, nobody knows
- A way to put the very best spin on

STAKE
- Look what's really at stake
- The stakes are very high
- In order to win the stakes
- The stakes have just gone way, way up so enter now

STEP
- Three easy steps to enter
- All it takes to enter is one easy step
- Your first step toward winning

STOP
- There'll be no stopping you

- Stop look, buy a ticket, take a chance
- You just can't stop coming back

STRATEGY
- Your strategy for winning
- We'll help you plan your ticket strategy
- In this game, strategy is everything

STUFF
- Plus other cool stuff
- Look at all the great stuff you could win
- Lots of stuff up for grabs

SUCCESS
- The probability of success is terrific
- The success of winning is contagious
- You're helping to make this game a real success

SURE
- No such thing as a sure thing
- Enter now and be sure to win
- Participate enough times and you're sure to luck out
- It's the surest way to get a shot at the top

SURPRISE
- Surprise yourself
- You could be one of our early bird surprise winners
- Won't you be surprised when your number is drawn

SWEEPSTAKES
- Enter the dream sweepstakes
- Look alike sweepstakes
- Ask about our sweepstakes
- Just look at some of our past sweepstakes winners
- You're helping them come out ahead in the sweepstakes of life
- Enter the sweepstakes right now

SYSTEM
- Beat the system the easy way
- Yes, you can beat the system
- Try out your system for winning
- We set the system up in your favor

TEMPTATION
- How can you resist such a temptation
- Admit it, the temptation is just too

strong
- Give in to temptation, play the game now

TICKET
- The ticket that just keeps on winning
- Buy a ticket – and feel good all over
- If you haven't purchased a ticket in the last month, it's time
- When you buy a ticket, you are buying hope
- Your ticket to a really good time
- The more tickets you buy, the bigger the prize becomes
- Don't wait another moment to buy your ticket
- Your ticket to fun and profit
- Get your lucky ticket today
- To guarantee your ticket, please order by
- Ticket sales are booming

TRICK
- Teaching some old dogs a new trick or two
- There's no trick to it
- Loads of prizes, no tricks
- Pull off the trick of winning the grand prize

TRUST
- Trust your lottery money to us
- Buy from a trusted name
- Trust us to come up with something truly unexpected

URGE
- Give in to the urge to win
- I urge you to buy a ticket right away
- Nobody can resist the urge for long

VENTURE
- Join in a brave new venture
- It's a terrific new venture
- Venture into uncharted territory, buy a ticket

WATCH
- Watch us on TV and win
- This is the contest to watch for
- Always on the watch for great chances to win

WEALTH
- You could become independently

wealthy in a jiffy
- Guess your way to wealth
- All this wealth could be yours by tomorrow
- Imagine yourself this wealthy

WIN
- Imagine, you would win so much
- The best way of winning
- You could win today
- Win often, win big
- More ways to win every day
- You could win everything here
- Win some big ticket items
- Three ways to win
- This could be your big chance to win
- See how you can win
- A major win will change your life completely
- Every ticket has a great chance to win
- When you win, we'll call and tell you
- Your chances to win get better when
- Now you have a chance to win even more
- You could win the entire cash prize
- Here's how much your ticket purchase helps
- When you play, everybody wins
- Please help us all win
- Going boldly against the odds to win
- Win right away
- The easy way to win
- Guess who really wins
- Your next big win is right around the corner
- Last chance to win
- Every ticket has a chance to win
- A chance to win something every week
- If you would like to win like these shoppers have
- Enter today to win big
- Win instantly
- One lucky customer will win
- You'll have a chance to win a complete set

WINNER
- As a potential winner you have the option of receiving your prize money in several ways
- To obtain the most recent list of winners, just call
- Put yourself in the winner's circle

- Beat out the previous top winners
- Join the ranks of our many winners
- Everyone's a winner, whichever way you look at it
- One very lucky winner will receive all this
- If you're the lucky winner you'll receive
- Contest winners will be quickly notified
- Enjoy being the winner of

WINNING
- Here's how you keep on winning
- You'll love winning
- Odds of winning depend on the number of entries received
- We follow through with real winnings
- Winning can work for you
- Your best chance of winning
- Take a chance on winning
- Get used to winning
- Get serious about winning
- Could you get used to winning this often
- Hooked on the thrill of winning
- Just imagine how good winning will feel
- Everyone has a shot at winning
- Try your hand at winning

WONDER
- It's much more than a small wonder
- The wonder of winning
- You'll wonder why you never bought a ticket before

WORD
- The word is out about
- Pass the word – big winnings are here
- The last word in lotteries
- Through word-of-mouth, the news about this great lottery has been spreading across the country

WORTH
- Worth much more than the price of your ticket
- Can't calculate the worth of the help you give
- Judged not by its cost, but by its worth
- Imagine how much your ticket investment could be worth

Section Four

Telemarketing

BLITZ

- Let yourself get swept up in this telephone blitz
- We're conducting this telephone blitz in order to
- We're all geared up for a major telephone blitz
- It's the biggest telephone blitz in our history
- Take advantage of this one-day telephone blitz
- We're having this telephone blitz to get the good news to you faster

CALL

- Then call us immediately at
- Your call matters
- Call in now
- Which why you should immediately call the number on your screen
- Your call could be the best thing you've ever done for yourself
- Please call right away
- Call now and find out how you can get the jump on
- It all starts with a single phone call
- A single phone call can start so much
- We're waiting for your call
- So don't wait, make the call now
- Keep our staff busy with your calls
- Our staff is only too pleased to be receive your calls
- Surprise us with your call
- Your call is the key to it all
- Our operators are waiting to take your call
- Please call and let us add your name to our list
- Get up off the couch now and make that call
- Even the government is encouraging you to call in
- Check this out while you make your call
- I can only ask you to make that call
- Your call today is vital to your future
- Our research shows that many more of you should be calling
- Get your phone call in ahead of the rush
- Use your call to tell the world how important you consider
- Let us know what you think by calling
- We're on hold waiting for your call

- I know those calls will come in
- I just know you'll be calling
- With time running out, we won't be able to wait much longer for your call
- Call us please
- It's your call now
- I can see you right now, reaching for that telephone
- It could be the most important phone call you'll ever make
- We're strongly encouraging you to call
- How could any smart person not call
- If you believe this product could be for you, please call
- Perhaps the shrewdest phone call you'll ever make
- Please keep those calls coming in
- Calling all interested parties
- You may never make a more important call in your life
- Call now to have it all
- Call now and this magnificent offer can be yours

CALLER

- Be one of the first two hundred callers and receive this great premium
- Just think, you could be one of the lucky callers
- Turn yourself into a caller right now
- Every caller counts
- Only the first fifty callers will qualify
- We give all our callers the secret
- Since this offer came out, we've been swamped with callers wanting to buy
- So many callers have thanked us from their hearts for telling them about
- Callers like you are the ones who benefit

CARD

- Have your credit card ready when you call
- With the phone and your credit card you can get
- Just put these easy payments on your credit card and you won't even notice
- Just slip out your credit card and pick up the phone
- It's so easy when you have your credit card in your hand
- Though your credit card, you can have this wonderful product instantly

- The magic of your credit card gets it all for you

CHAIR
- Asking you to heave yourself out of your chair right now
- Don't just keep sitting in your chair
- Call us, then you can go sit in that easy chair
- No chair could be so comfortable that you couldn't get up for this
- I'm talking to all you people sitting in your comfortable chairs
- Don't just think about calling – get up out of that chair
- Get your butt out of that chair and call us right this minute
- Reach for that phone right next to your chair

CLOCK
- We're racing against the clock to get all your calls in
- We just can't let the clock beat us in this one
- Just look at the clock and know that time is running out on your chance to
- Don't let the clock beat you this time
- Every time that clock hand moves, your time to call running out
- We only have so much time to tell you about this wonderful product – and the clock is ticking
- Don't let the clock tick away your chance to benefit big

COMMITMENT
- Please make that commitment very quickly
- We take your commitment very seriously
- Once you call, our commitment to you is strong and firm
- You won't make a bigger commitment to yourself than this one
- Your commitment now is really a commitment to change your life
- Make the commitment right now, before you do another thing
- Join the hundreds of others making that all-important commitment tonight
- Put your commitment into action before the hour is up
- You'll be making a big commitment to your own future
- Commitments have been flooding in
- If you don't call, you won't have our iron-clad commitment to

CONTACT
- We're calling to keep in contact with our most important customers
- Pick up the phone and make instant contact
- We really want to make contact with you
- And we'll keep in contact with you until
- The quickest way to make contact is to just grab your telephone
- Some people think telephone ordering is a contact sport
- We can't tell you how pleased we are that you've made contact with
- We wish to contact customers by telephone just as soon as possible
- Your phone is still the best way to contact us

CONVENIENCE
- Enjoy the convenience that telemarketing offers
- Nothing can beat the convenience of your telephone
- We set it up this way for your convenience
- Convenience means everything for our telephone customers
- The most convenient way is to just pick up your telephone and call today
- The convenience of dialling us direct

COST
- We're calling you by telephone to keep costs down
- Save on costs by ordering by telephone
- There's practically no cost at all to you when you order by phone
- We even pay the cost of the call
- The telephone call doesn't cost you a penny
- Using your telephone is the most cost-effective way to
- Use your phone to cut costs
- A simple phone call will cost you nothing but a moment of your time

CREDIT CARD
- We encourage you to use your credit card

- Thank you just because you were nice enough to use your credit card tonight
- You can space the payments on your credit card
- Here's a way to use your credit card for something you really want
- A few easy payments on your credit card will get you all this
- Here's a use for your credit card that perhaps you haven't thought of before
- Using the telephone and your credit card, you can get valuable products quickly
- When you use your credit card here, you're using it to improve you life
- All you have to do is tell us your credit card number
- One of the best uses you could put your credit card to
- Please get your credit card out now and call
- You can buy so easily over the telephone by using your credit card
- And telephone giving offers you the convenience of using your credit card

CUSTOMER
- A telephone survey was tops in customer generation
- More customers responded via the telephone than ever before
- Initial telephone response gives us the prospect of a very customer good year
- Reaching the hard-to-reach customer by phone
- Customers reach a sales associate immediately
- Turning a casual caller into a customer isn't always easy
- Every customer counts, so call today
- We're making a special effort to reach customers like you by telephone
- More customers are phoning than ever before
- We want to turn you into a satisfied customer – fast
- Your telephone can turn you into a pleased customer
- More customers than ever are picking up their telephones

DATA
- Accurate, quality data collection is vital

- Your telephone data will be kept strictly confidential
- We give you the data you need over the phone
- We look after all your data very carefully
- Your telephone is the quickest way to get this data from us
- The data you provide by calling is absolutely essential

DEDICATE
- Our dedicated staff is sitting by the phone waiting for you this very moment
- Show how dedicated you are to improving your life by calling us
- We dedicate this segment to you
- We're dedicated to getting this product to as many of you as possible
- Believe me, we have dedicated people waiting for your call

DEPEND
- We depend on the telephone to get your order
- Your satisfaction depends on your phone call
- When you realize how many benefits to you depend upon this call
- Success and security for the rest of your life could depend on whether you call today
- It all depends on whether you take action immediately
- We know you depend on getting the best when you order by phone
- Everything depends on us getting your call before the deadline

DETAIL
- Call now for details
- Get the details directly over the phone
- All the details are right at your fingertips

DIAL
- It's urgent that you dial now to get in on this offer
- Have you got your dialling finger ready
- All you have to do is dial this number
- Lots of people are dialling in already
- It's the number everyone's been dialling
- As easy as dialling your phone
- Do touch that dial

- Dialling up a storm of savings and value
- When you dial, you truly are dialling for dollars
- As near as your dial
- I'm telling you, you just have to dial your phone
- Dial up big satisfaction by calling now
- Our operators are just waiting for you to dial
- It's so very easy to pick up that phone and dial now
- Nothing could be simpler and dialling us immediately

DIRECT

- Call us direct
- A direct line right through to
- In direct communication with you
- You can get through to us directly
- A friendly salesperson will speak to you directly
- Direct from your telephone to our warehouse
- Your phone put you in direct contact

DO

- The first thing you have to do is pick up that phone and call
- Now you can finally get around to doing something about
- The time to do something is now, this minute
- Making a phone call is so easy to do
- Do it now and feel the satisfaction
- Do it right now, while your phone is within reach
- The satisfaction of doing something fast

EFFECTIVE

- An effort to spread the word about the effectiveness of this fine product
- A way to make really effective use of your telephone
- Act effectively by phoning today
- It's the effective way to order
- Turn your telephone into an effective tool
- Buying by telephone is a very effective way to

EFFICIENCY

- The telephone enhances your efficiency enormously
- Telephone ordering is number one in efficiency and speed
- Your just call increased your efficiency

EXAMPLE

- The example of others can't help but encourage you to
- Now that you've seen all these examples, how can you not call
- And this is just one example of the benefits to you when you call to order
- How many examples do you need to convince you to call
- You won't find a better example of how effective a product can be
- Here's an example of what your telephone order gets you
- Your call is one of the best examples

GIFT

- We have a lot of fabulous thank you gifts to give out
- The sound of the telephone ringing is gift enough for us
- A purchase you'll be proud to show off because it says
- I know you'll find plenty of uses for this thank you gift
- The best gift is your phone call
- Wouldn't you like the beautiful gift you see here
- All you have to do is call and you'll receive this valuable gift
- And here's a free gift, no strings attached, to help you decide to call
- When you call, you'll receive this lovely gift along with your purchase

HEAR

- We need to hear from you
- The more of you we hear from, the sooner we can ship you this product
- We know you're hearing us right now
- Have you ever heard an offer as tempting as this one
- Just wait till you hear what we're going to tell you next
- Why aren't we hearing from you
- So let's hear from you within the next half hour
- Please show you can hear us by calling soon
- We're waiting to hear from you right

now

HELP

- Help is just a simple phone call away
- Here's something to help you make your decision to call
- The best way to help yourself out is to call us today
- We're trying really hard here to help you out
- A quick phone call is all it takes to get help
- When you pick up that phone, know we're waiting to help

HESITATE

- Please don't hesitate to pick up that phone
- If you're hesitating, just listen to this
- If you hesitate too long, this could all just slip away
- All those people out there who hesitated, they don't have this great product to show
- Think what you could miss if you hesitate any longer
- If hesitate, you're going to miss out
- The worst thing you could do right now is hesitate
- When a chance like this comes along, don't hesitate to grab it
- Reaching the last holdouts who are still hesitating to call

HOLIDAY

- Telephone marketing has become as much a part of the holiday season as street corner Santas
- Make that call now while you're in a holiday mood
- Make this phone call part of your holiday tradition
- In the holiday rush, save time and money by calling now
- Top off your holiday by telephoning
- A telephone campaign carefully aimed at the brief holiday season window

INPUT

- And while we're talking, we really want your input
- Dial now for instant input
- Come on, give us some input
- For just a little input over the phone, you'll reap untold rewards
- Your telephone can provide the quickest input of all
- I'm calling to get your input about

LIFE

- Your life could be changed forever by what you do in the next few seconds
- The most important telephone call of your entire life
- Only once or twice in your life will you see an offer like this
- Turn your life into a happening thing by calling now
- It's your life, so it's really up to you to call

LINE

- We're keeping a line open especially for you
- Not all of our lines are busy so there's still room for you
- Now you can get a line directly right into the heart of the action
- We want those lines humming with calls
- We've had to put in more lines to accommodate everyone trying to call
- We still have lines open waiting for your call
- We hear you – all the way down the line
- An easy way to keep a line on us
- We just can't keep the lines open much longer so hurry up and get your call in
- If the lines are busy with other eager customers, don't give up
- When we answer, we could be throwing you a lifeline

MARKETING

- Telephone marketing is becoming very big business
- Marketing by telephone keeps down the cost to you
- We almost can't believe the success of this marketing effort
- Keeping up our year-round telephone marketing effort
- Your call will prove the effectiveness of our marketing effort

MEMBER
- When you become a member, you become part of the family
- Become a member now and get and early-bird prize
- Members who join by telephone get a cash rebate
- Now you can become a member by telephone
- As soon as you dial that number you become a member, it's that easy
- The more members who join up tonight, the closer we are to our goal
- Call now for all the special privileges that come with being a member
- It's so very easy to become a member by phoning

MEMBERSHIP
- We want those membership numbers to go up
- Call in for your free membership now
- Now extending this membership offer to you by telephone
- We want you to be part of our membership drive
- Building up our membership means more value for you
- You can help our membership grow by calling right away
- We have to tell you just how important your membership is to us
- Each membership is a foundation stone of our savings club

METHOD
- The telephone has become a key method of buying because it is so convenient
- Phoning in now could be your preferred method of purchasing
- A method we want to share with you as soon as you call
- Reveal the method to you when you call
- Arranged an easy method of payment over the telephone
- Choose the easiest method of ordering by simply picking up your phone

MOMENT
- Could you spare a moment to talk to us
- A moment is all it takes to buy
- This very moment others are calling and signing up for

- Won't you take a moment and call
- The moment you order will be a very happy moment for you
- Inside of a moment you could be giving us your order
- What better way to spend a moment than by calling

NUMBER
- The number to dial if you want to say yes
- You've got our number, we want you to use it
- Our number is on the screen for you to dial
- One phone number you don't want to lose
- When you reach us, you will find a number of options to choose from
- Numbers are limited, so call in for yours before they're gone
- We're simply overwhelmed by the numbers of calls we've received from people like you
- The number of satisfied customers keeps rising by the hour

OPERATOR
- Our operators are waiting to help you
- Just tell what you need to a friendly operator
- Dozens of operators are standing by to answer your calls
- There's an operator waiting specially for your call
- A courteous operator will take your order immediately

OPINION
- A way of finding out your reactions and opinions immediately
- Make your opinion known instantly by dialling this number
- Your opinion really counts, so call now
- The very fact of your phone call registers your opinion with
- Just by making this call, you're stating your opinion loud and clear
- The fastest way to get your opinion across

ORDER
- Toll-free orders for
- We need those orders to pour in over

the telephone

- Can go to work instantly on your order
- Get your order in without a lot of fuss and bother
- Even the most modest order is welcome
- Our operators are waiting eagerly for your order
- The faster you order, the faster we get to work on
- What better way to order than to call now
- Success all built on the orders of satisfied customers
- Order from the heart and make a dazzling difference
- Thanks to all those who have already called in with your order
- You must order before the phone lines close
- Please order as soon as you can
- Please call right now with your order
- Please ring up now and get in your order
- This lovely premium is our way of thanking you for your phone order
- And that makes it a very affordable order for everyone
- Boy, it would be wonderful to take your order over the phone
- Your order tells us what you approve of and what you like
- Here are the good things your order will get for you
- It will be your order that we take care of right away

PEOPLE

- People of all sorts have come together tonight
- All over the country, people are picking up the phone right now to call
- I know you are one of those people who has a need and calls in at once to take care of it
- People reaching people instantly
- Join all the other smart people calling in to grab this offer
- People just like you are calling by the hundreds
- The calls show that hundreds of people are rushing to buy
- We want to reach people just like you
- Be one of the first people to call

PHONE

- Your phone call is so very important
- How we love to hear those phones ringing off the hook
- Please phone just as soon as you can
- A simple phone call away
- We really want to thank all the people who phoned in
- Your phone is a tool with which you can let us know
- If you're heading for your phone, keep on going
- Another minute just to give everyone an opportunity to get to that phone
- The phones are suddenly beginning to come to life
- I urge you to pick up the phone and do what your heart is telling you
- Without your phone call, right now, this offer will disappear
- Please, please phone in your order now
- Get on the phone and call right now
- Don't hesitate one more moment – pick up that phone
- We're waiting for you to phone

PLAN

- A unique mail/telephone purchasing plan
- It's a plan to help you choose through the telephone
- Participate in this ingenious plan by dialling now
- If you're planning to reach us, you better dial soon
- And you can be part of this terrific plan just by calling this number
- Make dialling us part of your success plan

POSSIBLE

- Your telephone makes it all possible
- Here's just a few of things your call makes possible
- You can make it possible, just by dialling this number
- Could you have imagined that your phone could make all this possible
- We've made it as easy as possible for you
- Because of the magic of the telephone, all this is now possible
- With one call, so much is possible

PREMIUM

- And when you increase your order, you will receive this beautiful premium
- This splendid premium set is all yours when you call to order the deluxe model
- This is the best premium we've ever offered
- Premiums galore for the day's first callers
- Offering a special premium when you call us in the next half hour
- Today your phone order brings an automatic premium

PROFESSIONAL

- Talented professionals work the phones
- Your call will be received in a very professional manner
- Busy professionals are now using the telephone enhance their business
- Telephone business is a very professional, efficient way to
- A knowledgeable professional will answer your call
- Call today, it's the professional thing to do
- A cheerful professional is waiting at the other end of the line
- The fastest way to professional help

QUESTION

- The telephone gets questions answered
- We'll be happy to answer any questions when you call
- Experts are waiting at the end of the line to answer your questions
- There's no question that you get best value by phoning
- Only a question of how soon you can call
- Get your questions answered fast by phone

RECEIVER

- Pick up the receiver now
- Reach for that receiver and call this number
- Just grip that receiver tight and make your order
- I know you're already holding that receiver, now just dial

RELATIONSHIP

- Telephone contact has helped so much in building up our relationships
- Building a warm relationship with you over the telephone
- The kind of relationship where you can just pick up your phone and call
- When you call, you're joining with us in a relationship that will benefit everyone
- The telephone is vital to our relationship with you

RESOURCE

- Your call will help give us give you the resources you need
- With your telephone call, you'll get the resources to
- The fabulous resource can be yours if you make that call
- Giving you the resources you need right over the telephone
- At the end of your telephone line, we are your best resource
- A wonderful resource right at your fingertips

RING

- We're waiting for our telephones to start ringing
- Ring us up now
- Your call will be a ringing success
- The telephone is ringing constantly
- Oh boy, we like to hear those phones ringing
- When you give us a ring, you're making yourself happy
- It's such a joy to hear all those telephones ringing at once
- As long as the phones are ringing we know you're there
- It's so wonderful to hear all those telephones start ringing
- Do you hear all the phones ringing in the background
- Give us a ring
- Listening eagerly for that first ring
- Each telephone ring means another satisfied customer
- Please keep those phones ringing

RESULT

- For faster results, call the center nearest you
- This single phone call could result in
- Just look at the results you'll get merely

by calling in to
- Giving you the results you want right over the telephone
- The sooner you call, the quicker you'll get these terrific results

SALE
- Please don't wait until the end of this sale – call now
- Don't hesitate until this sale is over
- You can only take advantage of this sale by telephone
- A sale designed to make it easy for phone-in customers
- Our annual telephone sale gives customers a chance at big savings
- Phone right now before this sale ends

SCRIPT
- Responsible for successfully scripting so many segments
- Your telephone response is part of the script
- Scripted so that you can't possibly lose
- I'm not just reading some script here, I'm speaking from the heart

SERVICE
- People much prefer a call selling goods and services
- Dial a service
- As a special service to you, we keep our phones open overnight
- Call for immediate service and advice
- This service is provided over the telephone for your convenience
- Calling to offer you a service not available anywhere else
- A trained service person will answer your phone call
- Get service faster by phone
- Instant service at your fingertips

SOLUTION
- Providing telephone-based solutions
- A massive telephone campaign was proposed as the solution
- Your call now is a vital part of the solution for you
- The solution is to pick up that telephone and punch our number
- The solution is to call this number

STAFF
- Our telephone staff will explain clearly
- Our telephone staff will be very glad to talk to you about
- We have lots of staff waiting to take your call
- Wouldn't it be great to have every last one of our staff busy with the phones
- Just the number of people who staff the phones indicates how devoted
- Our staff will be very happy to explain everything you want to know about
- You will instantly reach one of our eager staff
- Our staff is just waiting for the phone to ring
- Sometimes our staff just can't keep up with the calls

STANDARDS
- Dedicated to establishing ethical standards for telemarketing
- Show your confidence in these high standards by calling now
- When you call, you can be assured of the best standards yet
- We'll explain about our high standards when you call

START
- Your phone call is just the starting point
- Start something wonderful with your phone call
- Everything starts the moment we receive your call
- Dial now to start receiving this wonderful service

SUPPORT
- Your call sparks immediate support
- The telephone is our way of getting support to you quickly
- Fast support is always available by phone
- Our telephone support service is known for quality
- We'll support you all the way
- Give us a call, try out the excellence of our caller support

SURVEY
- Marketing efforts very fruitfully combined with a telephone survey

- Telephone surveys are a highly accurate, cost-effective way of reaching the most desired segment of the population
- Three out of four people surveyed said they preferred to order by telephone
- Please participate in the survey to help us find out how best to please you
- A telephone survey to learn your preferences

TALK

- We're waiting now to talk to you
- We really want to talk to you
- Talk to us
- Call and let us prove this offer is not all just talk
- Here's what the talk is all about
- Call us up and we'll talk about it
- This offer has really got people talking
- Let us talk to you for only a few moments and you'll enjoy
- You'll love talking to us

TEAM

- Call now and join our team
- Our telephone team is waiting to serve you
- Our team wants to hear from every one of you out there within reach of your telephone
- With each person who calls, our team gets happier
- This really is a team effort, so call as soon as you can
- As part of our team, it's your call

TECHNOLOGY

- Using the latest telephone and computer technology to serve you
- It's a simple technology, right at your fingertips
- Through the miracle of technology, you can get your order in at lightning speed

TELECOMMUNICATOR

- Good telecommunicators are more at a premium than ever
- The true measure of a telecommunicator is how much response is generated within a given time frame
- We're working hard to become superb telecommunicators

TELEMARKETING

- Telemarketing has turned out to be a very powerful tool
- Telemarketing can offer twenty-four hour service
- Telemarketing is an efficient way of defraying costs
- Through the miracle of telemarketing, you too can have

TELEPHONE

- The telephone is something you use day in and day out
- Through the telephone, you can now reach us twenty-four hours in the day
- Tonight, your telephone can turn into a magical instrument
- Your telephone is right beside you
- Your telephone is only a hand-reach away
- Your telephone is the easiest way to
- Did you ever dream your telephone could make such a difference in your life
- Your telephone call means immediate help for you
- Via high-capacity telephone hookups
- You can get so much simply by picking up the telephone
- Enjoy yourself on the telephone
- Go to your telephone and let us know what you need
- Your telephone can open magic doors

TELL

- Tell us anything you want
- Your call tells us how well we're doing
- Nothing is more telling than the number of calls received
- Tell us directly over the phone
- Waiting for you to tell us

THANK YOU

- If you've already called, thank you
- And this fine gift is waiting to thank you for your call
- Thank you for listening, thank you for calling
- Thank you so much for picking up your telephone and ordering

TIME

- Time is rapidly running out
- Just one more hour, then our time is gone

- Now is the time to make your call
- Now is the time to get up and act
- Don't let any more time go by without calling
- Soon there'll be no more time to make your call
- Isn't it time you picked up that phone
- Only a few minutes to go, but my goodness, time is slipping by so quickly

TOOL

- The telephone is your most efficient tool
- The telephone is your foremost tool to improve your life
- Through a simple, nearby tool like your telephone, you can

TOUCH

- Keeping continually in touch with our vital customer base
- Touching base with you by phone
- Reach out and touch someone new
- Your phone is the quickest way of getting in touch with us
- Just keeping in touch with you
- Get in touch by phone right away

TRAIN

- To hire, train and manage staff to execute an effective solicitation plan
- Our staff is trained to respond to your call immediately and answer all your questions
- A well-trained staff is key to the success of any telephone campaign

TRUST

- With telephone sales, trust becomes a bigger issue than ever before
- We're going to trust in you that you're going to your telephone right now
- I trust you're dialling as I speak
- Call the people everybody trusts
- So many people are trusting that you'll call today
- You can call with complete trust

TRY

- If you haven't been able to get through, please, please try again
- Don't give up trying because of a busy signal

- Give us a call and try it
- If you've always wanted to try this but didn't know how
- If you try to reach us now, you'll be sure to get through

VERIFY

- Potential customers may call to verify the facts of this marketing campaign
- Call us whenever you wish to verify
- We'll be glad to verify every fact over the phone
- Can easily verify it by calling this number

WAIT

- Don't wait another minute, please call now
- We can hardly wait for your call
- The longer you wait, the more chance you have of missing out on
- What are you waiting for, just call
- Do you want to be one of those who waited too long

WIRE

- We're really coming right down to the wire here
- Your last chance before we get right to the wire
- Calls are just burning up the wires
- The wires are humming with calls
- If you call right now, you can just get in under the wire
- We're really wired about this phone offer
- Call now to avoid all the barbed wire

WORK

- You telephone really can work wonders
- Working hard to take down all your information
- Make your call a working call
- Put your telephone to work for you
- To find out how simple it works, give us a ring
- When you call, we start working with you immediately to

YOU

- We have to please you
- People like you are our mainstay
- Everyone here is waiting to hear from

you
- You are the center of our universe right now
- You are the one who makes it all work tonight
- It's all happening because of you
- And we're still waiting for you to call

Section Five

Saying Thanks

ACCOMPLISH

- You accomplished so much under very difficult circumstances
- You have accomplished the impossible
- I only wish everyone could see what has been accomplished

ACCOMPLISHMENT

- What an accomplishment
- Taking enormous pride in your accomplishment
- Look forward to your accomplishments in the years ahead

ACHIEVE

- I know how hard you've worked to achieve this
- And you achieve even more in the future
- No one imagined you could achieve so much

ACHIEVEMENT

- Even the preparations were a real achievement
- This level of achievement is rarely reached
- We're proud and happy about your achievement
- Derive great pleasure from your achievements
- You have a good solid record of achievement
- Your achievements quickly came to my attention

ACKNOWLEDGE

- Acknowledging that there is still room for improvement
- We would like to acknowledge the following organizations
- First, I want acknowledge all the effort that went into
- Acknowledge your dedication and commitment in such a special way

ACKNOWLEDGEMENT

- I would like to make the following acknowledgements
- I really appreciate the acknowledgement of such a special occasion
- Really treasure your acknowledgement of all the contributions

ACTION

- To everyone who cares enough to take individual and collective action
- Thank you for taking such prompt and effective action
- I always find you where the action is

ADMIRE

- I want to tell you how much I admire you
- Someone who we understand and admire
- I admire your perseverance and commitment
- I respect and admire your work
- Can't help but admire you in every way

ADVICE

- You always give such good advice
- Thanks a lot for your excellent advice
- Your valuable advice made our success possible
- Thank you so much for all your help and advice

AGREEMENT

- Coming to a very quick agreement
- So glad that you and I are both in agreement
- There can be nothing but agreement about

APOLOGY

- Again my thanks and apologies
- Apologies for our absence
- I want to apologize for taking so long

APPLAUD

- I want to applaud your stand
- Every one of us applauds your decision
- The more we applaud, the more you deserve

APPRECIATE

- Making sure how much we appreciate you
- Your continued support is greatly appreciated
- Appreciate all who have helped and contributed
- I really appreciate the fact that I call on you at any time
- I appreciate your review of my proposal
- To let you know we appreciate all your hard work

- I deeply appreciate your invitation
- I appreciate your taking on the responsibility
- Always remembered, shared and appreciated
- Each of your gestures, no matter how large or small, was deeply appreciated
- It's about appreciating the little things in life
- For those who appreciate the best
- You'll appreciate the value
- You are so appreciated
- To show how much we appreciate your patronage
- We deeply appreciate your business
- We appreciate your business and wish you every happiness
- A way to show just how much we appreciate your business
- The faster your life moves, the more you'll appreciate
- Few things are more appreciated than
- I appreciate you enormously
- Appreciate your willingness to take risks
- You'll never know how much I appreciate
- Someone who truly appreciates you
- We appreciate how rare it is to find a real gem like you
- You are most appreciated

APPRECIATION
- Expressing my thanks and appreciation
- With warmest appreciation
- Just a little token of our appreciation
- We just can't show our appreciation enough
- A gesture of appreciation
- Every year my appreciation of you becomes stronger
- Appreciation from the heart
- I'd like to express our deepest appreciation for
- Thanks and appreciation
- A growing appreciation is developing
- Appreciation changes and increases
- On behalf of our organization, I wish to express our appreciation
- Just one more way to show our appreciation for your business
- There's never a better time to express our appreciation
- In appreciation of our continued association
- Showing a keen appreciation for
- Expressing heartfelt thanks and deep appreciation
- This is the kind of appreciation you get when you come to us for
- Constant appreciation in value is only one benefit of
- I want to show my appreciation for everything you have done
- As guilty as the next person in not expressing my appreciation

Appreciation: recognition, thanks, comprehension, gratitude, thankfulness, thanksgiving, acknowledgement, tribute, praise, applause
See also: THANKS, TRIBUTE

ASK
- Thanks for asking
- No matter what we ask, you always come through
- How comforting to know I can always ask this of you
- You helped out without being asked

ASSET
- You have proved an invaluable asset
- Find you such an asset to the company
- You are our chief human asset

ASSIST
- Thanks so much for assisting us
- You are always so ready assist
- The one person who can always be counted upon to assist

ASSISTANCE
- I sincerely appreciate the assistance and support you provided
- I hope you will let me know if I can be of assistance to you in the future
- I want to thank you for your prompt assistance in this matter
- Thank you for your consideration and assistance
- You always give assistance immediately

ATTENTION
- Thank you for calling our attention to this problem
- I appreciated your prompt attention

- Thank you for your attention to my views

ATTITUDE
- Reflected in your positive attitude
- Especially appreciate your cheerful attitude
- Your helpful attitude has made such a difference

AWARD
- Earned every one of your numerous awards
- This award is richly deserved
- So very happy to know you won this award
- Congratulations on winning such a prestigious awards

BENEFIT
- You will reap the benefits for many years to come
- The benefits of this achievement are tremendous
- Extending a thank you benefit
- Everyone has benefited from your presence

BEST
- Definitely one of the best
- You are the best we've seen
- I wish you all the best
- Best wishes for the coming year
- You are one of the best and brightest
- It's great to work with the very best
- Have the best of everything right here

BUSINESS
- I enjoyed doing business with your from start to finish
- Good luck in your business
- Appreciate the generous actions of local businesses during the emergency

CARE
- We know how much you care
- I'll never forget the compassion and professional care
- People who care are thinking of you today
- I was genuinely touched by how much you care
- Thank you for a day full of warmth and caring

- Please know that we care very much
- Thank you for caring so much
- The care and concern of friends like you got us through
- Thank you so much for your expression of caring
- Care for it as much as you do
- Want to thank you personally for caring
- Thank you for caring enough to do this
- Thanks for caring so much

CELEBRATE
- We truly have something to celebrate
- Thinking of you as you celebrate this wonderful occasion
- Now there really is something to celebrate
- Thanks for helping us celebrate
- Come help us celebrate
- I look forward to celebrating many more such anniversaries

CELEBRATION
- In this time of celebration
- This certainly is a cause for celebration
- We wanted to be part of your celebration
- So grateful you wanted to join our celebration
- The celebration would have been ho-hum without you

CHANCE
- We wouldn't have missed this chance to
- Thanks for taking a chance on us
- Without you, I wouldn't have had a chance to try
- Thanks turning this chance into a win
- Bless the lucky chance that brought you to us
- Thanks for giving me the chance to show what I can do

CHOOSE
- We're delighted that you've chosen us
- Just one more way of saying thank you for choosing
- Thank you so much for choosing us

COMMITMENT
- Your personal commitment contributed overwhelmingly to our success
- This biggest decision and the biggest commitment we've ever made
- A lasting commitment like yours is very

hard to find
- So happy to recognize your commitment

COMMUNITY
- You've never been to busy to give back to the community
- On behalf of the entire community, I want to convey our thanks
- Your relationship to others and your community has always been splendid
- You help with so many worthwhile projects in our community
- Recognize your outstanding contributions to our community
- Aware of your efforts to make our community a better place to live
- You have so many great ideas for our community
- You are a great resource to the community
- Touched by the care our community members demonstrated
- We are fortunate to have such dedicated people in our community
- Thank you for being partners with our community
- Making the community aware of these generous actions

COMPLIMENT
- Thank you for the kind compliment
- My compliments
- So much more than just a simple compliment
- You are the perfect compliment to our staff
- We have received many compliments throughout the community

CONCERN
- Thank you very much for your concern over our recent misunderstanding
- I want to express my concern
- Reflected in your genuine concern for others
- I thought a long time about how to convey my concern
- Thank you for you attention to my concerns

CONGRATULATE
- I want to congratulate and thank the committee for

- I congratulate you for passing such a significant milestone
- I look forward to congratulating you in person
- I want to congratulate you on your recent appointment

CONGRATULATIONS
- Congratulations are in order
- Congratulations and many thanks to
- I wanted to send you a personal note of congratulations
- Please accept my love and congratulations
- Congratulations on the wonderful news
- Congratulations and many good wishes
- Congratulations on reaching such a major turning point
- My congratulations and love are with you
- Thank you for your letter of congratulations
- Congratulations on spreading your wings
- Congratulations on opening your own business

CONTRIBUTION
- I hope you know how much your contribution helped
- You have made a significant contribution to our fundraising effort
- I would like to thank you for your generous contribution
- Your contribution is sure to be remembered for a long, long time
- I want you to know how much I value your contribution
- Wherever you go, you make an important contribution
- To recognize your personal contributions
- Judged on the contribution you have made to our lives
- You've made a genuine contribution
- Enabled us to make a valuable contribution
- Your contributions have been exemplary

COOPERATION
- Thanks so much for your cooperation
- Thank you for your cooperation in this matter
- Your cooperation made it all possible
- I would particularly like to commend

your spirit of cooperation
- Grateful for your cooperation and willingness to assist

COUNT
- I know I can always count on you and I'm so grateful
- I can always count on you to help convince others
- I can count on you to take appropriate action

COURAGE
- I've always admired your courage
- Thank you for facing this challenge with such courage
- You hung in there with courage and determination
- Always admired your inner strength and courage

CREDIT
- You deserve all the credit for
- The credit is all yours
- Credit for this huge success must go to
- I wish to give credit to all the generous individuals who donated their time and talents
- So much of the credit belongs to you

DAY
- A day we've marked to celebrate
- Hope you'll be here forever and a day
- You really made my day
- I know this is a really great day
- Congratulations on your special day
- Taking it, one day at a time
- You provided a day I shall never forget
- Today is your special day
- Wonderful to have a special day just to honor you
- So happy to share your special day
- Even though I don't see you every day
- An unforgettable day for all of us
- I'm counting the days until we meet
- Wishing you a super day and a wonderful year ahead
- Remember this day as one of the most important in your life
- Thanks for brightening the day
- The most spectacular day we have ever experienced

DEAR
- You are very dear to us all
- Success is sweet when so dearly bought
- Want you to know how dear you are

DECISION
- You had a major influence on our decision
- Applaud your decision to
- Your input really helped us make a critical decision

DECLINE
- As it is so late, we must decline
- At the last moment, I must decline
- So sorry to have to decline your kind invitation

DEDICATION
- Truly inspired by your energy and dedication
- Your dedication and outstanding accomplishments in the field of
- So impressed with your hard work and dedication
- Proud of your dedication and accomplishment
- I truly appreciate your time and dedication
- Your dedication and excellent qualifications
- Expressed dedication to the many causes publically espoused

DEED
- Your kind words and thoughtful deeds are precious
- So many caring words and deeds
- Too many splendid good deeds to name

DELIGHT
- Always a delight to be with
- I am delighted that your opinion is similar to mine
- I know how delighted you must be

DESERVE
- You really deserve a really special thank you
- You deserve the best
- You deserve a lot more than
- You deserve a medal
- Congratulations on well deserved

recognition

- I can't think of anyone who deserves this position more
- Well deserving of this prestigious recognition
- Deserve a resounding "thank you"

DETAIL

- You made sure every detail was perfect
- No detail was too small for your attention
- Absolutely loved every detail
- Your attention to every detail made the day run smoothly

DETERMINATION

- We are very proud of your determination
- Applaud your determination to stick to your own convictions
- Your strong determination to succeed

DONATION

- I want to thank all of you who made a donation or volunteered
- Thank you for your concern and your donation
- We appreciate your donations in support
- Thanks for you in-kind donations
- We are so very pleased to accept your generous donation
- Thank you for your caring donation

DREAM

- Never in my wildest dreams did I think you could pull this off
- Now we are seeing so many of those hopes and dreams come true
- You've worked very hard to make your dreams come true
- Now you have made your dream a reality
- Thank you for a dream come true
- The achievement is the fulfilment of a longtime dream

EASY

- You make the hardest tasks look so easy
- It's so easy to say thanks to you
- I know it hasn't been easy
- You made my path an easy one

EFFORT

- I know how much time and effort you invested
- Certainly clear that all the effort was

worth it

- Nobody puts more effort into things than you do
- The many new, exciting innovations made possible by your efforts and generosity
- Appreciate your dedication to team effort
- All the effort and sacrifice takes on new meaning
- Your fine efforts will be recognized soon
- Please continue your efforts on behalf of the cause
- Very much aware of your efforts
- My appreciation for your effort is enormous
- Thanks again for your efforts
- Want you to know we greatly appreciated your efforts
- We appreciate this gift of time and effort more than you can know
- Thanks for making it possible to join this great effort
- Your efforts are sincerely appreciated
- Very grateful for your outstanding efforts
- Thank you for all your efforts on our behalf
- Thank you for your extraordinary efforts

ENCOURAGEMENT

- I appreciate your encouragement
- Couldn't have done it without your encouragement and determination
- Always there with encouragement when it was needed most
- You probably don't realize how much your encouragement has meant
- Thanks to your support and encouragement
- Thank you for your encouragement, help and advice
- I am particularly grateful for your unfailing encouragement
-

ENJOY

- Everyone enjoyed themselves so much
- I enjoyed every minute
- So enjoy your irrepressible humor
- I so enjoyed being part of this adventure
- I thought you might enjoy this
- Just wanted to you know how very much I enjoyed
- I hope you enjoyed it as much as I did

ENRICH

- You've enriched our lives
- So enriched by your many kindnesses over the years
- Enriched by your strength, patience wisdom and guidance
- Enriched us in so many ways

ENTHUSIASM

- I've never seen so much enthusiasm
- Your enthusiasm will ensure your success
- I just had to write to express my enthusiasm for
- Thank you for your enthusiasm and participation
- We share your enthusiasm
- Look forward with great enthusiasm

EVENT

- It was lovely to see both of you at this event
- You guys really made this event
- Went above and beyond to make this event a success
- So many guests said it was the best event they'd ever been to
- Resulted in the most spectacular event ever
- One of the most successful events we've ever had
- This is a real landmark event
- The event will be complete if you are there
- No one throws parties or events like you
- Thanks for helping make the event bigger and better than ever
- Thank you for making this event run so smoothly
- One of those lucky enough to be present at this event
- Your continued interest and participation in this exciting event

EVERYTHING

- So thank you so much for everything
- Many thanks for everything you and your staff did
- I just wanted to thank you again for everything
- You made everything just perfect
- Everything was excellent

EXPERIENCE

- It has been a powerful and positive experience
- I thank you personally for such a supportive and educational experience
- The experience wouldn't have been the same without you
- I know we've experienced difficult times and disappointments
- You always generously share whatever you have learned from your own experience
- Sharing a universally cosmic experience
- So exciting to be part of the experience
- We have shared so many outstanding experiences
- A truly new experience for most of us

EXPERTISE

- You alway lend additional insight and expertise
- An enthusiastic audience and very appreciative of your expertise
- We need you expertise
- The professional expertise needed on this crucial project

FAITH

- You have restored my faith in humanity
- Your faith in me means so very much
- You always had faith in the outcome
- Thanks for reminding me to have faith
- Thanks for keeping the faith when everyone else gave up

FAMILY

- My family and I will never be able to thank you enough
- My family and I would like to thank you
- You made us feel part of the family
- I wish to thank my loving family which has put with so much effort
- How fortunate to be part of such a warm, caring family
- A family with so much to give
- Looking forward to making you part of our family
- Our thoughts are with you and your family

FEELING

- My feeling is one of sublime happiness
- My feelings about it amount to a state of

euphoria
- I don't want to leave a single caring feeling unsaid

FRIEND
- I now consider you a good friend
- All your friends are there for you
- So lucky to have friends like you
- Counting on you as a friend
- Wonderful to be with such dear friends again
- Once again reminds me of what a good friend you are
- Not only as a partner but as a friend
- Have known you as a personal friend for years
- We look forward to meeting a dear friend
- You have become such a dear and valued friend
- We were friends long before this situation occurred
- Thanks for being my friend
- Thank you for telling friends about us
- Thanks for being such a loyal friend

FRIENDSHIP
- Our friendship and love are always here for you
- Thinking of our many years of friendship
- Such a comfort to know you are a dear friend
- Thanks for your friendship in bad times and good
- I value your friendship

FUTURE
- I am very excited about the future
- You'll be seeing more of us in the future
- You ensure there's a great future ahead
- Now you can create the kind of future you want for yourself

GENEROSITY
- We're blown away by your generosity
- We can never repay you for such generosity
- Thanks for your generosity
- Your generosity is awesome
- Your generosity springs directly from your heart

GENEROUS
- One of the most generous people in the entire city
- Thanks again for all your generous help
- Always so generous with your time and your expertise

GESTURE
- A simple gesture of thanks
- Please join us in a gesture of appreciation
- What a kind and wonderful gesture

GIFT
- It's clear you spent a great deal of time and care in choosing our gift
- A great comfort knowing the gift has been put to good use
- Your gift fitted perfectly
- Thanks for your very thoughtful gift
- No gift is really ours until we have thanked the giver
- Your generous gift is greatly appreciated
- I really value your gift
- Your gift will grow more precious every year
- Your gift was a memorable keepsake
- Thank you for the lovely gift
- Your gift will always remind me of you
- Each time I see your gift, I think of you
- As always, you picked out the perfect gift
- We wish to honour you by offering this gift in your name
- Just a small token gift to thank you for
- Thank you for sending me such a lovely gift
- Thank you for the exquisite gift
- Each time I look at your beautiful gift, my spirits lift
- I'm so glad you chose the gift you did

GIVE
- If it were up to me, I'd give you everything
- You give richly of your time, talent and resources
- Thank you for giving us such a terrific treat
- A gift that gives over and over
- We thank you for the things you gave us
- If giving makes life happy, you must be very happy indeed

GOAL
- Your participation and cooperation has helped us achieve our goals

- A time to think of your goals for the years ahead
- You've certainly achieved your goals
- Good luck in your pursuit of this very worthwhile goal
- You have made many sacrifices to achieve your goal
- Always a genuine interest in our goals

GOOD

- You make me feel so good
- Had such a good time last night
- Thank you for doing such a good turn
- We never forget a good turn
- Good food and good fellowship
- It feels so good just to know you are there
- It was so good of you to help out
- To recognize all the good you are doing
- I just can't say enough good things about

GRATEFUL

- We're grateful for you every day
- I wanted to tell you right away how grateful we are
- So many good things to be grateful for
- Feeling grateful but with no one to thank
- We are so grateful for everything we receive
- I am very grateful to you for
- I just want to convey to you how very grateful I am
- You were there for me and I'm deeply grateful
- I am eternally grateful

GRATITUDE

- I would like to express my deepest gratitude for
- To each and every member we would like to express our sincere gratitude and understanding
- How can I pack a lifetime of gratitude into a single letter
- Our attitude is one of gratitude
- Gratitude is one of the most beautiful virtues
- Gratitude is the mother of all other virtues
- Gratitude is the greatest form of courtesy
- I want to say everything in the language of gratitude
- We humbly express our gratitude

- Our gratitude knows no bounds
- The heartfelt gratitude of those in need

GREAT

- We think you are great
- The crowds thought you were great
- Great to know we have such dedicated people in time of need
- It was really great to have you there
- A few words from a very grateful guest

HAND

- Such a comfort to be in your capable, caring hands
- Hand in hand, we can meet the future
- Always ready to reach out a helping hand
- Thanks for giving us a hand when the going was tough

HAPPY

- I'm so happy for you
- We are so happy you arrived safely
- Happy to be so well matched
- I'm so happy for you
- You've made me very happy
- How proud and happy you must be

HEART

- You will always have a special place in my heart
- My heart prompts me to add these words
- You are always in our hearts
- The key is in our hearts
- You touched all our hearts in a very special way
- May you soon have all your heart's desires
- A helping hand and a willing heart
- Thank you for making our hearts so much lighter
- You always share right from the heart

HELP

- You've been such a big help
- You really helped us through
- Let me know if there's anything more I can do to help
- Want to help you through this difficult time
- Offer whatever help will be of value to you
- If I may help you in some way
- Always willing to help

- Thank you for your help
- We felt you did a splendid job
- Is there anything we can do to help or ease the burden
- You are a very special help to us
- Thank you again for your help and support
- I want to thank you again for all your help
- You help us a lot
- Always more than willing to help us out
- You really went all out to help
- It goes without saying it was great of you to help

HONOR

- I cannot tell you how pleased and honored I am
- I can't think of anyone more deserving of this honor
- An honor you richly deserve
- I can think of no better way to honor you
- So pleased and honored you could join us

HOPE

- Turned out even better than we could have hoped
- With high hopes and a fresh start
- A time when hopes rise for peace and understanding
- Thank you to everyone who urged me not to give up hope

HOSPITALITY

- Thank you for your gracious hospitality
- You give new meaning to the word "hospitality"
- Thank you for your wonderful hospitality during my visit
- Your warm hospitality made us all feel so at home

HOST

- Thank you for hosting such a marvellous educational experience
- Never met a more thoughtful host than you
- You are the best host ever
- Thanks for so skilfully hosting such a pivotal event
- Wish all hosts were as considerate as you

HUG

- Consider this a hug
- On days when you really need a hug
- Hearing from you is as good as a hug

IDEA

- I always look forward to hearing your ideas
- Thank you for coming and sharing your ideas
- Your hard work and creative ideas have already helped improve
- Your ideas are always so creative
- Hiring you was the best idea yet

IMPRESS

- I particularly wanted you to know how much I am impressed
- So impressed about how are able to balance both sides
- Impressed by your clear and reasoned arguments
- All were impressed by your artistry

INFORMATION

- Everyone enjoyed hearing the information you had at your fingertips
- Thanks for the valuable information
- We had such a great time trading information
- Thank you for making such vital information available

INSPIRE

- You are so inspiring
- It's inspiring to see so many new faces this year
- You inspired me
- I felt inspired after we met

INTEREST

- Just thought you'd be interested in this
- You always have our interests at heart
- We appreciate your interest
- Thank you for your interest and response
- Thank you for your continued interest and support
- I have followed your progress with great interest
- Persuade you to continue your interest
- Thank you for your kind interest
- Thank you for your interest in our products

- Thank you for your interest in staying updated
- Excited by your interest in
- I know you are particularly interested
- I would like to take a moment to confirm my strong interest in

JOB

- Please accept my congratulations on a job well done
- The job you did for us was truly special
- A great pleasure to work with you on this recent job
- Thank you for doing such a wonderful job
- You really do a great job
- You've done a wonderful job
- When we want to job done, we always call on you
- Each of you did an outstanding job
- Appreciate the excellent job you are doing
- Your presence makes our job easier
- I think you have done a super job
- My compliments on a job well done
- Dedicated and proficient in your job duties

JOIN

- It was a great pleasure to join you
- Thanks for letting me join in
- You joined us on a real voyage of discovery
- Thank you for joining our team

JOY

- It is a joy to know what a wonderful person you've become
- I wish you joy – and more joy
- You are someone who brings joy into our lives
- I remember with joy the time when
- Even though we cannot be present to share in the joy
- Thanks for bringing laughter and joy

KIND

- You are one of a kind
- Always there with a kind word and a helping hand
- Thank you very kindly
- Thank you again for being so kind

KINDNESS

- Thank you very much for your kindness
- Your kindness and good ideas will be sorely missed
- Your many kindnesses will be remembered
- How can anyone forget such kindness
- Sincere thanks for the thoughtful kindness you have shown
- Thank you for you kindness, gentleness and words of encouragement

KNOW

- Thanks for wanting to know something about this
- I know how much planning went into making this day a success
- Wanted you to know you are always in our thoughts
- Please let me know if you can use some help
- We feel as though we know you personally
- Although I do not know you well
- You will be so pleased to know
- I don't know how you do it

LETTER

- I know how hard it was to write that letter
- This is the easiest letter I've ever had to write
- I wanted to write a letter of appreciation
- This letter of thanks is very important to me
- It's not often I get to write a thank you letter for
- Thank you for your recent letter
- Your letter made all the difference
- My first priority was to write this letter of thanks

LIFE

- You've changed our lives forever
- I wanted to tell you how much I liked it
- I know this is a very exciting time in your life
- Knowing you has changed my life
- You've shared some of the happiest moments in my life
- Privileged to mark one of life's most precious moments
- Thank you for letting me be part of your

life
- Thank you for bring new life and hope to us all
- We look forward to hearing all about your new life
- The ability to laugh and keep life in perspective
- Convey my gratitude to a mentor who made such an impact on my life
- Filled with dignity and enjoying life to the fullest
- Life is so much easier because of you
- You help us celebrate life
- You are the best part of my life
- You fill our lives with sunshine

LOOK
- I look forward so much to working with you again
- Look forward to continuing our dialogue
- Look forward to lots of interesting
- Look forward so much to seeing you soon
- I look forward to introducing you
- We are looking forward to a great victory
- Now you can look back and access your accomplishments

LOVE
- I send you my love
- I love you all
- My love and wisdom always follow you
- Making us feel so loved
- You've always had our love and our pride
- You are a testament to the power of love
- You've always been there to love, guide and protect

LUCK
- Good luck with your efforts
- Good luck with your campaign
- Luck has nothing to do with it
- The fabulous good luck of finding you
- Just my luck

LUCKY
- I count myself lucky to know you
- Know how lucky we are to have you on board
- What a lucky day when you arrived
- We are very lucky to have you at all

MEET
- Very happy to have met and shared with you
- I look forward to meeting with you back home
- We enjoyed meeting with you about
- I can't wait to meet you
- Thank you for meeting with me so soon
- I can't tell you how much I enjoyed meeting you
- So glad I finally had the opportunity to meet you
- I've never met anyone like you
- What a pleasure it was to meet you
- Though I have yet to meet you personally
- It seems we met you only yesterday
- Thank you for meeting with us so promptly
- Planning a mutually convenient time to meet
- I am very grateful for our meeting

MEMBER
- Every member is exceptional
- A very responsible member of our community
- All our members were delighted

MEMORABLE
- You put such a memorable event together on short notice
- You help us relive a memorable day
- Your gift was such a memorable keepsake

MEMORY
- Such a nice memory
- A joyful memory shared by all
- So happy to have this for our memories
- Now I have one more fond memory
- Thanks for the memory
- You have honored a precious memory
- You bring back so many fond memories
- Given us memories we will always cherish
- I want to thank you for the treasured memories and those yet to come

MESSAGE
- Your message was so meaningful
- Thank you for your message of appreciation
- Everyone is very interested in your

message
- Thank you for taking the time to bring us such an important message

MILESTONE
- Congratulations on reaching such a milestone
- You've passed a very impressive milestone
- A real milestone in your growth

MIND
- You've been on my mind a lot lately
- Thank you for keeping an open mind
- Thanks for keeping me in mind

NOTE
- Thanks again for your note and your interest
- I'm sending you this little note to thank you
- Your personal note made me feel touched and remembered
- Your note really cheered me up
- Your note was a very special reminder of how much you care
- Your note said just what I was feeling
- Just a short note to thank you for
- I really appreciated your note
- A thoughtful note is even better than a gift

OCCASION
- How could we let such a significant occasion pass without acknowledgement
- This is one occasion that really means a lot
- One occasion I really look forward to
- An occasion I'll always remember with fondness
- Take pleasure in helping you celebrate this special occasion
- Such joyous occasions require substantial planning
- This occasion is very special to me too
- I know this is a solemn and joyous occasion
- Thanks for making the occasion so meaningful
- Ensure a memorable occasion for everyone
- Thank you for making the occasion so special

- You made the occasion so much fun

OFFER
- Very gratified by your offer
- Thank you very much for this offer
- I am really excited about this new offering

OPPORTUNITY
- Thanks for talking to me about this wonderful opportunity
- Very glad to have the opportunity to
- I welcome the opportunity of continuing our association
- Now so many new opportunities are opening to you
- A rare opportunity to touch hearts
- Thanks for the opportunity to grow in new ways
- I would appreciate the opportunity to serve
- An excellent opportunity to meet
- Saved us from missing this fabulous opportunity
- How gratified to be offered this opportunity
- Thanks again for the opportunity to
- Thank you for offering this exciting opportunity
- Thank you for the opportunity to serve you
- I would like to take this opportunity to express my thanks for
- Thank you for creating an additional opportunity

PARTICIPATE
- I would like to thank everyone who participated
- We would like to take this opportunity to thank you for participating
- I just wanted to thank you for letting me participate
- We hope you will continue to participate
- I encourage everyone to participate and contribute

PEOPLE
- I wish to extend a very special thank you to people who have gone out of their way
- It's wonderful to work with such an outstanding group of people

- Strongly committed to serving the people
- You always take care of people first
- If it wasn't for people like you, I don't know what I would have done
- Activities would not be possible without the generous support of our members
- People are still talking about it

PERFECT

- Having you this close makes the occasion perfect
- You proved yourself the perfect companion
- You made everything perfect

PERFORMANCE

- Your performance has been unfailingly superior
- Performance is consistently first class
- Thank you for the magnificent performance
- Your performance has always been a big reason for our success

PERSON

- Simply put, you are the best person
- You are a swell person
- You were the right person to ask
- What a remarkable person you are
- You were certainly the right person to handle this difficult assignment
- Persons whose accomplishments earn special recognition
- Knew you were just the person we were looking for

PERSONAL

- I wanted to write to you personally to convey my thanks
- Permit me to extend a personal thanks and welcome
- Thank for discussing this with me personally
- A very personal thank you
- I so enjoy getting personal mail from you
- How much I personally, and collectively, thank you

PLEASE

- So glad to hear you're pleased
- I hope this gesture of thanks will please you
- I was extremely pleased to learn

PLEASURE

- It was such a pleasure to have spoken with you
- Such a pleasure to see you moving up quickly
- Taking much pleasure in your accomplishments
- As always, it is a pleasure dealing with you

POSITION

- I am very excited about this position
- Thank you for considering me for this position
- Look forward to discussing this position with you

POSITIVE

- How wonderful to hear something so positive
- Your involvement has been such a positive
- I'm positive you have what it takes

POSSIBLE

- Without your help, the job would have been impossible
- It wouldn't have been possible without you
- You made it all possible
- I look forward to the possibility of working with you

POTENTIAL

- Justified our trust in your potential
- Gratifying to see so much potential finally realized
- With such a great deal of professional potential

PRESENT

- What a lovely present
- Thank you all again for such a fabulous present
- You dream up the most original presents
- I wanted to be present when you were honored

PRESENTATION

- Everyone loved the whole presentation
- Your presentation was both entertaining and informative
- A presentation delivered with the

confidence of someone thoroughly familiar with this complex subject
- Your presentation was so enjoyable it seemed to end all too soon

PRIDE
- I take great pride in my long association with you
- Your pride in taking such a big, important step
- Great pride in all that you are and will become
- You can't imagine the pride we feel in you
- You can look back with pride
- With great pride we say thank you to
- I was gratified to see the level of personal pride expressed

PRIVILEGE
- I can't tell you how privileged you make me feel
- Such an honor and a privilege to shake your hand
- A privilege like this doesn't come every day
- Such a rare and special privilege
- Privileged to know such a special person

PROGRAM
- I'd like to express my appreciation for the fine program you presented
- I am very impressed with programs currently in place
- Delighted with the facility and the programs you are offering

PROJECT
- Undertaking an important national project
- Thank you for sponsoring such a worthwhile project
- I appreciated the chance to look over this project

PROMPT
- Thank you for contacting me so promptly
- Your prompt action saved the day
- You are always prompt and considerate
- Prompt service is always much appreciated
- Your unfailing promptness is appreciated

PROUD
- You have right to feel proud
- You must be so proud
- I'm so proud of you
- We are so proud of you on this wonderful day
- I know how proud you must be
- Proud to know such a thoughtful, compassionate person
- I know that you are proud of yourself

RAVE
- I just want to rave about you
- There were raves about the
- Your performance produced nothing but raves

RECOMMEND
- I do not hesitate to recommend
- Like to recommend you to all our friends
- I won't hesitate to recommend you
- We will recommend you at every chance

RECOMMENDATION
- I would like to thank you for your favourable recommendation
- Pleased to offer this recommendation
- Delighted to give my personal recommendation

REGRET
- It is with particular regret I must decline
- I regret we will be unable to attend
- I'd like to express my sincere regrets

RELATIONSHIP
- I hope we'll always have a close, loving relationship
- Let's make this relationship permanent
- Always deepening your relationship
- Now that we have such a wonderful working relationship

RECOGNITION
- Equal recognition for all involved is well deserved
- It took a lot of time and effort to reach this kind of recognition
- What a perfect recognition of your outstanding contribution

REMEMBER
- Helped make it something we'll

remember forever
- We will always remember what you have so kindly done
- Thank you for remembering
- You always remember the important things
- Each time I remember, it brings a smile
- I want to say something that will be remembered long after this occasion is over
- You are remembered
- How thoughtful of you to remember in such a special way
- It was so good of you to remember

RESPECT
- To communicate our great respect for
- Deeply respected, professionally and personally
- Respected as a consummate artist at what you do
- I want you to know how much I respect you
- Won the respect of all who work with you

RESPONSE
- I really appreciate your prompt response
- Thank you for your candid response
- Thank you for your compassionate response
- Thank you for your quick response
- Want to thank you for your great response
- I was really touched by the enthusiastic response
- Your fast, on-the-scene response was genuinely appreciated
- The depth of response has been remarkable
- Thank you for your diligent response

RESPONSIBILITY
- One of my primary responsibilities is to thank you warmly
- Must salute the large responsibilities you have volunteered to take on
- Taking on new responsibilities for your community
- A time to reflect on our ongoing responsibility
- Demonstrating a strong sense of responsibility

SERVICE
- A free service for you and your family to enjoy
- Savings on service you might need in the future
- Avail yourself of this service
- A low price that still gives you personal service
- We offer services to the general public
- I'm very impressed with the services you offer

SHARE
- That's one memory we will always share
- It was truly a joy to share
- I can't wait to share this day with you
- I look forward to sharing a very special evening
- It meant a lot to have you share
- Thank you for sharing your wisdom and experience
- Work becomes a joy when shared by you

SHOUT
- You make us want to cheer and shout
- Shout your virtues from the rooftops
- Time to do a little shouting about you

SKILL
- You are making the best use possible of your skills
- Glad you have the opportunity to use your talents and skills in your new position
- Thanks for all your organizational skills

SMILE
- There's always room for a smile
- You make me smile just thinking about you
- We really appreciate your friendly smile
- With sleeves rolled up and smiles all around

SORRY
- You'll never be sorry
- Sorry! We'll be right back
- We're sorry for the mistake
- I'm so sorry to have to do this
- Sorry to take so long to congratulate you
- Sorry to learn of your recent troubles
- So sorry you couldn't share our day

SPEAK

- Thank you for speaking out so powerfully and effectively
- Thank you for having the courage to speak out publically
- Thanks for daring to speak up in support
- You are speaking our language
- Thank you for taking the time to speak to me so kindly
- I appreciate the opportunity to speak with you personally

SPECIAL

- So nice to be thought of in a very special way
- Acknowledge a very special relationship
- You are a very special person
- You are very special to us
- Let it be known you are special
- You are part of a very special group
- It really means something special to me
- Love and special strength sustains you
- Reflect on the special times we have spent together

SPIRIT

- How comforting to know you are always with us in spirit
- Your actions spring straight from the spirit
- Always admire your strong and soaring spirit

SPONSOR

- And now a word about our sponsor
- Please visit our sponsors
- I am very honored to sponsor
- I couldn't have handpicked a better sponsor
- A huge thank you to our loyal sponsors
- Thanks to our conference sponsors
- We'd like to thank our sponsors for their generosity
- Thank you for being our sponsor

STAFF

- I would like to take this opportunity to commend your staff
- I want to compliment your staff for their superb effort
- Please pass on our thanks to all your friendly staff
- Thank you and your staff for working so hard
- The efficiency with which your staff worked was truly memorable
- Your staff was very professional and friendly
- Your cheerful, efficient staff contributed so much
- Comforted by the efforts of your staff
- A terrific addition to our staff
- I would like to express my appreciation for the kindness and consideration of your staff

STAY

- So glad you chose to stay
- Your excellent hospitality made our stay very pleasant
- If you are ever in our area, please feel welcome to stay with us
- Thank you so much for our wonderful stay
- Thanks so much for making our stay such an enjoyable one
- We thoroughly enjoyed our stay
- Thank you for the kindness extended to me during my recent stay
- One more time I thank you for our lovely stay
- Your staying power

STORY

- We have many delightful stories to tell
- Your success is a story in itself
- We would love to hear all your stories

SUCCESS

- You have made this project such a big success
- You played a big part in creating this smashing success
- Your help ultimately resulted in success
- Thanks to everyone who helped make the weekend such a great success
- You have a secret formula for success
- I'm crowing about your level of success
- I have every confidence in your continued success
- You made the event an outstanding success
- Thanks for everything you did to make this such a resounding success
- Such a great success

SUGGESTION

- Your ideas and suggestions are greatly appreciated
- Thank you for your comments and suggestions
- Thank your for your creative suggestions
- Your suggestion made such a difference

SUPPORT

- You are always willing to offer support when you can
- Thank you so very much for your continued support
- Any time of the day or night when we need support
- Would like to thank those people and organizations for your support
- Thank you for your advice and support
- You are tremendous source of support and solace
- Our community would like to thank those people and organizations for their support
- Thank for your continuing support of our fundraising activities
- I wish to thank everyone for their support and kind words
- I would like to thank you for all the support and compassion you extended
- The respect and support you share
- Thanks for your support
- In facing such a challenge, your support has been invaluable
- Receiving your support was terrific
- Thank you for your beautiful gesture of support
- Your support means a great deal to me
- Happy to give you our wholehearted support
- Thank you for your comfort and support in my time of trouble
- Thank you for your generous cooperation and support
- Thank you to our foundation support
- Thanks to everyone who helped and supported
- You continually strength our support network
- Really appreciate your ongoing support

SURPRISE

- I have been very pleasantly surprised
- What a wonderful surprise greeted me

- Imagine our surprise
- Your success is certainly no surprise to us
- Each day brings new discoveries and surprises
- Surprised and delighted

TALENT

- Offering the talent and capabilities that so clearly demonstrate
- You certainly have the talent for finding unique things
- And now your talents shine even more brightly
- Always seeking new talent to enhance
- Your talent and genius produced something magical

TALK

- Thanks so much for talking to me today
- I look forward to talking with you further
- I appreciated the opportunity to talk directly to you
- I look forward to talking with you again
- Thank you for talking to me in response to my inquiry
- Thank you for talking to me so kindly

TEAM

- Can always count on team support
- Delighted that the team accomplished so much
- Your team was very disciplined and professional
- You fit so beautifully as a member of our team
- You are such an asset to our team

THANK YOU

- A big thank you to all
- A resounding thank you for
- A special thank you just for you
- A really big thank you is needed here
- A little thank you note to
- Oh, thank you
- Thank you for your patience
- Our way of saying thank you
- Thank you for allowing us access
- Thank you for checking us out
- Thank you for coming
- Thank you for answering so soon
- Thank you for applying
- Thank you forever

- Thank you for your business
- Thank you for your patience
- Thank you for your patient response to my questions
- Thank you once again for
- Thank you for your feedback
- Thank you all
- Thank you for your correspondence
- Thank you for this shot of realism
- Thank you for fanning the flame
- Thank you to everyone who sent a message
- Thank you for making us your first choice
- Thank you for your order
- Extend a heartfelt thank you from all of us
- There are many ways to say thanks you, none of them adequate
- We send a deeply felt thank you to
- Thank you for the pleasant evening
- We have what they'll thank you for
- Welcome and thank you so much for
- You've done so much, I hardly know how to thank you
- Thank you for not giving up in the face of overwhelming odds
- What a difference a simple "thank you" makes

THANK

- But first, I have to thank so many of you
- I wanted to thank you as soon as possible
- I just can't thank you enough
- I want to thank you and stay in touch
- I want to publically thank
- I do so want to thank all of you
- I wish to thank everyone who has contributed
- I want to thank some specific people for their help
- I want to thank each and every one of you
- Just wanted to thank everyone who has written in and provided insight
- Most of all, I want to thank
- Once again, I have to thank you for
- Thanking all who have helped and contributed
- How can I ever thank you for all you've done for me
- The first order of business is to thank
- We would like to thank the following people
- We're thanking our loyal customers with this fabulous, limited-time offer
- Your family will thank you
- Just wanted to take a minute to thank you
- I don't know what I can do to thank you enough
- No one grows tired of being thanked

THANKFUL

- I am so thankful for people like you
- If there's one thing for which we can be thankful
- One thing for which we are abundantly thankful
- Thankful not for what you have in your wallet but what you have in your heart
- There's always something to be thankful for
- Deeply thankful for all the good things we have
- Thankful we are living in a country where

THANKFULNESS

- Thinking of you, I am filled with thankfulness
- Thankfulness knows no bounds
- Overflowing with thankfulness

THANKS

- Please convey my profound thanks to all
- Thanks for sinking your teeth into this
- A special thanks to all our clients
- A big, big thanks
- Thanks for too much to count
- A personal thanks
- Thanks for being so upfront
- A quick note of thanks
- Thanks for the memory
- A shower of thanks
- A cartload of thanks
- A truckload of thanks
- As a small token of our thanks
- Bags full of thanks
- Bottomless thanks
- Bursting with thanks
- But thanks to all of you
- Extra special thanks
- First, let me send my heartfelt thanks
- Give more than thanks
- Heaps of thanks
- Thanks for helping recapture the magic

- Heart deep thanks
- I'm sending my thanks just for you
- Sending my special thanks to those who
- It's our way of saying thanks for being a customer
- It's thanks to you and yours that
- It's our way of showing thanks for
- Just our way of saying thanks
- Just a quick word of thanks
- Just wanted to say thanks
- Many thanks to you
- My heart goes out to you in thanks
- Our company thanks you
- Saying thanks is very special to me
- So worthy of thanks
- So long! And thanks
- Special thanks go out to each one
- Special thanks go out across the board
- Thank for giving your all
- Thanks to our product, you never have to
- Thanks for the valuable information
- Thanks so much for taking the time to
- Thanks for sharing
- Thanks for giving me a hand
- Thanks very much
- Thanks for being such a big help
- Thanks a bunch
- Thanks a million
- Thanks again for the chance to
- Thanks to our crew for
- Thanks for putting me back togther
- Thanks for being one of the good guys
- Thanks for the giggle
- Thanks for being so cool
- Thanks for being a true friend
- Thanks and good wishes
- Thanks for the idea
- Thanks a lot
- Thanks a heap
- Thanks for doing your very best
- Thanks for making so much possible
- Thanks for taking the time to
- Thanks for taking a moment to
- Thanks for stopping by
- Thanks to all who helped
- Thanks for the idea
- Giving thanks for all that we have
- Thanks is going out to all those who
- Thanks for the visit
- Thanks for life
- Thanks for a wonderful, enriching experience
- Thanks for the fascinating discussion
- Thanks to all who worked so hard
- Thanks to all our partners and sponsors
- Thanks for allowing this event
- Thanks, but no thanks
- Thanks for rescuing us
- Thanks be to
- Thanks for the smash hit
- Thanks again for a great time
- Thanks for signing up
- Thanks for the ride
- Thanks for everything
- Thanks a lot, man
- Thanks for the magic
- Thanks to all participants
- Thanks for sharing your observations
- Thanks again for choosing us
- Thanks to all those who have been active
- Thanks for the help everyone has given
- Thanks for letting me join in
- Thanks to you
- Thanks to the person who did the original work
- My heartfelt thanks to you
- Thanks to new technological advances
- Thanks for lending a sympathetic ear
- Thanks for your deeply valued business
- Thanks to you
- Thanks for putting a smile on so many faces
- Here's a world of thanks
- Thanks! Come back soon
- Thanks! You really made my day
- The list of thanks is in chronological order
- Very many thanks
- Many thanks for looking after us so well
- Way cool thanks
- We owe a great big thanks to
- We've made it big, thanks to you
- With thanks this week to
- You deserve so many thanks for
- You inspire sincere and grateful thanks
- Let us give thanks
- Thanks for making all the pieces fall into place
- I would like to extend my sincere thanks
- We can never say thanks often enough
- More thanks than words can ever say
- Thanks for everything

THINK

- Thank you so much for thinking of me
- You really made me stop and think

- I want you to know I'm thinking of you
- Always prodding us to think and learn
- When I think of you, I think of laughter
- Thank you for thinking of us
- I think of you a lot
- Thanks for thinking of us today
- I think of you especially at this time
- I was thinking of you the other day

THOUGHT

- I so enjoyed hearing your thoughts and ideas
- Thanks for your unique creative thoughts
- I wanted to share these thoughts with you
- With just a little extra thought, you give so much
- Our fondest thoughts are with you
- Thanks and warmest thoughts
- You are never far from our thoughts
- You are so often in our thoughts
- Comments were well thought out and clearly articulated
- Thank you so much to all who sent positive thoughts
- Special thoughts go out to you
- Warm thoughts are with you

THOUGHTFUL

- One of the brightest, thoughtful, most conscientious people I know
- A pleasant and thoughtful person
- Thoughtful people say thanks in a thoughtful way
- Thoughtful enough to carefully evaluate the issues

THOUGHTFULNESS

- Again, our thanks for your thoughtfulness
- I will think of you and remember your thoughtfulness
- Thanks to your kind thoughtfulness
- I'll always remember your thoughtfulness

THRILL

- I'm thrilled to be able to tell you
- I feel absolutely thrilled that
- I'm so thrilled for you
- We are thrilled that you are here at last

TIME

- I really appreciate that you took the time
- Thanks for taking the time to talk to me
- I thank you most sincerely for your time, energy and enthusiasm
- Thank you for taking time out of your busy day
- Your gift of time and of yourself
- I would like to thank all the people who gave so much of their time
- We had the best time
- I know this is an important time for you
- This must be a tough time for you
- This is a time to cherish
- One more time, thanks
- Cannot recall a time when you haven't been there
- Before too much time has gone by
- A great time was had by all
- This is a good time to look ahead
- Thank you for your cheerful support through good times and tough ones
- This is such a meaningful time
- Though times were not always easy
- It's always a treat to spend time with you
- You obviously took a lot of time and trouble to
- Looking forward to spending some time together
- Thank you for your time and consideration
- Thank you for taking time from you busy schedule
- Thank you for your time
- Grateful for your time and careful preparation

TOGETHER

- Working together, we are unbeatable
- Thanks for pulling it all together
- Together, we did it

TOKEN

- Presented with the following token of our thanks
- I want to give you this small token of our appreciation
- This small token cannot begin to show our gratitude

TOUCH

- I am so touched and grateful
- Appreciate all the nice touches you added
- Thanks for adding that special touch
- Whatever you touch turns out right

- You seem to have the magic touch
- You added just the right touches
- You touched my life deeply
- I sincerely hope you will keep in touch
- Let's make a mutual effort to stay in touch
- Gratified and deeply touched by all the help
- Thanks for staying in touch

TRIBUTE
- Pays tribute to
- Paying tribute to fifty years of
- A real tribute to you
- A tribute to the virtues you stand for
- The entire program was a tribute to
- As a tribute to our customers we're offering
- We want to pay tribute to you with this
- A tribute to honor your loyalty and

See also: APPRECIATION, GIFT

UNDERSTANDING
- Thanks for being patient and understanding
- Thanks to you, I came away with a keener understanding
- Your comments gave me a good understanding
- Your understanding and support mean such a lot
- Your excellent approach enhanced our understanding
- I deeply appreciated your understanding
- Thank you for your assistance and understanding
- My sincere thanks for your understanding

VENTURE
- You have devoted a significant portion of your time to this venture
- You gave us the courage to venture out
- You made this venture possible

VISIT
- You are the main reason we think of our visit so fondly
- Thank you very much for visiting us on the Web
- Thanks to all of you who came to visit
- Thank you for visiting our online store
- Your visit was like a shot in the arm

- Thanks for making my visit so memorable
- We so enjoyed your visit
- I always enjoy your lively visits
- Your visit was a most enjoyable one
- Your visit brought big changes here

VOICE
- I would like to add my voice to the many others who support your position
- Together, our combined voices have a powerful effect
- Thanks for standing up for our right to a voice

VOLUNTEER
- Our volunteers are the best in the world
- A volunteer like you doesn't come along every day
- With volunteers like you, we'll always come through
- You're the star on volunteer appreciation day
- Thank you for so generously volunteering your time and knowledge
- Thanks to everyone who so graciously volunteered
- Always among the first to volunteer
- Thank you for volunteering so much
- Thank you to our members and volunteers
- You always step up to volunteer

WAIT
- I can't wait to come back
- Finally, all the waiting is over
- Waiting for someone like you to come along
- Now that you are here, the waiting is over
- We can't wait to express our gratitude

WAY
- The world's best way to say thank you
- The ideal way to express your thanks and appreciation
- Only one of thousands of ways to say thanks
- Now you are really on your way
- The beauty of your gentle, caring ways
- Always something special about the way you do it
- Thanks for going out of your way to help

- You showed us the way
- Thanks for being there along the way

WELCOME

- We welcome the opportunity to
- Thank you for making me feel welcome
- Thanks for your very warm welcome
- Your welcome still warms my heart

WISH

- Wishing you all the very best
- Warmest wishes are coming your way
- May your fondest wishes come true
- I wish you all the best
- I only wish you could have been there to see
- I wish you all success in your endeavours
- Your good wishes are my reward
- Sending you my best wishes
- I want to express my personal good wishes
- I sincerely wish you well in your future plans and enterprises
- I wish I could have been there to see
- How I wish we could be present

WITHOUT

- What would we do without you
- Without you, we couldn't have done it
- I never want to try it without you
- Can't imagine life without you
- Our team wouldn't have been a team without you

WONDERFUL

- It's wonderful to be spoiled for a while
- Thanks for being truly wonderful
- I know we will have a wonderful time
- You are truly wonderful
- People still tell me what a wonderful time they had
- Because of you, it really is a wonderful world

WORD

- There are no words to express what you have done for us
- Thank you for being absolutely true to your word
- You are never at a loss for words
- In facing such a debt of gratitude, I am lost for words
- Thank you for your always thoughtful and comforting words
- It's easy to find words to
- It's very hard to find the words to express
- Words fail me now
- Sincere words express something significant
- A few sincere words can have so much impact
- Even though I'm not good with words
- Your caring words made all the difference
- Thank you for your encouraging words
- Your kind words helped me cope

WORK

- So that all this hard work will not be in vain
- I know how hard you worked to make this happen
- You have always been so supportive of our work
- Thanks for working under near impossible conditions
- I look forward to working with you again
- Keep up the good work
- Your intervention enabled all of us to work together effectively
- Thanks to you, work is proceeding ahead of schedule
- Expressed great interest in working with you
- Look forward to continuing to work with you
- A work of the heart is a work of art
- Working with you makes the day fly by
- Your hard work makes everything so easy for us
- Thank you very much for your excellent work
- Without your hard work we would never have finished in time
- We really count on such help as yours
- I know it was not an easy environment to work in
- You were terrific to work with

WORLD

- Bravely facing a world full of challenges
- You make the world a little better
- The world is better for having you in it
- I believe you really will change the world

WRITE

- It's about time I wrote to thank you
- The desire to write about this in a personal way
- I wish I could write something clever
- It's hard to write when every word means so much
- Thanks for writing to me out of the blue
- Thank you again for writing
- I know I don't always take the time to write
- Though I've thanked you in person, I just had to write as well

YEAR

- Some of the most exciting and productive years of my life
- I hope each of you has a fantastic year
- What a great year we've had because of you
- I hope the next year brings you even more success
- Here's to another great year
- This is a very special time of year
- It's that time of year again
- Look forward to many more wonderful years together
- The years have passed so quickly
- A thanks that lasts all year
- Finally, the culmination of years of planning
- I can't tell you what the past years have meant to me
- I look forward to sharing another wonderful year with you
- Looking forward to doing it again next year

Section Six

Saying No

ABLE
- Sorry, I won't be able to
- At this point in time, our staff is not able to accommodate your request
- Really wish I was able to help you out
- Already doing more than we are able

ACCEPT
- Far too expensive for me to accept
- Much I would love to accept this honor
- Regretfully, I am unable to accept

ACCOMMODATE
- Just can't accommodate you
- Schedule won't accommodate another addition
- Much as we would love to accommodate you

ACKNOWLEDGE
- First, let me acknowledge everything we owe to you
- Though we acknowledge our debt, we must decline
- Acknowledge your needs in this area

ACTION
- Regret concerning this action is all the stronger because
- Certain actions are simply beyond the scope of
- Do not feel this action is the right one

See also: **COMMITMENT, PLAN**

AFFORD
- Can no longer afford to invest
- We can no longer afford such a luxury
- Doesn't afford us the freedom to

See also: **BUDGET, PAY**

AGREE
- Since we are unable to agree on this matter
- I'm sure you'll agree that it's impossible
- Whether or not you agree with our final decision

See also: **DECIDE, JOIN**

ALTERNATIVE
- Glad to help you find out what the alternatives are
- Be more than happy to suggest some viable alternatives
- Ask that you find an alternative source
- You might consider alternative action soon

Alternative: selection, choice, option, pick, preference, substitute, other choice, backup
See also: **CHOICE, OPTION**

APOLOGIZE
- We apologize for the inconvenience
- First, let me apologize
- Apologize for saying no at this late date
- We can only apologize for our position at this time

APOLOGY
- Express personal apologies and regrets
- Though a simple apology may not be enough
- Decline with many regrets and apologies

APPOINTMENT
- Have a previously scheduled appointment on that date
- As the two appointments conflict, I must cancel yours
- Do not have an appointment time available that week

See also: **BOOK, CONFLICT**

APPROPRIATE
- Just wouldn't be appropriate
- Far more appropriate for you to do it
- Appropriately chastened by my inability to include you at this time
- Happy to point you in a more appropriate direction

See also: **CORRECT, JUSTICE, RIGHT**

ASK
- Thank you for asking, but
- Have you thought about asking someone else
- Cannot do what you ask at this time
- Why not ask another party instead
- How very kind of you to have asked
- How I wish you had asked a day earlier
- Please don't ask for something I don't want to do

See also: **NEED, REQUEST**

AVAILABLE
- Sorry, I'm not available that evening

- Really wish I was available to help
- That item is no longer available
- Please accept a substitute for an item that is not available

Available: accessible, handy, usable, attainable, at one's command, at one's fingertips, ready, present, obtainable, on call, at one's disposal, reachable, at hand, on tap, convenient
See also: CONVENIENT, FREE

BACK

- Be okay if I get back to you later
- Let me check my calendar and get back to you
- Wish I could back you in this
- We realize that now is a very bad time to back away

See also: RETURN, WITHDRAW

BELIEF

- That goes against our beliefs
- Belief in eventual success is just not strong enough
- Must stand by my beliefs and decline participation
- Since you operate with an entirely different set of beliefs

See also: CONCERN, GOAL, IDEA, POLICY, POSITION

BENEFICIAL

- Not so beneficial as I had originally thought
- The hard decision will be most beneficial to you in the end
- Our participation would not be beneficial

BEST

- Think it best to pursue our interests elsewhere
- It's best if we don't do it now
- A parting of the ways is best for both of us
- Not the best course to consider at this time

BETTER

- Cannot help but feel there is a better way
- You will have better prospects elsewhere
- Will clearly do better elsewhere
- This is not the better choice

BOOK

- Unfortunately, I'm already booked
- Wish you had tried to book me sooner
- Booked too far ahead to give you a date
- Not a single booking space available

See also: BUSY, SCHEDULE

BUDGET

- Operating on a very tight budget that does not allow
- Current budget constraints make it impossible
- Afraid our budget can't stretch that far

See also: FUNDS, PAY

BUSY

- Afraid I'm busy that day
- Much too busy to take on one more chore
- Never dreamed I'd be so busy I'd have to say no
- And we're going to get busier still

Busy: engaged, occupied, on duty, working, involved, tied up, employed, preoccupied, diverted
See also: ACTION, BOOK, CONFLICT, SCHEDULE, STRETCH

CAN'T

- I'm afraid I can't
- Realistically, I can't
- It's not often we say we can't do it
- Sometimes, we just can't live up to expectations

See also: REFUSE, UNABLE

CANCEL

- Regretfully, I must cancel the arrangements
- Cancelling at such a late date is not usual
- Cancel our sponsorship of this program

Cancel: withdraw, void, annul, quash, vacate, discharge, erase, nullify, cease, override, overrule, discontinue, negate, stop, break off, countermand, veto, revoke, rescind, recall, renounce, take back, disclaim, reverse, abrogate, disown, deny, retract, abnegate, relinquish, defect, back pedal, back track, neutralize, offset, make up for, write off, clear, eliminate, wipe the slate clean, absolve
See also: CAN'T, DECLINE, REFUSE, WITHDRAW

CANCELLATION
- Requesting a cancellation and a refund
- The cancellation was simply unavoidable
- I realize a cancellation at this late date is very inconvenient

CANDID
- It's time to be candid
- After a candid assessment of the situation, I can no longer continue
- The candid answer is no
- Let me be perfectly candid with you

See also: HONEST

CHANCE
- May I have another chance later
- Thank you for giving me this chance, even though I can't do it now
- Just cannot take such a chance
- Chances are, this course of action is unlikely to succeed

See also: OPPORTUNITY

CHANGE
- Looks as though we need to make a change
- I'm afraid a change of plan is necessary
- You understand that sometimes painful changes must be made

See also: ALTERNATIVE, DIFFERENCE

CHOICE
- Feel I have no choice but to
- Have no choice to find an alternate source
- All other choices have been cut off
- This tempting choice is not open to us

See also: ALTERNATIVE, OPTION

CLAIM
- Your claim is in error
- Other duties claim me
- After much examination, you claim is invalid
- With so many claims upon me, I must refuse

Claim: demand, challenge, right, assertion, birthright, due, appeal, petition, plea, entreaty, title, stake, interest

CIRCUMSTANCES
- Personal circumstances make it impossible
- If only circumstances were different
- Due to a most unfortunate set of circumstances
- Never thought we'd find ourselves in such circumstances

See also: CONDITION, POSITION, SITUATION

COMMIT
- I'm really over-committed this week
- It wouldn't be fair to you to commit
- Can't commit to this particular arrangement
- Already have far too many commitments to take this on

See also: PROMISE

COMMITMENT
- I don't have time for a formal commitment
- Can't take on the commitment right now
- Have far too many other commitments at the moment
- Unable to provide the required commitment level
- Suffering from over-commitment now
- Have commitment overload this month
- Have a prior commitment I cannot break

Commitment: assignment, authorization, pledge, assurance, obligation, responsibility, warrant, guarantee, word, promise, mission, task, job

See also: GOAL, PRIORITY, PROMISE

COMMON
- We have plenty of other things in common
- Though we have common interests, we cannot take common action
- We no longer support a common cause
- No longer have this objective in common

CONCERN
- I was very concerned to receive
- Have many concerns about this plan
- I know how much you are concerned about this
- Concerned by the impossible timeline

CONDITION
- These conditions are unacceptable
- Do not find the conditions to our liking

- Cannot agree under those conditions

CONFIDENCE
- Flattered by your confidence in me, but
- Have confidence you will understand our reluctance
- Have lost confidence in your ability to
- Out confidence is no longer firmly fixed in this project

See also: STRENGTH

CONFLICT
- Unfortunately, there is a conflict with another commitment
- Regret the conflict in scheduling
- Unable to overcome such a stubborn conflict
- A conflict our best efforts cannot resolve

Conflict: clash, disagree, discord, contest, contend, discord, jar, oppose, contradict, diverge, feud, collision, battle, struggle, lock horns, squabble, wrangle, at variance, at odds, differ

CONSIDER
- Considering the potential damage, we must decline
- Cannot possibly consider it at this time
- Would like to consider another course of action
- Now is not the right time to consider this

See also: PLAN, THINK

CONSIDERATION
- Unable to give favorable consideration
- My decision is based on personal considerations
- After much consideration, we must turn this down

CONVENIENT
- It's just not convenient
- Perhaps at some other, more convenient time
- Unfortunately, there is no convenient time
- I'm sure you'll find a more convenient choice

See also: AVAILABLE

CORRECT
- Having failed to correct the situation
- Feel the correct action is no action
- More of the same will not correct this problem

See also: CHANGE, RIGHT

COST
- The costs are out of line with the results
- The cost does not justify the action
- Will cost too much for us to commit

See also: EXPENSE, PAY

COUNT
- Know you can always count on me, but
- I'm afraid you'll have to count me out
- I know how much you were counting on this
- Down for the count

DEADLINE
- The deadline will soon be here
- Can no longer meet such unrealistic deadlines
- Deadlines are too tight to allow this project
- With deadlines rushing upon us, we must bow out of this one

See also: SCHEDULE, STRESS, STRETCH, TIMING

DECIDE
- I need time to think about it before I decide
- Ultimately, I have decided against participating
- Though it was very hard to decide, we must step away

See also: CONSIDER, PLAN, THINK

DECISION
- My decision is based on personal considerations
- This decision is not intended to reflect adversely
- Particularly dismayed at the decision
- Please remember this is only one decision

See also: CHOICE, OPTION

DECLINE
- Must respectfully decline
- My decision to decline is motivated by
- It is with particular regret I must decline
- The benefits seems to be in decline

See also: NO, PASS, REFUSE,

WITHDRAW

DIFFERENCE
- These differences only make us more dynamic – and incompatible with you
- Prevented by a strong difference of opinion
- The differences are just too great
- Since we have, to date, failed to work out our differences

See also: CHANGE, DISAGREE, STRETCH

DIFFICULTY
- A previously unsuspected difficulty has appeared
- After assessing the difficulties, we regret we are unable to take this on
- Simply too many unforeseen difficulties in the way

DISAGREE
- Much as I hate to disagree
- It just disagrees with me
- I can't disagree that you really need help

See also: CONFLICT, DIFFERENCE

DISCONTINUE
- Sadly, the day has come when we must discontinue
- Changed circumstances force us to discontinue
- Wish to discontinue immediately

DISCOVER
- Have unfortunately discovered I am not cut out for this
- Upon discovering new information, we must alter our position
- Discover we are not suited to be partners

See also: FIND

DUTY
- It is my unfortunate duty to inform you
- Have too many duties
- Wish I could take on this duty
- Not equipped to assume such an awesome duty
- I wouldn't be doing my duty if I agreed to such a contract

EARLY
- If only you had let me know earlier
- Far too early to make such a commitment
- Telling you of our decision as early as possible
- It's early days for such a big leap into the unknown

EMERGENCY
- An unexpected emergency has forced cancellation
- Only in an emergency like this would I refuse
- In this emergency, all obligations must be waived

Emergency: crisis, urgency, accident, pinch, extremity, juncture, exigency, unforeseen circumstance, difficulty, mess, fix, bind, squeeze, straits, pass, hot water, pickle, crunch, plight, dilemma, perplexity, impasse, predicament, corner, imbroglio, hole, stew

See also: MESS, SQUEEZE, STRETCH

ENJOY
- Would have enjoyed it so much
- Can enjoy this at another date
- Know you'll enjoy working with someone else instead
- Sorry to miss something that promises to be so enjoyable

ENSURE
- Must ensure this does not happen again
- In order to ensure fair treatment to all
- Can no longer ensure complete safety for everyone

EXPENSE
- Expenses are mounting up at an unacceptable speed
- In light of our recent budget, we can no longer justify the expense
- The rising expenses are just too much for us right now
- Can no longer afford so many extra expenses

See also: COST, PAY

FAIR
- Wouldn't be fair to take that on
- This arrangement is not fair to either of us
- In order to be fair, we will not enter
- **See also: CORRECT, JUSTICE, RIGHT**

FAMILY
- It's just with family this time
- My family is my priority
- Family obligations have to come first
- Family commitments and illness make it impossible

FAREWELL
- Fond farewell has to be said
- There always comes a time for farewell
- Let's make this a warm farewell

Farewell: goodbye, aloha, so long, sayonara, bon voyage, swan song, adieu, departure
See also: **PART, WITHDRAW**

FEEL
- Don't feel I'd be able to
- Sorry you feel that way
- Sorry, I just don't feel right about doing this
- Feel very badly about this impasse

Feel: sense, intuit, have a hunch, feel in one's bones, perceive, know, understand, note, discern, sympathize, commiserate, comprehend
See also: **KNOW, UNDERSTAND**

FIND
- Have to find someone else this time
- Find it impossible to
- Must ask that you find another person to fulfil these duties
- Much as I wish I could help, I cannot find the time to take on this additional commitment

See also: **DISCOVER**

FIT
- Just can't fit you in at this late date
- Really wish we could fit you in
- No longer fitting that
- Is not a fit for us any more

See also: **CORRECT, RIGHT**

FOND
- I'm not really fond of
- Must part on a fond note
- Too fond of you to do this

FREE
- The first was free but now there is a fee
- Can no longer provide this service for free
- Will not be free on the day you have designated

See also: **AVAILABLE**

FUNCTION
- With regret, I conclude I can no longer function as
- Will not function as desired
- Our function here is over
- This arrangement cannot function to everyone's satisfaction

FUNDS
- Simply do not have any funds to spare
- Seeking only a sound investment of funds
- Experiencing difficulty raising the necessary funds

See also: **AFFORD, BUDGET, PAY**

GIVE
- Cannot give more than one hour to this project
- More than we can give at this time
- Have already given our maximum

GOAL
- Must say no in order to pursue other goals
- Is not included in this year's goals
- Our goals are no longer mutual

See also: **COMMITMENT, INTEREST, NEED, PRIORITY, PROJECT**

HAND
- Really like to lend a hand, but
- Our hands are tied in this matter
- Many other hands will reach out to help
- Have none on hand at the moment

See also: **AVAILABLE, HELP**

HAPPY
- I'd be so happy to do this for you, but
- Will be very happy to assist you another time
- Happy to direct to someone equally skilled

HELP
- I'd love to help but I don't have the time
- Really wish I could help you
- Really hate to refuse such basic help

Help: assist, aid, accommodate, boost, oblige, pitch in, chip in, befriend, cooperate, lend a hand, endorse, maintain, join in, stick up for, stand by
See also: ASK, HAND

HONEST
- Now is the time to be honest with you
- I'm afraid this is very honest feedback
- Withdrawal is the only honest course of action
- The honest answer is no

See also: CANDID, FAIR, JUSTICE

IDEA
- Just not my idea of a fun project
- I know your idea is really great, but
- No way we can combine such opposing ideas
- Have to work hard to come up with another idea

IMPOSSIBLE
- It's absolutely impossible
- Now impossible to fulfil this longstanding agreement
- Proving impossible to continue
- Thank your for your inquiry, but we regret it is impossible to

Impossible: unthinkable, illogical, preposterous, contradictory, insoluble, unresolvable, inoperable, beyond one's power, incurable, intractable, impracticable, inaccessible, out of reach, unviable, insuperable, inadmissible
See also: CAN'T, INAPPROPRIATE, NO, UNABLE

INAPPROPRIATE
- It would be inappropriate to speculate
- Inappropriate at this time
- Not appropriate for us to interfere

Inappropriate: unsuitable, unfit, ill-adapted, uncongenial, out of keeping, unfair, inequitable, incongruous, inadvisable, out of character, disadvantageous, inexpedient, disproportionate, imprudent, untimely, impertinent, inopportune, out-of-bounds, out-of-line, out-of-order, untoward

INFORM
- It is with deep regret I must inform you

- Wish to inform you as soon as possible that we are declining
- Only fair to inform you of our contrary position

See also: NOTIFY, TALK, TELL

INITIATIVE
- Take the initiative in sorting this out
- Our new initiatives cannot include
- Taking the initiative in ending our long and fruitful association

INTEREST
- Deeply appreciate your interest
- In your best interests, I decline
- No thanks, I'm not interested
- Neither our interests nor yours are served here

See also: GOAL, PRIORITY, PROJECT

INTERPRETATION
- What surely must be an improper interpretation
- Our interpretations seem to differ markedly
- Afraid we have a completely different interpretation

INVITATION
- Sincerely hope you will favor me with another invitation in the future
- You invitation has arrived at an inopportune time
- This is one invitation I really hate to turn down

JOB
- Always sad when a job comes to an end
- Can no longer do such a demanding job
- It's a job for someone more skilled and daring
- Just not up to the job any more
- Other tasks prohibit me from doing an excellent job

See also: PARTICIPATION, WORK

JOIN
- Regret that I won't be able to join you
- Sadly unable to join in your new venture
- Would love nothing better than to join in
- Not everyone is able to join the enterprise

See also: PARTICIPATION

JUSTICE
- Don't feel I could do it justice
- Another colleague could do it greater justice
- Justice is not served by such an action
- In all justice, we just can't participate

Justice: fair play, equity, impartiality, neutrality, open-mindedness, evenness, fairness, propriety, honor, goodness, sincerity, frankness, legitimacy, lawfulness, validity, integrity, truth, probity
See also: CORRECT, FAIR, RIGHT

KNOW
- Feel you should know up front
- Want you to know as soon as possible about our decision
- Deep down, you know it is impossible
- Known for some time now that this will not work

See also: UNDERSTAND

LIKE
- Sorry, I don't particularly like that kind
- Cannot bring myself to like it
- Is not arranged to our liking
- Afraid we can't configure it your likng

LOVE
- Would really love to, but I can't
- We can't, but do you know who would love to
- Any other time we'd love a visit
- Much as I'd love it, other commitments intervene

MARCH
- Not quite marching to the same band
- No longer marching in step
- Our company is marching in a different direction

MARK
- Sometimes, we just can't come up to the mark
- The mark may be set a bit too high for us
- Mark us down for another day
- You certainly get high marks for trying

MATTER
- Ask that you attend to this matter immediately
- After giving the matter considerable thought, I must withdraw
- A very serious matter that can no longer be ignored

See also: CIRCUMSTANCES, PROBLEM, SITUATION

MIND
- I won't change my mind
- Need to change my mind about that
- Really hope you won't mind this sudden change
- Mind very much being unable to help

See also: REGRET

MINUTE
- Just don't have another minute to spare
- There aren't enough minutes in the day
- If only I had a few extra minutes, I could squeeze you in

See also: BOOK, SCHEDULE, TIMING

MISTAKE
- The mistake has been on our part
- Feel it would be a mistake to begin
- In order to prevent future mistakes
- A mistake even to think about doing this

Mistake: error, fallacy, flaw, fault, inaccuracy, omission, oversight, blunder, bungle, botch, boner, boo boo, screw-up, goof, blooper, clinker, misunderstanding, miscalculation, misconception, misjudgement
See also: PROBLEM, WRONG

NEED
- Must consider our own needs first
- Cannot fulfil your needs today
- Your needs are greater than our ability to meet them
- Not right for our needs

NO
- It's really tough to say no
- Really must say no this time round
- Much as I'd like to say yes, I must say no
- I've said no and I really mean it
- No, I really don't want to
- I know how much you'd like me to agree but I have to say no

No: not at all, by no means, no how, nothing of the kind, not so, not in the least, nowise, not by a long shot, in no case, not in a million years, by no stretch of the imagination, under no circumstances, in no way, shape or form, nothing doing, absolutely not, not on your life, certainly not, are you kidding, nay, negative, no-go

See also: DECLINE, REFUSE, WITHDRAW

NOTHING
- I know nothing can make up for
- Nothing would have pleased me more than to be able to help
- There's nothing for it but to say no

NOTIFY
- Undertaking now to notify you of this difficulty
- Will notify you in writing right away
- Notifying you of our regretful inability to participate

See also: INFORM, TELL

OBSTACLE
- Too many obstacles in our way
- An obstacle too large to overcome
- A much bigger obstacle than we had originally supposed

Obstacle: obstruction, barrier, hindrance, impediment, stumbling block, hurdle, snag, catch, drawback, jam, liability, fly in the ointment, *cul-de-sac*, congestion

See also: DIFFICULTY, PROBLEM, STALEMATE, WALL

OFFER
- At no time was any such offer made
- Must decline your fine offer
- Thank your for your offer, but we must refuse
- Must turn down your very kind offer

ON
- I've got so many things on
- Wouldn't want to take this on
- Time to move on to other ventures

OPINION
- We are experiencing a difference of opinion here
- We have a different opinion and must stick to it
- In my opinion, our involvement would

not be fruitful

See also: CONSIDERATION, IDEA, THINK

OPPORTUNITY
- Let's look at this opportunity together again later
- Regret to pass up such a great opportunity
- Hope you'll give us the opportunity to help another time
- How gratified I was to be offered such an opportunity even though I must refuse

See also: CHANCE, OPTION

OPTION
- That is no longer an option
- Is not one of our options this month
- Leaving you free to pursue other options
- Unable to choose this option

See also: ALTERNATIVE, CHOICE

OTHER
- So many other things I need to do
- Prevented by other commitments
- Other obligations claim me
- If only we didn't have other duties

PART
- Can no longer take part
- Do not wish to be a part of this program
- Really wish we could be part of this
- Must part after a long and profitable association

PARTICIPATION
- Our participation would not be beneficial at this stage
- Know you will go on successfully without our participation
- Unable to promise our participation for this coming year

PASS
- Thanks, but I'll have to pass
- Sorry to have pass up such a tempting opportunity
- Too bad we have to pass up such a great party
- We'll have to give it a pass

See also: DECLINE, NO, REFUSE

PAY
- Not financially able to pay

- The investment would not pay off
- Unable to pay such an excessive amount

See also: AFFORD, BUDGET, FUNDS

PERSON
- I'm not the best person to help you with this
- Another, more expert person, is who you need
- We have chosen a more qualified person
- There are many other persons more suitable to this job

PERSONAL
- Personal circumstances make it impossible for me to assume these duties
- This decision was not a personal choice
- Must go with my personal instincts

PLAN
- Not able to plan that far ahead just now
- Now that our plans have changed drastically
- New plans take us in an entirely different direction
- Thanks, but I already have a business growth plan
- Let's plan to make it possible next time

POLICY
- Your stipulation would be a violation of our policy
- Our policy just can't extend to cover this
- Though your request is a worthy one, it is not our policy to accept
- Our policy applies only to local organizations
- Had no idea of the new policy
- Have a policy about not lending money
- As I already said, it is our policy only to donate to

Policy: course of action, plan, strategy, game, custom, habit, way, tactics, protocol, utility

POSITION
- I am not in a position to cope
- No longer in a position to continue
- Our position has changed radically in recent months

PRIORITY
- Just committed to other priorities right

now
- Doesn't fit in with our current priorities
- Is not a priority in the coming season

See also: GOAL

PROBLEM
- Together, we can sort out this problem
- I really have a problem with that
- To solve this problem, we must acknowledge it
- Would like to clear up this problem at once
- You will not have a problem finding someone else
- May just make the problem worse

Problem: question, bone of contention, issue, dispute, point of dispute, maze, poser, mystery, puzzler, enigma, knot, stickler, conundrum, predicament

PROJECT
- Not taking on any more projects
- Couldn't really do the project justice
- This project just isn't for us
- Funding is limited to projects of known value
- Working on too many other projects at the moment

PROMISE
- Have already promised too much
- Cannot make a promise I will be unable to keep
- Promised to be elsewhere on that date
- Can't promise anything right now

See also: COMMITMENT, DECISION

RAINCHECK
- Afraid I must ask for a raincheck
- Look forward to claiming my raincheck soon
- This time I'll take a raincheck please

READY
- Just not ready yet
- Not ready to take so serious a step
- Feel you are ready to do it on your own
- Despite heroic efforts, we just can't be ready in time

RECOMMEND
- Let me recommend someone else

- Thank you for recommending me, but I unable to
- Very flattered that you recommended me, however

REFER

- Let me refer you to a colleague
- You were referred to us in error
- Be glad to refer you to someone else better fitted
- You are referring to a service we no longer provide

REFUSE

- Really hate to refuse, but
- Must refuse this one
- Sometimes, the only proper thing to do is to refuse

Refuse: reject, say no, thumbs sown, decline, pass up, abstain, abnegate, stand aloof, deny, forbid, not budge an inch, resist, nay say, repel, rebuff, prohibit, exclude, turn one's back, set one's face against, disallow, cast aside, disapprove, frown upon, keep back, begrudge, spurn, back off, back away
See also: DECLINE, NO, WITHDRAW

REGRET

- It is with great regret I must say no
- Really regret not being able to help out
- My regret is all the stronger

Regret: lament, deplore, rue, grieve, mourn, bemoan, miss, long for, sorrow, remorse, worry, pang, discontent, remorse, contriteness
See also: APOLOGY, SORRY

REQUEST

- Unfortunately, it is impossible to comply with your request
- Though your request is a worthy one
- The item you requested is not available
- You can imagine my shock at this request

See also: ASK, NEED

RESIGN

- Official notification of my intent to resign my position
- Due to personal circumstances, I have decided to resign
- The time has come to gracefully resign

See also: REFUSE

RESOLUTION

- Withholding payment pending satisfactory resolution of this problem
- Have voted in a resolution against it
- The resolution cannot be favorable to you
- The resolution involves a parting of ways

Resolution: conclusion, verdict, advance, solution, answer, end, result, point, issue, finding, outcome, upshot, unscrambling, cracking

RESOLVE

- See no way to resolve this conflict
- Must resolve it by ending the partnership
- Only with great difficulty can we resolve the problem

RESPECT

- Really respect your decision, but
- With the greatest respect, I beg to differ
- Out of respect to you, I want to be very clear

RESPONSE

- Since, to date, I have received no response
- The response had so far been quite unsatisfactory
- Our response must be negative

RESPONSIBLE

- Will no longer be responsible for charges incurred
- Not responsible for the outcome
- Not prepared to be responsible for so much

RETURN

- Unfortunately, I must return your gift
- In view of the diminishing returns, this cannot continue
- With many apologizes, I must return earlier than planned

RIGHT

- Not right for me any more
- The timing is not right
- Something is just not right about this option
- Telling you now is the right thing to do

See also: CORRECT, FAIR, JUSTICE

RISK
- Is too much of a risk right now
- Cannot justify the risk
- The risk is more than we can accommodate
- Can't risk my game for this action
- Don't want to risk my health

Risk: danger, hazard, liability, jeopardy, vulnerability, exposure, uncertainty, precariousness, unpredictability, leap in the dark, gamble, menace, threaten, engagement

ROOM
- Do not have room to store the item
- Just can't make any more room in our schedule
- Just don't have room to manoeuvre
- Really wish we had room for you

SCHEDULE
- Not scheduling anything new
- My schedule is already jam-packed
- I wish there were a spot free on my schedule
- Just too many conflicts already on our schedule

SHAME
- What a shame we can't do it
- Such a shame that you must refuse
- Cannot be shamed into doing it

SITUATION
- You will understand the difficult situation we're facing
- Another situation requires my full attention at this time
- Only a situation like this could force me to cancel
- This untenable situation has to change

See also: CONDITION, OPTION, PROBLEM

SOLUTION
- Can find no immediate solution
- This solution just doesn't work for us
- Please try to find an alternative solution
- Need a better solution to this
- Afraid we are not the solution you need for this
- The only solution is to cancel immediately

SORRY
- Very sorry to have to say no
- So sorry to refuse
- Sorry, but no thanks
- No one is sorrier than I to have to back out

See also: APOLOGY, REGRET

SOUND
- Doesn't sound like something that may be for me
- Feel the plan is not completely sound
- Don't want to sound negative, but I must say no

SQUEEZE
- Won't be able to squeeze this one in
- Really in a squeeze right now
- Already squeezing the most out of every minute

See also: EMERGENCY, STRETCH

STALEMATE
- Please do not view this as a stalemate
- It's the only way to break this unfortunate stalemate
- Looks as though we have arrived at a stalemate

Stalemate: deadlock, standstill, impasse, stop, halt, deathblow, checkmate, blockage, check, stand-off, draw, blind alley, perplexity, blockade, block, bar, thwart, dead heat, stay

See also: OBSTACLE, PROBLEM

STRESS
- Puts an unacceptable amount of stress on the system
- The stress is just too much
- We're already stressed to the max
- Cannot accommodate that amount of stress

STRETCH
- Stretched too much to accept your wonderful invitation
- Stretched beyond our maximum already
- Just can't stretch to include it
- Getting involved is too much of a stretch

STRONG
- Not one of my strong points
- Really not strong in that field

- Will be able to make a strong contribution without us

SUCCESS
- Really wish you success anyway
- Sure to be a great success without us
- Certain that success is already guaranteed

SUITABLE
- No longer suitable for our needs
- Not suitable for your requirements
- Cannot find a suitable replacement

See also: CORRECT, RIGHT

TALK
- Wish we could have talked about it earlier
- Unable to go beyond the talking stage
- Much has changed since we last talked about this

TASK
- Currently have three tasks waiting
- Unable to take on one more task
- Cannot do that task today
- That's a task for someone else

See also: COMMITMENT, JOB

TELL
- Let me tell you what I can do
- It's time to tell you the bad news
- Want to tell you as soon as possible that we can't

See also: INFORM

TERMINATE
- It is in our mutual benefit to terminate the agreement
- I am hereby terminating my contract with you
- At year end, we will be terminating this arrangement

Terminate: complete, conclude, end, finish, cease, discontinue, expire, wind up, run out, lapse, drop, abort, sign off

See also: FAREWELL, PART

THINK
- I don't think so right now
- No longer think this is necessary
- We don't think we can go along with this
- Don't think this proposal will work out

TIME
- It just isn't a good time right now
- This is not an okay time
- Tell you if I can spend time later
- Barely have time for my own commitments
- Time is really limited
- My time is already committed
- I just don't have the time to help
- Simply do no have any time to spare

TIMING
- Just a case of unfortunate timing
- If the timing weren't so bad for me
- Hope you will forgive the timing
- It all boils down to timing
- Afraid the timing is wrong

UNABLE
- Let you know we'll be unable to attend
- So sorry we are no longer able to
- I shall be away and unable to come

See also: IMPOSSIBLE

UNDERSTAND
- I know you'll understand
- Please understand how much we want to, even though we must refuse
- Not in a position to understand this way of doing things
- You understand why I must say no

See also: FEEL, KNOW

UNDERSTANDING
- Your understanding is deeply appreciated
- Our understanding has come to an end
- Understanding will go a long way here

UNEXPECTED
- I have been unexpectedly called out of town
- Too unexpected to be acted upon
- Something really unexpected has come up

Unexpected: unforeseen, sudden, unpredicted, unanticipated, unlooked-for, surprising, unusual, unintended, untimely, out-of-line

See also: EMERGENCY

VALUE
- I deeply value working with you
- I really value being asked

- This refusal in no way reflects upon your value
- Really hate to refuse such a valued customer

VIEW
- Opposing views are to be expected
- Differing views can sometimes create strong feelings
- In our view, a much different course is called for
- The view looks quite different from here

See also: OPINION

WALL
- Up against a stone wall here
- I'm afraid the wall is too high
- The walls are closing in on us
- We're looking at a wall without a door

See also: OBSTACLE

WARN
- We are constrained to warn you
- Must warn you of the coming termination
- Our last warning was a serious one
- Warn you that we are likely to be already fully booked

WISH
- Wish I couldn't but it's just not possible
- Truly wish I could help you out
- However, our best wishes will be with you
- Now matter how much we wish to help
- Only wish I could agree
- Wish this had never occurred

WITHDRAW
- Regret to inform you we must withdraw immediately
- Assume there will be no problem with this withdrawal
- Hard as it is to withdraw, we must do it soon
- So sorry to be forced to withdraw at this late date

WORK
- Doesn't work for me at this time
- Already working on some other things
- Just isn't working out
- I know you'll be able to work around this obstacle

- Work together to find suitable replacements

See also: FUNCTION, PARTICIPATION

WRONG
- Afraid you're asking the wrong person
- It would be wrong of me to commit
- Wrong to tell you I could
- Clearly, something has gone wrong somewhere
- Just the wrong place and the wrong time
- Really wish I were wrong about this

Wrong: incorrect, inaccurate, mistaken, amiss, imprecise, unfounded, abominable, dead wrong, whacko, misguided, wrong-headed, improper, unseemly, irrelevant, blunder, misstep, omission, lapse, abuse, transgress, cheat, slander, offend, trespass, insult, put down, amiss, out of whack

See also: IMPOSSIBLE, INAPPROPRIATE

Section Seven

Apology

ACCEPT
- Please accept our belated good wishes and sincere thanks
- Please accept our very sincere apology
- I hope you'll accept this very sheepish repentance

ACCEPTABLE
- Please let me know if this is acceptable
- Would really like to make an acceptable restitution
- Renewing our efforts to make our service truly acceptable

ACCIDENT
- You were very kind to say it was an accident
- I agree that this accident was entirely preventable
- In order to make up for this unfortunate accident

ACT
- I'm finally getting my act together
- Truly apologize for how I acted
- Acted in a very inappropriate manner
- There is no excuse for how I acted

See also: BEHAVIOR

AMENDS
- Tells us how we can make amends
- Make amends at your earliest convenience
- Making amend in the only way we know how

See also: FORGIVE, MAKE, SOLUTION

ANSWER
- Sorry I've taken so long to answer your letter
- Answer you in a more acceptable manner
- Certainly we don't always have all the answers
- Will keep at it until we find the right answer

See also: RESPOND

APOLOGIZE
- We apologize for the inconvenience
- Apologize for this regrettable incident
- Sorry, sorry, sorry – I apologize
- Just cannot apologize enough for this catastrophe
- I apologize for adding to your work
- We apologize for getting back to you so late
- How can I apologize more sincerely

Apologize: beg pardon, ask pardon, atone for, make up, regret, repent, make amends, lament, rue, eat humble pie, mitigate, palliate, extenuate, justify, excuse

See also: REGRET, SORRY

APOLOGY
- This is my apology in advance
- Please accept our apologies for our absence
- Express personal apologies and regrets to each
- A sincere apology is all I can offer
- You certainly deserve an apology
- I am enclosing my apologies
- A simple apology may not be enough
- I know an apology hardly makes up for my huge error
- Apologies for our absence
- I want to apologize for taking so long

Apology: expiation, confession, repentance, plea, defence, excuse, claim, advocacy, extenuation

ASSURE
- Assure you it will not happen again
- Rest assured that we will take care of the matter
- Hope you are now assured of our sincere intentions

ATTEND
- Sorry that I cannot attend
- Failed to let you know we would be unable to attend
- Unfortunately must attend another function

AWARE
- Really should have been more aware of the consequences
- Thank you for making us aware of this problem
- Now aware of how much I have offended
- Please be aware of how contrite I am

BEHAVIOR
- Such behavior is not in keeping with our

policies
- Deeply embarrassed by such uncouth behavior
- Want to apologize for my appalling behavior

See also: ACT

BETTER
- I promise to do better next time
- Really ought to have done better
- Feedback like yours helps us get better

CIRCUMSTANCES
- Explain the circumstances that caused us to disappoint you
- Circumstances refused to cooperate
- More than just a victim of circumstances

See also: SITUATION

COMPENSATE
- Know that nothing can compensate for the frustration and annoyance
- Hope we can compensate by
- Naturally, you will be fully compensated for this oversight

COMPLAINT
- We take every complaint very seriously
- Will act upon your complaint at once
- Have found your complaint a valid one

CONFIDENCE
- Make every effort to restore your confidence in us
- Deeply regret we did not live up the confidence you placed in us
- Let us show you your confidence has not been misplaced

CORRECT
- Will do whatever is necessary to correct the situation
- You observations were correct
- Expect the problem to be corrected very soon
- Please tell us what we can do to correct this error

See also: AMENDS, RIGHT

COUNT
- Count on us to make sure it will not happen again
- Hope I can still count you among my

dearest friends
- Counting the days until this is put right

CUSTOMER
- Without satisfied customers, our business would vanish
- What can we do to keep you as a valued customer
- As a customer, you are very, very important to us

DAMAGE
- I feel very bad about the damage
- We will repair any damage immediately
- Hope our reputation has not been damaged permanently in your eyes
- Scrambling to make amends, now that the damage has been done

See also: INCIDENT, PROBLEM, OVERSIGHT, SITUATION

DAY
- I realize we both have had a bad day
- Hope to make amends before the day is out
- Soon be able to forget this day ever happened
- Never thought a day like this could come

DECLINE
- As it is too late, we must decline
- At the last moment, I must decline
- So sorry to have to decline your kind invitation
- With deepest regrets, we are forced to decline

See also: APOLOGIZE, REGRET, SORRY

DELAY
- I apologize for the delay
- I know that delays caused much frustration
- So sorry for the unnecessary delay
- Promise there will be no such delays in the future

DIFFICULT
- At the moment, it will be difficult for me to do this
- This is a difficult but necessary letter to write
- Sometimes it is very difficult to admit we

are wrong
- I know I've made the situation more difficult for you

See also: PROBLEM

DISAPPOINT
- Would never intentionally disappoint you
- How disappointed you must feel
- I am as disappointed as you
- Want to apologize for a disappointing performance

DISAPPOINTMENT
- I share your disappointment
- Deeply regret your disappointment
- May you never suffer this kind of disappointment again
- So sorry to cause you disappointment

Disappointment: setback, failure, miscarriage, fiasco, shipwreck, defeat, letdown, disillusionment, chagrin, frustration, bitter pill, sorrow

See also: FRUSTRATION

DISMAY
- Imagine my dismay when I realized
- No wonder you were shocked and dismayed
- Dismay is the proper response
- News of the error caused great dismay

DISTRESS
- Particularly distressed when a customer feels we have failed to provide services promised
- I can certainly imagine your distress
- Deeply regret having caused you any distress

EMBARRASS
- You can't imagine how embarrassed I was to discover
- This is a very embarrassing letter to write
- I don't know which of us was the more embarrassed

EMBARRASSMENT
- Hope I have not caused you embarrassment
- Regret any embarrassment it may have caused
- Apologize for embarrassment to our community

ERROR
- Discovered I was indeed in error
- Mean to rectify the error as soon as possible
- Will do whatever we can to erase this shocking error
- Hope you will overlook this unfortunate error

See also: MISTAKE, OVERSIGHT

EXCUSE
- Although it was certainly no excuse
- I have no excuse to offer
- I beg you to excuse the offense
- Please accept out excuses

EXPECTATION
- Let us know should our product ever fail to meet your expectations again
- Regret that I was unable to meet your expectations
- You expectations were not too high

EXPENSE
- We will be happy to reimburse your out-of-pocket expenses
- Sorry you have been put to all this expense
- It seems expenses just got out of hand

EXPLAIN
- Will call tomorrow to explain the unfortunate train of circumstances
- Hope I can explain in a satisfactory manner
- Just can't explain what went wrong

EXPLANATION
- Really have no good explanation
- The explanation offered was not good enough
- Want to make sure you are given a full explanation

FEEL
- No wonder you felt let down
- Will continue until you feel the problem has been solved
- Feel certain we can do much better next time
- No one can feel more remorseful than

myself

FORGET
- Horrors! I completely forgot
- How could I have forgotten your birthday
- Really in the doghouse for forgetting
- Once again, I forgot
- Hope you will forget the incident ever took place
- I haven't forgotten you
- I have no excuse; I simply forgot

Forget: lose sight of, cease to remember, draw a blank, overlook, pass over, wink at, neglect, let alone, never mind, leave behind, omit, ignore, disregard, close the eyes too

FORGIVE
- Please forgive me for taking so long
- Very much hope you will forgive me
- Forgive me for being in such a hurry

Forgive: absolve, excuse, condone, overlook, make allowances for, pass over, look the other way, waive, indulge, let off the hook, cancel out, delete, erase, reprieve, wipe the slate clean, bury the hatchet, make peace, let bygones be bygones
See also: AMENDS, APOLOGY, RECONSIDER, REGRET, SORRY

FRUSTRATION
- I know nothing can make up for the frustration and time lost
- Hope you forgive us for all the frustration caused
- Your frustration was completely our fault
- No wonder you felt so very frustrated
See also: DISAPPOINTMENT, ERROR

GUILTY
- Feel guilty for having let this situation continue
- Look this way to see the guilty party
- Guilty as charged

Guilty: culpable, at fault, wrong, illicit, reproachable, blameworthy, amiss, contrite, red-handed, caught with one's hand in the cookie jar
See also: WRONG

HECTIC
- Things have really been hectic
- In the hectic rush, this vital detail has been overlooked
- Got lost in the hectic rush

HURT
- I can see why you might feel hurt
- Had no intention to hurt you in any way
- Unfortunately, some were hurt in the process
See also: DAMAGE. FRUSTRATION

INAPPROPRIATE
- Remarks were inappropriate and do not reflect our beliefs
- My behavior was completely inappropriate
- Quite inappropriate for that setting

INCIDENT
- Hope we can put this unfortunate incident behind us
- An incident that didn't need to happen
- Want no more incidents like this one
- Assure you such an incident will not happen again
See also: ACT, BEHAVIOR

INCONVENIENCE
- We apologize for any inconvenience
- The inconvenience was inexcusable
- Want to compensate you for the inconvenience suffered
- Sorry for the difficulties caused by this inconvenience

INQUIRY
- Certainly this matter warrants an inquiry
- According to our inquiries, your complaint is perfectly justified
- Assure you our inquiry will be timely and thorough

INTENTION
- My intentions were the best
- Realize that good intentions are not enough
- The best of intentions did not prevent this calamity
- It is our intention to rectify the deviation as soon as we can

KNOW
- I don't know what got into me

- If only we had known about the difficulty
- Really should have known better
- Didn't know it would come out this way

LUCK
- Just my luck that I must miss you
- Hope to turn this bad luck into good
- Determined to turn our luck around
- We admit this was more than just rotten luck

Luck: chance, serendipity, happenstance, fortune, lot, fate, fluke, contingency, accident, how the ball bounces, how the cookie crumbles

MAKE
- You must let me make it up to you
- Will do just about anything to make it better
- It's time to make amends

See also: AMENDS

MESS
- So sorry for my part in this mess
- I really messed up this time
- Will take care of this mess very speedily
- Promise to clean up this messy problem pronto

See also: EMBARRASSMENT, INCONVENIENCE, PROBLEM

MISTAKE
- Once again, I'm sorry for the mistake
- Hope you will forgive the mistake on my part
- Will attempt to rectify any mistakes

See also: ERROR, FRUSTRATION, OVERSIGHT

MISUNDERSTANDING
- Profoundly regret our recent misunderstanding
- Discover it has all be a sad misunderstanding
- So easy for misunderstanding to develop

NOTHING
- I know nothing can make up for
- Nothing I can say or do can erase
- Make sure all our efforts haven't been for nothing

Nothing: naught, none, diddly squat, no clue, nix, zilch, not a scrap, *nada,* no hint

OBLIGATION
- Fully recognize our obligation to
- Thank you for pointing out our obligation in this matter
- Now under even greater obligation to you

Obligation: necessity, promise, duty, requirement

OVERSIGHT
- Will correct this oversight at once
- I assure you this oversight was not intentional
- Hope you will forgive this oversight
- Please know that we are working to remedy this oversight at once
- To think, this all began with a perfectly innocent oversight

See also: APOLOGY, DAMAGE, ERROR, FORGIVE, GUILTY, REGRET, SORRY

PERSONAL
- Personally dispatched a staff member to look into the matter
- Cannot personally attest to
- Will take personal responsibility for this disaster

POINT
- You are quite right to point out
- So glad you pointed out the error
- Hope to turn thing around at this point
- Really has gone beyond the point of no return

PRIDE
- Take pride in our work and are particularly distressed when
- Until now we've taken great pride in our efficiency
- I can understand just how your pride was wounded
- I'm putting my pride totally aside

PROBLEM
- To ensure this problem will not recur
- Responsibility for this problem is entirely our own
- Promise to clear up this problem immediately

- Despite our best efforts, this problem keeps recurring
- This is one problem that won't happen again

See also: FRUSTRATION, ERROR, INCONVENIENCE, MISTAKE, OVERSIGHT

PROVE
- Only proves we are both stubborn
- Let us prove we've really changed
- Now is the time for us to prove otherwise
- Please give us another chance to prove our worth

RECONSIDER
- I hope you will please reconsider
- Ask that you reconsider your position
- Please reconsider your decision to
- I beg you to reconsider

See also: FORGIVE

REGRET
- I immediately regretted my hasty action
- Regret to inform you I must withdraw
- Hard to tell you just how much I regret
- First, let me express my profound regret for this incident
- It is with particular regret I must decline
- I regret we will be unable to attend
- I'd like to express my sincere regrets
- My only regret is that I couldn't thank you sooner

See also: APOLOGY, GUILTY, SORRY

RESPOND
- Sorry I have been such a slow poke in responding
- Should have responded to you much earlier
- Unfortunately, we failed to respond in time
- Wanted to respond right away to your dissatisfaction
- You responded with justified criticism

See also: ANSWER

RESPONSE
- Obviously most unsatisfactory in failing to reach response targets
- Apologize for any delayed response
- The response should have been much faster

RIGHT
- Now appears that you were right all along
- Plan to do right by you no matter what it takes
- Now see that it is the right thing to do

See also: CORRECT

SATISFY
- Will not be satisfied until I return it to its original condition
- Will do everything we can to satisfy you
- Won't stop until you are completely satisfied
- Our aim is to send every patron home satisfied

Satisfy: gratify, please, content, appease, gladden, resolve, solve, persuade, reassure, pacify, placate, fulfill, answer, assure, compensate, reimburse, atone for, make reparation, pay back

SERVICE
- Sorry to learn our response to your service needs disappointed you
- Will work harder to improve this service in the future
- You are certainly entitled to better service than this

SITUATION
- Will reevaluate the situation at once
- Do our very best to change this unhappy situation
- Very sorry for allowing this unfortunate situation to develop
- Never thought to find ourselves in a situation like this

SOLUTION
- Value your business and hope this solution is satisfactory
- Let's work toward a solution together
- For a solution we can all live with
- A speedy solution to this impasse is called for
- After several tries, I think I've finally found a solution

See also: AMENDS

SORRY
- Very sorry to hear about

- So sorry to hear you have been taken ill
- Very sorry to discover a member of our staff was rude
- Extremely sorry to lose you
- So sorry for the times I let you down
- First, let me say how sorry I am
- You'll never be sorry
- Sorry! We'll be right back
- We're ever so sorry
- I'm so sorry to have to do this
- Sorry to take so long to congratulate you
- Sorry to learn of your recent troubles
- So sorry you weren't able to share our day
- So sorry we can't be there to celebrate with you
- Can't tell you how sorry I am that this happened
- No one is more sorry than we are

Sorry: guilty, repentant, apologetic, abject, humbled, rueful, remorseful, chastened, sheepish, embarrassed, distressed, dejected, downcast, crestfallen
See also: APOLOGIZE, EMBARRASS, GUILTY, REGRET

STEP

- Taking steps to ensure it never happens again
- Should have taken that step long ago
- One more step on the road to reconciliation
- If we each take a step, we'll meet in the middle
See also: ACT

TELL

- Thank you for telling us of your dissatisfaction
- As soon as you told us, we went into action
- Only wish you had told us sooner
- Want to tell you how sorry I am
- Don't know what to tell you, except to apologize again

THANKS

- Again, my thanks and apologies
- Thanks for being so understanding
- Convey our thanks for all your patience
- A time when thanks is just not enough
- Apologize for not thanking you right away

TOUCH

- Sorry I haven't kept in touch
- Promise to keep in touch from now on
- This won't happen again, touch wood
- If I had kept in touch, this problem wouldn't have happened

TRY

- I will try my very best to
- Will try to do better in the future
- There's nothing for it but to try harder
- When trying is just not good enough
- Promise to keep trying until I succeed
Try: attempt, undertake, seek, venture, aim, strive, struggle, bend over backward, push, test, experiment, prove
See also: PROVE

UNFORGIVABLE

- Completely unforgivable to have behaved like that
- Such bad service is unforgivable
- An unforgivable injustice has just been committed
- Hope this act is not permanently unforgivable
Unforgivable: inexcusable, unpardonable, unjustifiable, scandalous, unwarranted, reprehensible, deplorable, low, atrocious, beastly, odious, disgraceful, rotten, shameful, despicable
See also: DAMAGE, MISTAKE, WRONG

UNFORTUNATE

- Unfortunately, I've just become redundant and can't help you
- Working hard to change this unfortunate problem
- A very unfortunate situation all round
- Nothing could have been more unfortunate than this
See also: HURT, UNHAPPY

UNHAPPY

- Just very sorry you are unhappy with
- Pains us to know you are unhappy with the service
- Cannot afford even one unhappy customer
- I'm very unhappy to learn you are

unhappy
See also: UNFORTUNATE

VALUE
- Value your friendship too much to
- Can't put a value on how much you mean
- Please accept this item of increased value in compensation
- Really don't want to lose value in your eyes

WISH
- Certainly wish this had never occurred
- Really wish to patch things up
- Dearest wish is for us to be friends again
- Wouldn't wish this on anyone, much less a friend like you

WORD
- Find us at a very distressing loss for words
- Sadly, we did not live up to our word
- Words can hardly convey how upset I feel
- Deeply regret going back on my word

WORK
- Hope we can work this out together
- This time we are determined to make it work
- Have been working to fix it since the moment we found out
- We're working on this as fast as we can
- For a long time, thing just haven't been working between us

WRITE
- Writing to say how sorry I am for what happened
- Taking this opportunity to write and apologize
- Please forgive me for not writing sooner
- This is the hardest letter I've ever had to write

Write: pen, inscribe, jot down, dash off, scribble, compose, type, keyboard, note
See also: INFORM

WRONG
- Will use whatever power we possess to right this wrong
- Ready to admit I was wrong
- According to the proverb, two wrongs don't make a right
- Completely wrong to insist
- I now realize I couldn't have been more wrong
- Do everything possible to wipe out this wrong
- Clearly, you have been wronged

See also: ERROR, MISTAKE

YEAR
- Hard to believe a whole year has passed
- Apologize for letting another year go by without
- Hope to put this troubled year behind us
- This certainly has been a year for misunderstandings
- Let's make this a year of reconciliation

Section Eight

Name that Sale

Name That Sale!

1) Select anything from Part One. Such as **"Blitz"**. Use it alone or
2) Match with anything from Part Two, such as **"Holiday"**.
3) Combine to produce **"Holiday Blitz"**.

Part One:

- AUCTION
- BASH
- BAZAAR
- BLAST
- BLITZ
- BLOWOUT
- BONUS
- BUCK BUSTER
- CARNIVAL
- CELEBRATION
- CLEAN OUT
- CLEAN SWEEP
- CLEAR OUT
- CLEARANCE
- CLOSE OUT
- CRAZINESS
- DAYS
- DEAL
- DISPERSAL
- DOORCRASHER
- EVENT
- EXCHANGE
- EXPLOSION
- FAIR
- FEST
- FESTIVAL

- GALA
- GIVEAWAY
- JAMBOREE
- KNOCK DOWN
- LIQUIDATION
- MADNESS
- MANIA
- MARATHON
- MARKET
- MARKETPLACE
- MELTDOWN
- MONTH
- OFFER
- OVERSTOCK
- RIOT
- ROLLOUT
- PARTY
- SALE
- SALE-A-BRATION
- SALE-A-THON
- SPLASH
- SPECTACULAR
- SPECIAL
- SPIN OUT
- WEEK

Part Two:

- Adventure
- Annual
- Annual Spring/ Summer/Fall/Winter
- Baby
- Bachelor
- Back to School
- Bake
- Bankruptcy
- Beachcomber
- Beat the Heat
- Beat the Blahs

- Before the Snow Flies
- Best Brand
- Best Buy
- Bi-annual
- Big and Tall
- Big, Big
- Big Chop
- Big Deal
- Big Little
- Big Savings
- Big Value
- Birthday

- Blowout
- Boatload
- Bonanza
- Boxing Day
- Boxing Day Preview
- Buck Buster
- Cargo
- Cash
- Cash and Carry
- Cash Back
- Cash Only
- Cashing Out
- Celebration
- Centennial
- Children's
- Christmas
- Clean Out
- Clean Sweep
- Clear Out
- Clearance
- Clearing
- Clearing House
- Close Out
- Closing
- Clubhouse
- Coast to Coast
- Cool Yule
- Country-wide
- Customer Appreciation
- Cutback
- Cut Rate
- Designer
- Discount
- Doorcrasher
- Downsizing
- Driveway
- Early Bird
- Early Morning
- Easter
- Elephant
- Emergency
- Empty Nest
- End of Season
- End of Summer/Winter
- Everyday
- Exclusive
- Expansion
- Factory Outlet
- Factory
- Fall
- Farewell
- Father's Day
- Final
- Fire
- Founders Day
- Fresh Air
- Frosty Friday
- Garagezilla
- Giant Spring/Summer/Fall/Winter
- Gigantic
- Going Out of Business
- Good Luck
- Good Sport
- Good Time
- Goodbye
- Grab and Run
- Grand Opening
- Grand Reopening
- Great Escape
- Half Price
- Halloween
- Happiness
- Happy Dance
- Hello Spring/Summer/Fall/Winter
- Hodge Podge
- Holiday
- House Warming
- Hungry Man
- Infants
- Infants and Toddlers
- Inside Outside
- In-store
- Inventory
- Inventory Blowout
- Inventory Clearout
- Investment
- Jumble
- Kids Galore
- Kids First
- Larger Than Life
- Lawn
- Leasing
- Leisure
- Liquidation
- Lots of Fun
- Lotsa Loot
- Lovers Only
- Lucky
- Lucky Saturday
- Lucky Day
- Madness
- Mail-in Rebate
- Mania
- Manufacturer's Clearance
- Manufacturer's Overstock
- Marathon

- March Break
- Mega
- Mid-month
- Midsummer
- Mid-week
- Midwinter
- Mid-year
- Midnight Madness
- Million Dollar
- Month End
- Monster
- Mother's Day
- More for Less
- Moving
- Moving In/Out
- Mystery
- Name Your Price
- National
- Neighborhood
- New Arrivals
- New Stock
- New Year
- No Worry
- Odd Size
- Odds and Ends
- Odd Lot
- Once in a Lifetime
- One Day
- One of a Kind
- Opening
- Out of this World
- Outlet
- Oversize
- Overstock
- Parking Lot
- Payday
- Penny
- Planeload
- Posh
- Pre-season
- Preview
- Price Basher
- Price Chopper
- Price Smasher
- Price Magic
- Public
- Purrrfect
- Rainy Day
- Recession
- Red Tag
- Relocation
- Remnant
- Renovation
- Retirement
- Roadside
- Rummage
- Sale of the Month
- Salvage
- Saturday Sale Fever
- Save a Dollar
- Save More
- Scratch 'n Save
- School's Out
- Scrooge
- Seasonal
- Secret
- Semi-annual
- Seniors
- Share the Wealth
- Shop Crazy
- Shop Till You Drop
- Shopfest
- Shopaholic
- Shopper Reward
- Sidewalk
- Smash Hit
- Smart Shopper
- SOS
- Special Purchase
- Spin Out
- Spring
- Spring Break
- Spring Cleaning
- Store-wide
- Street
- Summer
- Summertime
- Super
- Super Duper
- Super Holiday Special
- Super Saturday
- Super Saver
- Super Size
- Super Special
- Super Special Madness
- Surprise
- Switched On
- Tailgate
- Takeover
- Tax
- Tent
- Thank You
- Thanksgiving
- The Big One
- Three Day
- Time Out

- Tiny Tots
- Top of the Line
- Toy Express
- Trainload
- Trinket and Treasure
- Triple Value
- Truckload
- Two For One
- Ultimate Power
- Unbelievable
- Vacation Start-up
- Valentine's Day
- Value Added
- Van Load
- Water Damage
- Warehouse Clearance
- Warehouse
- Welcome spring
- White
- White And Bright
- White Elephant
- Wholesome
- Winter
- Wintertime
- Women's Day
- Worry Free
- Yard
- Yard and Garden
- Worry Free
- Year End
- Yearly
- You Won't Believe It
- Yuletide
- Yule

Section Nine

Exclamations

- 24 hour service!
- A classic!
- A new way to save!
- A dream come true!
- A-1!
- A name you can trust!
- Above the crowd!
- Absolutely thrilling!
- Absolutely free!
- Access guaranteed!
- Act now!
- Action-packed!
- Add up the value!
- Admit it!
- Adults only!
- All new!
- All you need!
- All on sale!
- All taste, no waste!
- All you can eat!
- All work is guaranteed!
- All-time low!
- Almost perfect!
- Always free!
- Always in stock!
- Always fresh and hot!
- An absolute must!
- An incredible secret!
- And that's not all!
- And free delivery too!
- Any questions!
- Apply today!
- Ask the experts!
- Attention pet lovers!
- Attention!
- Avoid the rush!
- Avoid disappointment!
- Award winning!
- Awesome!
- Back by popular demand!
- Back page deals!
- Bang on savings!
- Bank on us!
- Bargain bin!
- Bargain alert!
- Bargains galore!
- Be first in line!
- Be cool!
- Be convinced!
- Be our guest!
- Be the first!
- Be your own boss!
- Be the best!
- Beat the heat!
- Become a believer!
- Believe it!
- Below market value!
- Best in its class!
- Best grade!
- Best buy!
- Best ever!
- Best of all!
- Best service!
- Best buy anywhere!
- Best prices guaranteed!
- Best in show!
- Best selection!
- Best prices!
- Best service!
- Better taste!
- Better value!
- Better hurry!
- Better than ever!
- Big sale!
- Bigger and better!
- Bigger than ever!
- Biggest sale ever!
- Blockbuster!
- Bonus offer!
- Bonus time!
- Brand names, low prices!
- Break out now!
- Breathe easy!
- Buck buster!
- Buy, sell and trade!
- Buy one, get one free!
- Buy direct!
- Buy now, pay later!
- By invitation only!
- Call for details now!
- Call us today!
- Call today!
- Call our toll-free number!
- Call us first!
- Call right away!
- Call for reservations!
- Call immediately!
- Call now!
- Can you dig it!
- Caring for you!
- Carnival of savings!
- Cash savers!
- Cash in!
- Cash and carry!
- Cash back!
- Catch the action!

- Celebration savings!
- Celebrity endorsed!
- Celebrity favorite!
- Charge it!
- Cheaper than dirt!
- Check it out!
- Check us out today!
- Check these deals!
- Child's play!
- Clean up today!
- Come see what we are doing!
- Coming soon to an outlet near you!
- Coming soon!
- Command performance!
- Company's coming!
- Completely installed!
- Complimentary gift!
- Congratulations!
- Consumer's choice!
- Cool cash!
- Cool!
- Count us in!
- Count yourself in!
- Count on us!
- Coupon offer!
- Courteous service!
- Crazy days!
- Crazy!
- Creativity plus!
- Custom made!
- Customers wanted!
- Day or night!
- Deal discounts available!
- Deal of the month!
- Dealers wanted!
- Delivery service!
- Dial that phone!
- Direct savings to you!
- Discount prices!
- Discount outlet prices!
- Do it now!
- Do it!
- Do it right!
- Does it really work?
- Dollar days are here again!
- Don't take chances!
- Don't guess!
- Don't be left out!
- Don't hesitate!
- Don't change that channel!
- Don't pay for six months!
- Don't miss this special offer!
- Don't miss out!
- Don't miss it!
- Don't delay!
- Don't forget!
- Don't touch that dial!
- Done!
- Doorcrasher offer!
- Double your money back!
- Dream up!
- Dreams can come true!
- Dynamic duo!
- Earn your diploma!
- Easier access!
- Eat or be eaten!
- Effective immediately!
- Embrace temptation!
- Ends this week!
- Ends Saturday!
- Enrol today!
- Enter now!
- Environmentally friendly!
- Environmentally sound!
- Everybody's doing it!
- Everyday low prices!
- Everyone's favorite!
- Everything included!
- Everything must go!
- Everything on sale!
- Exclusive benefits!
- Exclusive!
- Factory outlet!
- Factory to you!
- Factory direct!
- Famous brand names!
- Fantastic deals!
- Fashion revolution!
- Fast and easy!
- Fast track value!
- Fast, reliable service!
- Fast forward!
- Fast, friendly service!
- Faster service!
- Featuring!
- Feel great and have fun!
- Feel the difference!
- Final week!
- Final notice!
- Final 3 days!
- Final days!
- Final blowout!
- Find out what's cooking!
- Finest quality!
- First quality!
- Fit for a queen/king/prince/princess!!

- Flat rate!
- Free estimate!
- Free gift!
- Free coupons!
- Free preview!
- Free with any purchase!
- Free with every purchase!
- Free catalogue!
- Free sneak peek!
- Free trial!
- Free rewards!
- Free special reports!
- Free trial offer!
- Free consultation!
- Free layaway!
- Free delivery!
- Free bonus!
- Free home delivery!
- Free registration!
- Free inspection
- Free!
- Fresh baked!
- Fresh brewed!
- Fresh from the oven!
- Fresh start!
- Fresh!
- Full steam ahead!
- Fun! Fun! Fun!
- Future shock!
- Get involved!
- Get it fast!
- Get yours now!
- Get on board now!
- Get it together!
- Get set, go!
- Get it done fast!
- Gt clicking!
- Get dialling!
- Get organized!
- Get involved!
- Get the complete set!
- Get the whole series!
- Gets things moving!
- Give us a call today!
- Give yourself a bonus!
- Go figure!
- Go green and save!
- Go green now!
- Go team!
- Go the distance!
- Go for broke!
- Go for it!
- Going, going, gone!

- Going fast!
- Good news!
- Goof proof!
- Grab you chance!
- Grade A!
- Grand opening!
- Great taste, great price!
- Great buy!
- Great news!
- Great gifts for grads
- Greener, cheaper, better!
- Green, greener, greenest!
- Guess what!
- Guess again!
- Half price!
- Half off!
- Happy New Year!
- Happy holidays!
- Head start!
- Heed the call!
- Held over!
- Help yourself today!
- Help yourself!
- Here they come!
- Here to help!
- Here's your chance!
- Here's how it works!
- Here's what you get!
- Home run!
- Hot buys!
- Hot new products!
- Hot list!
- Hot deals!
- Hot!
- Hotline to value!
- Hottest deals!
- Hottest thing going!
- Howlin' good!
- Huge inventory clearance!
- Huge market demand!
- Huge price drops this week!
- Huge end-of-season savings!
- Huge spring sale!
- Hundreds of styles!
- Hurry in!
- Hurry, hurry, hurry!
- Hurry in now!
- Hurry!
- Important announcement!
- In business thirty years!
- In just seven days!
- In stock daily!
- In the spotlight!

- In-store coupons!
- Incredible value!
- Incredible performance!
- Incredible profits!
- Inflation fighter!
- Inside scoop!
- Instant rebate!
- Intelligent savings!
- Introducing!
- Introductory deal!
- Introductory interest rate!
- Introductory offer!
- It really works!
- It works!
- It's amazing!
- It's remarkable!
- It's back!
- It's true!
- It's here!
- It's a special secret!
- It's a great time to buy or sell!
- It's hot!
- It's a first!
- It's your lucky day!
- It's basic!
- It's that easy!
- It's a surprise!
- It's time for a change!
- It's a buy!
- Join the party!
- Join the excitement!
- Join up now!
- Just for you!
- Just released!
- Just think of it!
- Just imagine!
- Just for the fun of it!
- Just arrived!
- Just in!
- Just off the truck!
- Just rarin' to go!
- Just reduced!
- Just released!
- Keep them safe!
- Keeping in touch!
- Kick start your future!
- Kid stuff!
- Kids participate free!
- Know it all!
- Last chance!
- Lead the pack!
- Less is more!
- Let us help!
- Let the game begin!
- Let's be friends!
- Lets you be you!
- Licensed tradesmen!
- Lifetime guarantee!
- Lifetime warranty!
- Lighten up!
- Limited time offer!
- Limited quantities!
- Limited time only!
- Liquidation sale!
- Listen up!
- Long live value!
- Look no further!
- Look here!
- Look what's new!
- Look sharp!
- Look better!
- Look for this symbol!
- Look no further!
- Look!
- Lots of action!
- Low price!
- Lower prices guaranteed!
- Lowest price of the year!
- Lowest prices!
- Loyalty rewards!
- Macro savings!
- Made for you!
- Made to order!
- Mail call!
- Mail-in rebate!
- Maintenance free!
- Make it possible!
- Make history!
- Make it happen!
- Make some waves!
- Make your dollar go further!
- Make money!
- Make the break!
- Making room for new stock!
- Members first!
- Merry Christmas!
- Micro prices!
- Mix it up!
- Money-back guarantee!
- Money in your pocket!
- More in your pocket!
- More please!
- More great values!
- More value than ever!
- More famous brands!
- More information!

- More money back!
- More great news!
- More free!
- More powerful than ever!
- More great buys inside!
- Most value!
- Most wanted!
- Multiple choice!
- Must go!
- Must see!
- A name you can trust!
- Name your price!
- Need help?
- Never before!
- New every day!
- New on the market!
- New arrivals!
- New lower prices!
- New low price!
- New version!
- New product!
- New and improved!
- New price!
- New low prices every day!
- New and improved!
- New collection!
- New this year!
- New!
- Newly renovated!
- News flash!
- Nice curves!
- No mixing required!
- No startup costs!
- No compromise!
- No cost to you!
- No end in sight!
- No fee!
- No extra cost!
- No kidding!
- No gimmicks!
- No wonder!
- No sweat!
- No problem!
- No way!
- No catch!
- No money down!
- No waiting!
- No annual fee!
- No restrictions!
- No deposit required!
- No strings!
- No hidden costs!
- Nobody beats our prices!
- Nobody knows it better!
- Nothing else to buy!
- Now you're talking!
- Now on!
- Now reduced!
- Now better than ever!
- Now open!
- Now discounted!
- Now available at leading stores!
- Now on sale!
- Now is the time!
- Now's your chance!
- On sale!
- On with the show!
- One low price!
- One of a kind!
- One week only!
- One-stop shopping!
- Only at this location!
- Only the best!
- Open 7 days a week!
- Open letter!
- Open house!
- Order immediately!
- Order today!
- Order yours today!
- Original formula!
- Our lowest prices ever!
- Our best!
- Outstanding credentials!
- Party time!
- Pay less!
- Pay no premium!
- Peak experience!
- People pleaser!
- Perfect timing!
- Picture this!
- Picture perfect!
- Play it safe!
- Please call us!
- Please respond immediately!
- Please order today!
- Power to the people!
- Price drop!
- Price guarantee!
- Price war!
- Priced for you!
- Priced to go!
- Priced to move!
- Priced to sell!
- Priced for quick sale!
- Prices slashed!
- Priority service!

- Product update!
- Purpose driven!
- Quality guaranteed!
- Quick results!
- Quick fix!
- Quick 'n tasty!
- Re-usable!
- Reach for the stars!
- Read on!
- Read all about it!
- Ready to install!
- Ready to use!
- Ready in an hour!
- Really hot!
- Really, really big savings!
- Red hot bargoons!
- Red hot prices!
- Red hot savings!
- Reduced again!
- Reduced!
- Reply today!
- Reply now!
- Right on!
- Rise and shine!
- Round the clock!
- Rush out and buy one!
- Rush shipment!
- Safe and gentle!
- Safe and easy!
- Safety first!
- Sale starts today!
- Satisfaction a must!
- Saturday only!
- Save dollars today!
- Save more!
- Save, save, save!
- Save this ad!
- Save big!
- Save today!
- Save!
- Savings alert!
- Season's greetings!
- See and compare!
- See you soon!
- Seeing is believing!
- Sells for less!
- Send no money!
- Send no money now!
- Senior's day!
- Sensitive service!
- Set me free!
- Seventh heaven!
- Shop by phone!
- Shop 'n save!
- Shop till you drop!
- Shopper's heaven!
- Show special!
- Show off!
- Sign up today!
- Simply heaven!
- Simply fab!
- Smart tips!
- So close to home!
- So alive!
- So call today!
- Something for everyone!
- Sparkling value!
- Special presentation!
- Special invitation!
- Special buy!
- Special extended!
- Special purchase!
- Special edition!
- Special offer!
- Special introductory offer!
- Special discount offer!
- Specialists!
- Specially priced!
- Spectacular values!
- Start smart!
- Starting today!
- Stay informed!
- Stay cool!
- Stepping out!
- Still free delivery!
- Stock up and save!
- Stock up now!
- Stock up while you can!
- Stop traffic!
- Stop!
- Stop! Look!
- Super savings!
- Super savers!
- Super buys!
- Super special madness!
- Super cool!
- Super special combos!
- Surefire!
- Surprise!
- Switch and save!
- Take the plunge!
- Talented experts!
- Talk about a full plate!
- Talk about service!
- Taste the best!
- Tenth action-packed week!

- Terrific buy!
- Thanks a million!
- That's impossible!
- That's a promise!
- That's right!
- That's all there is to it!
- The right stuff!
- The word is out!
- The call of the wild!
- The pro's choice!
- The king is back!
- The one and only!
- The big one!
- The end is near!
- The simple solution!
- The pleasure is yours!
- There is no competition!
- There's plenty more!
- Think big!
- Think again!
- Think savings!
- This week's events!
- This can be yours!
- This is for you!
- This weekend only!
- This month's specials!
- This Saturday only!
- Three years to pay!
- Thumbs up!
- Time limited offer!
- Time is running out fast!
- Timeless beauty!
- Today's super seller!
- Today's the day!
- Top quality!
- Totally freaky!
- Tried and true!
- Try now!
- Try something wild!
- Try it free!
- Try this!
- Try it for free!
- Two months to pay!
- Two in one!
- Unbeatable value!
- Unbeatable buy!
- Under new management!
- Unlimited use!
- Unprecedented value!
- Updated daily!
- Valuable information!
- Value guaranteed!
- Wait no longer!
- Wake up!
- Wake your spirit!
- Wake-up call!
- Walk-in special!
- Warehouse clearance!
- Warning!
- We install too!
- We appreciate you
- We can't wait!
- We did it!
- We confess!
- We promise!
- We will beat any advertised price!
- We deliver too!
- We have the solutions
- We sell excitement!
- We even pay the postage!
- We deliver!
- We guarantee it!
- We do it all!
- We got you covered!
- We'll come to you!
- We're the best!
- We're back!
- We've got it all
- Week-long savings!
- Welcome y'all!
- What style!
- What a feeling!
- What a deal!
- What next!
- What a catch!
- What a find!
- What next!
- What a natural!
- What a pleasure!
- When they're gone, they're gone!
- While quantities last!
- While supplies last!
- Why buy new!
- Why pay retail!
- Why wait!
- Wild!
- Win it!
- Win big!
- Win!
- Work at home!
- Work smarter!
- Works great!
- World's greatest!
- Wow, look at the sales!
- Wow!
- You can do it!

- You win!
- You got it!
- You ain't seen nothin' yet!
- You can too!
- You come first!
- You can say that again!
- You could be a winner!
- You deserve it!
- You want it!
- You'll be amazed!
- You'll love it!
- You'll be glad you did!
- You'll love this!
- You've got it made!
- Your privacy is guaranteed!
- Your best buy!
- Your complete shopping guide!
- Your invitation!
- Your choice!

Section Ten

Reply Coupons

- As a valued customer, I will also be entitled to receive, for free examination
- As seen on TV
- Bill me in full
- Bill me later
- Bill me in three months
- Bill me at big discount prices
- Bill me only when I'm fully satisfied
- Choose a payment method
- Choose the one best for you
- Choose one of three options
- Clip and save/mail/win
- Complete and mail this postage-paid reply card
- Complete all information
- Count me in
- Count on my order
- Enroll me under the terms outlined in this advertisement
- Enroll me under the terms outlined here
- Enroll my whole family in the club
- Enter me to win one of these incredible products
- Four easy payments of
- I am free to choose from any category
- I want to switch to
- I may cancel at any time
- I will enjoy three added bonuses
- I am under no obligation
- I may cancel my membership without prior notice
- I must be thrilled with the results or I get my money back less postage and handling
- I would like to get more information sent to me free of charge on the advertised product or service
- I understand this information is free, and I am under no obligation to purchase
- I understand I need send no money now
- I wish to enter the search which closes on
- I wish to receive my product on
- I am interested in knowing more about
- I can't wait! Send me the products I've checked in a package that doesn't say what's inside
- I may return any product within thirty days for replacement or refund
- I purchase only products I wish to own
- I would like to get more information sent to me free of charge
- I am free to choose from any category
- I am entitled to 50% off
- I am most interested in these items
- I understand the mailing of this card places me under no obligation
- I need send no payment now
- I understand I qualify for the seniors and pensioners discount
- I understand there is no sign-up or monthly fee
- I understand I am completely free to cancel at any time
- If I continue as a member, I will receive
- If you decide to purchase more than one product, please take note of the following volume rates
- It's easy to get savvy about
- I'd like to get my hands on a free sample
- Just complete and mail the form below
- Mail cheque or money order payable to
- Mail before expiry date
- Mail this rush coupon today
- Mail this card today
- Mail this rush order form today
- My signature authorizes
- My main interest is
- My satisfaction is guaranteed
- My signature is all that's needed
- No purchase necessary
- No membership required
- No money required
- No payment for three months
- Not available in any retail store
- Offer expires on this date
- Complete and mail the postage-paid reply
- Order your free kit which includes
- Payment enclosed
- Phone or fax for faster response
- Phone orders accepted
- Photocopy this form for a friend
- Please send the following titles
- Please send me my free
- Please fill out the information below so we can direct our communications
- Please send your cheque or money order to this address
- Please enter me into the contest to win a complete
- Please rush – at no risk or obligation – a free copy of
- Please accept my membership in
- Please start my subscription immediately
- Please fill out the order form and mail it to the address listed below

- Please help us keep our records up to date by telling us if you have recently moved, or of any other change in information
- Please print clearly
- Please include all vital information
- Please have a specialist phone me about
- Please, tell me more about the programs
- Please check off the service offer(s) you would like
- Please accept my enrollment and send me
- Please check off which product you wish to purchase
- Please makes cheques payable to
- Please read this important information and sign below
- Please take a minute to answer the following questions, so we can better provide solutions
- Please register me for the
- Please complete the information below
- Please send me, by first class mail
- Please call me at the time specified below
- Please fill my order first
- Please send me the free starter kit
- Pre-register before this date
- Reply now for a full-color catalogue
- Reserve your place today by filling in your name and address
- Reserve the following dates for me
- Return order form to
- Return with payment to
- Return your entry immediately
- Risk-free guarantee
- Rush me the all-new system immediately
- Rush me all ten right away
- Rush me these products now
- Send my friend a
- Send me the next one available
- Send today for your free catalogue
- Send my free bonus as soon as you receive my order
- Send no money now
- Send this amazing product at once
- Send for the information on
- Send me more information now
- Send for our free brochure
- Send me the product and bill me only
- Sign me up for one full year of
- Ten day trial coupon
- These offers valid at participating outlets
- This information is confidential and will be used for the sole purpose of

- determining how to serve you better
- Three easy ways to sign up
- To order, use this coupon or a separate sheet of paper
- Under terms of this offer I agree to buy
- Use the attached coupon and save
- Yes, I want to participate
- Yes, enter my subscription to
- Yes, I want to know more about
- Yes, please reserve for me
- Yes, I want to save on
- Yes! Please send me
- Yes! I want to join immediately
- Yes! I would like to order
- Yes! I want to train to become
- Yes! I want to beat the rush
- Yes! I've earned special status
- Yes! Please enter my order for
- Yes! I'd like to find out more about
- Yes! I request access to
- Yes! Send my system in a plain package
- Yes! My career needs a boost
- Yes! Please rush me more details about
- Yes! Please give me all the facts about
- Yes! Please send me the product
- Yes! Put me down for all three
- Yes! I want to give a one-year gift subscription for only
- Yes! Please give me all the facts about
- Yes! I want to switch to
- Yes! Start my subscription now
- Yes! I'd like to give a one-year gift subscription to the person named below
- Yes! I want admittance to
- Yes! I want to subscribe and save fifty percent off the cover price
- Yes! I want the best products at the best prices
- Yes! Save me a seat.
- Yes! I want to get my finances in shape
- Yes! Continue to deliver my
- Yes! I'd like to know what's going on
- Yes! Sign me up for
- Yes! I've waited long enough
- Yes! Please send me your catalogue listing other available products
- Your comments would be appreciated
- Your cooperation is deeply valued

Section Eleven

Envelope Teasers

- A chance to win thousands of dollars in cash
- Accepting the special card that's been enclosed in your name can help change your life
- Additional special offers waiting for you
- A whole new world has been introduced to me
- A big smile is enclosed
- A quiz that could save your marriage
- A world of thanks
- A program to protect you
- A message from president
- Absolutely radical news inside
- Access the world
- Almost too hot to handle
- An exceptional offer
- An invitation for you and a guest
- Annual report
- Answering your call
- Are you getting the rewards you deserve
- Are you ready to be counted
- Are you ready for the big time
- Are you paying too much for
- Are you ready to say yes
- At work for you
- Be one of the first 200 to respond and you could win
- Big change inside
- Bonus offer included inside
- Bringing the arts to life
- By invitation only
- Campaign for fairness
- Can you guess what's inside
- Celebrity quote from letter signer
- Change of life inside
- Complimentary certificate
- Confidential
- Confidential documents inside
- Confidentially yours
- Consider this
- Could you pass this test
- Critical message for you and your family
- Dare to open this message
- Date sensitive information
- Delivered by hand
- Don't put this aside and miss your chance
- Don't wait another minute
- Don't open this letter
- Don't open unless
- Enclosed: Terrific news about
- Enclosed is a special update

- Exclusive bonus offers for survey responders
- Fifty ways to help your bank account
- Final round
- Final offer
- Find out what you can expect
- For the future of your children
- For a very special someone
- Forty ways to boost your bank account
- Forty ways to love your home
- Free trial with enclosed coupon
- Free gift inside
- Free information
- Free sample
- Free this week only
- From your friendly neighbor
- From your neighborhood service center
- Get started now
- Get your early bird prize now
- Get your free gift. Details inside
- Go ahead, take a peek
- Good news
- Greetings
- Guaranteed tax free
- Guess what's inside
- Guess what
- Hand delivered materials enclosed
- Help stamp out high interest rates
- Help enclosed
- Helping you save even more
- Here is the information you requested
- Here's your list, please check it twice
- Here's your special invitation
- Here's our secret
- Here's your chance to get what so many others have
- Here's what the future looks like
- Holiday gift tags inside
- Hot news
- Hot stuff
- I am delighted to send you this letter
- I promise to send you a package of money-making offers
- I'd hate for you to miss out
- If you're feeling the heat, we can help
- If you want to breathe easy
- Important information about your taxes
- Important, updated information enclosed
- Important: registered documents enclosed
- Improving your odds
- In response to your need
- Inside – important information about

your
- Inside: How you can avoid a crippling debt
- Instant gratification inside
- Instant prize
- Instant win certificate
- Introducing a whole new world
- Investment opportunity
- Is this letter too hot to handle
- Joy inside
- Just a note to tell you we care
- Last chance to enter
- Last chance to win
- Listen to this
- Look inside to save
- Look inside to discover
- Look inside for great earning potential
- Look inside and find a smile
- Looking for some answers? Take this test
- Make sure you're not missing out
- Make sure you have a chance to win both
- Make your life more than just a game of chance
- Meet a new neighbor
- Message from the artistic director
- News flash
- News you've been waiting for
- No annual fee
- Now you can be included
- Offers not available to the general public
- Official documents enclosed
- Only special people receive this letter
- Open and save
- Open up for love
- Open and discover how you can win
- Open for business
- Open to find out how you can benefit
- Open so the whole family can enjoy
- Open for pleasure
- Open before your next meal
- Open at once
- Open this quick
- Open up for big savings
- Open for a change
- Our thanks
- Our reach goes round the world
- Pay off your bills fast
- Pay days are here
- Peek inside now
- Please check inside right now
- Please don't delay

- Please don't throw this survey away
- Please look inside for more details
- Please open right away
- Please don't throw away this letter
- Please tear open immediately
- Please reply by
- Please return as soon as possible
- Please R.. S. V. P.
- Pleased to meet you
- Postage is already taken care of
- Preferred client update
- Premium enclosed
- Presenting three new ways to save
- Printed matter
- Privacy strictly protected
- The programs that protect you
- Project happiness
- Project love
- Proud to present
- Reach round the world
- Read this before you spend another dollar
- Really great news inside
- Really quick answers inside
- Reserve your place today
- Responding to your query
- Rush order
- Rush
- Sample products on offer
- Seasons greetings
- Secure the future of your children
- See New York on a budget
- See for yourself
- See inside
- See how easy it is to earn
- See inside for review of
- See why we've had such an outstanding response
- See how much fun summer can be
- See what you're missing
- See inside to learn how you can save
- Simply fill out and drop in the mail
- Something to think about
- Special gift enclosed
- Special package
- Special offer inside
- Specially for you
- Stand up and be counted
- Stop! Look! Act!
- Strictly confidential
- Surprise, surprise
- Take a moment to read about your future
- Taking your concerns seriously

- Tear into this
- Tear this letter open fast
- Ten inspiring ideas
- Ten good reasons to join up
- Test your love meter
- Thanks for your interest
- Thank you for your time today
- The better alternative
- The enclosed survey will interest you
- The letter that will change your life
- The lowest rate you'll ever see
- The most fun letter you'll get all year
- The enclosed survey will interest you
- The letter that will change your life
- This could be your big chance
- This is really more important than you realize
- This letter may save your life
- This letter may save your investments
- Time limited offer! Act now
- Time critical action needed
- Time sensitive data inclosed
- Time to make your mark
- Too valuable to miss
- To find out why, look inside
- To thank you for your patronage
- Trust enclosed
- Urgent: test results
- Urgent communication
- Urgent news
- Urgent
- Urgent communication
- Up close and confidential
- Valuable coupons and special offers inside
- Wake up call inside
- Wake up to
- Wanna know a secret
- We dare you to open this letter
- We want to thank you
- We'll reward you for your time
- We're waiting to hear from you
- We've increased your benefits
- Welcome to our second decade
- What is it
- When help is needed
- When you really need some help
- Why more people select us
- Why save a little when you can save a lot
- Winning form enclosed. Please return within ten days
- Yes, I want to be financially independent
- Yes, I will accept more savings
- You are automatically entered to win
- You are entitled to special savings, coupons, trial offers and a chance to win
- You asked for proof
- You can count on us
- You are pre-approved
- You could be a winner
- You have been chosen
- You need to read this
- You're eligible for our main draw
- You're special. Here's proof
- You're a guaranteed winner
- You've never been closer to winning
- You've won big
- Your answers are important
- Your cooperation is greatly appreciated
- Your window of opportunity
- Your concerns finally addressed
- Your dividend statement is enclosed
- Your help package
- Your points are building
- Your personal membership card
- Your invitation is enclosed
- Your call to battle
- Your special invitation to participate
- Your satisfaction guarantee
- Your dreams can come true
- Your personal diary inside
- Your ticket to savings inside
- Your surprise package
- Your reservations are inside
- Your order form inside
- Your discount card has arrived
- Your free passport to
- Your six point plan for
- Your best chance to win a million dollars
- Your guide to the best
- Your mystery gift enclosed
- Your ticket to a new life
- We are seeking people like you
- Well worth your while
- Would you please read and fill out the enclosed survey

Section Twelve

**Beginnings
and
Transitions**

- A clear indication that
- A dramatic shift in
- According to the myth
- Add to that
- Additionally
- Advocating a dramatic departure from
- Again and again
- Also indicated
- Also
- Although, to be perfectly honest
- An apt description of
- And then there's
- And you know what
- And in preparation for
- And best yet
- And while you're at it
- And best of all
- And you must remember
- Anyway
- Apparently
- Apropos to
- Arguably
- As you read this crucial message
- As an added bonus
- As a matter of principle
- As a result
- As an example
- As you can see
- As further analysis shows
- As you know
- As a matter of fact
- As well
- Assuming that
- Assuredly
- At one point
- At first glance
- At the end of the day
- At this time
- Be certain that
- Because ultimately
- Behind the scenes
- Believe me
- Best of all
- Better still
- Beyond that, however, is
- But then
- But on the other hand
- But there it is
- But you know what
- But most importantly
- But thanks to
- But as usual
- By virtue of
- Candidly speaking
- Categorically
- Certainly
- Contributing to the shift away from
- Cost-effectively
- Covered exclusively by
- Did you know that
- Diplomatically
- Don't ever forget that
- Either way
- Elsewhere
- Equally important is
- Especially when
- Essentially
- Even better yet
- Even as you read this ad
- Even now
- Ever faithful
- Every minute, every day
- Examples include
- First and foremost
- Firstly
- For starters
- For openers
- For example
- For emphasis
- For the first time ever
- Fortunately
- Frankly
- From time to time
- Granted
- Happily
- Has always been our calling card
- Here is a perfect example
- Honestly
- How otherwise could we
- However
- In and around
- In all honesty
- In this regard
- In conjunction with
- In brief
- In keeping with
- In all likelihood
- In a nutshell
- In essence
- In particular
- In accordance with
- In the tradition of
- In the beginning
- In addition
- In the first place
- In many instances

- In case you're wondering why
- In conclusion
- In so many instances
- In anticipation of
- In the meantime
- In any case
- In recent years
- Inasmuch as
- Indisputably
- Initially
- Invite you to
- Inviting as it seems
- It really comes down to this
- It all adds up to
- It also explains a lot about
- It is estimated that
- It is impossible to even estimate
- It also explains why
- It's not just a plan to
- It's interesting to note
- It's obvious by now
- It's even more unthinkable that
- It's no coincidence that
- It's imperative that
- It's a foregone conclusion
- It's essential that
- It's quite obvious that
- Just in case
- Just between us
- Just one example is
- Keeping in mind
- Last year alone
- Last thing
- Lastly
- Lessons can be drawn from
- Let us assure you that
- Make no mistake about it
- May we introduce ourselves
- Meanwhile, back on the farm
- More recently
- More certain than ever
- More efficient than ever
- Moreover
- Most sincerely
- Most importantly
- Most of all
- Naturally
- Needless to say
- Nevertheless
- No one likes to
- No doubt about it
- Not if you want to
- Of course
- Of course, on the other hand
- Often, all it takes is
- Okay, here's the scoop
- On one hand
- On the other hand
- On second thought
- On behalf of
- On a scale of one to ten
- On a positive note
- On the home front
- On an absolute scale
- Once and for all
- Once again
- One of the strongest pieces of evidence
- One way or the other
- One guess would be
- One good example is
- Only natural that
- Overly optimistic projections can
- Please be sure to
- Please read on
- Presumably
- Primarily
- Provide access to
- Putting essentials first
- Quite a plus
- Quite simply
- Rationally speaking
- Realistically
- Regardless
- Rest assured, however, that
- Revealed by further analysis is
- Right now
- Secondarily
- Secondly
- Shortly
- Simply put
- Since our founding back in
- Sometimes
- Speaking of which
- Starting from the top
- Surely, however
- That distinction is reserved for
- The list goes on
- The operative word is
- The most intriguing thing about this is
- The scoop is
- The truth is
- The way we see it is
- The prognosis is
- The crowning touch
- The important thing is
- The irony is that

- The other day
- The data are quite clear on
- The thing is
- There's no such thing as
- There's no denying that
- Thirdly
- This being case
- Thousands, to be exact
- To commence
- To start with
- To commemorate
- To be honest
- To put it mildly
- To begin with
- To say the least
- To improve matters
- Today
- Truth to tell
- Truthfully
- Ultimately
- Undeniably
- Understandably
- We want you to know
- We pride ourselves on
- We watched in admiration as
- What's more
- When it comes to
- Whether you're concerned about
- With this in view
- With that in mind
- Without quibbling too much
- You understand that
- You have the option to
- You can call it what you like
- You can be sure that
- You may wonder if
- You might want to consider
- You might conclude that
- You should also know that
- You may not know this, but
- You even have the choice of
- You see

Section Thirteen

Colors

AUTUMN

- Auburn
- Bay
- Brandy
- Brass
- Brick
- Bronze
- Copper
- Copperplate
- Desert fox
- Ember
- Flower pot
- Fox
- Henna
- Hennaberry
- Irish setter
- Maple
- Ochre
- Prairie sunset
- Pumpkin
- Red cedar
- Redwood
- Roan
- Rum
- Russet
- Rust
- Sorrel
- Sunburnt
- Sunset
- Terra cotta
- Tiger eye
- Titian
- Vixen

BEIGE

- Almond
- Alpaca
- Antelope
- Army
- Bamboo
- Beige
- Biscuit
- Bisque
- Bistre
- Blonde
- Buckskin
- Buckwheat
- Buff
- Camel
- Chamois
- Champagne
- Danish blond
- Desert
- Desert rat
- Driftwood
- Dun
- Dusk
- Dust
- Ecru
- Eggshell
- Fawn
- Flaxen
- Honey
- Khaki
- Lion
- Lynx
- Marsh grass
- Natural
- Neutral
- Nude
- Puma
- Raffia
- Sable
- Sand
- Sandstone
- Seagrass
- Tan
- Tawny
- Taupe
- Viking blond
- Wheat
- Wicker

BLACK

- Andiron
- Anvil
- Asphalt
- Basalt
- Beetle
- Bile
- Black bear
- Black current
- Black
- Black ice
- Blackberry
- Bolt
- Bull
- Bunker oil
- Burnt
- Charcoal
- Cinderblock
- Cinder
- Clinker
- Coal
- Crow
- Crude oil
- Ebony
- India Ink
- Ink
- Iron
- Jet
- Jetty
- Loam
- Midnight
- Moonless
- Murky
- Noir
- Oil
- Oil patch
- Old rubber
- Panther
- Persian lamb
- Raisin
- Raven
- Scorched
- Skunk
- Sludge
- Smoky
- Soot
- Swart
- Thunderhead
- Tractor tire
- Transmission oil
- Truffle
- Whaleback

BLUE

- Adriatic
- Alice
- Agate
- Aqua
- Aquamarine
- Azure
- Baby
- Blowfly
- Blue mould
- Blueberry
- Bluebird
- Capri
- Cerulean
- Chevy
- Cobalt
- Cornflower
- Cote D'Azur
- Dagger
- Deepwater
- Forget-me-not
- Heaven
- Heron

- Horizon
- Ice blue
- Indigo
- Lapis lazuli
- Loyalist
- Marine
- Midnight
- Morning glory
- Navy
- Ocean
- Pacific
- Peacock
- Patriot
- Periwinkle
- Police
- Porcelain
- Powder
- Robin's egg
- Royal
- Sea
- Sky
- Spode
- Teal
- Tory
- True
- Turquoise
- Ultramarine
- Wedgewood
- Woad

BROWN
- Acorn
- Ale
- Allspice
- Almond
- Amber
- Anchovy
- Armadillo
- Augean
- Bannock
- Bark
- Barley
- Barracuda
- Bay
- Bayou
- Beagle
- Beaver
- Beech
- Beer
- Beetle
- Biscuit
- Bisque

- Boa constrictor
- Bog
- Boredom
- Bouillon
- Bracken
- Briar
- Brown sugar
- Brunette
- Burlap
- Burnt sienna
- Caffeine
- Calfskin
- Cappuccino
- Caramel
- Carob
- Chestnut
- Chimpanzee
- Chocolate
- Cider
- Cigar
- Cinnabar
- Cinnamon
- Cinnaspice
- Clove
- Cocoa
- Coconut
- Codfish
- Coffee
- Cognac
- Cookie
- Cordovan
- Cork
- Cowhide
- Dune
- Earth
- Earthwood
- Falcon
- Fawn
- Fresh bread
- Ginger
- Ginger snap
- Guitar
- Hazel
- Hickory
- Honey
- Honey mead
- Irish whiskey
- Jackrabbit
- Java
- Leather
- Macaroon
- Mahogany

- Maple
- Mincemeat
- Mink
- Moccasin
- Mocha
- Mongrel
- Monkey
- Mud
- Muskrat
- Nut
- Oak
- Ochre
- Oil
- Old spice
- Ox hide
- Peanut butter
- Pecan
- Pigskin
- Porcupine
- Quail
- Raisin
- Rattlesnake
- Rawhide
- Reindeer
- Rust
- Sandalwood
- Scotch whiskey
- Seal
- Sepia
- Sherry
- Shipping crate
- Shoe leather
- Sienna
- Snakeskin
- Snuff
- Spice
- Stout
- Tabby
- Taffy
- Tan
- Tea Stain
- Tea
- Teak
- Terra cotta
- Toast
- Tobacco
- Toffee
- Umber
- Vandyke
- Walnut
- Whiskey

CLEAR
- Cloudless
- Colorless
- Crystal
- Crystalline
- Diamond
- Diaphanous
- Glassy
- Gossamer
- Ice
- Ice cube
- Lambent
- Laquer
- Limpid
- Lucid
- Pellucid
- Pure
- Sheer
- Stainless
- Starlight
- Transparent
- Translucent
- Uncolored
- Vermouth
- Vitreous
- Vodka

GENERAL
- Balloon
- Bird of paradise
- Chevy
- Fiesta
- Hollyhock
- Horizon
- Iridescent
- Jube Jube
- Lollipop
- Neon brights
- Nordic
- Notice-me
- Pale
- Pastel
- Pastels
- Primaries
- Two-tone

GREEN
- Acid
- Alfalfa
- Algae
- Alligator
- Aloe
- Alpine
- Amazon
- Amphibian
- Aphid
- Apple
- April
- Asparagus
- Avocado
- Bamboo
- Bottle
- Broccoli
- Cabbage
- Camouflage
- Celery
- Chartreuse
- Chlorophyll
- Crocodile
- Cucumber
- Dill pickle
- Dinosaur
- Emerald
- Forest
- Frog
- Garden hose
- Grass
- Hazel
- Holly
- Hunter
- Iguana
- Ivy
- Jade
- Jungle
- Kale
- Kiwi
- Leaf
- Leek
- Leopard frog
- Lettuce
- Lichen
- Lily pad
- Lime
- Lizard
- Marsh
- Mint
- Moss
- Olive
- Parsley
- Pea
- Philodendron
- Pine
- Pond scum
- Reed
- Relish
- Puke
- Romaine
- Sage
- Sagebrush
- Sap
- Sea
- Snow pea
- Spinach
- Spruce
- Swamp
- Verdant
- Veridian
- Verdigris
- Watermelon
- Weed
- Willow

GREY
- Abbey
- Accomplice
- Adulterer
- Aluminium
- Ambush
- Amnesia
- Ash
- Bailiff
- Barn board
- Barred rock
- Battle
- Battleship
- Bilge water
- Burnt Silver
- Cement
- Chrome
- Chromium
- Cinder
- Clay
- Cloud
- Deadwood
- Dolphin
- Driftwood
- Dust
- German silver
- Granite
- Greystone
- Grime
- Grit
- Gunmetal
- Haggis
- Haze
- Hippopotamus
- Hoary
- Iceberg
- Iron

- Iron ore
- Jailor
- Lard
- Lead
- Lichen
- Militia
- Mole
- Moonbeam
- Moonstone
- Mould
- Mouse
- Mushroom
- Nickel
- Pewter
- Porridge
- Powder
- Pudding
- Putty
- Sea
- Seal
- Shadow
- Shark
- Silver fox
- Silver
- Silverbright
- Slate
- Smoke
- Steel
- Sterling
- Stingray
- Stone
- Storm
- Toad
- Toadstool
- Tuna
- Zinc

JEWEL
- Amber
- Crystal
- Diamond
- Emerald
- Garnet
- Opal
- Rhinestone
- Ruby
- Sapphire
- Topaz
- Zircon

MIXED
- Agate

- Appaloosa
- Blaze
- Brindle
- Calico
- Cat's whisker
- Checkered
- Cosmic
- Dapple
- Fleck
- Freckle
- Gingham
- Hazel
- Leopard
- Marble
- Masquerade
- Mosaic
- Motley
- Mottle
- Opal
- Paint
- Painted brick
- Patchy
- Particolor
- Pepper
- Piebald
- Pied
- Pinto
- Plaid
- Porcelain
- Pot pourri
- Salt and pepper
- Snake eye
- Speckle
- Spotty
- Sprinkle
- Stained glass
- Stripe
- Stipple
- Stud
- Tabby
- Tiger
- Tigereye
- Tortoise shell
- Variegated
- Zebra

ORANGE
- Apricot
- Bittersweet
- Cantaloupe
- Carrot
- Cat's eye

- Mango
- Marmalade
- Papaya
- Persian melon
- Pumpkin
- Sundog
- Sunset
- Tangerine
- Tiger

PINK
- Acne
- Adonis
- Affronted
- Baby's bum
- Blush
- Bo-peep
- Bougainvillea
- Cheerleader
- Coral
- Dawn
- Flamingo
- Fuchia
- Geranium
- Magnolia
- Melon
- Orchid
- Peach
- Pill
- Pimple
- Placenta
- Raspberry
- Rose
- Roseate
- Rosette
- Salmon
- Shrimp
- Spun
- Sunset
- Toenail
- Tuna
- Watermelon

PURPLE
- Amaranthine
- Amethyst
- Aster
- Aubergine
- Bacchanalian
- Beet
- Bilberry
- Blackberry

- Boisonberry
- Bordeaux
- Burgundy
- Chokeberry
- Chokecherry
- Eggplant
- Elderberry
- Fuschia
- Grape
- Heather
- Heliotrope
- Hyacinth
- Imperial
- Iris
- Juniper berry
- Lava
- Lavande
- Lavender
- Lilac
- Liver
- Magenta
- Maroon
- Mauve
- Missouri currant
- Morning glory
- Mulberry
- Pomegranate
- Peony
- Plum
- Port
- Puce
- Rowanberry
- Royal
- Sapphire
- Sugarplum
- Violet
- Wine
- Wisteria

RED
- Alder
- Alizarin
- Apple
- Bacon
- Barn
- Baroness crimson
- Beef
- Beet
- Berry
- Bleeding
- Blood
- Bloodshot
- Bloodstone

- Blush
- Bolshevik
- Brick
- Cardinal
- Carmine
- Carnation
- Catsup
- Cerise
- Cherry
- Chinese
- Claret
- Cochineal
- Corrosion
- Crimson
- Dried blood
- Ferrari
- Fiesta
- Fiery
- Fireweed
- Flame
- Gangrene
- Garnet
- Geranium
- Grenadier
- Hereford
- Holly berry
- Hollyhock
- Imperial scarlet
- Lava
- Lipstick
- Lobster
- Macintosh
- Madder
- Moroccan
- Nuclear holocaust
- Ochre
- Ox blood
- Pigeon's blood
- Pimiento
- Pimple
- Pomegranate
- Poppy
- Rampage
- Raspberry
- Raw
- Red squirrel
- Rhode Island
- Roof tile
- Rooster
- Rouge
- Ruby
- Ruddy
- Rose hip

- Ruddy
- Russian
- Salamander
- Santa
- Scarlet fever
- Scarlet
- Strawberry
- Sumach
- Sunset
- Tomato
- Turkey
- Venetian
- Vermillion
- Watermelon

WHITE
- Acadian mist
- Alabaster
- Albatross
- Albino
- Alkali
- Arctic
- Arsenic
- Ash
- Birch
- Blanche
- Blanc mange
- Blank wall
- Bleach
- Blossom
- Bridal
- Bride
- Bright
- Buttermilk
- Candescent
- Chalk
- Cherry blossom
- Chicken thigh
- China
- Coconut
- Cotton
- Cream
- Creme
- Daisy
- Damask
- Drywall
- Fang
- Flour
- Freesia
- Frost
- Froth
- Garlic
- Gauze

- Gull
- Ice cube
- Ice
- Iceberg
- Icing sugar
- Iridescent
- Ivory
- Lightning
- Lily
- Marshmallow
- Milk
- Mist
- Molar
- Moonbeam
- Mother-of-pearl
- Nacre
- Natural
- North Pole
- Old lace
- Opalescent
- Orchid
- Oxide
- Oyster
- Pearl
- Pasty
- Picket fence
- Polar bear
- Porcelain
- Powder
- Ptarmigan
- Pure
- Rice
- Salt
- Sea foam
- Seagull
- Shell
- Smile
- Snow
- Snowdrop
- Spotless
- Surf
- Tooth enamel
- Ultrabright
- Vanilla
- Waterfall
- Waxen
- Wedding
- Wedding veil
- Wedding dress
- Whipped cream
- White hyacinth
- Zinc

YELLOW

- Ale
- Amaranth
- Amaryllis
- Amber
- Antique gold
- Applesauce
- Aureate
- Banana
- Baroque Gold
- Beer
- Bumblebee
- Butter
- Cadmium
- Cheddar
- Chrome
- Citrine
- Citron
- Citrus
- Corn meal
- Corn
- Crocus
- Daffodil
- Dandelion
- Duck
- Egg yolk
- Flaxen
- Honey mead
- Gilt
- Ginger
- Gold
- Goldenrod
- Gouda
- Jaundice
- Jonquil
- Lemon
- Mango
- Margarine
- Marigold
- Marmalade
- Mustard
- Old gold
- Omelette
- Persimmon
- Pineapple
- Primrose
- Saffron
- School bus
- Slicker
- Solar
- Straw
- Sulphur
- Sun gold

- Sun
- Sunbeam
- Sunflower
- Sunrise
- Topaz
- Tulip
- Vinegar

Section Fourteen

Power Words

Ablaze
- Afire
- Blazing
- Blistering
- Conflagration
- Fiery
- Fire
- Fire-breathing
- Flame
- Furnace
- Heated
- Hot
- Hotter
- Hottest
- Ignite
- Incandescent
- Kindle
- Red hot
- Scalding
- Scorching
- Searing
- Sizzle
- Sizzling
- Smouldering
- Sparks
- Spitfire
- Torchy

Able
- Affect
- Capable
- Capacity
- Pragmatic
- Resourceful
- Self-starting
- Self-monitoring

Abound
- Abundance
- Abundant
- Ample
- Bonanza
- Crammed
- Double
- Endless
- Enriched
- Enriching
- Excessive
- Expansive
- Extensive
- Free-flowing
- Full
- Full-blown
- Full-bodied
- Full-featured
- Fully-loaded
- High-yield
- Lavish
- Liberal
- Loaded
- Luxuriant
- Numerous
- Packed with
- Plentiful
- Plenty
- Superabundance
- Trimmings
- Triple
- Unconditional
- Unending
- Unstinting

Absolute
- Absolutely
- Ageless
- Everlasting
- Forever
- Perpetual
- Universal

Absorbent
- All-weather
- Astringent
- Flesh
- Geometric
- Low-slung
- Material
- Molded
- Non-greasy
- Oil-free
- Ouch-free
- Patented
- Pre-owned
- Prefinished
- Retouch
- Retractable
- Rubberized
- Stackable
- Triple-sealed
- Woody

Accelerated
- Break-neck
- Chop chop
- Fast forward
- Fast

Fast-acting
- Fast-acting
- Fast-paced
- Faster
- Fastest
- Fleet
- Flying
- Gallop
- High-speed
- Hurry
- Overdrive
- Presto
- Prompt
- Quick
- Quick 'n
- Quicken
- Quickest
- Race
- Racing
- Racy
- Rush
- Same day
- Speeded-up
- Speedy
- Stampede
- Swift
- Time-saving
- Velocity

Accent
- Accentuate
- Acknowledge
- Attention
- Emphasize
- Highlights
- Juxtapose
- Limelight
- Notice
- Notice-me
- Privilege
- Selected
- Spotlight
- Target

Accept
- Acceptance
- Accepting
- Forgive
- Forgiving
- Profound
- Spiritual
- Tolerance
- Tolerant

Access
- Accessible
- Accommodate
- Automatic
- Available
- Built-in
- Convenient
- Frequent
- Handle
- Handy
- Handy for
- In-store
- One stop
- Portability
- Portable
- Receptive
- Suitable for

Accessory
- Accompanied by
- Blend
- Companion
- Compatible
- Complimentary
- Cross reference
- Juxtapose
- Matching
- Shared
- Simultaneous
- Supporting
- Symmetrical
- Together

Acclaimed
- Acknowledged
- Celebrated
- Established
- Recommended

Accolade
- Admire
- Admiration
- Adoration
- Applause
- Kudos
- Laurels
- Praise
- Rave

Accurate
- Impeccable
- Impeccably-crafted
- Made-to-measure
- Meticulous
- Perfect
- Perfectionist
- Perfectly
- Precise
- Precision
- Scrupulous

Achieve
- Achievement
- Achiever
- Feat
- Peak
- Performance
- Reach

Action
- Action-packed
- Activate
- Adventure
- Aggressive
- Bounce
- Bouncy
- Bounding
- Contagious
- Doer
- High-performance
- Made-for-adventure

Actual
- Genuine
- Honest-to-goodness
- Palpable
- Real
- Real-life
- Real-world
- Reality
- Template
- Valid
- Verified
- Virtually
- Visibly

Adage
- Buzzword
- Language
- Medium
- Statement
- Verdict
- Vernacular
- Word

Adapt
- Adaptable
- Adaptation
- Adjustable
- Adopt
- All-purpose
- Amenable
- Convertible
- Diverse
- Ever-evolving
- Flexible
- Interchangeable
- Malleable
- Multi-
- Multi-dimensional
- Multi-function
- Multi-media
- Multi-purpose
- Multi-use
- Multifaceted
- Reversible
- Transitional
- Upgradability

Add
- Add-on
- Addition
- Additional
- Adopt
- Alternate
- Bonus
- Conjunction
- Extra
- Plus
- Supplement
- Topped with
- Upgrade
- Upload

Addictive
- Hooked
- Habitual
- Shopaholic

Adept
- Astute
- Attune
- Brain trust
- Canny
- Clever
- Discerning
- Expertise
- Flair

- Hone
- Genius
- Intelligent
- Knack
- Learn
- Mastermind
- Proficient
- Savvy
- Sharp
- Sharpest
- Skillful
- Smart
- Sophisticated
- Talented
- Tricky

Adore
- Adored
- Bask
- Beloved
- Care
- Caring
- Cherish
- Compassionate
- Cult
- Darling
- Dear
- Dearest
- Fondness
- Heart
- Heartfelt
- Indulgent
- Kind
- Love
- Worship

Advance
- Advanced
- Advancement
- Ahead
- All-new
- Au courant
- Avant-garde
- Breakaway
- Breakthrough
- Cutting-edge
- Early
- Early bird
- Educated
- Enhancement
- First
- Forward-looking
- Fusion

- Future
- Futuristic
- Ground-breaking
- Initiate
- Initiative
- Innovation
- Innovative
- Latest
- Leading-edge
- Modern
- Modernist
- New dawn
- New
- New-age
- Newborn
- Newest
- Nouveau
- Novel
- Novelty
- Pioneer
- Promise
- Promising
- Prototype
- Revolutionary
- Space age
- Trial run

Advertise
- Boast
- Boost
- Broadcast
- Conjure
- Develop
- Download
- Exponent
- Hustle
- Promote
- Represent
- Upload

Advocate
- Auxiliary
- Help
- Helper
- Helpful
- Helping
- Welcome
- Welcoming

Aesthetic
- Artistic
- Beautify
- Beautiful

- Beauty
- Cute
- Good-looking
- Handsome
- Knockout
- Looker
- Lovely
- Loveliness
- Prettiest
- Pretty
- Stunning

Afford
- Affordable
- Available
- Buyable
- Cheap
- Cost-effective
- Deposit
- Inexpensive
- Low cost
- Save
- Savings
- Thrifty
- Value

Age
- Century
- Eon
- Era
- Millennium
- Period
- Years

Age-defying
- Ageless
- Taut
- Younger-looking
- Youthful
- Youthfulness

Aged
- Ancient
- Antique
- Colonial
- Nostalgic
- Old
- Oldest
- Reminiscent
- Retro
- Retro-minded
- Timeless

- Time-honored
- Veteran
- Vintage
- Vintage-inspired

Aggressive
- Aggressiveness
- Audacious
- Audacity
- Bold
- Boldness
- Brash
- Brave
- Courageous
- Daring
- Dash
- Dashing
- Derring-do
- Edgy
- Energetic
- Nervy
- Sass
- Sassy
- Spirited
- Tiger
- Venturesome
- Verve
- Unabashed

Agile
- Agility
- Flexible
- Sinuous
- Supple

Aim
- Destination
- Goal
- Intention
- Target

Alchemy
- Enchanting
- Enchantment
- Enchantress
- Incantation
- Incantatory
- Magic
- Magical
- Mysterious
- Mystery
- Mystical

- Secret
- Sorcerer
- Sorceress
- Spell
- Spellbinding
- Spellbound
- Witchery
- Wizard
- Wizardry

Alert
- Alive
- Avid
- Go-ahead
- Lifelike
- Magnetizing
- Never dull
- Watchful

Alike
- Coattails
- Copy
- Duality
- Emulate
- Equal
- Equivalent
- Imitate
- Interchangeable
- Look-alike
- Mimic
- Similar
- Tantamount

All-in-one
- All-out
- Complete
- Head-to-toe
- Total
- Total-body
- Totally
- Whole
- Wholly

All-inclusive
- All-time
- Every
- Everything
- Everywhere
- Panacea

All-star
- Compelling
- Five star

- Highest
- Must
- Must-have

Allow
- Let
- Release
- Treat

Allure
- Alluring
- Attractive
- Beautiful
- Compelling
- Enticing
- Handsome
- Lovely
- Sharp-looking

Alone
- Loner
- Monopoly
- One of a
- One-of-a-kind
- One-touch
- Only
- Original
- Originality
- Particular
- Particularly
- Private
- Single
- Single-minded
- Single-mindedness
- Singular
- Solitary
- Solo
- Unique
- Unmistakable

Alp
- Apex
- Beyond
- Conqueror
- Hero
- Superachiever
- Jackpot

Alternative
- Counterculture
- Demimonde
- Alternate reality

Amazing
- Astonishing
- Awe-inspiring
- Dazzling
- Dizzying
- Drop-dead
- Extraordinary
- Eye-popping
- Incredible
- Knock down
- Knockout
- Mind-boggling
- Outrageous
- Sensational
- Shattering
- Smashing
- Spectacular
- Staggering
- Startling
- Stunning
- Stupendous
- Traffic stopper
- Unbelievable
- Uncanny

Ambiance
- Ambient
- Atmosphere
- Aura
- Bathed in
- Limpid
- Misty

Ambiguity
- Contrary
- Counterpoint
- Opposite

Ambition
- Ambitious
- Aspiring

Amenity
- Asset
- Comfort
- Convenience
- Goody

Amok
- Boffo
- Funny
- Giddy
- Hilarious
- Howling
- Out-there
- Outrageous
- Pandemonium
- Socko
- Uproarious
- Whoop-up

Angle
- Perspective
- Leaning
- Pitch
- Slant
- Tendency

Announce
- Declare
- Proclaim

Anticipate
- Discover
- Find
- Intrigued
- Rediscover
- Reinvent

Appeal
- Appealing
- Crisp
- Dandy
- Delight
- Effortless
- Elegy
- Enviable
- Evocative
- Eye-catching
- Fashionable
- Gold
- Golden
- Good
- Picturesque
- Precious
- Preferred
- Quaint
- Yearn

Appetite
- Desire
- Eagerness
- Hunger
- Yearning
- Zest

Appointed
- Esteem
- Motherhood
- Respect
- Respectful
- Revere
- Reverence

Appreciate
- Appreciation
- Blandishment
- Compliments
- Compliments of
- Generous
- Gratifying
- Gratitude
- Thank you
- Thanks

Architectural
- Build
- Building
- Cantilevered
- Edifice
- Form
- Pavilion
- Place
- Precinct
- Setting
- Situate
- Situation

Aristocratic
- Arrogant
- Blue chip
- Diva
- Imperious
- Privileged
- Swish

Aroma
- Aromatic
- Breathable
- Fragrant
- Musky
- Nosegay
- Perfume
- Scented
- Sweet
- Unscented

Arouse
- Catapult

- Intensify
- Jazz
- Juicy
- Lightning
- Revved up
- Rocket
- Strike
- Surrender
- Zing

Art
- Artful
- Artfully
- Artistry
- Creative
- Creativity
- Picture
- Portrait
- Sculpture
- Skill

Ask
- Aspire
- Challenge
- Compare
- Estimate
- Inquire
- Reckon

Assemblage
- Collect
- Collectible
- Collection
- Crowd
- Gather
- Gathering
- Menagerie
- Portfolio
- Stock

Assemble
- Deliver
- Furnish
- Install
- Provide
- Serve
- Service

Associate
- Association
- Buddy
- Friend
- Pal

Assorted
- Assortment
- Eclectic
- Ensemble
- Guesswork
- Harlequin
- Medley
- Mixed bag
- Random
- Scattershot
- Sprinkling
- Variety
- Variation

Assure
- Bonded
- Certainty
- Certified
- Cinch
- Complete
- Ensure
- Guarantee
- Ingrained
- Insured
- Licensed
- Patented
- Proof
- Surefire
- Truth
- Warranty

Astronomical
- Celestial
- Comet
- Cosmic
- Extraterrestrial
- Galaxy
- Heavenly
- Stellar
- Supernova

Attract
- Draw
- Entice
- Inviting
- Lure
- Pull

Attribute
- Credit with
- Feature
- Trait

Austere
- Bare
- Bare-bones
- Minimalist
- Monastic
- Skinny
- Spare
- Stark
- Stripped-down

Authorized
- Legit
- Legitimate
- Official

Avail
- Effective
- Equipped
- Functional
- Functionalism
- Functionality
- Serviceability
- Use
- Useful
- Usefulness
- Utilize
- Work

Award-winning
- Deserve
- Deserving
- Esteemed
- Highly-regarded
- Reputed
- Respectable

Awe
- Impress
- Interest
- Interesting
- Reverence
- Veneration

Baby
- Childish
- Childlike
- Germinate
- Infant
- Kid-friendly
- Kid-pleasing
- Playable
- Playpen
- Young

- Youth

Back
- Encourage
- Endorse
- Hearten
- Resonate
- Support

Background
- Heritage
- Historical
- History
- Legacy
- Story

Badass
- Beast
- Impudent
- Maverick
- Prowl
- Prowler
- Renegade
- Revolutionary
- Restive
- Roughneck
- Runaway
- Street-smart

Balance
- Range
- Setting
- Spectrum

Ball
- Bat
- Flag
- Page
- Shoot
- Texture
- Wall

Ballad
- Cavalier
- Celebrate
- Celebration
- Gala
- Ode
- Poem
- Poetry

Banish
- Discontinued

- Elimination
- Fewer
- Impossible
- Improbable
- Less
- Minimize
- Nadir
- Never
- No
- Notorious
- Overstatement
- Preventable
- Prevents
- Reduce
- Regardless
- Unacceptable
- Zero

Baronial
- Baroque
- Deluxe
- Grand
- Fancy
- Majestic
- Ornate
- Palatial
- Swanky

Base
- Foundation
- Solid footing

Basted
- Bittersweet
- Buttery
- Chewy
- Confection
- Creamy
- Delicious
- Flavor
- Flavorful
- Fruity
- Gourmet
- Mouth-watering
- Nutrient
- Nutrition
- Nutritional
- Nutritious
- Organic
- Palette
- Recipe
- Relish
- Savory

- Scrumptious
- Slice
- Smack
- Smothered
- Succulent
- Sun-ripened
- Superfood
- Tangy
- Tasteful
- Tastefully
- Tasty
- Yummy

Battle-tested
- Die-hard
- Durable
- Durability
- Endurance
- Endure
- Indelible
- Indestructible
- Indispensable
- Lasting
- Lastingly
- Longer-lasting
- Longest
- Stamina
- Staying power
- Tireless

Beckon
- Call
- Elicit
- Influence
- Invite
- Solicit
- Overture
- Induce
- Lure
- Persuade
- Invite

Bedazzle
- Bright
- Brightest
- Brilliance
- Brilliant
- Burnished
- Gilded
- Glistening
- Glitter
- Glittering
- Glitzy

- High-shine
- Phosphorescent
- Scintillating
- Shimmer
- Shimmering
- Shine
- Shiny
- Sparkling
- Sun-kissed
- Sunny

Bedecked
- Decorative
- Decorator-inspired
- Embellished
- Fancy
- Ornament
- Ornamental

Bedew
- Dew
- Dewy
- Greased
- Moist
- Moisture-rich
- Sheen
- Slick
- Wet-look

Beef-up
- Boost
- Booster
- Deepen
- Enhance
- Enhancing
- Enrich
- Enriching

Befriend
- Friend
- Friendship
- Social
- Sociable

Begin
- Beginning
- Catalyst
- Dawn of
- Debut
- Inaugurate
- Initiate
- Introduce

- Introducing
- Introductory
- Self-starting
- Springboard
- Start
- Start-up
- Trigger
- Unfold
- Unleash

Beguile
- Captivate
- Charm
- Charming
- Captivating
- Charisma
- Charismatic
- Please
- Pleaser
- Suit
- Winsome

Behold
- Look
- Scope out
- See
- Spot
- Spy

Believe
- Believer
- Optimist
- Optimistic

Benchmark
- Example
- Hallmark
- Identity
- Measure
- Metaphor
- Model
- Namesake
- Reference

Best
- Best-ever
- Finest
- Master
- Masterpiece
- Masterwork
- Maximum
- Olympian

- Olympic
- Optimum
- Optimal
- Optimize
- Premium
- Prime
- Purest
- Smartest
- Supreme
- Tiptop
- Tops
- Unbeatable
- Unrivalled
- Unsurpassed

Best-loved
- Bestseller
- Notable
- Notch above
- Noteworthy
- Remarkably

Better
- Excel
- Improve
- Improvement
- Refine
- Refinements
- Finer
- Mainstream
- More

Big
- Biggest-selling
- Bigtime
- Cataclysmic
- Colossal
- Considerable
- Enormous
- Epic
- Epoch
- Extra-big
- Extra-long
- Extravaganza
- Extreme
- Fat
- Gargantuan
- Giant
- Gigantic
- Ginormous
- Grand
- Grandeur

- Great
- Heroic
- High-capacity
- Huge
- Humungous
- Imposing
- Jumbo
- Large
- Large-scale
- Legion
- Lofty
- Major
- Mass-produced
- Mind-boggling
- Monster
- Monstrous
- Mountain
- Olympian
- Outsize
- Overriding
- Oversize
- Sizable
- Sky-high
- Titanic
- Tower
- Ultra strong
- Ultra
- Vast
- Whopper
- Whopping

Bioforce
- Chemical-free
- Earth bound
- Earth
- Earth-friendly
- Earth-safe
- Earthy
- Eco-friendly
- Environment
- Habitat
- Lake
- Life
- Live
- Living
- Mother
- Motherly
- Natural
- Naturally
- Nature
- Ocean
- Rooted
- Sea

- Solar
- Summer
- Sun
- Sunshine

Blast
- Blast-off
- Boom
- Booming
- Bursting
- Dynamite
- Earth-shaking
- Explosion
- Explosive
- Fireworks
- Flare
- Pow
- Pyrotechnic
- Rocket
- Thunder
- Thundering
- Thunderous

Blend
- Combine
- Combination
- Fuse
- Mix
- Integrate
- Incorporate
- Medley
- Merge
- Merger
- Synergistic
- Synthesis
- Synthesize

Bliss
- Carefree
- Cheers
- Euphoria
- Glad
- Hallelujah
- Happiness
- Happy
- Joy
- Joyful
- Joyous
- Light-hearted
- Merriment
- Merry
- Rejoice
- Rejoicing

Blockbuster
- Blowout
- Champion
- Outstanding
- Overwhelming
- Towering
- Winner
- Winning

Bloom-crazy
- Blooming
- Bouquet
- Floral
- Flowery

Boast
- Brag
- Flaunt
- Pride
- Proud
- Record

Bodacious
- Clingy
- Erotic
- Flirt
- Flirty
- Flirtatious
- Hearthrob
- Hunk
- Hunky
- Kissable
- Lusty
- Mega-sexy
- Orgy
- Provocative
- Seduce
- Seductive
- Sensuous
- Sexiest
- Sexy
- Sinuous
- Siren
- Slinky
- Sultry
- Sybaritic

Bohemian
- Iconoclast
- Maverick
- Outlaw
- Rebel
- Rebellion

- Rebellious

Bolt
- Chug
- Click
- Quiver
- Rack up
- Rap
- Smack

Bombast
- Bombastic
- Exaggeration
- Puffery
- Rant

Bond
- Destiny
- Fate
- Guarantee
- Pledge
- Warranty

Boundary
- Bounds
- Circumscribed
- Edge

Boundless
- Countless
- Endless
- Limitless
- Unlimited

Branch
- Branching
- Multiply
- Proliferate
- Propagate

Bravo
- Hit
- Home-run
- Win

Break
- Contrast
- Controversial
- Drift away
- Drifts
- Open
- Out of this
- Out

Breakable
- Delicate
- Fragile

Breathless
- Breathtaking
- Galvanic
- Rapture
- Rapturous
- Thrill
- Thriller
- Thrilling
- Tingle
- Viva
- Vive
- Vivid

Breeze
- Breezy
- Brio
- Bubbly
- Festive
- Fizz
- Fizzy
- Jazzy
- Perk
- Perky
- Pizzazz
- Snazzy
- Zip
- Zippy

Bridge
- Byway
- Country
- Distance
- Hub
- Journey
- Map
- Odyssey
- Vacation

Broad
- Colonial
- Empire
- Global
- International
- Internationally
- National
- Nationally
- World
- Worldwide

Broad-based
- Inclusive
- Rangy
- Wide

Brooding
- Delirious
- Extremist
- Madly
- Madness
- Manic
- Obsess
- Obsessed
- Obsession

Brouhaha
- Hubbub
- Melee
- Noise
- Riot
- Scrap

Buccaneer
- Catch
- Capture
- Cavalry
- Control
- Force
- Kingmaker
- Militant
- Military
- Outperform
- Overcome
- Piratical
- Prevail

Buckbuster
- Bucks
- Budget
- Cash
- Cash in
- Cash
- Commercial
- Cost
- Dollars
- Earn
- Financial
- Invaluable
- Invest
- Investor-owned
- Millions
- Money tree

- Money
- Moolah
- Non-refundable
- Payoff
- Pocketbook
- Precious
- Pricey
- Profit
- Profitable
- Recession-proof
- Refundable
- Spendable
- Valuable
- Value
- Value-driven
- Value-packed

Bulletproof
- Firm
- Heavy-duty
- Husky
- Industrial
- Reinforced
- Resistant
- Robust
- Rock
- Rugged
- Shock-absorbing
- Solid
- Steely
- Strenuous
- Strong
- Stronger
- Strongest
- Sturdy
- Sturdiness
- Substantial
- Tough

Busy
- Buzzing
- Countdown
- Enthusiastically
- Hardest-working
- Industry
- Nurse
- Push
- Shopfest
- Street smart

Calculate
- Design
- Order

- Organize
- Plan
- Plot

Calm
- Calming
- Candle light
- Cradled
- Casual
- Easy-going
- Mellow
- Nonchalance
- Relax
- Relaxing
- Serene
- Serenity
- Settle
- Soothing
- Still
- Stillness
- Tempered
- Tranquil
- Tranquility
- Unfazed
- Unhurried

Careful
- Discretion
- Guard
- Protect
- Protectant
- Preventative
- Risk-free
- Safe
- Safety
- Sanctuary
- Shield
- Worry-free

Caress
- Contact
- Cradle
- Cuddle
- Embrace
- Hug
- Intimacy
- Nestle
- Tuck
- Warm

Carnival
- Escapade
- Festival

- Festivity
- Jubilee
- Party
- Party along

Carry away
- Heady
- Head-turning
- Inebriate
- Intoxicate
- Intoxicating
- Passion
- Possessed
- Transport
- Swoon

Celebrity
- Celebrity
- Famous
- Headliner
- Idol
- Luminary
- Memorable
- Newsworthy
- Noteworthy
- Prominent
- Recognized
- Repute
- Reputation
- Sought-after
- World famous

Center
- Genre
- Hub
- Headquarters
- Showroom
- System

Centerpiece
- Center
- Crown
- Crowning
- Culmination
- Heart
- Peak
- Pinnacle
- Preeminent
- Primary
- Top
- Tops
- Topped with
- Zenith

Ceremony
- Courtesy
- Development
- Event
- Holiday
- Scenario

Chain
- Line
- Link
- Succession
- Unbreakable

Chameleon-like
- Change
- Changeable
- Intervention
- Modify
- Modified
- Metamorphosis
- Reappraisal
- Restructure
- Revised
- Transform
- Transforming
- Translate
- Versatile
- Versatility

Champagne
- Creme de la creme
- Cushy
- Decadent
- Fancy
- Luxurious
- Luxury
- Magnificent
- Opulence
- Opulent
- Rich
- Splendor
- Sumptuous

Chance
- Factor
- Opportune
- Opportunity
- Potential
- Test

Chant
- Lyrical
- Melodic

- Musical
- Operatic
- Song
- Tinkling

Character
- Inborn
- Inherent
- Personality
- Quality
- Temperament

Charged up
- Crackle
- Dynamic
- Electrifying
- Energetic
- Energize
- Energy
- Galvanize
- Power up
- Supercharged
- Vibrate
- Voltage
- Zap

Chase
- Headlong
- Pursue
- Pursuit

Check out
- Evaluate
- Examine
- Explore
- Look for
- Quest
- Search
- Seek
- Unravel

Cheeky
- Contagious
- Impish
- Infectious
- Kicky
- Saucy
- Whimsical

Chi-chi
- Chic
- Cyberchic
- Elegant

- Elegantly
- Fashion
- Fashion-conscious
- Natty
- Sporty
- Supercool
- Super stylish
- Style
- Stylish
- Trend
- Trendy
- Trendoid

Chivalrous
- Chivalry
- Fervor
- Gallant
- Inspiration
- Inspire
- Inspiring
- Intense
- Nostalgic
- Romantic
- Sentimental

Choice
- Choose
- Choosey
- Decide
- Decidedly
- Decision
- Determine
- Favorable
- Fave
- Favorite
- Inclination
- Judgement
- Pick
- Picky
- Prefer
- Select
- Selection
- Selective

Chuckle
- Giggle
- Laughs
- Laughter
- Smile
- Smiling

Circle
- Encircle

- Spin
- Rotate
- Surround
- Turn

Civic
- Correct
- Obey
- Right

Civil
- Civilized
- Courteous
- Courtesy
- Formal
- Ladylike
- Kind
- Polish
- Polished
- Polite
- Reasonable
- Sophisticated
- Stylized
- Suave
- Urbane

Clarifying
- Contemplate
- Justification
- Rational
- Reasoned
- Reflect
- Reflection
- Sense
- Sensibility
- Simplicity

Clarity
- Clear
- Crystal
- Transparent

Class
- Kind
- Sort
- Species

Classic
- Classy
- Dress
- Dressy
- Eloquent
- Exquisite

- Grace
- Graceful
- Gracious
- Hauteur
- Refinement
- Signature

Classify
- Context
- Interpret
- Motif
- Pattern
- Theme
- Topic
- Typical

Clean
- Clean-cut
- Cleanse
- Flawless
- Hygienic
- Immaculate
- Pristine
- Pure
- Purer
- Purest
- Purifying
- Sanitary
- Stainless
- Sterling
- Untouched
- Virgin

Close-up
- Confidential
- Face-to-face
- First-hand
- Intimacy
- Intimate
- Intricate
- Lock-in
- Nuances
- Personal
- Personalize
- Privacy

Cloud-light
- Downy
- Fluffy
- Gentle
- Gentleness
- Lighten
- Lightest

- Puffy

Cloud-soft
- Featherweight
- Light
- Lightweight
- Ultra light

Collaborate
- Collaboration
- Collaborative
- Compatibility
- Compatible
- Complementing
- Coordinate
- Harmony
- Harmonize
- Marriage
- Mediate
- Participate
- Partnership
- Reciprocate
- Share
- Team up

Coloration
- Colorful
- Monochrome
- Psychedelic
- Two-tone

Comeback
- Reborn
- Refund
- Restorative
- Restore
- Resurface
- Resurrect
- Return
- Revive

Comfort
- Cool
- Ease
- Friendly
- Refreshing
- Forgiving
- Serendipitous
- Serendipity

Comfy
- Comfortable
- Cosy

- Easy-to-wear
- Familiar
- Informal
- Ergonomic
- Lounge

Comic
- Frivolity
- Froth
- Fun
- Fun-loving
- Funhouse
- Funny
- Hopscotch
- Joke
- Kidding
- Quip
- Wry

Commanding
- Exciting
- Stirring

Commission
- Duty
- Function

Commitment
- Devoted
- Devotee
- Devotional
- Dutiful
- Faith
- Faithful
- Loyalty
- Patriotic
- Trust

Communication
- Flyer
- Letter
- Message
- Offer

Competition
- Provocation
- Rival
- Rivalry
- Victory

Competitive
- Entrepreneurial
- Enterprise

- Venture

Complete
- Completely
- Comprehensive
- Filled
- Extensive
- Extra
- General
- In-depth
- Stranglehold
- Thoroughly
- Throughout
- Ubiquitous
- Unabridged
- Unfiltered
- Utterly

Compliant
- Comply
- Compromise
- Controllable
- Options
- Pliable
- Programmable

Component
- Detail
- Dose
- Part
- Portion

Computer-friendly
- Computerized
- Cyber
- Cyberpal
- Wired

Conceivable
- Concept
- Idea
- Instinct
- Thought

Condition
- Conditioning
- Fitness
- Tone
- Workout

Conjure
- Construct
- Create

- Form
- Formative
- Formulate
- Formulated
- Made
- Magic up
- Make
- Produce
- Render
- Whip up

Connect
- Connection
- Continuous
- Join
- Link

Conquer
- Conquering
- Hard-earned
- Hard-won
- Overcome
- Prevail
- Succeed
- Triumph
- Triumphal
- Triumphant
- Unconquered
- Victor
- Victory
- Win

Conservative
- Consistency
- Consistent
- Constant
- Continually
- Dependability
- Dependable
- Fail-proof
- Goofproof
- Guaranteed
- Proven
- Reliable
- Rely
- Stable
- Steady
- Time-tested
- True
- Warranted

Consider
- Consideration

- Deduce
- Preconceive
- Think about
- Understand
- Understanding

Consummate
- Exact
- Particular
- Precise
- Precision
- Spot on

Contemporary
- Modern
- State-of-the-art
- Up-to-date

Content
- Peace
- Peaceful
- Peacemaker

Contour
- Form
- Proportions
- Shape
- Shaped
- Shapely

Contribute
- Donate
- Give
- Hand out

Convenience
- Ease
- Easier
- Easiest
- Easy
- Easy-to-use
- Effortless
- Elementary
- Immediate
- Instant
- Instantly
- Low-maintenance
- Low-tech

Costly
- Expensive
- High
- High-priced

- Pricey

Coverage
- Evidence
- Recognition
- Testament
- Testimony
- Witness

Covet
- Coveted
- Desire
- Desirable
- Long for
- Necessitate
- Need
- Require
- Want
- Wanted

Craft
- Crafted
- Fashioned
- Hand-formed
- Hand-picked
- Well-made

Craze
- Crazy
- Fad
- Insane
- Loony
- Nuts
- Nutty
- Wacky

Create
- Improvise
- Invent
- Invention

Creditable
- Credit
- Respected
- Tested
- True
- Truly
- Trustworthy
- Truthful
- Verify
- Veritable
- Virtual
- Virtually

Crescendo
- Suspense
- Tension

Critical
- Critically
- Crucial
- Crunch
- Urgency
- Urgent
- Urgently
- Vital

Crowd-pleasing
- Pleasing
- Popular
- Promotable

Crucial
- Important
- Highlight
- Limelight
- Mission-critical
- Momentous
- Spotlight
- Vital

Cue
- Hint
- Indication
- Invitation
- Sign

Cultivate
- Develop
- Exponential
- Grown up
- Growth
- Plow

Current
- Currently
- Now
- Presently
- Up-to-the-minute

Custom
- Habit
- Observance
- Ritual
- Tradition

Cut above
- Exceptional
- First
- First class
- Grade A
- Superb
- Superior
- Superlative
- Top form
- Top drawer
- Top quality
- Top-rated
- Topnotch
- Tops
- Transcendent
- Unprecedented
- World class
- World-beater
- World-beating

Dance
- Danceable
- Dancing
- Flowing
- Fluid

Danger
- Hazard
- Peril
- Risk
- Warning

Darling
- Honey
- Huggable
- Lovable
- Love-struck
- Loved
- Lover
- Sweet
- Tender

Decorate
- Embellish
- Ornament

Dedicated
- Determined
- Diligent
- Disciplined
- Dogged
- Effort
- Highly-motivated

- Insistence
- Perseverance
- Persistence
- Relentless
- Remorseless
- Uncompromising
- Undaunted

Deep
- Discreet
- Hidden
- Profound
- Sensible
- Serious

Defining
- Especially
- Exclusive to
- Exclusive
- Special
- Specialize
- Specially
- Specialty
- Specific

Definite
- Distinctive
- Distinction
- Exceptional
- Extraordinary
- Rare
- Singular
- Special
- Uncommon
- Unusual

Definite
- Definitive
- Firm
- Undeniable

Deliberate
- Fixed
- Inevitable
- Stubborn
- Unmoving

Delight in
- Enjoy
- Relish

Demanding
- Imperative

- Instrumental
- Locked-down
- Necessary
- Prerequisite
- Requisite

Demonstrate
- Depict
- Display
- Eye-opening
- Examination
- Expose
- Exposition
- Gallery
- Present
- Preview
- Reveal
- Revelation
- Show

Deserving
- Excellence
- Excellent
- Merit
- Quality
- Quality-crafted

Desirable
- Enticer
- Enticing
- Highly-prized
- Intrigue
- Intriguing
- Magnet
- Magnetic
- Tantalizing
- Tease
- Tempt
- Tempting
- Yummy

Diaphanous
- Sheen
- Billowy
- Floating
- Gauzy
- Invisible
- Misty
- Peekaboo
- See-through
- Sheer
- Transparent

Different
- Distinct
- Divide
- Division
- Spin-off

Diminutive
- Jewel-like
- Little
- Microfine
- Petite
- Small
- Tiny

Distill
- Distilled
- Elixir
- Essence
- Infusion
- Quintessential
- Seminal
- Ultimate

Distinctive
- Impressive
- Remarkable
- Significant

Dive
- Flow
- Gush
- Pool
- Plunge
- Splash
- Spurt
- Wave
- Well

Divine
- Elysian
- Heavenly
- Nirvana
- Paradisial
- Sublime

Domestic
- Domestically
- Home
- Homey
- Home-style
- Homebody
- Homecoming
- Hearth

- Lair
- Nest
- Oasis
- Refuge
- Sojourn

Door
- Doorway
- Enter
- Gate
- Gateway
- Key

Drama
- Dramatic
- Dramatically
- Theatrical
- Vignette

Drench
- Flood
- Flooded
- Free-flowing
- Overflows
- Poured

Dynamo
- High-energy
- High-intensity
- Mega-hot
- Raging
- Rockin'
- Sizzling
- Super-powered
- Torqued

Ecstacy
- Ecstatic
- Gripping
- Rhapsodic
- Rhapsody

Efficient
- Efficiency
- Energy-saving
- Practiced
- Well-oiled

l

Element
- Essence
- Fundamental
- Lasting
- Substance

- Root

Elevate
- Radical
- Speechless
- Transfix
- Transported

Eloquent
- Eloquence
- Express
- Fluent
- Hail
- Voice

Elusive
- Ethereal
- Intangible
- Flighty
- Remote
- Retire
- Retreat
- Untouchable

Emotion
- Emotional
- Evoke
- Evocative
- Excite
- Excitement
- Experience
- Feel
- Feeling
- Haunting
- Moving
- Touch
- Touching

Emperor
- Imperial
- King
- Kingpin
- Prince
- Princely
- Princess
- Queen
- Queenly
- Regal
- Royal

End
- Final
- Finale

- Finish
- Last
- Sold-out
- Ultimate
- Utmost

Enlighten
- Illuminating
- Inspirational
- Smarten
- Vision
- Visionary
- Vista
- Wisdom
- Wise
- Wiser
- Wisest
- Wise up

Enliven
- Invigorate
- Lively
- Peppery
- Peppy
- Psyched
- Stimulate
- Stimulating
- Stimulation
- Vivacious
- Zingy

Enthral
- Enrapture
- Hypnotic
- Hypnotize
- Magnetizing
- Mesmerize
- Rivetting

Example
- Model
- Paradigm
- Replica

Exotic
- Rare
- Uncommon
- Unusual
- Weird

Expanded
- Expandability
- Extended

- Extra
- Plus

Expert
- Expertly
- Master
- Mistress
- Proficient
- Virtuosity
- Virtuoso

Fab
- Fabled
- Fabulous
- Fairy tale
- Fantastic
- Fantastical
- Imaginary
- Marvel
- Marvelous
- Wonder
- Wonderful
- Wondrous

Fearless
- Fierce
- Fight
- Feisty
- Ferocious
- Roar

Flair
- Impact
- Punch

Florid
- Fat
- Flourish
- Plump
- Plush

Flourish
- Grow
- Increase
- Swell
- Thrive

Fly
- Flight
- Leap
- Leapfrog
- Soar
- Wind

- Wings
- Zoom

Foremost
- Front runner
- King
- Leader
- Leadership
- Leading
- Pacesetter
- Premier
- Premiere
- Star
- Top of the top
- Topdog
- Tops
- Uncontested
- Undisputed

Fortunate
- Fortune
- Positively
- Productive

Frank
- Frankness
- Honest
- Honesty
- Integrity
- Open
- Truly

Free
- Freedom
- Open
- Receptive
- Receptiveness
- Uncensored

Free trial
- Freebie
- Gift
- Unload

Fresh
- Fresh-picked
- Freshen
- Fresher
- Freshest
- Freshly

Funky
- Kitsch

- Kitschy
- Nifty
- Playful
- Playfulness
- Quirky
- Trippy
- Whimsical

Geek
- Mouse potato
- Nerd
- Propeller head

Glamorous
- Glorious
- Gorgeous
- Lush

Gleam
- Glimmer
- Gloss
- Glossy
- Lambent
- Lustre
- Lustrous
- Moon
- Moonlight
- Moonshine
- Patina
- Polished
- Smooth
- Translucent

Graphic
- Obvious
- Seen
- Visible
- Visual

Groove
- Groovy
- Hip
- Hipper
- Hippest
- Hipster
- Smooth
- Super cool
- Yuppie
- Zone

Habit
- Methodical
- Regular

- Reliable
- Step-by-step
- Way

Hale
- Healthy
- Healthy-looking
- Hearty
- Rosy
- Shapely
- Tonic
- Vital
- Wholesome

Halt
- Quench
- Relief
- Restrain
- Restraint
- Stop

Hammer
- Implement
- Physical
- Practical
- Tool

Handful
- Heap
- Load
- Pile
- Trove

Heavy
- Heavy duty
- Heavyweight
- Hefty
- Mass
- Massive
- Weighty

Hegemony
- Domain
- Kingdom
- Realm
- Region

Height
- Heights
- High
- Higher
- Tallness

Highroad
- Highway
- Path
- Road
- Swath
- Track
- Trail
- Trajectory

Homage
- Honor
- Reverence
- Tribute

Horsepower
- Potency
- Potent
- Power
- Power-packed
- Powered
- Powerful
- Pressure
- Prowess
- Rigorous
- Steam
- Steamroller
- Strength

Hotline
- News
- Scoop
- Wired

Humanity
- Soul
- Soul mate

Humble
- Modest
- Neat
- Nice
- Nicely

Hybrid
- Interface
- Hodgepodge
- Pastiche

Icon
- Idol
- Landmark
- Symbol

Idea
- Info
- Information
- Low-down
- Scoop

Ideal
- Ideal for
- Idyllic
- Perfect
- Perfecting
- Perfection

Idiosyncrasy
- Idiosyncratic
- Independence
- Independent
- Individual
- Individualist
- Individually

Imagine
- Imaginative
- Imagination
- Intuition
- Intuitive
- Sensibility

Indefinable
- Indescribable
- Mysterious
- Secret

Indigenous
- Local
- Native

Invincible
- Irresistible
- Unbeatable

Jewel
- Nugget
- Treasure

Lean
- Slender
- Slim
- Svelte
- Thin
- Trim
- Wiry

Legendary
- Renowned
- Storied

Lifetime
- Long-range
- Preserve
- Preservation

Linger
- Hang on
- Remain
- Stay

Long
- Lanky
- Sky-high
- Tall
- Tiptoe

Magnificent
- Out-there
- Rewarding
- Smash
- Smash hit
- Splendid
- State-of-the-art
- Stunner
- Super duper
- Super

Mature
- Maturity
- Ready
- Ripe

Meaningful
- Memorable
- Persuasive
- Remember
- Resonance
- Resonant
- Resonate
- Unforgetable

Means
- Medium
- Method
- Modus operandi
- Way

Mission
- Plan

- Purpose
- Strategy

Modest
- Modesty
- Unassuming
- Understated
- Undertones
- Unfussy

Monochromatic
- Muted
- Neutral
- Subtle
- Subtlety
- Understated

Move
- Relocate
- Peripatetic
- Shift
- Shuttle
- Tumble

Norm
- Normal
- Regular
- Standard

Own
- Possess
- Possession

Pleasure
- Satisfy
- Satisfaction

Position
- Order
- Profile
- Presence
- Stance
- Stand

Practitioner
- Expert
- Renderer
- User

Problem-solving
- Solution
- Troubleshoot
- Troubleshooter

Progress
- Progressive
- Spearhead
- Tomorrow
- Uncharted

Project
- Extrapolate
- Series
- Scientific
- Statistically

Purveyor
- Salesperson
- Seller
- Staff
- Vendor

Quicksilver
- Volatile
- Volatility

Quiet
- Silent
- Still
- Stillness
- Whisper
- Whisper-quiet
- Whisper-smooth

Radiant
- Shining
- Star-studded
- Starry
- Star-struck
- Sun-loving
- Sunny
- Twinkling

Raging
- Rambunctious
- Rampage
- Reckless
- Riot
- Riotous
- Rip snorting
- Rip roaring
- Unsettling
- Untamable
- Untamed
- Wild
- Wilder
- Wildest

Ready
- Ready-made
- Ready-mixed
- Ready-to-use
- Ready-to-wear

Reborn
- Recapture
- Reconfigure
- Reconstruct
- Reconstruction
- Recreate
- Refinance
- Reignite
- Remodel
- Revival
- Revive

Recondition
- Regenerate
- Regeneration
- Reinvent
- Reinvigorate
- Rejuvenate
- Rejuvenating
- Rejuvenation
- Renew
- Revitalize
- Revitalizing
- Self-renewing

Recycled
- Refillable
- Removable
- Renewable
- Replacement
- Reusable

Reliable
- Steady
- Trustworthy
- Unshakable
- Unsinkable
- Unswerving
- Unwavering

Remedy
- Results
- Reward
- Solution
- Success
- Successful
- Yields

Repository
- Storage
- Store
- Treasury
- Vault

Resilience
- Resiliency
- Resilient
- Responsive
- Responsiveness

Room
- Roomy
- Latitude
- Space
- Spacious
- Capacious
- Wide open

Rustic
- Pastoral
- Simple
- Simplicity
- Unpretentious
- Unstudied

Satiny
- Glossy
- Seamless
- Silkier
- Silky
- Sleek
- Sleeker
- Slick
- Smooth

Seal
- Imprint
- Sheath
- Stamp
- Wrap

Soft
- Downy
- Soften
- Touchable
- Velvet
- Velvety

Sponsor
- Sponsored

- Support

Spontaneous
- Surprise
- Unexpected

Storm
- Stormy
- Tempest
- Tempestuous

Stuff
- Substance
- Texture

Swell
- Swing
- Swirl
- Swoop
- Tumble

Thumbs up
- Vocal
- Wow
- Wowed

Wash 'n wear
- Washable
- Waterproof
- Wear-resistant
- Wearable
- Weatherproof
- Wrinkle-free

Well-balanced
- Well-established
- Well-prepared
- Well-set

Fundraiser's Phrase Book

The *Fundraiser's Phrase Book* provides you with thousands of winning phrases designed for the nonprofit professional.

INSIDE YOU'LL FIND:

* Hundreds of ways to ask for help, support, donations, gifts, assistance, aid, sponsorship, MONEY, members, volunteers and much more

* All the "trigger words" that send donors running for their check books

* Columns of creative, donor-friendly salutations as well as clever envelope teasers and urgings your lapsed donors and members can't resist

* Help to communicate in a warm, one-to-one manner, giving that one-of-the-family feeling so essential in getting your message across with powerful emotional punch

* Ideas! Ideas! Ideas! The book acts as an natural idea bank. Use the phrases to jump start your imagination, come up with exciting new concepts and revitalize your work.

Terrific for
* Impressive Letters
* Dynamite Speeches
* Friendly Newsletters
* Convincing grant applications
* Persuasive Proposals
* And Fundraising Packages that Really Work

"Building blocks you can actually use in your letters, proposals or presentations...an easy escape hatch when you just can't find the right words yourself."
Canadian Fundraiser

Check this book out at:
www.hamilhouse.com

1001 Ways to Say Thank You

Thousands of Dynamic Phrases to Help You:

Appreciate, Applaud, Celebrate, Cheer on, Congratulate, Encourage, Honor, Inspire, Recognize, Sympathize, and Thank
with Warmth, Grace and Ease

Everyone loves to be thanked. And thanking others makes you feel terrific. A sincerely declared thank you is a powerful thing. It brings smiles, binds the heart and sometimes moves to tears.

In personal life, you show family and friends how much you care. In business, politics or charitable endeavor, your gratitude oils the wheels, tells colleagues and contributors they are appreciated and conveys how strongly you recognize the efforts of others.

Now you need never be at a loss for what to say as you express appreciation.

INSIDE YOU'LL FIND:

* Thousands of ways to thank, congratulate, appreciate, cement friendship and express love

* All the "triggers" that set friends, family, associates, customers and others smiling and thinking of you

* Huge choice of dashing signature lines

* Attention-getting exclamations to emphasize your feelings

* Ideas! Ideas! Ideas! The phrases naturally contain hordes of bright ideas which you can easily adapt to your own special needs

* Sample Letters! Find an example for just about every occasion to make your thank you notes even faster and more effective

* Special sections to help you with apology and condolence

Check this book out at:
www.hamilhouse.com

Printed in the United States
214803BV00004B/29/P

9 780968 085394